Social Psychology:
Identities and Relationships

Editors:
Kopano Ratele
Norman Duncan

UCT
PRESS

Social Psychology:
Identities and Relationships

© 2003 UCT Press
P O Box 24309, Lansdowne, 7779

ISBN 1-919713-83-2

Project management: Liesbet van Wyk
Copy editing: Stuart Douglas, Boltupright
Proofreading: Andrew van der Spuy
Indexing: GM Kettley
Photographs (text): Zenzo
Cover design: Pumphaus Design Studio
Photographs (cover): Sunday Times
DTP and design: Charlene Bate
Printed and bound in the Republic of South Africa by Paarl Print, Oosterland Steet, Paarl

Contents

Part 4: Sexualities and Masculinities: Histories and Future Possibilities

Contributors

Floretta Boonzaier completed her BA degree at the University of the Western Cape, and her BSocSc (Honours) and MA degrees at the University of Cape Town. Her interests include issues of race and gender construction, violence against women and qualitative research methodology. She is currently a PhD candidate and Research Associate in the Department of Psychology at the University of Cape Town.

Lindsay Clowes is a historian who lectures in the Women and Gender Studies Unit at the University of the Western Cape. Focusing on change in gender relations over time, her most current research explores change in the social construction of masculinities and femininities in the South African media in the mid to late twentieth century.

Anthony Collins lectures in the Psychology Department, Natal University. His interests include critical psychology and post-colonial studies and film.

Cheryl de la Rey was previously Executive Director at the National Research Foundation and associate professor of psychology, University of Cape Town. She is currently the deputy vice-chancellor at the University of Cape Town. She is the co-editor of *Contemporary issues in human development: a South African focus* and *'Race', racism, knowledge production and psychology in South Africa.*

Norman Duncan has been Associate Professor and head of department in the psychology department, University of Venda for Science and Technology and is currently Associate Professor at the Institute for Social and Health Sciences at the University of South Africa and editor of the *South African Journal of Psychology.* He is co-editor of several texts, including *Contemporary issues in human development: a South African focus, 'Race', racism, knowledge production and psychology in South Africa* and *Discourse of difference, discourses of oppression.* Racism and the development of authorship capacitation initiatives constitute the primary areas of his research interests.

Vijé E. Franchi is currently Senior Lecturer and Researcher at the University of Lyon 2, and member of the Laboratorie, d'IPSE Université Paris-Nanterre. Her research, community and clinical interventions have addressed issues related to the politics of intercultural identity among minority nationals, the mediation of 'racialised' conflict in organisations undergoing structural transformation, racism and self-articulated self-representation, and the primary prevention of risk behaviours among socio-politically disadvantaged youth.

Derek Hook lectures in the School of Human and Community Development at the University of the Witwatersrand, Johannesburg. A co-editor of *Body politics: power, knowledge and the body in the social sciences, Psychopathology and social prejudice* and *Developmental psychology,* he maintains a variety of research interests, stretching from the socio-political contexts of development to the politics of identity and the fledgling field of critical psychology.

Annik Houel is Professeur, Directrice du Département de Psychologie Sociale, Institut de Psychologie, Université Lumière-Lyon 2, Her interests are in gender. She is the author of *L'adultère au féminin et son roman* (Armand Colin, 1999) and *Le roman d'amour et sa lectrice: une si longue passion, l'exemple Harlequin* (L'Harmattan, 1997). She is co-author of *Chronique d'une passion, le mouvement de libération des femmes, Lyon, 1970–1980* (L'Harmattan, 1989, with C. Guinchard, B. Lhomond and M. Bridoux) and *Crime passionnel, crime ordinaire* (PUF, 2003).

Rafiq Lockhat is a Senior Lecturer in the Department of Psychology at the University of the Western Cape. He has been co-director of the Bathuthuzele Youth Stress Clinic and a regular commentator on youth-related topics. He is the current vice-chairperson of the South African Society of Clinical Psychology.

Vuyisile Mathiti lectures in Psychology at the University of the Western Cape. His research interests cover social identity, indigenous knowledge systems, and sports psychology. His current research and community work is on HIV/AIDS and mentoring projects involving young people, using music therapy and other diversion programmes.

Patricia Mercader, Social Psychology Professor at Lyon 2 University, specialises in gender studies and pedagogy for mature students. She is the author of *L'illusion transsexuelle* (L'Harmattan, 1994), co-author of *Chronique d'une passion, Le mouvement de libération des femmes, Lyon, 1970–1980* (L'Harmattan, 1989) and *Crime passionnel, crime ordinaire* (PUF, 2003), and editor of a forthcoming book about training in psychology.

Nthabiseng Motsemme has taught at the Department of Industrial Psychology at the University of the Western Cape and is currently associated with the Department of Sociology at the University of South Africa (UNISA) where she is also PhD candidate. She has an MA in Culture, Race and Difference from Sussex University. Her research interests include feminist theory and cultural studies. She has written on shifting identities during the post-apartheid era and women and the Truth and Reconciliation Commission.

Cheryl-Ann Potgieter is an Associate Professor in the Department of Psychology, University of Pretoria. Her teaching and research interests are in the areas of research methodology, feminist psychology and transformation issues related to the higher education sector. She is professional editor for *Health South Africa* and is a member of the editorial committee of the *Journal of Lesbian Studies*.

Kopano Ratele teaches in the Department of Psychology and Women and Gender studies programme at the University of the Western Cape. His current areas of interest include epistemology, critical studies of men and masculinities, discursive psychology, sexualities and research methods.

Mohamed Seedat is Associate Professor of Psychology and Director of the University of South Africa's Institute for Social and Health Sciences and its Centre for Peace Action. He has been centrally involved in several priority national research initiatives and collaborative cross-disciplinary research projects. He serves on several editorial boards and international conference organising committees, acts as external examiner on numerous masters- and doctoral-level research reports, and provides consultancy to various agencies in the psychology, injury prevention and development fields. He has published several articles in the areas of community psychology, racism, psychohistory and community development, and is chief editor of the first South African community psychology text, *Theory, Practice and Methods in Community Psychology: South African and Other Perspectives.*

Tammy Shefer is Associate Professor of Psychology and Director of Women and Gender Studies at the University of the Western Cape. She is co-editor of *Contemporary issues in human development: a South African focus* and *Discourse of difference, discourses of oppression.* Her major teaching areas are in epistemology, research methodology and discursive feminist psychology.

Helga Sobota is a Sociologist and Directeur des Affaires Culturelles, Ville de Grenoble. She specialises in gender studies. She is co-author of *Chronique d'une passion, le mouvement de libération des femmes, Lyon, 1970–980* (L'Harmattan, 1989, with C. Guinchard, B. Lhomond and M. Bridoux) and *Crime passionnel, crime ordinaire* (PUF, 2003).

Garth Stevens is a Researcher at the Institute for Social and Health Sciences at the University of South Africa. Understanding the causes, consequences and prevention of violence, as well as the study of the newer manifestations of racist ideology, constitutes the focus of his research interests.

Shahnaaz Suffla is trained as a Clinical Psychologist and is a Senior Lecturer/Student Counsellor at the Institute for Counselling at the University of the Western Cape, where she is involved in service delivery, research and the training of intern psychologists. Her research interests include women's health, peace and safety promotion, violence prevention, health systems research and issues related to social, community and peace psychology. Her research partners include the University of South Africa's Institute for Social and Health Sciences. She is on the editorial board of *African Safety Promotion: A Journal of Violence and Injury Prevention,* and is currently the chairperson of the Western Cape Branch of the Psychological Society of South Africa.

Tanya Swart is a Researcher attached to the Institute for Social and Health Sciences at the University of South Africa. Identity, racism and violence comprise her principal research interests.

Ashley van Niekerk is a Researcher at the Medical Research Council of South Africa. He is co-editor of *Contemporary issues in human development: a South African focus* and *'Race', racism, knowledge production and psychology in South Africa.*

Contexts and Concepts

PART ONE

Introduction: A Psychology of a Society

Kopano Ratele

OUTCOMES

The aim of this chapter is to introduce this book by:

- indicating some questions that confront a society such as ours and which the book deals with
- examining a number of definitions and brief critical remarks on them
- offering our understanding of social psychology
- sketching the context of the book
- summarising the sections and chapters in the book.

THIS CHAPTER has six objectives. The first is to examine a story and to ask how we make sense of this and other stories. Secondly, the chapter contemplates what social psychology is all about, noting a few definitions of the sub-discipline, and identifying very briefly some of the problems implicit in some of the notions these definitions deploy. Thirdly, the chapter presents a discussion of what social psychologists actually do, and more importantly, what they perhaps ought to be doing. Next, the chapter seeks to orient readers to this volume by describing the context that informs and the plan that underlies the volume. It does this by identifying the themes around which the text is built. Lastly, the chapter offers a series of thumbnail sketches of the different sections and chapters of the volume.

Making sense of stories

Consider the following story:

> Louis and Loraine have been seeing each other for ten months or so. Anticipating problems, they have a secret marriage. According to Louis, getting married to Loraine was the happiest day of his life. But his world was soon to fall apart when his parents told him Loraine would not be welcome in the family home. Although Louis said he loved his new wife, he decided to divorce her after his family

threatened to cut him off if he remained married to her. The 29-year-old Louis did not earn enough money to support himself and his wife and relied on his retired parents, Dries and Lettie de Beer. In fact, the parents accompanied and sat with Louis through the interview with Prega Govender (Sunday Times, 13 June 1999) who recounts the story. The father said Louis only told them about his marriage four days after he and Loraine Ramsamy secretly exchanged wedding vows at a marriage registry office. 'Over my dead body will he be allowed to bring her into our house,' he said. 'He would also not be welcome in our family if he decided to live with her elsewhere.' The parents said their son's marriage to Loraine had split their close-knit family. 'We come from a very conservative Afrikaner family,' Dries de Beer said. 'We are not racists, but at the same time we cannot ignore our strong Afrikaner values and traditions. Our customs differ tremendously from Loraine's, and I can't see how this marriage will work.' Dries de Beer told the journalist that one of his sons who lived in Cape Town has close ties to the extra-parliamentary Afrikaner Weerstand Beweging, the white ultra-rightwing grouping. This son had threatened to stop visiting them if Louis brought his new wife to the family home. Dries de Beer told Govender, 'I have four sons [besides Louis] and a daughter to think of, and I have to listen to them as well. At my age I cannot risk antagonising them just because of Louis.' Another son, the father's namesake, said he had warned Louis to stay away from Loraine. According to him, 'Warning bells went off when, four days after meeting my brother last year, she asked him to marry her. And when I heard that they had married without our knowledge I almost exploded. Family members were not given the chance to object to the marriage in court. It is not a question of race. My best friend is an Indian, but Loraine lied to us. Besides, she's older than Louis,' Dries jnr. said. Govender writes that speaking in the presence of his brother, Dries jnr., and his parents, Dries and Lettie, a subdued Louis said, 'After my parents told me my marriage had upset them, I decided to ask for a divorce. I cannot go against my parents' wishes. I am on their side.' However, a heartbroken Loraine is said to have vowed not to give up her Louis. She said, 'Ours was a marriage made in heaven. I know that his family is forcing him to ask for a divorce but I will never give him up. Our dream has been to live together in marriage, but it seems we are still in apartheid times' (Sunday Times, 13 June 1999).

The Social Sciences and Humanities are, in effect, about trying to make sense of and explain social and human phenomena through producing and analysing stories or narratives out of bits of data.

There are several ways of framing and interpreting stories. And in a certain sense social psychology, like other disciplines, concerns itself with framing and making sense of stories such as the one presented above. In effect, disciplines in the Social Sciences and Humanities are about trying to make sense of and explain social phenomena through producing and analysing stories or narratives out of bits of data. Or, perhaps more narrowly, the Social Sciences and Humanities are about *(re)arranging* stories or discrete bits of data according to methods valued by its constituent disciplines, so as to make some sense of the social world.

Disciplines are about framing phenomena and telling stories about them in order to make sense of the world.

Defining a field of inquiry

The manner in which students of human behaviour approach a situation such as that described in the story presented above is determined by their definition of their own field of inquiry. In addition, of course, the approaches adopted by social scientists are influenced by certain paradigmatic and ontologic assumptions, what they consider as *true knowledge*, their theoretical orientations, and the methodologies that they favour. However, more about this later.

For now we need to note that how we comprehend or make sense of stories to a significant degree is determined by the disciplines that we study or in which we are located. While there are really no bold lines that separate one Social Science discipline from another, academic or disciplinary territoriality is a fact. Our disciplinary location frequently determines how we apprehend and attempt to understand stories such as the one presented above. For example, in attempting to make sense of this story, a sociologist would most probably focus on the functioning of the Afrikaner family; a feminist or gender analyst might pay particular attention to the gender and sexual politics that structure the interaction of the males and the females in the story; psychologists might focus on the behavioural elements of the story; and psychologists of a psychoanalytic persuasion would probably focus on the unconscious, intra-psychic dynamics of the characters in the story. How these social scientists each define their field and view their own expertise plays an important part in the kinds of questions they would ask of and the answers they would look for from the people involved in the situation. That is also to say, their formulation of their field of inquiry offers them a way of looking, directing their attention to certain things and making them uninterested in or even blind to others.

Contesting stories, redefining fields of inquiry, redrawing disciplinary boundaries

You will agree that how we make sense of any story is never an uncomplicated process. It is not as though when friends tell us stories, we always listen to them with complete attention; or that we are interested in every aspect of the story; or that we believe everything about their stories; or indeed, that we view these stories only through our disciplinary lenses.

Reflect for a moment on what you thought about and felt on reading the story of the De Beer family and Loraine Ramsamy. Did you think that, despite their claims to the contrary, the De Beers are racist, or did you feel that they were merely expressing their right to be with people like themselves? Or, on reading this story, did you think, 'Racism is still a problem in South Africa'? Or did the thought perhaps cross your mind, as your read this story, that Louis and Loraine's love affair could be a form of resistance against the way South African society is structured? Did you have any questions about the source of the story, what it conveys, or the way it is written; or did you accept the story as typical of the South African context? Do you think everyone would respond to this story in the way that you did?

Obviously, on integrating the story into this chapter, I had rearranged the version originally presented by Prega Govender. Even Prega Govender in all likelihood (re)arranged the interviewees' responses to her questions in order to tell *a particular* story. I think that we can safely assume that, in narrating the story in the way that she did, she left out bits of information that she did not consider relevant and included information that she thought her readers would be interested in.

The point of all this is that how we make sense of or tell a story is never completely impartial or an unedited representation of 'what actually happened'. For this reason, stories of the same events inevitably differ and rarely go uncontested. Similarly, different fields of study investigating the same phenomena usually differ in the stories they tell about those phenomena. Their representation of these phenomena is often subject to intense contestation. We presently turn our attention to the roots and influences of, and intra-disciplinary contest within, social psychology – the field of study that forms the framework for the present volume. Before we even get into social psychology, though, it must be noted that just like differences around stories, definitions of the contents and limits of a field of study rarely go uncontested. This is

6

especially true in times of what has been referred to as disciplinary crises (Parker, 1989). The encouragement of interdisciplinary scholarship has also meant many an old border has been blurred, and the stories that get told about phenomena more complex. Newer disciplines like cultural studies, bio-informatics, public health, and men's studies, and older ones like African studies, women's studies, international relations, and African American studies, for instance, which tend to be inter-disciplinary in character, are interested in several divergent aspects of a situation at once. However, it is important to note that there are very few disciplines, including 'older' ones like psychology, that have just sprung up, without developing out of other disciplines.

The roots and influences of social psychology

Social psychology has roots in both psychological and sociological thinking. And the field of study is characterised by influences from both psychology and sociology, as well as the tensions that have resulted from the convergence of these ostensibly diverging fields.

> Social psychology has roots in both psychological and sociological thinking. It is characterised by influences from both the fields of psycho-logy and sociology, as well as tensions resulting from the convergence of the two fields.

The emergence of social psychology as a field of study within the broader discipline of psychology took place nearly one century ago with the publication of the first two books containing the term 'social psychology' in their titles. The sociologist E.A. Ross (1908) wrote the first of these publications and, in the same year, the psychologist William McDougall (1908) penned the second.

While it is generally accepted that Ross and McDougall's publications marked the beginning of social psychology as a substantive sub-discipline in psychology, writers such as Worchel *et al.* (1988) stress that the sub-discipline has its roots in, and maintains a strong connection to, not only sociology and psychology, but several other disciplines as well, including economics, philos-ophy, political science, history, business and management sciences, education, architecture, medicine, and law. This volume too sees social psychology as borrowing its insights from and lending them to various cognate disciplines, as well as 'common sense' (see Figure 1.1 for a visual representation of this link between social psychology and other cognate disciplines and 'common-sense'). Moreover, this volume departs from the assumption that, given the multiple origins and effects of its objects of study, social psychology of necessity has to be open to inter-disciplinary influence and has to maintain an inter-discipli-nary orientation.

Consistent with this general orientation, the contributors to this volume do not confine themselves to narrow psychological and sociological perspectives, nor indeed, to a narrow psychosocial perspective. Instead, they harness research findings and theoretical understandings from a range of disciplines and research traditions in order to explain the social phenomena constituting the focus of their chapters, paying special attention to the symbolic and the social, political and inter-personal forces structuring these phenomena. For instance, Chapter 14 employs feminist and specifically poststructuralist theory and research to examine heterosexuality. Chapter 18, which explores how violence can be understood and prevented, emphasises the benefits of using a public health model in conjunction with social and psychological frameworks. An historian writes Chapter 15, which offers an historical account of a set of representations of masculinity and homosexuality as articulated in relation to race. (In regard to history, we should note at this point, it is also important in other ways. A psychology of a real, living society, rather than a hypothetical one, cannot but be interested in where that society has been and what histories have shaped the objects of study. Some theorists have spoken of social psychology as history [Gergen, 1973; 1996].)

What is social psychology all about?

US social psychology has been, and still is 'before us, ahead of us, and around us', as Serge Moscovici (1972) said.

Traditionally, social psychology has studied a fairly wide range of topics, including the topics covered in this volume. However, as you will agree, some of the issues dealt with in this volume have thus far not received the kind and degree of attention due them. One of the reasons for this perhaps is related to US (and to some extent, Western European) domination of social psychology. US social psychology has been, and still is 'before us, ahead of us, and around us', as Moscovici (1972:18) said on behalf of Western European social psychology, the other dominant influence on social psychology internationally.

The dominant orientation in social psychology that has emerged from the US is ensconced in and gives substance to ideological positions that valorise notions of what has been termed 'self-contained individualism'.

According to Foster (1991:6) the dominant orientation in social psychology that has emerged from the US is ensconced in and gives substance to ideological positions that valorise notions of what has been termed 'self-contained individualism'. Moreover, this orientation is essentially positivistic, with a strong bias toward experimental research. However, after the late 1960s, European social psychologists increasingly began to question this orientation with its sharp focus on the individual and experimental research, and its patent neglect of the 'social' in social psychology. Consequently, a social psychology began to emerge in Europe that manifestly focused more sharply on the social, as opposed to the individual (see Tajfel, 1972). Harré, Moscovici, Secord and Tajfel ranked amongst the foremost proponents of this European orientation.

Foster (1991) identifies a third geographically linked orientation, namely, an explicitly political orientation that has emerged particularly from low-income and globally marginalised countries. This social psychology favours the study of issues-related oppression and the application of social psychological insights in ways that will enhance the living conditions of people, particularly marginalised groups. Hussein Abdilahi Bulhan (in Foster, 1991) can be considered a key proponent of this orientation (see Chapter 6 in this volume for a discussion of the work of Bulhan).

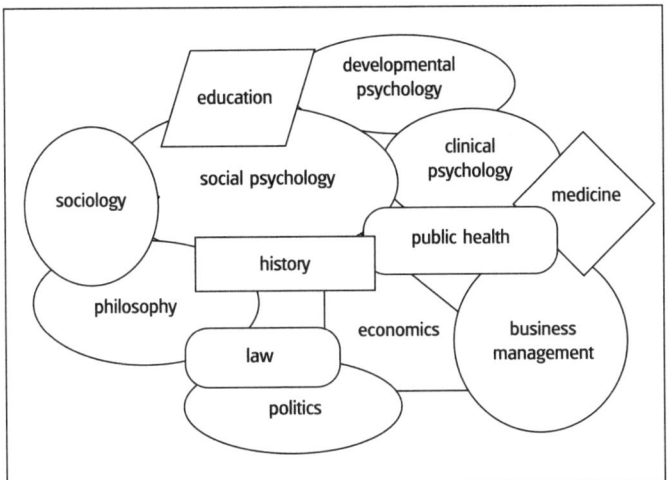

Figure 1.1
The influences and ties of social psychology

Where can South African psychology be located in relation to these orientations? It is difficult to say, as no substantive research has been conducted on the issue. A cursory examination of social psychology publications that have emerged from South Africa over the last eight decades or so seems to indicate that for the better part of the twentieth century South African social psychology has been heavily influenced by both the US and Western European variants of social psychology. The 1980s and 1990s, however, saw an increasing visibility of a variant of South African social psychology that could be seen to fall into the third orientation identified above (see Seedat, 1990).

Although there has been social psychological research since the beginnings of psychological studies in South Africa in the early twentieth century, and specifically since the 1920s, the present volume is only the second one to be published on social psychology out of South Africa. The first volume, published in 1991, consisted of a collection of 14 chapters by 12 South African psychologists and was edited by Donald Foster and Joha Louw-Potgieter.

Contest around what social psychology is about

As should be clear from the preceding discussion, social psychology is a contested field of study. This is illustrated *par excellence* by the existing definitions of the sub-discipline. In this regard, consider the following selection of definitions.

According to Baron and Byrne social psychology is 'the scientific field that seeks to understand the nature and causes of individual behavior and thought in social situations' (1997:6). In an earlier edition of the textbook, the authors defined social psychology as a field of study that focuses on 'the manner in which the behaviour, feelings, thoughts of one individual are influenced and

According to Baron and Byrne social psychology is 'the scientific field that seeks to understand the nature and causes of individual behavior and thought in social situations' (1997:6).

Social psychology is a field of study that focuses on 'the manner in which the behavior, feelings, thoughts of one individual are influenced and determined by the behavior and/or characteristics of others' (Baron & Byrne, 1981:7).

McGrath (1970:1), defined social psychology as the study of how human behaviour is influenced by the presence, behaviour, and products of other human beings, individually and collectively, past, present, and future.

Sherif and Sherif (1969:8) defined social psychology as 'the scientific study of the experience and behavior of the individual in relation to social stimulus situations'.

Traditionally social psychology has sought to understand an individual's thoughts, feelings and actions in relation to other individuals' thoughts, feelings and actions.

determined by the behavior and/or characteristics of others' (Baron & Byrne, 1981:7).

McGrath (1970:1), in an even earlier text, defined social psychology as the study of how human behaviour is influenced by the presence, behaviour, and products of other human beings, individually and collectively, past, present, and future. He saw social psychology as 'an interdisciplinary field of study analogous to the field of biophysics', located between psychology and sociology. It is 'that part of psychology which is concerned with human behavior in relation to the social parts of the environment', and which 'deals with human behaviour as it is influenced by the presence, beliefs, actions, and symbols of other men [sic]' (*ibid.*:9).

Prior to McGrath (1970), Sherif and Sherif (1969:8) defined social psychology as 'the scientific study of the experience and behavior of the individual in relation to social stimulus situations'. Along similar lines, Aronson (1984:6), in *The Social Animal*, would define social psychology as studying 'the influences people have upon the beliefs of others'. According to him, the social psychologist studies social situations that affect people's behaviour. Focusing on the relational, Kenneth Gergen and Mary Gergen (1981:5) present social psychology as a sub-discipline 'devoted to the systematic study of human interaction and its psychological basis with a focus on the "individual actor" and the "internal" processes of the individual.' Perhaps the most circulated definition of social psychology is that by Gordon Allport. Allport (1968) defined social psychology as an attempt to understand and explain how the thought, feeling, and behaviour of individuals are influenced by the actual, imagined, or implied presence of others.

As suggested earlier, definitions are never neutral, nor innocent. Take for instance the concept of 'the individual' in some of the definitions above. While this concept is central to the dominant representation of psychology, it is not unproblematic. Indeed, as Russel Spears and Ian Parker (1996) observe, individuality is the grand illusion of psychology.

Perhaps it should be noted here that a focus on the individual *per se* is not necessarily problematic. For example, for certain groups of people engaged in socio-political struggles for the recognition of their human dignity and for the right to be viewed and treated as individuals, the valorisation of the individual, in itself, may not constitute a problem. However, the historical prioritisation of the individual and individualism in a discipline that ostensibly seeks to understand the social is unquestionably problematic.

Another notion that is not as unproblematic as it seems is that of 'science'. As evident in the definitions provided above, 'science' is the status that many social psychologists, including Baron and Byrne (1997) and Sherif and Sherif (1969), claim for social psychology. As Sherif and Sherif (*ibid.*:8) argue, while 'policy makers, religious leaders, novelists, and commentators on the social scene cannot be held accountable for adhering to the ground rules of communicability and reproducibility of methods that permit verification – *social psychologists* are.' Similarly, Baron and Byrne posit that 'many persons seem to believe that the term science refers primarily to fields such as chemistry, physics, and biology. Such persons may find somewhat puzzling our view that social psychology, too, is scientific ... Although the topics that social psychologists study are very different from those in the physical or biological science, the methods we employ are similar in nature and orientation. For this reason, it makes sense to describe social psychology as basically scientific in nature' (1997:6–8). However, the narrow conceptions of 'science' that have dominated psychology (i.e. as being neutral, exact, aspiring to find absolute truths, above politics) make this aspiration of social psychology to be a science somewhat problematic (see Seedat, 1990).

To get back to the definitions of social psychology, it is perhaps worth reiterating that definitions are never entirely neutral and innocent, because how a discipline is defined determines what it regards as worth studying, as well as which questions it asks and which answers it seeks. And the questions it asks and the answers it searches for serve as lenses through which it perceives and analyses objects, events, processes, interactions, and relationships. In general, a definition of a discipline directs the attention and activities of those working within it. It determines what is important to look for, where to look for it, and how to go about looking for it. Having accepted a definition, some aspects of objects, events, processes, and so on become salient while others do not.

While there are common threads linking the many extant definitions of social psychology, most of these definitions are also fairly different in very

Social Psychology is a sub-discipline 'devoted to the systematic study of human interaction and its psychological basis with a focus on the "individual actor" and the "internal" processes of the individual' (Gergen & Gergen, 1981:5).

Gordon Allport (1968) defined social psychology as an attempt to understand and explain how the thought, feeling, and behaviour of individuals are influenced by the actual, imagined, or implied presence of others.

important ways, and therefore can be quite confusing to the student entering the field. Drawing on the work of other left-leaning psychologists, such as Kenneth Gergen and Michael Billig, and emphasising the differences, disagreements, and dissensions within social psychology, Foster (1991:4) perspicaciously characterises the sub-discipline as follows, and thereby offers us a route out of the immobilising range of divergent definitions of the sub-discipline:

> In the present view, social psychology is not a static and unitary field, discipline or endeavour. It has changed, and will change of over historical times ... It becomes transformed across national, interdisciplinary and other contextual boundaries ... It is 'policed', guarded and altered within institutions and organisations of varying and changing degrees of power: universities, professional societies, journals and publishing houses. Depending on its particular emphasis it claims different heroes and fools; its identity is structured by varying histories which mark some successes and others failures. Social psychology is a human invention and creation, and like other human endeavours is subject to indefinite possibilities of debate and challenge ... yet simultaneously is subject to social, historical and cultural contexts.

A social psychology of an actual, living society

At times it seems that social psychologists, like other categories of psychologists and social scientists, are interested more in legitimating their claims to knowledge and their social authority than in confronting actual problems that face the societies in which they live and work. Perhaps this is truer for contexts other than the USA, for as Moscovici (1972:19) observes,

> The real advance made by American social psychology was not so much in its empirical methods or in its theory construction as in the fact that it took for its theme of research and for the contents of its theories the issues of its own society. Its merit was as much in its techniques as in translating the problems of American society into sociopsychological terms and in making them an object of scientific enquiry.

Even in the US, though, the social and other psychologies that were legitimated and practised have tended to suit and address mostly the problems of the economic, social, and political majority, viz the White middle-class in general, and the male of that race-sex class in particular. The tragedy for social psychology internationally is that social psychologists in the USA have for a long time set the tune for the discipline; a tune that many researchers and educators from other parts of the world have been content to dance to.

What Henri Tajfel said about the identity crisis and the challenges to its social authority that European social psychology faced back in the 1970s applies to us. Here we note that Parker (1989) has observed that the crisis of social psychology is a *permanent* one, and that there is not one, but a number of criss-crossing dilemmas that the discipline faces. In any case, Tajfel's point was that social psychology 'is a discipline which, in principle, should be able to contribute a great deal to the interpretation of contemporary social phenomena' as its 'aim is the explanation of social life of individuals and of groups' (1972:1). If this is what social psychology should be doing, then the sub-discipline is unquestionably under-achieving in the South African context.

Any *social* psychology must, by definition, be *a* psychology of *a* society – that is to say, to be truly social, it must be concerned with specific contexts, contexts inhabited by real, living people; people inhabiting bodies, living in specific communities, with particular histories, not abstractions. What this implies is that if there is person called a social psychologist, sitting in an office somewhere in Grahamstown or Pretoria, furiously writing clever articles on people she or he has never interacted with, and wanting to pass these articles off as saying something worthwhile about real South Africans, that expert really cannot expect to be taken seriously. Indeed, such a person cannot have much respect for the people and society she or he is writing about. However erudite that 'social psychologist', he or she cannot have the development of a social psychology relevant to the society in which he or she is located at heart.

A psychology that wants to be taken seriously by the society it seeks to address cannot but be rooted in that society, yet should also avoid ingratiating itself with the powerful social groups.

If social psychology has not grown out of the social context it seeks to understand and engage with, and if it regards itself as the psychology of every society on earth, then it cannot be a psychology that is appropriate for any one social context. In relation to this, Wetherell (1996:1) argues, 'just as there is no *the* history, say of the national liberation, there is no *the* social psychology'. This does not mean, as you may come to agree on reading the different chapters in this book, that we have to throw up our hands and write off social psychology. For, as will become apparent from a reading of the chapters contained in this volume, social psychology has some value.

The value of social psychology, or any psychology for that matter, is judged by the extent to which the society it seeks to address takes it seriously. To be taken seriously by the people it seeks to address, social psychology will have to learn to be genuinely social, without being overly sociable. This, in other words, does not mean a social psychology has to be a lackey of the ruling ideas or classes of society. In fact, a *social* social psychology must challenge the ruling ideologies. But it has to be rooted in society.

A social psychology that wants to be taken seriously will know that it is important to work towards a more ethical society, a society that values the dignity of people and positive human relations. While social psychologists get on with the work of building theory and doing research, they will also step out onto the streets to work with communities and individuals to help them deal with the obstacles, the pain, the distortion, the injustice that confront them in their society. They will want to go beyond the trauma to see how humans can live better. Our responsibility, as scholars and students, to our society (despite its brutal history) is to ensure that we do not limit ourselves to talking from and working at the margins. We need not be at the margins, except as a deliberate *tactical* move. Our responsibility is to employ social psychology to work towards better racial, gender, economic, cultural, and interpersonal relations.

Any social psychology must be a psychology of an actual society of real living people with embodied psyches in relationship to one another, existing in specific communities, with particular histories.

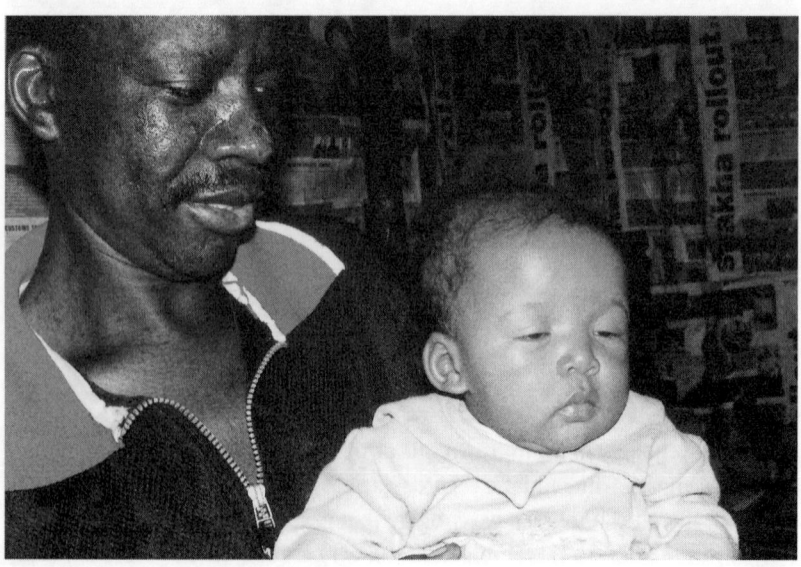

About this volume

Having noted the fact that social psychologists study a wide range of topics, the idea of this volume has been to look at some of those topics that are most pertinent to social psychology in South Africa. But perhaps it is important to clarify that statement. To suggest that a range of topics make up a discipline needs clarification as topics do not really of themselves constitute a discipline. The truth is, no amount of subjects in and of themselves constitute and can exhaust a discipline: there are always new topics to pursue; topics falling out of favour; new ways of looking at old topics. More importantly, social psychology, or, for that matter, anthropology, sociology, or gender studies, are not shopping lists of topics. Neither is social psychology a textbook that must start with the biological bases of behaviour, sensation and perception, through language, learning, and cognitive process, and intelligence, development, to personality theory, stress, and ending with psycho-pathology and therapy and social behaviour, with a sprinkling of boxes on sex, gender, culture, and race. Similarly, social psychology is not a bunch of chapters that must include the self, attitudes, persuasion, experimental research methods, statistical analyses, social cognition, attributions, self-perception, and self-schemata, non-verbal communication, self-concept, inter-personal attraction and anti-social behaviour, inter-group conflict, the nature of crowds, social influence leadership, decision making, and territoriality.

A discipline, as suggested earlier, is constituted by 'looking' at and 'thinking' on the subjects it eventually chooses to study. 'Looking' and 'thinking' in this instance is another way of talking about perspective or approach and frameworks of understanding. To say 'looking' and 'thinking' is shorthand for saying the sum of philosophical grounds, of *ontology, paradigmatic assumptions, epistemology, methodologies* and *techniques.* Fields of study are constituted by how they define the nature of reality; by what their exponents count as knowledge in their defined area of study; by the models which they follow in practising their discipline; and how those who work in the area approach their chosen topics of study (Mouton, 1996; Terre Blanche & Durrheim, 1999).

But talking of ways of seeing and understanding triggers the notion of ideology. In this regard Spears and Parker (1996) have called psychology an ideology and an activity of the adherents of the *psy-complex* in Western societies and those caught it is grip. Psy-complex is a term that they take from the sociologist Nikolas Rose. It is used to refer to 'the set of theories and practices which reproduces the society from the base up, from the individual out' (Spears & Parker, 1996:1). Spears and Parker here are showing that 'psychology is more than just an academic discipline but rather that it filters out' from university halls and professional journals and conferences into the everyday world, its concepts used in a range of contexts from advertising to television sitcoms and glossy magazines (*ibid.*).

Social psychologies from three continents

A: From the USA

The following list of contents is from Robert A. Baron and Donn Byrne's (1997) *Social Psychology*. The book is in its eighth edition. It is classical in the sense of being from the United States of America. These are the list of contents:

1 The Field of Social Psychology: How We Think about and Interact with Others
2 Social Perception: Understanding Others
3 Social Cognition: Thinking about Others and the Social World
4 Attitudes: Evaluating the Social World
5 Aspects of Social Identity: Establishing One's Self and Gender
6 Prejudice and Discrimination: Understanding their Nature, Countering Their Effects
7 Interpersonal Attraction: Initial Contact, Liking, Becoming Acquainted
8 The Joys and Sorrows of Close Relationships: Family, Friends, Lovers, and Spouses
9 Social Influence: How We Change Others' Behavior – and How They Change Ours
10 Prosocial Behaviour: Helping Other People
11 Aggression: Its Nature, Causes, and Control
12 Groups and Individuals: the Consequences of Belonging
13 Social Psychology and Society: Legal and Organizational Applications
14 Social Psychology in Action: Applications to Health and Environment

B: From South Africa

The second list is from Don Foster and Joha Louw-Potgieter's *Social Psychology in South Africa*, published in 1991. This is an edited collection of writings by different contributors, dissimilar from the more traditional textbooks, such as that by Baron and Byrne, authored by only one or two scholars and teachers. Foster and Louw-Potgieter's text has the distinction of being the first and only textbook on social psychology from this country. While content lists can tell you only so much, do note the differences between the list of contents of the Foster and Louw-Potgieter volume and that of Baron and Byrne. The list of contents is as follows:

1 Introduction, by Don Foster
2 Inter-group relations: Theories and positions, by Cheryl de la Rey
3 Historical perspectives: Psychology and group relations in South Africa, by Johann Louw and Don Foster
4 Methodological perspectives, by Graham Tyson
5 Attitudes and related concepts, by Don Foster and Elizabeth Nel
6 Prejudice and racism, by John Duckitt
7 Social cognition and attributions, by Gillian Finchilescu
8 Social comparison and relative deprivation: Perceived justice and intergroup attitudes, by Ans Appelgryn
9 Contact and change, by Johan Mynhardt and Alheit du Toit
10 Language and identity, by Joha Louw-Potgieter
11 Social influence I: Ideology, by Don Foster
12 Social influence II: Majorities and minorities, by Colin Tredoux
13 Social influence III: Crowds and collective action, by Don Foster
14 A note on attitude measurement, by Don Foster

C: From the UK

The third list of contents is from *Social Psychology: Identities, Groups and Social Issues* (1996), edited by Margaret Wetherell. The book is part of the social psychology course offered at the Open University, called 'Social Psychology: Personal Lives, Social Worlds.' This, unlike the book from the USA, is a collection of writings by different scholars, and similar to (though different from) Foster and Louw-Potgieter's volume. Again, although lists can tell you only this much and no more, what do you think are the differences among the three lists? Below follows the contents list of the Wetherell volume:

Introduction, Margaret Wetherell

1   Themes in experimental research on groups from the 1930s to the 1990s, by Hedy Brown
2   A psychodynamic perspective on group processes, by Helen Morgan and Kerry Thomas
3   Attitudes, social representations and discursive psychology, by Jonathan Potter
4   Group conflict and the social psychology of racism, by Margaret Wetherell
5   Individuals and institutions: The case of work and employment, by Diane Watson
6   Life histories/social worlds, by Margaret Wetherell

Paradigm, ontology, epistemology, methodology

'Paradigm' refers to *an exemplar, a model case, or a central overall way of understanding, of thinking, of looking, of approaching phenomena* within which a social psychologist or other social scientist normally works. The paradigm *dictates what types of explanations* a social scientist finds acceptable.

Ontology is a branch of metaphysics concerned with the study of what exists. It differentiates between what *really exists* and what only *appears to exist* and investigates the ways in which entities such as numbers, physical, social, or psychological objects may be said to exist. In Social Science we tend to use ontology more in another sense, to mean the assumptions about *what is there* or *what is not there*, assumptions about existence that underlie our systems of ideas, theories, or concepts.

Epistemology refers to the branch of philosophy that concerns itself *with the theory of knowledge*. Major issues for epistemologists have traditionally been the nature, derivation, and scope of knowledge as well as the reliability of claims to knowledge.

Simply, methodology refers to *the study of method*. It is a demonstration of how a study is organised. Methodology covers the aims, specific method, procedures, and sample. Generally, in studies students are required to complete for higher degrees, one is supposed to spell out one's methodology, going into details about the *specific method* one used in getting data and in analysing it (Speake, 1979; see also Mouton, 1996; Terre Blanche & Durrheim, 1999).

At the same time as looking at and thinking about certain issues pertinent to our context therefore, some of which have received inadequate attention from social psychology, this volume attempts to push the disciplinary borders of social psychology. By marshalling social psychological frameworks to examine issues that other more traditional social psychology texts have thus far avoided, this volume seeks to deepen and broaden the limits of social psychology, and in the process to contribute to the shaping of the sub-discipline in a manner that will make it more reflective of, and responsive to, the South African reality.

It has been noted that some time ago the French theorist Serge Moscovici (1972) argued that any advance European social psychology would make would be because social psychologists on that continent turned to *their own reality*, towards the maxims from which they must derive their own scientific consequences. In his view, as we well know here, 'the fact that social psychology is almost exclusively American is a handicap' (*ibid.*:19). What we sought with this volume, therefore, was to bring together scholars who would foreground and identify a specific and real problem and examine it in their contributions. Having done so they would write their way through the identified problems. They would use up-to-date empirical findings and theoretical work. And they would offer solutions by the end of their contributions, even if these were only tentative.

Importantly, however, we were desirous for authors to approach their objects of study from a socially and politically informed perspective. This was to be achieved, not by means of the add-and-stir approach, and certainly not by relegating society and politics to the margins of the volume, as is the case in volumes where authors have a few boxes on sex, gender, culture, race and other such 'non-psychological' topics to appease the barbarians waiting at the gates. This tends to be how many of the psychology textbooks from the United States of America used in our universities deal, or do not deal, with social and political information.

In approaching their topics, the contributors to this book depart from the premise that their topics have histories, that all social psychological phenomena have a political element, and yes, that these topics *become* topical because of particular conditions and get salience from specific cultural milieu. The authors thus give special consideration to how, for instance, the trajectories of their objects of study intersect and are structured by, *inter alia*, poverty, socio-political change, sexuality, race, and gender. Here the aims were to make the study of psychology in general and social psychology specifically less closed and more engaging, less sterile and alienating and more useful and enjoyable, especially for the people who have historically not been able to read about themselves and their communities in psychology textbooks. These people, in our thinking, include students from rural, poor, and working-class backgrounds, Blacks, females, and gays and lesbians.

Summary of sections and chapters

In talking about how people make sense of and tell stories, I asked you to reflect on whether you thought the story of the family de Beer and Loraine Ramsamy was about racism or not. I asked whether you believe racism may still be a problem in post-apartheid South Africa or not. If it is, I asked, how does it manifest itself and how is it reproduced? And then I asked if you would say the love affair and secret marriage of Loraine and Louis was a form of resistance or not. This last question is related to the questions asked in Chapter 5, namely, whether instances in our country's past, where a person got him- or herself reclassified as White (when they had been officially classified Coloured) or Coloured (when they had been officially categorised Black), could be considered as a form of resistance, or whether all 'passing' or race-changing must be considered a collusion with or submission to oppression.

Now, it has been noted that one of the aims of this volume of chapters is to focus on and address questions that face us today in our society and communities from a social psychological perspective. The questions in the preceding paragraph are some of those. Other questions asked in the volume are whether we can get any help from the work of Frantz Fanon, the psychiatrist from Martinique who wrote *Black Skin, White Masks* on these and other questions of identification, relational life in the post-colony, and resistance? Of what utility is his notion of pathologies of liberty to understanding our condition? How does socio-political transition affect age, race and gender identities? What are the sources of violence against women, and how do women resist such violence? What are the convergences and differences between feminist and psycho-dynamic theories, and how do they enable us to understanding intimate partner homicide? Is there a relation between intimacy and identity? Is lesbianism foreign to African societies and what are the dominant ideas of men, women and heterosex? What discursive strategies have been deployed to construct homosex as deviant? How has heterosex been constructed as normative in the South African media in the past? How does a society achieve reconciliation and what is the role of political leaders, as distinct from other members of society, in this process? What are the factors related to children being on the streets? Is violence preventable?

These, then, are some of the questions the volume examines. They are consequential questions in that they are at the centre of a range of historical, social, political and psychological problems South Africa and other societies like ours are confronting today. These questions knock at the door of traditional social psychological methods and analytical frameworks. They force us to stay in touch with developments beyond the blurry boundaries of the discipline, if, that is, we want to deepen our understanding of our objects of study. And the responses the contributors to this volume offer to the questions are as trenchant as many provided by other social psychologists or social scientists.

You will see that each chapter begins with certain learning objectives towards which the authors work. You will also see that chapters include useful photographs, boxes, illustrations, exercises, and questions. The intention with these learning aids is to enliven learning and, of greater importance, to foster independent, critical thinking. Nevertheless, or perhaps because we found it desirable to inspirit the text with instructional aids, you will also find that the chapters are scholarly, that they are critical, that some are densely written, and that different chapters may approach the same subject from differing perspectives. The debates are at times overt and at other times implicit. This is an important aspect of the volume that should perhaps be emphasised. The intention of this volume is of course to introduce students to, and instruct them in, the issues and debates that go into making social psychology. However, at the same time, the contributors to this volume (most of us being university teachers and researchers) seek to develop radical citizens and foster free thinkers, and so to expose the differences in perspective and the often-unarticulated debates between themselves. In this respect, intellectual dissension and critical dialogue among ourselves is more than acceptable.

The present chapter is one of two making up Part I of the volume, which essentially focuses on what social psychology is and what to do with it. In the other chapter in this section, Anthony Collins writes on research methodology in social psychology.

While race and racial identification are themes that traverse the better part of the entire volume, Part II of the volume is dedicated to looking at different aspects of this theme, from racial identities in the (post)colony and racism, to bodies, self-definition and racial classification. This is the bulkiest of the five parts of the volume. This should be so, given that racial identity, racial prejudice, discrimination, and an oppressive racist economic and socio-political structure have been at the basis of our lives and troubled our psyches and inter-personal relationships for so long. In Chapter 3 Cheryl de la Rey and Norman Duncan cast a wide-angle look at racism. Chapter 4, by Norman Duncan, focuses on 'race' and racism in the media. In Chapter 5 Kopano Ratele examines bodies, apartheid, and national freedom. In Chapter 6 Derek Hook looks at the work of Frantz Fanon in relation to racial identity in (post)colonial contexts. Garth Stevens and Rafiq Lockhat's chapter (7) is on Black adolescent identity during and after apartheid. Chapter 8 is co-authored by Vijé Franchi and Tanya Swart, and focuses on identity dynamics and the politics of self-definition.

Part III of the volume deliberates on issues of inequality, intimate relations, and gendered violence. The first chapter (9) in this section is by Floretta Boonzaier, and offers a critical review of the literature on woman abuse. Chapter 10 provides an international perspective, specifically a French perspective, on the same problem, namely, that of violence against women. In this chapter,

Patricia Mercader, Annik Houel, and Helga Sobota analyse what are frequently referred to as 'crimes of passion' in relation to gender inequality. Chapter 11, which is written by Nthabiseng Motsemme, focuses on Black women's identities. Kopano Ratele authors Chapter 12, which deals with mixed relations.

Part IV provides a critical look at the histories, present circumstances and future possibilities around sexualities and masculinities. In Chapter 13 Cheryl Potgieter writes on lesbianism. Tammy Shefer examines the notion of heterosexuality in Chapter 14. Chapter 15, by Lindsay Clowes, an historian, looks at the histories and relationship of 'race', masculinity, and homosexuality. The chapter is anchored in representations of these issues in the old *Drum* magazine.

The last section of the volume, Part V, provides a direct look at socio-political change. Chapter 16, by Shahnaaz Suffla and Mohammed Seedat, focuses on political leadership in the context of reconciliation. In Chapter 17 Vuyisile Mathiti turns to a problem that has come to trouble many of us, literally spilling out onto the streets – children on or of the streets. The last chapter (18) is by Garth Stevens, Mohammed Seedat and Ashley van Niekerk. Moving from description and analysis to social action, this chapter offers critical ways to understand and prevent violence.

Some of the overarching intentions and aims of the volume

Some of the overarching intentions of this volume are that after reading it and any of the chapters one would be able to:

- understand and describe for oneself what social psychology is all about
- have a deeper appreciation of the deep and complex inter-connections of the inner, intra-psychic, private life and the outer, socio-political, public life
- discuss identities and relational life more critically
- evaluate the true value of social psychology to one's self and society
- follow and understand the key concepts and theoretical and empirical facts of social psychology in general and those deployed in any one chapter
- enter into a critical discussion around concepts, theories and research findings detailed in the different chapters

- intelligently and critically apply social psychology to enduring, everyday social problems
- apply the insights offered by social psychology to different community contexts
- respond to the exercises at the end of the different chapters
- pursue a particular issue raised in a chapter that one found interesting or troubling by undertaking further research on it in order to better understand it
- recognise that knowledge in general is provisional and related to power, and
- understand that psychological knowledge is historically contingent, socio-politically embedded, and related to power.

Exercises for critical engagement

Note: you will gain optimal benefit from the exercises if you do them with one or two other people.

1 With your chosen partner, read the story of the De Beer family and Loraine Ramsamy. After going through the story, you should each write your own version of the story. Write the story in your own words, as though you are relating it to your partner. After having written the story, swap stories and consider the following questions:

2 What did you render significant in your partner's story that you think was not so significant in the story as told by Prega Govender? Did s/he present it as the story of the De Beer family and Loraine Ramsamy, as it was presented in my version, or did s/he present it as the story of Louis and Loraine? Was the relationship between men and women more important in your partner's story, or was the relationship between fathers and their sons or that between Whites and Indians/Asians more important? What aspects of the story were most important in her or his presentation?

3 Read the textbox on 'Social psychologies from three continents' again, as well as the definition given in here and in other books on social psychology. Among the three psychologies, tell your partner which is your preferred one and why. Among the definitions you have read, tell which is your preferred one and why. Each of you must now write down your own succinct definition of social psychology, before showing it to one another.

4 We have argued that social psychology is not a collection of topics. Having said that, and having had you define what social psychology is all about for you, put together a list of twenty subjects that you would write a textbook on if you were to be so inclined.

Recommended reading

Baron, R.A. & D. Byrne (1997). *Social psychology*, 8th Edition. Boston: Allyn and Bacon.

Foster, D. & J. Louw-Potgieter (Eds.) (1991). *Social psychology in South Africa*. Johannesburg: Lexicon Publishers.

Parker, I. (1989). *The Crisis in Modern Social Psychology – and How to End it*. London: Routledge.

Wetherell, M. (Ed.) (1996). *Social Psychology: Identities, Groups and Social Issues*. London: Sage.

Social Psychology and Research Methods

Anthony Collins

OUTCOMES

After having studied this chapter you should be able to answer the following questions:

- What are the advantages and disadvantages of experimental design as a research method in social psychology?
- How do discourse analysts understand the nature of language and how does this differ from traditional views of language?
- What are discourses, and why should we study them?
- What important discourses have been identified in local research on gender and HIV/AIDS?
- Based on this research, what can be done to reduce the spread of HIV/AIDS in South Africa?
- What can you do with discourse analysis methods, and what can't you do with them?

SOCIAL PSYCHOLOGY has a long history of debate about the best ways of doing research. From the outset, the academic discipline of psychology was defined in terms of its commitment to scientific methods, and social psychology followed this example. This meant that the ideal research design was the scientific experiment: the researcher created a controlled environment where s/he could change one detail and observe the effects that followed. A good example of this kind of research design is Milgram's famous investigation of obedience to authority (Milgram, 1963; 1974). Milgram asked volunteers to take part in what they were told was an investigation into the effects of punishment on learning. The volunteers had to give electric shocks to learners whenever they made a mistake in recalling words from a list. In fact the learners were just acting and no real shocks were being given – what was really being investigated was how far the volunteers would go in obeying the experimenter's instructions even while they thought they were giving increasingly painful and dangerous shocks. This obedience to authority was what was really being measured (*ibid.*).

Experimental design in social psychology

An experimental design allows a researcher to create a controlled situation where s/he can ensure that the results are not influenced by uncontrolled factors.

Confounding factors: Influences beyond the experimenter's control that change the results of an experiment in unknown ways.

Why is this a good example of an experimental design? It allows the experimenter to create a controlled situation where s/he can ensure that the experimental results are not being influenced by other outside factors. Confounding factors – influences beyond the experimenter's control that change the results – could be kept to a minimum as it was easy to ensure that conditions were the same each time the experiment was run: the same instructions, the same learners' reactions, and so on. The only changes were those that were deliberately introduced by the experimenter, so it was easy to conclude that it was those changes that caused the different results. Hence, clear relationships of cause and effect could be identified.

Very importantly, the results could be quantified. Human social life doesn't always just happen in convenient isolated units, so it is very important for the experimenter to turn it into specific behaviours that can be observed and measured. In this case, the degree of obedience to authority could be directly translated into the voltage at which the volunteers refused to carry on giving shocks. There was thus no need to get into the murky area of trying to interpret their internal psychological states or make inferences about their motives. Thus the experimenter could claim that the results were objective – based on simple direct observation, without having to resort to subjective interpretations that would be hard to verify. Also, because the results were in measurable units, statistical methods could easily be used to show various relationships between the findings.

It was also a good experimental design because it was easy to create variations on the original experiment to see what the effects would be. This is exactly what Milgram and others then did: in different versions they changed the person giving the instructions from a scientist to a civilian, they introduced physical contact between the person giving and the person receiving the shocks, and they had other volunteers in the same room refuse to give the shocks. Each change had different results and they were thus able to draw important inferences about what factors make people more or less inclined to obey authority. A further advantage of this design was that it was easy to reproduce, and anyone anywhere else could repeat exactly the same experiment to verify the results.

A quick examination of mainstream social psychology journals shows that this experimental ideal is still the goal of most research in the field. In fact, one is sometimes left wondering if most research is not more about the idea of experimental design and related displays of statistical calculation than about understanding the most urgent questions regarding human social life. Against this trend it has been argued that experiments are sometimes trivial because in the attempt to create controlled conditions, the situations that are produced are so artificial and unlike the everyday world that they undermine the meaningfulness of the results. The criticism here is that the experiments might not have ecological validity, that is to say, that the findings in the laboratory might not hold true in the complex social worlds in which people live their actual everyday lives.

Beyond experimental design

Many alternatives have been proposed. It has been argued that social psychologists could instead focus on studying people in their ordinary social worlds. The clear advantage here is that it avoids the contrived artificiality of the laboratory, but by the same token it loses the element of control and it becomes harder to determine exactly what causes are responsible for exactly what effects. It has been suggested that perhaps social psychologists should be less concerned with measuring behaviours and take note of the fact that what is essentially human and psychological about people is that their actions are meaningful, and that it would thus be more appropriate to study how people understand what they do, rather than treating them as machines that just respond automatically to external stimuli. It has also been proposed that social psychologists move towards a much more encompassing notion of the social – not just how individuals can influence other individuals in small social groups, but how people can be deeply influenced by the entire culture, society and history in which they find themselves.

The aim here is not to explore these arguments and the many different theoretical approaches and research methods that have emerged from them, although they make a fascinating area for further study. Instead I will exclusively focus on one of the recent approaches that has tried to respond to these problems and that is becoming increasingly influential amongst people who believe that a social psychology that is serious about tackling the challenges of contemporary South African society will need to move beyond is roots in USA-based and -derived experimental science.

Although it is relatively easy to move from experimental design to naturalistic observation, the shift from observing individual behaviours to investigating broader social processes is a more complex one. It is easy to measure behaviour, but it is not so easy to observe a meaning or a social process. Social psychologists have also tended to shy away from broad social theories that attempt to explain relationships between people and their social worlds. Thus, many of the critical challenges to traditional social psychology have focused on the need to develop a stronger theoretical framework in this area. Although there is little agreement on the best way to proceed, the example below will illustrate how discourse analysis has been found useful by some social psychologists.

Although it is relatively easy to move from experimental design to naturalistic observation, the shift from observing individual behaviours to investigating broader social processes is a more complex one. It is easy to measure behaviour, but it is not so easy to observe a meaning or a social process.

Social psychology should study people in their ordinary worlds.

If we want to find out about people's experience rather than just their behaviour, speaking is probably the best, if not the only, tool we can use.

Language and discourse analysis

I wish to begin by arguing that if we want to find out about people's experience rather than just their behaviour, speaking is probably the best, if not the only, tool we can use. Language is after all, a specialised tool developed precisely for people to communicate their experiences with each other. While question-naires and interviews have long been an established way of doing this kind of research, more recently an approach known as *discourse analysis* was developed by people interested in studying the relationship between society and the individual.

Discourse analysis or conversation analysis

Confusingly, there are two different approaches in psychology, both called discourse analysis. It is not necessary that you understand the complex technical differences between them, but just in case you encounter them later in your studies, it might be useful to state that the version I am referring to here comes from cultural studies and looks at how language structures people's thought in ways that reflect the particular social system. The other version, also called conversation analysis, draws on linguistics and is less concerned with the way the social world is organised and how this affects people.

To understand discourse analysis, we need to grasp some important ideas about language that are very different from our traditional understandings.

Discourse analysis attempts to work out from what people say what underlying system of ideas is structuring their thoughts, words and experiences.

The traditional view assumes that reality consists of things (like dogs, cats and rats) that exist independently of our perceptions of them, and that words are just useful name tags that people use to refer to them. Similarly these things have properties and interact in specific ways that we can observe and then describe using language. In this view, science is the business of making rigorous observations and then carefully building theories to explain these observations. The important concern is that the observer should see and describe exactly what is taking place in the external world, and not allow his or her perceptions to be influenced by any errors, distortions or personal bias.

Discourse analysts take an alternative view, and argue that language is not simply a set of labels that we use to refer to things we experience, but rather that languages are systems of organisation that shape the way we experience things in very important ways. They organise our perceptions and thoughts by giving us the categories, concepts and systems of explanation that we use to interpret sensory information. Experience is not just the awareness of what is going on outside us, but an interpretation of those things. Our cultures give us these interpretations by providing us with language, which is here taken in the very broad sense of not only words, but all the symbols, myths, customs, rituals and systems of explanation that we use to make the world meaningful.

To give a very simple example, the word *dog* is not simply a convenient label for those four-legged things that yap when we walk past. Rather, it is because we have the word *dog* to think with that we automatically see idiotic Maltese poodles, vicious Rottweilers, and friendly Labradors as a fundamentally similar group of creatures, quite different from, say, cats or rodents. Another culture might have a completely different system of organisation, where instead of differentiating dogs, cats and rodents it might have categories which rather differentiate friendly animals (including spaniels, Siamese cats and domesticated mice), and dangerous animals (like pit-bulls, tigers and cane rats). In this culture, creatures within each of these two groups (friendly vs. dangerous) would automatically be experienced as having more in common with each other than they have with members of the other group, and the differences we make between the various members of each group would seem quite arbitrary, strange and unnecessary. The real difficulty is for us to imagine that our system is not the only possible one, and to realise that the main reason we tend to think that ours is more sensible, obvious or correct, is simply because it happens to be more familiar to us.

The next important idea is that if languages do not simply label the objects in the world, they do reflect something else that was not fully appreciated before: the way in which that society structures the experiences of individuals. For instance, a racist society will provide categories for dividing people into racial groups. When members of this society are in the presence of others, their experience will be shaped by those racial categories. They will not be aware of this process, but will simply experience people as belonging to particular races – race will be seen as an intrinsic property that can be clearly observed in people, and it will not be noticed that it is in fact a set of social categories that are shaping what is being seen. The racist society will probably also provide a whole system of explanation of these racial categories, with details of the qualities of each race, where they came from, what their position in the society is or should be, and how different races should interact with each other. Here again, any given individual will not necessarily be consciously aware of these ideas, but will automatically use them for thinking, and their experience of others will be structured by these ideas.

These clusters of ideas are what we call *discourses*. In doing discourse analysis we attempt to work out, from what people in a particular group say, what underlying system of ideas is structuring the way they think and experience things. These individuals are usually not consciously aware of the discourse, and the researcher has to notice the patterns in what is said in order to identify the structure that is shaping the way they think. Unlike a survey which investigates how many people say a particular thing, discourse analysis tries to get underneath the specific things that are said, to understand the way underlying organisation of ideas produces the beliefs or behaviours that people report. So a survey might find that, for example, despite awareness of AIDS, 38 per cent of sexually active South African university students say that it is not necessary to use condoms when having sex with a partner with whom they have a long-term relationship. Discourse analysis would try to go further than this claim, getting people to talk more about relationships, sex and related matters and then examine the patterns that emerge and how these reflect whole systems of thinking that shape their sexual experiences and behaviour. This analysis might then be able to identify underlying cultural ideas, such as romantic love, showing how it includes feelings of trust and safety that cause individuals to misjudge their risk of HIV infection, leading them to unsafe sexual practices in their long-term relationships.

Discourse analysis is of course not limited to spoken accounts – it can be done on material where meaning can be uncovered, be it written articles, adverts, TV programmes, fashion trends, social customs, or any other behaviour where underlying conventions shape the meanings of what is done.

One of the difficulties in doing discourse analysis is that we tend to take the way we think as being just common sense, so obviously true and right that we can't even ask questions about it. To do discourse analysis we need some distance from which to critically reflect on our own thinking. This can be done in various ways, for instance by contrasting the way a society has thought about something at different periods in time, by comparing different cultures, or by looking from a different position within the society. It is often easier for an outsider or someone from a marginalised group to see what the underlying patterns are than for a person for whom everything seems natural and familiar.

It is important to note that in any society there are different discourses contradicting and competing with each other. Contradictions exist between groups and within individuals. For instance, although racism was a dominant discourse in South Africa for a long time, there was at the same time a contradictory discourse of universal human rights, and another of Black consciousness. Different individuals juggled these competing discourses

---

Discourses are systems of meaning that operate at individual, social, cultural and historical levels and inform how we interpret and understand our lived experiences. They are not the speeches and conversations, but the broad patterns of talk, systems of statements, or clusters of ideas that underlie and inform particular speeches and conversations.

In doing discourse analysis we attempt to work out, from what people in a particular group say, what underlying system of ideas is structuring the way they think and experience things.

Discourse analysis is of course not limited to spoken accounts – it can be done on material where meaning can be uncovered, be it written articles, adverts, TV programmes, fashion trends, social customs, or any other behaviour where underlying conventions shape the meanings of what is done.

differently depending on aspects of their experience. For instance, it was easier for Whites to identify with racist discourse which justified their social privilege, than for Blacks, to whom it was degrading. Nonetheless, some White South Africans identified with universal human rights against racism, and some Black South Africans in certain ways internalised the negative images of themselves circulated by apartheid. But more than this, individuals had to resolve the tensions between these discourses within themselves in various ways, and might have found themselves using different discourses in different situations or creating hybrid mixtures to try and negotiate their way through the problems of everyday life. For instance, as an employee, someone might support equality in the workplace, but as a father, the same person might fall back on racist ideas regarding who his daughter should date.

Discourse analysis has been especially useful for developing social critiques because of the way in which it goes beyond what people think to show the hidden implications and consequences of their thought, and because it not only highlights contradictions and shortcomings, but in so doing also creates the possibility of thinking differently from the way we ordinarily do.

Discourse analysis has been especially useful for developing social critiques because of the way in which it goes beyond what people think to show the hidden implications and consequences of their thought.

Two research examples

Two recent South African studies which we will now discuss investigated discourses of gender and AIDS in South Africa. Because HIV infection is very easy to avoid but expensive to treat and still cannot be cured, from the outset of the pandemic it was believed that providing people with information about prevention would be the best course of action. Education programmes had already been in place for some time, but what become clearer during the 1990s was that simply providing people with information about how HIV was transmitted and the medical consequences of AIDS would not automatically lead them to avoid situations where there was a high risk of HIV infection. Although people increasing came to know that AIDS was an incurable sexually transmitted disease that could very easily be avoided by either not having sexual intercourse or simply by using condoms when having sex, many continued to have unprotected sex and HIV continued to spread very rapidly.

Another aspect of the pandemic that became clearer during this period was the ways in which the social and economic structure of the society was affecting the spread HIV/AIDS. Poor people were at a higher risk for a number of reasons including their often already impaired health from poor nutrition, conditions of urban overcrowding with poor sanitation, and lack of access to both medical treatment and current health information.

It became important to investigate why AIDS education programmes where not working as well as had been hoped, and to examine the social and psychological factors affecting the spread of the pandemic. With this in mind,

Strebel and Lindegger (1998) did a study of discourses of women and AIDS in the Western Cape. They ran 14 *focus groups*, mostly with women recruited from a variety of different settings including clinics, community organisations, domestic workers, tertiary education students, and teachers.

Focus group

A focus group is a small group, usually of about six to twelve people, that has a focused discussion on a particular issue in which all group members are encouraged to participate and openly share their feelings and ideas. For research purposes, the discussion is often tape-recorded and then written up for analysis.

A similar study based on this one was later done by Hoosen and Collins (2001). The second study closely followed the methods suggested by Strebel and Lindegger (1998), and the striking similarities in the results strongly supported the original. However, the Hoosen and Collins (2001) study was with women from a poor community in KwaZulu–Natal, where HIV infection rates were known to be very high at that time. The study included a wide range of age groups and different situations with respect to relationships and children.

While the first study found that most of the women had a good idea of what AIDS was and the principles of how to avoid infection (but that these principles were more difficult to put into practice), the second study contradicted most previous research. The second study discovered that many of the women in fact had only a little knowledge of HIV and how to prevent sexually transmitted diseases. But the study made very similar findings to the first study in revealing how difficult it was for women to put the knowledge they did have into practice. This may indicate that there are large differences in levels of AIDS awareness in different areas, perhaps especially between rural and urban areas. It is worth noting that researchers, especially in universities, often research whoever is closest at hand, meaning that more research is done on students and their immediate social groups than on the general population. Hence, groups from different economic, cultural or geographical contexts are often not included in research, producing unrepresentative results.

The research identified two important groups of ideas in what was being said about why people did or did not practice safe sex, namely discourses of power and discourses of responsibility. Firstly, there was a discourse of male power, a whole set of ideas that revealed the underlying belief that men have the right to decide what happens in relationships, specifically that they can put themselves and their partners at risk by having multiple sexual partners and refusing to use condoms, and that the women simply have to accept this behaviour. Several factors were found to work together to produce this power.

Because of social discrimination, women were more likely to be unemployed, to be less educated, and have fewer and worse paid employment opportunities, which made them economically dependent on men and thus forced by them to tolerate abusive behaviour. In addition, certain ideas about masculinity supported these arrangements: the idea that men cannot help having multiple sex partners because of an uncontrollable sex drive that they need to express, the idea that men need to prove their manhood by having many different sexual encounters, and the idea that men need to prove their virility by having children, so they can reasonably object to the use of any contraception. There was also distressingly widespread acceptance of the idea that men could physically assault their partners if their partners objected to this behaviour.

At the same time there was a discourse of women's power. In their accounts, the women were not just victims or objects of a male sex drive, but could make their own decisions and sexual choices, both when it came to choosing sexual partners and in asserting themselves within relationships. At the same time it was made clear that the main problems they faced were created by the social position of women, and that the entire society needed to continue changing to give women equal rights and opportunities. There was also an indication that women as a group had the power to act collectively to change their situation, as they had in previous political struggles.

There was a discourse of women's power in Hoosen & Collins' (2001) study that revealed that women as a group had the power to act collectively to change their situation.

The other significant discourse to emerge was the discourse of responsibility. It was understood that individuals all need to take responsibility for their own sexual practices to protect themselves and others. It was understood that women need to be more assertive in raising issues of safe sex, such as insisting on the use of condoms and limiting promiscuity. There was also a reference to traditional practices of non-penetrative sex as a safe-sex alternative. At the same time it was clear that taking this responsibility was not always easy, and that several factors worked against it. Not only did women sometimes find that they themselves were reluctant to raise sexual issues and use condoms, but they faced the problem that often men not only fail to take responsibility for safe sex, but even actively resist changing their dangerous behaviours. Women found themselves not only economically and emotionally vulnerable at the hands of men who threatened to leave them if they insisted on safer sex practices, but often feared being physically beaten by their partners if they asserted themselves.

The gender roles provided by society in some ways empowered women by making them think about themselves as caregivers who needed to take responsibility for health issues, but also worked destructively by allowing men to be irresponsible, and even to be threatening and violent in asserting their lack of concern. The social position of women also made them more likely to be unemployed, less formally educated and trained with job skills, and paid less when they did have work. In addition they were more likely to have the responsibilities of caring for children and elders. For many this meant that they had to submit to their partner's dangerous and abusive behaviour out of sheer economic necessity and lack of social support. For these reasons women often felt individually powerless, but also at the same time felt strength in the solidarity of their shared social position, and the possibility of collectively engaging in social change.

This research made it clear that avoiding AIDS is not simply a matter of education, nor simply of understanding the psychology of the individual's reaction(s) to AIDS education, but rather of understanding the social arrangements which empower and disempower people. This means simultaneously understanding how people get the basic material necessities of survival, including examining social arrangements such as inequality in the workplace and the overall distribution of wealth in the society, and at the same time looking at the ways in which discourses structure their thinking about who they are and can be, such as the way in which ideas of gender lead men to be irresponsible and women to be submissive. The important thing to understand is how these two sides influence each other, and to grasp the ways in which discourses both reflect a system of social organisation and shape the identities of the individuals within that system.

This means that psychologists need to address not only the psychological problems of specific individuals, but also the problems in the psychological effects of the way the society is organised. In attempting to change sexual practices, they need to intervene in the different discourses that shape people, using

Avoiding HIV/AIDS is not simply a matter of education nor simply understanding the psychology of the individual's reactions to HIV/AIDS education, but also of understanding the social arrangements which empower and disempower people.

the positive possibilities against the negative. This means changing the emphasis in gender roles to safe sex as an expression of female care giving and away from risky practices that result from feminine submission. It also requires changing masculinity towards responsibility for protecting others rather then the irresponsible assertion of a 'male sex drive'. It would also entail arguing against the idea of condoms as a disruption to sexual intimacy, and instead present safe sex as a form of caring appropriate for intimate relationships. Thus this analysis leads us to both critique gender arrangements, and to use aspects of current thinking to bring about transformation in people's behaviour.

What discourse analysis can and cannot do

In these examples, discourse analysis was useful because it allowed the researchers to go beyond the idea that safe sex behaviour is simply a rational response to knowledge of HIV transmission. It also went beyond the idea that behaviour is simply caused by psychological attitudes and beliefs, and instead highlighted how the culture and society provide people with both the actual conditions in which they live, and the fundamental ideas that structure how they experience themselves and the situations they have to deal with. It further showed that these ideas are not simply abstract concepts, but shape the very way that people experience who they are and what they can do. In this case it determined something a basic as whether individuals could choose to practice safe sex.

But discourse analysis also does not allow us to reduce everything to social conditions – we cannot simply say that women don't use condoms because they are economically dependent on men. Nor can we argue that society creates discourses that control people like puppets.

Beyond discourse analysis? How the social psychologists got their facts: A post-colonial tale – part 1[1]

This is script for a video, prefaced with an explanation, which was developed as the opening lecture of an introductory course in social psychology. The aim of the video was to destabilise the ways in which social psychology is imported and marketed as an authoritative body of knowledge, typically without reflecting too deeply on the problems and limitations it might face in being implemented in local contexts. As explained here (in the preface), the strategy chosen was not to contest the arguments and findings of social psychology, but rather to subvert its method of self-presentation. Hence the video is a children's fable, a post-colonial 'Just So' story, this time told by the native, about the process of colonisation by the Western academy.

> The history which bears and determines us has the form of a war rather than that of a language: relations of power, not relations of meaning (Foucault, 1980:160)

The empire strikes back[2]

In any war over a domain of academic knowledge, a crucial site of tactical engagement is the introductory textbook. For it is here that the basic training takes place: it is the ritual of initiation that defines the battleground for the hearts and minds. The textbook is a crucial ideological apparatus in the maintenance of the bureaucracies of academic knowledge. Ostensibly its aim is to provide an introduction to the content of a particular field. In fact, its role is to constitute that field by offering a narrative that produces an effect of coherence – presenting a clearly bounded, internally consistent, meaningful and authoritative network of practices, circumscribing the domain and organising the content of the field. Not simply reflecting the field, but (re-)producing it.

The real lesson of the textbook is hidden, which serves primarily to make it unassailable. While seeming to present an overview of significant theories and research findings, it is in fact presenting the exemplars that covertly structure what is admissible in the field. Specifically, it claims to present content, while in fact trading in

method. It is not the arguments but the rules of argument; not the findings, but the research designs, that are being set in place.

As with all initiation, it is a lesson in power: not just a humiliation, but a practical assertion of who must be respected. And a second lesson: the only way to engage it is to attempt to systematically become that authority by submitting to it and proceeding to ascend its internal hierarchies. You will be assimilated. Resistance is futile. Like the nation-state, under normal conditions disciplines tacitly agree not to engage in acts of war, leaving each one to occupy itself with its own domestic administration and policing. The discipline is thus protected from outside attack by implicit non-aggression pacts, and from inside attack by the establishment of the rules of engagement that radically limit the modes of internal opposition.

Conventional war implies that the adversary accepts the rules of engagement. But in the case of an oppositional grouping that lacks a fully developed institutional military apparatus, there is the possibility of guerilla war. The guerilla army, knowing it is massively outgunned, articulates new rules of engagement. The effectiveness of the guerilla war is determined by the degree to which it manages to analyse and attack the hidden mechanisms of power, while winning popular support by exposing the way those mechanisms of power are in fact being used against the domestic population. The guerilla attack on social psychology can proceed using these very principles. Rather than accepting the tacit rules of argument and research procedures of the discipline, it should seek both to reveal these regulations, and to reveal them for what they are: the mechanisms by which the discipline excludes radical internal critique and maintains its domestic policing against other possible modes of organisation.

In the case of the introductory textbook, the attack should not contest the arguments and findings on their own terms, but expose the hidden rules of rationality and assumptions about research methodology by which it asserts its authority. This entails identifying an underlying conceptual hierarchy, in which certain terms and concepts are taken as markers of authority, while others are rendered dubious and illegitimate. Some elements may include:

science	myth
history	story
rational	emotional
objective	situated/subjective
facts	interpretations
first world	third world
man	woman
White	Black
adult	child
serious	humorous
dispassionate	manipulative
etc.	

The textbook presents its narrative as the history of scientific findings. Here science is precisely that method that avoids the mistakes of religion, superstition and myth. While these systems of ideas offer interpretations, science offers the facts. The facts are established most securely by experimental design and statistical inference. Scientific methods allow unmediated access to the material world that exists prior to human perception, and thus eliminates the distortions of subjective experience. In this way it claims the ultimate authority: it is, quite simply, and by definition, true.

The textbook's narrative is first of all rational, and emotion would be out place. It is serious and dispassionate, neither entertaining nor deliberately designed to shift your thinking in a specific way. It is told by nobody in particular and to everybody in general, as it is simply the neutral vehicle of objective truth. This is its authority, its condition of truth.

While we can show how deeply people are influenced by discourses, it is also clear that discourses don't exist except inasmuch as they are used by actual people in specific situations, and that people also have the ability to change and challenge discourses, to use different discourses against each other, or to use different parts of a discourse against other parts. Thus, while women can feel powerless to insist on safe sex practices because they believe they should be sexually submissive, they can also be motivated to change this because of their responsibilities towards their children. While they can feel powerless because of their economic dependency, they can also feel empowered by their ability to act collectively and challenge their oppression.

It is necessary to move away from the simple idea of a mechanical cause, and instead look at the ways in which systems are sustained by complex factors that interact with each other: how social conditions produce ideas, as well as how ideas produce social conditions; how beliefs shape behaviour but also how behaving in specific ways shapes what people can believe about themselves. Discourse provides a key concept in bringing these elements together, filling the gap between the social structures and individuals, without attempting to reduce either one to the other. It thus provides a useful tool for a social psychology that attempts to take both society and individuals seriously, avoiding the reductionism that has so often limited the scope of traditional scientific research in the field.

While people are influenced by discourses, discourses do not exist except as they are used by actual people in specific situations, and people have the ability to change and challenge discourses.

Beyond discourse analysis? How the social psychologists got their facts: A post-colonial tale – part 2

In the face of this apparently seamless fortification of knowledge, what is the guerilla to do? The first strategy is to reject the terms. In other words, and against this formidable seriousness, to play a joke. Against this science, a myth. Against this abstract truth, a local situated account. Against this dispassionate information, a deliberate intervention. Against this rational adult history, an imaginary children's story. Against the invisible White male voice, a Black woman speaking: not to a universal audience, but for our children. Against the tanks in the streets, some graffiti scribbled on the walls:

Many years ago, before you were born, even before your grandparents were born, maybe when your great-great-grandparents were still living, the greedy people in a faraway land devised a new plan for making money. The people of this land were crazed by money, and had tried everything to get richer and richer. They had gone around the whole world, taking everything they could find and selling it. Often they even sold things they had stolen back to the people they had stolen them from. So shameless were these people, that they even stole people and sold them, shipping them across the sea and selling them like animals to work in the fields and factories.

They kept inventing new things to sell, and made machines that could make things faster and faster so that every day there was more to sell. These machines were hungry and had to be fed all the time, so the people of this land had to look further and further for the materials to feed the machines. They spread all over the world, invading many countries, taking what they could find and forcing the inhabitants to work for them to make supplies for their devouring machines.

But our story is about a new way of making money that they invented. These people had realised that some kinds of knowledge were useful for making money, especially the technical knowledge that could be used for making new machines and new things to sell. So they became great scientists, with knowledge of all the material things in the world. And although they neglected the wisdom of other matters of life, their scientific knowledge brought them great power and wealth, riches and splendour which had never before been seen in this world. But even then they were not content, so some of them devised the plan to make money out of understanding people.

Now every culture has its ways of understanding people, and its wisdom about human matters, but these people wanted a different kind of knowledge. They had wise elders with knowledge of philosophy and religion, but they wanted their knowledge of people to be like their scientific knowledge. This knowledge should not just be the wisdom of their culture, based on everyday truths observed by people in their daily lives, or the results of debates amongst the wisest of them. It should instead be based on the experiments of scientists, like their knowledge of machines and material things in which they had already excelled. It should not just bring them sympathetic ways of understanding people, but rather technical and scientific ways of understanding how to change people.

They realised that if they could tell those in charge of the factories how to make the people who work for them work harder and more efficiently, and those in charge of countries how to make their citizens more obedient and productive, their knowledge would be worth a lot of money. So they grouped together and invented a new profession, which they called psychology.

Now all this took place in Europe and the United States of America about one hundred years ago. This new profession of psychology quickly became powerful, especially in the United States, where industry was growing at a rapid rate, and the new techniques for making workers more productive were very popular with the bosses. But the real success of this psychology came with the outbreak of fighting between some of these countries. We must remember that these people were not only insatiably greedy, but inclined to great violence, and just when it seemed that they had finished conquering all the other countries of the world, they turned on each other. Believing, as they did, that they were the centre of the world, they called this terrible outbreak of White-on-White violence World War I.

In this war the American army recruited many thousands of new soldiers, and then had to work out how to fit each person into a job they could do properly. This was difficult as these Americans were mainly an uneducated bunch, many of whom could not even read or write, and some who hardly spoke English. Here the new psychologists showed themselves to be useful. Taking the idea from IQ testing, which had already been developed for placing learners in different classes, they made tests for assessing people and streaming them according their skills and abilities, and thus helped assign the new troops into suitable positions. It soon became clear that this skill could be just as useful in the workplace, and out of this testing the field of industrial psychology was born. For the psychologists who had been dealing with emotionally disturbed people, the war was also good for business, and they had many victims of shell-shock (or post-traumatic stress disorder as it has become known) whom they could now treat and use to develop their treatments. These years were so important for American psychology that by the end of World War I, they could proudly announce that:

> As we have put more psychology into this war than any other nation, and as we have more laboratories and more men than all others, we should henceforth lead the world in Psychology ... the future of the world depends in a peculiar sense upon American psychologists (Hall, 1919:49).

As psychology grew from strength to strength, it had to show how it was different from other professional approaches to studying people. Just as it had claimed to be better than philosophy because it used experimental methods, psychology also tried to make itself separate from other area of study like anthropology, sociology, and politics by studying individuals on their own rather than groups of people. This concern with the individual fitted very well with the culture of these Europeans and Americans, who were an individualistic, selfish and uncaring people, with little sense of community. Their greedy and aggressive nature made them compete against each other to try and be richer and have more possessions, and those that were very successful in this striving liked the psychological approach most of all, because it told them that they were successful because they had greater abilities and

higher intelligence. This let them ignore the fact that the rich almost always started out with wealth and privilege, and that the poor were poor not because of laziness or stupidity, as the rich liked to believe, but because their society did not offer them the same opportunities that the wealthy were given.

So psychology carried on ignoring the problems in the culture and society, and instead looked for problems inside each individual. Psychology became powerful, as it always had friends among the privileged, and in each country the psychologists formed professional societies so that they could control who could become psychologists and how much they would get paid. Psychology grew to have large departments in the universities, with a multitude of researchers publishing in many different academic journals, and developed specialised knowledge and training in several professional areas such as clinical, educational and industrial psychology. Only a privileged few could complete these training programmes, with the hope of lucrative career ahead of them.

But because psychology was concerned only with studying individuals, a problem remained. It is obvious to us that people live in a social world, but the psychologists, having cut themselves off from the other social sciences, did not know how to think about this properly. This was a common mistake in their culture, and their greatest philosophers had said 'I think, therefore I am', not realising, as we all do, that we do not just exist in our thoughts, but in our culture, and in our relationships with those around us. Psychologists had turned this mistake into a profession, and now had to try and think of ways of solving the problems it created.

Thus, in their discipline the psychologists invented a small area called social psychology, to investigate how social groups influence individuals. They avoided questions about how cultures and societies work, and concentrated instead on studying small groups of people. Because they wanted to seem scientific, they devised experiments to examine how people would behave in different situations. Although they did many thousands of different experiments, nobody really seemed very interested in the results, and it was only after the next major outbreak of White-on-White violence (this time they called it World War II) that things started getting interesting.

This long and brutal war left the Europeans and Americans in a state of shock. Finally they realised that the science and technology that they had believed would solve all their problems could also be used destructively, and that the brutal methods that they had developed for conquering other parts of the world could just as easily be used at home. They were especially shocked by the concentration camps, realising with horror that they could treat each other the way they had previously only treated other races, and by the atomic bomb, which gave them the ability to destroy each other completely.

Finally the social psychologists became interested in why they could inflict so much harm on each other, and why violence was so common in their societies. They designed new experiments to investigate these problems, several of which became quite famous because of their disturbing results. One such experiment was done by Stanley Milgram (1963), in which he asked people to take part in a study of punishment and learning. To repeat what is outlined at the beginning of this chapter, the participants were told to give stronger and stronger shocks to learners every time they made a mistake remembering groups of words. Milgram really wanted to see how severely the participants would shock the learners before refusing to carry on with the experiment. Most of the people he asked beforehand thought that the participants would not give very strong shocks at all, but in the actual experiment most of them carried on making the shocks stronger and stronger until they were giving extremely dangerous and potentially lethal shocks to the learners when the experimenter finally told them to stop.

Another psychologist called Philip Zimbardo (1974) and his associates did a study of how people's behaviour is affected by the social roles in which they find themselves. Zimbardo's researchers got students at the elite Stanford University to set up a mock prison, where some of them played the parts of prisoners and others were guards. The participants started acting as if

their parts were real, and after a few days Zimbardo had to stop the whole study because the guards were becoming so abusive to the prisoners, who had quickly become scared and depressed.

In another famous study, Muzafer and Carolyn Sherif (Sherif *et al.*, 1961) and their colleagues took some young boys to a holiday camp to study the ways in which conflict between groups developed. The boys were divided into two groups who competed for prizes in various games and activities. The Sherifs and their colleagues found that the boys from the different groups became increasingly hostile to each other, and that this hostility carried on even when they were not competing with each other any more, and that it was very difficult to find was of reducing this conflict once it had started (Sherif & Sherif, 1969).

You might think that these disturbing findings made the social psychologists start worrying about the consequences of their culture, built as it was on ruthless competitiveness and exploitation. But this was not the case. Because they did not know how to think about culture and society, they just assumed that they had discovered the universal laws of human nature, which applied to all people everywhere. They believed that all people would behave in the destructive ways that they had seen in their experiments. They never thought about the fact that almost all their studies were done on and with middle-class White American men, and usually university students at that. But soon afterwards, some voices of discontent started to be heard in American society. Black Americans and women had grown angry that they did not have the civil rights that America so proudly claimed for all its citizens. The official discrimination against women and Blacks was challenged, and as they gradually managed to take up professional and academic positions in the field, the White men who had always run psychology were faced with criticism about the way they had assumed that their limited perspectives could explain all of human existence.

At the same time there was a bit of a squabble going on between American and European psychologists. The Americans had always been greatly impressed with the advances of the physical sciences, and had thought that the only way for psychology to become a respected field was to use the methods of the physical sciences as guidelines for their work. That is to say, that they should at all times use experimental methods in their research. Now the European psychologists argued that there were two problems with this belief. Firstly, an experiment relies on results that you can see and measure, which is a problem when you are trying to understand people, because you can't see and measure their thoughts and feelings. So all you can study is their behaviour, and it was argued that restricting yourself to examining behaviour without being allowed to talk about people's experiences meant missing the whole point of studying psychology. Secondly, the Europeans argued that people need to be understood in the social environment in which they exist, not just as isolated individuals in artificial laboratory settings. They were more influenced by ideas from the social sciences, like sociology and anthropology, than by the physical sciences. So the European social psychologists wanted to study people in real-life situations, and speak to them about their experiences.

The European social psychologists wanted to find out more about how people think, and were more willing to pay attention to the influence of culture and society in these matters. They said it was more important to study things like language and ideology, to find out how society shaped the way people think. They showed that the way in which people think about themselves and the world they live in was greatly influenced by the culture and society in which they live. These findings were very interesting, but the European social psychologists kept trying to justify their work by getting caught up in complicated philosophical arguments about language and the nature of reality, and so most of the time people didn't really understand what they were talking about.

In any case the American social psychologists were not very concerned with these arguments. Although they also wanted to make their work relevant for current social issues, nobody really paid much attention to them, and they had to get on with the business of making money. All that was left for them to do was to design more and more experiments and publish them in academic journals, which nobody else really read. But at least this helped them to get jobs in universities, teaching learners about all these experiments that they had done. Some of them even wrote big textbooks, with glossy pages and pictures, telling of all the things they had found. They sold these textbooks all over the world (even here), where university lecturers prescribed them for students of psychology. If you look around, you are sure to see them.

So now when you see learners weighed down with big books on social psychology, looking very confused by all the strange ideas, you can explain to them where these things come from, and tell them our story of how the social psychologists got their facts.

Exercises for critical engagement

1 Suggest several other areas where discourse analysis would be a useful research method. Briefly explain how you would go about doing the research in each case.

2 The chapter suggests that it is difficult for people to see the discourses which they use in their thinking. Can you identify some examples of this kind of 'common sense' that people simply take for granted? How are you able to identify them more easily than other people?

3 What additional discourses (over and above the ones identified in the research) do you think might affect safe sex behaviour in your community. How can you identify these discourses?

4   The research suggests that people need to think differently about what it means to be men or women. How is it possible for psychologists to try and get people to change in this way?

5   Based on the research and theories in this chapter, make practical suggestions for an intervention to reduce HIV infection.

Endnotes

1   The 'Post-colonial tale', Parts 1 and 2, first appeared in an article in *Psychology in Society* in 2001. Permission to use this is gratefully acknowledged.

2   At the initial presentation at the South African Psychology Congress, a member of the audience argued that the video was problematic in representing a paranoid account of the emergence of social psychology. At the time (and suspecting the unwitting invocation of the rhetorical rule developed for deligitimising oppositional discourse), I somewhat facetiously defended the importance of paranoid interpretations. A double task then emerged: how to write an introduction to the video script for this publication, and how to explore the utility of a paranoid standpoint. Methodologically, there was also the problem of avoiding replicating the rhetorical structure of academic writing, which is one of the things that the video sought to problematise. Given that military paranoia seems to be the prototypical paranoia of our age, the solution presented itself: it must surely be an *act of war*.

Recommended reading

Bannister, P., Burman, E. & I. Parker (Eds.) (1994). *Qualitative Methods in Psychology: A Research Guide*. Buckingham: Open University Press.

Breakwell, G., Hammond, S. & C. Fife-Shaw (Eds.) (1995). *Research Methods in Psychology*. London: Sage.

Burman, E. & I. Parker (1993). *Discourse Analytic Research: Repertoires and Readings of Texts in Action*. London: Routledge.

Burr, V. (1995). *An Introduction to Social Constructionism*. London: Routledge.

Foucault, M. (1980). 'Power/knowledge'. In Gordon, C. (Ed.) *Power/Knowledge: Selected Interviews and Other Writings by Michel Foucault, 1972–1977*. New York: Pantheon Books.

Hepburn, A. (2002). *An Introduction to Critical Social Psychology*. London: Sage.

Parker, I. (1989). *The Crisis in Modern Social Psychology – and How to End It*. London: Routledge.

Parker, I. (1992). *Discourse Dynamics: Critical Analysis for Social and Individual Psychology*. London: Routledge.

Parker, I. & the Bolton Discourse Network (1999). *Critical Textwork: An Introduction to Varieties of Discourse and Analysis*. Buckingham: Open University Press.

Potter, J. & M. Wetherell (1987). *Discourse and Social Psychology: Beyond Attitudes and Behaviour.* London: Sage.

Potter, J. (1996). *Representing Reality: Discourse, Rhetoric and Social Construction.* London: Sage.

Terre Blanche, M. & K. Durrheim (Eds.) (1999). *Research and Practice: Applied Methods for the Social Sciences.* Cape Town: UCT Press.

Wetherell, M. & J. Potter (1992). *Mapping the Language of Racism: Discourse and the Legitimation of Exploitation.* London: Harvester Wheatsheaf.

Willig, C. (Ed.) (1999). *Applied Discourse Analysis: Social and Psychological Interventions.* Buckingham: Open University Press.

Wilton, T. (1997). *Engendering AIDS: Deconstructing Sex, Text and the Epidemic.* London: Sage Publications.

Race, Racism and Identities

PART TWO

Racism: A Social Psychological Perspective

3

Cheryl de la Rey & Norman Duncan

OUTCOMES

After having studied this chapter you should be able to:

- define racism
- distinguish between the concepts 'racism', 'racial prejudice' and 'racial discrimination'
- describe the key social psychological perspectives on racism and related phenomena
- identify the strengths and weaknesses of some of the key social psychological perspectives on racism and related phenomena, and
- provide your own views on how racism can be combated.

This chapter provides an overview of a selection of psychological explanations of racism. It aims to describe the various theories and approaches to the study of racism and also to assess their usefulness in attempts to eradicate racism. Collectively, these approaches contain various insights which could be harnessed in our attempts to understand, so as ultimately to deal with, the problem of racism as well as its psychological and social sequelae. Before presenting these theoretical positions emerging from psychology, however, we will firstly present a brief discussion of the differences between the concepts 'racism', 'racial prejudice' and 'racial discrimination', specifically because these terms refer to closely related and interwoven processes, and because they are frequently erroneously conflated (see Katz & Taylor, 1988).

Racial prejudice, racial discrimination and racism

What is racism?

Racism is a notoriously difficult concept to define. This is undoubtedly a consequence of the complexity of the phenomenon as well as its constantly changing manifestations (de Waal Malefijt, 1976; Miles, 1989). Nonetheless, for the purposes of this chapter we will define racism broadly as an

Racism:
An institutionalised system whereby certain racialised groups are systematically dominated or marginalised by another racialised group or other groups.

institutionalised system whereby certain racialised groups are systematically dominated or marginalised by another racialised group or groups. As was evident in the two most notorious systems of racism witnessed in recent world history, namely, apartheid and Nazism, the inequalities and abuses that the phenomenon seeks to entrench are primarily legitimated or justified, and consequently, reproduced by means of the systematic inferiorisation or 'negativisation' of dominated racialised groups. Thus, within these systems, Blacks and Jews, for example, were constructed as racially 'inferior' to White South Africans and 'Aryan' Germans, respectively, and therefore deserving of the abject subjugation and abuse to which they were routinely subjected in their countries of birth.

While the twentieth century was witness to some of the most dramatic and worst excesses of racism in the form of apartheid and Nazism (most notably, institutionalised racial segregation and the disenfranchisement, institutionalised economic exploitation, widespread imprisonment, as well as the systematic persecution of those deemed 'racially inferior'), it also announced the demise of these signally ignominious manifestations of state-sponsored racism. However, while the world has witnessed the demise of both these repulsive systems of state-sponsored racism this unfortunately does not mean that racism is something of the past. Indeed, as various writers have commented in recent years, racism remains a deep-rooted and pervasive problem in contemporary society (Dovidio & Gaertner, 1986; Miles, 1989; van Dijk, 1987). In South Africa, for example, the fact that Blacks still constitute the majority of the poorest sector of the population, the under-representation of Blacks in the most powerful positions within the business sector, and the continued under-representation of Blacks in most of our national sports teams attest to the fact that many apartheid-era racialised patterns of privilege (i.e. racism) remain a ubiquitous reality in this country (May *et al.*, 2000; *Saturday Star*, 6 June 1998). The ongoing reality of racism in South Africa is also illustrated by the ever-present and growing threat of military-style violence on the part of White rightwing movements hankering after the unearned and unfair privileges and political power that their skin colour had afforded them under the apartheid system.

In South Africa, for example, the fact that Blacks still constitute the majority of the poorest sector of the population, the under-representation of Blacks in the most powerful positions within the business sector, and the continued under-representation of Blacks in most of our national sports teams attest to the fact that many apartheid-era racialised patterns of privilege remain a ubiquitous reality in this country.

Certainly, the racism that currently confronts us in South Africa is articulated less crudely than had been the case a decade or so ago. However, it can be argued that this is less a function of the dissipation of racism in contemporary society than it perhaps is a reflection of the changing articulation of the phenomenon. Various writers have in fact commented on the changes that racism has undergone in recent years. We will briefly consider the views of some of these writers here.

According to Essed (1987) and Eyber *et al.* (1997), one of the major ways in which racism as ideology has changed over recent decades relates to the fact

While a significant number of South Africans today reject the apartheid labels used to categorise them as 'Coloured', 'Indian' and 'African', for various reasons a significant number of people also use these categories and their associated identities at various times.

that it is increasingly being articulated within a discourse of 'culture' and 'cultural difference'. Here a brief comment on ideology might be apposite. According to Eyber *et al.* (1997:38) ideology refers to 'all the beliefs, common-sense understandings and practices' that legitimise a specific status quo. Racism as ideology attempts to justify the racial inequalities in society. Initially, of course, it attempted to justify these inequalities through notions of the innate inferiority and superiority of different 'races' (Miles, 1989). However, as Essed (1987) argues, as scientists around the world increasingly began to admit that notions of racial inferiority or superiority could not be defended on scientific grounds, racist beliefs and practices were increasingly reproduced through, and justified on the grounds that they were essential for the preservation of the *Other's* culture. Furthermore, 'racial' inequality was increasingly justified as being a function of 'cultural difference'. Certain South African rightwing White supremacist movements' claim to the right to preserve their cultural values and practices, as a justification for 'racial' exclusivity and for their attempts to regain some of the benefits they had enjoyed under the apartheid system, can be seen as an example of the use of culture to legitimate racist objectives. Essed (1987) refers to the increasing trend in contemporary society towards harnessing notions of 'culture' and 'cultural difference' as a medium and justification for claims to benefits for racialised in-groups and the continued domination or marginalisation of racialised out-groups, as the *culturalisation* of racism.

In the United States, Sears (1988) delineated the concept of *symbolic racism* to describe changes in the articulation of racism during recent decades. Sears observed that following the civil rights movement in the United States,

> *Ideology:*
> 'All the beliefs, common-sense understandings and practices' that legitimise a specific status quo (Eyber *et al.* 1997:38).

Racism is about unequal relations of power in all spheres of society.

Symbolic racism includes the denial of the continuing patterns of racial inequality that prevail in racist contexts, resentment over mechanisms aimed at redressing these patterns of inequality, and antagonism towards demands for the elimination of racism in its various manifestations.

traditional forms of racial hostility and discrimination were no longer particularly visible. Instead, he noted the emergence of newer forms of racial prejudice and -discrimination, which he termed symbolic racism (*see* McConahay in Jones, 1997). In brief, symbolic racism includes the denial of the continuing patterns of racial inequality that prevail in racist contexts, resentment over mechanisms aimed at redressing these patterns of inequality, and antagonism towards demands for the elimination of racism in its various manifestations. The denial of racism as a feature of symbolic racism is also dealt with by van Dijk (1987), who argues that denial in fact is a central element of racism in its newer guises.

While none of the writers referred to above provide a comprehensive account of the newer manifestations of racism, they do provide us with a description of some of the more salient features of contemporary articulations of the problem, and in so doing equip social scientists with some basic conceptual tools that can be employed to understand and deal with the issue as it is currently evolving.

What is racial prejudice?

Racial prejudice: 'Feelings of antipathy based on a faulty and inflexible generalization' (Allport, 1954:280).

Allport (1954:280), one of the first researchers in psychology to investigate the phenomenon of racial prejudice, defined it as '[feelings of] antipathy based on a faulty and inflexible generalization. It may be felt or expressed. It may be directed towards a ['racial'] group as a whole, or towards an individual because he [sic] is a member of that group.'

Many other definitions of racial prejudice, like Allport's definition, conceptualise it as consisting of a set of generally negative cognitions about and affective or emotional responses to members of other groups (Bobo, 1988). Important to note here is that while racist prejudice may be felt or expressed towards the individual, it is felt or expressed towards that individual, not really as a function of his or her personal traits, but as a function of his or her membership of a specific racialised group. Furthermore, the phenomenon is generally conceptualised as a set of negative cognitions and beliefs that do not remain fixed but undergo constant change as a function of changes in broader society and because of social pressure (Smitherman-Donaldson & van Dijk, 1988). For example, in South Africa, some of the 'old-fashioned' openly bigoted apartheid-era beliefs concerning the intellectual, moral and physical inferiority of Blacks seem to have shown a decided decline in recent years, while generalisations about the *'cultural distinctiveness'* of Blacks seem to have become increasingly prevalent (Shefer, 2000). Important to note, however, is that while its belief base might undergo change, the affective component of racial prejudice generally remains essentially negative.

What is racial discrimination?

Unlike racial prejudice, which is defined in terms of feelings and beliefs, racial discrimination is generally described as that which is *'actionable'* (Jones, 1997:10). Essed (1986:11), for example, defines racial discrimination as social 'acts, verbal, non-verbal, and paraverbal, that result in negative or unfavourable consequences for the dominated racial-ethnic groups, in particular'. Furthermore, she defines racial discrimination as the behavioural manifestation or enactment of racial prejudice (*ibid.*). While this understanding of racial discrimination is widely accepted, many psychologists add the important caveat that while racial prejudice frequently leads to discriminatory behaviour, the latter does not necessarily flow from the former (Dovidio & Gaertner, 1986). As various studies have illustrated, even the most prejudiced people, in their quest to act in a socially desirable manner and in an effort to present a positive image of themselves and their group, will go to great lengths to avoid expressing and enacting their prejudices (van Dijk, 1987). Moreover, as will become clear in the following paragraphs, discrimination is not always motivated by prejudice.

Traditionally, two forms of racial discrimination have been distinguished, namely, direct and indirect racial discrimination. *Direct racial discrimination* refers to unequal treatment based on racial or related criteria (Essed, 1986). In apartheid South Africa, examples of this form of discrimination were widespread. Consider, for example, the vast differences in the quality of

> Unlike racial prejudice, which is defined in terms of feelings and beliefs, racial discrimination is generally described as that which is *'actionable'*.

> Direct racial discrimination refers to unequal treatment based on racial or related criteria

Indirect racial discrimination, refers to the tendency to adhere to the 'equal treatment' of different racialised groups under systematically unequal conditions, which leads to the creation or perpetuation of patterns of racial inequality.

Unlike blatant or direct discrimination, which manifests in unequal treatment that is intentional, visible, and easily documented, subtle discrimination is often not visible and obvious (especially not to those benefiting from it). It may be intentional or unintentional and it often is difficult to prove.

Paternalism and condescension refers to behaviour that is superficially polite and nice but which treats members of the target group as though they are children, lacking in some things or otherwise inferior. Speaking loudly and slowly when addressing Blacks constitutes one example of this form of subtle discrimination.

educational, health and housing facilities available to Blacks and Whites. The facilities enjoyed by Whites, in most cases, were infinitely superior to those of Blacks. *Indirect racial discrimination*, on the other hand, refers to the tendency to adhere to the 'equal treatment' of different racialised groups under systematically unequal conditions, which leads to the creation or perpetuation of patterns of racial inequality (*ibid.*). In other words, indirect racial discrimination refers to the unwillingness or failure to discriminate in favour of dominated or marginalised racialised groups so as to redress extant 'inertial' patterns of inequality (Nell & van Staden, 1988). Examples of this form of discrimination, which is particularly prevalent in contemporary South Africa, would include the selection, employment and promotion practices of certain institutions (such as certain institutions of higher learning in this country) with an over-representation of White staff members, particularly in positions of authority. Frequently, the criteria utilised to recruit, select and promote potential employees in these institutions, while not explicitly racial, are stacked against groups such as Blacks. In most cases these institutions proudly claim that they do not practice racial discrimination because they would employ and promote anyone who meets certain 'objective' institutional requirements. However, to the extent that these criteria and existing staffing practices do nothing to alter extant racialised staffing patterns, it can still be argued that these institutions are practising (indirect) racial discrimination.

With the expansion of research on racial discrimination and changes in social and historical context, recent years have seen the development of a wider vocabulary to describe emerging manifestations or forms of racial discrimination. *Subtle discrimination* is one such form of discrimination. Unlike blatant or direct discrimination, which manifests in unequal treatment that is intentional, visible, and easily documented, subtle discrimination is often not visible and obvious (especially not to those benefiting from it). It may be intentional or unintentional and it often is difficult to prove. Together with indirect discrimination, subtle discrimination is becoming the dominant mode in which racism currently manifests itself. Ways in which subtle discrimination is normally expressed include: first, *paternalism and condescension:* this is behaviour that is superficially polite and nice, but paternalistic in that members of the target group are treated as though they are inferior, or 'lacking' in something. Speaking loudly and slowly when addressing Blacks (no matter how well they speak and understand the language in which they are addressed) constitutes one example of this form of discrimination. Second, *supportive discouragement:* this occurs when mixed messages about one's abilities, intelligence or accomplishments are conveyed. Consider here, for example, the person who constantly complements the work of Black colleagues but not that of White colleagues. In South Africa this is frequently a result of the fact that the latter's competence is always taken for granted, while the former is invari-ably expected to fail. Third, *stereotyped humour:* this refers to the telling of jokes that are based on stereotypes and the imitation of accents to create humour (Benokraitis & Feagin, 1995).

> Stereotyped humour refers to jokes that are based on stereotypes and the imitations of accents to create humour.

While the concepts of subtle and indirect discrimination overlap consider-ably, they differ in the sense that the concept of indirect discrimination most frequently is used to refer to what Nell and van Staden (1988) would refer to as 'inertial' institutional practices.

Earlier we stated that 'racial' prejudice and 'racial' discrimination are closely associated with the functioning of racism. However, as implied, not all forms of 'racial' prejudice and discrimination are racist. The question that consequently arises here is: When do 'racial' discrimination and prejudice become racist? We attempt to answer this question below.

Racism, racial prejudice and race discrimination: How they are related

According to the definition presented earlier, racism can be seen as referring to all those institutionalised practices, discourses and processes that lead to the production or perpetuation of the domination of one racialised group (or groups) by a dominant racialised group (or groups). In other words, racism is closely linked to relations of domination. If it is accepted that racism is linked to institutionalised relations of domination between racialised groups, then 'racial' prejudice and discrimination are racist only to the extent that they are systematically linked to broad institutional structures and practices that seek to bring about or perpetuate the subjugation or marginalisation of one or more racialised groups by another racial group or groups (Biko, 1988; CAL, 1987). This is in effect the view held by Jones (1986:280), who defines racism as the transformation of 'racial' prejudice and discrimination, 'through the exercise of power against a racial group ... by individuals and institutions, with the intentional or unintentional support' of an entire culture, society or broad institutionalised practices.

> Racism is closely linked to institutionalised relations of domination between racialised groups.

This distinction between racial prejudice and discrimination, on the one hand, and racism, on the other, is important not only for the sake of concep-tual clarity, but also because it lays the basis for effectively dealing with the problem of racism. Failure to appreciate the distinction between these terms could easily lead to equating dominant group prejudice and discrimination with those of the dominated (the illusory narrative of shared victimisation that hooks [1996] speaks of), thereby obscuring the uniquely systematic and destructive manner in which racism impacts on the lives of the latter (*ibid.*). It could also lead to equating instances of non-systemic or contingent expres-sions of prejudice and discrimination with racism, which is systemic and widespread. Lastly, and very importantly, it could easily lead to anti-racist interventions being misdirected, for example, in the sense of them targeting the prejudices and actions of the victims of racism, rather than the institutional practices that perpetuate racism and pose a greater threat to equality and social progress than the essentially defensive prejudices and discriminatory behaviours of systematically marginalised and subjugated racialised groups.

Here it might be apposite to say something about the notion of *reverse racism*. Very frequently, dominated racialised groups' defensive prejudices and discriminatory behaviours are characterised as reverse racism. This character-isation is problematic for at least one reason. As the discussion presented above should illustrate, theoretically, racial prejudice and discrimination only amount to racism in instances where they enjoy broad institutional support. In the case of dominated racialised groups this is rarely the case (Essed, 1986; 1987). Thus, representing their reactive prejudices and discriminatory actions in relation to those who marginalise and oppress them as racist is not entirely accurate. As Biko (1988:39) argued in relation to many Blacks' negative responses to Whites during the apartheid era, '[t]hose who know, define racism as discrimination against another for the purposes of subjugation and maintaining subjugation. In other words one cannot be a racist unless he [sic] has the power to subjugate. What blacks are doing is merely to respond to a situation in which they find themselves the objects of white racism.'

> Representing the reactive prejudices and discriminatory actions of the dominated racialised groups in relation to those who discriminate against them as racist is not entirely accurate.

The individual, the group and society[1]

As should be clear from the preceding discussion, racism is a social and systemic, rather than individual problem; and it refers to broad social and systemic or institutionalised practices, rather than individual actions. However, it cannot be denied that the individual plays an important role in the perpetuation of racism, for it is frequently the individual who performs acts of racism and who serves as principal executive agent of institutionalised racism (Essed, 1987).

Various theories on the psychology of racism have grappled with the issue of the relationship between the psychology of the individual and broader societal systems and institutions. Attempts to explain the causes and func-tioning of racism, and why some people endorse and enact racism while others do not, vary in terms of where these theories locate the source of the problem, as will be seen in the examples discussed below.

Racism as a function of personality

> Traditionally, social psychological theories have tended to focus primarily on the individual in trying to explain the causes of racism.

Traditionally, social psychological theories have tended to focus primarily on the individual in trying to explain the causes of racism. This orientation is perhaps best illustrated in the frequently expressed idea that racial prejudice is the source of racism and that it can be linked to a definite personality type. In South Africa, studies formulated and conducted within this orientation have conventionally focused on the personality profile of particularly White Afrikaners, who traditionally were seen as extremely prejudiced, and therefore, the major cause of racism and related problems in this country.

Adorno and his colleagues originally developed the idea that there is a specific personality type that is predisposed to racial prejudice (Adorno *et al.*, 1950). Based on a comprehensive study of the dynamics of anti-Semitism, these theorists argued that prejudice and racism developed from a particular personality syndrome, which they labelled the 'authoritarian personality'. Specifically, they posited that the authoritarian personality syndrome is characterised by the following nine traits: *Conventionalism, Authoritarian Submission, Authoritarian Aggression, Anti-intraception* (an opposition to the subjective, the imaginative), *Superstition and Stereotypy, Power and 'Toughness', Destructiveness and Cynicism, Projectivity* (the projection outwards of unconscious emotional impulses), and *Sex* (an exaggerated concern with sexual 'goings-on').[2] Adorno *et al.* (1950) stressed that the syndrome does not necessarily lead to prejudice, but that it predisposes the individual to racial prejudice (de la Rey, 1991).

In essence, the development of the authoritarian personality was described in terms of certain assumptions flowing from Sigmund Freud's psychoanalytic theory. Adorno *et al.* (1950) claimed that racism or racial prejudice could be traced back to the individual's early childhood experiences. Specifically, they maintained that a strict, rigid pattern of parental discipline early in life leads to feelings of hostility towards parents. However, society generally discourages the expression of negative feelings towards authority figures. Consequently, children repress their inner feelings of hostility and set out to obey their parents – and later, other figures of authority – slavishly in reaction to these unacceptable feelings. However, as negative affect cannot be repressed forever, children ultimately seek out safe targets at which to direct their hostility. Often, visibly 'different' out-groups become the targets of their projected hostility, which ultimately is transformed into racial prejudice and racism (de la Rey, 1991).

Since its publication, this account of the development of racial prejudice, and by extension, racism, was the subject of intense critique, particularly with regard to issues of research methodology. Of central relevance here, however, is not so much the technical strengths and weaknesses of the study by Adorno *et al.*, but the argument that racism is essentially a function of personality traits. Specifically, the notion that racial prejudice is merely a consequence of an authoritarian personality is much too simplistic to be of any use in our attempts to understand this complex social phenomenon. A study conducted by Pettigrew (1958) in the United States and South Africa illustrated the importance of considering broader social factors in the development of racial prejudice. He found that White South Africans and Whites from the Southern

> Adorno and his colleagues originally developed the idea that there is a specific personality type that is predisposed to racial prejudice (Adorno *et al.*, 1950).

> The notion that racial prejudice is merely a consequence of an authoritarian personality is much too simplistic to be of any use in our attempts to understand this complex social phenomenon.

states of the United States of America scored high on an anti-Black scale. However, in terms of authoritarianism scores, they did not differ significantly from their peers. He consequently argued that in social contexts in which racial prejudice is normative, broader social factors are more significant than personality factors in determining racial prejudice. Despite this finding, however, the 1960s and 1970s witnessed the generation of a fairly large number of South African studies and publications which appeared to support the idea of racial prejudice and racism as a function of the personality traits of Whites (Louw-Potgieter, 1988). These studies typically sought to correlate certain personality traits (e.g. authoritarianism) with levels of racial prejudice (de la Rey, 1991).

Louw-Potgieter (1988) argues that the 'personality-oriented' approaches to the analysis of inter-group relations within South Africa have led to politically conformist psychological research and discourses which have been incapable of providing adequate explanations of the genesis and functioning of racism. Specifically, by focusing on the individual, these approaches fail to account for the social structures and processes implicated in the reproduction of the phenomenon. Various writers have also argued that by focusing on the prejudices of certain groups of individuals, these approaches have also played a key role in the perpetuation of the popular myth that racism is a problem of only certain people and that it is not as widespread and deep-rooted as it really is. For example, in the context of apartheid South Africa, we know that racism was not caused by and did not benefit only White Afrikaners or conservative Whites. All Whites benefited from apartheid racism, and because of this, many were complicit (to varying degrees, obviously) in its perpetuation.

Notwithstanding the individualism of the 'personality-oriented' approaches, they do point to some insights that may be worthy of further consideration, for example, the suggested intersection between certain intra-psychic dynamics and racism, a link which is stressed in recent studies of racism as ideology (Stevens, 1997). Eyber et al. (1997) suggest that the further exploration of this link between individual dynamics and racism could perhaps contribute to our understanding of the uneven levels of racial prejudice and discrimination exhibited by different members of dominant groups benefiting from racism.

Racism as a consequence of competition over resources

Unlike the approaches focusing on the link between racism and personality, the realistic conflict theory (RCT) proposes a group-based approach to understanding the causes of racism. RCT basically suggests that incompatible goals or competition between racial groups over scarce resources leads to hostility and conflict, and that superordinate goals or cooperative activities between these groups induce social harmony (Sherif, 1966). According to this approach, therefore, racial conflict and racism result from inter-group

Unlike the approaches focusing on the link between racism and personality, the realistic conflict theory (RCT) proposes a group-based approach to understanding the causes of racism.

competition over scarce resources such as land, employment, schools, and housing. Interestingly too, the theory posits that the extent of racial conflict and racism would diminish when there is cooperative inter-group activity in the attainment of superordinate goals such as the elimination of crime and other threats to social stability (de la Rey, 1991).

Realistic conflict theory identifies the unequal distribution of resources as a key determinant in the functioning of racism.

RCT has been applied in various settings to deal with the problem of racism. In the case of desegregated schools in the United States of America, for example, Aronson and his colleagues (Aronson *et al.*, 1978) tried to deal with prejudice in these settings by replacing the typical competitive classroom activities with more cooperative activities involving groups of learners. They hoped that this intervention would lead to a reduction in prejudice. Their intervention ultimately led to a reduction in racial prejudice and discrimination (de la Rey, 1991).

Generally, RCT has had a very positive impact on the application of social psychological theory to dealing with prejudice and discrimination in real-life settings. Very importantly too, the theory correctly identifies the unequal distribution of resources as a key determinant in the functioning of racism. However, it must be recognised that the theory's focus on superordinate goals as a means of dealing with the problem of racism is somewhat problematic. If the source of racism lies in the unequal distribution of resources, surely the solution is in redistribution, not merely in the creation of superordinate goals.

Racism as linked to categorisation, identity and comparison

A significant experimental finding that the mere division of individuals into groups constituted a basic condition for the appearance of bias against members of other groups led to the development of the social identity theory (SIT). SIT posits that social categorisation forms part of a fundamental cognitive process known as *categorical differentiation* (Tajfel, 1959; 1981). More specifically, the theory holds that because we cannot process the infinite array of information present in our environment, the individual tries to make sense of the world by categorising objects and people into groups (de la Rey, 1991).

According to SIT, the phenomenon of accentuation is central to social categorisation. Accentuation refers to the process whereby the similarities within a group and the differences between groups are exaggerated or accentuated. In racist societies, for example, one can frequently discern the tendency to accentuate similarities within 'racialised' groups. Hence familiar statements such as, 'They [Blacks/Whites] are all alike' or 'You've seen one, you've seen them all', made in relation to members of out-groups. This accentuation of intra-group similarities is inevitably accompanied by an emphasis on the differences between groups: 'We're not like them, we're very different'; 'Our cultures are not compatible'. The perception of social groups (more so than is the case with the perception of objects) is characterised by an evaluative (positive or negative) and an emotional (feelings of like, hate) component. The process of accentuation is believed to be related to the development of racial stereotypes (de la Rey, 1991).

We do not merely place others into social categories; we also identify ourselves in terms of social categories. The statements 'I am White', 'I am Black', and 'I am South African', all reflect the individual's identity in terms of belonging to some categories and not to others. SIT argues that our membership of groups, such as 'race' groups becomes internalised so that it forms part of our self-concept. Who we are (the self-concept) comprises both elements that are uniquely individual and idiosyncratic (personal identity) and elements that we share with others by being members of groups (social identity). Through social identity, group memberships are internalised and become part of the individual's internal, subjective identity. Therefore, any comment or action (positive or negative) directed at the group will also have an impact on the individual (de la Rey, 1991).

A fundamental hypothesis of SIT is that every person has a need to be regarded positively; in other words, to have a positive self-concept. How do we assess whether our group is positively distinctive? According to SIT, we compare our group to others using some dimension that we value. The comparative dimensions used may include skin colour, material resources, political power, moral codes and cultural characteristics. If the outcome of this comparison were negative, the need for a positive social identity would not be met. This would then motivate the individual to undertake some action to achieve a change in the relations between the groups. Such action could include attempts to valorise in-group characteristics or, where possible,

Our membership of groups, such as 'race' or 'cultural' groups, becomes internalised so that it forms part of our self-concept.

attempts to be assimilated into the dominant out-group or to reverse the *status quo*. Important to note, however, is that people will only strive towards changing the relations between groups if they perceive such change as possible (i.e. if they perceive 'cognitive alternatives' to prevailing group relations).[3]

One of the most valuable contributions of SIT is its attempt to offer explanations for the divided, hierarchical nature of social reality and the impact that this has on people. Furthermore, insofar as its analysis of the social order incorporates social change, SIT marks a departure from earlier psychological theories of inter-group phenomena, which tended to view the social order as relatively static. Very importantly too, through its emphasis on the role of social processes (rather than focusing only on intra- and inter-personal processes) in inter-group phenomena, SIT has been able to transcend many of the limitations of earlier psychological accounts of these phenomena. Despite its manifest strengths, SIT also has several shortcomings, its primary shortcoming being its apparent failure to provide an understanding of the role played by ideology in structuring power relations between groups (including racialised groups), and how this influences the process of social categorisation, as well as perceptions of the Self (or the in-group) and the Other (or the out-group) (de la Rey, 1991).

Nonetheless, SIT offers us several informative pointers regarding the functioning of racism, chief of which are the following. Firstly, the theory indicates that using the category 'race' to make sense of the world (however innocent the intention), at the outset already, could lead to the individual developing a certain measure of negative bias towards members who belong to other 'races' (Sears, 1988). Secondly, the theory shows us how 'race' as a social category becomes internalised as part of people's self-concept, and how this impacts on their perceptions of themselves and others. Thirdly, and very importantly, SIT indicates that those whom the ideology of racism seeks to subjugate, largely because of the intensely disruptive effects of the ideology on their

Black:
This term designates a racial category on the basis of the latest South African census criteria. 'Black' refers to people who are often labeled African, however, many people who are not Black consider themselves, and are often considered by others, to be African. Given South Africa's racial legacy, 'Black' also can be defined by exclusion and negation – it is a referent that does not include 'Coloured', 'Asian/Indian', and 'White'.

'Coloured' refers to a racial category derived from apartheid classification, but used in the latest South African census. Used as a positive assertion of identity, 'Coloured' celebrates diversity and an inclusive, hybrid history. Deployed in counter-distinction, 'Coloured' brackets people who are neither Black nor White, nor for that matter Asian/Indian.

psychological well-being, will inevitably attempt to escape or to counter the impact of the ideology. Whether the strategies that they will employ to do so can be considered socially and psychologically productive or not will of course depend on the alternatives available to them.

Social constructionism

The social constructionist perspective on 'race' and racism, a relatively recent development, denotes a break with earlier views through its claims that the identities harnessed by, flowing from, or developed in opposition to, the phenomenon of racism are not fixed, nor static, but shifting or in flux and socially constituted through language. In support of the notion of 'race' categories and racism as changing and historically specific, we may refer to how, at different times in history, people have moved in and out of certain 'racial' categories. South African history provides a rich source of examples, perhaps the most illustrative being the racial category, 'Coloured'; a peculiarly South African distinction. The *Population Registration Act* of 1950 legally constituted the category, 'Coloured', as a person who is not White or native (Black). This category is under continual contestation. In present-day South Africa, individuals who during the apartheid years were classified as Coloured, variously refer to themselves as Black, 'so-called Coloured', 'Coloured' and Coloured. Scrutinising instances of racial naming brings to the fore the idea that 'race' and racial identity are discursively constructed and that these constructions change over time and space. As Frankenberg (1993) uncovered in her study of Whiteness, 'race' is not a trans-historical or trans-contextual essence, it changes over time and context. By breaking with the notions of 'race' and racial identity as fixed essences, constructionism opens up spaces for new ways of theorising the complexities, changing forms, ambiguities and contradictions that mark present-day realities.

The view that 'race' is a socially constructed rather than an inherently meaningful category is consistent with a growing agreement in the vast literature on 'race', namely, that 'race' is an empty signifier, that is, that it has no ontological status. As reflected in the work of Carrim (2000), Foster (1991) and Miles (1989), the understanding of 'race' as empty signification has permitted, in the social sciences in general and psychology in particular, a conceptualisation of racisms in the plural as historically situated and shifting, and as necessarily relational, in the sense of specifying Self and Other in relations of domination and resistance.

Psychological consequences of racism

Various scholars (e.g. Bulhan, 1985; Fanon, 1990; Frye, 1992; hooks, 1996; Manganyi, 1973; Memmi, 1982; Stevens & Lockhat, 1997) have written extensively on the psychological impact of the social and material consequences of institutionalised racism on the lives and psychological integrity of Black people. Fanon's writings on the psychology of oppression have been especially influential. Basing himself on both a sociological and psychoanalytic analysis of colonialism, Fanon suggested that racism can be considered a form of systemic vertical violence aimed at (re)producing relations of racial domination. He argued that in contexts characterised by racism, the dominated 'race' is kept in subjugation, not only by means of brute force and social stratification, but also through its own internalisation of the dominant group's racism. This frequently results in the dominated being reduced to accomplices in their own subjugation. Fanon's account of the functioning of racism added substantially to understandings of the effects of racism on the psyche of dominated groups (see Chapter 6). However, his theory has been criticised for not paying sufficient attention to the manner in which gender and socio-economic class positionings mediate the impact of racism. For example, in South Africa, as we know, racism has a qualitatively different impact on the lives of middle- to upper-income Blacks than on the lives of lower-income Blacks.

The social constructionist perspective on 'race' and racism argues that identities harnessed by, flowing from, or developed in opposition to, the phenomenon of racism are not fixed nor static but shifting or in flux and constituted through language.

In South Africa, Manganyi (1973) argued that exposure to racism over a prolonged period of time frequently results in dominated groups internalising the messages and representations of themselves and that of the dominant group conveyed in the ideology. The internalisation of these messages can lead to intense intra-psychic distress against which marginalised and dominated racialised groups have to defend themselves; and as Manganyi (*ibid.*) points out, the latter frequently defend themselves, not by attacking the source of their distress, namely, institutionalised racism, but by turning inward against themselves and their communities. Hence the high levels of all forms of abuse evident in many oppressed and marginalised communities.

Exposure to racism over a prolonged period of time frequently results in dominated groups internalising the message and representations of themselves and that of the dominant groups conveyed in the ideology.

Frye (1992) argues that for the targets of racism, being confronted by instances of racism often results in psychological double binds. She describes these double binds as positions in which the individual is faced with limited, mutually contradictory emotional response options, each precipitating a penalty or negative consequence. In contexts such as South Africa, where social interaction is over-determined by racism, double binds are quotidian experiences in the lives of racially oppressed and marginalised groups. Frye (1992) gives the example of how social pressure is often brought to bear on oppressed people to be 'agreeable', even when confronted by incidents of racism. However, by being agreeable when confronted by racism, the dominated risk creating the impression that they are docile and acquiescent in their own oppression – an impression which they obviously would want to avoid. On the other hand, not being agreeable exposes them to being labelled as angry, aggressive and dangerous, which feeds into one of the more dominant representations of the dominated contained in the ideology of racism, namely, that the latter are 'difficult' and a threat to social stability.

Psychological double binds: Positions in which the individual is faced with limited, mutually contradictory emotional response options, each precipitating a penalty or negative consequence.

Double-bind experiences of any kind are considered to rank amongst the most psychologically disruptive experiences. In her collection of essays titled *Killing Rage: Ending Racism*, hooks (1996) poignantly describes how the reality of the routine assault and harassment (and the double binds embedded in these experiences) to which Black people are exposed in racist societies can ultimately drive the individual to the point of '*killing rage*'. She defines *killing rage* as the accumulated repressed anger that builds up in the individual as a result of repeatedly being subjected to racist abuse. Echoing the views of Fanon (1990) and, to a certain extent, Mangayi (1973), hooks (1996) argues that this rage can be turned inward (and manifest in all forms of addictions), it can be turned against 'safe' targets (such as other victims of racism), or it can be directed at members of the dominant racialised group.

In view of the above, there can be no denying that racism can be profoundly destructive as far as the psychological well-being of racially oppressed and marginalised groups is concerned. However, as hooks (1996) cautions, the destructiveness of this social scourge should not be used to cast dominated groups into the role of victims, as their construction primarily as 'victims' inevitably feeds into extant racist discourses caricaturing them as 'people with problems' or 'people who cannot deal with their problems', and ultimately, therefore, 'people who are problems'. Moreover, constructing racially oppressed and marginalised groups as victims negates their agency, and more specifically, their daily struggles against, and their triumphs over, racism and its inimical consequences (Essed 1991; hooks, 1996).

While acknowledging the power of human resilience and agency, we wish to caution against a growing tendency in psychological literature to focus mainly on the resilience of the targets of racism and to ignore the manifestly deleterious impact of the phenomenon on the lives of many people. Like hooks (1996), we believe that focusing only on the resilience of people and their triumphs over racism could easily result in the development of a discourse that constructs people who unavoidably succumb to the adverse effects of racism as weak, or indeed, abnormal. To a certain extent, this could, in turn, lead to the silencing of racially marginalised and oppressed groups by making it increasingly difficult for them to acknowledge and disclose 'the ways in which living in a [racist] society and being the constant targets of racist assault and abuse are fundamentally psychologically traumatic' (*ibid.*:134).

In recent years, especially since the demise of formal apartheid, there has been much public talk about the impact of racism on White people in South Africa, in particular the claim that apartheid was damaging for White people too. Admittedly, any system of oppression, through its inherent divisiveness and violence, has a negative impact on all people who fall within its ambit. Frye (1992) uses the metaphor of a caged bird to illustrate the impact of systemic racism on both the oppressed and the oppressor. She points out that the

> There can be no denying that racism can be profoundly destructive as far as the psychological well-being of racially oppressed and marginalised groups is concerned.

> While acknowledging the power of human resilience and agency, we wish to caution against a growing tendency in psychological literature to focus mainly on the resilience of the targets of racism and to ignore the manifestly deleterious impact of the phenomenon on the lives of many people.

barriers erected by oppression, like the bars of the birdcage, negatively structure the lived reality of those on either side of the barriers. Given that within such a bounded system people are cut off from one another as humans in vital relationship with one another, there is dehumanisation on both sides of the barriers. But the impact on each side is fundamentally different. Being inside the cage means a loss of freedom; being outside means being in a position of control over the cage's lock and keys, and therefore, the Other's lack of freedom. This metaphor draws attention to the significance of power inequalities as a fundamental feature of racism. Therefore, even if apartheid did have negative consequences for White people as human beings, these effects cannot be equated with the suffering endured by Blacks as a result of the brutal system of institutionalised racism that was apartheid. Moreover, as hooks (1996) argues, the focus on the pain and suffering of Whites in current public discourses on the effects of racism (of which there is much evidence in South Africa), could easily result in the reinforcement of the 'centredness' of Whites (and the further marginalisation of Blacks) in extant constructions of the human condition – thereby reaffirming the central racist narrative that the experiences of White people are more important than those of Blacks.

> Even if apartheid did have negative consequences for White people as human beings, these effects cannot be equated with the suffering endured by Blacks as a result of the brutal system of institutionalised racism that was apartheid.

Just as racism does not affect dominant and dominated racialised groups in the same manner, it also does not affect the dominated in a uniform manner either. Thus, in South Africa, while all Black people generally are adversely affected in myriad ways by racism, the phenomenon has affected and continues to affect those labelled by the past apartheid government as Coloured, Indian/Asian and African (Black) in significantly different ways. According to the logic of past apartheid divide-and-rule policies, each of these groups were assigned different regimes of entitlement in this country. The result was that while Indians/Asians and Coloureds were significantly worse off than Whites, they were given access to many more economic, social and political privileges than Africans (Blacks). These patterns of inequality still prevail to a large extent (May *et al.*, 2000).

> Just as racism does not affect dominant and dominated racialised groups in the same manner, it also does not affect the dominated in a uniform manner either.

In a similar manner, socio-economic class also mediates the manner in which racism impacts on the lives of Blacks in this country. Specifically, the manner in which middle- and upper-income Blacks are affected by the phenomenon differs substantively from the manner in which lower-income or indigent Blacks are affected by it. Middle- and upper-income groups also have greater access to various forms of support (e.g. counselling, professional networks and legal resources) to help them deal with the effects of racism than do lower income groups.

> Socio-economic class mediates the manner in which racism impacts on the lives of Blacks in this country.

Eyber *et al.* (1997) and hooks (1996) argue that gender also serves as a significant mediating factor as far as the impact of racism is concerned. For example, in a British study conducted by Green (in Eyber *et al.*, 1997), it was found that in a 'multi-racial' school setting Black boys are more likely than any

In recent years there has been much public talk about the impact of racism on white people, in particular the claim that apartheid was damaging for white people too.

other children to elicit a negative interaction style from their teachers. White boys, followed by White girls and Black girls, respectively, were more likely to elicit positive responses from their teachers. Another study by Rubovitz and Maehr (in Eyber *et al.*, 1997) found that Black boys who performed well academically were particularly prone to hostility from their teachers. However, while Black boys appear to be more prone to negative social responses than Black girls in multi-racial settings, hooks (1996) finds that society tends to take Black males' accounts of their experiences of racism more seriously than Black females' accounts of the same experiences.

Given the potentially harmful impact of racism on the well-being of people, it is important that intervention strategies be devised to deal with the problem in all its manifestations.

Dealing with racism: Psychological perspectives

Over the years, both in South Africa and in countries such as Brazil, Britain, Canada and the United States, there have been numerous attempts at translating psychological theory and research into effective programmes of intervention. Overall, these initiatives have been identified as 'tricky' at best (Aboud & Levy, 1999) as they have not shown consistent success in eliminating the problem. The selection of intervention strategies examined here flow from the theoretical perspectives dealt with in this chapter. Despite the limitations of many of the interventions, each of them contains elements that could be used effectively. These strategies do not necessarily draw on any single one of the theories described; instead they draw on multiple perspectives. Of the various psychological perspectives on racism, the 'personality-oriented' perspective, the contact theory (Allport, 1954), and the social identity theory have most commonly been used in the design of anti-racist intervention strategies. By way of illustration, we present a discussion of a limited selection of these intervention strategies.

Contact between groups

The contact theory has been fairly widely applied at the level of programmatic interventions. The main idea behind the contact theory is that contact between members of different groups will produce positive changes, such as reduced racial discrimination and harmonious inter-racial relations. However, research shows that contact *per se* will not necessarily improve inter-group relations. Instead, a successful outcome will only result if certain other conditions are also present. Allport (1954) pointed out that social status is a critical factor when contact is used as a means of reducing discrimination and prejudice. Specifically, he argued that contact is only helpful in reducing discrimination and enhancing inter-racial relations when those in the contact situation enjoy equal status. Subsequently, other researchers have identified additional critical factors, including strong institutional support for positive inter-racial relations, as well as cooperative interaction – aimed at the attainment of shared goals – between members of the different groups within the contact situation.

> The main idea behind the contact theory is that contact between members of different groups will produce positive changes, such as reduced racial discrimination and harmonious inter-racial relations.

Translating these ideas into intervention strategies has proved difficult, and the findings have not been consistently positive. For example, it has been found that contact in racially integrated social settings, such as workplaces and classrooms, sometimes leads to a hardening of stereotypes and an increase in racial hostility. Also, it has been noted that while inter-racial contact may reduce an individual's hostility towards some individuals of another 'race', this does not automatically translate into a decrease in hostility towards the other 'race' group as a whole.

Nonetheless, the literature reports some successes in certain environments where the contact situations have been structured in ways that take account of the critical factors identified above. In appropriately structured school environments, for example, it has been shown that bringing learners of different 'races' and levels of achievement together in small groups that work cooperatively on assignments can produce positive outcomes (Khmelkov & Hallinan, 1999). However, for this type of intervention to work, the institutions in which contact occurs have to be committed to promoting positive 'race' relations by ensuring that the institutional environment and discourses are conducive to inter-group tolerance and positive attitudes.

Stereotype reduction

In the early 1990s, the central assumptions of the social identity theory were applied in the development of a stereotype reduction programme in South Africa (Louw-Potgieter *et al.*, 1991). The programme sought to establish norms for acceptable and unacceptable inter-group behaviour and attitudes among people working together in organisations. Using experiential learning exercises, the programme specifically aimed to empower people to understand, recognise and then intervene effectively in changing stereotyping. Further, it incorporated techniques to illustrate that all humans are capable of racial prejudice discrimination but that the consequences are destructive for all.

While useful as a means of demonstrating to people how destructive racial prejudice and discrimination can be, as an anti-racist intervention strategy, the long-term success in changing stereotypes has not been systematically assessed. As Louw-Potgieter *et al.* (1991) point out, evaluations of programmes of this type are very difficult, as assessing impact requires sophisticated pre- and post-intervention measures. Moreover, the myriad manifestations of a problem such as racism render it difficult to assess impact overall. It should be noted that focusing on stereotype reduction is a very limited way of dealing with the very complex phenomenon of racism.

> While useful as a means of demonstrating to people how destructive racial prejudice and discrimination can be, as an anti-racist intervention strategy, the long-term success in changing stereotypes has not been systematically assessed.

'Therapeutic' interventions

Since the demise of formal apartheid, the assertion that racism no longer constitutes a serious problem in South Africa has become a disturbingly common refrain in public discourses, particularly in the discourses of those who continue to benefit from past institutionalised racist practices. Proponents of this view frequently argue that if racism exists, it exists only in the psyches of a few 'sick' individuals. In keeping with this argument, a range of anti-racist interventions aimed at 'curing' racist individuals of their prejudices have been developed over the last few years (Eyber *et al.*, 1997). Broadly based on the 'personality-oriented' perspective of racism, these interventions normally take the form of workshops where individuals examine their racial prejudices and consequently the manner in which they may contribute to racism. By recognising people's insecurities (however unfounded they may be), these workshops attempt to provide a non-threatening and non-judgmental forum in which participants can confront and deal with their prejudices. In short, therefore, these workshops are a bit like psychotherapy sessions aimed at 'healing' people of their prejudices (*ibid.*).

In the sense that they typically locate racism in the individual (and specifically 'sick' individuals), and that they do not take into account the broader social institutions and practices that feed into and reinforce the phenomenon, intervention strategies based on the 'personality-oriented' perspective are undeniably of limited value. However, as Eyber *et al.* (1997), argue and as previously noted, this does not mean that these strategies are completely valueless. Trying to help people deal with their prejudices may not eliminate racism, but if appropriately implemented, can certainly contribute to broader interventions aimed at dealing with the problem (*ibid.*).

There is much more that can be said in relation to anti-racist strategies that have emerged from the extant social psychological research on racism. However, given space constraints, we have to restrict our discussion to the above-mentioned interventions.

Conclusion

Psychology has produced various explanatory frameworks of and solutions to the phenomenon of racism. However, largely because they misapprehend or gloss over the complexity of the phenomenon, most of these explanatory frameworks have failed to provide adequate accounts of the functioning of the phenomenon, and have therefore generated a range of responses to the phenomenon that have generally been – to put it mildly – less than successful.

Racism does not only impact on the psychological reality of the individuals who fall within its ambit but simultaneously entrenches itself as a defining thread within the social and economic fabric of their world.

Because the problem of racism is so complex and multifaceted, we need explanatory frameworks of and solutions to the phenomenon that are equally complex and multifaceted. In short, we require explanatory frameworks and solutions that take into account the constantly changing manifestations of racism as well as the systemic, social, cognitive and emotional factors that sustain the phenomenon – explanatory frameworks and solutions that venture beyond the familiar boundaries within which psychology has traditionally worked.

Exercises for critical engagement

1 How does social psychology assist us in our understanding of racism?
2 Discuss racism in South Africa today. Does it exist and if so, how?

3 According to bell hooks (1996), when racism is the focus of public debate, those who participate and are heard are males. Discuss the implications of this statement for: 1) our reading of the existing literature on racism, and 2) for future research and writings on racism in South Africa.

4 Design an intervention programme that will assist in addressing the problem of racism in South Africa.

Endnotes

1 This section is based in part on a presentation to the South African Human Rights Commission National Conference on Racism and Related Forms of Intolerance (Duncan & de la Rey, 2000), as well as a chapter previously written by de la Rey (1991).
2 See Duncan and de la Rey (2000) for the full definitions of these terms.
3 See de la Rey (1991) for a more detailed discussion of this issue.

Recommended reading

Biko, S. (1988). *I Write What I Like*. London: Penguin.

Boonzaier, E. (1988). '"Race" and the race paradigm'. In Boonzaier, E. & J. Sharp (Eds.) *South African Key Words: The Uses and Abuses of Political Concepts*, pp. 58–67. Cape Town: David Philip.

Donald, J. & A. Ratansi (1992). *Race, Culture and Difference*. London: Sage.

Fanon, F. (1990). *The Wretched of the Earth*. London: Penguin Books.

hooks, b. (1996). *Killing Rage: Ending Racism*. London: Penguin Books.

Miles, R. (1989). *Racism*. London: Routledge.

Stevens, G. (1997). *Understanding 'Race' and Racism: A Return to Traditional Scholarship*. PRC Occasional Publications Series. Bellville: UWC.

'Race', Racism and the Media

4

Norman Duncan

OUTCOMES

After having studied this chapter you should be able to:

- explain the link between discourse and racism
- distinguish between overt and inferential racism
- identify some of the discursive strategies by means of which racism is currently perpetuated through the media, and
- generate some solutions to racism in the media.

THIS CHAPTER will explore how racism generally is reproduced by and through the mass media.[1] More specifically, it will examine the manifestations of racism in the mass media in South Africa during the 1990s. You will remember that it was during the 1990s (and particularly during the late 1990s) that the role of the media in the reproduction of racism was placed firmly at the centre of political and public debate and scrutiny in South Africa. It is largely for this reason that the 1990s was selected as focal period or period of reference for the discussion contained in this chapter. I have also selected the 1990s as focal period because, while it is sufficiently recent for the reader to recognise the events from that period which will be referred to or discussed in this chapter, it is simultaneously sufficiently distant in the past to provoke less of the defensiveness that is usually associated with most discussions of the phenomenon (see *Sunday Business Times*, 19 March 2000; Smith, 2000).

I introduce this discussion with the following series of events, which to a certain extent can be seen to have served as catalyst for the above-mentioned scrutiny and debate.

Towards the end of 1998, two local Black professional organisations, namely, the Black Lawyers Association (BLA) and the Association of Black Accountants of South Africa (ABASA) submitted a complaint to the South

African Human Rights Commission (SAHRC) in which they accused the main-stream mass media of 'violating the fundamental rights of black people' in this country, and more specifically of racism (Mona, 1999:58). Partly in response to this complaint, the SAHRC subsequently announced its intention of initiating an inquiry into racism in the media (SAHRC, 2000).

Both the complaint submitted by BLA and ABASA, as well as the SAHRC's proposed inquiry immediately precipitated an avalanche of protests and heated debate in the media (*Mail & Guardian*, 20–27 November 1998). Of particular interest here are the positions adopted by various local newspapers in this debate. On the one hand there were those newspapers, such as *The Star*, which supported the BLA and ABASA's claims and the SAHRC's planned inquiry, arguing that media racism still constituted one of the more serious social problems in the South African media and therefore that it warranted an inquiry (*ibid.; The Star*, 17 November 1998). On the other hand, however, there were those newspapers, such as the *Mail & Guardian* and the *Citizen*, which argued that the BLA and ABASA's claims of media racism were moti-vated by hidden political agendas and that the SAHRC's planned Inquiry into Racism in the Media was at best ill-advised (*Mail & Guardian*, 20–27 November 1998; Mona, 1999). According to this group, not only were the BLA and ABASA seeing racism where it did not exist but the SAHRC's proposed inquiry eventually would merely serve to undermine the freedom of the press in South Africa. Specifically, the *Mail & Guardian* posited that an inquiry of this nature ultimately would only serve to intimidate the media into becoming 'more quiescent and acquiescent' (*Mail & Guardian*, 20–27 November 1998).

The position adopted by the latter group of newspapers throws into relief two important questions that can perhaps be considered as central to any current discussion on racism in the South African media. Firstly, given the profound impact which institutional racism had on South African society, can any institution or individual (even at this stage in this country's history) claim never, in any way, to have been complicit in the functioning or reproduction of the phenomenon? Secondly, should media freedom be privileged over and above the media's obligation to contribute towards the elimination of racial stigmatisation and persecution as dictated by Article 4 of the *International Convention on the Elimination of Racial Discrimination* (ICERD) (United Nations, 2000)? Both these questions will be addressed later in this chapter. However, of greater importance at this point perhaps is to consider the concep-tion of racism that informs this chapter.

What is racism?

While much can be said about racism, in view of space constraints, only four of the key features of the phenomenon most relevant to the ensuing discussion will briefly be introduced here.[2] *En passant*, the identification and characterisation of these features had been informed by readings not only in social psychology, but also in a range of other disciplines, including sociology, gender studies, and language studies.

Firstly, racism is inextricably linked to processes involving the marginalisation and domination of 'racialised' groups, that is, processes entailing 'systematically asymmetrical relations of power' between different groups constituted as 'races' (Thompson, 1984).[3] For example, in South Africa, as indeed in many other countries in the Western world, and broadly speaking, racism has predominantly manifest itself in processes involving the social, political and economic domination or marginalisation of people of colour by Whites or people of European origin.

Secondly, as is the case with other ideologies, the ideology of racism always attempts to justify and conceal the unequal relations of power that it seeks to engender and maintain. One of the principal manners in which this is done is through the differential representation of the dominant and dominated racialised groups, with the dominant racial groups usually represented as 'superior' (and, therefore, entitled to their dominant position in society) and dominated racialised groups represented as 'inferior' and a threat to social order (and consequently, 'deserving' of their inferior position in society).

Thirdly, like other ideologies, and as an explanatory system that aims at legitimising inequality, racism is dynamic and subject to a process of constant change. According to Bozzoli (1987), this process of continuous change is a consequence of various social and political pressures challenging the inequalities that the ideology attempts to sustain, as well as the various arguments employed within the ideology to sustain these inequalities (see Foster, 1991; Sharp, 1997). For example, at the beginning of the twentieth century, Whites in South Africa frequently attempted to justify their domination of Blacks on the basis of the latter's supposed genetic 'inferiority'. As this justification increasingly came under attack for its scientific untenability (Laville, 2000), Whites increasingly took to justifying their oppression of Blacks on the basis of the supposed 'cultural differences' between Blacks and Whites. However, the elements of this 'cultural differences' discourse are frequently built onto, or an extension of, the elements contained in the 'racial inferiority' discourse.

Fourth, and very importantly, the ideology of racism has a consistently negative impact on the lives of its targets. Here it is worth noting that very few extant scholarly works or definitions of racism make any significant reference to the impact of the phenomenon on the lives of its victims. Perhaps this is due to the widespread contemporary myth that racism no longer constitutes a significant problem internationally. Or perhaps it can be seen as an indication of the extent to which researchers in the area of racism have themselves been influenced by extant racist discourses which do not only seek to inferiorise the

Racism is inextricably linked to processes involving the marginalisation and domination of 'racialised' groups, that is, processes entailing 'systematically asymmetrical relations of power' between different groups constituted as 'races' (Thompson, 1984).

As is the case with other ideologies, the ideology of racism always attempts to justify and conceal the unequal relations of power that it seeks to engender and maintain.

Like other ideologies, and as an explanatory system that aims at legitimising inequality, racism is dynamic and subject to a process of constant change.

The ideology of racism has a consistently negative impact on the lives of its targets.

targets of racism, but (as part of the ideology's 'legitimatory' and 'concealing' functions) also to negate the impact of the ideology on their lives (Skutnabb-Kangas, 1990).

Racism is not a phenomenon that merely seeks to justify the domination and marginalisation of certain 'races'. Rather, it is a phenomenon that consistently operates 'to the detriment of its victims'.

Whatever the causes for this omission, it is essential that it be recognised that racism is not a phenomenon that merely seeks to justify the domination and marginalisation of certain 'races'. Rather, it is a phenomenon that consistently operates, as Memmi (1982:147) observed, 'to the detriment of its victims' (my translation).[5] This constant is indelibly inscribed in the history of marginalised or dominated racialised groups in many parts of the world. Consider here, for example, the social and psychological consequences of the processes of enslavement, segregation, and bondage that characterised the reality of people of colour for so many years in North America (hooks, 1996). Think too of the effects of the policies and practices of exclusion and genocide to which people of colour and people of Jewish origin have been subjected in many parts of Europe over many centuries (van Dijk, 1990). In Africa, consider the economic, political, social and psychological effects of the institutionalised processes and policies of racial exclusion and domination to which Blacks had been subjected since the arrival of European colonisers on this continent (Bulhan, 1992; 1985).

As justification for the oppression of Blacks because of their supposed genetic inferiority came under attack for its lack of scientific grounds, Whites increasingly took to justifying their oppression of Blacks on the basis of supposed cultural differences between Blacks and themselves.

Although relatively few in number, various writers (e.g. Bulhan, 1985; Cooper, 1990; Fanon, 1990; Goldberg, 1988; hooks, 1996) have written fairly extensively on the extremely deleterious effects of racism on the social, economic, political and psychological reality of people of colour. Given the specific focus of this chapter, however, these sequelae of racism will not be explored here. Suffice it to state, therefore, that the ideology has had a profoundly and consis-

tently destructive impact on both the lived and internal reality of racially dominated groups.

Discourse and racism

> In our information age, words have no innocence. Language is our weapon, our
> primary tool for dealing with the world around us ... Language can be sly,
> manipulative and cunning: it can be ably employed to dominate and oppress
> (*The Star*, 16 January 2000).

Discourse – that is, meaning expressed in speech and writing (Thompson,
1984) – is central to the functioning and reproduction of racism as ideology.
This is because it is largely through discourse that justifications in defense of
processes of racial domination, marginalisation and exclusion are formulated
and transmitted (Steenveld, 2000b; Thompson, 1984; Williams, 1997).

Discourse is central to the functioning and reproduction of racism as ideology.

The interpretation of the role of discourse in the reproduction of racism
that informs this chapter is loosely based on what Thompson (1984) and
wa Machwofi (1998) refer to as a '*critical*' and '*conflict-based*' perspective on
discourse, respectively. To accept a critical perspective on discourse, according
to wa Machwofi (1998:10), is to 'recognise the inevitable conflict arising from
the differing perspectives of seeing the social world'. It is also to recognise that
people (and the institutions in which they are located, such as the media)
produce various conflicting realities that in large measure are a function of
their desires, affiliations, interests, and so forth (wa Machwofi, 1998).

A critical perspective on discourse also acknowledges that ideological
discourse (i.e. discourse that serves to [re-]produce relations of domination)
reflects extant conflicts between various social groups, as well as attempts to
control these groups' positions in society (see Williams, 1997). Thus, within
this framework, discourse is seen as inextricably linked to, and infused with,
power (Barthes, 1964). However, while discourse is seen as infused with power,
it is acknowledged that this power is relatively variable. In the words of
Thompson (1984:132), 'different ... groups have a differential capacity to make
meanings stick'. Moreover, as will be argued later in this chapter, dominant
groups (including dominant racialised groups) and the elites linked to them,
partly as a result of their influence and control over large sectors of the media,
have the power to ensure that the meanings which they give to social
phenomena and experiences are the ones that attain prominence and widespread acceptance (see Billig, 1976).

Furthermore, as should be clear from the above, within this perspective,
discourse is seen as more than merely a medium employed to convey information. People (including media workers) do other things with their discourse as
well. They may mobilise it to attack and vilify others and to defend themselves.
They may also employ it to represent the Self and the Other in ways that will

facilitate the control and subjugation of the latter (Macdonell, 1987; Williams, 1997). Discourse, as Williams (1997) argues, is often commandeered to assign places to human bodies in existing or envisaged social hierarchies.

However, while discourse is normally used with specific intentions, it often escapes the control of those who articulate it, and – largely as a result of its plurivocity – generates various unintended consequences (Wetherell & Potter, 1988). In the words of Wetherell and Potter (1988:168), once pronounced, discourse has repercussions 'which may not have been formulated or even understood' by its producers (see de Beer, 1997). Thus, sometimes even the most innocuous remarks have the potential to be racist. This is one of the more crucial points which have to be borne in mind when addressing the issue of media racism: it matters little what individual media workers' intentions are when they (re-)produce certain discourses. What is important is the effect of these discourses. Thus, if these discourses can be construed as bolstering or reproducing extant racial inequalities, they can be considered racist.

After this somewhat protracted (but necessary) detour, I will now take a closer look at the role of the media in the reproduction of racism in South Africa. At the outset, let it be stated that the position adopted in this chapter (the defensive protests of certain sectors of the media notwithstanding) is that the media in South Africa have played, and indeed continue to play, a central role in the perpetuation of the ideology (*Mail & Guardian*, 20–27 November 1998). This position is in fact supported by the research and views of a range of media workers and academics (e.g. Braude, 1999; Mandaza, 2000; Media Monitoring Project [MMP], 1999; Mokoe, 2000; Steenveld, 2000a; 2000b; 2000c; Whitfield, 2000) who, in 1999 and 2000, responded to the controversy that had surrounded SAHRC's Inquiry into Racism in the Media, as well as the events leading up to it, in submissions to the SAHRC (2000) and a special issue of the *Rhodes Journalism Review* (2000).

Obviously, during the pre-1990s, the media's role was easily detectable; for then most of the media contributed fairly explicitly (albeit to varying degrees) to the justification of racial inequality in this country (Braude, 1999; Whitfield, 2000). Such explicit racism, which Hall (1995) refers to as *overt* media racism, included explicit racial vilification through the construction of stereotypical and blatantly prejudiced representations of certain 'racial' groups,

> Discourse is often commandeered to assign places to human bodies in existing or envisaged social hierarchies.

Special issue of *Rhodes Journalism Review*, August 2000.

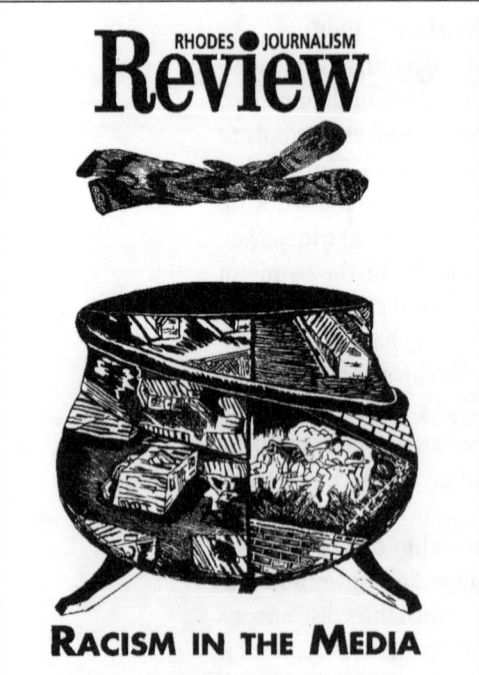

RACISM IN THE MEDIA

incitement to racial discrimination and conflict, and the media's tendency to grant extensive and favourable press to individuals and groups explicitly promoting racist views and policies, while suppressing or attacking the views of anti-racists and marginalised or dominated groups (see *Mail & Guardian*, 20–27 November 1998).

While overt racism was certainly still discernible in the media in South Africa (particularly in the conservative print media) during the 1990s (see Diederichs, 1997; Williams, 1997), since the early 1990s, it increasingly gave way to subliminal or what Hall (1995) would refer to as *inferential* racism. According to Hall (1995:20), inferential racism refers to 'those apparently naturalised representations of [people,] events and situations ... whether "factual" or "fictional", which have racist premises and propositions inscribed in them as a set of *unquestioned assumptions*' (emphasis added). To a certain extent, inferential racism can be seen as a logical development in the evolution of the ideology of racism. This is because the assumptions of overt racism have become so sedimented or embedded and 'naturalised' in Western society, that they can be communicated and internalised without being explicitly articulated. Largely because it does not make explicit the racist assumptions on which it is based, inferential or subliminal racism is very difficult to identify; hence certain newspapers' near-arrogant position that they are in no way complicit in racism. Since it is difficult to identify, it is also difficult to deal with. Consider here the example of a certain newspaper that runs a series of articles that consistently portrays Black people negatively and Whites positively, but without overtly employing traditional stereotypes to 'negativise' the former or to valorise the latter. Because of the ambiguity of its articulation within these articles, many people might not challenge this form of racism, and as a consequence allow it to insidiously reproduce itself. On the other hand, those who do challenge it are very likely to be attacked by particularly the beneficiaries of racism for seeing racism where there is in fact no racism. To a certain extent this was reflected in the responses of certain groupings in the media to the ABASA and BLA complaint to the SAHRC (referred to earlier). As soon as these groupings became aware of the complaint, they immediately started a campaign of public disparagement aimed at the complainants and the SAHRC, accusing them of willful mischief mongering and provocateurism, and they produced a range of very plausible arguments to support this accusation.

In spite of the fact that media racism is becoming increasingly implicit and difficult to distinguish, van Dijk (1990) identifies several patterns in media discourses which, he contends, allows for the perpetuation of racism. A consideration of some of these strategies, as well as a cursory assessment of the dominant discourses maintained by the South African media, will reveal that there is substance to the BLA and ABASA claims that during the 1990s, racism

According to Hall (1995:20), inferential racism refers to 'those apparently naturalised representations of [people,] events and situations ... whether "factual" or "fictional", which have racist premises and propositions inscribed in them as a set of *unquestioned assumptions*'.

was still very evident in at least the mainstream print media in South Africa, albeit in an increasingly sophisticated form. Here it must be noted that in the discussion to follow, the assessment of the dominant discourses maintained in the South African media will largely be based on the research and observations of various academics and media workers, rather than on a single empirical study. We now turn our attention to some of the discursive strategies identified by van Dijk (1990).

Representations of the 'Other'

As stated earlier, one of the primary ways in which racism is justified is through the negative representation of the 'Other'. As also mentioned above, prevailing social norms have made the explicitly racist stereotyping characteristic of overt racism increasingly untenable. However, this does not mean that, in racist societies, dominated or marginalised 'races' are no longer 'negativised'. On the contrary, there are various ways in which the 'negativisation' of certain groups is perpetuated, and the media play an important role in this process. For example, research indicates that in White-dominated societies, a number of negative stereotypical themes are favoured by the media in news reports and recreational stories (such as television drama series) featuring people of colour. These topics include violence, crime (especially drug-related crimes, theft and corruption), industrial conflict, cultural differences and 'ethnic' conflict. Reflecting on patterns of reporting in the print media in South Africa during the 1990s, Mokoe (2000:15) observes somewhat despairingly that the only time when black people appear to 'make the headlines is when something negative occurs, but on the whole, they are never ... depicted as pioneering crusaders'. According to Bertelsen (2000), this was particularly the case when the black subject had left-leaning political affiliations.

> One of the primary ways in which racism is justified is through the negative representation of the 'Other'.

Conversely, the topics normally favoured in media reports featuring Whites included the economy, education, social affairs, sporting achievements and culture (see van Dijk, 1990). Furthermore, when Whites were implicated in crime or other misdemeanours by the media, they, unlike Blacks, were easily rehabilitated by the self-same media (Mokoe, 2000). Here the highly 'mediatised' 'scandals' or 'incidents' involving the cricketers, Makhaya Ntini and Hansie Cronjé, serve as a case in point. As observed by Mokoe (2000), the Black cricketer Makhaya Ntini was relentlessly vilified in the media as a 'rapist', 'not fit to represent his country', and a 'bad role-model' – even after having been acquitted of a rape charge lodged against him. However, the self-same media that had crucified Ntini forgave his White counterpart, Hansie Cronjé, who had admitted to having committed serious fraud, fairly quickly.

Along similar lines, Mandaza (2000:23) describes how White fascist leaders of the old order, like P.W. Botha, had been allowed by the media of the 1990s to 'retire almost victoriously ... their glaring atrocities ... concealed under the flimsy cloak of reconciliation', while Black leaders were 'being demonised beyond recognition, their historic sacrifices almost forgotten'.

The ideological function of such differential 'casting' of Whites and people of colour in the media should be clear. Here it must be noted, however, that due to the emergence of increasingly influential Black political and economic elites in this country in the 1990s, a growing number of media reports featuring Blacks also dealt with fairly positive topics. Nonetheless, such reports continued to be overshadowed by reports featuring Blacks in relation to the stereotypical themes mentioned above – or not at all (MMP, 1999; Mokoe, 2000; see van Dijk, 1990).

While the dominant representations emerging from media reports during the 1990s obviously differ substantially from the 'old-fashioned' racist representations of blacks as 'barbaric', 'savage', 'child-like', etc. (Kuper, 1974; *Rhodes Journalism Review*, 2000), through the fairly consistent association of Blacks with negative topics, they nonetheless constructed Blacks as a negative *'Other'* and thereby arguably contributed to the justification and consequent perpetuation of extant patterns of racial inequality (Whitfield, 2000).

Other techniques (i.e. techniques other than the association of Blacks with negative topics) frequently employed by the media to 'negativise' Blacks include the types of photographs and film footage, and the lexical registers favoured in relation to Blacks (van Dijk, 1987; Williams, 1997). For example, in a study on media reportage on political violence in South Africa in 1993, it was found that when newspapers reported on the death of Whites in incidents of political violence, they most often used very emotive terms, such as 'the brutal' or 'callous murder'. However when they reported on the death of Blacks in similar circumstances, they would most often use words emanating from the lexical register of animals – words such as 'the killing' or 'slaughter of people' (see Duncan, 1996; see also van Dijk, 1991).

Along similar lines, MMP (1999) found that the media generally tended to 'depersonalise' the death of Black people. Consequently, when reporting on the deaths of Blacks, the media would often only concentrate on the number of the people who died, and provide no details of the circumstances and histories of the individuals who had died. This was in stark contrast to the reporting conventions employed when covering the death of Whites (*ibid.*). This process of 'depersonalisation' was also reflected in the manner in which images of the dead were used. Specifically, the MMP (*ibid.*) found that graphic images of dead bodies were more common in stories that dealt with the death of Black people. Indeed, in some instances, the same pictures were used to 'illustrate' totally unrelated incidents of violence. The MMP (*ibid.*) very plausibly argues that one of the consequences of the constant use of images of dead bodies to represent the death of Black people is that it normalises the death of Blacks and ultimately reduces the viewer's or reader's sympathy for them.

In the United States, Johnson (1994) found that when the electronic media covered stories about crime, they usually used footage of Blacks regardless of whether the stories involved Blacks or not. Needless to state, this differential usage of photographs and footage in reports on violence and other negative events or issues, if it takes place consistently and over a long period of time, ultimately leads to Blacks being constructed as violent in the public psyche and Whites as their eternal victims (Kern-Foxworth in Johnson, 1994).

Denial

According to van Dijk (1987), denial constitutes one of the key means whereby the media currently contribute (unintentionally, as well as intentionally) to the reproduction of racism. In essence, the discursive strategy of denial perpetuates racial inequality, not by openly advocating racial inequality, but by claiming that racism is less widespread than it is, or else that it does not exist. Thus, the strategy of denial perpetuates racism through concealing extant patterns of racial inequality. An examination of media reports of the 1990s reveals that the denial of racism seems to have been a fairly central feature of the dominant media discourse of the period (Duncan, 1996).

One of the principal ways in which the media normally attempt to negate the existence or extent of racism is through the use of distance markers when reporting on instances of racism. Consequently, when black people accuse institutions or individuals of racism, their accusations are normally inserted between quotation marks or are accompanied by words such as 'claimed' and 'alleged' (Duncan, 1996). In this regard, consider the following excerpts from a selection of media reports published in the late 1990s:

> SOUTH AFRICAN PLAYERS FACE SANCTIONS OVER RACISM CLAIMS. South African cricketers Pat Symcox and Fanie de Villiers face disciplinary action over *alleged* racist remarks made to spectators during the second Test against Pakistan in Durban last weekend (Agence France-Presse, 1998:1).

> Human Rights organisations yesterday joined President Mandela in condemning the *killing* of six-month-old Thobile Zwane – who was *allegedly* shot by a [White] farmer (*Sowetan*, 15 April 1998).

By using distance markers such as those contained in the quotations presented above, it would appear as if the writers of the articles in question wished to disassociate themselves from these reports and the accusations of racism contained in them (van Dijk, 1989). Through this act of *discursive distantiation*, these writers simultaneously also appear to cast doubt on, or question, the authenticity of the reported accusations of racism.

Here it can be noted that denials of racism in the media have far-reaching implications because they often help to construct the discursive context in which processes aimed at reversing extant patterns of racial equality (such as

According to van Dijk (1987), denial constitutes one of the key means whereby the media currently contribute (unintentionally, as well as intentionally) to the reproduction of racism.

affirmative action processes) are branded as 'unnecessary' or even as 'reverse racism' (van Dijk, 1990). In the 'new' South Africa of the 1990s, the oft-repeated belief that since apartheid laws had been scrapped, racism was largely something of the past undoubtedly played a significant role in the articulation of such media denials of racism.

Smith (2000) argues that the frequent usage of the strategy of denial in the media in the recent past can perhaps be viewed as a consequence of defensiveness on the part of particularly White media workers in response to recent public acknowledgements of the horrors of the apartheid order. Nonetheless, because media reports using the discursive strategy of denial contribute to the obfuscation of the nature and extent of racism, they can be seen to aid in the perpetuation of the phenomenon. As hooks (1996) and Essed (1987) note, media reportage which obfuscates the functioning and extent of racism effectively renders attempts to deal with the problem more difficult, and in this sense perpetuates the phenomenon (see van Dijk, 1990). The following strategies can be seen to contribute to the perpetuation of the phenomenon for more or less the same reason.

Mitigation

Mitigation, a 'milder' version of the previous strategy, refers to the use of rhetorical devices such as 'down-toning' and euphemisms aimed at minimising the culpability of groups and institutions accused of racism. For example, very frequently, the media will report processes and acts that are undeniably racist as merely incidents of 'discrimination', 'bias', 'prejudice' 'conservatism' or 'intolerance' (van Dijk, 1990). This strategy too, was fairly widespread in the media during the 1990s (Duncan 1996). Consider here, for example, the following headlines that appeared in *The Star* during early 1999:

> Racial intolerance [and] cultural ignorance are among causes of classroom tension (*The Star*, 5 March 1999).

> US study initiates probe into possible racial bias over heart bypass surgery (*The Star*, 11 January 1999).

> VRYBURG: THE SORE STILL FESTERS. Racial tensions at this North West school reflect the situation in South Africa ... (*The Star*, 11 March 1999).

Given that racism is generally seen as a more serious social infraction than discrimination, bias, prejudice, 'cultural ignorance' and intolerance (which are normally seen as individual 'aberrations' or 'deviations'), such reportage, van Dijk (1990) argues, can be seen as an attempt to mitigate the culpability of those accused of racism. Accusations of racism are frequently also mitigated by quoting the accused's explanations of these processes and acts at length and ignoring the experiences of those who lodge the accusations.

Mitigation refers to the use of rhetorical devices such as 'down-toning' and euphemisms aimed at minimising the culpability of groups and institutions accused of racism.

Another manner in which the impact and extent of racism in South Africa were mitigated in the media during the 1990s, according to Seepe (1998), was through its representation as a problem that was incidental and essentially caused by small, insignificant groups of right-wing extremists. The problem with this representation of racism obviously is that it ultimately denied the fact that racism constituted one of the more significant problems that characterised the South African social landscape during the period under consideration. By downplaying or concealing the extent of racism, it *a priori* questioned or censured whatever interventions may have been instituted to deal with the problem, and in the process, therefore, aided in the perpetuation of the phenomenon.

Reversal

Reversal refers to situations where those who lodge accusations of racism are themselves frequently accused of racism, or else of being 'oversensitive ... intolerant, and ... seeing racism where there is none' (van Dijk, 1990:4).

This strategy goes beyond the mere denial and mitigation of racism by reversing accusations of racism. Specifically, reversal refers to situations where those who lodge accusations of racism are themselves frequently accused of racism, or else of being 'oversensitive ... intolerant, and ... seeing racism where there is none' (van Dijk, 1990:4). Here the media's general response to the BLA and ABASA complaint to the SAHRC is a case in point. Thus, the victims of racism are represented as the 'real racists'. Needless to state, this strategy should be seen as an integral aspect of the manner in which the ideology of racism attempts to 'negativise' its targets, for as van Dijk (1990) argues, being accused of racism, in contemporary society, constitutes one of the most negative evaluations any individual or group can be subjected to.

The media's apparent preoccupation with the problems experienced by middle-class White South Africans during the 1990s (see Braude, 1999) is another example of this strategy. Hardly a day went by during that period (and to a certain extent, today still) without the public being bombarded with the most detailed reports of how White farmers were killed, how (White) South African citizens' confidence was being eroded by the prevailing crime rates; how the property of Whites was being devalued as a result of squatter problems; and how difficult it had become for Whites to procure stable employment, etc. (Braude, 1999; MMP, 1999). Now, it is not the intention here to imply that these reports in themselves were problematic. On the contrary: as the media so frequently argue, it is their duty to inform the public of whatever problems compromise the social stability and the well-being of South Africans. However, it was the media's sudden and significantly heightened sensitivity to these problems (Mandaza, 2000), which had affected Blacks for decades (without eliciting similar levels of protest from the self-same media), that could be called into question. Furthermore, the manner in which these reports were framed also poses a problem. In most of these reports the problems experienced by Whites were invariably presented as a consequence of the policies of the present (Black-led) government, or of the actions of certain Black individuals or groups (e.g. new policing policies, Black crime syndicates, Black squatters, anti-racist activists, and affirmative action appointees) (Braude, 1999; MMP, 1999). The implicit accusation therefore was that the problems experienced by Whites were a result of Black 'racism'.

During the 1990s, attempts to target specific marginalised Black groups, such as Coloureds, Zulu speakers, and Indians/Asians as the 'real racists' in South Africa, constituted a particularly distorted and cynical expression of this strategy. For example, research shows that prior to, and following the 1994 general elections the media appeared to consistently play up the Coloured issue in relation to the housing problems, the outcome of the elections and problems concerning the implementation of affirmative action programmes in the Western Cape (Pickel, 1996). More specifically, these problems were most often presented as being a result of 'Coloured racism'. This tendency on the part of the media to focus on the 'racism' of marginalised Black groups[6] obviously results in the focus being shifted from the real cause of these problems, namely, institutionalised racism which, in South Africa, initially had been put in place to secure White privilege.

'Naturalising' inequality and blaming the victims

This strategy, which intersects with all the strategies discussed above, refers to the media's tendency to report on racialised patterns of socio-economic inequality without attempting to examine the structural causes of such inequality (MMP, 1999). During the 1990s, this frequently resulted in the perception that extant racialised patterns of unemployment, poverty, and ill health were 'inevitable' and as a consequence no-one was to blame for the invidious circumstances of the victims of racism (see wa Machwofi, 1998). It is therefore not surprising that so many people, particularly during the 1990s, perceived affirmative action programmes aimed at correcting racial inequality as 'unfair'; for if no-one was really to blame for under-privileged position of Blacks, then the preferential treatment they received as a result of these programmes would obviously also be perceived as unfair. Frequently, where media reports did make mention of the structural causes of racialised patterns of inequality, they neglected the historical (apartheid) origins of these patterns. Consequently, the persistence of these patterns was construed as being a result of the ineptitude of the government of the day. The resulting implied message obviously was that the present (predominantly Black-led) government was responsible for the prevailing processes of racial inequalities. As a result, the attention was effectively drawn away from the key causes of racism.

Naturalising inequality and blaming the victims is a strategy that refers to the media's tendency to report on racialised patterns of socio-economic inequality without attempting to examine the structural causes of such inequality.

Identify the racism

Row over 'racist' council. Crisis in Durban over NP motion

Durban – The crisis over the appointment of four Durban city councillors of colour deepened today with a controversial new bid by a National Party member to include 12 more nominated councilors.

Councillor Mr. Johan Krog drafted notices of motion calling on the council to allot 12 further seats to the African National Congress, Inkatha and the civic movement.

This is being seen as an effort to defuse mounting opposition, including threats of strikes and breakdowns in negotiations.

But the ANC has rejected the idea as 'racist tokenism' and plans are going ahead for concerted action against the council. The municipal employees' society promises to bring the city to a standstill 'if the council persists in its foolishness'.

In theory, Mr. Krog's motion means the council could have 16 new councilors, mostly 'non-white', but appointed, not elected.

'Totally unacceptable', was the response of Mr. Mike Sutcliffe, ANC local government convener for Southern Natal.

'We reject outright this racist attempt to hand out a few token seats,' he said, adding that the ANC would continue planning concerted action against the council.

Mr. Nad Murugan, general secretary of the Democratic Integrated Municipal Employees Society, Natal's biggest municipal trade union, said the proposal was 'unacceptable'.

'If the council thinks the leaders of the community will insult their constituents by accepting co-option into such a racist set-up, they are more stupid than I imagined.

'My union will bring this city to a stand-still if the council persists in its foolishness,' he said, indicating that the public transport system would be the first target.

The grim threats by the ANC and its allies have prompted growing concern in the city's business community (*Argus*, 17 July 1992).

'Taxi rabies' fuels killer disease

It's hard to control stray dogs brought to settlements from rural areas.

For many South Africans, there is the real danger of being bitten by a rabid animal, as the disease expands into areas previously considered rabies-free. Over the past five years, some 272 districts – 75 per cent of all magisterial districts in South Africa – have recorded one or more cases of rabies.

Traditionally, KwaZulu–Natal and the Eastern Cape were rabies hotspots, but now the disease is appearing in Mpumalanga and in new areas in the Eastern Cape. In other regions like the Northern Province, rabies is often diagnosed in mongooses, jackals, bat-eared foxes, cats and other domestic animals.

Part of the reason for the spread of rabies into these new areas is that over the past couple of years we have had what is termed 'taxi rabies', resulting from the movement of people and dogs from rural areas into informal settlements. Stray dogs roam around these settlements, which are difficult to control, says Professor Robert Swanepoel, of the National Institute of Virology (*Saturday Star*, 19 June 1999).

Possible reasons for media racism

A range of factors contributed to the role played by the media in the reproduction of racism during the period under consideration, as well as currently, some of which are briefly discussed below.

Firstly, South African media workers (i.e. journalists, reporters, and producers) would acknowledge that racism is deeply embedded in South African society and that few people are consequently left untouched by the influence of this ideology. Furthermore, they would have to acknowledge that given that they do not function in a social vacuum, they too might have internalised aspects of the ideology. Indeed, as Essed (1987) observes, in racially stratified societies, racism has a profound impact on intellectuals such as media workers, as well as their intellectual productions. Here it is important to note that in the South African context, Black media workers are not immune to the effects of racism and that they too can become important agents in the reproduction of racism, even anti-Black racism. As the African National Congress (2000:21) in its submission to the SAHRC Enquiry into Media Racism argued, 'Many contemporary ... [Black] journalists help to sustain ... racist images ... because they too have absorbed the white stereotype of the black savage'. In this regard, Legum (in Steenveld, 2000a:11) posits, 'racism means that all people's relationships, even with themselves are influenced by ["race"]'. This leads to the next important factor contributing to the media's role in the reproduction of racism in South Africa.

It is important to note that in the South African context, Black media workers are not immune to the effects of racism and that they too can become important agents in the reproduction of racism, even anti-Black racism.

During the 1990s, the media sector in South Africa was still dominated by large conglomerates owned primarily by Whites – and with primarily White males in key decision-making positions (Boloka, 2000; Diederichs, 1997; Haffajee, 1998; *Mail & Guardian*, 20–27 November 1998). Given that the overwhelming majority of the members of this elite had benefited significantly from institutionalised racial discrimination, Seepe (1998) argues, it could consequently be expected that the media would, to varying degrees, have continued to aid in the perpetuation of racism in this country (see van Dijk, 1987). Admittedly, Blacks were gaining increasing control of the media during that period, either at an editorial level or through acquiring shares in companies linked to the big media conglomerates (Haffajee, 1998; *Mail & Guardian*, 20–27 November 1998). However, such control was limited. Moreover, as Haffajee (1998:41) observed, 'the ... media are big businesses and their new owners are only just getting their hands onto the levers; for that reason we have not seen major changes in the ... [media]'.

A third factor contributing to the media's role in the reproduction of racism is related to this institution's reliance on what van Dijk (1987) refers to as *White expertise* when reporting on 'race'-related issues. Analyses of media reports indicate an undue reliance on the opinions of White elites or, as Seepe (1998:3) puts it, the systematic 'marginalisation of black thought and input', in reports dealing with 'race'-related issues, i.e. issues that affect Black people most adversely (see van Dijk, 1987). This tendency to constantly defer to *White expertise* and to ignore the experiences of the targets of racism, van Dijk (1990:9) argues, to a large extent is a reflection not only of the media's confidence in this expertise, but also of their 'negative prejudices about the credibility and reliability' of Blacks as sources of information. This is consistent with the views of Matisonn who, in an article published in 1998 (*Mail &*

Contributing to the media's role in the reproduction of racism is this institution's reliance on what van Dijk (1987) refers to as *White expertise* when reporting on 'race'-related issues.

Guardian, 20–27 November 1998), argued that newspaper editors frequently avoided Blacks as key informants in matters pertaining to racism because they perceived the latter as too '*partisan*' as far as racism was concerned. In the South African context, Whites have generally not been subjected to racism in the same manner that Black people have and, as previously noted, given that Whites have in the past generally benefited from institutionalised racial discrimination, this tendency, during the period under consideration, frequently led to the emergence of accounts of racism which only told 'half the story' and which themselves contained a myriad of racist messages (Seepe, 1998).

Here it needs to be noted that the fact that media workers play such a central role in the reproduction of racism does not necessarily mean that they do so consciously, or that they do not at times attempt to challenge the ideology (MMP, 1999). That would be too simplistic a perception to be of much use in explaining the dynamics of this very complex phenomenon and its ancillary discourses (Alexander, 1985).

Given that media workers do not constitute a homogeneous group and that they are differentially *subjected* by the ideology of racism, their discourses are frequently relatively variable. Indeed, their discourses at times reflect various decidedly anti-racist elements (MMP, 1999; van Dijk, 1987). Consider here, for example, the pivotal role played by some sectors of the media in unmasking apartheid excesses in the past. In fact, it was in view of the potential threat that the media posed to the apartheid order that previous governments mobilised a myriad of external restraints or checks to ensure its control over the media. Here the censorship laws of the apartheid era immediately come to mind (e.g. the *Publications Act,* 1974 and the *Suppression of Communism Act,* 1950). While restraints such as these could ultimately not halt the demise of the apartheid regime, it cannot be denied that they had a profound influence on the prevailing ethos in media institutions (Whitfield, 2000).

The impact of media racism

Racist messages transmitted by the media are much more powerful and destructive than racist messages produced in interactive or interpersonal situations. This is so for a number of reasons, three of which are mentioned below. Firstly, the racist messages transmitted by the media reach many more people than racist messages produced in other situations, such as in conversations and discussions in class-rooms and meetings (de Beer, 1997). As de Beer (*ibid.*) argues, the mass media constitute an integral and pervasive aspect of our daily lives. We are confronted by the media 'from the moment breakfast television or the morning newspaper greets us, through thousands of advertising and other mass communicated messages during the day, until we watch the late-night movie' (*ibid.*:6). Even people who do not watch television, listen to the

> Racist messages transmitted by the media are much more powerful and destructive than racist messages produced in interactive or interpersonal situations.

radio, or read newspapers are exposed to the messages transmitted through these media, for they have contact with those who are exposed to television, the radio and newspapers and who in various ways relay the messages they receive from the media (*ibid.*).

Secondly, unlike racist discourses relayed in 'dialogical' situations, racist media discourses (because they are inscribed) are very difficult to erase, and as a result continue to 'live' long after they have been produced.

Thirdly, the media are generally viewed as much more authoritative or credible than many other sources of information. Thus, people tend to believe what they hear from or read in the media. It is for this reason that van Dijk (1987) found that people more often than not justified their racist beliefs and actions on the basis of messages conveyed by the media. *En passant*, it is important also to note here that the media are not only potentially destructive in terms of the apparent credibility of their justifications for racial inequality, but also because of the likelihood that dominated and dominant groups will internalise the negative identities and characteristics which the media attribute to them – particularly if this is done consistently and over a protracted period of time. As a reading of Goldberg (1988:23) suggests, through their interaction with other discourses, media racist discourses play a crucial role in defining human subjectivity and molding 'the subject's relations with others'. However, people do not always succumb to the influence of the media, for as Williams (in Gross, 1995:67) puts it, hegemony 'is never either total or exclusive. At any time, forms of alternative or directly oppositional politics and culture exist as significant elements in the society.'

One of the ways in which people may oppose media 'negativisation' would be to ignore the media, but given the pervasiveness of the mass media this strategy is not very feasible or successful.

Oppositional strategies

There are various ways in which people may oppose media racism. The most obvious form of opposition would be to ignore the mass media so as to avoid being influenced by the manner in which they systematically negativise marginalised groups. However, given the pervasiveness of the mass media in contemporary society, and given that the mass media constitute an important source of entertainment and information for large groups of people, this strategy is not always very feasible or successful (Gross, 1995; *Mail & Guardian*, 20–27 November 1998).

A second oppositional strategy that is sometimes used by groups consistently negativised by the media is the appropriation and subversion of media representations of these groups. This strategy operates primarily

by means of the appropriation and exaggeration of media stereotypes of marginalised groups (Gross, 1995). The African American sitcom, *In Living Color* (Schulman, 1995) and the South Africa sitcom, *Fishy Fêshuns,* are striking examples of this strategy. What these sitcoms essentially do is to evoke and exaggerate dominant-group stereotypical representations of Black people in order to subvert them. Such appropriation of racist stereotyping is of course an age-old strategy utilised by dominated groups to challenge their domination (Schulman, 1995). However, to a certain extent this strategy is a double-edged sword, because while it aims at exposing, so as to undermine, racist stereotypes, it has the potential of reinforcing racist bigotry and narrow-mindedness (Schulman, 1995).

The ultimate strategy that can be employed is for marginalised groups to become the creators of their own representation in the media. This strategy can obviously only be optimally successful if these groups are adequately represented at all levels of mass media production and control.

The ultimate strategy that can be employed to oppose media racism is for members of marginalised groups to become producers of their own representations in the mass media, like the columnist John Matshikiza and disc jockey 'The General'.

Dealing with media racism

Given the media's enormous power, as well as the fact that this power is unfortunately frequently used in the reproduction of racist ideas and the pre-formulation of justifications of racial inequality, it is important that preventative measures, including legislation, be put in place to ensure that this power is used responsibly (Johns, 1995).

Right to freedom of expression vs right to dignity and equality

The nineteenth edition of the *Rhodes Journalism Review* contains a range of articles by 25 media workers and academics reflecting on the question of media racism in South Africa as well as the events leading up to SAHRC's Inquiry into Racism in the Media. The overwhelming majority of these academics and media workers concluded that, until the end of the 1990s at least, racism was still a significant problem in South Africa. Yet, newspapers like the *Mail & Guardian* want us to believe, firstly, that the problem is not as significant as it is made out to be; and secondly, that establishing an inquiry to examine the problem would merely lead to the stifling of media freedom. It is to the latter point that we now turn our attention.

What should take precedence: the right to media freedom or freedom of expression, or the right to dignity and equality?

According to Steenveld (2000c) the hegemonic view amongst certain sectors of the South African community appears to be that freedom of expression should be untouchable in a democracy. This view is based on the following assumptions:

- Self-expression is an essential human characteristic. Consequently, preventing people from expressing themselves is a violation of people's freedom and autonomy.

- For democracy to function optimally, people must have access to a range of views – which freedom of expression allows for (*ibid.*).

The underlying argument for an absolute freedom of expression is that 'sharing/contesting/debating ideas [is] the basis of a democracy' (Steenveld, 2000c:26). However, in the event of one accepting this argument, the question which then logically comes to mind is: What happens to people's right to dignity and equality (and therefore, not to be subjected to racism) in cases where freedom of expression leads to racist utterances? The literature reflects various answers to this question. Lawrence (in Steenveld, 2000c), for example, implies that freedom of expression is not possible if the individual's right to dignity and equality is not guaranteed. As he puts it, 'there can be no free speech when there are still masters [/madams] and slaves' (in Steenveld, 2000c:26). Specifically, he reasons, in situations characterised by systematically asymmetric relations of power between groups, those with most power generally benefit most from unlimited freedom of expression, and they use this advantage to maintain the status quo – even if this would mean reproducing racist discourses.

Conclusion

In this chapter we have examined the ideology of racism and how it is perpetuated via the media. In this examination we have also seen that racism, as perpetuated through the media, is becoming increasingly covert. Consequently, it is becoming increasingly difficult to identify, and therefore, to combat. For this reason, it is argued in this chapter, current manifestations of media racism are particularly destructive. Nonetheless, because racism is not an inevitable aspect of human – and consequently social group – functioning, it can be eliminated. In view of the potentially damaging consequences of the phenomenon, it is incumbent upon all of us – particularly those of us who, through our exposure to social psychology, have some understanding of social processes and dynamics – to contribute to efforts to eradicate it.

Cover of *Chimurenga*

Courtesy of *Chimurenga*

Southern trees bear strange fruit
Blood on the leaves and blood at the root
Black bodies swinging in the southern breeze
Strange fruit hanging from the poplar trees

Pastoral scene of the gallant south
The bulging eyes and the twisted mouth
Scent of magnolias, sweet and fresh
Then the sudden smell of burning flesh

Here is fruit for the crows to pluck
For the rain to gather, for the wind to suck
For the sun to rot, for the trees to drop
Here is a strange and bitter cry

Exercises for critical engagement

1 Identify the discursive elements that can be construed to perpetuate racism in these two reports that appeared in the printed media during the 1990s. Provide a discussion detailing why you would consider these discursive elements to be racist in nature.

2 What are your views regarding the question posed above, namely: What should take precedence, the right to media freedom or freedom of expression, or the right to dignity and equality? In response to the South African Human Rights Commission's Inquiry into Racism in the Media, the *Mail & Guardian* argued that the problem is not as serious as it is made out to be. This is a common element in the discourses of many South African media companies, despite the fact that various studies indicate that racism is still a significant social problem in South Africa. How would you explain such denial?

3 Why would legislation alone not suffice in attempts to combat racism in the media? Based on extant social psychological theories and research (see Chapter 3 for a summary of these theories and research), what measures would you propose to combat media racism in South Africa?

Endnotes

1   In this chapter, when the term 'mass media' is employed, it will broadly refer to all forms of the print media (such as newspapers, magazines, and popular literature) as well as electronic media (such as the radio, television, cinema and the Internet), which have a mass audience (Nodoba, 2002).

2   For a more detailed discussion of racism, see Chapter 3, this volume.

3   Here the reader is referred to Laville (2000) for an informative critique of the use of 'race' as a taxonomic system to classify human groups.

4   In this chapter I employ the terms 'people of colour' and 'Blacks' interchangeably (and fairly arbitrarily) to refer to 'other-than-White' groups when the need arises to refer to these groups collectively. I take cognisance of the fact that many people, for a range of reasons, are not comfortable with either of these terms, the chief reason being that these terms often serve to homogenise the people which they are meant to designate. However, despite the criticisms that their usage will predictably provoke, I will, at various points in this chapter, be constrained to employ these collective labels in the development of some of the arguments put forward in this chapter. In any event, they are preferable to the term 'non-White' (which effectively transforms people of colour into a negative Other), traditionally used as a collective label to refer to people of colour.

5   All translations provided in this chapter are the author's own.

6   An accusation that, at a theoretical level at least, is fairly problematic (see Essed, 1986; 1987; Steenveld, 2000a).

7   See chapter by de la Rey and Duncan in this volume for a summary of these theories and research.

Recommended reading

Diederichs, P. (1997). 'Newspapers. The fourth estate'. In de Beer, A.S. (Ed.) *Mass Media for the Nineties. A South African Handbook of Mass Communication*, pp. 71–100. Pretoria: van Schaik.

Essed, P. (1987). *Academic Racism*. Amsterdam: CRES Publications.

Hall, S. (1995). 'The white of their eyes'. In Dines, G. & J.M. Humez (Eds.) *Gender, Race and Class in Media*, pp. 18–22. Thousand Oaks: Sage.

hooks, b. (1996). *Killing Rage: Ending Racism*. London: Penguin Books.

Rhodes Journalism Review (2000). *Racism in the Media*. Grahamstown: Rhodes University.

South African Human Rights Commission (SAHRC) (2000). *Faultlines: Inquiry into Racism in the Media*. Parktown: SAHRC.

Van Dijk, T. (1989). 'Structures and strategies of discourse and prejudice'. In van Oudenhoven, J.P. & T.M. Willemsen (Eds.) *Ethnic Minorities. Social Psychological Perspectives*, pp 115–138. Amsterdam: Swets & Zeitlinger.

Van Dijk, T. (1987). *Communicating Racism. Ethnic Prejudice in Thought and Talk*. Newbury Park: Sage.

Bodies and Apartheid

Kopano Ratele & Tamara Shefer

OUTCOMES

After having studied this chapter you should be able to:

- understand the interest in bodies among scholars and in the wider cultural arena
- give your own interpretation of the meaning of 'race' re-classification
- describe how discourse constructs bodies and explain how bodies get inserted into social, sexual, political, cultural and economic structures
- engage in a discussion of how apartheid represented and used bodies, and
- discuss critically the way in which anti-apartheid struggles, in particular, the Black Consciousness Movement (BCM), challenged apartheid's construction of bodies.

THIS CHAPTER has two foci. The first is to show the importance of the body to the history, economy, politics, and social psychology of the country. To this end, the chapter describes how the body was one of the crucial elements in conceiving and entrenching the policy of segregation, as well as in the struggle for democracy and freedom. The chapter explores how both apartheid and aspects of the national liberation movement were actively engaged in defining the meaning of *the body*.

The second focus is to describe how apartheid and the national liberation movement were out *to win bodies*, that is, to use bodies towards particular political and ideological goals. Thus, in addition to possessing, prevailing over, or converting minds, psyches, or what might be referred to as souls, bodies were utilised by both apartheid and the national liberation movement in very specific ways. This latter focus is of course not entirely separate from the former, since the objective of defining what the body is and what parts of the body stand for (the construction of knowledge), and that of capturing it or *deploying* it for certain ends (achieving power), are supportive of one another.

As Foucault (1979), who theorised the complex relationship between knowledge and power, argues – where one is, the other will be found. In both cases the intention is to reveal how the body was another terrain on which the political, economic, and social oppression and struggle for democracy was grounded, and where subjugation immediately happened and got directly challenged. The body was arguably one of the primary targets of state power, segregation law, police brutality, as well as Black resistance. Writing about the factors that have prevented the full development of conceptions of the African self, Achille Mbembe (2002:246) observes 'the centrality of the body in the calculus of political subjection'. The body, then, in a manner of speaking, is the space on which the battle for South Africa, or South Africa's soul, was waged.

> Under the system of apartheid the body was one of the primary targets of governmental power, segregation law, police brutality, as well as Black politics.

This chapter begins by illustrating how the body seems to have come into fashion in academic and cultural sectors, and shows how there are different paths to approaching an understanding of the body in society. The chapter then goes on to embark on its own path, which is to unpack how the body was constructed and used within apartheid South Africa. This task starts with a description of the connection between body and 'race' by signalling a familiar but intriguing aspect of the history and politics of our country, that of 'race' re-classifications. Next, the chapter turns to the matter of difference, leading on to how the body gets socialised, or more specifically, racialised, with a focus on the role of knowledge in constructing the apartheid body. The chapter ends off with a look at how the body was theorised and politicised within the struggle against apartheid. This section highlights in particular the work of the BCM in re-constructing the Black body as part of a psychological and political resistance to the oppressive racialisation and negative construction of Black bodies in the apartheid system. The chapter shows how the BCM re-interpreted the body, resisting apartheid modes of racialisation, while at the same time seeking to attain psychological liberation, which hinged on a bodily reclamation. The chapter concludes with some comments about the shifting context of the racialised body in the new dispensation, highlighting the relevance of changing political discourses as well as new, critical theories of identity and embodiment within academic knowledge production.

Contextualising the body

It has been said that the body is in scholarly and cultural fashion. While it is not possible to give a full description of the multiple debates around the body here, the following text box sketches some examples of this renewed interest in the body (see, for example, Benson, 1997; Butchart, 1998; Butler, 1993; Clark, 1993; Edwards & McKie, 1997; Gilman, 1993; Grosz, 1994; Nast & Pile, 1998; Sherlock, 1993; Shilling, 1997; Terre Blanche *et al.* 1999; Turner, 1984; Zarkov, 1997).

The body in fashion

The body, it has been said, is in fashion (Davis, 1997a; 1997b; Morgan & Scott, 1993), and there are enough signs, both in popular culture and academia, to support the claim: the body does seem to be everywhere. For instance, in 1999, Orlan, the French artist known for her body art, was invited to come to South Africa to talk on her work. The invitation was by a group of critical scholars who run what is known as the Qualitative Methods Conference. The interest of this group in bodies does not start with Orlan, though, as the 1996 edition of the conference was devoted to method and the body (see Hook, 2001; Terre Blanche et al., 1999). This conference's focus on bodies, exemplified by Orlan's presence as a keynote address speaker, is representative of a growing interest in the body in the contemporary inter-disciplinary academic world. Such an interest appears to be reflected in the social world, particularly popular culture, as well. The body appears on the covers of the glut of magazines which have flooded our everyday consciousness and shop shelves since the opening up of our society. It is on the minds of local writers, journalists, artists, and academics who have shown interest in the body. In addition to international magazines, local magazines, especially what are called mainstream women's magazines, such as *True Love, Fair Lady, Elle South Africa, Cosmopolitan*, and *Femina*, are full of articles and images about the (female) body; the 'man' editions of the above (*Tribute Man, Cosmoman, Elle Man*) also deal with (male) body matters. A male magazine, focusing on health issues, *Men's Health*, usually carries an image of a well-exercised male body on its cover, as well as 'tons of' advice on workouts, and other matters relating to how readers can get a toned, firm abdomen, thighs, calves, biceps, triceps, back, buttocks, and other attractive bits of the body. The weekly newspaper *Mail & Guardian*, devotes a column to similar and other related issues, called 'Body Language'. In addition to Orlan, a number of local artists, among them Steven Cohen and Mark Hipper, have done work focused on the body: questioning it, presenting *transgressive* ways of thinking about bodies, being playful about it, and generally trying to represent bodies. Thus, it may appear as though, as a society and a world, we have suddenly realised we have bodies, and bodies are interesting subjects.

It is evident that outside of the popular obsession with the physical body (both male and female nowadays), there is also a growing body of knowledge production in the area of the body. We should not, however, be lulled into thinking this sudden and proliferating excitement reveals the body, at last, for what it truly is. That bodies have suddenly been found to be interesting does not make it easy to understand them, and almost certainly not their present histories and futures. In fact, this sudden interest and focus on the body might confuse and make it harder to appreciate the complexity of the body and how it has been represented and constructed in our social worlds. The body has always been a core element within universal economic, political, cultural, and personal struggles. Indeed, the re-classification figures presented below are intended to be read from this vantage: as a first indication how, when, and where the body has been (and continues to be) crucial, as it were, to life, politics, love, and all the other important things.

But it could be asked: if the body is said to be *in* fashion in academic and culture circles, where, when, and how was it *out*? The body, to be sure, has never really been totally *out*. At the same time, the body was never looked at directly, nor been obviously and totally *in*. What this means is that there has always been theoretical, research, and cultural work, after a fashion, on the body, but it has always been somewhat on the margins of academic work.

Perhaps more than any other thinker, the French philosopher René Descartes caused the greatest trouble in respect to how we think about the body. In his second meditation, from the well-known work *Meditationes de Prima Philosophia* (which appeared first in the seventeeth century), Descartes asked himself the question: 'But what, then, am I?' His answer: 'A thing that thinks' (Descartes, 1968:106). Perhaps just to be sure, in his sixth and last meditation, Descartes would say, '... I rightly conclude that my essence consists in this alone, that I am a thinking thing, or a substance whose whole essence or nature consists in thinking' (*ibid*.:156). In other words, Descartes succeeded in distancing thought or knowledge from the body, and in establishing a hierarchy between body and mind in his maxim 'I think, therefore I am' – that is, without thought (or consciousness) there is no material I or me (body). Such a philosophical paradigm has dominated Western thinking, placing thought or the mind in a position of superiority over the body (now also associated with emotion), and reproducing the classic mind-body dualism in which knowledge or the mind becomes disembodied. In this view, the body is decentred, marginalised, and devalued. It is not suprising, then, that historically there has been a strong association between those who have power and the mind or thought, while those historically oppressed have been strongly associated with the body (such as women, Black people, and children).

The keen interest in the body in the academy and society, highlighted in the media examples in the earlier text box, thus implies that traditional work, especially that by Western scholars, has always played a kind of hide-and-seek with the body – where most of the game was hiding rather than seeking the body. Western social science and Western culture, following Western philosophy, has tended to be 'indifferent, even hostile, to bodily matters' (Morgan & Scott, 1993:12). The legacy of Descartes, to social scientists in general, and social psychologists in particular, has been to privilege rationality and the psyche. Bodies, seen as irrational, or at best, non-rational, have been largely ignored, treated obliquely, trivialised, considered risqué, and generally disparaged (Greer, 1999; Schiebinger, 2000).

It is thus the *character* or bias of this body work to extend the metaphor that is being referred to by commentators when they claim the body is on the agenda. For the most part, that body characterisation is traceable to Judeo-Christian thinking, and as we suggested to Descartes. This is the same characterisation of the (absent) body that lies at the centre of scholarship and culture, and that also formed the core of the policies of apartheid.

In his sixth meditation, from his *Meditationes de Prima Philosophia,* the French philosopher René Descartes said "... I rightly conclude that my essence consists in this alone, that I am a thinking thing, or a substance whose whole essence or nature consists in thinking', and thus managed to help to distance thought from the body.

'Race' re-classification

As already mentioned, the focus in this chapter is on the connection of body, racial oppression, and national freedom struggles. The path we are following here is one that allows us to see how moments, events, policies, and struggles, performances, consciousness, and interactions get *embodied or disembodied*. One of the questions this route enables us to answer is whether it is ever possible to have any existence, or consciousness, and politics, that is not socialised, not *embodied*. It equips us to think how the body is related to 'race', and therefore political oppression and liberation. In other words, it enables us to examine how our bodies were (and indeed are) inserted into, talked about, legislated, and struggled for, within our society and politics. The path we have struck, then, is one that leads us to appreciate the racial (dis-)embodiment of actions, identities, affiliations, relationships, languages, and events. To achieve this understanding, it is important to go back in time and explore an intriguing example from our past of how the body got to be a crucial element within the edifice of apartheid.

In 1984, 795 people officially changed their 'race' classification. In 1985, the figure was 1 167, and in 1986, 1 102 (RSA, 1986; 1987). Most 'race' re-classifications happened in two categories: from Coloured to White, and from African (Black) to Coloured. For instance, of the 795 re-classifications approved in 1984, the majority were of Coloureds who changed to White (518), followed by Africans (Blacks) who changed to Coloured (89), together making up 77 per cent of the re-classifications. Of the 1 167 re-classifications approved in 1985, again the majority were Coloureds who changed to White (60 per cent) followed by Africans (Blacks) who changed to Coloured (21 per cent). In 1986, the number of Coloureds who officially changed their 'race' to White dropped dramatically (314) in comparison to the previous years, while the number of Africans (Blacks) who moved to the Coloured category increased (387).

What do these figures indicate? Do they mean that under apartheid more Coloureds had difficulties than Africans (Blacks), and Africans (Blacks) had more difficulties than Whites, with their classification? Do they imply that persons classified White were more satisfied with their 'race', their bodies, or themselves than persons classed Coloured and African (Black) were? Or do they mean more Coloured and African (Black) people were likely to be wrongly classified to begin with and to be the worst affected and afflicted by their classification? When a subject applied to have him- or herself re-classified, did it mean the initial classification did not fit him/her, and more specifically, did not fit him- or herself (see the text box on the body and the population)? Where does the problem lie: with the idea of classifications, or with the notion of 'race', or with the way we see bodies, or with our selves?

First, the figures tell us that more Coloureds and Africans (Blacks) than Whites had problems with their legal racial categorisation. A principal reason for this is that the categories or identities of 'race', like the categories of sex or gender, are not equal. Being classified White meant you were *officially* superior to 'non-Whites'. A person classified White was therefore less likely than a person categorised 'Coloured' or 'African' (Black) to want to change their classification because the latter were by law inferior categories. Indeed, persons classified as White may have worked to protect their White identity (see Lelyveld, 1987).

Second, the figures suggest that there was a lot of official 'race' changing during apartheid – official 'race' changes, because it is likely that there was 'unofficial race changes' – racial movement that was outside the law. This, as has been pointed out by many commentators, shows the perverse importance of 'race' to our past lives, and in many respects, to our present existence. One interesting interpretation of these racial metamorphoses, though, is that it was possible for apartheid officials to classify a person erroneously, to be mistaken about 'what' individuals are. Apartheid, in other words, got it wrong; it did so from the very start, and many, many times over.

There is a third suggestion that follows from the last interpretation of the numbers that is even more directly related to our purposes. This is that there may have been something wrong not merely with apartheid's system of racial classes, but with the idea of racial cataloguing itself (as suggested in Chapter 3). The idea of raced bodies is itself spurious (Miles, 1989), yet it served a very particular ideological and political function in apartheid South Africa. The re-classification figures highlight both the rigidity of a system that insisted on categorising people, in particular groups that represented differential access to power (both economic and political), as well as a fluidity and weakness in the system – apartheid made some mistakes (people could prove they had been wrongly classified), but more importantly, it was possible to move from one category to another. There are many stories of apartheid South Africa in which people who possessed certain physical characteristics could appropriate these to switch their classifications so as to gain access to a different world (as in the case of a previously classifed, but light-skinned, Coloured woman, who married a White man and became classified White in order to inhabit a White world).

The racial body

The body was an important item on the social, political, and economic agenda of apartheid. But the importance of the body goes beyond the apartheid system and regime to other kinds of government, political and economic systems, and national movements. Indeed, the national freedom project in our country also

A person classified White was therefore less likely than a person categorised 'Coloured' or 'African' (Black) to want to change their classification because the latter were by law inferior categories.

There was a lot of official 'race' changing during apartheid – official 'race' changes, because it is likely that there was 'unofficial race changes' – racial movement that was outside the law.

had its own social and political economies of the body. Thus, Turner (1984) has said that the body is or has been at the *centre* of social, political and, of course, economic struggles. This was no less true in this country. The difference between the national freedom movement and the apartheid state in this respect is that each appropriated the body for different kinds of 'truths'.

The body was an important item on the political, economic, and social agenda of apartheid.

To see the body as an important point on the national agenda means to understand that the apartheid state and the national movement for freedom were also defining the 'truth' of the body – in other words, constructing for us the 'truth' about what is a good and acceptable body, and what is a bad and unacceptable one. In this way the body became a medium for the development of particular discourses. It was recast as something critical in social relationships; it became critical in defining group membership; it defined who was a citizen and who was a subject; who was White, who 'non-White'; who the oppressor and who the oppressed; it was right in the middle of governance and resistance.

In a society such as we have (had) in this country, the socialisation of the body (making the body critical in social relations) is concurrent or at least culminates with its 'racing' or racialisation. Miles (1989) uses the term 'racialisation' to refer to a dialectical process by which meaning is attributed to particular features of the human body in order to construct difference and legitimise inequality on the basis of 'race'. Put differently, a racial discourse selects certain biological and somatic features as a basis for classifying people. Those chosen characteristics are given meaning and special significance. Bodies thought of in this way become a sign of the existence of some other phenomenon, for example, in some contexts the Black body has signified the unbridled sexuality of Black people. As a result of racialisation, the body – as a biological feature of an individual – may be assigned to a general category of people.

In a society such as we have (had) in this country, the socialisation of the body (making the body critical in social relations) is concurrent or at least culminates with its 'racing' or racialisation.

But it is imperative to remain aware that racialisation is not confined to the physical characteristics of people. It encompasses social, political, and cultural processes in which people take part, as well as the structures and institutions that result from such participation. What this means is that the oppression of Black people and the privilege of White people were and are tied to their bodies. Perhaps it is easy to see this, but an appreciation of the process of racialisation leads us to note that racism therefore interests itself in the bodily aspects of hated groups, and not just in ideology (see Chapters 3 and 4). It is important, then, that we note that the struggle against that oppression is both physical and ideological.

The body and knowledge

When apartheid sought to construct the body as naturally racialised, to persuade individuals and society to perceive and experience the human body as biologically raced, the knowledge system had already provided the scaffolding on which the socio-political programme could be hung. The related historical impact of *Social Darwinism*, the *eugenics movement*, and *differential psychology and intelligence tests*, manifest in support of *essentialist* theories of the body, including a reductionist discourse on the Black subject who was, and is, fundamentally and naturally different from the White subject.

The apartheid state utilised its institutions and processes dedicated to creating and transmitting knowledge to help in organising the relationship between itself and the individual body, as well as between and among bodies of people. For example, all schooling was racially segregated, with Black education governed, among other pieces of legislation, by the *Bantu Education*, the *Education and Training*, and the *University Extension* Acts. Furthermore, the academy and popular media tended to play critical roles in creating and reproducing particular 'truths', especially when considering the work once done at the National Institute of Personnel Research, the South African Broadcasting Corporation, and the Human Sciences Research Council, colleges, universities, and even newspapers.

The discipline of psychology has produced some very important tools that were used to justify racialisation and apartheid (see Nicholas and Cooper, 1990; Jansen, 1991). Psychology largely gave itself over to be used to propound views of Blacks as a primitive, inferior species, limited intellectually and culturally. In helping to constitute raced bodies, and identifying and producing explanations for these, psychology in effect contributed to the social and political problem of the Black body (and to a degree, and distinctively, of the White body). In another way, the discipline of psychology assisted the social, political, and cultural formation of apartheid by furnishing it with a specialised language of essence, difference, and hierarchy.

Social Darwinism is a set of ideas based on an erroneous conception and application of Charles Darwin's theory of evolution of species by natural selection. It argues that the physical, intellectual, psychological, and moral traits of human beings can and should be improved through selective breeding.

Eugenics movement is a social and scientific movement that developed in the 1800s and drew heavily on the work of Francis Galton. It suggested that, like intelligence and beauty, illiteracy, wealth, and poverty are genetically inherited. Galton, who coined the term 'eugenics', in turn had borrowed liberally from the ideas of his cousin, Charles Darwin. In Galton's words, 'eugenics' meant the 'science' of improving humans by giving the more suitable races or strains of blood a better chance of prevailing over the less suitable.

95

It is against this background that questions have to be asked about the authorship of knowledge. Such inquiries have often thrown into bold relief the unspoken character of the resulting knowledge and those whom it serves. Such examinations become extremely important against the background of current renewed racist psychology and scholarship, especially evident in the recent attempts to illustrate essential IQ differences between Black and White people, highlighting the continuing attempt to bring *scientific* evidence of the inherited inferiority of Blacks (see Terre Blanche & Durrheim, 1999). Note should also be taken of the somewhat wider acceptance that, notwithstanding claims of empirical observation, of objectivity and valid knowledge, psychologists (as well as other social scientists) bring to their work their own assumptions and beliefs about human nature and society. Science, as many writers are now acknowledging, is a social activity. The concepts and constructions of psychology, and not only the context of discovery but the context of justification as well, are socially embedded.

The White, masculine, and class character of the academic process becomes clear when we ask who is in charge of and shapes that process (see, for example, Evans, 1990). White authors of advanced knowledge sometimes do not have to offer explanations to buttress the interest of their 'community', whatever it is. The physical fact of Whiteness – the White bodies of the writers – gets associated with superiority, or at least, with superior knowledge, with learning, with 'intelligence'. These things reinforce each other while conferring and confirming the intellectual backwardness and the inferiority of the Black subject. That Whites dominated the knowledge production system became, then, both a mechanism for and an effect of a hierarchical racial structure, simply because the dominant ideas were the ideas of the dominant group. That Whites controlled the intellectual discourse, as they equally commanded other spheres of South Africa, insured the reproduction of the social relations of racialised power (Pityana, 1992).

The apartheid body and identity

We have suggested that in our country, and not too long ago, the single most important official determinant of identity – who we are, where we can live and be educated, who we can have sex with or marry – was the classification of the body as belonging to this or that 'race'. Being born in or living with a skin of a particular colour, as a White or Black some-body (or, as those who were classified as Coloured were defined, neither a Black nor a White some-body), was, as it were, an absolute determinant. We inherited three central beliefs about our bodies and identities from the fathers of apartheid and, to an extent, those closely and formatively involved in the liberation project.

Differential psychology refers to the psychology of individual and group differences, which revolves on measuring differences in aptitudes, abilities, interests, and personalities.

In our country, and not too long ago, the single most important official determinant of identity – who we are, where we can live and be educated, who we can have sex with or marry – was the classification of the body as belonging to this or that 'race'.

96

First, we were to understand that bodies of differing colours led (had to lead) to different and often opposed identities. A person's body determined, or at the least was related to, a certain and enduring identity. Africanness (Blackness), Colouredness, Indianness/Asianness, and Whiteness (as well as femaleness and maleness, naturally) were and are not socially constructed, deriving as they do from a non-negotiable, unchangeable biological reality. Africanness (Blackness), Colouredness, and Whiteness are natural, physical facts. They cannot be experienced except as physiological makeup and realities. Is it a wonder that rather than, for example, socialisation, or class, or gender, the Coloured, Indian/Asian, African (Black), and White physical bodies were overriding in determining group participation?

Second, South Africans were to see, talk about, perceive, and experience the body as mono-racial. A child was not allowed to be both Black and White, even if s/he had a White parent and a Black parent. Apartheid, in other words, did not have space for what are called bi-racial individuals.

The third part of the inheritance, flowing from the first two, was an understanding that the distance between raced bodies was immutable. Attempts by individuals to close the distance, so to speak, were discouraged by social sanction and indeed prohibited by law.

This way of looking at, seeing, talking about and experiencing the human body, as well as the resulting identities and selves, was and is bred by determinist and essentialist discourses. Biology, for the essentialising apartheid discourse, was destiny. In this way, not only the state, but also society and culture, came to use the body and its codes to define difference and thus force identity on individual subjects.

This way of looking at, seeing, talking about and experiencing the human body and our selves that was adopted in the apartheid era led to some strange ends. The absurdity of the body of apartheid can be seen in the incredibly entangled, and in certain cases bizarre, apartheid laws. Take, for instance, what the group areas laws, whose major aim was to segregate space, said about women who challenged its objective. These laws stated that any White woman who married or cohabited with either a native (African or Black) or a Coloured man was transformed into either a native (African or Black) or a Coloured. How was this possible, and how did a White woman one day experience herself as White and then as Coloured or native (African or Black) the next day? This is not mere contradiction. It is an illogic bordering on madness, a madness, as we said, that was inaugurated at the moment of apartheid's bodily insertion of people into its structures and institutions. Yet it helps, paradoxically, to work (with other moves) in undermining, for example, Blackness and Whiteness as identities and explanatory categories.

The body and the population

The 'body problem' is attributable to significant historical, economic, political, and social events. Such events inform how individuals subsequently come to think and feel about themselves and others, how they behave in everyday life, and how they relate to their social conditions. Events construct, or reconstruct, our cognitions, emotions, and practices, but perhaps more fundamentally, our bodies.

In our country, one of the most significant events was the enactment of the *Population Registration Act*, No. 30 of 1950. The ostensible aim of this Act was 'to make provision for the compilation of a register of the population of the Union' (Statutes of the Union of South Africa, 1950:275). But what the government concretised with this law were the primary mechanisms by which successive White governments in South Africa would define many matters about the body. The body was thought or made to have something to do with identity, and particularly racial and ethnic identity. With the *Population Registration Act*, the government set down one of its main tools to connect body and 'race' and ethnicity. The object of this law was then not to provide the expressed innocuous register of the population of the country, but to re-produce categories of and relations (of inequality) between the subjects/objects of the apartheid state. Although there were several contradictions between different laws and policies, as well as numerous alterations to the official language and terms used to refer to subjects, this Act may be taken to underpin or originate many of the more recent and even contemporary body and identity struggles. Even

where a longer history is considered when examining who we are and who others are, it seems to us that we are forced to negotiate our way past the definitions contained in this one particular law.

Section 1 of the Act is devoted to defining, among others, the terms 'Coloured person', 'native' (African or Black), and 'White person'. A Coloured person is defined as 'a person who is not a White person or a native [African or Black]'. A native (sic) (African or Black) is said to be 'a person who in fact is or is generally accepted as a member of any aboriginal race or tribe of Africa'. A White person is taken to be 'a person who in appearance obviously is, or who is generally accepted as a White person, but does not included a person who, although in appearance obviously a White person, is generally accepted as a Coloured person' (Statutes of the Union of South Africa, 1950:277).

Because they can be seen, bodily features get appropriated as the basis for the social order. But the features are already 'accepted' as or 'appear' to be parts of a 'raced' body. There is no-body except the Black, the White, the Coloured. The body of a 'race' or tribe or ethnic group is thus made the basis for a regime of 'truth'.

> Every person whose name is included in the register shall be classified by the Director as a White person, Coloured person or a native [African or Black], *as the case may be*, and every Coloured person and every native [African or Black] whose name is included shall be classified by the Director according to the ethnic or other group to which he belongs (Statutes of the Union of South Africa, 1950:279, our emphasis).

Bodies, law and resistance

Notwithstanding the hierarchical nature and oppressiveness of 'race' categories, to those without the 'White bodies' at least, it is important to note that some individuals willingly applied to have themselves re-classified, besides those who were reported to authorities by neighbours, colleagues, or enemies and consequently racially 'tested'. That individuals applied to have their racial classes changed means that subjects would readily submit to the law, and that the law, like other disciplines, was productive (Foucault, 1973). This suggests that even when a piece of legislation may be unjust and vile, quite a few of us will construct ourselves, 'fit' our bodies, and shape our lives, in accordance with the law. It suggests that people will 'extradite' or 'hand over' their bodies and those of others to the legislator, the leader, the movement, the medicine man, disciplines, culture, and fads, in order to have access to power.

Body extraditions should be seen as covering a wider range of practices than merely getting re-classified (which always incorporates de-classifying), or 'passing' as a member of another 'race'. They extend to such acts as body building, exercising, dieting, navel and tongue piercing, 'nose jobs', 'scarification', 'strengthening oneself' by putting medicine under the skin (*ho phatsa*), lipo-suction, face-lifts and circumcision. All of these highlight ways in which the body is acted on, frequently through invasive techniques, in order to gain access to social power, achieved through looking like the socially acceptable ideal body in a particular cultural context.

Pass:
Let oneself be known as a member of a racial or ethnic group other than one's own.

We said the problem of the body for the subjects of apartheid began where the body became the target of its structures (such as government policies, job reservation for Whites, laws on separate schooling, residential areas for different 'races', and segregated worship). The interesting aspect of this is that these structures, these laws, practices and policies, were themselves based on certain interpretations of the body. The point here is that the subject of apartheid thus *became or got known through his/her body*.

To offer examples other than the ones about 'race', the apartheid government banished political activists like Robert Sobukwe, Winnie Madikizela-Mandela, and so on. It detained and imprisoned others such as Zeph Mothopeng, Walter Sisulu, Fikile Bam, and many others. It 'neutralised' or 'eliminated' terrorists like Steven Biko, Solomon Mahlangu, and so on. Forms of torture, such as applying electricity to the testicles, beating up and severe physical abuse, keeping prisoners on their feet for days on end, the 'helicopter', etc. were focused on the body. And apartheid segregated living and public spaces along racial lines in order to separate Black bodies from White bodies.

The body was therefore both the target of apartheid as well as the projectile, at the base of its oppressive laws. The body, to put it differently, is the terrain on which the edifice of apartheid was erected and the object at which its rule was first and foremost directed. This means that classification and change, segregation and superiority, prohibition and permission, imprisonment and freedom, murder and protection, all followed from the construction of a body as Black and White. Most of all, though, these things followed from the fact that the body was taken as the natural basis of 'truth'.

The body and discourse

The body, we said, was fundamental to apartheid structures and governance, as it is to government or governance and to power generally. What we also need to explain is how this is accomplished. It is accomplished *discursively*, that is through discourses that construct meaning in our culture. By this we do not just mean that the body is important as a target when, for instance, a government restricts its movement through a banning order, or when the police come to arrest you and throw you in gaol, or when the body is tortured so that the 'truth' can be revealed, or when the body is killed because it is somebody. We mean that the body is a target of discourse (see Chapter 2 for a discussion of discourse).

Discourse, or more accurately language or any language-like system, provides the framework not only for the meaning made of bodies, but also our entire social worlds and even our identities. Language is there at the beginning. Individuals are born into a language. Language structures their bodies, not just their actions and thoughts. This idea leads us to understand that apartheid itself was a discursive project. If one appreciates this, it becomes easy to appreciate the discursive insertion of bodies. The most important consequence of apartheid as a discursive practice levelled at human bodies was the construction and differentiation of bodies along racial lines. Therefore, the importance of the body and its features to the apartheid regime becomes clear inasmuch as definitions of 'races' have historically referred to bodily characteristics. It is now an easy step to understanding why social, political, and economic structures in a racially divided world would be and indeed are interested in bodies.

Redescribing oppression and freedom

Looking back at the struggle against apartheid, there are a number of key theoretical and political moments in which the body was brought into view. One of the early prominent African psychologists, Chabani Manganyi (1981), began theorising about the body through his focus on the existential experience of being Black in the world. He argued that the struggles of oppressed people are primarily struggles of human beings with existential questions (questions about the meaning of life and their own place in the world). These questions of course incorporate questions of embodiment, or at least of the bodied or sensational experience. Thus, in another way, Manganyi would say, the problems of, for example, Blackness or masculinity, arise out of the fact that humans *live in a body*, are *partly body* (in addition to being partly psyche), and *have a body*. The problem of the body is in this way always there, and always the same, for it is inherited by individual humans at birth, when they come into the world.

Existentialism: The view that the problem of being takes precedence over essence and knowledge in philosophical investigations.

Is it ever possible to divorce the problems individuals have with their bodies from how societies, cultures, economies, and polities come to see bodies? In the introduction to a little book of essays called *Body*, which explores different parts of the body, the editors, Fiffer and Fiffer (1999:xi) say that 'it may be our minds that govern us, our souls that guide us, but it is our bodies on which our histories are written, in which our stories are embedded'. The body is a canvas on which the pasts are tattooed, narrating its own story. Simultaneously, the way we see the body is a consequence of historical construction and social embedding of the body. By this it is meant that social, cultural, political and economic institutions and processes – for example, language, knowledge, laws of apartheid, the idea of democracy, media, work, etc. – are not merely focused on, used, and employed to transform the body in their own interests, but actually to construct a particular kind of embodiment, a certain manner of thinking and feeling about the particular body and inhabiting it.

It may be our psyches that govern us, but it is our bodies on which our histories are written and in which our stories are embedded.

Blood and 'race'

Both the governments of South Africa and the United States of America still force people to choose their identities by placing a cross in one of the racial categories, boxing people in identities labelled, for example, Black or White. While the question did appear in the media and political debates around the first post-apartheid census, the Central Statistical Services went ahead and included the question of race in the question-naire. The seriousness of the issue was officially explained away by saying people can choose not to make a choice. In the case of the USA, the question is becoming contentious, even (or especially), it appears, among the African American 'community'. The issue is not simply about the census of 2000 recognising the growing number of citizens in that country who see themselves as multi-racial, but, says Charles Byrd, of the treat-

ment by the National Association for the Advance-ment of Coloured People's (NAACP) of people of mixed race in America as a 'wholly owned subsidiary of Black Inc.' The NAACP has previously acknowledged that about 70 per cent of those labelled Black might properly be defined as of mixed ancestry. The reasons for this classification revolve around the 'one drop rule' (*Sunday Times*, 30 March 1997).

The 'one drop rule' refers to the definition in the United States of America of a Black as any person with any known Black ancestry. This means that a single drop of Black blood makes a person a Black. The 'one drop rule' (also known as the one Black ancestor rule, the traceable amount rule, and the hypo-descent rule), applies only to Black Americans and not to any other group in America, and is accepted by both Blacks and Whites in that country. (A reading of Davis' (1992) book *Who is Black? One Nation's Definition*, is instructive for understanding the definition of Blackness in that country.) To show the effaced ambiguities, the forced identity of racialised bodies, of how White racism defined Blackness and Whiteness – which have their parallel in apartheid – a case reported in Davis' book will be cited:

In 1948 a young man called Davis Knight was sentenced to five years in jail for sleeping with a White woman in Mississippi. In his own defence Knight said that he was not aware that he was Black, that he had, as it were, any Black blood. The state, however, successfully demonstrated that indeed he did, his great-grandmother being a slave girl. Second is the case of Susie Phipps. Phipps had been denied a passport because she had put White on her application form, though, it was shown, she was Coloured – the designation on the birth certificate she had never seen indicating Coloured. Phipps said her classification as Coloured came as a shock since she had always thought she was White, had lived as a White, married, divorced, and married for the second time as a White. The state claimed it could prove that Mrs Phipps was three-thirty-seconds Black, which was more than enough Blackness for the court in 1983 to declare her to be Black.

Black conscious bodies

It could be argued that it was the Black Consciousness Movement (BCM) of the late 1960s and 1970s that brought the role of the body to the forefront within the broader struggle against apartheid. The BCM defined Blacks as those who by law or tradition were politically, economically, and socially discriminated against, and who as such constituted a unit in the struggle towards realising their aspirations (essentially escape from oppression). In making the term 'Black' include Africans, Indians/Asians and Coloureds, the movement was making a bold statement, especially, as some writers have said, when one notes that the two older liberation movements had not defined the oppressed in this form. However, this is not exactly true – unless one opts for a simplistic reading of references to 'Blacks' and 'Whites' in the preamble of the Freedom Charter, as well as the Pan Africanist Congress's definition of Africans. In any event, for SASO (South African Students' Organisation, one of the key BCM organisations, of which Steve Biko was a founder member and first president), Black was not a skin pigmentation but a reflection of a mental attitude. Black was meant to define or describe those working against the socio-political system and towards liberation.

The BCM provided an alternative to the psychological complicity of the Black person with White oppression. It gave to the Black man and woman redefined racial subjectivities that would encourage solidarity with and commitment to all of the oppressed. Under the BCM, 'Black' encompassed and encouraged all those who were working towards social, psychological, and political liberation themselves. Biko (1996) and his comrades addressed the racist social psychologies of the political economy of apartheid, working against the erosion of the oppressed's sense of self and worthiness. The BCM was an inward-looking movement, preoccupied with the Black psyche. Blackness was not seen as a biological category (as the White government saw it), but as a psychological and social construct that was to be affirmed, associated with pride and worth. The Black consciousness philosophy suggested a discourse unique to the victims of White oppression, a discursive response elicited by what Cornel West (Gates & West, 1996:80) calls 'the whirlwind of white supremacy – that is, a response to the vicious attacks on black beauty, black intelligence, black moral character, black capability, and black possibility'. The call to a Black consciousness was a politically determined social psychological call on Black people to close ranks, to identify with and love Blackness, and a call to act accordingly. However, one should note that militant Black consciousness activists wanted to distinguish between committed Blacks and the educated middle-class whose Blackness was only skin deep, which is reflected in the slogan, 'We are *Black* students, not Black *students*.' Not to be White did not necessarily mean to be Black.

> The Black Consciousness Movement defined Blacks as all those who by law or tradition were politically, economically, and socially discriminated against, and thus the term 'Black' included Africans, Indians and Coloureds.

Criticisms have been levelled at the 'race' consciousness of the BCM as reverse racism. Such criticisms represent a knee-jerk response that does not adequately engage with the theoretical and political writings of the BCM. Another criticism made about Biko and his comrades' work has been that it was a tacit submission to defeat as well as being an agreement with the system. A third criticism was that they were causing resentment, when they need not have, while widening what was called the racial gap. Biko's (1996) own writings, and those of his comrades and admirers, deal more than adequately with these old criticisms.

A more interesting response to the BCM gesture is that apartheid's ideology of White superiority itself created the conditions for a Black consciousness, for Black solidarity is a necessary and legitimate response to White racism. In other words, Black consciousness is a legitimate spawn of and mirror image to racism and segregation. This position is more interesting, for it appreciates the imperatives that called for the Black move, for the need for unity around 'race' in the ranks of the oppressed.

The problem with this response is that it assumes that there is an *a priori* category of people called Black, among whom a positive consciousness could always be engendered and nurtured, in order to fight against an *a priori* White oppressor. The answer to this is that there is no stable Blackness grounded on a natural body; there is no Black community as much as there is no White one, outside of social, cultural, economic and political programmes which aim at inserting subject bodies into racial structures. Whiteness and Blackness do not constitute communities, except of racialised bodies and identities. In other words, White communities and Black communities, in the absence of a racist or colour-conscious cultural, economic, political and social formation, are impossible. Of course, the bequests of racial zoning of apartheid, racial superiority and inferiority, and social group membership get added to the meanings of bodies to construct Whiteness and Blackness. Whiteness and Blackness are discursive but also embodied locations that are culturally, socially and politically produced and linked to relations of domination (see Frankenberg, 1993).

Biko (1996) had a penetrating insight into the psychological, social, and political set-up of his time and situation. Through the contribution he and his colleagues made, the oppressed were revitalised from political impotence into programmatic psychological, social, and political work. What Biko and his comrades left behind was a recognition of the need for a coherent political identity for all the oppressed to organise around a uniting consciousness, in this case of Blackness. The stretching of Blackness to include people classified as Coloured, Indian/Asian, and Bantu/African, though not unproblematic and contested, had a liberating effect. What it did achieve was to free many from the categories defined by apartheid. Yet, at that moment it also imprisoned bodies in other categories.

What we are at pains to show is that however politically, socially, culturally, and psychologically liberating Blackness is, it also imprisons the body in another way. The body remains the ground for political activity, providing for the development of *liberating* Black psychologies, true, but ideologies grounded in the body, nonetheless. In searching for true Black identity, for racial authenticity, the spectre of essentialism and determinism is (re-) awakened, and with liberation come brand new boxes in which to put new identity crosses. In critiquing the notion of Blackness given to us by the historically critical moment of Black consciousness, we keep watch over the tendency of society and individuals to objectify conceptions and analysis. We open ourselves to the constant change that attends our situation. Even what may appear at first liberatory and advantageous should be critiqued to reveal the historical and cultural embeddedness of understandings and actions. Radical scholars and activists need to stay continuously sensitive to the taken-for-granted and its imprisoning possibility.

Conclusion

To differing degrees, the classification of bodies inherited from the past was actually always problematic for the apartheid establishment, the broad liberation movement, and for individuals. The problems were present from the very beginning. For the new post-apartheid society, or at least part of it, the difficulty has an added twist. Things called by the same name, having attained a constancy of sorts, are starting to lose their sameness. This breaking up of bodies will be interpreted by some as inimical to a continuing struggle. This is possibly correct at some level. For instance, for the African National Congress-led government, it might herald the loss of political influence. On the other hand, what the erosion of sameness of identity might be pointing to is an alteration in the relationships between individuals and their bodies and others.

The politics of Africanness, Colouredness, Blackness, Whiteness, Indianness, and Asianness, which could serve politicians well for the next one or two national elections, is ill-equipped in the long run to deal with what Henry Louis Gates Jr. terms the dilemma of intra-racial disparities. Clearly, the condition of apartheid, a time of an extremely brutal police state, and the present, with a predominantly Black government, are dissimilar. Different times demand different forms of analyses. The body labels of pre-1994 are increasingly being destabilised and fragmented. The politics of body and identity are changing with the opening up of our society but also because the nature of loyalties and collective conflicts is changing. What we are witnessing, at least, is a shift in the signification of bodies. This transformation in political, cultural, and social psychological meanings given to bodies is changing with and because of the movement in body discourse, made possible, in turn, by the new order. At another level, the increasing influence of critical projects in the academy, including postmodern, post-colonial, feminist theories and others, are motivating a radically different appreciation of bodies or the body.

Exercises for critical engagement

1   Why do you think there were more people who changed their 'races' in some years than in other years?

2   What are some of the factors, in addition to those covered here, that you think influenced individuals to change their 'race', and what role do you think sex or gender, class and geographical location, played in race re-classification?

3   For senior students, if you can find somebody who was re-classified under apartheid to talk to about their identity, bodies and/or experiences, it would make a good research project or long paper.

4   The representations of bodies we find over time in magazines and newspapers (such as *Drum, Fair Lady*, the *Star* and *Sunday Times*) are not the same. Using photographs from different decades of any one magazine or newspaper of your choice, mention and discuss some of these changing representations.

Recommended reading

Biko, S. (1996). *I write what I like.* London: The Bowerdean Publishing Company.

Davis, F.J. (1992). *Who is Black? One Nation's Definition.* Pennsylvania: Pennsylvania State University Press.

Schiebinger, L. (Ed.) (2000). *Feminism and the body.* Oxford: Oxford University Press.

Shilling, C. (1997). 'The body and difference'. In Woodward, K. (Ed.) *Identity and Difference*, pp. 63–120. London: Sage Publications/The Open University.

Terre Blanche, M., Bhavanani, K. & D. Hook (Eds.) (1999). *Body Politics: Power, Knowledge and the Body in Social Sciences.* WITS: Histories of the Present Press.

Turner, B.S. (1984). *The Body and Society.* New York: Basil Blackwell.

Frantz Fanon and Racial Identity in Post-Colonial Contexts

6

Derek Hook

OUTCOMES

After having studied this chapter you should be able to:

- define the concept of identity
- qualify what is meant by 'the post-colonial'
- explain concepts of racial alienation, cultural dispossession and double consciousness, as well as Fanon's ideas of 'lactification', 'pathologies of liberty' and the lack of synchrony between culture, nation and family
- discuss the identity-dynamics of racism, including the notions of essentialised identity and the binary logic of whiteness and blackness, and
- explain and elaborate Bulhan's stages of marginal identity and his ideas of cultural 'in-betweenity'.

Thinking post-colonial identity

THIS CHAPTER will focus on a particular approach to the question of identity, an approach that may be characterised as *post-colonial*. Identity here will be understood as that set of social and cultural understandings through which we come to *know* and *experience* ourselves. These understandings play an important role in constituting *who we are* – that is, in who we, and others, *understand ourselves to be.*

There are four important aspects of this approach to identity that are worth emphasising. Firstly, this definition presents identity as *necessarily social* – as contingent on a variety of social factors, be they material, political, economic or ideological. I am talking here both of *social meanings*, on the one hand – ways of talking, ways of making sense of the world – and of *actual structural conditions* of day-to-day life, that is, the material circumstances that define and limit where and how one lives. Secondly, given that identity has here been understood in terms of experience and self-knowledge – terms that seem reasonably flexible and mobile – we can see that this approach views identity as potentially shifting, *as open to negotiation and change.* Then again,

> **Identity:**
> A set of social and cultural understandings through which we come to know and experience ourselves.

107

and this is the third point, given that this approach emphasises the *contingency* of identity on a variety of social and political factors, on relations of power, we need to understand that *identity is not simply free-floating or arbitrary*, but is significantly *delimited and conditioned by social (and material) relations of power*, by ideology and by historical patterns of privilege. Fourthly, we might say that individual or group identity has a given amount of cultural resources available to it. Here we are referring to a collection of narratives, values, ideals, types of knowledge, discourses, social practices and beliefs, which are *shared*, and which maintain a sense of sameness, or continuity, across different contexts within that culture. This is the framework *without* which, as Bulhan (1979) notes, social identity fails to have meaning. What is important to understand about this *cultural dimension* to identity is that it is not equally shared across society. Different groupings of people – and this is especially so in situations of cultural dominance – have differing resources of identity available to them.

Integral to the critical perspective on identity that this chapter will put forward are questions of race, culture and power, all of which play an important role in the works of the revolutionary writer Frantz Fanon (1968; 1970; 1986; 1990), around which an increasing body of contemporary scholarship has come to centre (see particularly Alessandrini, 1999; Gordon *et al.*, 1996; Read, 1996). Fanon was a psychiatrist and revolutionary, born in the French colony of Martinique, who dedicated much of his life to the liberation of

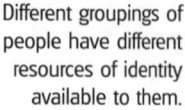

Different groupings of people have different resources of identity available to them.

Algeria from France (see Julien, 1996; Macey, 2000a). Amongst others, he was responsible for the massively influential books *Black Skin, White Masks* (1986, originally published 1952) and *The Wretched of the Earth* (1990, originally published 1961). The first of these texts will form the basic touchstone of this chapter. Also important here is the writing of Hussein Abdilahi Bulhan (1979; 1980a; 1980b; 1985), who has provided one of the most valuable commentaries on Fanon. Bulhan's work will also feature strongly in what follows.

Identity is necessarily social, open to negotiation, but not simply free-floating, and has a given amount of cultural resources open to it.

Defining the post-colonial

A further qualification that needs be made here concerns a definition of 'the post-colonial'. As both Ashcroft *et al.* (1995) and Williams and Chrisman (1994) have reiterated, this term has come to mean many different things to many different people, so much so that the term is in danger of losing its effective meaning altogether. Perhaps the most basic use of the label of 'post-colonial' is simply to indicate the historical period immediately following the age of European colonial expansion, an age which began its decline at roughly the end of World War II. This is the period in which colonial powers increasingly began to grant independence to former colonies. (It should be noted that this itself was often a period of great conflict and violence, however.) Importantly, however, the granting of independence does not simply bring colonial politics to an end. As Ashcroft *et al.* (1995:2) warn: 'All post-colonial societies are still subject in one way or another to overt or subtle forms of neo-colonial domination, and independence has not solved this problem.' So although the terms of Fanon's analysis are principally those of the colonial situation, they still usefully inform post-colonial periods, which are never fully separable from their colonial past.

Post-colonial refers to the historical period following European colonial expansion when former colonies gained political independence. But in addition, post-colonial means a particular critical orientation to understanding the relationship between the coloniser and colonised.

More than just a historical period, the term 'post-colonial' denotes a particular critical orientation to understanding the relationship between colonisers and colonised, and the psychological, material and cultural effects of these relationships. Indeed, in this respect, *post-colonialism* – as a particular *theoretical* form of reading and critique – pays particular attention to the relationship between *the personal-subjective* and *the socio-historical* domains in the construction of individual identity. Van Zyl (1998) provides one of the most useful shorthand definitions of the post-colonial from within a South African perspective. She views post-colonialism as *a critical perspective* that aims to understand the relationships of *domination* and/or *resistance* that manifest when one culture (typically Western) 'owns' or controls another (typically Eastern or African) culture, *even after the era of formalised colonialism has ended* (*ibid.*). Key concerns in this connection are issues of cultural dispossession/integration, racial identity and the self–other dynamic of inter-group relations, all of which are discussed by Fanon.

It is important we realise the importance of this approach to South Africa. For, as Bertoldi (1998) points out, apartheid may be considered a particular extension or variation of the basic politics and conditions of colonialism. Similarly, Wolpe (1975) considered South Africa a 'colonial society of a special type', and saw apartheid as a form of 'internal-Colonialism'. In a similar way, we might consider the current post-apartheid period as a particularly South African variant of the broader post-colonial era. An important word of caution stems from this last point. I am not here seeking to reduce the current historical period of post-apartheid South Africa simply to a 'post-colonial' characterisation. There are clearly unique historical circumstances present within post-apartheid South Africa which differentiate it from other post-colonial contexts. Similarly, broader political forces like globalisation, as one example, and the growing and differing intersections between race, class, gender, ethnicity, religion, as another, would seem to call for more detailed forms of analyses than those outlined here, under the label of 'the post-colonial'. Furthermore, again emphasising the lack of any rigid demarcation between the colonial and the post-colonial, we need be aware that certain dynamics of race, racism and identity formation that were present in apartheid South Africa no doubt *still* feature in what counts as a *post*-apartheid situation. In view of this, I suggest that 'the post-colonial', as either historical period or critical perspective, should not be viewed as *all-encompassing*, but rather as one element within many potential others through which we may read, attempt to understand, and critique, the social-political life in previously colonial contexts.

One last qualification: we should beware of attempting to apply too easily, too directly, the terms of Fanon's analysis to the South African situation. Ultimately we should undertake our own forms of analysis and critique of racial identities in the *particularity of the post-apartheid South African context*. However, this is not to say that Fanon's concepts do not provide us with a valuable starting point, a basic conceptual vocabulary that we can draw on, where appropriate. (Both Fanon [1986; 1990] and Bulhan [1979; 1980a; 1985] do in fact make repeated reference to apartheid South Africa in their writings.)

Post-colonialism: A theoretical perspective that seeks to understand the relationships of domination and/or resistance that manifest when one culture 'owns' or controls another culture even after the era of formal colonialism has ended.

How racial oppression affects identity

The *lived experience* of the Black man/woman

The task Fanon sets himself in *Black Skin, White Masks* is that of describing, as vividly as possible, *the lived experience of the Black man*. In attempting to do this, Fanon is not merely looking at experience in the banal everyday sense of the term. The notion of experience here suggests a deep engagement with the world around the subject, a profound sense of feeling and 'living through' the social conditions that define a particular time and place (Macey, 2000a). One way of understanding how Fanon means 'lived experience' here is through the idea of a *political consciousness*, that is, an acute awareness both *of how one is crucially a part of the world and its conditions* – and not easily separated from them – and a critical attention to exactly how much of that world is conditioned, or even determined, by political circumstances (such awareness and attention forms the basis of one's political project).

Such a political consciousness entails a careful consideration of what Fanon, following Sartre, refers to as *facticity*, in other words, those seemingly 'concrete' factors that define my situation in the world, such as the actual physical environment in which I live, the time of my birth, my class membership, the facts of my nationality, my body, my race, etc. These are the conditions within which I live, that cannot simply be transcended, merely 'wished away'. In fact, it is vitally important that they not be under-estimated when one starts to formulate one's political project. A broader understanding of what 'lived experience' means to Fanon helps us think about exactly why, for him, identity is always in dynamic negotiation with the world around it, always in relation to other people, structures and conditions, and remains eternally potentially changeable, despite the facticity of these elements.

Racial alienation

The search for Black identity, and racial identity, is the abiding concern of *Black Skin, White Masks*. Although for Fanon both White and Black races are locked within the constraints of colour, his particular emphasis, as Wyrick (1998) suggests, is on the formation, meaning and effects of 'Blackness'. Fanon is trying to understand both Blackness *and* Whiteness, *as inseparably linked*, and as always in relation to one another. If *lived experience* is the basis on which Fanon begins his exploration of racial identity in colonial contexts, then *racial alienation* proves to be his chief problematic. It is this notion – of alienation – that provides Fanon with his principal means of 'thinking' racial identity and its cultural challenges within colonial contexts. 'Alienation', is a very dense theoretical concept, one with a formidable history. As such, it is important that we be clear on how Fanon used the term. Both Zahar (1969) and Bulhan (1985) will be useful to us here, although principally the latter.

Alienation is a dynamic concept, one which relates experience to social conditions in a way that enables us to produce critique (Bulhan, 1985; Zahar, 1969). It is also a concept with a certain amount of synthesising power, by which I mean to say that it can be applied in a number of different levels of experience (Zahar, 1969). Bulhan (1985) introduces his qualification of the term by emphasising its usefulness as a means of linking *personal-subjective* and *socio-historical* domains. Already, then, we get a sense of the importance of the term to Fanon; it gives us a way of thinking the connections – or articulations – between the *internal world of the individual subject*, and the *external world of the constraining social, economic or political structures* that surround and contain that individual.

Estrangement

A second basic aspect of the notion of alienation is the idea of estrangement. This idea features centrally in what is perhaps the best-known account of alienation, that of Karl Marx. For Marx, alienation is the result, particularly characteristic of modern capitalism, of the separation of the worker from the products of his or her labour. In his conceptualisation, what the workers produce they do not own or ultimately have control over. Their labour hence takes on a life of its own, which is alien, and even threatening. The products produced by the worker are lost to her or him and appropriated by the employer, which leads to a sense of estrangement and alienation on the part of the worker. This alienation of labour leads, as Macey (2000b) summarises, to a loss of reality, to the situation where human beings are estranged from their own bodies, from the natural world and from their potentially universal essences.

The concept of alienation then emphasises a sense of rupture in the relationship between the self and those things, objects and people around us. This estrangement is not only that of the self from the world, but also, in a very powerful way, *that of the individual person's estrangement from him- or herself.* Here it is important to pay attention to how Fanon adapts the concept of alienation to suit his purposes. For Marx, the root causes of alienation reside in the substructure of society, and particularly in the alienation of productive labour engendered by a capitalist mode of production. Therefore, when the worker's labour is alienated, so too is his or her 'humanness'. In different terms, because of alienated labour, the being of the worker remains alien to him and all others.

The concept of *racial* alienation seeks to show the sense of separation in the relationship of the Black self and things, objects and others around itself.

For Fanon, *race*, and the various social practices and meanings attached to it, proves to be the pivot of alienation, rather than productive labour. As Bulhan (1985) rightly notes, Fanon's application favours *psychological* and *cultural* dimensions rather than *economic* and *class* dimensions. Clearly, as a psychiatrist, Fanon was interested in an exposition of alienation from a *psychological* perspective (*ibid.*). As individuals, we can then be estranged, from our 'humanness', from our own body and sense of self, from a sense even of belonging to our people, *all on the basis of race.* In many ways, this is perhaps the most consistent theme throughout *Black Skin, White Masks,* that of dehumanisation, that of the inability, because of various forms of racism and cultural dispossession, to settle on any kind of authentic identity.

The pathology of the colonial context

The juxtaposition of the Black and White races in post-colonial contexts creates, for Fanon, a collective form of mental illness, a 'massive psycho-existential complex' (1986:12). I must be clear on what Fanon means here; he is by no means suggesting that racial contact is inherently pathological, that races should not seek contact. Rather he means to emphasise how problematic, *pathogenic* even (in the sense of inducing psycho-pathologies, inauthentic forms of identity), such racial contacts prove to be in contexts in which one racial group maintains a powerful degree of aggressive dominance over the other. (And this dominance may be realised in concrete physical, economic or cultural terms.) In such contexts, the potential for psycho-pathology, at least in the sense of compromised identity formation, is omnipresent. Hence Fanon's assertion that 'a normal black child who has grown up in the bosom of a normal family will be made abnormal by the slightest contact with the white world' (1986:117).

Pathogenic:
Causing or tending
to cause disease,
illness, or
psychological
disturbance.

One of Fanon's most profound points in the thinking of Black identity is to suggest that the material effects of racism and colonialism have large-scale *identity effects.* We need to think of colonialism, and for Fanon (1986; 1990), its lingering after-effects, not only as a means of appropriating land and territory, but of appropriating culture and history themselves, that is, as appropriating the means and resources of identity. Here we get a sense of how the material practices of colonialism, to use Wyrick's phrase (1998), *translate a denial of history into a displacement of culture and language.* The colonisation of a land, its people, its culture, in short, is a 'colonising of the mind', in Ngugi wa Thiong'o's (1986) famous phrase.

Cultural dispossession: Alienation through language

One of the most direct routes of racial alienation is through the adoption of the language of the oppressor. To speak a language, for Fanon, is 'to assume a culture, to support the weight of a civilization' (1986:17–18). More than this, the colonised Black subject 'will be proportionately whiter – that is, he will come closer to being a real human being – in direct ratio to his mastery of the [coloniser's] language' (*ibid.*:18). Fanon here is emphasising the role of language within the objectifying and dehumanising qualities of colonial practice. He is also aware, however, of the two-part process of alienation, whereby the process of assuming another's culture typically necessitates the giving up of one's own.

Simply put, the Black man or woman's mastery of the coloniser's language may increase their acceptance by Whites, but it alienates them from their root culture – taking on of the coloniser's language can erase their own cultural memory. An assumed language can both reinforce feelings of racial inferiority in the colonised, and emphatically mark their dislocation from the black community. In Bulhan's words: 'The fact of having to speak nothing but the other's language when this other was the ... oppressor was at once an affirmation of him, his worldview, and his values; a concession to his framework; and an estrangement from one's history, values and outlook' (1985:189).

Lactification

What starts to become apparent here is the idea of the possibility of moderating one's race, of lessening the degree of one's Blackness, a desire which Fanon refers to as *lactification*, toying with the word's associations to milk and Whiteness. He considers this, the wish to be White, to be a very powerful – and damaging – desire in colonised subjects, so much so that he poses (then answers) what is perhaps *the* question of racial identity and desire for the Black colonised subject: 'What does the black man want?... The black man wants to be white' (1986:8–9).

This is a pathological desire that is forced upon Black subjects by White civilisation and European culture. The effect of racist culture is to affirm supposedly global standards of value, which are really those of a select White American/European/Western group, as universal. In other words, the Black subject is, right from the start, 'predetermined' to fall short of these norms, by virtue of how culturally specific they are. 'Black people, then, abandon themselves individually and collectively in quest of white acceptance. The quest is inherently and ultimately futile; it results primarily in solidifying deep and disturbing feelings of inferiority' (Wyrick, 1998:29). This notion of internalised kinds of inferiority, of socially induced inferiority complexes, is one of the most important ways in which Fanon thinks about the damage, on the level of identity, the mass victimisation, enforced by dominant racist cultures on those they colonise. It is in this connection that he quotes Aimé Césaire: 'I am talking of millions of men who have been skilfully infected with fear, inferiority complexes, trepidation, servility, despair, debasement' (Fanon, 1986:12).

Practices of hair-straightening, skin-lightening, the attempt to earn a White spouse at all costs, and the enthusiastic adoption of the accent and language of the oppressor, all of these are examples of *inauthenticity* for Fanon. They are voluntary kinds of masking, symptoms of what is wrong in the colonised subject's psyche. These are negative bids at identity – processes of negation – that constantly *affirm* the coloniser's culture as the superior term, and dismiss the colonised culture as inferior. Importantly, these are *self-objectifying* practices in which the Black subjects comes to implement a kind of racism *from within*, so to speak, *upon themselves.* It is due to these internally reproduced kinds of racism that Fanon (1986:8) asserts that 'I propose nothing short of the liberation of the man of colour from himself.'

'Degrees' of race: The whitening of the Black subject

What Fanon's idea of lactification suggests, perhaps contrary to our expectations, is that race need not work simply as an 'all or nothing' category. In certain instances, it would seem that we are working with a *hierarchy* of racial identities, with *degrees* of Whiteness and Blackness. The Black subject hence, for Fanon (1986) becomes proportionately White, and closer to being a real human being, in direct ratio to his or her mastery of a White language, his acquisition of White culture, the attaining of a certain level of wealth. Put differently, one might say that the dynamics of race intersect with dynamics of class, such that it is understood that 'one is white above a certain class' (Fanon, 1986:44). European accents, figures of speech, fashions, modes of dress, all of these come to act as 'signals of class', which contribute, in the colonised subject, to a feeling of equality with the European, to an apparent *lessening* of one's Blackness. As true as these observations might seem one should point out that where racial categories have been essentialised (as to be discussed below) then race becomes an inescapable category. So even if one is able to lessen considerably one's Blackness, one will never be totally White, totally accepted by the colonising culture. Of course it is also important to mention here that a dynamics of race is overlaid not only by dynamics of gender, class and sexuality, but also by a dynamics of ethnicity, such that Fanon notes that in the Antilles it was understood that Senegalese were considered to be *more Black*, so to speak, that is less civilised, than the native inhabitants of Martinique. In this sense one is able to see how a racist culture begins to set up levels of separation, differential degrees of Blackness, in this case, *hierarchies of prejudice*, within a given population.

Dispossessed identities

To be the subject of cultural oppression/racism, is to be continually fed with cultural understandings *which are not our own*, which are primarily hostile towards us, *and which consistently de-evaluate us and our culture.* It means to exist in a state of few or no cultural resources of my own, because they have been eradicated by the cultural imperialism of the coloniser. More than this, it means to internalise the coloniser's stereotypes as a means *of knowing self.* Simply put, for each step with which I try to understand myself, I am actually further alienated, because I am using pre-determined and loaded terms that always dispossess and devaluate me, and serve the dominant group culture.

What Fanon is here attempting to impart to the critical consciousness of his readers is an awareness of the continual sense of dissonance within the colonised subject, which occurs between ego and culture, self and society. There is a continual mismatch here – a sense of alienation rooted in race, or how race has been *socially produced* and *practiced* within a given culture – which results in a dislocation between the ideals, the norms of the valorised Western culture, and what I, by distinction, am (namely the *other* of all of these values). This constant and recurring slippage is pathogenic, it causes a deeply-rooted sense of inferiority, a constantly problematised sense of identity which is split and at war with itself, causing 'pathologies of liberty' as Fanon (1990) calls them.

'Double consciousness'

Black identity is hence typically marked by self-division, and can be characterised as a kind of *double consciousness*, which is essentially the result of the attempt *to configure Black identity within the coordinates of (racist) White culture*. For Fanon then, the Black subject has two dimensions, one with the other Black man/woman, and another with the White subject. As previously noted, the more the colonised subject comes to succeed in the culture of the coloniser, the more he or she is distanced from the home culture, the more the difference, the incomprehension and the disharmony between the two sides is increased. This situation presents as a double bind; despite the costs in terms of cultural alienation of identifying with the world of the coloniser, this colonising culture will never accept the colonised subject completely. And of course it is understandable that the colonised subject would want to speak the language of the oppressor, to attain competence in his or her culture, because it 'can open doors which were still barred to him [sic] fifty years ago' (Fanon, 1986:38). Fanon dramatises this double bind with the following comment: 'I'm beginning to wonder *if I haven't been betrayed by everything around me*, as the white people do not recognize me as one of their own, and with the black people virtually rejecting me' (cited in Macey, 2000a:197, own emphasis).

> ### What is 'double consciousness'?
>
> Double consciousness has become a useful, shorthand critical term used to evoke a sense of *looking at one's self through someone else's eyes*. Gilroy (1994; 2000) describes it as a state of 'being and not belonging', *of being an outsider on one's self* by virtue of the fact that the various norms, templates and categories for understanding and making sense of self have been set by a dominant class to which one does not belong. The term originates in the writing of W.E.B. du Bois (1995), who suggested that marginal groups in society are denied a 'true self-consciousness' because the dominant culture constantly devalues them, looks at them, their history and their traditions, with contempt. As a result they feel a divided sense of self, a *double consciousness*, with an allegiance to the valued world of their family and traditions, but also looking at themselves and their world through the eyes of the dominant culture.

Synchrony between culture, nation, family

Alienation of the sort of which we have been speaking happens at multiple levels, many of which reinforce one another. As a way of emphasising the depth and complexity of such alienation, Fanon expounds briefly on the ideal situation, on what it means to be 'at home' within a culture, nation and family. Here, as Bulhan (1985) paraphrases him, the family and the nation turn on the same axis; both are governed by essentially the same values, laws and principles. In such a situation, the values children internalise, the parental rules they observe, the forms of self-expression they are permitted, all of these guide them along a normative course of socialisation (*ibid.*). An ego-syntonic view of the self arises, as does a shared sense of belonging, hence 'The child grows in ... [a] stable family constellation and later emerges from that intimate circle to encounter a wider social world governed by similar values, laws, and principles' (*ibid.*:190).

Hence, where goes the nation, so follows the family, and ultimately the child. In short, these senses of home, of belonging, and meaning – all of which of course are vital sources of identity – are commensurate and resonant, echoed and reiterated across the levels of family, nation, culture. Situations of social or political oppression present us with a very different picture. Here one finds, in Bulhan's (1985:190) words,

> The colonial situation fosters ... neither continuity between the nation and family nor synchrony between the family and the identity of its members. The social structure exists primarily for the purpose of exploitation. Violence, crude and subtle, brought it into existence and maintains it. This violence, pervading the social order, in time affects the life of the colonized in a most fundamental way. The indigenous social structure is dislocated. The family institution subsequently is disrupted. The identity of its members also is constantly assaulted. In situations of prolonged oppression ... the oppressor had long obliterated the culture, language, and history of the oppressed. It is here less a question of discontinuity of the social structure and the family and personal identity than of a massive swamping of the family and a profound intrusion into the psyche.

Violence internalised

I am speaking here not only of how family structures are destroyed by oppressive systems, such as that of the migrant labour as necessitated by policies of separate development within apartheid South Africa. I am also speaking of how families may be destroyed from within. Bulhan (1985) here is referring to a traumatic tearing apart – one that exists within individual identities also – which occurs as a result of violent and oppressive cultural dislocations. What Bulhan is speaking of here is an extremely insidious process of negation in which one's loved ones and family members have 'unwittingly been enlisted as instruments of the prevailing social order' (*ibid.*:191).

Bulhan's objective, obviously extending Fanon, is to emphasise the overwhelming and ubiquitous violence of the colonial social order. Even if family conflicts of the sort described above are avoided, colonised subjects will sooner or later 'come up against massive social forces that undermine and sometimes overwhelm their development' (Bulhan, 1985:191). In this way the transition from childhood to adulthood, from the intimate circle of the family to broader spheres of social interaction, almost unavoidably involves personal conflicts and turmoil.

What is so valuable about the way in which Bulhan (1985) has elaborated Fanon's basic position is that it conveys how unavoidable some or other kind of conflict is within the marginalised identity of the colonial subject. Put slightly differently, we might suggest that the identity of the oppressed subject has violence at its core, a violence that duplicates itself on the level of how that individual attempts to know and experience self, between the individual and significant others, within families, within intimate relationships.

In closing this section, it is important not to over-emphasise Fanon's pessimism. While it is true that he argued that the disjuncture between what happens in the Black family and broader (racist) society may lead to psychic disarray, Fanon, specifically when writing on the Algerian family, also implied that the disruption of the Black family which is provoked by racism simultaneously also serves to co-create with various other processes the conditions for the destruction of racism. For Fanon, racist oppression does not only lead to inestimable psychic maiming, but the phenomenon ineluctably also generates the conditions for its own undoing. Indeed, it is sometimes within the contexts of the worst and ostensibly most invincible forms of racist oppression that the seeds of a new social order are sown.

The 'identity dynamics' of racism

Blackness essentialised

Fanon's analysis suggests that race often comes to act as an *essential* and *determining* quality of identity, perhaps *the* essential and determining quality of identity. European existentialist Jean-Paul Sartre, a prodigious influence on Fanon's writings, famously announced that 'existence precedes essence', meaning to suggest, amongst other things, that we should not tie our identity, or that of others, to predetermined qualities, prejudices or stereotypes. The experience of living as a minority (racial or otherwise) within a dominant or racist culture is to live the reverse of this adage – to live the experience of our '*essence preceding [our] existence*'. In this connection Fanon (1986:111–12) relates an incident where a White child sees him on a train:

'Look, a Negro!' It was an external stimulus that flicked over me as I passed by ...

'Look, a Negro!' It was true. It amused me ...

'Mama, see the Negro! I'm frightened!' Frightened! Frightened!

Here Fanon feels himself radically objectified, imprisoned by his race. His subjectivity, along with his ability to represent or define himself, is evaporated, destroyed. Hence, 'it is not I who make a meaning for myself, but it is the meaning that was already there, pre-existing, waiting for me' (1986:134). The Black subject, as such, becomes 'the eternal victim of an essence, of an appearance for which [he or she] is not responsible' (*ibid.*:35).

What is particularly important for Fanon here is the *inescapability of an individual's Blackness*. He refers to Sartre's thoughts on anti-Semitism, which suggest that because Jews have come to internalise the stereotypes others have of them – even if only to try and contest them – they have become 'over-determined' from within. They have come to understand themselves in the objectifying terms provided by the racist and hostile culture in which they live. There is a crucial difference here, though: whereas the Jew can 'be unknown in his Jewishness ... [and can] go unnoticed', because, after all, he is White, the Black subject cannot but be seen and identified, hence defined by his race. What Fanon is emphasising here is that Blackness comes to function as a fixed essence both in speech *and appearance*, one comes to 'speak' one's race, as well as to visually embody it. One cannot mask one's race, conceal it. Hence one is 'overdetermined from without' (Fanon, 1986:16). The evidence of the Blackness of a person's identity is there, unalterable, to 'torment ... pursue ... disturb ... anger' the Black subject (*ibid.*:117).

Qualifying, categorising, problematising the racial subject

What Fanon is suggesting here is that racist thinking defines individuals not only in terms of their race, but in terms of all the associations, stereotypes and values that such racial categories involve. All of these associated qualities themselves come to be virtually inescapable, *essentialised* qualities of identity. Fanon's point here is apt. If we want to problematise a woman, a Black man, a homosexual, or any minority, we do it exactly on the basis of what is taken to be most essential about them. So women are problematised on the basis of their femininity (which is, seemingly, by 'nature' irrational), Black people on the basis of their Blackness (which is by 'nature' primitive, dangerous, unintellectual), the gay man on the basis of his gayness (which is by 'nature' perverse and/or promiscuous), etc. These qualities are taken to be unchanging and timeless, and come to be locked into circular and self-confirming ways of thinking about particular types of personhood. Put differently, these ways of thinking, these prejudicial discourses, give birth to categorical ways of thinking, which come to order our world.

What we see operationalised here are the prejudicial terms of privilege and dispossession which systematically protect and idealise one (dominant) class of people, while derogating or problematising another (dominated) class. Hence the tendency always to qualify 'the other'; the White woman is referred to as *a woman*, the Black man as *a Black*, the Black woman as *a Black woman* whereas the White man is thought of as just *a person* (Edley & Wetherell,

1995). The Black subject, the woman, the gay person, etc. always needs be understood *through* the terms of these categorical groupings, that is through how they are thought to *differ* from the norms of the dominant culture. Put differently, this is a categorical fixing of certain identities that ties them to a set of prejudicial stereotypes. Note of course that dominant classes are not qualified in this way – they are not to be understood in terms of such a prejudicial fixing of identity – their acts, achievements, characteristics need not be understood against, or in terms of, such a basis or essence.

How Whiteness defines Blackness

The trauma of Blackness, as Wyrick (1998:37) puts it, paraphrasing Fanon, 'lies in its absolute Otherness in relation to white men'. Not only then must the Black man be Black, 'he must be black in relation to the white man' (Fanon, 1986:110). What Fanon is driving at here is the fact that the racial categories of Whiteness and Blackness are necessarily related to one another in the sense that they are *mutually dependent* terms, each coming to define and delimit the other. Simply put, the apparent superiority of Whiteness requires *the systematic devaluation of Blacks*. It is in this sense that Fanon (1986) argues that it is 'the white man who creates the black man' – his meaning here of course is not literal, his suggestion is rather that the White man creates the Black man as *an object of racism.*

    In order to present itself as a superior term, Whiteness relies on something other than it, something it defines as inferior and problematic, and against which it may be qualified as preferable, morally, intellectually, culturally superior. *Black Skin, White Masks* is full of references to what Fanon calls a *Manichean way of thinking,* that is a binary logic which splits all concepts into pairs of opposites, one which is negative (typically *Black*), one which is positive (typically *White*). Fanon hence underscores an important logic of racist thinking, and at the same time demonstrates how the racist, in an odd sort of way, comes to be reliant on the object of his or her hatred and racism as a means of qualifying and affirming his or her own supposed superiority.

Manicheanism:
A way of thinking, based on the religious system of Persian founder Manes, that believed in the supposed primeval conflict between light and darkness, God and Satan.

    In the same vein, Fanon's suggestion is that Blackness does not come to be experienced as a predominant dimension of identity – and certainly not in the derogatory sense implied by racism – in pre-colonial contexts. It is only after contact with White culture that the native is 'led to ask himself whether he is indeed a man ... because his reality as a man has been challenged' (Fanon, 1986:98). His supposed inferiority only comes into being through the mediation of the White other. Blackness is hence predicated on the fact *of not being White*. In Fanon's own words: 'I begin to suffer from not being a white man to the degree that the white man imposes discrimination on me ... robs me of all worth, all individuality' (*ibid.*).

Blackness is predicated on the fact of not being White, according to Frantz Fanon.

Identity development in oppressive contexts

Stages of marginal identity

Bulhan (1979; 1980a; 1980b; 1985) has usefully extended Fanon's work by proposing a stage theory of identity development in oppressive contexts. Clearly, these stages hold only for those racial, cultural or minority 'others' who have experienced prolonged periods of oppression or alienation, although this oppression need not necessarily be characterised by physical violence. Each stage in this theory of identity development is essentially a mode of *psychological defence*. What we view at each level is a struggle between two ways of being in the world, two kinds of knowing and acting. Put slightly differently, each stage represents a mode of existence and of action in a hostile, unaccommodating, or alienating world. Furthermore, and as a result, each stage is characterised by its own particular risks of alienation and its own distinct social rewards.

Psychological defence: Processes which defend or protect the self from threats or anxiety and whose major goal is to keep what is in the unconscious out of conscious awareness.

Bulhan refers to the first stage of this form of identity development as *capitulation*. The defensive mechanism that predominates in this stage is *identification with the aggressor*. What occurs here, as has been described above, is the individual's increasing *assimilation* into/by the dominant culture, an assimilation that results in his or her increased detachment from the root culture. For this reason Bulhan (1980a; 1985) argues that this stage involves a pattern of *compromise*. Here cultural and racial alienation is at its highest; the standards, values and ways of knowing and understanding our self are almost exclusively those of the dominant culture. This stage involves 'relegation to objecthood' (Bulhan, 1979:260). Accordingly, the potential for an interiorised sense of identity, for tendencies to self-estrangement and auto-destruction, is very high. As a result, psycho-affective injuries are frequent and extreme. Fanon (1990) refers to these marginalised or colonised subjects as 'without horizon', anchorless, colourless, rootless.

'*Revitalisation*' is the term with which Bulhan (1980a; 1985) names the second stage. This is a period characterised by a powerful reactive repudiation of the dominant culture. The defense mechanism entailed here is that of the *romanticism of the indigenous or accommodating culture*. The example Bulhan (1985) gives here is the literature of negritude, which, as explained above, is a celebratory approach to Black Africanness and its distinctive forms of expression and culture. This stage is thought to involve a pattern of *flight* from the dominant culture. A transitional phase, this level of identity development can be painful and difficult to accomplish; it remains nonetheless necessary, however, if viable forms of racial and cultural identity are to be established (Bulhan, 1979). The possibilities for cultural and racial alienation have been alleviated here somewhat, chiefly because of the availability of new cultural resources of identity that are not wholeheartedly owned and defined by the oppressive socio-political domain.

The third stage is that of *radicalisation*. It signals an 'unambiguous commitment to radical social change' (Bulhan 1985:193), and is characterised by a willingness to *fight*, to claim a just and equitable place for ourselves within our current social-political location. The pattern of adaptation in this stage is that of *synthesis*. Here the emergence of individuation and autonomy becomes a real possibility for the colonised/marginalised subject. Bulhan (1979; 1980a; 1985) considers this to be a period of potentially revolutionary action, one in which the individual or group significantly understands and in fact changes the root causes of social reality.

The dynamics of cultural 'in-betweenity'

Bulhan (1979; 1985) warns that one should not conceptualise these stages in a static fashion: 'whether considered as stages, tendencies, or patterns, it is important to note that none of them exist in a "pure state" nor is any one ... exclusive of the others' (1985:194). All three of these stages are taken to coexist in each marginalised individual, with one or another being dominant in a given moment, situation or era. Ordinary people will remain in the phase that is prevalent in their particular time and social milieu (Bulhan, 1979; 1985). Furthermore, Bulhan (1985) suggests these stages may characterise a given generation, which, for example, remains in a position of *capitulation* during a particular historical era. Because these stages overlap, and because they refer to historical eras and groupings as much as to individuals, Bulhan (*ibid.*) prefers to represent them not in a separable, sequential fashion, but together, as cultural trajectories, directions, that are linked in a relationship of dynamic tension.

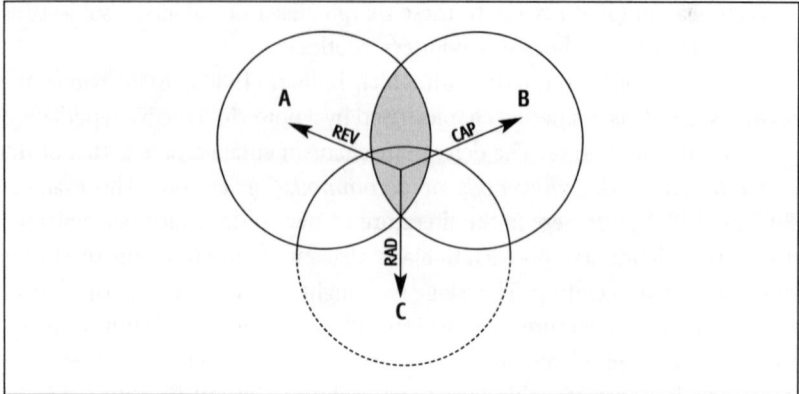

Figure 6.1
Bulhan's (1985) dynamics of 'cultural in-betweenity': (A) the dominated culture,
(B) the dominating culture, (C) the emerging culture. The shaded area represents
spaces of cultural overlap, confrontation and/or mutual influence.
The arrows indicate different routes of identity development or adaptation within
marginal groups in oppressed contexts, REV (revitalisation), CAP (capitulation) and
RAD (radicalisation).

Bulhan's (1985) diagrammatic representation of these stages (above) consists of
the following – three overlapping circles, one of which represents the dominated culture (A), another the dominating culture (B), and a third culture (C),
as of yet unformed and which is still coming into being. The three arrows REV
(revitalisation), CAP (capitulation) and RAD (radicalisation) indicate the
patterns of reaction or stages of identity development of marginal groups in
oppressed contexts. The dominated culture (A) is made up of all the values,
beliefs, norms and ideals that have historically characterised that culture,
despite the fact that they are under threat by the dominant culture. The
dominant culture (B) is that vast system of knowledge, representation, values
and politics that has come to be imposed on the oppressed in a variety of
different ways. The third, emerging, culture (C) is partly made up of a synthesis
of aspects of the dominant and dominated cultures. It is more than just this,
however. Part of the reason that Bulhan (1985) represents this new culture with
broken lines is to suggest that this situation of cultural hybridity brings with it
the potential to form new, unique, hitherto unprecedented cultural forms.

The shaded areas in the diagram indicate the region of cultural contact – or
'cultural in-betweenity' as Bulhan (1979; 1985) refers to it – typically characterised by confrontation and/or mutual influence. These spaces of cultural
overlap vary greatly according to time and place, depending, obviously, on the
type and strength of one culture's oppression of another. As Bulhan (1985:193)
points out, frequently it is less a question of overlap of cultures than 'the oblit-
eration of one and the supplanting of the other'. Bulhan is particularly

interested in this area of 'cultural in-betweenity', in which 'new' and 'old', 'modern' and 'indigenous' coalesce, 'one modifying the other and each losing in consequence its original character' (*ibid.*:193–4).

Critiques of Fanon

Before closing, it is important to draw attention to certain shortcomings within Fanon's theory of racial identity. In this regard one of the most obvious problems with Fanon's work, despite its heightened sense of race-based oppression, is its implicit, and at times quite *explicit* sexism. A large part of *Black Skin, White Masks* deals with the question of sexual desire across the lines of race. For Fanon it is the case that the Black female's desire to marry a White man is inauthentic, it is a detestable example of negative, self-depreciating identity. The Black male subject's desire for the White female subject is portrayed in very different terms, as containing an almost redemptive political value: 'When my restless hands caress those white breasts, they grasp white civilization and dignity and make them mine' (Fanon, 1986:63). Fanon has been rightly criticised for this sexist double-standard in his work (Fuss, 1994; McCulloch, 1983; Wyrick, 1998).

While Fanon portrays the Black female's desire to marry a White man as a detestable example of negative, self-depreciating identity, he depicts the Black male subject's desire for the White female as containing an almost redemptive political value.

Fanon is sometimes criticised as representing the colonial relationship as one of *complete dominance and control* (Moore-Gilbert, 1997; Young 1990). The claim here is that Fanon undervalues the various forms of resistance and opposition that colonised individuals and groups can offer colonisers, and that he stereotypes the nature of these relationships. The first part of this suggestion is not always true, although a book like *Black Skin, White Masks* does spend far more time emphasising the degree and dynamics of colonial/racist control, than it does the possibility of resistance. *The Wretched of the Earth* is a useful counterpoint here, in that it is exactly a revolutionary text focusing on the possibility, and in Fanon's terms, the *inevitability* of an eventual overthrow of, colonial dominance. Perhaps the point is that whereas *Black Skin, White Masks* rather pessimistically prioritises relations of domination and control in its analysis – because it does not want these processes to be *underestimated* – *The Wretched of the Earth* far more optimistically prioritises the prospects of revolutionary resistance.

A further criticism of Fanon is to argue that he himself involves essentialist and static categories – 'the Black', 'the White', 'the colonised', 'the coloniser', and so on, as Caute (1970) suggests. To a certain extent this is true. Fanon does appear to make sweeping observations and remarks at this level, and does seem to tie certain categories of personhood to certain necessary forms of experience, or identity. The strongest version of this critique is to suggest that Fanon enforces a kind of victim blaming, by emphasising how Black subjects, in their grasping at White culture are making only 'inauthentic' and self-objectifying bids for identity. The idea that Black subjects perpetuate a form of internal racism against themselves seems to do much the same.

It could be argued that the reason that Fanon makes the kinds of arguments that he does is exactly to emphasise the insidious and pervasive nature of the effects of racism on identity, effects that had not previously been examined, and particularly not from a perspective of *internalised psychological damage*. Does this mean that the terms of Fanon's analysis may be somewhat stark, somewhat caricatured, that his understanding of the 'Black subject' allows for little diversity within itself? Very possibly, but many would argue that Fanon provides us with the *starting point* for the analysis of post-colonial contexts, one that is elaborated on in increasingly sophisticated terms by later postcolonial theorists such as Homi Bhabha (1994). Similarly, Fanon's objective is not to do further racist damage by recourse to a form of victim blaming, but to warn those he empathises with precisely of the damaging effects of internalising racist, objectifying terms of identity. Hence one might argue that Fanon's project is a fundamentally liberatory one.

Conclusion

This chapter has discussed marginal identity in post-colonial contexts. Such forms of identity, it has been suggested, are necessarily social, and exist in negotiated states which are at the same time informed by cultural resources and delimited by them, especially in those cases where forms of oppression have obliterated, undermined or devalued such cultural resources. The chapter has tried to illustrate what a political consciousness meant to Fanon, and to describe the dynamics of oppressed identities, particularly with reference to the ideas of racial alienation and cultural dispossession. Also important here were ideas of double consciousness, of racist disruptions of identity, or 'pathologies of liberty' as Fanon called them. Questions regarding the essentialisation of racial identity, of the mutually dependent relation of Whiteness and Blackness, and of the ways in which categorical thinking and prejudicial discourse problematise minority identities, were also discussed. The chapter closed with a brief elaboration of Bulhan's stages of marginal identity development in oppressed contexts, and with a description of his notion of the dynamics of 'cultural in-betweenity'.

It is worth noting that how Fanon has thought of the problems of Black identity in hostile cultural environments may inform how we understand marginality in society more generally. Of great importance here is Fanon's assertion that in the presence of a dominant and/or oppressive culture, minority groups, who do not significantly share in the power holding of a society, must make sense of themselves, *understand* themselves in terms of the racist and inferiority-inducing terms and values of that society, terms that are evaluative and pre-set so as to affirm Whiteness over Blackness, masculinity over femininity, heterosexuality over homosexuality, and so forth. *Black Skin, White Masks* is nothing if not this, a dramatisation of such a process of *ongoing* psychic damage, where exactly the practices of identity are beset *with a systematic devaluation of self.* Just as we should not underestimate the extent of such oppressive practices on identity, however, so we should not underestimate the possibilities of resistance to them, of cultural revitalisation and radicalisation as forms of social change. Without this lesson, we have not properly grasped Fanon.

Steve Biko and Black Consciousness in South Africa

One of the most important Black leaders to oppose the apartheid government in the late 1960s and early 1970s was Steve Biko. Biko was the founder of Black Consciousness in South Africa, a movement that both echoed, and was strongly indebted to, Fanon. Biko's view of Black Consciousness called for the *psychological* and *cultural* liberation of the Black mind as a prerequisite for political freedom — in his own words: 'mental emancipation as a precondition to political emancipation' (Biko in Arnold, 1972:xx). Hence a large part of the struggle, for Biko, was exactly 'the *psychological* battle for the minds of the black people' (*ibid.*, emphasis added). As Biko described it in May 1976:

Black Consciousness refers itself to the Black man and to his situation ... [to the fact that] the Black man is subjected to two forces in [South Africa]. He is first of all oppressed by an external world through institutionalized machinery, through laws that restrict him from doing certain things, through heavy work conditions, through poor education – these are all external to him – and secondly ... the most important, the Black man in himself has developed a certain state of alienation. He rejects himself, precisely because he attaches the meaning White to all that is good ... (Biko in Arnold, 1979:22).

In opposition to such self-negating ways of thinking, Biko called for solidarity among Blacks, emphasising the need for oppressed groups to identify with *themselves* and to advance the liberation struggle on this basis. The challenge confronting Black consciousness was to reverse years of negative self-image and to replace it with an affirming and positive – if not *angry* – Black identity. 'Black' here, as Arnold (1979:xxv) points out, was more a state of mind than an expression of origin: 'The use of the word was a deliberate attempt to lay both the intellectual and emotive base for ultimate political unity between the Africans [Blacks], Coloreds and Asians[/Indians] of South Africa.' 'Blackness' here is a form of solidarity, a collective form of hope and security, a way for Black people to 'build up their humanity' (Biko in Arnold, 1979:34).

The key strategy of Black Consciousness was *conscientisation*. Conscientisation involves what Biko referred to as 'protest talk', talk about circumstances of oppression. It involves the repeated attempt to

> make reference to the conditions of the Black man and the conditions in which the Black man lives. We try to get Blacks in conscientization to grapple realistically with their problems ... to develop what one might call an awareness, a physical awareness of their situation ... to be able to analyze it, and to provide answers for themselves (Biko in Arnold, 1979:33).

Black Consciousness was an extremely positive form of politics, one which maintained that the very conditions of oppression were what would often bring a group of people together, embolden and invigorate them in their resistance to power. In Biko's own words (in Arnold, 1979:xx):

> The call for Black Consciousness is the most positive call to come from any group in the Black world for a long time ... The quintessence of it is the realization by blacks [that] ... they have to use the concept of group power ... Being an historically, politically, socially and economically disinherited and dispossessed group, they have the strongest foundation from which to operate. The philosophy of Black Consciousness ... expresses group pride and the determination by the Blacks to rise and attain the envisaged self.

One of the most powerful lessons of Black Consciousness for Biko is contained in 'the realization by Blacks that the most potent weapon in the hands of the oppressor is the mind of the oppressed' (in Arnold, 1979:xx). This, of course, is a weapon that can be reclaimed.

Exercises for critical engagement

1   Is it the case that race can exist as a matter of degree? Motivate your answer with examples.

2   Think of other forms of 'double consciousness' and use them to further illustrate the concept.

3   If it is the case, as Fanon suggests, that Whiteness defines Blackness, is it also the case that Blackness defines Whiteness?

4   Bulhan is careful to qualify that his stages of identity development can also be applied to an entire nation. At what stage of development would you locate post-apartheid South Africa, and why?

Recommended reading

Bulhan, H.A. (1985). *Frantz Fanon and the Psychology of Oppression*. New York & London: Plenum Press.

Fanon, F. (1968) [1961]. *Toward the African Revolution*. New York: Grove.

Fanon, F. (1970) [1959]. *A Dying Colonialism*. New York: Grove.
Fanon, F. (1986) [1952]. *Black Skin, White Masks*. London: Pluto.
Fanon, F. (1990) [1963]. *The Wretched of the Earth*. London: Penguin.
Macey, D. (2000a). *Frantz Fanon: A Life*. London: Granta.

Acknowledgements

I would like to thank Peace Kiguwa, Garth Stevens and Norman Duncan for their critical input on earlier drafts of this chapter. I am also indebted to the Center for the Study of Public Scholarship at Emory University; it was during a fellowship granted by the Center to the author that final work on this chapter took place.

7 Black Adolescent Identity During and After Apartheid

Garth Stevens & Rafiq Lockhat

OUTCOMES

After having studied this chapter you should be able to:

- describe the possible factors influencing Black adolescent identity development during and after apartheid
- show the impact of apartheid capitalism, violence and racism on Black adolescent identity development and mental health
- critically locate the process of Black identity development within a framework of personality theory
- critically apply Erikson's theory of psychosocial development to the South African context
- sketch factors that contribute to the dilemma facing Black adolescents in the process of attaining healthy levels of identity congruence and integration, and
- discuss Bulhan's theory of identity development of oppressed people and its application to our context.

I°T IS NOT hard to convince most observers of African politics and societies that the South Africa of the 2000s is not the same country as that of the early 1990s and before. The transition of the country from apartheid rule to democracy has not only had a profound impact on its legislated political arrangements, but has also redefined interpersonal, social, cultural, and arguably, to an increasing degree, economic relations. The consequences of the transition are then being felt not only at a large, macro- or group level, but reverberate at a micro- or inter-personal and intra-psychic level as well.

Many psychologists agree that intra-psychic, inter-personal and inter-group processes are all embedded within socio-historical contexts (Bulhan, 1985; Erikson, 1963; Tajfel & Fraser, 1978). In addition, many would agree also that shifts, or perceptions of shifts, within these contexts are likely to induce changes in inter-group, inter-personal, and intra-psychic processes. It is these potential psychological changes that this chapter looks at. It is important that

Black adolescents should not be viewed as a homogeneous grouping with a unitary experience.

the chapter not be read as the ultimate truth. No chapter, or book for that matter, can provide an exhaustive analysis of all shifts at all levels of psycho-social functioning. For these reasons, the chapter should be read as exploring possible ways in which specific social psychological processes may be affected by transitions, and more specifically, that which our country has recently undergone.

Debates about Black identities

In recent years there has been a proliferation of social and psychological literature characterising Black children and adolescents as the victims of the politics of liberation, resistance and transformation (Malepa, 1990; Mhlambo, 1993). However, equally vociferous have been the critics of these positions, who have opposed the unitary nature of these analyses, and who have rather highlighted the resilience and adaptation of Black adolescents within the process of social transformation (see Dawes, 1994).

One of the ways of framing the debate around Blackness in general, and Black youth and adolescent identity specifically, is to note that the different arguments reflect the shifting, multiple and contradictory character of identity. Another way is to think of the debate as mirroring the difficulties that many Black people are experiencing in the process of self-definition. Once again though, it is important to note that we do not view Black people or Black adolescents as a homogeneous and coherent group with a unitary experience of Blackness or adolescence. Nevertheless, the Black adolescent experience referred to is that which is formed, entrenched or re-formed over and against the facts of an historical oppression and institutionalised racism during the apartheid era, and the Black adolescents we are talking of are those who were engaged in various forms of liberation politics.

Now it is clear that many of the facts that helped to shape, cement or reshape Black identities prior to the first democratic elections have changed fundamentally. To explore some of the effects of these socio-historical changes on Black adolescent identity development, the chapter begins by locating the process of identity development within a framework of personality theory. It then goes on to examine the influence of what is characterised as apartheid-capitalism on Black adolescent identity development, with particular reference to the impact of violence and racism. Third, the chapter outlines several ideological, economic, social and political factors that continue to contribute to the dilemmas facing Black adolescents in the process of attaining healthy levels of identity congruence and integration in post-apartheid South Africa.

> One of the ways of framing the debate around Blackness in general, and Black youth and adolescent identity specifically, is to note that the different arguments reflect the shifting, multiple and contradictory character of identity.

Understanding adolescence

In spite of the wide range of personologists who have theorised about psycho-logical development, there are relatively few who have focused specifically on what may be seen as perhaps the most important social psychological task of adolescence – *identity development*. One of these few personality theorists is Erik Erikson. Erikson's (1963) psycho-social theory of human development has also proven to be highly influential in thinking about adolescence and indi-vidual identity development in general. This theory of psycho-social development built on and revised Sigmund Freud's theory of psycho-sexual development, and in the process contributed to the formation of what is today known as Ego Psychology.

Erikson's theory is important in one more respect: it is arguably the only one to address adolescence as a specific developmental phase within a coherent and integrated life-stage framework. What follows below, though, should not be regarded as a comprehensive account of identity development theorisation, but only a brief delineation of the theoretical framework utilised in this chapter. It is within this framework that we locate the process of adolescent identity development among Black South Africans during and after apartheid.

Erikson's theory of psycho-social development

Erikson's (1963) psycho-social theory of personality development is perhaps the most commonly known theory to address adolescence as a specific devel-opmental stage, and to look at it within a larger, coherent and integrated framework of life stages. His theory is based on several psycho-social stages, in which internal psychological needs and drives are mediated by various social influences. At each stage there is a new developmental crisis or challenge to resolve, with either a positive or negative outcome. Generally, positive outcomes lead to mental health and negative ones to maladjustment.

Erikson's stages also include an emphasis on the distinct developmental tasks of identity formation in adolescence. In this period between puberty and early adulthood, adolescents engage in self-definition and discover their *sexual, occupational* and *ideological* identities. This is done through com-bining certain aspects of earlier childhood identifications with the adoption of certain socio-historically influenced systems of values, norms and standards. This process therefore involves a relatively unique integration of both intra-psychic and socio-historical aspects into the person's developing personality (Erikson, 1968). This developmental task essentially incorporates the conflicts related to negotiating between ego identity versus role confusion.

Erikson furthermore noted the importance of several concepts such as the *psycho-social moratorium* and *identity foreclosure* in the process of identity formation. In fact, he conceptualised adolescence as a psycho-social moratorium in which society provides a period of grace for adolescents to experiment and pursue various identities. The *premature conclusion* to this process, in which self-definition is attained without exploring different possible identities, is what he termed *identity foreclosure* (Erikson, 1968).

Erikson's stages of psycho-social development

Erikson defines eight major life stages in terms of the psycho-social problems or crises that must be resolved.

Stages & ages	Psycho-social crisis	Significant question	Favourable outcome
Birth–1	Trust versus Mistrust	Can I depend on others?	Trust and optimism
2–3 years	Autonomy versus Doubt	Can I do it?	Sense of self-control and adequacy
4–6 years	Initiative versus Guilt	Am I good?	Purpose and ability to initiate one's own activities
6–12 years	Industry versus Inferiority	Am I competent?	Competence in intellectual, social and physical skills
Adolescence	Identity versus Role confusion	Who am I?	An integrated image of oneself as a unique person
Early adulthood	Intimacy versus Isolation	Am I likeable/loveable?	Ability to form close and lasting relationships; to make career commitment
Middle adulthood	Generativity versus Self-absorption (stagnation)	Am I a good parent and worker?	Concern for family, society and future generation
Late adulthood	Ego integrity versus Ego despair	Has my life been worth it?	Sense of fulfilment and satisfaction with one's life; willingness to face death

Erikson's 6th stage of psychosocial development is characterised by the ability to form close relationships or not.

Erikson has been most successful in analysing a combination of internal psychological drives and needs, as well as the demands of the external social world of the adolescent (Rosenthal, 1987). For a long time he was one of the few theorists to place a particular emphasis on the adolescent period of human development. In spite of criticisms below, this work has enhanced our understanding of the development of adolescent identity as part of overall individual identity. In addition, the references to the importance of socio-cultural factors in his theory (though we think it does not deal adequately with the particulars of these factors) are what lead us to our comments about Black adolescent identity development.

Erikson on Black psycho-social development

Even though Erikson's (1963) theory may be an elegant framework for comprehending adolescent identity development within a social context, and has led to many writings on personality development, it has a number of shortcomings. For one thing, the theory is unable to explicitly and adequately address the impact of prolonged structural oppression. For another, it cannot account for social and political situations other than orderly ones, for example, situations such as cultures in transition, countries at war, or societies in the middle of a humanitarian crisis. Yet another shortcoming, though not restricted to Erikson's theory, is that the theory is applicable to certain contexts only and therefore cannot fully and generally comment on people (such as Black South Africans) other than those on whom the theorist based his work. Last, Erikson says little about sexuality and gender in identity development, as though men and women go through exactly the same life crises, and in the same order.

James Marcia's theorisation of identity status in adolescence

James Marcia (1966; 1980) is another personologist who focuses on identity formation in adolescence. In Marcia's view there are a number of *identity statuses* out of which individuals work. Each identity status is a result of a combination of the presence or absence of a crisis and a commitment regarding identity. Unlike in Erikson's theory, Marcia's identity status is not a stage that an individual goes through but rather an orientation to the world which may occur at a particular time in the individual's life. Four possible statuses result from these combinations:

	No crisis	Crisis
No commitment	*Identity diffusion* (no struggle for identity, and no obvious concern about it)	*Identity moratorium* (active struggle for a sense of identity)
Commitment	*Identity foreclosure* (uncritical adoption of parental or social values)	*Identity achievement* (successful achievement of a sense of identity)

As can be seen from the above, what is referred to as *identity diffusion* refers to a state resulting from two absences: an absence of crisis about identity and an absence of commitment to an identity. People who have a diffuse identity do not know what they want to do with their lives and do not want to find out. Their state is one characterised by a sense of directionlessness and apathy. The individual refuses to face him- or herself and the challenges of making a life. It may be said that 'they are just going along'. Though they may manage to steer clear of the struggles of commitment and the future, steering clear of identity in the present may lead to future challenges.

In *identity moratorium* one is in the middle of a crisis about who one is and is not. The individual is searching, and so there is a deferment of commitment. The individual is experimenting with possibilities, for example, by going to work abroad, taking a year to travel the world, or, as people would say, 'doing something different'. This experimentation can be useful when one decides to commit to a life course, but one should guard against the lack of commitment going on forever.

In contradistinction to moratorium, with *identity foreclosure* there has not been a struggle. Rather, there is a commitment to an identity, social values, and a life. Such commitment is therefore seen as premature. The individual has avoided making an informed and active choice. His or her commitment is not a questioning one.

Identity achievement may be seen as an antithesis to identity diffusion in that the latter results from two presences: a presence of commitment to an identity, after the presence of a struggle for identity. Identity achievement means a person has arrived at a sense of who he or she is following a search of what he or she can be.

The historical development of apartheid-capitalism, or more generally, a 'racial' economy in South Africa, is well documented (see Chapters 3, 4 and 5). So have the social, economic and political relations and consequences thereof been comprehensively demonstrated. We refer here specifically to the long-ruling White National Party's choice of institutionalised racism as embodied in the 1948 apartheid policy (Terreblanche & Nattrass, 1990), the social impact of racist policies and legislation (Wolpe, 1988), the economic gains for the majority of Whites (Callinicos, 1987; O'Meara, 1983; Saul, 1986), and the resulting downward economic pressure on the majority of Black South Africans (Alexander, 1985; Brecker, 1994). The links between these social and economic consequences and the psychological outcomes have frequently been alluded to, but not made explicit enough by social scientists.

But it is now widely understood that the psychological sequelae of apartheid on Black people in general, and on Black adolescents specifically, have been profound. One of the most important aspects of that understanding is that the socio-historical context of apartheid was so determinative for Black people because of the extreme violence of the policy. Where traditional definitions of violence tended to emphasise overt physical actions or abuse, and therefore did not consider ostensibly 'non-violent' acts or omissions which may have violent consequences, violence is now seen as a much broader phenomenon. One of the theorists who worked according to this viewpoint is Bulhan (1985). His own definition is that violence is 'any relation, process, or condition by which an individual or group violates the physical, social and/or psychological integrity of another person or group' (*ibid.*:135). Following from this definition, any situation of oppression is therefore underwritten by violence.

Bulhan's (1985) definition allows both overt and covert acts or omissions, which may have direct or indirect violent consequences, to be incorporated into an analysis of oppressive situations. The definition permits us to see poverty, forced removals, lack of access to health services, separate and unequal education, and lack of adequate housing, over and above political tortures and murder, as part of the same violence. The much higher levels of poverty among Black South Africans (as opposed to White South Africans), generated by apartheid-capitalism, are then seen as part of the same, systemic onslaught. The same can be said for forced removals and relocation of different 'racial' groups through the *Group Areas Act* and *Land Acts*, which resulted in the destruction of many Black communities and families (Richter, 1994). Estimates are that during the period from 1960 to 1983 more than five million people (primarily Black) were either victims of forced removals or were threatened with forced removals (Duncan & Rock, 1995). Turning to the unequal distribution of basic health services, the evidence of this violence is the higher rates of physical illness, mental illness and mortality among Black people (Bulhan, 1985; Reynolds, 1989; Wilson & Ramphele, 1989).

Bulhan's modes of psychological defences

As we saw in the previous chapter, according to Bulhan there are three modes of psychological defences which occur in stages (Bulhan, 1979; 1985). The first stage is *capitulation*. Capitulation refers to a situation where the person increasingly assimilates into the dominant culture while simultaneously rejecting his or her own culture. The second stage is termed *revitalisation*. It is characterised by a reactive disavowal of the dominant culture and a concurrent romanticism of the indigenous culture. *Radicalisation* is stage three. It consists of an unambiguous commitment towards radical change. For the oppressed to reclaim their identity after prolonged oppression, the imposition of the oppressor has to be rejected, and the system must be prevented from determining the parameters within which identity is defined (Bulhan, 1979).

Bulhan's (1985) theory thus offers another perspective in assisting in understanding Black adolescent identity development. Again though, Bulhan's theory does not provide a comprehensive framework in which to see Black adolescence. Indeed, as yet no personality or social psychological theory provides us with a complete framework in which to analyse all of Black adolescent identity development in South Africa. Read in conjunction though, Erikson's (1963) and Bulhan's (1985) work offers productive elements towards such understanding. Before going on to this discussion, however, a brief account of the South African social formation and its impact on Black adolescents prior to the April 1994 general elections is appropriate.

The violence of apartheid against education, health and family life

South Africa has been distinguishable by a strikingly unique and integral relationship between 'race' and social class. Several writers have suggested various theoretical characterisations of this socio-political economy. In addition to the one we have been employing, that of *apartheid- or 'racial' capitalism* (Alexander, 1985; Legassick, 1980; Wolpe, 1988), the other notable characterisation is what was called *the internal colonialism* or *colonialism of a special type* thesis (Marquard, 1957; Slovo, 1989). Rather than discussing the merits of these varying characterisations, it is sufficient to state that there appears to be general agreement that the ideology of racism has developed alongside certain processes of capitalist accumulation in South Africa. The resulting oppressive conditions have had profound economic, structural, social and psychological consequences for the majority of Black people.

These social and psychological consequences arose, in particular, out of a situation where state repression, counter-violence, inter-personal and intra-personal violence became endemic to the society. For example, it is reported that from mid-1985 to 1989 between 8 000 and 9 000 children were detained for political reasons (Duncan & Rock, 1995). During 1984–1986, 300 children were killed, 1 000 wounded, 18 000 arrested for protesting, and 173 000 were awaiting trial, under house arrest, in 're-education camps', and exposed to various acts of abuse by the security forces. With regard to counter-violence, an unknown number of young people who went into exile to undergo military training were co-opted and incorporated into what were called community self-defence or self-protection units.

At the level of intra-community violence, over 46 000 children were displaced due to conflict during the period from 1991 to 1994. In addition, a conservative reflection of over 26 000 crimes against children were reported to the South African police between 1989 and 1991 alone (Duncan & Rock, 1995; also see Lockhat & van Niekerk, 2000, for a more comprehensive discussion of this topic).

As indicated above, education was not the same and not equal. Educational services reflected the historical implementation of 'Bantu Education'. This had a bearing not only on the number of Blacks receiving education, but also on the number of Blacks who were able to succeed at secondary and tertiary levels of education (Reynolds, 1989; Wilson & Ramphele, 1989). State expenditure on each White pupil was almost triple that for each Black student. In the period 1984–1985, for instance, just over 20 per cent of eligible Black students were accepted into tertiary educational institutions, while approximately 50 per cent of eligible Whites gained access to such institutions (Duncan & Rock, 1995).

Black adolescents: Damaged or resilient?

The deleterious psychological consequences of this socio-historical context on Black South Africans have been shown by several authors. For example, Wilson and Ramphele (1989) found that higher unemployment rates in various Black communities resulted in many able-bodied adolescents resorting to self-destructive behaviour in the form of substance abuse. In terms of the incidence of psycho-pathology, higher rates of depression were also reported as a direct consequence of unemployment. In addition, the lack of access to educational services has resulted in poorer academic performance and consequently fewer prospects for social upliftment among Black adolescents (Reynolds, 1989). Letlaka-Rennert (1990) argues that the lack of material resources for Blacks has, in part, resulted in reduced levels of emotional involvement between many Black children and adults. Other authors such as Duncan (1991) and Richter (1994) have also written substantially about these effects on the Black family (see Lockhat & van Niekerk, 2000).

Several authors have, however, suggested that Black children and adolescents should not only be characterised as victims of the socio-historical context, but that there should be acknowledgement of the fact that they also display resilience and fortitude. Even though they may therefore be predisposed to a host of negative effects, this is not necessarily a logical outcome for all of them (Dawes, 1994; Levett, 1988; Swartz & Levett, 1989). Dawes (1994) elaborates on this argument, and suggests that biomedical discourse tends to assume a natural and predetermined outcome for all children exposed to violent events. He says that this discourse does not consider that there may be several mediating factors that determine the extent of children's subjective experiences of stress. In this way, children who are survivors of violence are constructed as 'innocent, passive victims' (Dawes, 1994:190), and their role as active participants within the socio-historical context is denied.

Contradictory expectations

In our view, the different characterisations of Black South Africans as either 'damaged' and 'lost' on the one hand, or 'resilient' and 'hardy' on the other, are aptly illustrated when exploring the contradictory influences of apartheid-capitalism on Black adolescent identity development. As we saw, according to Erikson (1963), the primary task that the adolescent must negotiate successfully is the development of congruence between the self-image (i.e. the evaluative component of one's conscious personal experiences) and role expectations of the environment; including independent judgement, emotional independence, assurance of economic independence, preparation for occupational and family life, socially responsible behaviour and a value and ethical system. Whether or not these tasks are central to adolescent development, clearly their successful negotiation has been hampered among Black South African adolescents. For example, contradictory role expectations were encouraged by capitalist ideology, on the one hand, and a racist ideology, on the other. Black adolescents have been exposed to the imagery of personal success and progress, the symbols and values that encourage individual achievement and social mobility, but simultaneously have been refused access to any significant material resources that allow for this (Duncan, 1996; Foster, 1991; Stevens, 1996). In our view, these contradictions have impeded the development of healthy self-concepts (i.e. the general self-representation based on personal experiences that one is consciously aware of) and healthy levels of independent judgement among Black adolescents.

> During apartheid Black South African adolescents were confronted with contradictory role expectations – on the one hand those of a capatalist ideology, and on the other, a racist ideology.

The widespread destruction of Black family relations may also have contributed to increased emotional insecurity among Black adolescents and consequently difficulties related to emotional independence during and after adolescence (Letlaka-Rennert, 1990). Cooper (1990:2) supports this in arguing that, 'the black family has been steadily denuded of its ability to provide a structured, nurturing ambience where the creativity and full potential of the developing child can be fostered. Interactions and relationship patterns have been eroded and are steadily breaking down.'

Erikson's (1963) psycho-social moratorium, as we said in respect of his theory in general, did not apply to the majority of Black adolescents. Economic independence was frequently not attainable, preparation for occupational and family life was commonly viewed as preparation for psychological and material enslavement, and value and ethical systems that emerged were often in direct conflict with those of the status quo, resulting in further alienation. In view of these potentially negative psychological consequences, it is no surprise that Black adolescents in this historical period were often characterised as victims.

However, to dismiss these adolescents purely as victims denies the dynamic, adaptive and dialectical nature of human subjectivity (Henriques *et al.*, 1984). Whilst the repercussions of these events for children should not be underestimated nor negated, the heightened politicisation of adolescents during the period 1970–1990 in South Africa offered a temporary reprieve for certain Black adolescents from the extremely negative impact of South African society. Politicisation provided a framework in which to generate meanings for social experiences and to challenge them, and simultaneously offered a 'home' to many Black adolescents who had originally experienced disintegrated family life. Furthermore, it actively promoted a common social identity through identification of a common 'enemy', common oppressive experiences, and common objectives. In addition to fostering various counter-ideologies, a culture of collectivity, social support, and structural containment may have acted as a partial buffer against the many stressors of South African society.

Within Erikson's (1963) stage of Identity Formation versus Role Confusion, many of the developmental challenges that may have been difficult for Black adolescents to negotiate within their everyday experience in South African society were negotiated differently through the process of political activism. In essence, this process also assisted in reducing the levels of alienation among Black South African adolescents. This is akin to what Bulhan (1985) refers to as the process of radicalisation, in which there is clear rejection and active opposition to the status quo, and where a commitment to radically restructure the social relations entrenches itself among the oppressed. However, with regard to Erikson's (1963) and James Marcia's (1966; 1980) concept of identity foreclosure, it is unclear what the long-term impact of being prematurely forced into choosing between capitulation and political radicalisation may be for Black South African adolescents. It could be postulated that the limited choices and rigidity of these choices may have provided many Black adolescents with an extremely limited range of options in post-apartheid South Africa.

Radicalisation.
The third phase, tendency, or pattern in Hussein Abdilahi Bulhan's theory of identity development is characterised by synthesis and unambiguous commitment toward radical change (see p 124).

With regard to the meanings ascribed to violent events, Dawes (1994) highlights the case of young South African political activists – who at times were referred to and defined themselves as the *young lions*. These young lions were elevated to the status of freedom fighters, and experiences of confrontations with the state security apparatus were seen as a symbol of their commitment to radical social transformation. As such commonsense interpretations and meanings become entrenched within the everyday consciousness of people, they have a profound impact on their everyday material practices and frameworks of understanding social realities (Thompson, 1990). In spite of the potentially negative impact of violence on Black people, several authors have suggested a number of factors that may reduce this impact and even help survivors to redefine their experiences more positively. These include the degree of social support, family integration, extent of perceived trauma, a variety of personal factors and the particular meanings that survivors ascribe to these events (Dawes, 1994; Straker, 1992).

Black adolescent identity after apartheid

Apartheid has effectively been dismantled as a legislated system, and no longer manifests itself politically and socially. But it is an arguable point whether the majority of South Africans view the objective material conditions as dramatically altered. It is not far-fetched to say that the historical interpenetration and mutual reinforcement of racist domination and capitalist exploitation in the development of the South African political economy continue to have economic and social psychological effects on the lives of the majority of Blacks (Alexander, 1992).

In its turn, the new political dispensation has had severe and unforeseen impacts on Black people in general, and Black adolescents in particular. With regard to adolescents, virtually overnight they have been required to change their life scripts from the 'young lions' to, perhaps, 'young entrepreneurs'. This has meant that they have had to redefine their identities once again. For one thing, they now have to define themselves in terms of the most prevalent social norms and values – many of which have not altered significantly since the apartheid era. They are therefore having to define themselves according to many of the norms and values which they may have opposed and rejected during the 1980s. These contradictory prescriptions for adolescents may well be contributing to role confusion rather than identity integration (Erikson, 1963).

One of the shortcomings of Erik Erikson's theory of psycho-social development is that it is unable to adequately address the impact of prolonged structural oppression.

In fact, while apartheid-capitalism no longer exists, a 'racialised' capitalism is still firmly entrenched (Alexander, 1992). In essence, this implies that many Black adolescents are being prescribed roles that are consistent with a capitalist framework, but which are frequently unattainable due to the racist legacy of South African society. This double bind has been compounded by social and economic programmes such as the *Reconstruction and Development Programme* (RDP), and the *Growth, Employment and Redistribution Policy* (GEAR), that have proven and continue to prove to be ineffective in reducing inequities in resource distribution (Bond, 1994). Effectively, the common 'enemy' that provided the reference point for many Black adolescents against which to collectively define themselves is no longer particularly visible or obvious in post-apartheid South Africa.

It must also be remembered that the young lions experienced the sudden loss of long-standing role models (e.g. the death of Chris Hani, the public censuring of and recent legal verdict against Winnie Mandela, the co-option of the late Peter Mokaba into a high-ranking government position, etc.). Furthermore, in spite of the national and provincial youth commissions, the shortage of directed programmes for adolescents, together with the collapse of extra-parliamentary political structures (Becker, 1994), has left many Black adolescents feeling directionless and uncontained.

With the open acceptance of Western economic models in the era of globalisation, the influence of Western ideologies is now greater than before, and has also been granted increased legitimacy. Within an Eriksonian (1963) framework, this shift would also contribute to role confusion, rather than identity integration. In a society that is becoming increasingly atomised and individualised, these adolescents must necessarily develop an identity that allows them to cope with their changed social realities. In apartheid South Africa, it was partly due to a shared political consciousness that many adolescents were able to develop a collective identity that resisted and challenged the pervasive racist ideology. The new role models, economic structures and dominance of Western ideologies, however, have now encouraged an ideological shift from collectivism to individualism. Out of the debris of collective struggle is emerging a culture of rampant individualism, what could be referred to as a 'Coca-Cola' culture. This culture embraces Anglo–American competition, 'looking out for number one', and individualistic aspirations in general. To call it the 'Coca-Cola' culture is apt in that Coca-Cola is perhaps the most successful brand in the world, considered as one of the most notable international symbols associated with Western individualism and, in particular, North American culture.

'AmaComrades' or 'AmaCoconuts': New identity hurdles

In an article entitled 'Ticket between two worlds' (*Sunday Times*, 10 November 2002), reference was made to the fact that Soweto youngsters who travel across Johannesburg to and from former Model C or private schools everyday are labelled 'AmaBhujwa' (bourgeoisie). As schools come to terms with the challenges that change has brought about, pupils find themselves embroiled in a different kind of battle – an emerging class divide that goes beyond the general 'race' paradigm commonly used in South Africa to explain economic inequalities. The language of the new order mirrors a growing hostility between those who travel to the suburbs for their schooling and those who have remained behind. 'Comrade', like 'young lion', is the affectionate term that was employed to express camaraderie and a sense of common purpose. It seems that around school yards and on university campuses, 'comrade' has undertones of those who remained (with 'the people'). On the other side are the 'AmaCoconuts' or 'cheese boys/girls'. These are pejorative labels for those who have left, run away from townships, or 'turned away' from their people. 'AmaCoconuts' refers to the fact that one is Black outside yet White inside, while 'cheese boys/girls' are those who have the luxury of eating cheese while others do not have anything. Other labels attached to them are 'Model Cs'. This article testifies to the hurdles that adolescents and young people have to negotiate in a post-apartheid South Africa.

What needs to be understood is that these shifts among Black adolescents, from political and social activism to a 'Coca-Cola' culture and individualism, are not merely determined by the new socio-historical context, but that many Black adolescents are actively embracing the latter as a means of maintaining their material and psychological integrity. The cynicism related to not being able to experience tangible benefits in the 'new' South Africa; the double bind as a result of confusing and contradictory role prescriptions; the lack of structural containment and programmes to allow for the development of healthy independence and judgement; have all contributed to even fewer healthy options for Black South African adolescents than before. What we now also encounter is a proliferation of gangsterism, substance abuse, anti-social behaviour (*Cape Times*, 9 April 1997; *Mail & Guardian*, 4–10 April, 1997) and an emerging ethnic separatism (Stevens, 1996), to mention but a few of the other possible trajectories that Black adolescents have opted for in attempting to either collectively redefine themselves or to deal with the double bind of the 'new' South Africa.

The 'Coca-Cola' culture

In addition to the foregoing, there is an increasing presence of Western ideological symbols at all levels of the social and cultural fabric. These symbols present themselves through language, accent, recreational activities and popular culture in the form of movies, clothes, music and so on. Many Black adolescents are now actively adopting an identity that allows them to cope to some degree in this new socio-historical period, but that simultaneously also marginalises and alienates them further from their own social realities. This in itself constitutes a form of ideological and social oppression (Bulhan, 1985). Not only does it undermine the containing culture of collectivity established in the 1970s and 1980s, but this process of acculturation frequently results in the historically oppressed experiencing a psychological tension related to them straddling different worlds that all become increasingly alien (Bulhan, 1980).

At a theoretical level, these shifting identities resemble Bulhan's (1985) understanding of capitulation. But perhaps these shifts should be seen from another perspective. This perspective shows that material conditions have

Capitulation:
The first stage of Bulhan's theory involves increased assimilation into the dominant culture and a simultaneous rejection of one's own culture. This stage is based on the defensive mechanism of identification with the coloniser or powerful subject.

forced many black adolescents who were previously committed to radical social transformation into a process of *deradicalisation*. The role of Black adolescents is perceived differently in post-apartheid South Africa, that is to say, from being 'young lions' to a more controlled and accommodating social category within the new dispensation. This process of deradicalisation has taken the form of vilifying and even physically repressing activities of Black adolescents in a new generation.

In some respects, it seems that life after apartheid has not been able to fulfil a range of expectations for the historically oppressed. Indeed, many young and old Black people may be experiencing greater difficulties adjusting to the contradictions within the process of social transformation. That the transformation of our society has had a simple, straightforward positive effect on Black life and on Black adolescence is a simplistic argument. The current socio-historical context tends to encourage a rejection of collectivism and even community, rather inviting Black adolescents to embrace individualism. Ironically, it appears that it is this very individualism that is contributing to several difficulties pertaining to social adjustment and identity integration among Black adolescents in post-apartheid South Africa.

It is clear that Black adolescent identity development during apartheid was affected in a contradictory manner, and that the extreme positions of 'damage' versus 'resilience' are too simplistic. Rather, it may be more useful to conceptualise these adolescents as experiencing multiple and sometimes contradictory social realities, and that the *changing nature* of identities has allowed for varying degrees of personal integration (Campbell, 1995; Henriques *et al.*, 1984). In a similar vein, while the post-apartheid country has generated greater opportunities for the historically disadvantaged populace, it also impresses on Black adolescent identity development in a complex and often ambiguous manner.

What needs to be recognised is that the impact of social influences on identity formation is more complex and nuanced than had been conceptualised by most personologists – many of whom did not adequately address the role of subjective agency in this process. South Africa, both under apartheid and after apartheid, has presented certain contradictory challenges and obstacles to the development of Black adolescent identity. One of the current strategies utilised by Black adolescents in this ever-changing socio-historical context is the active adoption of what has been referred to above as the 'Coca-Cola' culture, in an attempt to function more optimally within this context.

Exercises for critical engagement

1 In this chapter it has been argued that a Black person who went through adolescence in the 1990s, after apartheid, had very different experiences

from an individual who went through adolescence before the 1990s, during apartheid. To prove whether this argument holds, access two Black individuals who are willing to talk to you about their experiences while growing up. One of them should of course have been an adolescent after 1990 and one an adolescent in the 1980s, preferably during the height of state repression. After talking to both, what themes are raised by each individual (e.g. apartheid, political struggle, 'race', economic hardship, personal relationships, popular culture, clothes) more often? Using what you have read in this chapter and your own knowledge, try to *explain the differences or similarities in responses.*

2 To what extent do you think that differences between White and Black adolescent identity development still exist in contemporary South Africa, and conversely, to what extent do you think that there are increasing similarities between White and Black adolescent identity development in contemporary South Africa? When responding to this question, consider the recent apartheid past and differences and similarities in Black and White adolescent identity formation. Are there carry-overs from this past that significantly impact on the present? Think carefully about how new economic arrangements impact on the formation of Black and White middle and upper classes, and how this in turn brings greater complexity to the social psychology debate about class, 'race' and adolescence. Also, consider the degree to which 'racial' integration is or is not occurring in the 'new' South Africa as a result of new economic arrangements, and how this influences Black and White adolescent identity development today.

3 To what extent, in your opinion, is Erikson's theory of psycho-social development *inapplicable* (i) to the Black adolescent experience in apartheid South Africa, and (ii) to the Black adolescent experience after apartheid?

4 This chapter has indicated certain factors that young Black people have had to face up to if they want to attain healthy levels of identity congruence and integration. One of these factors is perhaps that young Black people have had little access to *resources* to 'be all they could be'. With *your own life* or *the life of someone in your family* in mind, and with more *specificity*, (i) detail for yourself some of the factors that you think disallowed you to 'be all you could be', and (ii) detail for yourself some of the resources that helped you to get where you are today.

5 Is being politically radical off the social agenda? With reference to Bulhan's theory of identity development of oppressed people, respond to this question by thinking about radicalisation. Do you think being radical is important or not? Think about what you regard to be a well-adjusted South African and what you regard as 'healthy' about your identity in relation to what is 'healthy' in your community and society.

Recommended reading

Bulhan, H.A. (1985). *Frantz Fanon and the Psychology of Oppression*. New York: Plenum.

Dawes, A. & D. Donald (Eds.) (1994). *Childhood and Adversity*. Cape Town: David Phillip.

Duncan, N. & B. Rock (1994). *Inquiry into the Effects of Public Violence on Children: Preliminary Report*. Sandton: Goldstone Commission.

Erikson, E.H. (1968). *Identity: Youth and Crisis*. New York: Norton.

Lockhat, R. & A. van Niekerk (2000). 'South African children and mental health: A history of adversity, violence and trauma'. *Ethnicity and Health*, 5(3/4):291–302.

Marcia, J.E. (1980). 'Identity in adolescence'. In J. Adelson (Ed.) *Handbook of Adolescent Psychology*, pp. 159–187. New York: Wiley.

8

Identity Dynamics and the Politics of Self-Definition

Vijé E. Franchi & Tanya M. Swart[1]

OUTCOMES

After having studied this chapter you should be able to:

- understand the origins of modern preoccupations with the self and identity in psychology
- define and distinguish different theoretical approaches (content versus process) to identity in social psychology
- understand culture and identity
- describe the dynamic and inter-cultural model of identity, and
- articulate the issues at stake in defining self-identity for young adults in post-apartheid South Africa (a contextual and political approach to the study of identity).

THIS CHAPTER outlines a theoretical framework for understanding identity dynamics that represents an alternative to the more widespread content definitions of identity, and examines the politics of self-definition in the context of broader socio-political changes in South Africa. However, before presenting this theoretical framework and examining the issues at stake for defining identity in post-1994 and present-day South Africa, it is worthwhile to identify the origins of psychology's Eurocentric preoccupation with the self and with identity. This assists us in narrowing down a theoretically viable definition of the self and identity, concepts for which there is little consensus in the field of social psychology. Following this, the chapter proceeds to critically examine self-definition within the context of the recent political and socio-economic processes that characterised the transition from an apartheid state to one of democratic governance. These broader contextual factors form the changing 'intentional world' (Shweder, 1990) in articulation with which individuals negotiate the meaning and value of old and new identities. Shweder (1990:2) argues that:

> A socio-cultural environment is an intentional world ... because its existence is real, factual and forceful ... [inasmuch as] a community of persons whose beliefs, desires, emotions, purposes and other mental representations are directed at it ... are thereby influenced by it ... What makes their existence intentional is that such things would not exist independent of our involvements with them and reactions to them; and they exercise their influence in our lives because of our conceptions of them.

These factors constitute key elements that determine the issues at stake for self-definition. We draw on the findings of studies on identity among university students in local South African institutions (Franchi & Swart, 2003; Swart, 2001) in order to illustrate some of the issues at stake for self-definition – especially with reference to the use of the 'racial' categories and linguistic markers of apartheid, or the reference to the post-1994 ideals of non-racial, unified, and reconciled citizenship.

In many parts of the world, especially those influenced by European philosophical traditions, the self and identity are thought of as entities that each person develops and has, and whose defining features both distinguish the individual from, and allow her or him to identify with, others.

Self-definition occurs inter-subjectively and always involves processes of *power*. The negotiation of the value and meaning of self-identity takes place within a particular context defined by its spatial, temporal, and symbolic boundaries, which is invariably constructed through differences and inequalities among individuals and groups. In South Africa, self-identity is constructed and re-constructed against the backdrop of structurally entrenched asymmetries (on the basis of 'race', class and gender), created and maintained through historical processes (such as apartheid, struggle politics, and the negotiated transition to a liberal democracy). Within this context, identity is not only defined by, but functions to re-define, contest, legitimate or transform social and historical processes.

We argue that the specific meaning associated with the recruitment of 'racial', linguistic, national, ethnic, cultural, gender and class signifiers of self-identity – rather than reflecting either the continued salience of 'race' as an identity signifier in post-apartheid society, or the so-called orientation of the self towards the norms and values of a particular 'cultural' affiliation group – needs to be understood as variable, shifting in concert with the changing meaning and politics of identity definition in a given 'intentional world'. It reflects that which the individual experiences as being at stake in the act of self-definition in a particular context and at a given time, which is itself contingent upon shifting internal and external factors. This is especially important in view of the historical centrality of 'race' as a determinant of the unequal distribution of economic and power-political resources in South Africa. It is also important given the intersection of theories of 'race', 'nationality' or 'ethnicity', and 'language' in the way that the apartheid ideologues conceptualised South Africans (see Alexander, 2001), as well as the present-day connection between language, 'ethnicity' and the 'racial' categories of apartheid. We conclude by cautioning against an interpretation of identity in terms of its 'contents' – that is, the markers used to self-articulate self-identity – as this is only likely to contribute to further reifying identity in apartheid ('racial') or post-apartheid (non-racial, unified national) terms. The dynamic nature of identity, its shifting contextually defined meanings, and the political function of self-definition necessitate remaining open to new and different possibilities for self-definition, and attentive to their shifting significance against an ever-changing subjective and socio-political landscape.

The philosophical origins of modern preoccupations with the self

In many parts of the world, especially those influenced by European philosophical traditions, the self and identity are commonly thought of as entities that each person *develops* and *has*, and whose defining features both distinguish the individual from others, and allow her or him to identify with others. The limitations and usefulness of such ideas are better understood by identifying the origins of the social sciences' preoccupation with the constructs of the self and identity throughout the twentieth century.

Solomon (1988) traces the origins of the importance accorded to the self in modern continental philosophy back to Socrates and Protagoras. These philosophers had argued that humanity must be the focus, if not the limit, of human inquiry. Descartes later brought subjectivity and the self into the philosophical limelight, by placing the emphasis on human experience and introspective reflection, the nature of the identity of the self, and the importance of the first-person standpoint. However, the *transcendental importance of the self* was only recognised by the continental philosophical community in the nineteenth century, when Kant elevated the status of the self from that of 'just another entity in the world' to that of 'the entity that creates the world' (Solomon, 1988).

The reflecting self was seen to know not only itself, but in knowing itself was seen to know all selves, and the structure of any and every possible self. These same assumptions were later taken up in psychoanalysis, when Freud developed a theory of personality based on introspective reflection. He demonstrated that it was possible to know the innermost layers of his own self and use this knowledge to uncover and know the selves of others. More importantly, this view legitimated the assertion that the structures of one's own mind, culture, and personality are in some sense necessary and universal for all humankind. This is one of the sources of psychology's ethnocentric, ahistorical assumption that theoretical paradigms of human development and functioning derived from Europe- and American-based research are universally applicable.

Although these philosophical premises significantly shaped the approaches adopted by anthropology and psychology in the earlier part of the twentieth century, each sub-discipline in the social sciences generated its own particular epistemological framework for investigating and conceptualising the nature and workings of the human self. For instance, psychoanalysis and the broader field of clinical psychology continued to give primacy to subjective experience and the first-person standpoint – the 'I' (the self as subject) is considered to be the only valid standpoint from which the 'me' (the self as object) can be truly known. In contrast, cognitive and social psychology focused on the observable, measurable, conscious aspects of self (the cognitive self-schema) thought to be responsible for processing self-relevant information and organising behaviour.

Perspectives on the self, identity and identity dynamics
Current conceptions of self and identity

The literature abounds with different definitions of self and identity. The definitions presented here are drawn from the psychoanalytic and phenomenological perspectives, as well as from the fields of clinical psychology, experimental social psychology, and cognitive psychology.

Some theorists highlight the spatial and temporal embeddedness of the self or identity. From a psychoanalytic perspective, Winnicott (1960) described the *sense of a continuity of self* across time and space – the self is perceived as retaining its singularity in spite of changing external and internal factors and the interaction between them. Anzieu (1985), a French psychoanalyst, addressed this question from the standpoint of the ego's experience of a separation between its outer and inner worlds, given by its outermost envelope, the *human skin*. In addition to providing a protective envelope, the skin is experienced as the point of interface and separation between internal and external realities, and procures a subjective experience of the *self as bounded*.

However, beyond this experience of the self as a set of coordinates in space and time, individuals extrapolate their uniqueness and singularity from the experience of their internal life as inhabited by private thoughts and feelings. It is perhaps, above all, this awareness of an embodied, unfolding, innermost private life that procures what Erikson (1968:19) called a feeling of identity – that uncanny subjective sense of '*sameness and continuity*', of being whole, separate and unique.

From a phenomenological perspective, Rom Harré (1998:4) defines this feeling of identity in terms of the individual's 'sense of self'. He argues that a sense of self is not the substantial referent of the word 'I'. It is not an essential and bounded entity, nor '*the ego's intuition of itself* as an object, as could be inferred from the use of the word 'me' – it is not the 'me' that the 'I' knows. Rather, 'to have a sense of self, is to have a sense of one's location as a person ... It is to have a sense of one's point of view, at any moment a location in space from which one perceives and acts upon the world, including that part that lies within one's own skin' (*ibid.*). In sum, the sense of self or singularity of experience is not an entity but a *site* from which to perceive and a location from which to act. For many theorists, this sense of self extends to the collection of attributes, experiences, thoughts, motivations, attitudes, feelings, and behaviours that one identifies as particular to oneself. It is equally shaped by those social, cultural, historical and political factors that characterise the contexts within which individuals negotiate their personal and social identities – namely, the sense of that which is unique and that which is shared in the experience of identity.

Rosenberg (1990:51) points out that 'the notion of identity structure as an organised multiplicity of constituent identities is a common one in contemporary psychology and sociology'. Drawing on empirical research in clinical psychology, he defines the psychological content of these constituent identities as 'an amalgam of personal characteristics, feelings, values, intentions and images that a person experiences *through* this identity' (our emphasis and translation). While this theoretical model postulates the existence of multiple identities, their psychological contents are seen as inter-related and constitute an organisational unity called identity structure. According to Rosenberg (1990), the unity of the self is not a phenomenological sense of unity but the structure of identity created by the structural and functional characteristics of the self.

In the field of experimental social psychology, Hazel Markus (1977) demonstrated the role of self-schemata in organising and making use of self-related information. This served as the basis for numerous empirical studies, such as Markus & Herzog (1991) on the role of the self-concept in aging;

Markus and Kitayama (1991) on culture's influence on the self and the implications for cognition, emotion and motivation; Markus and Oyserman (1989)
on the role of self-concept in gender and thought; and, Markus *et al.* (1990) on
the role of the self-system in competence.

According to Markus (1977:64), self-schemata are 'cognitive generalisations about the self, derived from past experience, that organise and guide the
processing of self-related information contained in the individual's social experiences.' The self-concept can be conceptualised as a subjective theory of the
self that both integrates and reflects self-relevant knowledge and understanding, and that organises future action. Markus and Wurf (1987)
emphasise the multifaceted, dynamic, active, socially embedded, and socio-
cultural nature of the self-system. 'Multifaceted' refers to its content and
structure, while 'dynamic' refers to the continually shifting array of accessible
self-representations in the self-concept. The self-concept is seen as 'active' in
that self-schemata function to both represent the self to the self (the self as
object of knowledge or 'me'), and constitute the locus from which the person
perceives and acts (the self as subject or knower, 'I'). Finally, all self-knowledge
is socially and culturally derived.

From a perspective of cognitive psychology, Ulric Neisser's (1988:35)
taxonomy of types of self-knowledge helps clarify some of the apparent contradictions inherent in conceptualising the self 'as a unitary object ...
simultaneously physical and mental, directly perceived and incorrectly
imagined, universal and culture-specific.' This framework postulates the existence of different types of self-knowledge, each of which originates from the
cognitive processing of a different type of self-relevant information, and
performs a separate though inter-related function. (See Gore *et al.* [1999] for
an in-depth analysis of this taxonomy.)

The 'Ecological Self', which emerges through the processing of perceptual-
type information, allows the individual to situate the self within a physical
environment. The 'Interpersonal Self', on the other hand, has its origins in the
earliest signals through which the human infant establishes emotional contact
with other human beings (usually the primary caretakers). By engaging in
'immediate unreflective social interaction' (Neisser, 1988:41), this self nurtures
and maintains inter-subjectivity with others. The 'Extended Self' is the site of
autobiographical construction, and reflects the part of personhood that is
contained in self-related memory and projection. The 'Private Self' is derived
from the awareness of one's unshared personal experience. The fifth type of self-
knowledge, the 'Conceptual Self', most resembles the self-concept as defined
above. Gore *et al.* (1999:378) define Neisser's (1988) 'Conceptual Self' as:

> The cognitive network of theories and assumptions with which the person reflex-
> ively locates herself in the surrounding world. It includes the wide variety of
> 'ethnopsychologies' (i.e. local understandings concerning the regularities of self,

Self-schemata:
Cognitive generalisa-
tions about the self,
derived from past
experience, that
organise and guide
the processing of
self-related informa-
tion contained in the
individual's social
experiences.

Self-concept:
A person's theory of
him- or herself that
integrates and
reflects self-relevant
knowledge and
understanding and
organises future
action.

emotion and experience) around the world, and encompasses social roles (e.g. graduate student), presupposed internal entities (e.g. the soul) and socially significant dimensions of difference (e.g. intelligence). In addition, this Conceptual Self is responsible for integrating each of the other selves into a coherent tapestry of experience: 'the result is that each of the other four kinds of self-knowledge is also represented in the Conceptual Self.

Individual agency versus cultural determinism

Despite the obvious differences in the focus of their inquiries and in the methods they use to apprehend the self, neither clinical nor social psychology has completely abandoned the basic assumption that there is universality and necessity in the fundamental modes of human experience (Franchi & Andronikof-Sanglade, 1998): the fundamental structure and functions of the self remain constant across nations and ages, in spite of the recognised influence of 'socio-cultural', historical and political factors.

This view is rejected by theorists who conceptualise the self as embedded in, and constructed through, its dialectic articulation with pre-existing semiotic resources. As Hallowell (1955:89) put it, 'culture [plays] a constitutive role in the psychological adjustment of the individual to his world'. It provides certain 'basic orientations' to the self that shape self-awareness and enable the individual to 'act intelligibly in the world he apprehends'. This view has inspired numerous theoretical and empirical attempts – notably in cross-cultural psychology – to demonstrate the embeddedness of identity in the frameworks of meaning provided by culture (e.g. Gore et al., 1999; Markus & Kitayama, 1991; Oyserman, 1993). Equally important, it inspired a renewed interest in the development of ethnic identity (e.g. Atkinson et al., 1983; Gay, 1985; Marcia, 1980), processes of ethnic identification (e.g. Oetting & Beauvais, 1991; Weinreich, 1989a; 1989b; Weinreich et al., 1991), and ethnic self-identification (Aboud, 1987; Phinney, 1990) among minority youth. Some epistemological difficulties inherent in approaching the study of identity in South Africa from an 'ethnic' or 'cultural' identity perspective are evident.

First of all, research on ethnic identity has focused primarily on minority youth – that is, youth who are nationals of a particular country by birth, but who continue to be treated by the dominant society as outsiders or as second-rate citizens by virtue of a designated 'immigrant', 'racial', 'religious', or 'linguistic' identity. While this would be the case of the majority of youth in South Africa during apartheid, the historical and political context in South Africa differs markedly from the European and American contexts in which most of these studies were undertaken. Moreover, as Bekker (2001:2) points out, 'ethnic identities are constructed and manipulated, not "given". Though they may often be considered and even experienced as ascribed, this does not detract from their constructed nature.' Bekker (2000:4) stresses that 'ethnicity is a relational concept – it has to do with insiders and outsiders. It is often useful to speak of ranked ethnicity, where one group is perceived to be super-ordinate to another.' The constructedness of so-called 'ethnicity' in South Africa needs to be examined in the specific context of apartheid, racial oppression and the ideology of racism.

Secondly, research on minority identity development and the self across cultures has tended to focus on the child's negotiation of a sense of self with each of the two domains of reference within his or her immediate social environment, namely, the family and public micro-systems of the school, health and social services, the neighbourhood and a religious 'community'. The trend has been to conceptualise identity as caught between these different socialising systems, and the child as being socialised into the values of each separately and with differing degrees of success. Within these paradigms, it is usually the family's or the community's so-called 'ancestral culture' which is accorded the main role in the development of ethnic identity, notably through early primary identification with caretakers. On the other hand, ethnic self-identification (identifying oneself in terms of 'ethnicity', 'nationality', 'culture', 'religion', 'language', or 'race') is usually explained in terms of the individual's instrumental desire for greater integration within mainstream society, social mobility or power (for example, certain identities may be adopted as a way of gaining admission into a particular group, educational institution, or organisation). Such approaches have been criticised for defining identity in reified cultural terms (Franchi & Andronikof-Sanglade, 2001), and focusing on the 'cultural' aspects of inter-group relations to the exclusion of the socio-political and historical factors that underpin and maintain asymmetrical relations between minority and majority groups (defined in terms of access to power-political resources).

Lastly, it is becoming increasingly difficult to identify examples of mono-cultures in most twenty-first century societies. The internal diversification of cultural groups through movements of migration, immigration, political exile, unification of states and countries, and economic and cultural expansion has created an unprecedented number of multi-cultural contexts in which young people are now raised at the interface of a host of different 'partial' cultures, which are themselves embedded in systems of asymmetrical relations and competition for symbolic, political and material resources. In these contexts, the very processes of attachment and primary identification underpinning the emergence of a sense of self (and later the definition of identity) need to be understood in inter-cultural terms (Franchi, 1999). The asymmetrical power relations among minority and majority socialising systems – which are historically constructed through socio-political processes such as colonisation, decolonisation and apartheid – create the political, symbolic, temporal and spatial coordinates of an inter-cultural meso-system. It is in articulation with

> The internal diversification of cultural groups through movements of migration, immigration, political exile, unification of states and countries, and economic and cultural expansion has created an unprecedented number of multi-cultural contexts. Young people are now raised in these contexts at the interface of a host of different 'partial' cultures, which are themselves embedded in systems of asymmetrical relations and competition for symbolic, political and material resources.

That the internal structure of identity is inter-cultural is evident from the fact that the contents reflect an awareness and experience of the self as belonging to a number of different reference groups at once and to none completely.

the competing and conflicting demands and imperatives of this meso-system that the child develops a sense of self and negotiates an identity that provides both meaning and value for the self. The internal structure of self-identity – understood in line with Rosenberg's (1990:51) definition as 'an organised multiplicity of constituent identities' – is in itself inter-cultural (Franchi & Andronikof-Sanglade, 2001). This is evident insofar as the psychological contents of its constituent identities reflect an awareness and experience of the self as belonging to a number of different reference groups, while at the same time belonging to none completely or essentially; as moving and translating between their codes, values and expectations; as alternating the cultural viewpoints through which each of these groups perceives the world, while retaining a meta-perspective (a representation) of the relativity of the respective logics of each; and as insider and perpetual outsider of a number of reference groups whose asymmetrical dynamics – socio-economic, political and historical processes – determine the issues at stake for self-definition. In this context, the structure of self-identity cannot be conflated with the content of self-definition: the structure of identity reflects the inter-cultural epistemology of the self that guides the individual's reflexive and political rewriting and rethreading of a situated self-narrative in response to the complex interaction of personal and contextual identity imperatives and stakes.

Identity dynamics and the politics of self-definition

Towards a definition of identity dynamics

We turn now to a more in-depth examination of the processes underpinning the construction and regulation of identity dynamics in post-apartheid South Africa. Before looking more closely at the particular issues at stake for self-definition among youth in a changing South African context, it is necessary to define what it is exactly that we mean by identity dynamics and what difference there is between this approach and those defined by social and cognitive psychology, for instance. Lastly, this section outlines the reasons for choosing to focus on the politics of self-definition in the post-1994 socio-economic and political context.

The term identity dynamics seeks to highlight a process-driven approach to the study of identity, in particular the process underpinning the negotiation of meaning of identity in a given context.

We use the term *dynamics* in association with *identity* to highlight a process-driven approach to the study of identity. This approach differs from those that define identity as a composite or collection of self-relevant contents (that is, traits, attributes, characteristics, or features), some of which are considered to remain stable across the lifespan, and others to be subject to fluctuation. Process definitions of identity highlight the processes underpinning the negotiation of meaning and value for identity in a given context. They focus on those internal and external factors that influence the identity negotiation process – namely, the issues at stake for self-definition in a given context – and consider the product of these processes (that is, the particular way in which a person defines the self) as variable and relative to these issues.

Let us take the example of a person who states: 'I am a Xhosa male', for instance. The content approach would consider that the person defines himself to be, at all times and across all contexts, primarily 'a Xhosa male'. A process definition of identity, on the other hand, would ask 'what, in the current context – namely, in the individual's external and internal environment and in the interaction between them – is prompting the individual to define himself in this way?' Another related question would be: 'what is the person doing by defining himself as a Xhosa male?' In other words, how is he acting upon (or influencing) his environment by self-articulating self-identity in terms of 'ethnicity' and gender, rather than nationality or professional role, for example?

A person's sense of identity may be seen as deriving from those experiences that are most recurrent in the self – ideas, attitudes, feelings.

Drawing on the work of Carmel Camilleri (1990), we define identity as a complex dynamic that emerges and is transformed through intra-personal and inter-personal processes that are socio-politically and historically embedded. A person's sense of identity is derived from those experiences that are most recurrent in the self (ideas, attitudes, feelings). Moreover, it is represented through shared meanings, and derives its value through a process of negotiation with others within a particular socio-historical context. The individual creates and maintains this sense of sameness, coherence, and continuity of self by incessantly re-negotiating self-identity to either accommodate or integrate new and different self-relevant experiences. According to Camilleri (1990), identity dynamics are organised around two primary goals, namely: to preserve the meaning associated with the self (the person one thinks one is and

Identity can also be defined as a complex dynamic that emerges and is transformed through intra-personal and inter-personal processes that are socio-politically and historically embedded.

recognises oneself to be across time and contexts), and to negotiate inter-personal recognition for the value of one's identity (self-esteem and the esteem of others).

Drawing on the above theory, and for heuristic purposes, it may be useful to conceptualise identity dynamics as a complex system created through the dynamic tension between separate yet inter-related dimensions of self, namely:

1 the self as one defines oneself to be in the present (present self-articulated identity),
2 the self as one thinks one ought to be (identity ideals),
3 the self as others portray one to be (attributed or designated identities),
4 the self as one is expected to be by the groups within which one claims membership (e.g. 'cultural' ideals for identity),
5 the self as one represents oneself to be in the past (past identities), and
6 the self as one aspires to become, or fears becoming, in the future (identity threats and aspirations).

The glue that connects these constituent dimensions of the self is derived from the processes that continually re-negotiate a sense of sameness in the face of difference. Differently stated, the individual makes use of a range of more or less conscious strategies in order to reduce the discrepancies that arise between these different dimensions of identity (for instance, between current self-artic-ulated identity and the identity designated by society; or between past self-conceptions and the shared 'cultural' ideals of a group in which one claims membership). This is done with the aim of preserving the meaning and value attributed to one's self-identity both by oneself and by others. It is not the particular meaning associated with who one is that matters. Rather it is the sense of continuity of self, as remaining relatively constant in spite of impor-tant developmental and contextual changes, that is important. On the other hand, the value that the individual attributes to her or his self-identity will depend both on the degree to which current self-articulated identity corre-sponds with the ideal self, and the degree to which it corresponds with the identity attributions and ideals that others ascribe to the self. It is important to note that these dimensions of identity are deeply subjective, and are under-stood to be more a matter of the narratives that a person constructs about the self than some objective entity *per se*.

To understand this more clearly, let us examine the ways in which processes of representation and self-representation work. Firstly, self-represen-tation is *relational* since one defines oneself as either similar to or different from others, through processes of empathic identification and contra-identifi-cation with one's identity referents (Weinreich, 1989a; 1989b; Weinreich *et al.* 1991). Identity referents are those people whom the individual takes either as models or as negative examples for self-identity. They are often people whose opinions matter in the ways in which we come to see ourselves, for example, friends, family members, peers, professional colleagues, society, and community leaders.

Moreover, self-representation is based on a process of differentiation – 'me' is defined in articulation with that which is 'not-me'. The definition of one's self-identity depends on the definition of another's identity as other. In this sense, self-definition can be used to either underscore differences between self and other or, conversely, to highlight similarities and reinforce common group identities.

According to Stuart Hall (1996), identities acquire their particular meaning through the language and symbolic systems – namely, the labels and signifiers – that are used to represent them. The meaning and value of particular identity labels are negotiated with others in one's environment and are contingent upon the socio-historical and political context in which they are used, as well as the person who uses them. For example, in the context of South Africa's apartheid ideology of 'racial' segregation and oppression, 'Black' as an identity signifier could have very different meanings depending on whether it was used by the dominant group or by oppressed groups in the Black Consciousness movement or in the liberation struggle. In the first case, 'Black' would probably be used to signify the person's difference and inferiority with regard to the speaker, as well as to legitimate asymmetrical relations between the parties. In the second instance, it would probably be used in the spirit of contesting the fragmentation of the identity of a 'racially' oppressed majority in South Africa through the use of a variety of different 'racial' signifiers. The possibility of using self-definition to either assert group membership or set oneself apart from a constructed other brings us to one of the central concerns of this chapter, namely, the politics of self-definition in post-apartheid South Africa.

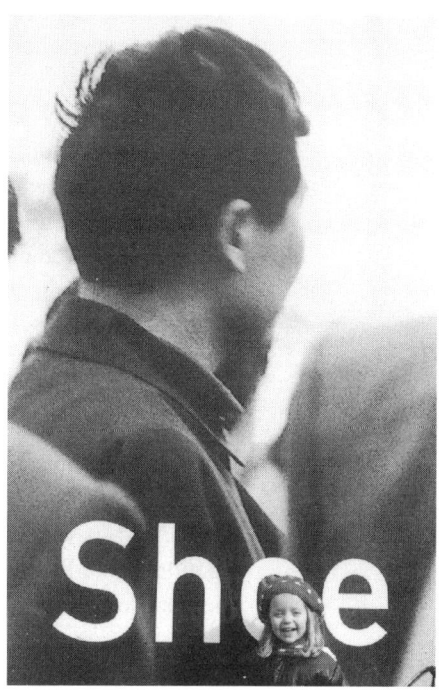

Self-representation is relational and is based on a process of differentiation.

What's at stake for identity negotiation in South Africa?

As mentioned earlier, identity dynamics always involve processes of power. These include the power to define oneself in one's own terms, the power to ascribe identity definitions to others, the power to contest historically constructed and inter-personally imposed identity categories and attributions, and the power to accept or reject so-called cultural conceptions, ideals and expectations that a particular group has for one's identity. However, as Alexander (2001:149) correctly points out, 'the decisive categorising power lies with the dominant group or groups. It is in their interests that the social hierarchy (casts, classes, 'races', gender categories, language groups, etc.) is established, and it is in their interests to keep it that way'.

The Jamaican-born cultural theorist Stuart Hall sees identities as acquiring their particular meaning through the language and symbolic systems that are used to represent them.

Although the birth of the psychological self is traced back to the developmental stage, when the individual first perceives the self as separate from the other, self-definition only occurs much later in development, and is usually associated with the onset of puberty and the developmental tasks of adolescence (Erikson, 1963). The politics of self-identity is not only a matter of negotiating self-identity inter-personally, with those who form one's primary relational environments (e.g. primary caretakers, siblings, and family) and secondary relational environments (e.g. neighbours, close friends, schoolmates, university peers, work colleagues, and so forth). Rather, it entails a taking up of historical, political, cultural, and socio-economic issues within one's intentional world, and negotiating ways of acting on this world that both defines the meaning and value of who one is, and determines the relative power of the location from which one can act on self, other, and one's life.

The following section examines the way in which self-articulated self-identity is taken to represent a privileged site of identity politics in post-apartheid South Africa. The selective use of 'racial', 'linguistic', 'ethnic', 'national', 'religious', 'gender', 'social class' or professional identity markers is taken to reflect not only an individual's struggle to define the meaning and value of the self in articulation with the ideals and projected attributions of the other (Franchi, 2000), but also to re-assert either the legitimacy of, or the continued 'struggle against, European economic, social, cultural, racial and political domination' (Mandaza, 2001:133). Mandaza (*ibid.*) emphasises the importance of considering 'not only the historical, socio-economic bases of the key determinant of identity in Southern Africa – i.e. *race*, but also the issue of class and ethnic identity, including other derived identities, such as those of "colour"'. While this would require, as Mandaza (*ibid.*) correctly notes, 'some focus on the nature and extent of the social engineering that characterised white racial domination – and *apartheid* – in Southern Africa; and an account of the complex interrelationship between race, colour and class identity in the Southern African context, including *ethnic* or "tribal" identification and *conflict*', space limitations and the focus of this chapter do not permit us to explore these further. Rather, we turn now to an overview of some of the macro-changes that impact on the issues at stake for self-definition in the current South African context.

Historical change and the issues at stake in self-definition

The transition from a racist apartheid system of governance to a liberal democratic polity was accompanied by significant and far-reaching macro-level changes in social, political, economic, and cultural life in South Africa (Stevens & Lockhat, 1997). Amongst the most noteworthy of these are:

- The ratification of the 1996 Constitution guaranteed the rights and liberties of all South Africans for the first time in over 350 years.

- An 18-month Truth and Reconciliation Commission (TRC) was established and mandated to recover South Africa's 'historical truth', and 'foster reconciliation' through the healing of survivors of gross human rights violations (through contained testifying, land restitution and financial reparations), and the healing and rehabilitation (social and moral) of their perpetrators (through truthful 'confession' and the granting of amnesty).

- Affirmative action measures were implemented in the public and private sectors with the aim of proactively redressing past discrimination in the internal labour market and promoting employment equity and equal access to resources. Formal labour market discrimination is addressed in the *Employment Equity Bill* (December, 1997) and includes factors related to the participation in the labour force and the central and occupational allocation of labour in terms of recruitment, promotion and training.

- A new language policy was adopted, which recognises the official status (executive, legislative and educational) of the nine indigenous languages of South Africa, in addition to English and Afrikaans, the two languages endorsed during apartheid (Finchilescu & Nyawose, 1998).

These macro-level and constitutional changes have an impact on micro-level changes in youth's perceptions of the issues at stake in defining identity. In attempting to unravel these issues, it is necessary to look beyond stated national imperatives and apparent advancements in constitutional, social and economic policy since 1994, towards some of the political and socio-economic compromises that underpinned the negotiated settlement between the National Party and the African National Congress, and that were at the base of the TRC.

At face value, the new democratic dispensation intended to: remember, eradicate and reverse the oppression and inequalities of the past; proactively prevent all forms of present and future discrimination; and recognise and preserve the 'cultural' diversity and multi-lingualism of present-day South African society. However, the processes of consigning individual and collective experiences and trauma to memory are selective, and they serve particular political agendas and understandings of the socio-economic and political situation at any given moment in history. This means that the ways in which certain parts of the country's apartheid past were remembered, and others not, had an impact on the politics of self-definition. Equally important, the continued 'racialisation' of processes of remembering, redistributing resources, and charting future life possibilities in South Africa, as well as the implications of the 'tension between the explicit constitutionally enshrined principles of the promotion of multilingualism in South Africa, and the concurrent practical commitment to the hegemonic status of English' (Alexander, 2001:144) are among the many issues that inform the meaning that processes of identification and self-definition come to acquire for youth in South Africa today. More specifically, they influence the way in which young people, whose experiences of past and present South Africa continue to differ markedly in accordance with their belonging to historically privileged or oppressed groups, integrate past, present and future self-understandings and identity narratives, as well as gain access to cultural capital and power-political resources.

Transition, or a story of negotiated political, social and economic compromises

The negotiated settlement reached between de Klerk's National Party and Mandela's African National Congress implied a number of costly political compromises and even costlier social and economic compromises (Marais, 1998) for the majority of South Africans. These included:

- the agreement to share political power for the first five years of the transitional democracy, within a free-market framework,

- the undertaking to protect minority rights and to allow White civil servants to retain their positions in the state bureaucratic structures, and

- the decision to grant amnesty to all activists, politicians and soldiers, in exchange for the full disclosure of their contributions and participation in gross human rights violations and atrocities.

In this process, the TRC emerged as a key player in legitimating and entrenching the socio-economic and political compromises of this transition (van der Walt et al., 2003).

TRC, memory and the politics of self-representation

The TRC set in motion a process that translated the imperative to remember the apartheid past. Its aim was to create a new national consciousness that incorporated the differences among previously separated groups, weaving them into one and the same social and political fabric. While the process permitted many to directly or vicariously speak and gain recognition for the atrocities witnessed and experienced during apartheid, it could be argued that this process also entrenched the fragmented view of subjectivities produced by 'racial' segmentation during the apartheid period, and has reinforced the subjective understanding of 'separate oppressions', expressed in the 'ranking of pain and disadvantage' according to the old 'racial' categories of apartheid. The Truth and Reconciliation process can be seen to have constructed the identity of different groups of South Africans in ways that must now be dealt with in order to move towards the political ideal of a democratic society built on equality, human rights, and social and economic prosperity. Present-day self-narratives reveal the effects of racialising identity and politicising 'racial' identity in the years prior to and following the new democratic dispensation in South Africa.

The ideology of racism and the racialisation of identity

While the racial groups that underpinned the organisation of every aspect of life under the apartheid regime are clearly fabricated political and socio-linguistic categories, their impact on present identity politics is far more difficult to unravel. This is especially the case in view of the racialisation of historical, material, socio-economic process after the official end of apartheid in 1994. Bundy (2000) speaks of the ways in which the *racialised* divides salient during apartheid were taken up, maintained, and rewritten in other discourses which performed essentially the same function, that being to maintain a passivity towards addressing exploitative social and economic conditions. He charges the African National Congress (ANC) with strategically retreating from addressing issues of land and wealth redistribution in order to ensure that the 'structural foundations of a two-nation' (*ibid.*:11) society could be sustained through the transition from apartheid to democracy.

In summary, it can be said that the recognition and reversal of past inequalities and apartheid trauma and oppression, and the construction of a sentiment of national unity capable of reworking 'racially-constructed' differences into a vision of a meaningful and valued national identity, were short-circuited by such factors as the new democratic government's failure to place apartheid as a system on trial and oblige its authors to make civil and economic reparations for their crimes, the elision of socio-economic and land reform issues, the failure to address pre-labour discrimination through affirmative action measures in the areas of training, human resource development, and education, and the foregrounding of national imperatives of 'non-racial' unity and reconciliation over individual and community imperatives for the recognition of individual and collective oppression and loss, the uncovering and healing of past wounds and the socio-economic rehabilitation of the survivors and their families. Pre-labour discrimination refers to the creation and maintenance of historical disadvantage through unequal access to assets,

Pre-labour discrimination refers to the creation and maintenance of historical disadvantage through unequal access to assets, financial credit, economic opportunity and human resource development, the dispossession of land and the politically orchestrated devastation of solid social capital (family structure, human relations and community life).

financial credit, economic opportunity and human resource development, the dispossession of land and the politically orchestrated devastation of solid social capital (family structure, human relations and community life).

The politics of self-definition

In this last section we examine the politics of self-definition for youth confronted with the legacy of an apartheid past, the disillusionment of a negotiated and transitional present, and the indeterminacy of a future which holds little certainty but a wide range of possibilities. The articulation between social, political, and economic contextual factors in South Africa and identity dynamics amongst young adults is examined by drawing on examples from studies of self-articulated self-identity amongst a student population in South Africa (Franchi & Swart, 2003; Swart, 2001).

The study on which we focus was undertaken in 1998, among 544 students of differing 'cultural' and 'linguistic' backgrounds enrolled in universities, mostly within the Gauteng province of South Africa. The study examines the challenges presented to identity by macro-level factors within the country, especially in terms of their impact on self-definition in 'cultural', 'ethnic', 'racial', 'linguistic' or national terms. In particular, the study looks at the extent to which post-apartheid society offered young adults new and different possibilities for constructing their identity, or whether 'race' still constituted a central defining feature of *self* and *other* representations. Respondents' open-ended self-identity assertions were examined in light of their reported desire to stay in South Africa, and their perceptions of being able to succeed (both personally and professionally) as compared to other South Africans. An empirically derived grouping variable – 'language orientation across contexts' – was used to distinguish between previously advantaged and disadvantaged South Africans. This variable was derived as a summation of the use of one (monolingual) or more (bilingual or multi-lingual) of the colonial (English and Afrikaans), vernacular or immigrant languages across family, social and university life-contexts.

Categories used to code present self-concept

In this study, respondents were asked to complete the open-ended sentence: 'I am ...' in order to tap their present self-concept. Their responses were coded into the following categories:

1 *Intra-personal positive*: This category included self-statements such as 'I am artistic' or 'I am intelligent'. This category was used in 72.6 per cent of cases.
2 *Intra-personal negative*: This category included self-statements such as 'I am absent-minded' or 'I am a procrastinator'. This category was used in 65.4 per cent of cases.

3   *Inter-personal positive*: This category included self-statements such as 'I am a good listener' or 'I enjoy being around people'. This category was used in 36.9 per cent of cases.

4   *Inter-personal negative*: This category included self-statements such as 'I am difficult to approach' or 'I am violent'. This category was used in 30 per cent of cases.

5   *Relational subject position*: This category included self-statements such as 'I am a wife' or 'I am an oldest child'. This category was used in 14.9 per cent of cases.

6   *Interest/activity/occupation*: This category included self-statements such as 'I am a reader' or 'I volunteer for the police'. This category was used in 24.3 per cent of cases.

7   *University-related*: This category included self-statements such as 'I am a student at Wits' or 'I am completing a degree in Education'. This category was used in 25.2 per cent of cases.

8   *Beliefs/values/worldview/politics/class*: This category included self-statements such as 'I am a socialist' or 'I am a feminist'. This category was used in 29.4 per cent of cases.

9   *Physical (including age)*: This category included self-statements such as 'I am 20 years old' or 'I am tall'. This category was used in 27.9 per cent of cases.

10 *Gender*: This category included self-statements such as 'I am male' or 'I am a woman'. This category was used in 34.8 per cent of cases.

11 *Nationality/birthplace*: This category included self-statements such as 'I am a South African' or 'I was born in South Africa'. This category was used in 18.8 per cent of cases.

12 *Language/religion/culture/ethnicity*: This category included self-statements such as 'I am a Tswana-speaker' or 'I am a Muslim'. This category was used in 30 per cent of cases.

13 *Racial identity/race-related*: This category included self-statements such as 'I am White' or 'I am Coloured – father White and mom Black'. This category was used in 24.3 per cent of cases.

Results of the study showed that there was a general paucity of direct references to 'racial', 'cultural' and national identity markers in respondents' self-articulated self-conceptions, a finding that remains open to several interpretations. This finding may be indicative of attempts to define identity beyond the narrow confines of 'racial' categorisation, in ways that were perhaps limited during apartheid. This may reflect a desire to align with the ethos of the new democratic South Africa, and attempt to embrace a unified national identity, whilst simultaneously recognising individual differences. Furthermore, the transformations of post-apartheid South Africa may present these youth with new identity challenges and concerns which may be more prominent for self-representation, in which 'race' no longer fulfils a salient or central function. However, it may be more realistic to hold that the legacy of decades of 'racial' oppression has not dissipated as a consequence of the demo-cratic transition. While based on a constructive sentiment and the imperative for national unity and reconciliation, an ethos of non-racialism to a certain extent elides the remnants of apartheid. The absence of 'racial' self-descriptors in self-articulated forms of identity amongst South African students may in fact represent what Carrim (2000) refers to as a 'silencing' of 'race'. According to Carrim (*ibid.*), this results from the 'fear of losing privilege', the 'fear of continuing with the ways of the past' or the 'fear of civil war'. For those who continue to benefit from 'racially-constructed' privileges, the silencing of 'racial' identity is seen to fulfil the strategic function of self-presenting as aligned with the new dispensation's non-racial ethos and the ideals of national unity and reconciliation, at a time when the focus on 'racial' identity would serve to expose and denounce the illegitimacy of this privilege. In other words, the attempts to *deracialise* identity representations amongst historically advantaged South African students may well be related to their fear of losing the socio-economic status that continues to afford them greater opportunity relative to the historically disadvantaged majority.

The findings also suggest that making overt references to 'race' is no longer considered to be acceptable when self-reporting identity amongst South African students. This tends to be corroborated by the finding that, while 'racial' markers were infrequently used, implicit references were consistently made to an apartheid history and its implications for the present and the future. These were expressed through future identity representations (e.g. civic/political commitment to South Africa; making a difference/charity work/idealistic change; the fear of being a victim of crime/the desire to leave South Africa; the fear of becoming a racist or of being a victim of discrimina-tion), the motivations given for wanting to leave the country (e.g. crime rate, insecurity, fear, politics), and the reasons cited for perceived opportunities to succeed, get a job, and achieve future happiness in the new South Africa (e.g. affirmative action and lack of future employment prospects). Referring to these concerns in self-articulated self-identity attests to the difficulties that present-day youth experience in coming to terms with South Africa's history of 'racial' oppression, and the legacy of personal and collective trauma, in the face of the present move towards non-racial, democratic nationhood. The relative salience of indirect references to apartheid oppression/privilege and post-apartheid transformation in the self-conceptions of historically privileged and oppressed language orientation sub-samples suggests that students in post-apartheid South Africa are likely to be grappling with a process of negotiating the multiple and conflicting personal and social meanings of 'racially-constructed and de-constructed' past, present and future locations of the self and the other.

> Youth in the new South Africa have difficulties in coming to terms with the country's history of racial oppression and the legacy of personal and collective trauma, in the face of the present move towards non-racial, democratic nationhood.

Categories used to code future identity aspirations

In this study, respondents were required to write down four things that they hoped to be, expected to become, or wanted to achieve for themselves in the next few years in order to tap their future identity aspirations. Their responses were coded into the following categories:

1 *Health-related:* This category included future identity aspirations such as the desire 'to be well and healthy' and to 'stop smoking'. This category was used in 5.7 per cent of cases.

2 *Intra-personal:* This category included future identity aspirations such as the desire to 'be satisfied with life' or 'be successful'. This category was used in 31.8 per cent of cases.

3 *Inter-personal:* This category included future identity aspirations such as the desire to 'be loved by people around me' or 'have more close friends'. This category was used in 18.2 per cent of cases.

4 *Marriage/relationship:* This category included future identity aspirations such as the desire to 'be a good husband' or 'be married or with a serious boyfriend'. This category was used in 30.5 per cent of cases.

5 *Becoming a parent:* This category included future identity aspirations such as 'having children and being a good mother' or to 'be a mother'. This category was used in 15.1 per cent of cases.

6 *Leisure/travel:* This category included future identity aspirations such as to 'be able to travel' or to 'be travelling the world'. This category was used in 18.9 per cent of cases.

7 *Graduation/university-related:* This category included future identity aspirations such as the desire to 'graduate' or to 'be an LLB student'. This category was used in 39.3 per cent of cases.

8 *Related to career/occupation:* This category included future identity aspirations such as the desire to 'be a psychologist' or to 'have a good job'. This category was used in 77.6 per cent of cases.

9 *Material objects/wealth:* This category included future identity aspirations such as the desire to 'have financial independence' or 'have a car, have a house'. This category was used in 29.4 per cent of cases.

10 *Making a difference/charity work/idealistic change:* This category included future identity aspirations such as the desire to 'help the illiterate' or to 'be charitable'. This category was used in 6.8 per cent of cases.

11 *Not a crime victim/safety/leave SA:* This category included future identity aspirations such as the desire to 'be safe' or to 'be settled down in a safe country'. This category was used in 3.1 per cent of cases.

12 *Language/religion/culture/ethnicity:* This category included future identity aspirations such as the desire to 'be more culturally involved' or to 'grow as a Christian'. This category was used in 4.4 per cent of cases.

13 *Civic/political commitment to SA:* This category included future identity aspirations such as the desire to 'correct the past by social awareness' or to be a 'good citizen'. This category was used in 2.4 per cent of cases.

Categories used to code future identity threats

In this study, respondents were required to write down four things that they were afraid of becoming, would like to avoid becoming or wanted to change about themselves in the next few years in order to tap their future identity threats. Their responses were coded into the following categories:

1   *Health problem/death-related:* This category included future identity threats such as 'being HIV positive' or 'being sick'. This category was used in 18 per cent of cases.

2   *Intra-personal:* This category included future identity threats such as 'not being faithful to myself' or being 'unhappy'. This category was used in 71 per cent of cases.

3   *Inter-personal:* This category included future identity threats such as 'hurting others' or being 'hated by people'. This category was used in 47.1 per cent of cases.

4   *No relationship/homosexuality:* This category included future identity threats such as 'being single', 'not getting married' or being 'homosexual'. This category was used in 13.8 per cent of cases.

5   *Pregnancy/single parent/bad parent:* This category included future identity threats such as being 'a mother before I'm married' or being 'a terrible parent'. This category was used in 6.8 per cent of cases.

6   *Not travel/no leisure/not being able to move:* This category included future identity threats such as being 'in the same place too long' or being 'restricted in activities'. This category was used in 2.9 per cent of cases.

7   *Graduation/university-related:* This category included future identity threats such as being 'a university drop-out' or 'failing university'. This category was used in 17.5 per cent of cases.

8   *Unemployment/bad job prospects:* This category included future identity threats such as 'being unemployed' or 'failing at my career'. This category was used in 29.4 per cent of cases.

9   *Material poverty:* This category included future identity threats such as 'being homeless' or 'being destitute'. This category was used in 18 per cent of cases.

10 *Delinquency:* This category included future identity threats such as becoming a 'drug and alcohol abuser' or 'being a criminal'. This category was used in 14 per cent of cases.

11 *Victim of crime/discrimination/racist/negative about SA:* This category included future identity threats such as being 'worried about crime' or becoming 'racist'. This category was used in 0.9 per cent of cases.

12 *Language/religion/culture/ethnicity:* This category included future identity threats such as fearing 'stigma attached to my culture' or 'being too Western'. This category was used in 4.8 per cent of cases.

13 *Civic/political commitment to SA:* This category included future identity threats such as being 'politically active' or being a 'victim of government corruption'. This category was used in 7.7 per cent of cases.

Students' constructed self-identities in the present study clearly reflect the socio-historical divide in their respective backgrounds, when examined by their language orientations across life contexts. For example, bilingual English, Afrikaans, Zulu, Xhosa and other vernacular language speakers made more frequent mention of identity threats related to *delinquency* and *graduation* than the other two groups. The members of this sub-sample are more likely than the other two groups to share an historical background of 'racial' discrimination under apartheid, with all that this entails in terms of pre-labour market discrimination (Mhone *et al.*, 1998) and psychological trauma. Respondents in this group, all of whom would be defined as 'Black' according to Black Consciousness (BC) criteria, used 'racial' and 'cultural' identity markers the most often when defining their self-concept. Moreover, their concurrent use of 'racial' and 'cultural' markers appears to suggest an orientation both towards the past (which may reflect a positive identification with 'Black' identity gained from the BC Movement, or the internalisation of apartheid's 'racial' categorisation), and towards the present (in terms of the discourse of recognising 'cultural' differences in present-day South Africa and the focus on affirmative action practices). Respondents in this group also made reference to *language/religion/culture/ethnicity* when self-defining their future identity aspirations as South Africans, suggesting an attempt to align themselves with the 'recognition of culture(s)' in the new democratic dispensation.

From a different perspective, the more frequent use of 'cultural' and 'racial' identity markers amongst 'historically oppressed' South Africans appears to confirm Duncan's (2001) finding that there was a greater acceptance of the existence of 'racial' differences, and a greater emphasis on 'cultural' differences between 'Black' groups and amongst 'Blacks' in the post-1994 period than during the apartheid regime. The more frequent use of 'ethnic' or 'cultural' markers suggests that 'cultural identity' may be made salient when an individual identifies with more than one reference group and is faced with negotiating identity at the interface of their respective identity ideals and competing expectations and attributions (Franchi, 1999). Moreover, in the context of South Africa's transition from apartheid to democracy, some respondents may use 'cultural' or 'ethnic' markers to articulate 'racially-constructed difference', without reverting to apartheid terminology. Alternatively, the use of 'cultural' markers may represent a contestation of the homogenising practice of 'racial' categorisation both in the past and in the present. These two possibilities could be seen to stem from the potential for 'culture' or 'ethnicity' both to exclude and to articulate belongingness (Adam, 1995).

The more frequent use of ethnic or cultural markers in the post-1994 period may be salient when individuals identify with more than one reference group and are faced with negotiating identity at the interface of their respective identity ideals and competing expectations.

Bilingual speakers of English, Afrikaans, Zulu, Xhosa and other vernacular languages showed the highest levels of commitment to staying in South Africa, defined their future identity aspirations in terms of making a difference in South Africa more often, and perceived relatively greater equality of opportunities to succeed in the 'new' South Africa, in comparison to their classmates. This suggests a greater willingness on their part to embrace the democratic ideals and changes, and the perception that present-day South Africa offers opportunities for what was a 'racially-defined' minority during apartheid. However, the self-reported future identity fears of students in this group highlight the historical disadvantage that continues to undermine their access to economic and social resources.

Monolingual English-speakers (the majority of whom are likely to have been categorised as 'White' under apartheid) also made frequent use of overt 'racial' self-concept markers, and showed a similar orientation towards the past. These findings corroborate those of Smith and Stones (1999) as well as the increased 'racial' identification amongst English-speaking 'White' respondents and 'Black' respondents found in a Markdata omnibus survey (cited in Bornman, 1999). The use of 'racial' markers can be taken to indicate an orientation towards identifying either with an apartheid past or with a future outside of South Africa. Sennet and Foster (1996) point out that 'White' English-speaking South Africans have historically shown a more diffuse sense of collective identity and have been characterised by internationalism and close links to mainstream Western culture, a relatively weaker commitment to South Africa and prolific international travel. Similar trends were found in the present study, with monolingual English-speakers perceiving less equality of opportunities to succeed as compared to other South Africans, often expressing a desire to leave the country, and making relatively greater use of intra-personal markers across their self-concept and future identity representations. These respondents also made significantly more mention of crime, safety, leaving South Africa, and being racist or negative about South Africa in their future identity aspirations and threats than bilingual speakers of English, Afrikaans, Zulu, Sotho and other vernacular Southern African languages. While bilingual speakers of English, Afrikaans, European and other immigrant languages made use of 'racial' markers significantly less often, they nonetheless made frequent use of intra-personal markers in their self-articulated self-concepts and future identities, and reported a similar desire to leave South Africa. The latter may be seen to reflect their perceived or imagined 'cultural' ties with an ancestral immigrant 'group of origin', their family or 'cultural' links with the international community, or their inability to anchor their future lives in the current South African context.

These findings may be seen to indicate the difficulty that members of these two groups experience in envisaging a place for themselves in the new South Africa, and a related tendency to emphasise negative aspects of the transition process and to aspire towards emigrating. On the other hand, discourses related to the lack of opportunity for future employment, happiness or security may also function to deny the implications of 'racial' oppression in the past and legitimate socio-economic inequalities in the present. The reasons given for wanting to leave suggest an unwillingness to forgo a position of privilege relative to the majority of South Africans, and a resistance towards aligning the self with the imperatives of the new democratic dispensation. The unwillingness or inability to locate the self in relation to the 'new' South Africa may also heighten identification with a colonial country of origin or an apartheid past, idealised through processes of nostalgic and evasive remembering.

While some students appeared to be disillusioned with perceived future opportunities to succeed, find satisfactory employment and be happy, the reasons cited for this seem to suggest that their disillusionment had more to do with group membership and a fear of losing the social status and economic privileges of the past than with current realities. The reasons given for perceiving opportunities to succeed as compared to other South Africans also suggest that these students may be grappling with a process of negotiating the tension between a 'liberal democratic' ethos of individualism (evidenced through the mention of reasons such as personal effort, capabilities, interests, and intra-personal factors), collective concerns related to a socio-political legacy of apartheid (socio-economic constraints, crime, unemployment, and 'racial' identity), and current imperatives to recognise and redress past injustices (by instituting policies of affirmative action), foster reconciliation among historically-constructed 'racial' groups, and achieve national unity.

Overall, overt 'racial', cultural and national markers were not the most central defining features of identity amongst the South African students sampled. In this regard, present-day South Africa appears to offer youth a range of identity possibilities that include, but are not restricted to, 'racial', 'cultural' and national representations. However, the question remains as to whether the self-description categories available to young people in South Africa merely constitute new ways of re-writing or disguising the 'racial' discourses of the past, or whether these identity options offer new ways of conceptualising the self and the other. Nevertheless, the use of both direct and indirect references to 'racial', 'cultural' and national issues reflects South Africa's past and present historical context, and highlights many of the challenges facing students as they seek to define themselves in current-day South Africa. Moreover, the variation in the use of these markers by language orientation is sufficient to contrast different sub-groups' location of themselves with regard to past, present and future-orientated understandings of the self and the other.

Patterns in the differential use of 'racial', 'cultural' and national identity markers, as a function of language orientation across contexts, appear to suggest that these markers have less to do with a substantive core of identity, or a source of 'authenticity' which is central to self-definition, and more to do with the particular way in which the members of each sub-group locate the self in relation to their experiences of past, present, and future understandings of identity. They testify to the ways in which identity representations are embedded within the understandings of the self that are rendered possible by the broader social-political context of past, present and future. The construction of a location from which to speak and be identified by the 'other' reflects an individual's authorship over his or her orientation of self in the face of the subjective and collective implications of past experiences of apartheid, present understandings and the endorsement of social transformation, and the capacity to imagine a meaningful and valued location for the self in a future South Africa of non-racial integration.

For young South Africans straddling the remnants of an historically entrenched divide, their particular self-articulated self-conceptions in many ways interrupt, contest and question the homogenising practice of racial categorisation that characterised South Africa's past and that continues to divide the 'inter-cultural' social during the post-apartheid transition to an ideal of national unity and equality. They bear witness not only to the displaced and disjunctive present of desecrated, transplanted and enfranchised communities, but also to the absurdity of viewing 'racially-constructed' communities and ethnic identities as unchanged by historical process.

Conclusion

In this chapter we have sought to critically appraise the implications that some of the more recent socio-political and economic processes inherent in the transition from apartheid to democracy have for the negotiation of identity dynamics in present-day South Africa. The framework presented for such an analysis argued that identity dynamics are process-driven and need to be understood in the context of the intentional worlds in which they are constructed and in articulation with whose imperatives and stakes they are constantly re-negotiated.

Exercises for critical engagement

1   Think about how you would describe yourself and write this down as an answer to the question, 'I am ...'. Now think about how others perceive you and write this down. Does your own self-description differ from the ways in which others would characterise you?

2   Now think about the ways in which you would describe or locate yourself in cultural terms. Does this differ from the ways in which other people would perceive or describe you in cultural terms?

3   Now think about the next few years and write down four things that you would hope to be, expect to become or that you want to achieve.

4   Now consider the things you are afraid of becoming or would like to avoid becoming in the future, or those things about yourself that you would like to change, and write these down.

5   Examine your responses to the previous questions and discuss these with a classmate with reference to the material presented in this chapter. In what ways do these descriptions reflect South Africa's apartheid past or transformation process?

Endnote

1   This research was carried out with the support of a research grant provided by the French Institute of South Africa (IFAS). The ideas and opinions expressed in this article are those of the authors and do not reflect the views of this organisation.

Recommended reading

Gore, J.P., Miller, J.P., & J. Rappaport. (1999). 'Conceptual self as normatively oriented: The suitability of past narrative for the study of cultural identity'. *Culture and Psychology*, 5(4):371–398.

Hallowell, A. I. (1955). *Culture and experience*. Philadelphia: University of Pennsylvania Press.

Harré, R. (1998). *The Singular Self: An Introduction to the Psychology of Personhood*. London: Sage.

Intimacy, Inequality and Gendered Violence

PART THREE

Women Abuse: A Critical Review

9

Floretta Boonzaier

OUTCOMES

After having studied this chapter you should be able to:

- understand the differences between individual and social or cultural theoretical accounts of women abuse
- explain some of the basic tenets of a critical feminist perspective or of critical feminist perspectives on violence against women
- discuss how race, class, culture and other forms of difference intersect and influence the meaning of women abuse, and
- understand the feminist post-structuralist perspectives on women abuse.

VIOLENCE PERVADES women's lives and may occur in the context of intimate relationships or in the public sphere. These types of violence include (but are not limited to) sexual harassment, dowry-related violence, female genital mutilation, forced prostitution and women abuse (Jacobs & Suleman, 1999). Since the 1970s, *women abuse* (see definitions below) has been identified and constructed as a widespread social problem affecting all societies. Social scientists have increasingly turned their attention to theorising women abuse – paying attention to the varying definitions, the causes of the problem and appropriate intervention strategies. The earliest perspectives illustrate the individual-societal dualism that has dominated the discipline of psychology in general. More recently, increasing attention has been accorded to the broader context in which violence occurs. This chapter traces the dominant *discourses* that have been at work in the theoretical and empirical study of women abuse – charting the shift from an individualist-psychological focus to broader contextual and multi-systemic perspectives.

Discourses:
Broad patterns of talk; interpretive repertoires.

Concepts and definitions

In this chapter, the term '*women abuse*' refers to a form of violence directed at women in particular, which occurs in the context of intimate heterosexual relationships. women abuse is asymmetrical, perpetrated mostly by men against women. This form of violence includes emotional, verbal, physical, sexual and economic abuse, stalking, harassment and damage to property (Jacobs & Suleman, 1999). The use of the term 'women abuse' is intended to acknowledge the gender-specific nature of the violence and the power disparities between perpetrators and victims (Bograd, 1990).

'*Domestic violence*' is used to refer to violence encompassing any domestic relationship and may not be directed at women in particular. This type of violence may include violence against the elderly.

'*Violence against women*' is used to refer to the broader context of violence, which occurs in both the private and public spheres. This type of violence is gender-based and may include women abuse, dowry-related violence, femicide and sexual harassment.

Violence against women is a serious and widespread problem in South Africa. Reliable statistics, however, are difficult to establish, as incidents of violence are typically under-reported. Furthermore, there is no large-scale, national study on the incidence of women abuse in South Africa. Available estimates are based on police records, hospitals, social service organisations and various local studies. For example, in a study of 412 women attending a community health centre in the Western Cape, Jacobs and Suleman (1999) found that 48.5 per cent reported current or past abuse by male partners. Abrahams *et al.* (1999) employed a quantitative methodology (involving structured interviews) to describe the incidence of reported violence amongst working men in Cape Town. They found that more than 40 per cent of the sample (of 1 394 men) reported having physically or sexually abused their partners. Vetten (1999) investigated the nature and extent of abuse in a sample of 269 women who presented at helping agencies in Cape Town, Johannesburg and Durban, and found that large proportions of women experienced emotional, physical, sexual and economic abuse, and that 42.5 per cent of the sample had experienced multiple forms of abuse. In a study conducted in three provinces, Jewkes *et al.* (1999) found that 30 per cent of the 1 306 women surveyed reported violence from male partners. Reports of physical, financial and emotional abuse were very common and resulted in a range of injuries. The above estimates provide an indication of the magnitude of the problem of women abuse in South Africa.

International statistics attest to the fact that women abuse is a widespread problem that affects all societies. For example, a 1993 Canadian survey revealed that more than one quarter of a nationally representative sample of women experienced violence from current or past partners (Statistics Canada in Duffy, 1995). It is estimated that every nine seconds a woman in the United States is physically abused and that four women die per day as a result of women abuse (Domestic Violence Project/Safe House in Westlund, 1999). In a district in Kenya, 42 per cent of 733 women reported being regularly beaten by their partners (Raikes in Watts *et al.*, 1995). It is also estimated that 60 per cent of Tanzanian women are physically abused by their partners (Sheikh-Hashim & Gabba in Watts *et al.*, 1995). Given the magnitude of the problem of women abuse in Southern Africa and abroad, it is important to theorise and explore the multiple manifestations of, and solutions to, the problem.

Below I explore how women abuse has been theorised from an individualist perspective, where both abused women and abusive men are depicted as psychologically deficient. Learning theories locate the problem of women abuse within the individual's capacity to learn violent behaviour or the woman's capacity to learn helplessness. Given that an individual/psychological focus has a number of inherent flaws and limits our theorising of the problem, social or cultural theories of women abuse are posited in contrast. A review of family violence scholarship illustrates an increasing shift away from individualistic pathological preoccupations. This approach, however, still does not provide an adequate framework for theorising women abuse as it overlooks important issues such as gender and power inequalities. In this chapter, I argue that feminist multi-systemic perspectives allow for the inclusion of multiple constructs and the exploration of varying facets of violence against women. The chapter ends by introducing feminist post-structuralism and highlighting its value to theorising women abuse.

Individual/psychological perspectives

Women abuse as pathology

Individual-psychological theories have typically focused on psychological characteristics, personality development and childhood histories of abusive males. For example, abusive men have been described as extremely jealous (Hotaling & Sugarman, 1986), and having a low self-esteem (Hampton *et al.*, 1999), a heightened need for control, a low level of assertiveness and feelings of powerlessness (Hotaling & Sugarman, 1986; Petrik *et al.*, 1994). Violent men have also been described as more aggressive and dependent than their non-violent counterparts (Kane & Staiger, 2000). In addition to describing specific psychological traits, personality profiles of abusive men have also been offered (Holtzworth-Munroe, 2000). For example, abusive men have been described as evidencing borderline or antisocial personality characteristics (*ibid.*). These psychological characteristics and traits are said to predispose men to the use of violence against female partners.

Gender is a concept usually referring to the social construction of biological, or inherent, sexual differences between men and women. It is assumed that gender is social while sex is biological, though some theorists question this divide and whether there is anything outside of the social. It is also assumed by most gender theorists that the term encapsulates a notion of power inequality, in which, in patriarchal societies, the male gender is imbued with more status and access to power (social, political and economic) than the female gender.

Individual/psychological perspectives of women abuse typically focus on psychological traits, personality development and childhood histories of abusive males.

In a similar vein, the earliest psychological profiles of the victim also focused on pathology and deviance. Victim precipitation theories suggest that women possess particular characteristics that lead to their victimisation (O'Neill, 1998). Freudian constructions of femininity portrayed women as masochistically desiring or provoking abuse from their partners. In 1964 in the United States, Snell *et al.* (in Hydén, 1994) published an article based on a study of 12 couples where *wife abuse* had been present. They described the women as aggressive, efficient, masculine and sexually frigid, with controlling and dependent tendencies. Men in the study were described as passive, indecisive, impotent and alcohol-dependent. Snell *et al.* (*ibid.*) inferred that the combination of the passive man and aggressive woman was the cause of violence in those relationships. Discourses of psychological deviance or abnormality have pervaded the literature on women abuse. For example, women have been diagnosed with battered women's syndrome, self-defeating personality disorder and co-dependency (Westlund, 1999). Psychological practices reflect a preoccupation with the mental instability of women who have been abused, thereby deflecting attention away from the social and political contexts in which violence occurs.

Learning theories

Learning theories of women abuse assert that men learn the 'appropriateness' of using violence as a means of conflict resolution during childhood in the family of origin.

Learning theorists assert that violent behaviour is learned through childhood models in the family of origin. In terms of these perspectives, men learn the 'appropriateness' of using violence as a means of conflict resolution. Studies show a strong correlation between violence in the family of origin and the later perpetration of violence against female partners (Halford *et al.*, 2000; Hotaling & Sugarman, 1986). Witnessing violence in the family of origin is therefore said to predispose men to the use of violence against future partners, and the inter-generational transmission of abuse is thought to operate like a hereditary disease, passing on from each generation to the next (O'Neill, 1998).

Walker (1979; 1984; 2000) posited the theory of learned helplessness to describe the psychological disposition of women in abusive relationships. In terms of this theory, adapted from Seligman's experiments with laboratory dogs (in Walker, 2000), women are unable to escape from abusive relationships because they are deficient in problem-solving skills and they perceive their chances of escape as impossible – they therefore 'learn helplessness'. Walker also proposed a cycle of violence that describes different phases of the abusive relationship. Firstly, the tension-building phase may include minor violence or verbal abuse. The explosive or abusive phase is characterised by more severe abuse. This phase is followed by a calm, loving or honeymoon phase during which the abuser becomes apologetic and manipulates the woman with promises of change. In terms of Walker's proposition, the combination of women's 'learned helplessness' and the cycle of violence traps women in abusive relationships and explains why women often stay with abusive partners.

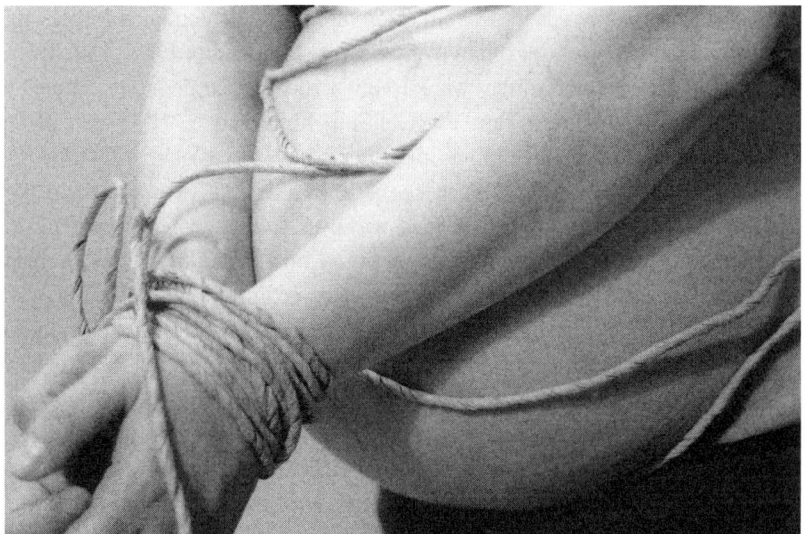

Learning theories view women as unable to escape from abusive relationships because they are deficient in problem-solving skills and perceive their chances of escape as impossible.

Walker's theories offered an alternative to explanations of abused women as masochistic or personality disordered (Walker, 2000). However, the passive representations of women in Walker's work cannot be overlooked. The learned helplessness model has since been contested, and studies (Hoff, 1990; Profitt, 2000) have shown a lack of support for its application to women's experiences (see also Chapter 10, this volume). More recent studies show how women employ various strategies at their disposal to resist violence from their partners. Some of these studies will be explored at greater length later in this chapter.

The perspectives outlined above propose that violence is a result of individual psychological characteristics, individual background factors or a simple interaction between individuals. An individualistic focus does not provide an adequate account of women abuse (or any other social problem) since it ignores broader social, cultural and historical contexts that colour and shape the meaning of the problem. Conceptualising women abuse as an aberration or indicative of underlying pathologies ignores the varying forms of violence and contextual influences such as culture, class, sexuality or race. If contextual factors are not accounted for, certain groups may not be deemed 'legitimate' victims and may be denied adequate protection from violence (Bograd, 1999). For example, the construction of the problem of 'lesbian battering' brought the experiences of those who might have otherwise been silenced to the foreground of research and advocacy (also see Chapter 17 on how the issue of street children became constructed and defined as a social problem).

Social or cultural accounts of women abuse

Family violence research

Family violence approaches to women abuse focus on the social context and family variables.

Family violence approaches focus on socio-demographic variables and family dynamics in an attempt to explain women abuse (Anderson, 1997). Data from violent and non-violent families were used in order to examine the prevalence of, and explain, violence in families (Gelles in Kirkwood, 1993). The 'violent family' rather than the 'violent individual' became the focus of investigation. In the *National Family Violence Surveys* (of 1975 and 1985) conducted in the United States, the Conflict Tactics Scale was used to measure the incidence of violence, and correlations were found between violence and variables such as age, cohabiting status, unemployment and socio-economic status (Straus *et al.* in Anderson, 1997). Higher rates of violence were found among younger, poorer, less educated, unmarried, African American, Hispanic and urban couples (Gelles in Anderson, 1997). This model argues that these groups are structurally predisposed to violence since there are higher frustrations associated with a lower socio-economic status (O'Neill, 1998). Violence is therefore viewed as an expressive release of the frustrations associated with issues such as poverty and unemployment. Other sociologists of the family contend that the structural features of the family make it more likely that conflict will occur in the home (Farrington in O'Neill, 1998) since family members engage in frequent, personal interaction with each other.

By acknowledging social and demographic variables, these perspectives shifted the emphasis away from an exclusive focus on the psychology of the violent or violated individuals to a focus on the social context in which violence occurs. However, the risk of reifying the 'violent family' based on these socio-demographic variables is great, and there is a danger of attributing violence to the inherent characteristics of particular strata of society. These studies also found similar rates of violence by husbands and wives. These findings led to the assumption of *sexual symmetry* in domestic violence (i.e. that women and men are equally violent). This supposition has been vehemently criticised by feminist researchers (Dobash & Dobash, 1979; Dobash *et al.*, 1992; Saunders, 1990), who contend that methodological flaws in the survey techniques as well as the use of the Conflict Tactics Scale did not allow for the exploration of whether women used violence in self-defence. Dobash *et al.* (1992) asserted that the scales simply focused on the violent acts and did not measure the actor's intentions. This critique also lends credence to a broader critique of the utilisation of quantitative methodology in the field of women abuse. Since the Conflict Tactics Scale focused only on the violent incidents, the broader context and meanings attached to the violence were overlooked. Many family violence approaches therefore ignored gendered power relations, and women's acts of self-defence were concealed in the statistics generated by these

Sexual symmetry: The contention that, within the family, husbands (men) and wives (women) are equally violent.

methods. Although these studies consider the unequal distribution of power in society by focusing on a range of socio-demographic variables, they are 'gender-neutral' and consider violence to be a problem of both sexes (Bograd, 1990).

The family violence theoretical approaches are therefore unlikely to provide an adequate explanation of women abuse. Anderson (1997) used self- and partner-reported data from the *National Survey of Families and Households* in the United States in an effort to integrate family violence and feminist theoretical approaches. She found support for both theoretical approaches, in that elements of the structural environment such as age, cohabitation, education and income resources were associated with women abuse. However, these risk factors differed by gender, with men being more likely to engage in violence against their partners. It follows that, although structural elements are important, an analysis of women abuse cannot be successfully accomplished without the critical interrogation of gender and power inequalities.

Although researchers who focus on the family context in which women abuse occurs have helped in shifting the emphasis away from an exclusive focus on the psychology of violent men, there is a risk of attributing abuse to inherent characteristics of particular strata of society.

Feminism/Feminist: This is an umbrella term for a large and diverse body of work that broadly explores women's subordination in male-dominated societies. It should be noted that there is no unitary feminist theory or methodology, but what all feminist work has in common is the broadly defined goal of challenging gender power inequality.

A feminist multi-systemic analysis of women abuse

From a feminist perspective, women abuse is viewed as a reflection of unequal power relationships rooted in patriarchy (Dobash & Dobash, 1979; Yllö & Bograd, 1990). A patriarchal culture maintains the domination of men in the family and society at large. As discussed earlier, feminist researchers proposed that the national survey techniques ignored the gendered context in which violence occurred, and that gender was seen as only one of a number of demographic variables. As a counter to this critique, family sociologists asserted that a feminist focus on patriarchy was limited by a single variable analysis

Feminist analyses of women abuse aim to show the unequal power relationships between women and men rooted in patriarchy.

(Anderson, 1997). Contemporary feminist analysts respond by exploring the intersections of multiple systems of power and oppression (Bograd, 1999).

Recent scholarship on gender and violence recognises the saliency of multiple sites of power and inequity by shifting away from the analysis of patriarchy as the only source of women's oppression. There are a number of research endeavours that show how women's experiences of violence are complicated by issues such as race (Callaghan *et al.*, 1997), class (McCloskey, 1996; Miles-Doan, 1998; Tiefenthaler & Farmer, 2000), sexuality (Shefer *et al.*, 2000; Wilkinson & Kitzinger, 1993), culture (Abraham, 2000; Haj-Yahia, 2000; Horne, 1999; Lui, 1999; McWhirter, 1999; Perilla *et al.*, 1994; Zaman, 1999) and other forms of difference. For example, Bograd (1999) discussed race, class, sexual orientation and gender, showing how they shape and colour the meaning of women abuse, and how a lack of attention accorded to these constructs could result in the invisibility of certain victims of violence. The shifts in theorising women abuse have mirrored Black feminist challenges to a narrow Western feminist preoccupation with patriarchy as the only form of oppression. As Mama (1996) noted, Black feminists have called for an integration of race, religion, class, sexuality, culture and other forms of difference into the analyses of violence against women. Below, I review recent empirical work that takes account of the broader context of women abuse by examining the confluence of multiple forms of difference and oppression.

Woelz-Stirling *et al.* (1998) investigated the high prevalence of women abuse in marriages between Filipino women and Australian men. A large proportion of Filipino women immigrated to Australia and married permanent residents of the country. These marriages were characterised by high rates of violence that were often unreported. The authors recognised a number of factors contributing to violence in these relationships. They examined the unequal distribution of power within the marriage, as well as within society. Filipino women married mostly for economic security and Australian men had the image of Filipinas as powerless, subservient and compliant, creating a power imbalance in the relationships. The marriages were often stigmatised, and women were reluctant to report incidents of violence that could further stigmatise their marriages. The powerlessness of Filipino women within the home and society therefore accorded men more control and made it relatively difficult for these women to leave abusive situations. Filipino women's decisions to stay were further complicated by their Catholic values, which discouraged divorce.

Religious and cultural practices frequently reinforce and sanction violence against women. In South Africa, Govinden (1997) focused on the abuse of women in Christian homes. She illustrated how the 'Sunday best' culture of the church resulted in women remaining silent about abuse in order to project a respectable image to outsiders. Similarly, Giesbrecht and Sevcik (2000) examined the process of recovery for abused women situated in a conservative religious culture in Canada. They illustrated that although the church could provide social support and spiritual encouragement, the abuse was often minimised and denied. Boonzaier (2001) found that when women approached religious leaders for assistance with problems of violence, they were often persuaded to endure the violence and reconcile with their partners. Religious ideals script the role of the 'good woman or wife', emphasising qualities of femininity as tolerant, caring, nurturing and subordinate.

Recent feminist scholarship on gender and violence shows how women's experience of abuse is complicated by issues such as race, class, sexuality, culture, age, and other forms of difference.

Haj-Yahia (2000) explored the relationship between wife abuse and the socio-cultural context of Arab society. He conducted research with married Arab women in Israel, investigating their definitions of violence, awareness of the problem, justifications or condemnation of violence, awareness of risks and their perspectives on coping with violence. In his analysis, Haj-Yahia integrated masculine cultural constructions and the power accorded to men in Arab society. Values in this society emphasised family unity and reputation. In accordance with this, most respondents in his study advocated that women first approach their extended family for assistance with regard to women abuse. There was a strong emphasis on getting help from within the family and a stigma attached to seeking help from outside agencies. Similarly, Lui (1999) investigated women abuse in a rural village in southeast China. She revealed how institutions in Chinese culture reinforced the oppression and subservience of women. For example, historical cultural practices, such as the dowry system, reinforce the subordinate position of women *vis-à-vis* men. The family is viewed as the basic unit of society, resulting in strict cultural sanctions against divorce, and women suffer both economically and socially if they choose to divorce their abusive partners. As in the previous example, the family would mediate and try to reconcile the married couple, rather than encouraging the woman to leave the abusive partner. These studies show how the socio-cultural context shapes and impacts upon women's experiences of violence and how women are forced to negotiate the cultural and social boundaries and find alternative means of dealing with violence in their relationships.

An analysis of the socio-political and historical context is also important in theorising women abuse. In societies that have experienced large-scale, state-sponsored violence (for example, Chile under the dictatorship of Pinochet and South Africa during the apartheid period), there is an increased tolerance for the use of violence as a means of maintaining authority and control (McWhirter, 1999), and the use of violence (particularly against women) may become normalised. Dangor *et al.* (1996) conducted ethnographic interviews with 37 health-clinic employees, church members, community workers, students and professionals in South Africa. All the participants in their study commented on the relationship between the oppressive system of apartheid and violence against women. Within the authoritarian and violent system of apartheid women were particularly vulnerable, with Black women experiencing multiple forms of oppression (based upon race, class and gender). Vetten (2000) asserts that violence against women in South Africa should be analysed on multiple levels that include the power dynamics within South African society and apartheid's legacy of institutionalised violence. There are particular manifestations of violence against women that result from a unique interaction between race, gender and other forms of power to form complex dynamics of inequity and domination (*ibid.*).

The literature on culture and women abuse illuminates a range of issues that include the positions of women in different societies, cultural or religious justifications for violence against women, and varying definitions or forms of violence. In different cultures, women are oppressed to varying degrees. Women's positions range from blatant oppression, as in Bangladesh, where girls are discriminated against from birth (Zaman, 1999), to situations where societal institutions and cultural practices legitimise and sanction violence against women (Horne, 1999; Kozu, 1999; McWhirter, 1999). Ellsberg *et al.* (1999) cite an example where until recently, the Nicaraguan Penal Code did not criminalise the violent act, but rather the physical injury sustained by women who were abused by their partners. The injury sustained had to be severe enough to require 10 to 15 days to heal. In Nicaraguan society violence against women is widely accepted and justified. Clearly, social institutions also reinforce the subordination of women by denying them adequate legal protection from abuse.

To some degree, family violence approaches (explored earlier) addressed the relationship between socio-economic issues and women abuse. A critical

> The literature on culture and women abuse illuminates a range of issues that include the positions of women in different societies, cultural or religious justifications for violence against women, and varying definitions or forms of violence.

feminist perspective, however, acknowledges that particular groups may not be predisposed to violence due to their socio-structural positions alone. Instead, a range of factors has to be considered. According to Schornstein (1997), the highest reported incidence of women abuse is amongst the poor but this could be because they have little alternative but to seek help from public agencies. Middle- or upper-class women are more likely to have a range of options available to them. Studies that examine class issues (Miles-Doan, 1998; Schornstein, 1997) yield conflicting results but there is consensus that poor women's options are constrained by the lack of access to and assistance from social institutions. Richie and Kanuha (1997) examined the role of social institutions in the perpetuation of violence against women of colour. They asserted that the effects of racism systematically disadvantage Black women. In the South African situation, with the reality of poverty and racism, many women from underprivileged communities have limited options and support. According to Callaghan *et al.* (1997), women who are living in disadvantaged conditions are at increased risk of violence. Poor women often have limited access to social and institutional support and may be financially dependent on their spouses, thus limiting their options of leaving a violent relationship. The lack of institutional support is sometimes evident in the effectiveness of the police when assisting women with problems of violence in their relationships. South African researchers continually reflect upon the lack of efficacy and problems encountered when women attempt to obtain assistance from the police (Artz, 2001; Boonzaier, 2001; Nix, 1998). These examples show that violence against women is not an individual problem, and that social institutions play an important role its perpetuation.

An analysis of socio-political and historical context is important in trying to understand violence against women.

Medicine, like other social institutions, has also been implicated in the perpetuation of women abuse. Often, women first approach medical practitioners for treatment of injuries resulting from abuse by their partners. Some authors have focused on how medicine as a social institution perpetuates and sanctions violence against women, often resulting in secondary victimisation (Stark & Flitcraft, 1996). Jacobs and Suleman (1999) examined the prevalence and patterns of women abuse amongst women who presented at Mitchell's Plain Community Health Clinic in the Western Cape. They found that of 103 cases of abuse in the sample, only 31 were documented in the medical records. In addition, they found that health-care workers did not directly enquire about women's experiences of violence from intimate partners. Motsei (1993) found similar patterns of poor detection at Alexandra Health Clinic in Johannesburg. These findings point to the inadequacy of the health sector in terms of identifying and assisting women who have been abused.

The reviewed research, examining multiple sites of oppression and power, provides evidence for the inclusion of these constructs in the analysis of women abuse. The cultural domination of men creates expectations for both men and women. Historically, the family has been viewed as the basic unit of society, with males being afforded authority over women and children (Dobash & Dobash, 1979). Husbands are generally viewed as the heads of the households, with wives' roles scripted as obedient and subservient. Notions of male authority in the family are reinforced and supported by other social institutions, such as the law and religion, thereby sanctioning and legitimising a husband's violence against his wife. Thus, the beliefs and values surrounding masculinity, femininity, family and violence within the culture constitute and shape the problem of women abuse (O'Neill, 1998).

Hanmer (1996) suggested that the personal strategies employed by women to deal with violence are structured by the boundaries set by culture, religion, education, class and language. The decision to leave or stay with an abusive partner is therefore negotiated within a set of boundaries. Rather than focus on why women stay in abusive relationships, it may be more productive to consider how women negotiate these personal and cultural boundaries through an exploration of the macro-context of violence. In the final section of this chapter I examine some of the scholarship focusing on women's resilience and the strategies they employ to negotiate violent relationships. A focus on agency and resistance permits the re-visioning of the traditional script that depicts women as passive victims of patriarchy and other structural forces.

Agency, resistance and negotiation

The women abuse literature has shifted to a focus on women as 'survivors' rather than 'victims' of abusive relationships. Women are described as

> Historically, the family has been viewed as the basic unit of society, with males being afforded authority over women and children. Husbands are generally viewed as the heads of the households, with wives' roles scripted as obedient and subservient.

survivors who experience excessive trauma as a result of the abuse but who also use various strategies to resist and cope with abuse from their partners (Browne, 1997). From a psychological perspective, women were historically depicted as deficient in coping strategies, depressed and passive (Finn, 1985; Nurius *et al.*, 1992). As an alternative to these approaches, Banyard and Graham-Bermann (1993) postulated a gender analysis of women abuse that describes coping as a process, and that acknowledges the social context of abuse. This section reviews these shifts in the literature, recognising women's *agency* and the ways in which they respond to violence within particular social, historical and cultural contexts. This line of scholarship reconstructs certain responses (such as staying with or returning to an abusive partner), which had previously been defined as pathological, as active, reasoned coping mechanisms.

Agency refers to the capacity of a designated group's women, Blacks, poor people, etc.) to continue functioning and cope under subjection and within abusive and oppressive relationships.

Hoff (1990) conducted an in-depth study starting from the premise that battered women are survivors rather than victims. She explored women's experiences of violence while taking account of broader social and cultural issues. She suggested that the consideration of why women stay should involve an interaction between the meanings women attach to their experiences, the social and cultural context, women's social networks and the practical realities of their lives. Hoff (*ibid.*) found that almost all the women in her study expressed and channelled anger towards their abusive partners and not inward, as generally purported. This finding contradicts traditional views of battered women as passive, depressive and accepting of the abuse. Hoff (*ibid.*) also recognised that leaving an abusive partner is a process that occurs over time. The decisions and options for each woman varied, and Hoff (*ibid.*) showed how women were able to manage the violence and make decisions based upon their personal circumstances.

In a cross-national study in the United States and England, Kirkwood (1993) interviewed 30 women who left their abusive partners. She initiated her study from the perspective that women are survivors of abuse. Kirkwood (*ibid.*:135) used the term 'survivor' to describe women who take 'active positive action ... to continue functioning within an abusive relationship or to free themselves from abuse'. She described the shifts in power and control in abusive relationships where, at different times, women were either powerless or regained some measure of power and control. The regaining of control encompassed women's awareness that personal change occurred as a result of the abuse. Women experienced anger and fear as a result of this awareness. These emotions provided the impetus for action, which included leaving the abuser, gaining support from others, seeking resources or threatening the abuser. Women who leave abusive partners return with more experience, therefore, according to Kirkwood (1993), leaving and returning is accompanied by the gaining of more power and control. Like Hoff's (1990), her work showed how women's attempts to leave an abusive partner should be viewed as a process. Kirkwood (*ibid.*) also acknowledged that power within relationships is not unidirectional and that, at certain times in the relationships, women gained a measure of power and control depending on personal, cultural and social circumstances.

Lempert (1996) examined women's strategies for coping and surviving abusive relationships and conducted in-depth interviews with 32 women. She described a number of strategies employed by women initially to keep the violence invisible and later to achieve self-preservation. During the 'invisibility' phase, women utilised face-saving and problem-solving strategies to contain the violence. These included rationalisation, minimisation and self-blame. Self-preservation strategies included fantasies of suicide or murder (see Chapter 10 on abused women who kill their partners), telling others about the violence and seeking outside assistance. Lempert (*ibid.*) interpreted passive resistance as a strategy aimed at survival. She illustrated how women adapted their methods of coping to their immediate contexts and experiences. Based upon the success or failure of previous methods, women devised new strategies for coping. In Lempert's analysis, the 'spiral' of power and control (described by Kirkwood, 1993) is evident as women devised certain strategies in order to regain a measure of power in their lives. Similarly, Hydén (1999) examined the experiences of women who left abusive relationships. She proposed a distinction between psychological and physical break-up and asserted that some women psychologically distanced themselves from their spouses long before

> Psychological break-up refers to the situation where women establish psychological distance between themselves and their partners long before they physically leave the relationship.

they physically ended their relationships. The central themes explored in Hydén's study were fear and resistance. She explored fear as a constantly present emotion during the process of separation. Fear dominated the lives of many of the women in her study and served the purpose of protection and resistance. Hydén interpreted the act of breaking-up as a resistance strategy and she suggested that resistance in abusive relationships was always present but seldom shown openly. She therefore described it as a 'hidden transcript'. Hydén's study provides an implicit critique of the frequently stated question or accusation: Why do women stay in abusive relationships? Her decision to focus on the process of breaking up showed how leaving should not be considered as an isolated event and concurs with the assertions made by Kirkwood (1993) and Hoff (1990).

In her qualitative study, Baker (1997) focused on the level of agency of women in abusive relationships. She initiated the study from the premise that a new cultural script urged women to leave abusive partners, maintain restraining orders and cooperate with the police. From the perspective of a participant observer at a shelter, and through her analysis of interview and archival data, she illustrated how women employed active, reasoned strategies and resisted this dominant script. Many women in the study chose to stay in the relationship, ignored or lifted restraining orders and refused to call or cooperate with the police. Issues that mediated these decisions were fear of harassment from their partners, emotional connections to partners, children, economic dependence and a lack of institutional support or viable alternatives. Rather than pathologising women for not leaving abusive partners, Baker's study focused on their capacities for making reasoned choices. The study acknowledged that contextual issues were an important consideration in women's decisions to leave or stay with abusive partners rather than suggesting that women 'learn helplessness' and are unable to leave abusive partners.

Learned helplessness: Passive behaviour produced by being in an unfavourable situation such as an abusive marriage where one learns to think of it as unavoidable.

In one of the few local endeavours on the issue, Boonzaier (2001) conducted a narrative study with women who have experienced violence from their partners in Mitchell's Plain, in the Western Cape. She focused on *how* women stay in abusive relationships by examining the meanings they attach to their experiences and the intersections of gender, class and culture. In their narratives, women named their experiences of violation and abuse, explored the impact of abuse and discussed their strategies to cope with the violence. Women also constructed particular gendered identities for themselves and their partners. Hegemonic gendered identities were sometimes adopted or resisted and reflected contradictory subjective experiences. The study also showed how women in abusive relationships utilised a variety of strategies (both personal and social-institutional) to end the violence in their lives and challenged constructions of women as passive, submissive victims of abuse. Women's strategies and meanings were filtered through the particular socio-cultural context (characterised by violence, poverty and deprivation) within which their experiences occurred. In the study, the importance of the socio-cultural context was illustrated in the forms of violence that the participants chose to accentuate. A large proportion of the women centralised the issue of economic abuse and their concerns may have reflected aspects of the broader socio-economic environment such as the high levels of poverty and unemployment in Mitchell's Plain. The options available to women were also negotiated within these structural and material constraints. Some women questioned the effectiveness of applying for a protection order to end the abuse. Their situations were complicated by economic dependence on the abuser, which made it difficult for them to have their partners sent to prison.

Hegemonic gendered identities: The ruling ideas of how to be women or men.

Waldman (1995) investigated women abuse on two farms in the Western Cape, showing how these farms were characterised by male dominance exercised by the farmers and the male farm labourers. The farmers and the male labourers controlled most aspects of women's lives, including their labour and sexuality. Gender relations on the farms were characterised by high levels of violence. Waldman illustrated how women on these farms employed strategies to resist male control to a certain degree. Some women resisted male control

191

by deciding to remain single so as to maintain a measure of economic independence. Another form of resistance was related to the use of contraception. Although their partners discouraged its use, some women used contraceptives without their partners' knowledge. Waldman's study illustrated that women (even in blatantly oppressive situations) were sometimes able to make active choices about their own lives.

Abraham's (2000) study of South Asian immigrants in the United States focused on the intersections of ethnicity, race, class, gender and citizenship in women's experiences of intimate violence. By employing unstructured interviews with 25 participants, Abraham showed how these issues were implicated in women abuse against minority groups in the United States. Women faced difficulties in negotiating cultural norms that prescribed gender-stereotypical behaviour. The violence experienced from their partners was exacerbated by the lack of proper assistance from social institutions as well as fears surrounding their immigrant status. However, Abraham identified a number of coping or defensive strategies used by these women, challenging notions of the passivity and submissiveness of abused women. Women either employed personal resources or sought outside assistance. Personal strategies included placating and avoidance, talking back, using violence in self-defence, attempts at a degree of financial independence, and contemplating suicide. Abraham acknowledged that some strategies were self-destructive, but women often negotiated their options and sought alternative solutions (such as seeking help from friends, family, neighbours, police or the courts) when personal strategies failed. Although some strategies used by women may be self-defeating, they negotiate their options and employ alternative strategies at their disposal. For example, women who attempt to fight violence with violence often realise that it may result in further danger and they resort to other means necessary to deal with the abuse. Campbell *et al.* (1994) provided an example of how women's strategies were often successful. In their sample, women's attempts to stop the violence resulted in either the cessation of violence or termination of the relationship. On the other hand, Fleury (2000) showed that ending an abusive relationship does not necessarily end the violence and that women may often be at greater risk of violence after leaving their partners. Again, we see that women attempt to take control of their own lives to stop the violence or ultimately leave their abusive partners and have to negotiate cultural, social and personal circumstances.

Also in the United States, Profitt (2000) investigated how survivors of abuse made connections between their experiences of violence and political activism through examining the stories of 11 survivors involved in collective action as well as through interviews with educators and activists in the antiviolence movement. She examined the process of change in abused women who subsequently became involved in political activism to end violence against women.

Profitt's analysis and interpretation yielded six main themes, namely: the complexities involved in naming experiences of violation as violence or abuse, women's struggle with contradiction in shifting their consciousness, the psycho-dynamics evoked in the change processes, participants' development of a critical analysis of their personal experience and encounters with social institutions, changes in women's sense of self, and the relation between changes in women's consciousness and subjectivity and their participation in collective action for social change. Profitt's study is a valuable one, allowing us to recognise that women who have experienced violence from their partners are able to institute action to change their conditions and even develop an activist consciousness regarding violence against women. Profitt also acknowledged the effects of race, ethnicity, class, gender, sexuality and ability on women's experiences of violence.

Feminist post-structuralism and women abuse

A feminist analysis of violence against women takes account of the structural oppression of women. Central issues are male power and women's subservience. The line of scholarship reviewed above has illustrated that these positions are not static as women display agency and actively resist male dominance. This was exemplified in Gavey's (1996) study on sexual coercion. She argued that the traditional heterosexual account emphasises women's passivity and submission. However, her study showed that these scripts are often contradicted when women experience desire, pleasure and power in their sexual relationships. Based upon this, Gavey inferred that relationship power is not unidirectional and fixed. She also argued that, although it is necessary to acknowledge male dominance and female victimisation, we should also emphasise and theorise competing discourses that reflect the positions of resistance assumed by many women. Studies such as these have provided the foundation for a feminist post-structuralist analysis of gender and women abuse.

As an epistemological framework, feminist post-structuralism emphasises the

> A feminist analysis of violence against women takes account of the structural oppression of women.

Feminist post-structuralism, language, meaning and plurality

From a post-structuralist perspective, what an event means to a particular individual depends on the ways of interpreting the world and the discourses available to her or him at any particular social or historical moment. For example, the ways a woman will respond to and experience abuse are linked to her access to the ways of understanding (Weedon, 1987). These include her self-image and cultural or religious beliefs about masculinity and femininity and about marriage and family life. Therefore, if she endorses constructions of masculinity as inherently violent and blames the abuse on her own provocation, she will be more likely to accept the violence. The following quotations are taken from a study by Boonzaier (2001) and are used in order to illustrate this point.

... the woman isn't the head of the household. The man is the head of the household. The word of the Lord tells us that the man is the head of the household. We must serve the man and the man serves the Lord.

In contrast, if a woman views the violence as a reflection of unequal gender relations and an exercise of male authority and sees herself as blameless, she would be more likely to view the violence as unacceptable. Thus, the plurality of language and the lack of fixed meaning are emphasised, showing how any interpretation is temporary and contingent upon the context in which it is produced.

He's a man ... he always tells me, he's a man and I'm a woman and there's a big difference between us. A woman's got no willpower. She can be used. You can just do with her whatever you want to. That's one of the things we always used to quarrel about. He thinks the man and the woman must be, yes boss, no boss. And I said to him, 'I can't do that. I'm a person in my own right, you're a person in your own right. You can't make me be like your slave or submissive to you.' I know that I must be submissive to him because he's my husband but not to that extent that he wants me to be.

Source: Boonzaier, 2001

Researchers working from a feminist post-structuralist perspective have re-visioned the traditional psychological meaning of identity.

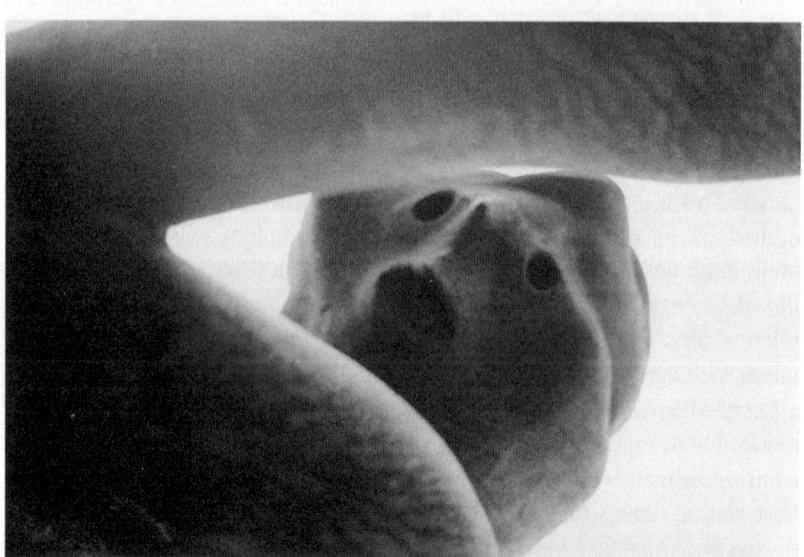

Feminist post-structuralism emphasises the deconstruction of taken-for-granted categories, calling into question notions that (gendered) identities are stable and coherent.

deconstruction of taken-for-granted categories, calling into question notions that (gendered) identities are stable and coherent (Gavey, 1997). Researchers working from this perspective have re-visioned the traditional psychological meaning of identity. For example, Mama (1995) rejected the concept of identity, which she described as psychologically constructed to be static and unitary. Rather, she posited the notion of subjectivity that acknowledges multiplicity, contradiction and change. Weedon (1987:32) characterised subjectivity as 'the conscious and unconscious thoughts and emotions of the individual, her sense of herself and her ways of understanding her relation to the world'. Similarly, Gregg (1993) defined subjectivity as a continuous process of experiencing the world and making sense of our experiences through an interaction of material, structural and inter-personal encounters. Post-structuralism posits a subjectivity that is fluid, contradictory and multiple. Realities, experiences, and meanings are neither fixed nor essential and are constituted through language, which also constructs subjectivity for the individual. Language offers us various subject positions (or a range of ways of interpreting our lives) that we can take up in order to construct our realities and meanings (Weedon, 1987).

However, meanings of experiences are not inherent in language. Instead, they are shaped or mediated by broader systems, institutions and relations of power (Parker, 1999). For example, the manner in which certain qualities such as passivity and aggression come to be defined as feminine or masculine is linked to patriarchal power dynamics which accords men power, control and dominance over women. These qualities by themselves have no inherent meaning; however, the way they are defined within particular communities is linked to discursive power relations. The social relations (of power) will determine the range of subject positions immediately open to any individual on the basis of gender, race, class, age and culture (Weedon, 1987).

There is a proliferation of studies addressing feminist issues from a post-structuralist perspective, opening up new possibilities for feminist scholarship on violence against women. Studies have focused on women's heterosexual desire and negotiation (Gavey, 1996; Shefer *et al.*, 2000), women's aggression (Squire, 1998) and narratives of romantic love (Jackson, 2001). These areas illuminate new possibilities for theorising about women abuse, which acknowledge multiplicity and variability in women's experiences. Critical South African researchers show the value of post-structuralist theorising in the areas of violence against women by problematising the relationship between male violence and constructions of masculinity (and femininity) in young adult relationships (Shefer *et al.*, 2000; Wood & Jewkes, 2001). For example, Shefer *et al.* (2000) explored the discourses students drew upon in order to discuss heterosexual relationships. They found that students employed varied discourses of power, control, coercion and violence and that heterosexual relationships are perceived as being bound up with gender inequality and violence. Shefer *et al.* (2000) also found that, although discourses of violence were 'normalised' within heterosexual relationships, some students drew upon alternative discourses challenging women's passivity and submission to male control (see Chapter 14 on heterosexuality in contemporary South Africa). The post-structuralist and discourse analysis literature show distinct connections between people's talk about violence and predominant forms of masculinity and femininity available within particular contexts, showing how cultural/social contexts set the scene for men's violence against women.

Conclusion

In this chapter, I have illustrated the dominant discourses framing women's experiences of, and responses to, violence from their partners. I have showed how recent scholarship has shifted away from earlier individualistic preoccupations with the psychological conditions of women and men. Recent theorising has acknowledged that, although violence against women operates in a patriarchal system of power inequity, women display agency and adopt various positions of resistance by negotiating personal, social and cultural boundaries. By recognising the confluence of culture, class, race, religion, sexuality and other forms of difference, we can avoid homogenising the experiences of women and open up avenues for the inclusion of multiple discourses of violence.

Exercises for critical engagement

1 Go to www.womensnet.org.za and find two articles on women abuse in South Africa.

2 Read the articles and identify the ways in which the problem has been theorised by drawing upon the theories discussed in this chapter.

3 Try to identify the contextual influences on the problem and how this may impact upon a woman's experiences of violence from her partner.

4 Find four magazine articles that explore gender issues in Southern Africa.

5 Read and analyse these articles and try to find evidence of support for gender-stereotypical roles or behaviour (e.g. male dominance and female submission).

6 Now, try to find examples of the ways in which gender stereotypes are challenged.

7 Conduct an Internet search and find three organisations addressing violence against women.

8 Assess the aims and objectives of each of these programmes.

9 Identify the services being offered to victims or perpetrators of women abuse.

10 Try to identify some of the theories that may form the basis for the programmes' interventions.

11 Based upon your knowledge of the programmes, briefly try to evaluate them. Consider which areas of the programmes may be improved. What services are lacking? How can these be addressed?

Recommended reading

O'Neill, D. (1998). 'A post-structuralist review of the theoretical literature surrounding wife abuse'. *Violence Against Women*, 4(4):457–490.

Park, Y.J., Fedler, J. & Z. Dangor, Z. (Eds.) (2000). *Reclaiming Women's Spaces. New Perspectives on Violence Against Women and Sheltering in South Africa*. Johannesburg: Nisaa Institute for Women's Development.

Weedon, C. (1987). *Feminist Practice and Poststructuralist Theory*. Oxford: Blackwell Publishers.

Yllö, K. & M. Bograd (Eds.) (1990). *Feminist Perspectives on Wife Abuse*. Newbury Park: Sage.

Acknowledgements

I would like to thank Cheryl de la Rey for valuable commentary and input on earlier drafts of various sections of the chapter. I am grateful to Shahnaaz Suffla for an insightful review and constructive suggestions. Funding from the University of Cape Town and the AW Mellon Foundation is gratefully acknowledged.

10 Gender Inequality, Family Relations and Crimes of Passion

Patricia Mercader, Annik Houel
& Helga Sobota[1]

OUTCOMES

After having studied this chapter you should be able to:

- discuss some facts and figures about the so-called 'crime of passion', or domestic and intimate partner homicide, especially in France (but North American research shows very similar results), and
- compare, confront and/or articulate an overall understanding of feminist and psycho-dynamic theories and debates about intimate partner homicide.

WHAT IS special in relationships between men and women? One of the answers to this question might be that it is the only relationship where the dominant and the dominated are supposed to, and in fact often do, love each other, whatever 'love' means for an individual. It is not surprising, therefore, that both sociologists and psychologists work to understand this relationship. Many of the former insist on the power dynamics of gendered, hierarchical relations between men and women, while the latter focus on the subjective aspects of object relations. As can be expected, the debate between these approaches is a very conflictual one.

One of the responses to the question 'What is so special about relationships of women to men?' is that they are one of the kinds of relationships where the dominated and the dominant are supposed to and in fact do love one another – however love is defined.

A social and feminist perspective

Feminist researchers basically see intimate partner homicide as the paroxysm of domestic violence, and they stress that in many cultures the husband battering his wife is a normal, and in some circumstances, even recommended practice. Of course, ostensibly, this is not the case in Western liberal democracies. However, in these societies the practice is so pervasive that the 'abnormality' of the phenomenon can be questioned. For example, in the United Sates, between 21 per cent and 34 per cent of all adult women will experience violence from a male partner (Koss *et al.*, 1994). The same can be said of lethal violence against women in intimate or domestic situations. According to the United States Federal Bureau of Investigations statistics (United States Department of Justice, 1996), over 30 per cent of female homicide victims are killed by their intimate partner. Between 1976 and 1996, over 30 000 women were victims of intimate partner homicide. Nonetheless, the social 'legitimacy' and the visibility of violence against women vary from one society to another.[2]

The idea that intimate partner homicide has more to do with 'normality', than with marginality is reinforced by the fact that the traditional predictors of homicide (social disorganisation, poverty, etc.) have an overall low predictive value in terms of intimate partner homicides, as well as domestic violence. Nevertheless, male batterers, men who kill their partners, and battered women (whether they kill or not) all have a history of violence in their family (Johnson, 1996), and their high power and control needs may arise from a sexist gender socialisation that is more accentuated than usual.

Therefore, feminists: 1) analyse intimate partner homicide as an asymmetrical phenomenon, caused by men's domination over women; and 2) consider that psycho-pathological or even merely psychological explanations (references to passion or jealousy, for instance) mask the social dynamics of the phenomenon, and more specifically the reality of domination. Research carried out in this field within this perspective over the past twenty years or so can be divided into two distinct themes, namely, studies dealing with femicide, and those focusing on battered women who kill. Most research, however, appears to focus on the latter.[3]

Femicide

According to Russel and Harmes (2001), the concept of femicide specifically designates the killing of females by males (or in some situations by females) *because* they are female. To a certain extent, this definition challenges the popular conception that the murder of a woman or a girl is a private affair or a pathological aberration. Furthermore, it highlights the understanding that when men kill women, power dynamics, and specifically the power dynamics underscoring misogyny or sexism, are always implicated. The killing of a

> Feminist researchers view intimate partner homicide as the paroxysm of domestic violence, stressing that in many cultures the battering of the wife by the husband is a normal, and in some circumstances, even recommended practice.

> The concept of femicide specifically designates the killing of females by males (or in some situations by females) *because* they are female.

199

woman by her partner is seen as femicide because power and control are salient contributing factors to the perpetration of the murder: batterers kill not because they lose control (of themselves, as the 'passion' explanation of the murder suggests), but because they want to exert control over their partner. Thus, symptomatically, women are more at risk of being killed just after leaving their partner. This can be seen as an extreme manifestation of particularly men's attempts to assert their ownership and control over the sexuality and reproductive capacity of their female partners (Wilson & Daly, 1992).

Battered women who kill

Studies generally show that female intimate homicides frequently take place within the context of abusive relationships. For example, it has been found that between 40 per cent and 55 per cent of female intimate homicides occur within the context of a male partner assaulting the woman. According to Walker (1979; 1989) abusive relationships are characterised by a cycle of violence consisting of three phases. Phase one is called 'tension building', and it includes verbal and minor physical abuse from the man, with the woman trying to placate him in order to prevent more serious abuse. Phase two consists of an acute battering incident. During phase three, termed 'loving contrition', the apologetic batterer assures the woman that the violence will not be repeated. He explains that the violence will not occur again, and that it would not have occurred, if only she had obeyed him. However, after this 'honeymoon' period, tension starts building again and the cycle recommences.

Abusive relationships are said to be characterised by a cycle of three phases: 1) a build-up of tension; 2) an acute battering incident; and 3) a loving contrition.

As the cycle of violence is repeated, the 'loving contrition' phase becomes shorter and shorter, and the violence becomes increasingly severe. According to Walker (1979, 1989), any woman may find herself in an abusive relationship with a man once, but a woman who has been exposed twice to this cycle and remains in the relationship presents the battered woman syndrome, characterised by learned helplessness. Repeatedly exposed to painful stimuli over which they have no control and from which there is no apparent escape, these women eventually cease trying to recognise or take advantage of available opportunities to transform their situation. In order to placate their jealous and possessive partners, battered partners often become increasingly isolated, and therefore progressively more dependent and vulnerable. It is important to stress that in this relationship the woman often tries to placate the man, frequently because of the widespread notion that the violence displayed by men towards their female partners is a response to a provocation; in other words, that the woman in some way seeks his violence.

The learned helplessness theory is meant to answer the question: 'Why do battered women stay in abusive relationships?' To a certain extent, it might in fact describe some of these women's feelings of helplessness and dependency

('Where could I go to?', 'How will I feed my children?', etc.). However, recent research tends to criticise this theory (Browne, 1987; Busch, 1999; Gondolf & Fisher, 1988). Battered women are no longer seen as resigned, but instead as active survivors thwarted in their attempts to leave by very real legal and social obstacles (mostly indifference, or even active hostility from the medical profession, the police, the justice system, and sometimes even from friends and relatives). Their psychological condition might be compared to that of victims of torture or of war, and may reflect similar symptomatology to post-traumatic stress disorder.

The above-mentioned research also stresses that leaving does not always efficiently end the violence, and in fact often precipitates more violence in the form of 'separation assault' (referring to the reality alluded to above; that women are often at greater risk of assault after they had left their partners). Focusing on the woman's helplessness, as the learned helplessness theory does, can be seen as yet another, and quite traditional, manner of stigmatising women.

Post-traumatic stress disorder: A diagnosis that is made of disturbed behaviour that is attributed to a major stressful event but that emerges after the event.

Justice and intimate partner homicide

It has been argued by feminist researchers and advocates that battered women who kill are actually in a situation of self-defense, even in the (not so rare) case in which, after a particularly threatening and intense outburst of violence from their partner, they kill him while he is asleep (Gillespie, 1989). This conception demands an extension of the notion of self-defense, which relies on an overall idea of 'reasonableness', e.g. the use of equal force (you can only use a weapon to defend yourself from an armed person) and the duty to retreat in the face of imminent danger (you must seek all means of escape before using deadly force). As indicated earlier, there are many reasons why women do not leave abusive relationships, including economic dependency, and the fact that leaving may lead to more violence.

There are those (including some feminist researchers and advocates) who think that the extension of the traditional conception of self-defense leads to the unequal treatment of men and women, since within the extended definition, self-defense is differentially evaluated according to the killer's and victim's gender. However, it can be argued that society on the whole being unequal, the extension of the traditional definition of self-defense is basically a way of striking a balance: the socialisation of women as gentle, weak, etc. makes them respond to violence in a specific way.

It has been broadly demonstrated that the judicial system is deeply influenced by gender bias.[4] More specifically, reasonableness is defined in male, and not female, terms. For instance, with the idea of provocation so often used by men in the case of *flagrante delicto* betrayal, English common law relies heavily upon a conception of the way in which a reasonable man is supposed to react; the only provocation invested with the same power to mitigate a killer's responsibility is a direct physical assault on that man himself or on a relative (Wilson & Daly, 1992). The new definition of self-defense reverses this idea of provocation, relying on a conception of the way in which a reasonable woman is supposed to react.

Ewing (1990) has argued that in the case of battered women who kill, one should consider the idea of psychological self-defense: the abuse is a life- or-death attack on her psychological self. This argument has been broadly criticised, even by feminists. Understanding the motivations for murder is different from excusing it, and it is ultimately patronising to women and so could result in abused women being further pathologised.

The influence of social evolution

In her ecological analysis, Stout (1992) examined intimate partner homicide in various states in the United States, and noted that intimate femicide tends to decrease under the following conditions:

- when the economic situation of women is 'average' (neither very favourable nor very unfavourable),
- in states that promote gender equality and social justice for women, and
- when shelters for abused women exist.

According to Stout (1992) after a period of substantial expansion in services for abused women, men's risk of being killed by their partners decrease significantly.

Furthermore, she observes that after a period of substantial expansion in services for abused women, men's risk of being killed by their intimate partners decreased significantly. However, women's risk of being killed did not. Thus, the expansion of services may have resulted in the protection of abusive men from defensive violence by their female partners, without succeeding in protecting women from the violence of their male partners (Gartner *et al.*, 2001).

As noted above, the traditional indicators of homicide generally are better predictors of female, rather than male, intimate partner homicide. There is only one exception: population density is negatively related to the rate of female intimate homicide, perhaps because the lack of population density provides a greater barrier to assistance and community support that could help abused women before lethal violence occurs (Jensen, 1996).

According to Jensen (1996), gender equality is the situation where men and women have equal access to valued resources, in particular economic equality, political and legal equality, and social equality.

Jensen (1996) provides a more definitive definition of gender equality than Stout (1992). According to her, gender equality refers to the situation in which men and women have equal access to valued resources. More specifically, she posits, gender equality can be conceptualised in terms of three categories, namely, economic equality (i.e. equality in terms of wages, economic opportunities, education, etc.), political and legal equality (i.e. equality in terms of representation in the political sphere, fair treatment by the legal and justice system, etc.), and social equality (i.e. equality in terms of social interaction, expected roles and behaviours, the acceptance of crossover roles and behaviours, etc.). She uses existing state-level indices to evaluate economic and political/legal gender equality, and constructs her own indicators to measure social gender equality, including measures of non-traditional living arrangements, such as divorce and men rearing children (The latter does not necessarily follow from the former). The assumption is that such variables reflect the degree to which traditional values are emphasised, and therefore indicate the levels of social freedom women experience. On this basis, she shows that the breakdown of traditional conjugal norms and expectations does more to decrease the rates of female intimate partner homicide than economic equalities between men and women as a whole – whether because it provides fewer restrictions for women who need to get out of abusive situations, or because non-traditional views of men's and women's partnership roles decrease the likelihood of abusive situations.

Under societal conditions of increased gender equality, traditional divisions of power in relationships may shift, influencing the levels of violence (including lethal violence) within relationships. For example, greater gender equality could be presumed to:

- increase intimate partner homicide by males seeking to re-establish control (the 'backlash' theory),

- decrease intimate partner homicide by males because of the greater resources available to women seeking to escape violent relationships (the 'resource' theory),

- increase intimate partner homicide by females who can more readily assert their power (the 'power corrupts' theory), or

- decrease intimate partner homicide by females who can escape relationships without resorting to homicidal self-defense (the 'resource' theory) (Dupong, 1999).

A psycho-dynamic approach

To understand the process leading to intimate partner homicide from a psycho-dynamic angle, one must articulate two broad fields of thinking: the dynamics of violence and the dynamics of object relations. As it is completely impossible to give even a rough overview of this field within the confines of this chapter, we chose to present some very basic texts which are (with a few exceptions) available in English.

Freud and love

In Freud's basically pessimistic view, the existence of violence is hardly exceptional in any kind of interpersonal relationship: 'The evidence of psycho-analysis shows that almost every emotional relation between two people which lasts for some time – marriage, friendship, the relations between parents and children – leaves a sediment of feelings of aversion and hostility, which only escapes perception as a result of repression' (Freud, 1921:101). To explain this ambivalence, in *Group Psychology and the Psychology of the Ego*, Freud makes reference to the numerous occasions of conflict of interest that arise in intimate relationships. *En passant*, his preoccupation with intimacy is intertwined with thoughts about how small differences lead groups to hostility: one cannot form a group (or a couple) without accepting a limitation on one's narcissism, and if a group or a couple lasts, a tension will always remain between similarities and differences, narcissism and libidinal bonds.

> Love as idealisation means that a considerable amount of narcissistic libido overflows onto the object until it eventually takes possession of the entire self-love of the ego.

In the same paper, Freud analyses love as idealisation, meaning that a considerable amount of narcissistic libido overflows onto the object until at last it takes possession of the entire self-love of the ego: the object has been put in the place of the Ego Ideal, as in hypnosis, and unlike in identification (in which the object is put in the place of the Ego), this idealisation coexists with what he referred to earlier as the universal tendency to debasement in the sphere of love – two currents (affectionate and sensual) have to be united. For

instance, some men cannot express sexuality except with a debased object, which means a splitting of the two currents, between mother and whore.[5] However, Freud does not provide any examples of women considering men as debased objects. Instead, he argues (somewhat neutrally) that, 'there are only a very few educated people in whom the two currents of affection and sensuality have become properly fused' (Freud, 1912:185).

Women's hostility towards their lovers is mentioned in *The Taboo of Virginity* (Freud, 1918). Some women show hostility towards the man after intercourse. Defloration is seen as a narcissistic injury, leading to a wish by the woman to castrate the man and keep his penis for herself. It is analysed again, in quite a different way, in his study on femininity (Freud, 1932). A woman's first experience of love is her highly ambivalent pre-Oedipal attachment to the mother. Sometimes, when a daughter turns to her father, the hostility of this relation remains with the mother, but it also happens that the hostility follows in the footsteps of the positive attachment and spreads to the new object. The woman's husband can therefore inherit hostility from both her father and from her mother. And, of course, for men and women, love has to do with jealousy, whether normal-competitive, projected (I am not tempted by unfaithfulness, my partner is), or delusional (e.g. homosexual, I do not love my partner, my partner does) (Freud, 1922).

Another trend of thought leads Freud to establish a typology of object relations, whether anaclitic or narcissistic. The anaclitic or attachment object choice is directly derived from self-preservation: love of someone who takes care of the subject, the woman who feeds the partner, the man who protects the partner. In the narcissistic object choice, the subject seeks himself or herself as a love-object, what he himself or she herself is, was, would like to be, or someone who was once part of him- or herself (Freud, 1914).

Psychoanalytic family and couple therapists later developed and transformed this typology. Eiguer (1998) and Eiguer *et al.* (1984) identify different types of couples, namely, narcissistic (or psychotic), perverse, anaclitic, and neurotic (or 'normal') couples. Narcissistic couples feel that love is a form of merging and aim at abolishing all the differences that threaten this view. Therefore, the relationship is marked by control, devalorisation, sacrifice, etc. Perverse couples focus on sexual scenarios, supposed to procure exceptional pleasure and value for those who experience this pleasure. The relationship is asymmetrical (sadistic–masochistic, voyeuristic–exhibitionist) and participation in the perverse scenarios is a necessary condition for the relationship. Anaclitic couples are confronted with a fear of abandonment, and see their relationship as a way of being jointly and individually stronger. They tend to avoid changes and conflicts. However, after a few years, their basic complaint is boredom. In neurotic couples, the other is seen as a whole object and loved because he or she is different. Conflicts arise from sexual jealousy and professional rivalry. In narcissistic and anaclitic couples – albeit in different ways – the object is seen as a potentially good parent for the subject; whereas in neurotic couples, the object is seen as a prospective good parent for the subject's children.

The Kleinian school and violence

The Kleinian approach to the development of the self and object relations is especially useful in understanding violence in general and intimate violence in particular. In Klein's view (1946), the infant evolves from merging with the mother to becoming a separate and integrated self by passing through two positions: firstly, the schizo-paranoid position, characterised by splitting (i.e. the satisfying part of the mother and the frustrating one are seen as two distinct imagos, the 'good mother' or 'good breast' versus the 'bad mother' or 'bad breast'); secondly, the depressive position, which entails an integrative

The anaclitic object choice is derived from self-preservation: love of someone who takes care of the subject, the woman who feeds him/her, the man who protects her/him.

The narcissistic object choice is derived from the subject seeking him- or herself as a love-object, what he himself or she herself is, or was, or would like to be, or someone who was once part of him- or herself.

Narcisstic couples feel that love is a form of merging and aim to abolish all the differences that threaten this view.

Perverse couples focus on sexual scenarios that are supported to procure exceptional pleasure and value for those who experience it.

Anaclitic couples experience a fear of abandonment, and see their relationship as a way of being jointly and individually stronger.

In neurotic couples the other is seen as a whole object and is loved because she or he is different.

experience of both the mother and the infant him- or herself as a whole person, both good and bad at the same time.

People who cannot bear the idea that good and bad coexist in the same person, subject or object, stay in the schizo-paranoid position, and fail to reach the depressive position. Many factors may make the integrative evolution impossible or more difficult. Following Klein, Winnicott (1960) shows how deeply the possibility of this integrative process is rooted in the early quality of the mother's care. A reliable empathic holding provides the child with an unobtrusive but necessary ego-support, and consequently a sense of continuity of being. *Failures* in maternal care (loss, but also intrusion) interrupt this continuity, which constitutes an experience of annihilation for the infant (Winnicott, 1960). This constitutes an unthinkable anxiety, for example, falling for ever, going to pieces, having no relationship to the body, or having no orientation (Winnicott, 1962).

To Bion (1962; 1963), violence has to do with the mother's function of containment: as container the mother is able to transform the child's incoherent emotional experiences (undigested sensations, called ß elements by Bion) into meaningful feelings and thoughts. This occurs if the mother can sustain intolerable behaviours long enough to decode and detoxify them (Bion, 1962; 1963). The mother's inability to contain ß elements exposes the infant to extreme experiences of annihilation. This extreme anxiety, experienced again every time the subject has to face object loss or the intrusion of the other in his or her psyche, is one of the most common sources of violent acting-out: the subject kills to avoid being annihilated. In other words, the subject acts 'crazy' to avoid going 'crazy' (Balier, 1988).

The Kleinian school views the infant as evolving from being merged with the mother to becoming separate and integrated by passing through the schizo-paranoid position and the depressive position. People who cannot handle the idea that good and bad coexist in the same person stay in the former position with its characteristic splitting and fail to have integrative experiences which are characteristic of the latter position.

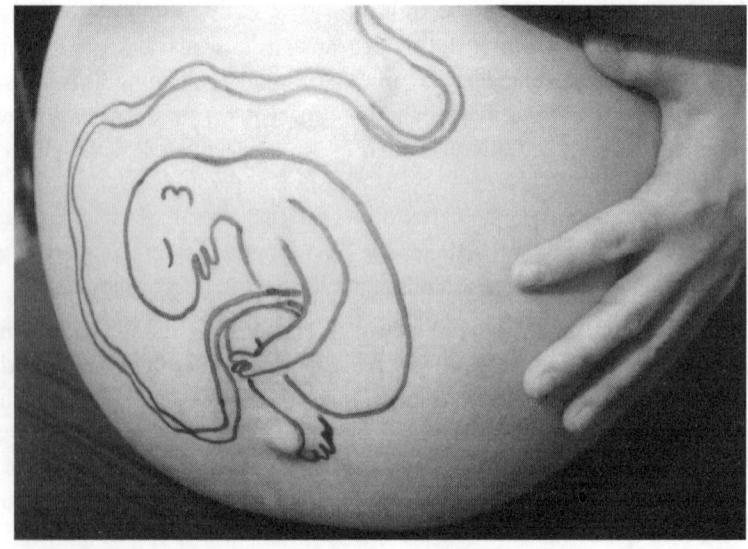

This tragic dependency of the subject upon external events and object relations is a symptom of his or her poor ego-relatedness. To Winnicott (1958), ego-relatedness depends on the subject's capacity to be alone in the presence of the mother, even (as is usually the case with adults) if her presence is represented by something else, or an atmosphere (for instance, when you feel so deliciously 'at home' in your worn-out pyjamas). This capacity to neither withdraw nor make direct demands for the mother (like, for instance, enjoying a concert with a friend) depends on the existence of a good object in the psychic reality of the individual. The relationship of the subject to this internal good object provides a *sufficiency of living* (Winnicott, 1958).

Ego-relatedness is also a condition for the subject to recognise, to feel concerned by, the object's subjectivity. The immature child has two mothers: the object-mother who satisfies the infant's needs (related to id-tension) and the environmental-mother, who wards off the unpredictable, and provides holding, handling, etc. The link between the destructive elements in drive-relationships to objects and the positive aspects of relating can be called concern. The object-mother is ruthlessly used (for instance, eaten), which causes anxiety to the infant (fear of loss). If she survives, and if the environmental-mother continues to be empathic and pleased by her interactions with the infant, then the infant can contribute to and sustain the relationship. This cycle leads to the capacity for concern. Failure in this cycle will lead to crude anxieties and crude defenses, such as splitting (Winnicott, 1963).

The process can also be stopped by deprivation, as in the case when an experience of loss is so long and intense that the child cannot keep the mother alive inside him- or herself. Deprivation leads to antisocial tendencies and attempts to reach back beyond the experience of deprivation to the lost object. So, individuals who fail to reach the depressive position evacuate unwanted parts of themselves onto the other (projective identification). The other is, up to a certain point, compelled to behave according to the projections she or he has received. This concept is most appropriate in understanding the interactive dynamics in the batterer–battered couple. He absorbs her violence, she absorbs his feeling of inadequacy, helplessness and self-contempt. But all these feelings, although suppressed and enacted in a polarised relationship, are actually shared by both partners. She can represent for him a powerful persecutory maternal figure, constantly reminding him of his own deprivation and his fear of abandonment. The more she identifies with his deprivation, the more she finds it difficult to leave him. Moreover, she is unconsciously aware of his dependency (on her) (Motz, 2001).

Battered women who kill project their murderous desires onto their partner (and others), and retaliate when it becomes unbearable. That which leads a battered woman to kill is her own perception of her situation, her subjective experience of degradation, isolation and terror. If a drunken man is

That which leads a battered woman to kill is her own perception of her situation, her subjective experience of degradation, isolation and terror.

threatening her life, and if there is a weapon at hand (for him to use to kill her or her to use to kill him), then there is a significant risk. More importantly, psychological abuse – the feeling of humiliation or degradation – increases feelings of self-loathing and worthlessness, and therefore suicidal feelings, which are deeply linked to homicidal acting-out.

Women who have had disturbed early experiences may be more likely to enact their violence than others (Browne, 1987). This is because they have not been able to integrate their murderous feelings: early maternal loss, parental violence, or a mother who cannot provide the containment of the infant's projection, thus allowing her or him to symbolise her or his feelings. This makes these women more likely to have an unplanned pregnancy in adolescence, to develop depression in adulthood, to be victimised in their intimate relationships, and to be disadvantaged in terms of alternative or escape solutions from an abusive relationship. When they engage in an abusive relationship, they develop learned helplessness (Motz, 2001).

Reconciling psychological research with egalitarian advocacy

The split between feminist and clinical approaches is an obstacle to a true understanding of the problem. We aim to articulate feminist and clinical approaches instead. We will do so with regard to the following specific questions: Why do so-called 'crimes of passion' occur? What kind of pain leads a man or a woman to kill his or her partner (or connected persons)? And, what underlying models can provide a deeper explanation of these crimes? Finally, we will compare the motives of men and women who resort to the murder of their partners.

The study reported here is based on an analysis of the 558 articles relating to 337 so-called 'crimes of passion' in two popular regional French newspapers (*Le Progrès* and *Le Dauphiné Libéré*) from 1986 to 1993. As we were interested in what is called a 'crime of passion', but could not accept *a priori* the notion of 'crimes of passion' as obvious, our selection criteria when choosing the cases were as follows: any crime involving people who are married, or live together, or 'go out together', or whose relationship is in any way based on love or sex. Most of the situations, therefore, concerned current or former intimate partners, but we have decided that some marginal cases were relevant and had to be included in the corpus: for instance, a man who kills the woman who refuses to have a relationship with him. Our definition is also broader than what many researchers call intimate partner homicide, because we have included multiple or different victims (and not only the partner as victim) in the final corpus of texts analysed. For instance, our definition includes a man whose wife announces that she will leave him, and who kills her, their children, and possibly himself; or a man who kills his wife's lover or his girlfriend's family (whom he sees as posing a threat to their relationship); or even a woman who kills her rival's daughter (because to her this is the worst form of punishment she can inflict on her rival). We have included homosexual relationships, but since only two situations concerned homosexuality (a woman prisoner who kills her cellmate and lover, and a man who kills his wife who is leaving him to live with a woman), our research admittedly essentially deals with heterosexual crimes. The notion of 'crime' is not obvious either. Most of the crimes reported were of course homicides or attempted homicides. However, we have included other kinds of crime, such as a man who explains that he has been left by his girlfriend and seeks revenge, kidnaps an unknown woman, threatens to kill her and then rapes her.

We have used this corpus in three different ways:

1   We have analysed the 337 crimes from a quantitative and sociological point of view, our primary goal being to compare men's and women's crimes, that is, who are they (e.g. age, socio-professional status, etc.)? What kind of relationships are they involved in (e.g. marriage, engagement, or cohabitation)? Who do they kill (e.g. partner, children, rival, others, etc.)? For what reasons do they murder (as far as we will ever know!)? And when, how, and where do they murder?

2   As about 50 of these crimes have been judged in the Lyon court, we have gathered all the documents constituting the inquiry into these specific cases. These include statements, testimonies, and forensic reports. This information provides an in-depth view of the cases, and constitutes the primary basis of our clinical approach. These documents are also interesting insofar as they inform us about the procedure and the institutional (and therefore social) treatment of such cases: for instance, whose testimony is *a priori* considered relevant? What do police officers or expert psychiatrists consider normal or abnormal, healthy or pathological behaviour in a man or a woman?

3   We have focused on the articles relating to a trial in the most popular of the newspapers (176 articles in *Le Progrès*) in order to study the social representations of 'crimes of passion', love, the couple, etc. through a discursive and narrative analysis.[6]

In our corpus, it was reported that men are most frequently the perpetrators of intimate partner homicide. Specifically, 78 per cent (264) of the perpetrators of intimate partner homicides are men, and 22 per cent (73) are women. Historically, this ratio seems fairly stable. For example, a study on intimate homicides in Paris in the nineteenth century reported a comparable figure, with 82 per cent of these homicides committed by men (Guillais, 1986). The proportion of male criminals is even greater if we include accomplices: 25 per cent of the women (17) in the present study had male accomplices, usually relatives, such as a brother, a father, a son, or a lover, and occasionally, a hired assassin. In this study it was also found that men killed more people in 'crime of passion' cases. For example, 72 of the women murderers whose cases were included in this study had one victim, while one of them killed three people. On the other hand, 60 of the men (23 per cent) whose cases were included in this study killed two to seven persons. In sum, 264 men killed 383 persons, including their partners and/or children, rivals, and their partner's or rival's family.

Obviously, masculine violence must be a primary focus in analysing this phenomenon, but one could also argue that the number of women murderers whose cases were examined in this study (22 per cent of the total sample) is a significant proportion, specially when we consider that the ratio of male to female criminals generally is 8:1 (Cario, 1997). Not surprisingly, female criminality takes place in private life spaces more than in public life spaces. It has been shown that, proportionally, women kill family members and intimate partners more often than men, although the overall total of victim–offender categories is higher for men than for women (Holmes & Holmes, 1994).

Establishing the motives in these crimes from journalistic data alone is, of course, very difficult. We generated our own typology (see Table 10.1) after reviewing all the available information, and found it impossible to decide in one-fifth of the cases.

Table 10.1

Motives	F Perpetrator		M Perpetrator	
Jealousy (whether the infidelity of the partner is actual or imaginary)	10	16%	111	53%
Actual, impending or feared estrangement from a partner	2	3%	115	55%
Hatred, quarrels, abuse, tyranny of the partner	31	55%	49	23%
The perpetrator does away with an obstacle to achieving his/her aims	10	16%	8	4%
Defending personal interests (financial, custody over children...)	6	10%	18	9%
Rejecting someone who makes an unwelcome advance	6	10%	3	1%
Feelings of devalorisation			12	6%
The perpetrator defends the loved one			4	2%
The perpetrator takes revenge on a stranger			11	5%

The percentages were calculated using the number of cases in which at least one motive is known, i.e. 211 cases of male homicide and 62 of female homicide. The same case can include a combination of two different motives.

The remaining cases clearly show that men and women do not kill for the same reasons. More than half of the men killed as a result of jealousy (whether their rival was real or imaginary), and more than half because their wife or partner was leaving them (three-quarters of the men gave one of these motives or both). Only one-quarter of the men killed because they found the relationship itself unrewarding and characterised by hatred, quarrels, and abuse. Conversely, more than half of the women killed as a result of abuse, and only two of them killed because their partner was leaving them. They were also married in more cases, and were more likely than their male counterparts to be living with their partners (70 per cent of the women and only 48 per cent of the men killed in a couple that was cohabiting). In the case of men, the importance of the theme of abandonment suggests that they see the couple as indissoluble, that the woman's decision to end it does not end the man's feeling of proprietorship (love as possessing or belonging to the partner) and that men keep trying to control the woman after she has left: 13 per cent killed their former partner.

Conversely, 82 per cent of the women killed their current partner (see Table 10.2). For example, after 24 years of marital life characterised by violence, Liliane L killed her tormentor as well as her two daughters. Jacqueline S murdered her husband, who had threatened to take her life six months earlier. Battered and kept under tight surveillance for years, she saw no other way out of her marital prison: 'If I had left, he would have found me.' Myriam F's case is similar: she had two children at the time she met her companion, and some time later had a third child with him. From this time onwards, he became brutal and violent towards her two eldest children. She killed him to put an end to the situation.

Table 10.2

Relation between the victim and the perpetrator	F Perpetrator		M Perpetrator	
Current partner	60	82%	180	68%
Envisaged partner	2	3%	8	3%
Former partner	5	7%	35	13%
Parent-child	0	0%	57	22%
Rival	1	1%	24	9%
Partner's or rival's family	2	3%	45	17%
Perpetrator's own family	3	4%	6	2%
Other	2	3%	27	10%
Grand Total	75	103%	382	144%

Percentages were calculated on the basis of the number of different cases and not the victims.

If men tend to kill more than one person, it is because they often choose different types of victims, a phenomenon which is much less salient among women. Besides their female partners, men's most likely victims are children. The age range of men's victims indicates that one out of six is younger than 16 years of age. In other words, and quite paradoxically, in the case of males, 'crimes of passion' do not merely concern the partners in the *'tête-à-tête'* love relationship. They are in fact a family matter. A group of people is implicated in the break-up of a relationship, and can sometimes be held responsible for it in the eyes of the perpetrator of such a crime. The case of D, which *Le Monde* referred to as *'le crime passionnel par excellence'* (the ultimate 'crime of passion') provides an interesting example. Rejected by the young woman whom he had been seeing for over a year and had hoped to marry, a young man of 23 decided to do away with her. The young girl lived with her parents, and her family intervened. Pascal D murdered his ex-girlfriend, her parents, her grandparents and one of her brothers, and injured the other brother, who managed to escape.

However, men are often their own victims: 19 per cent committed suicide immediately after committing the murder (and half of the suicides occurred after a collective murder). In the case of women, suicides are much less frequent, and occur a lot later. Only three women committed suicide, two of them in prison.

These figures definitely suggest that, on the whole, men and women kill their partners for very different reasons: women to get rid of their partners; men more often, and paradoxically, to 'keep' them. Therefore, they are perfectly consistent with the 'femicide vs. battered woman who kills' asymmetrical approach.

> On the whole, men and women kill their partners for very different reasons: women to get rid of their partners; men more often, and paradoxically, to 'keep' them.

The underlying models of love

When we approach the cases included in this study from a clinical perspective, we see that the deeper reason for the crime is the (often unstated) meaning the murderers attribute to love, the underlying models of love, family and the relationships they base their lives upon. And this model is the same for men and women: it is made of merging (love as annihilation of all differences) and proprietorship.

It is interesting to note, in conclusion, that these types of crimes arise in families that show similar characteristics to those of abusive and incestuous families. The drama develops over several generations, from the grandparents to the grandchildren, through the repetition of dysfunctional parenting. The parental identifications appear unclear and lacking (uncertain filiation, experiences of abandonment or of separation, losses [mourning], lack, etc.), and are constituted on the basis of rigid and violent models (archaic perceptions of the paternal role and of marriage as indissoluble, the playing out of a domestic tyranny). The family's internal functioning is persecutory, with each family member the object of control and appropriation, which forbids all search for autonomy. An adhesion to the all-powerful internal law of the family prevents recognition of the social law as one which is applicable to all members of the family. The family unit, constrained within a form of *huis clos*, tends to organise generations on the basis of the confusion/fusion of the sexes.

Conclusion

The study on which this chapter is based points to the complex interplay of social, intra-psychic and inter-generational factors in the development (or in consequence, the prevention and treatment) of violence in the sphere of gender and family relations. Any attempt to reconcile psychological research with egalitarian advocacy, to create links between feminist and clinical approaches, must understand how society encourages the merging and proprietorship model. For instance, in a story of a man who kills his wife and their children, a French newspaper, well-known for its leftist egalitarian stance, publishes the story under the title 'A family commits suicide' (*Libération*, 21 May 1993). This is a fusional representation of the family, one in which the paterfamilias's decision is considered as the decision of all members.

Exercises for critical engagement

1   Working with a partner, go to the *Sunday Times* website archives at www.sundaytimes.co.za or the web or physical archives of any other South African newspaper. Find twenty different stories of murders of intimate partners. After studying the stories, each of you should generate a typology of the cases as we have done in this chapter. When each of you has completed his or her typology, compare typologies, discussing differences and points of commonality. If applicable, describe the different or similar reasons men and women kill their partners.

2   Select half of the stories out of those you used in the previous exercise, and identify the ways in which the problem of intimate partner murder has been understood. Specifically, discuss with a partner whether each of the selected newspaper stories views the problem as one of power dynamics or hierarchical relations between men and women, or one involving the subjective aspects of object relations.

3   Working with a partner, select one story from your corpus of articles. One of you should write a 250-word analysis from a social and feminist perspective, and the other should write a 250-word analysis from a psycho-dynamic perspective. After having written your analysis, exchange your analyses and critique each other's work.

Endnotes

1   Many thanks to Vijé Franchi who spent some hours reviewing our English and translating some difficult sentences for us.
2   Consider here the apparent legitimacy of 'crimes of honour' in Arabo-Muslim societies, as opposed to the legal and social proscription of all forms of lethal retribution in other societies.
3   This is probably because it reverses the dominant stereotype of women.
4   For a South-African approach to these biases, see Mills (2001), who shows that this influence continues, notwithstanding the improvements introduced by the new constitutional order in South Africa, with its emphasis on the right to equality, and the formation of a Commission on Gender Equality in 1997.
5   If the woman is not seen as a whore, then she reminds them of the mother. Since sex with the mother is forbidden, she has to be debased to become an object of sexuality.
6   This part of the research will not be presented here. Readers interested in this aspect of the study are, however, referred to Mercader *et al.* (2003).

Recommended reading

Bion, W. (1962). *Learning from Experience.* London: Heinemann.

Bion, W. (1963). *Elements of Psychoanalysis.* London: Heinemann.

Busch, A.L. (1999). *Finding Their Voices: Listening to Battered Women Who've Killed.* New York: Kroshka Books.

Freud, S. (1914). 'On narcissism: An introduction'. *Standard Edition XIV*, pp. 73–102. London: Hogarth Press

Freud, S. (1921). 'Group psychology and the analysis of the Ego'. *Standard Edition XVIII*, pp. 65–143. London: Hogarth Press.

Klein, M. (1946). 'Notes on some schizoid mechanisms'. In *Envy and Gratitude and Other Works 1946–1963.* London: Hogarth Press.

Motz, A. (2001). *The Psychology of Female Violence.* Philadelphia: Taylor & Francis.

Black Women's Identities

11

Nthabiseng Motsemme

OUTCOMES

After having studied this chapter you should be able to:

- discuss some of the historical, social and cultural events and experiences that shape being Black and woman
- outline some of challenges Black women face in giving voice to their experiences
- discuss the contested notions of Blackness in post-apartheid, and
- describe some of the historical events and experiences that have shaped your own life.

THERE IS little doubt that the fall of apartheid has meant the possibility of negotiating new lives for Black people. At the same time, the demise of this system has thrown well-defined ways-of-being and of representing experiences into crisis. How so? As people grapple with life after apartheid and its effects on the present, questions around which stories of the past should dominate the present continue to be contested. These debates are concerned with how different voices struggle to shape ideas about both our present and past social and psychological realities. One of the aims of this chapter is to explore the various ways in which specific voices and experiences tend to be relegated to the margins of our social worlds and imagination. We will do this by centrering Black women's accounts of their lives which have historically been neglected or marginalised. The chapter thus traces the complex ways Black women negotiate voicing their social and psychological existences in the post-apartheid present.

But how do we map out these silenced and distorted voices? How are we to formulate ideas on what shapes Black womanhood in South Africa at this present historical moment? To begin this exploration, I will employ the insights of many Black feminists and womanists who have shown the importance of theoretical models that incorporate the intersection of race, gender,

Black feminists such as Angela Davis have shown the importance of theoretical models that incorporate the intersection of race, gender, class, generation, and culture to understand the lives of the oppressed.

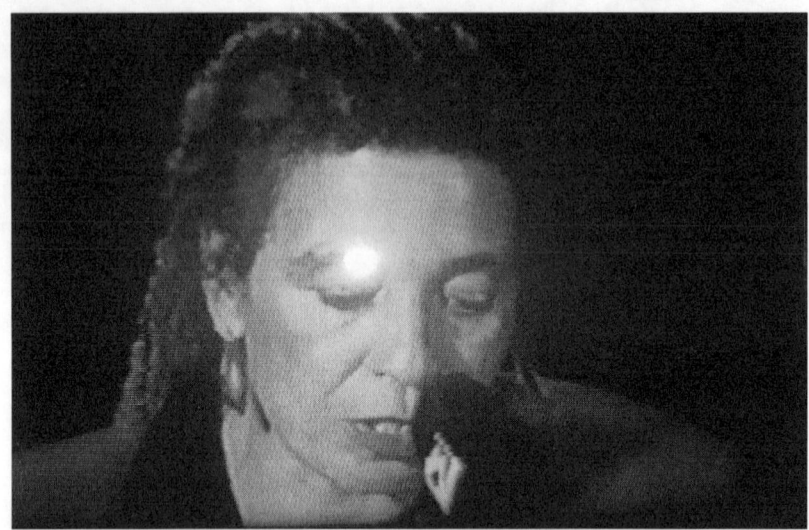

class, generation and culture, to understand the lives of the oppressed (Carby, 1987; Collins, 1990; hooks, 1990; 1995; Mohanty, 1988; Williams, 2000). These same authors have identified the importance of women voicing their experiences, as opposed to being silent, as pivotal in creating empowering spaces for women. While we will return to look at this issue more closely, for now it is important to note that these scholars have consistently shown that the denial of space for Black and poor women to represent themselves and their experiences meaningfully has brought about a sense of powerlessness in patriarchal and racist regimes.

The chapter starts by identifying ways in which Black women's voices are silenced and their experiences distorted. Here I discuss how various narratives, such as *nationalist narratives of resistance* and memorialising the past, can in fact act to muffle Black women's voices and diminish their lived experiences. In this discussion I will explore some of the emerging representations of women that surfaced at the Truth and Reconciliation Commission (TRC). I will then examine how power operates within racialised societies by discussing constructions of White womanhood and its relation to Blackness, particularly Black womanhood. These constructions are considered important in order to understand the ways in which forms of power or powerlessness operate, and how we reach situations in which White womenhood, but not Black womenhood, becomes an unidentifiable but normative female identity.

Following this, the chapter charts some historical events that have textured and shaped Black women's identities. These historical moments are discussed under three selected projects: first, apartheid's racial classification project; second, the national freedom project, as expressed through the Black Consciousness Movement (BCM); and third, the project of racial 'unity' in post-apartheid South Africa. It is important to stress that these are only some of the projects that provide the *discursive materials* for Black women's accounts of their past and present experiences. Finally, as I explore women's experiences it will become evident that they challenge the myth of an essential, unitary and static Black woman. These voices draw our attention to the competing meanings of Black womanhood, suggesting that these ways-of-being in the world are grounded in specific experiences, tied to defined locations at particular historical moments. That is, to be a Black woman varies temporally (*over time*) and spatially (*over space*). Throughout the chapter, Black women's creative power and agency to transform their lives and identities, even in the most limited and oppressive contexts, is highlighted.

Black women's experiences and silence

The idea that individuals' experiences cannot be understood through a single, all-embracing master narrative such as race, class, or gender has become widely accepted within the social sciences and humanities. This theoretical shift has been informed by the notion that structures of class, race, gender and sexuality cannot be treated as 'independent variables' since the oppression of each is inscribed within the other and constituted by and of the other (Brah, 1996). Responding to the homogenising impulse of western feminism (Carby, 1987; Christian 2000; Collins, 1990; hooks, 1990; Mohanty, 1988), Black feminists and womanists have advocated more inter-related ways of how discourses such as race, class, and gender simultaneously shape individual experience. As mentioned, within this framework the idea of speaking has been argued as important. This is based on the recognition that the denial of the right to speak

> The idea that individuals' experiences cannot be understood through a single, all-embracing master narrative such as race, class, or gender has become widely accepted within the social sciences and humanities.

> Responding to the homogenising impulse of White western feminists, Black feminists and womanists have indicated more interrelated ways of how discourses such as race, class, and gender simultaneously shape individual experience.

has brought about a sense of voicelessness amongst Black women in patriarchal, racist and capitalist regimes. The act of speaking is deemed empowering and silence is seen as undesirable. Patricia Williams (2000:421) outlines the negative effects of silence: 'It is the only image I have of Tawana – *with her mouth open* [own emphasis] – caught in a position of compromise of satisfying the pleasure and expectations of others, trapped in the pornography of living other people's fantasies.'

> Those who are the most marginalised have often used invisibility and silence as a means to protect themselves.

However, in privileging speech we need to be aware that those who are the most marginalised have often used invisibility and silence as a means to protect themselves. Valentine-Daniel (2000) observes that the capacity and ability to survive in zones of oppression gives life to subjectivity rooted in the mastery of hiding and not being seen. In this oppressive context, silence takes on meanings it was perhaps never intended to. It is transformed into a sign of defiance and self-protection (Motsemme, 1999). Therefore, we must realise that in encouraging women to speak, these acts of voicing may be liberating, freeing, yet full of anxiety for those who have been denied the occasion to tell their own stories. The dilemma then becomes this: in supporting women to break silences how do we ensure that racist and patriarchal legacies are simultaneously undermined?

In view of these assertions, giving voice to Black women's experiences of rage, humiliation and general oppression remains a complex exercise. One of the reasons why this is the case is because Black women's experiences and subjectivities have historically been formulated within a cautionary discursive framework, which has sought not to threaten an imagined Black solidarity. In post-apartheid South Africa, the pressure for Blacks to advance economic independence has made this discourse of unity even more compelling, if not coercive. For example, in the name of Black homogeneity and political solidarity, bringing to attention the inequities that continue to define Black female–male relationships is easily constructed as harmful to community, and discouraged from public official discourse. This discursive space of Black female–male relationships thus remains vividly coloured with silences and myths.

> Black women's experiences and subjectivities have historically been formulated within a cautionary discursive framework, which has sought not to threaten an imagined Black solidarity.

One such myth that continues to be perpetuated, despite widespread evidence to the contrary, is that racism is more oppressive for Black men than for Black women. Not only does such a myth warmly embrace patriarchal notions of masculinity, it is also used as a silencing device to label 'inauthentic' those Black women who resist the structures of patriarchy. This has resulted in some Black women deciding to assume consciously supportive and secondary roles that do not challenge Black men's power (hooks, 1995; Mandela, 1985; Ramphele, 1995a; 1995b). Relating her experiences of racism and sexism in the United States, bell hooks maintains that this patriarchal practice remains embedded within the culture of many Black homes and communities:

Many of us were raised in homes where black mothers excused and explained male anger, irritability, and violence by calling attention to the pressures black men face in a racist society where they are collectively denied full access to economic power ... They believed, as do many black men, that racism is harder on males than females, even though many of these women worked for low wages in circumstances where they were daily humiliated and mistreated ... and until black men face the reality that sexism empowers them despite the impact of racism on their lives, it will be difficult to engage in meaningful dialogue about gender (hooks, 1990:72).

In the case of South Africa, Mamphela Ramphele points to the ways Black women have precariously participated in sustaining some elements of the patriarchal structure to ensure the continuity of morally sustainable communities. She argues that ordinary women have negotiated this uncertain territory by carefully 'tread[ing] a fine line between affirming the manhood of their men-folk and supporting themselves and their children. The myth of the man as supporter, protector, provider and decision-maker was carefully nurtured in an attempt to protect the family and community from moral/ethical breakdown' (Ramphele, 2000:115).

> Mamphela Ramphele points to the ways Black women have precariously participated in sustaining some elements of the patriarchal structure to ensure the continuity of morally sustainable communities.

In addition, in the post-apartheid present, the growing assumption that Black women are advancing economically at the expense of Black men only entrenches conflict between men and women. Women who are perceived as too powerful or ambitious have either been labelled as menacing witches, cigarette-smoking whores, or frustrated lesbians. These hostile expressions are formulated against a backdrop where some formally educated Black women are seizing economic and professional opportunities and opening their own businesses. Many of these women who operate as independent consultants lament the extent to which some Black men assume they are willing sex partners. That one can encounter powerful and independent Black business-women runs counter to these men's ideas of femininity, and thus ideas of themselves as 'real' men. Mamphela Ramphele, the former Vice-Chancellor of the University of Cape Town and now one of the World Bank's Managing Directors, once observed that:

> [M]any of the women branded as witches are single parents who manage to live successfully without a man. People with problems will look for signs of taboos that have been crossed – Aha! You see that Mamphele is doing x or y and she's not supposed to do that. By breaking the taboo she has become the reason for your personal misfortune (*Mail & Guardian*, 27 October 1998: www.mg.co.za).

However, this is not at all peculiar to South Africa. In fact, these types of tensions between men and women have been noted in several countries undergoing gender role transformations where dominant forms of masculinity appear to be under threat (Connell, 1995).

Black women and the TRC

Some of the patriarchal practices outlined above take on new meanings when it comes to remembering resistance. It can be argued that there is a gendering of the struggle as contemporary memories of apartheid and even post-apartheid transition continue to be publicly shaped by men. The presence of women in the official resistance memorial constantly appears under the sign of exceptionalism. This is partly due to the fact that the discourse of liberation and freedom is understood within the geography of the public-political. And it is this restrictive understanding of the public-political which continues to confine women's participation in the liberation struggle to the private and feminised spaces of home and/or church. That the transition to democracy offered an opportunity for moments of terror and resistance to be fashioned in gendered terms has not been borne out.

When we shift our gaze to the TRC specifically, we note that narratives of loss and pain were filtered through the dominant prism of resistance, which favoured patriarchal notions of masculinity that foreground an imagined community of sacrifice and martyrdom. There are instances in women's testimonies where commissioners never failed to reassert traditional female stereotypes such as the strong matriarch in the reading of women's painful stories. Such an instrumentalising of female trauma was strategically used to construct a nation born out of tears. We must remember that a critical part of setting up the TRC was to facilitate the project of the nation building. So the tears and blood spilled in the name of the liberation struggle represent and communicate a powerful imagery critical for the making of a masculine nation free from any form of emasculation. This depiction of the nation should not be viewed as surprising as scholars have observed that most Black nationalist movements have ended up demonstrating their place within, rather than against, the patriarchal structure (hooks, 1990; West, 1992; Wiegman, 1995).

Another dominant representation of Black women in the TRC was one that privileges their experiences as victims. One such example can be located in Krog's (1998) book, *Country of my Skull*, where she observed in awe how the narratives of suffering of ordinary Black women during apartheid undermined men as the source of truth, transforming these very women into the true embodiment of truth, or rather suffering. But the question remains of what kind of truth is a Black woman's truth. Is it one that is negotiated, consensual, or collusive with patriarchy? Or is it a woman's truth defined in its own terms? Simply elevating the Black woman's voice to truth fails to open the production of knowledges that deepen our understanding of her historical expulsion. Fixing and framing the feminine in this way fetishises and institutionalises her marginality, once again (and ironically) eroding her agency.

There are other reasons why we must problematise such representations of Black women. First, they contribute to reinforcing the gross stereotype of her as the 'strong matriarch' or 'helpless victim'. Such stereotypes encourage static understandings of Black women's experiences and subjectivities. These representations are appropriated and reflected in various individuals' ideas about these women. Watching the proceedings of the TRC, this is what a White farmer from the Limpopo Province had to say: 'If I see another black woman crying, then I remember two Afrikaans expressions from my youth, "to cry like a meid" and to be "scared as a meid".' (Krog, 1998:190). While we could easily dismiss such articulations as irrelevant and flawed, this response would neglect to confront the effect these sorts of representations have in inserting Black women into the national consciousness in ways that are limiting. Allen Feldman (2000:61) makes the observation that 'in nationalist and ethnic politics the feminine is permitted to be image, but women are not readily positioned as authors of national imagery'. We need to consider that representing women as national objects risks capturing images that remove us farther and farther from the intimate experiences of their daily lives. One of the greatest dangers of the state-building project of the TRC has been to absorb, rather than transcend, familiar tropes of Black women that marginalise them even further. The image of Black women as victims, formalised in colonialism, extended in apartheid, and now confirmed by the TRC, becomes enlarged, permanent and fixed in post-apartheid public consciousness.

These frozen images of Black women do not help us to answer difficult questions such as what remains unspeakable to those who have been systematically dehumanised (Das, 1996; Nuttall, 2000; Sasaki, 1998). How do we 'hear' tears and recover silences that have been reinforced and deepened by racist and sexist discourses and legal practices? Do we as researchers have a right to uncover the origins of the stories of tears and silences? In what ways is this silence of daily trauma inscribed on the female body? How does this shape the subjectivities of women?

White women and Black women's voices

There is another layer we must unravel which contributes to the silencing or distorting of Black women's voices and bodies. This is the ideological construction of White femininity through racism and the forms of power it generates for White women. The articulation between forms of White femininity, womanhood and power is undoubtedly a critical one, particularly in view of how discourses of miscegenation were mobilised to advance violent racist ideologies such as *'swartgevaar'* (Black terror). In a racialised state, such as apartheid South Africa, White women were not fully in power but clearly exercised power in other spheres – initially the domestic and now, increasingly, the commercial and academic spheres. The iconic figure of the 'White madam' and her 'Black garden boys' and 'Black maids' remains a forceful image in both the past and present popular imaginations of South Africans. Sarah Nuttall captures this social imaginary when she relates: 'Nadine Gordimer once asked a black writer – "why do you always picture a white woman lounging next to a swimming pool? We are not all like that!" He replied "because we perceive you like that!" Gordimer admits that she has to take cognisance of that truth' (Nuttall, 2000:4).

In the post-1994 period, the figure of the lounging 'madam' or 'missus' and labouring Black woman continues to be partially represented in the popular *Madam and Eve* comic strip, which features weekly in the *Mail & Guardian*. This comic strip simultaneously reinforces and subverts this classical power relationship between White women and Black women in the context of the domestic sphere. But how are we to understand these subtle forms of power, produced in racial discourse, which continue to deface the Black woman's voice and body?

Carby (1987) offers an interesting account of how this marginalisation can be understood by linking notions of women's raced voices and bodies, and how these coalesce to form racially informed femininities and sexualities. She argues that, historically, the link of the reproductive body with racial discourse was further bound up and reinforced within the 'cult of womanhood' that was made up of four cardinal values: piety, purity, submissiveness and domesticity. Black womanhood was then polarised against White womanhood and defined in terms of 'lack' – absence of male protector, beauty, morality, home, and family. These were basically all the conditions considered necessary for 'true' womanhood to flourish. Within these assumptions of domestic ideals and White feminine beauty, the Black female being became associated with all that was against truthful and civilised (i.e. White) womanhood. In these instances 'true' womanhood and sexuality became ways to articulate the social complexities of race and racial hierarchy as projected on the Black female body. Examples include ways in which excessive and hyper-sexualised images, as witnessed in the symbolic and actual dismemberment of Saartjie Baartman's body parts (namely her buttocks and genitals), reduced Black women's bodies and sexuality to negative bodily truths. Other equally harmful and reductionist representations are those of respectable, asexual and suffering Black woman as reflected in Antjie Krog's 'various large mothers' covered in traditional head-wraps. These numerous reflections serve to fix Black women's positionalities, making it difficult for Krog to speak through them in her own terms.

If we focus on the issue of power, it becomes evident that the White woman's positions within racist discourse meant that she occupied a contradictory space where she was dependent on patriarchy but also not fully in power. However, this constraint within a racialised patriarchy also forged other forms of enablements and positive uses of power, which then generated specific forms of domination. In other words, power over Black women and

> Carby (1987) argues that historically the link of the reproductive body with racial discourse was further bound up and reinforced within the cult of womanhood that was made up of four cardinal values: piety, purity, submissiveness and domesticity.

men did not preclude the ways White women experienced constraint and domination. It is only when we adopt a more situated and inter-related notion of power that we can begin to appreciate the complex workings of our social realities. Therefore, to understand power as operating in the same manner across contexts and outside other forms of socially sanctioned hierarchies (applicable to race, sexuality, beauty, femininity and womanhood), would be to essentialise and mask the ways *disabling forms of power* continue to constrain Black women to fully express themselves in a largely *de facto* (no longer *de jure*) racially stratified society. Analysing the location of women in Nigerian Yoruba society, Bibi Bakare-Yusuf (2002) also maintains that it is only an interwoven and context-sensitive account of power that will enable us to understand the experiences of women's differentiated positionalities. She makes this interesting case for a more nuanced perspective on how power works:

> In line with recent theories of power (such as feminist and post-modern thought), I suggest that different modes of power are always working in terms of each other. No form of power, be it gender, race or class, has the same value from context to context and from time to time. No form of power is monolithic or univocal, existing in isolation from all other modes of social structuration. Rather, each variable of power acquires its specific value in the context of all other variables operating in a given situation. The consensus amongst many critical thinkers today is that the boundaries between different modes of power are often irreducibly blurred. For example, class difference works only in the way it does through a specific constellation of effects that are articulated in terms of race, gender, ethnicity, religion, geography and generation and *vice versa*. And of course, this pluralised, context-sensitive approach to class changes how we understand these differentiated positionalities in turn. Each mode of power is like a thread that creates a pattern of significance only when woven together with all other threads that combine in a specific situation (the family, the workplace, the city, the culture and so on) ... (Bakare-Yusuf, 2001:n.p.).

One can extend this insight to the South African context and argue that to assess some of the ways White women exercise(d) power (over) and domination, one must also understand how racial difference works through its intersection with sexuality, womanhood and femininity. Again, I must stress that placing a heavy reliance solely on race only adds to masking other forms of power relationships which have found their expression through racialised notions of beauty, femininity and sexuality. And it is by considering this conceptualisation of power that stresses both enabling and constraining possibilities (Bakare-Yusuf, 2002) that richer accounts of marginality and silencing of Black women can be presented.

However, there are efforts to situate the White women within South Africa's shifting landscape (Adler, 1998; Krog, 1998; Nuttall, 2001; Steyn, 2002; Whitlock, 1996). These accounts form part of an international move by scholars to deconstruct Whiteness and highlight the forms of privileges that it entails. However, a prominent feature in most of the South African works is the way that they rarely link White women's positionalities and the ways these are entangled in the distortion of Black female bodies and voices. They have, rather, unveiled Whiteness as another kind of racial specificity. And as Brah (2000) reminds us, it is imperative that we broaden our analysis of race and gender to include both Black and White women, as White women's privileged positions within racialised discourses (even when they share a class position with Black women) fail to be adequately theorised. The result of such a short-coming in analyses is that specific processes of domination remain invisible. Further, adequate and strong critiques will be important in challenging the normative and deferred position implicit in discourses of Whiteness. They will contribute towards dismantling what has been described as the structured invisibility that continues to define the concealed workings of racial discourse (Frakenberg, 1993).

It is only an interwoven and context-sensitive account that will enable us to understand the experiences of women's differentiated positionalities.

Black women and apartheid racial categories

The cataloguing of various races into distinct and registered types remains one of the most definitive features of the defunct apartheid regime. The obsession with racial distinctiveness, which was transformed into a systematic bureau-cratisation and normalisation of race (Posel, 2001), became the key structuring discourse in people's lives. Saul Dubow (1995) has suggested that this was part of a broader project of scientific racism that made the body the principal sign of race. Being classified into a particular race determined where one lived, where one went to school, which public facility one could access, with whom to have sex, whom to love and where to worship. All this was couched in the language of population groups, which reflected what Ndebele (1991) described as part of the 'spectacle' element of South African society.

This racial discourse was also inextricably and elaborately moulded with other signifiers of identity such as language, culture, religion, class, and social reputation. This moulding continuously destabilised racial discourse itself at particular historical times, thus making it difficult to read. In fact, recent readings of some segregationist pieces of legislation have revealed how the naturalising and protective discourse of apartheid was never static, but was rather characterised by change, often turning against itself (Posel, 2001). However, it is the colour Black as a visible characteristic which was to become a core concern in racist theorisation.

Frantz Fanon (1986) has described this obsession of the *epidermal schema* as reflecting the inscription of race on the skin and the ways this becomes a sign of racial and cultural difference (see Chapter 6). The development of a colour hierarchy between Black people when they accepted fixed notions of Blackness imposed by Europeans is a condition Fanon identified as part of the post-colonial condition that needed to be confronted. Within this colour hierarchy, to be *Black-skinned* or *light-skinned* becomes a critical site in making the meaning of 'race' real, and therefore becomes a form of *bodily truth*. These bodily truths are then extended and interiorised as social fact. The acceptance by Black people of 'dark-skins' and 'light-skins' to embody individual and social worth reflects the penetration of the racialisation project and its consequent domestication of Black bodies and psyches. In this instance we witness how colour gets valorised to such an extent that it produces a social order based on colour, which determines one's status, social mobility and social interactions. From that moment on colour becomes a key part of a visible economy of race that enables the viewer to ascertain a person's rightful place in the racial hierarchy (Wiegman, 1995). Of course these hierarchical arrangements remain trapped within Eurocentric discourses of racial purity ordered on the logic of vision (Oyewumi, 1997), forming new boundaries of exclusion between those defined as 'dark-skinned' and 'light-skinned'.

Black women and the BCM

The BCM became an important project for shaping the political and social consciousness of many young South Africans in the 1970s and beyond. It also changed the nature of Black resistance politics by providing an alternative vocabulary to articulate a counter-discourse of the *'Black experience'* within the apartheid racial structure (Sole, 1993). This Black experience would be premised on what the leading voice of the BCM, Steve Biko (1978), described as a collective consciousness of oppression. The underlying assumption of the

BCM was that Blacks shared a degree of compassion, depth of anger and militancy stemming from a shared oppression (Matshazi, 1996), which would form the basis for collective unity and action against White oppression.

However, the BCM was not only a social and political movement, but also a cultural and aesthetic movement. In this regard, the BCM was heavily influenced by Leopold Sedar Senghor and Aimé Césaire's *negritude movement*. This can be seen in its rhetoric, which focused on the *recovery* of a beautiful and heroic African past; the *rehabilitation* of the wounded Black body and its history; and the *transfiguration* of Blackness, which encompassed transforming Black from ugly to beautiful. We have all come across the famous Black Power slogan – 'Black is beautiful' – which can be traced back to this movement. It was argued that the conditions for the Black man to attain full selfhood (Mbembe, 2002) were, for Biko, attainable through a return to the past where Black legends and heroes would be restored back into history. This of course echoed Césaire's (1995) sentiments for a heroic return to the past. Indeed, Black Consciousness was and is tied with re-presenting the past. It was then within the waves of this Pan-Africanist intellectual tradition that Steve Biko wrote: 'part of the approach envisaged in bringing about "black consciousness" has to be directed to the past, to seek to rewrite the history of the black man and to produce in it the heroes who form the core of the African background' (1978:29).

Biko and his influences

From his writings it is clear that Steve Biko, the medical student, read a lot more widely than his prescribed textbooks on anatomy and physiology. Biko managed to get hold of other Black writers' words and was informed on what other social and political leaders before him and of his time were doing. Some of the well-known writers and leading voices he refers to in his works include leaders of national liberation movements such as Walter Sisulu, Nelson Mandela, Robert Smangaliso Sobukwe, and Govan Mbeki; 'homeland' leaders such as Lucas Mangope, Kaizer Matanzima, and Gatsha Buthelezi; and also Senghor, Frantz Fanon, Mahatma Gandhi, Odinga, Kenneth Kaunda, Hastings Banda, Kwame Nkrumah, Tom Mboya, Jomo Kenyatta, and of course Césaire.

Césaire may actually have influenced Biko more than we know. For instance, in two articles, 'White racism and black consciousness' and 'Fear – an important determinant', he refers in several places to the words of the poet-politician. In 'White racism and black consciousness', prepared for a student conference held in Cape Town in 1971 and sponsored by the Abe Bailey Institute for Inter-racial Studies, Biko directly quotes Césaire in two places. The first quote can be found in the opening lines of the article, where Césaire states: 'No race possesses the monopoly on beauty, intelligence, force, and there is room for all of us at the rendezvous of victory' (Biko, 1987:61). The second time Biko used Cesaire's reflections on the peculiar uniqueness of the Black situation:

'We Coloured men, in this specific moment of historical evolution, have consciously grasped in its full breadth, the notion of our peculiar uniqueness, the notion of just who we are and what, and that we are ready, on every plane and in every department, to assume the responsibilities which proceed from this coming into consciousness. The peculiarity of our place in the world is not to be confused with anyone else's. The peculiarity of our problems which aren't to be reduced to subordinate forms on any other problem. The peculiarity of our history, laced with terrible misfortunes which belong to no other history. The peculiarity of our culture, which we intend to live and to make alive is an ever real matter' (*ibid.*:67).

In another piece, Biko quotes the poet, chanting: 'When I turn on my radio, when I hear that Negroes have been lynched in America, I say we have been lied to: Hitler is not dead: when I turn on my radio and hear that in Africa, forced labour has been inaugurated and legislated, I say that we have certainly been lied to: Hitler is not dead' (1987).

But perhaps it is when the BCM leader quotes the line on racial monopoly from Césaire that we get the feeling that the latter's thoughts were quite important to Biko. On this occasion Biko is talking about Black envy of White society for the comfort it has usurped and at the center of which is: 'the wish – nay, the secret determination – in the innermost minds of most blacks who think like this ... to kick whites off those comfortable garden chairs that one sees as he rides in a bus, out of town, and to claim them for themselves'. From this he concludes in an appalled yet meditative tone, 'Day by day, one gets more convinced that Aimé Césaire could not have been right when he said "no race possesses the monopoly on beauty, intelligence, force, and there is room for all of us at the rendezvous of victory"' (1987:77).

It is important for us to note that the BCM programme of recovery, rehabilitation, and transfiguration was always focused on the Black *man*. Ideas of gender and class were rarely interrogated. In failing to scrutinise patriarchy, the BCM discourse, like many of the national liberation struggles that had come and gone before it, continued to *celebrate* restrictive feminine roles for women, which activists such as Winnie Madikizela-Mandela (1985) and Mamphela Ramphele (1995b) began to challenge. Nevertheless, we must also note that even though the BCM and other organs of liberation privileged a masculine Blackness, they did create spaces for women to generate new ways to express themselves.

The Black Consciousness Movement programme of recovery, rehabilitation, and transfiguration was always focused on the Black man; ideas of gender and class were rarely interrogated.

It was through participating within these new political spaces and negotiating their own realities within them that actually women such as Madikizela-Mandela, Ramphele, and a whole new generation of politically active Black women would refashion themselves and the future.

Black women and the transition to democracy

Thornton has argued that the transitional moment from apartheid to democracy brought about a fracture in the representation of identities since 'they are yet to be articulable' (1996:145). In this changing social and political context, old registers of race are being replaced by new ones, a replacement that itself exposes the instability of race (see Chapter 7). Further, as new modalities of identity and selfhood emerge, political and social identifications also become remoulded and realigned. For example, there are recent arguments that suggest that young Black South Africans are reading race in entirely new ways – through the prism of taste (Dolby, 2000) – impacting on how they view and map their social and political worlds.

It is well accepted that identification connects us to others. It is also this connectedness to others that we use to make claims about our place in the past as well as the future. For instance, when an individual identifies herself as 'a Xhosa woman' or 'a Muslim woman', she is connecting to a community that shares ideas of a historically rooted past. However, it is also on this terrain of identities and communities that we encounter many contradictions when the present is clearly not a straightforward extension of the past. While the transition embodied a historical rupture that enabled Black women to release themselves from the shackles of apartheid's racial and gendered categorisations, it also exacerbated dilemmas of the identification of 'who we are'. At this juncture of flux individuals and members of groups cannot but draw on conflicting constructions of origins, which consequently influence who and what (that is, the self) we identify as the authentic post-apartheid subject.

This post-apartheid subject is something President Thabo Mbeki (1998) often elicits in his speeches. In his famous speech 'I am an African' he talks about what it is to be a South African being. However, what is notable is that President Mbeki's subject appears to be inherently infused with a tension-ridden doubleness. For example, Chipkin has observed that 'this is the inherent tension in the politics of President Mbeki. On the one hand the nation is composed of Fanonian beings: those merely willing to be who they want. On the other it is composed of Black African Men!' (Chipkin, 2002:14).

This tension alerts us to the slippages of who qualifies as the 'authentic' South African being. Perhaps this contradictory subject lies at the heart of the South African social and political imagination, and may partially explain some of the contradictory utterances and political practices emerging in the

> While the transition embodied a historical rupture that enabled Black women to release themselves from the shackles of apartheid's racial and gendered categorisations, it also exacerbated dilemmas of the identification of 'who we are'.

post-1994 period. These are depictions that range from celebrating the country and its people as a rainbow nation, to those that characterise it as a country of two nations – one privileged and White, the other poor and Black. However, the question remains whether this constantly deferred subject (Derrida, 1978) is characteristic of the transitional moment, or a permanent feature of what it means to be a post-apartheid subject in South Africa, that is, a subject caught between the desire to erase race but simultaneously invoking it at every turn to define oneself and one's experiences.

We also need to keep in mind that the 'native-settler' encounter has been a violent, ambiguous and protracted exchange and struggle in Southern Africa. This is somewhat different to similar encounters in West, Central and East Africa, which saw fewer settlers, with even fewer settling permanently in these respective colonies. In South Africa particularly, there are Whites who continue to organise and agitate for a White homeland on what they argue is their native land where their blood was shed in one of the only 'White-on-White' wars in Africa, the South African War. These Whites come from sections of the Afrikaans-speaking group and are always contrasted in opposi-tional terms to those coming from the English-speaking group. These groups of Whites are constructed as different from each other because of divergent histories, languages and cultures. To complicate this scenario we need to take into account that South Africa has also attracted a large number of Portuguese, Italian and Greek communities who also occupied the privileged apartheid racial category of White. However, we must note that even within these groups of Whites, complex internal differences are visible. In addition, convergences across groups occur and are often expressed via social class, ideological and religious positionings, and lifestyles. So what are we to make of these competing claims to Whiteness? How, for instance, do such contested notions of Whiteness interface with emerging ideas of Blackness?

Complicating identity

But what does this all say about post-apartheid identities? It simply demon-strates that the taken-for-granted categories of Black and White in South Africa have always been unstable and more complicated than we imagined. To be Black or White is not fixed across time or place. For example, to be Black or White in South Africa signals different bodily and relational meanings as compared with another country such as Brazil. That is, a 'White' in Brazil might not be considered a 'White' by many South Africans. In this case we see how meanings of the colours Black and White shift and transform depending on specific geographical and historical contexts. Sansome (1997) reminds us that in countries such as Brazil, where there is a large percentage of Blacks, ways-of-being-Black are being formulated with exchanges and borrowings

> To be Black or White is not fixed across time or place.

from multiple sources such as the African, the global and, of course, the Brazilian cultural arenas. It is this playful yet oftentimes violent interplay and synthesis of symbols and practices which goes into forging new ways of being both a 'Black' and a 'White' Brazilian.

This brings me to a point that I must emphasise – the suppleness and transformatory character of identities. It also shows the creative ways we imagine our identities through language. In other words, the colour Black cannot be the only significant marker in identifying people since there are other things at work such as culture, class, generation and location in the making of Blackness, as in the making of Whiteness. A Black or White skin then becomes a necessary but insufficient signifier for the formulation of specific racist ideologies and practices, since its interpretation always runs alongside other social constructs. The meanings attached to skin colour thus change, making racial identities always wholly unstable (Mama 1995). Brah (1996) supports this view by suggesting that for visible racial markers to be effective, they need to articulate with other specific racist constructs, while Ratele (1998) makes the provocative assertion that the discourse of 'being Black' is not simply to be 'Black-skinned' but rather more importantly to be socially, culturally, politically and economically marked as other.

In thinking about identity, serious consideration must also be given to the effects of globalisation on the ways Blackness is being formulated (Erasmus, 2000). Globalising influences from fashion, music, various lifestyles and technology will surely be felt at the community level in South Africa, where the bonds of Blackness will be challenged in interesting ways. Along the busy roads of Johannesburg there are clear signs of how urban youth cultures, Black gay lifestyles and Black women are forcing us to see Blackness in new registers. These cultural and social transformations challenge the very idea of a singular, unchanging Black subject and an inevitably stable Black community.

Yet another marker of identity is language, which incorporates names, accents, and so on. Neville Alexander (1996), a South African educationalist working in language policy, comments on the extent to which language itself has become more complex after apartheid, as it is employed to operate within a context of promoting national unity while accommodating diversity. Take, for example, a woman who sounds like a person of colour but has a 'White surname', or one that looks Black whose home language is Afrikaans. These are apartheid's symbolic 'excesses', those individuals who failed to fit comfortably within the violent discursive world of apartheid's racial categories. The irony, as I have noted, is that these categories were far from fixed and at times near-irrational. However, on the surface apartheid was able to articulate a complete lack of accommodation for contradictions, and those who dared step outside its boundaries were quickly rejected and marked as unnatural, taking us back to racist explanations of inferiority based on biology.

> Sansome (1997) reminds us that in countries such as Brazil, where there is a large percentage of Blacks, ways-of-being-Black are being formulated with exchanges and borrowings from multiple sources such as the African, the global and, of course, the Brazilian cultural arenas.

> In thinking about identity, serious consideration must also be given to the effects of globalisation on the ways Blackness is being formulated.

What's in a name?

A simple act of changing a name and/or surname can alter the ways people see a person. In a study conducted by Motsemme (2002) one of the respondents, Busi, whose father is Mozambican and mother South African, commented on how neighbours from her township of Thembisa changed the way they perceived her after she changed her surname from the Portuguese Dos Santos to her mother's Setswana surname. In other words, a name shift can transform one from being viewed as an 'outsider' to an 'insider'; from a *kwere-kwere* to being a Black South African. The meaning of the term *makwere-kwere*, which has entered South African everyday speech, remains highly contested. In both official and popular discourse its meaning shifts from 'illegal alien' to 'foreigner' to 'African immigrant'. However, there appears to be a large consensus that the term refers to immigrants from other African countries. The origins of the term are also unclear. Rob Nixon, writing for the *Atlantic Monthly* (November, 2001), states, 'South Africans claim to hear "*kwere, kwere*" when immigrants open their mouths.' This has been disputed though. Some oral accounts claim that the term was used as far back as the early 1970s to refer to Xhosa-speakers who came from the eastern parts of the country to settle in largely Tswana-speaking communities located in the northern parts of South Africa (Matlapeng, pers.comm.).

In any event, in South Africa the tensions between those called *amakwere-kwere* and those that are 'authentically' South African have left many immigrants and refugees from other parts of the continent brutally injured (see *Mail & Guardian*, October 1997). These conflicts occur between ordinary citizens and immigrants who are seen as taking away South Africans' jobs, and the police who are tasked with enforcing the new immigration law. Random and often humiliating inspections and arrests by police have become commonplace on the streets of South African cities and along its borders. There are amusing incidents of mistaken police arrests of South Africans who were thought to be outsiders because of their 'dark looks' or because they

failed to say 'elbow', '*indololwane*', in isiZulu – a very tricky word if you do not speak isiZulu. The irony of this tactic used by police is that isiZulu is just one of eleven official languages recognised by the South African Constitution.

Other criteria used by police to identify 'illegal' immigrants include the location of vaccination marks (Klaaren & Ramji, 2001). Some South Africans will testify that they are able to tell the difference between a *ikwere-kwere* and a 'genuine' South African through differences in skin colour. Those who say they are able to do this argue that those coming from other parts of the continent are darker-toned than Black South Africans, though there are of course millions of dark-skinned South Africans. Secondary though significant and contributing markers include physical build, shapes of heads, fashion sensibilities, and ways of walking and talking. These everyday attempts to define those that come from within and outside South Africa's borders are further reflected in the increasingly restrictive official discourse of the *Immigration Bill*. This draft legislation, which was released in July 2000, increases government agencies' discretion in implementing migration legislation. Klaaren and Ramji (*ibid.*) argue that this shift of migration policing from exclusively border control to community policing will undoubtedly encourage undocumented assaults by police and anti-immigrant responses from local communities. Such moves will make it even more difficult for those African migrants escaping wars, famine and unemployment in the rest of the continent to enter and forge new lives in South Africa.

However, this terrain is complex, as South Africans themselves feel resentful of the shallow government promise of work, while retrenchments and restructurings dominate both business and the public sector's transformation logic. According to the International Monetary Fund's *International Statistics* (2000), South Africa's unemployment rate stands at a striking 37.5 per cent. In addition, the increased levels of reported xenophobia in South Africa must also be situated as a continuation of an apartheid legacy of 'separate development' and the ghettoisation of the African mind. We need to critically examine how this apartheid paradigm of isolation not only found its expression in the homeland system, but in other bureaucratic creations such as Bantu Education that had profound psychological effects for Blacks. This system of education was seen as an appropriate response to prepare Black children to learn only what was necessary to be useful human beings and in order to take their place in apartheid's racial hierarchy (Norval, 1996). Bantu Education became a response by Afrikaner nationalist intellectuals in the 1950s to what they saw as a broad and philosophically based missionary education. This system of education was seen as inappropriate as it denativised Africans and turned them into Black Europeans. Given its limited official intellectual scope, Bantu Education also encouraged a distorted view of Africa, where South Africa was geographically viewed as a separate appendage to the rest of the continent. This was essential in creating identities and subjectivities rooted in localised bonds that found a difficulty in articulating with a Pan-African consciousness. Prior to 1994, it was not unusual for Black South Africans to know little, if anything, about the political and cultural experiences of other parts of the continent. It is thus not surprising that narratives of 'outsiders coming from Africa', as South Africans will say, are coloured with images of the 'other', who descend from a separate place not seen as connected to them in any pre-imagined way. These historical, economic and political shifts point us to the cracks in the ways Blackness, South Africanness and Africanness are undergoing shifts and inevitably change.

Language can act as a site for inclusion and exclusion within Black communities (as within White communities).

Language can also act as a site for inclusion and exclusion within Black communities (as within White communities). It also helps to draw our attention to the ruptures that continuously occurred in apartheid. This refers to the notion that within the apartheid discursive world you could have a situation where *a woman who looked Black* with Afrikaans as her first language was simultaneously closer in cultural identity (via language) to dominant constructions of Whiteness, and closer in racial identity (via colour and physical features) to constructions of Blackness. In such a case there was no language to describe and make sense of this simultaneity, so new constructions, in which such individuals were likely to be regarded as social and psychological deviants, were invented. These negative characterisations and consequent normalisations had profound effects on those individuals who felt they could not 'comfortably' insert themselves into apartheid's racial logic. The formulation of their identities was thus often characterised by a sense of alienation and tension from themselves and their respective communities. However, it is also at these unspecified and thus under-theorised spaces that a creative, albeit painful, process of forging a multiplicity of new forms of selves and social identities was generated.

Finally, there is an interesting change that is taking place post-1994. This is the increase in the number of people officially replacing their English, or what are referred to as 'colonial' names, with Black ones. Some scholars have recognised that the act of naming for those who have been marginalised reflects a material and symbolic shift from being viewed as objects to subjects, from being 'christened' with names to self-nomination. The recently published book, *Call Me By My Name*, which provides a list of Zulu names and their meanings for Black babies, forms part of a broader authoring process by Black South Africans. However, it remains clear that more attention is needed to outline the complex ways identities are being fashioned through manipulations of language in post-apartheid South Africa.

Blackness and women's experiences

As mentioned earlier, the view of Blackness as an experience of a shared history of oppression among dark-skinned peoples became the key organising principle within the BCM. However, this term *experience* is not as straightforward as we might think, and is filled with shifting meanings for women, as it is for men. This becomes clearer when we look at how it is used by various women in very different ways. Two evocations are where being Black can be explained by calling on shared *experiences of exclusion and White domination*, or where Blackness is understood as encompassing shared *experiences of an integration of cultural and religious meanings* (Motsemme, 1999). It is important that these experiences are not necessarily viewed as mutually exclusive.

In the first instance the shared experiences of poverty and oppressive relationships with Whites become central in creating a unified image of Black womanhood. We have noted how this universalising impulse was strategically important in anchoring Black nationalist and aesthetic projects, where a shared experience of oppression was key in constructing a discourse on Black unity. This idea of Black womanhood is influenced by Pan-Africanism and radical Black feminist and womanist thought. In the second instance, cultural and religious motifs dominate and are crucial in mediating the experience of being a Black woman. For example, for a formally uneducated rural woman who came of age in the early 1940s as a rural labourer, an overtly political notion of Blackness, which a woman coming of age in the 1970s and 1980s might draw on to frame her experiences, was not a readily available discourse. The 1940s were times of extreme economic exploitation, where paternalistic relationships between Black servants/labourers and White landowners dominated. It is important to avoid generalisations in the absence of extensive research data, but an ordinary woman from earlier times might be less likely to invoke the term 'Black' in the politicised sense when she talks of people around her, and instead might make references to people – *abantu* – or community. This may reflect the extent to which 'Blackness' is understood and experienced as cultural rather than political.

In Motsemme's study (2002), one of the respondents, 65 year-old Ma Shusha, maintained that consumed by survival, motherhood and wifehood, there was little time left to participate in formalised political structures and events. She points to how these events were far removed from her world, and that public-political episodes were rarely discussed in her social circles. In fact, Ma Shusha's interview is filled with recollections of maintaining the everyday such as sweeping the house and yard, fetching water, preoccupations about the children, their education and food, the role of God and the church in her life, visits to her elderly mother, her father and husband's expectations of her; as opposed to the protest and political organising and education that mark the official nationalist and liberal historiography of South Africa in the 1960s. The questions women like Ma Shusha beg us ask are: What other factors shaped ordinary Black women's sense of womanhood in the 1950s and 1960s? How did these women construct their own identities?

Several studies have pointed to the ways women living under oppressive regimes tend to intertwine their recollections with the daily chores of family and work (Butalia, 2000; Passerini, 1992, Ross, 1996; Zur, 1998). This embeddedness in domestic and familial life becomes vital in organising their experiences and shapes their sense of self. Now this should not be taken to mean that women naturally belong to the domestic sphere (Ross, 1996). Importantly, what we also need to extract from such narrations is the agency that women enact through harnessing positive social and cultural meanings that are necessary for the delicate maintenance of relationships, and refiguring the home as a place of safety for children amidst brutal racist conditions. These are indeed demonstrations of *agency* and creative *work* by women. These ordinary women's voices require us then to actively acknowledge the extent to which the patient repair of relationships across generations and the protection of homes from a daily wounding and humiliating outside have largely been the silent but conscious work of women. Importantly, it is these processes that are vital in the building and sustaining of specific moral communities. So while a story such as that of Ma Shusha's sense of separation from public events is a story of ordinary and 'apolitical' life, it simultaneously forces us to rethink how women construct time, events and modes of selfhood during critical historical moments.

While it is necessary to avoid generalisations, an ordinary woman from the pre-1970s period might be less likely to invoke the term 'Black' in the politicised sense when she talks about herself and people around her, and instead might make references to 'abantu' or 'community'.

It is thus in historicising Blackness that we can better understand why the site of affirmation for some women can be found in a complex integration of selected cultural traditions and religious practices rather than, for instance, a political idea of Black Pride or Black Power. For some women cultural traditions and religious rituals, particularly those associated with marriage, birth and death, must be respected and maintained in order to give continuity and meaning to their otherwise fractured lives. In this instance the church plays a contradictory role in the lives of Black women, where it is born out of domination but provides an affirming space in their daily experiences (Abrahams, 2000). It addition, it offers a powerful alternative imaginary space of spiritual time, which becomes an important psychic reservoir for oppressed women to negotiate, attempt to rehabilitate and make sense of their traumatising present realities. The integration of cultural and religious symbols in some Black women's narratives thus provides us with a glimpse of the importance of the spiritual dimension in forging more empowering notions of self for those living under oppressive regimes.

Women's ways-of-being-Black may also draw on particular cultural values such as respect and trust. Returning to Motsemme's (2002) study, Ma Shusha nostalgically remembered earlier times when Black communities were cohesive and safe. It was then consistent that for her the current perceived lack of trust and loss of respect all point to a crisis in what it means to be Black. Ironically, as a 65 year-old Black woman, she continues to be cast as a living icon of the 'Black experience', yet in the interview she relates how she is increasingly unable either to understand or identify with the present changes occurring in Black community life. In fact, her narrative is filled with a sense of doubt of whether her idea of Blackness, governed by particular cultural and religious bonds, exists any longer. For her, modes of being Black encompass *a memory of experiencing a particular kind of community* that she sees as something of the past, no longer part of the present landscape.

On the other hand, another young marketing executive interviewed in the study, Nandi, who positioned herself as a 'privileged' Black – she always lived in a bigger house relative to others in the township and attended White private schools – revealed other important points to pay attention to in talking about Black womanhood and the authenticating practices that accompany this identification. In her narration Nandi situates herself as occupying a selfhood that is outside hegemonic definitions of what she called 'Soweto Blackness'. So what is this Soweto Blackness, or more generally this way-of-being-Black in one of South Africa's urban townships? This version of Blackness, which is linked to subjectivities integrally located in the township, constitutes *another form* of 'authentic Blackness'. But we must remember that we have already identified another 'authentic Blackness' which continues to be central in the production of Black aesthetic and nationalist discourses. This version draws heavily on notions of roots and cultural origins. In contrast, a major element shaping the discourse of 'Black township authenticity' is its complex interplay with practices of township survival and apartheid's ideology of oppression. It is this violent encounter between state repression and civilian resistance that gives shape to these myriad 'township-ways-of-being'. Nandi's utterance thus shows us the various ways people assemble specific markers to identify a Sowetan, or more generally what an urban township Black *ought* to look and act like.

Fake and genuine Blacks

In post-1994 South Africa the question of authenticity is once again being challenged as more affluent Blacks move from the township, or *ekasi*, into what were previously White-only suburbs. These individuals are commonly known as 'amabourgeois' or 'amacoconuts', and are seen as no longer 'authentic Blacks' but illusionary 'fakes' – able to pass as Black on the outside but authentically White on the inside (see Chapter 7). However, simply relying on geographical markers to distinguish between 'fakes' and 'genuine' township Blacks is itself unreliable as there may be individuals who live in the township but act or aspire to be 'amabourgeois'. Further, what happens when Whites begin moving to the townships? Who are they or, rather, what do they become in this context? Journalists Tangeni Amupadhi and Thokozani Mtshali in 1998 spoke to a few Whites who had opted to live in Soweto. These few Whites, most of them poor, outlined financial and cultural reasons for moving to Soweto.

Rudolf Thokozani Blignault, who continues to be mistaken for a policeman, maintains that the reason he moved to Soweto was 'When the *umlungu* (Whitey) sees you suffering, they don't even give you a bottle of water ... They'll just watch you die. Here in Soweto people will help you' (*Mail & Guardian*, 3 November 1998: www.archive.mg.co.za). And Sipho du Preez, a sangoma student who lives in Meadowlands, explains, 'You get freedom here – to beat drums, to dance and to slaughter a goat. People in the suburbs don't understand, they freak out' (*ibid.*). Helen Suzman's award as Sowetan of the Year (*City Press*, 2 June 2002) will also add to these everyday reported cases that confound what future meanings of township Blackness might be. As spatial, cultural, epidermal and shared meanings of oppression become unreliable, 'township Blackness' will also be contested and made anew.

Busi, another interviewee in Motsemme's study (2002), provides us with another reflection of this slippery boundary of 'authentic' township Black woman versus an 'inauthentic' one in her daily negotiations with living in the township, and her love for bohemian dress. Busi recalls how she is often told that she dresses like a White woman, and how some people in the township regard those who insist on speaking English to be simply striving to be White, or 'ibourgeois'. It is interesting to note that the terms 'White' and 'ibourgeois' are often used interchangeably. However, what is different in the ways these representations of 'Whiteness' are being mobilised in the post-apartheid era is that there are no longer merely entrapped in notions of race, privilege and affluence, but are being extended to incorporate social modes of dress, talk and interaction. For example, Busi's recollection outlines that for her neighbours some important representations of being a township Black also include speech and dress and how these coalesce to resonate with a particular fashion-style and way of speaking. These become the essential props for the performance of this version of Blackness. However, we need to note that even these carefully crafted modes of talking and ways of dressing are as fluid and unreliable as the constructs of language and fashion that constitute them. But what informs this style, this way-of-being-Black? The underlying assumption is that given a shared history of marginality these Black women will be able to 'naturally' comprehend and access these forms of cultural expression. But we must also place this discussion within the growing and rich youth cultures which appropriate *iscamtho* and *lokishi* or township styles as a fashion gesture to be globalised. *Iscamtho*, often contrasted with the Afrikaans-based *tsotsitaal*, refers to a Zulu urban dialect generally spoken by young men in Soweto. It is also an important defining feature of Black urban culture (For a more extended discussion on *iscamtho*, see Ntshangase, 1993). The critical aspect then is that if you cannot effectively assemble this timely script of being Black, you are seen as an 'inauthentic' Black woman and striving for Whiteness. Interestingly, in this case Whiteness is no longer something to be desired or aspired to, but rather a demonstration of a negative inscription on Black bodies and psyches.

What is involved in the process of being pushed outside symbolic definitions of 'authentic township Backness'? Nandi recalled experiencing a doubleness in her experience: 'I had to play more than one role, at school [read: White] I played the game and at home [read: Black] I played the game there' (Motsemme 2002:668). At this point of splitting, although she is skin-Black, others in her township do not recognise her as such. This is not just simply a matter of class, but also a making of a yet-to-be-specified Blackness. She explains how this process of transfiguration involves processes of trauma, assimilation and reinvention. Within these processes, other ways of experiencing Blackness are forged. Nandi's experience reveals that to be a Black woman is influenced by a number of factors and is never stable. In other words, there exist different ways of thinking through Blackness which result in several ways of experiencing being a Black woman. We can no longer ignore the extent to which mediating factors such as social class, language, location, culture, generation and lifestyle are reshaping the meanings of Black womanhood.

Conclusion

Women's narratives of their lives highlight the need for a layered approach to make graphic the complexity of their lives. This framework must ensure that these voices and bodies that have either been ignored or glorified to legitimate the public making of nation, for purposes of reproduction and to make racism compelling, are fully explored. We must continue to search for a critical impulse that allows us to explore the fears, desires and yearnings of these women. And given the constant fragmentation of Black women's identities, the need to find theoretical and methodological frameworks that will allow them to speak on their own terms becomes imperative. The question remains whether this is ever possible.

This chapter has shown how Black women's sense of being-Black is constantly being constituted out of social and historical experience. The many positionings women take up within different social contexts to make sense of their personal and collective experiences have also been shown. The idea that Black womanhood embodies a homogeneous and static discourse is challenged by women's narrations. They do this by illustrating how the meanings attached to 'being a Black woman' change over time and space, as it co-articulates with other social constructs such as social class, location and generation. The extent to which 'versions of Blackness' are emerging as a result of local, national and global changes has been mentioned, but requires fuller attention. Throughout the chapter, contextual meanings of power and authenticity have been inserted to expose the ever-changing frames in which Black womanhood is being imagined and formulated in post-apartheid South Africa.

Exercises for critical engagement

1   Briefly interview three Black women from different generations (for example, the first may be in her 60s; the second in her 40s and the third in her 20s), social classes (some may be middle-class and others working-class) and locations (urban vs rural or suburban vs township). Ask them what major social, cultural and political factors have shaped the construction of their identities. Take note of the simultaneous discourses that they refer to in the moulding of their identities.

2   Browse through a few Black magazines such as *Drum, Bona* and *True Love* from ten years ago, and then from a year ago. Do you notice any changes and/or continuities in the ways Black women are being represented in these popular media forms?

3   Read one of the following short autobiographies written by Black South African women to get a more textured and richer account of their lives and experiences:
    • Ramphele, M. (1995). *A Life.* Cape Town: David Philip.
    • Mashinini, E. (1989). *Strikes Have Followed Me All My Life.* London: The Women's Press.
    • Magona, S. (1992). *Forced to Grow.* London: The Women's Press.
    • Madikizela-Mandela, W. (1985). *Part of My Soul.* London: Penguin.

4   Trace the ways your own identity as a woman or man has been constructed by paying particular attention to the role of social processes such as social-isation, and social institutions like the family, school, church and others you may belong to and participate in. Think of 'common sense' lessons (explicit and implicit) that social processes and structures have taught you in becoming a woman or man.

Recommended reading

Back L. & J. Solomons (2000). *Theories of Race and Racism: A Reader.* London: Routledge.

Collins, P.H. (1990). *Black Feminist Thought: Knowledge, Consciousness and the Politics of Empowerment.* New York: Routledge.

hooks, b. (1990). *Yearning: Race, Gender and Cultural Politics.* Boston: South End Press.

Mama, A. (1995). *Beyond the Masks: Race, Gender and Subjectivity,* London: Routledge.

Mohanty, C.T. (1988). 'Under Western eyes: Feminist scholarship and colonial discourses'. *Feminist Review,* 30:61–89.

12 'Mixed' Relations

Kopano Ratele

OUTCOMES

After having studied this chapter you should be able to:

* discuss productions or representations of relationships and of 'mixed' relationships
* explain Coloured–Black 'mixed' relationships
* describe how intimacy and identity are intertwined, and
* understand how discourses of difference and sameness are employed in constructing relationships.

THE *PROHIBITION of Mixed Marriages Act* was promulgated in 1949, a year after the apartheid government came to power. It was repealed less than twenty years ago. The first 'mixed' couple to get legally married were Mr Protas Madlala and Ms Suzanne Leclerc. In spite of the law being repealed, Mr and Mrs Madlala, like other 'mixed-race' couples, were confronted with a set of incredible circumstances. Newspapers reported that Mrs and Mr Madlala considered emigrating. Among some of their reasons was that although Mrs Madlala was given a residence permit she was not allowed a work permit (South African Institute of Race Relations, 1987). Mrs Madlala ended up working in the Transkei, nearly 400km from Marianhill, where she had lived with Mr Madlala. While living in the township, Mrs Madlala had been unable to take the same bus as Mr Madlala into Durban (*ibid.*) because of the policy of segregating public transport, and there being no bus for Whites from Marianhill to Durban.

Another of the first legally married 'mixed' couples that faced similar problems were Raymond and Welheminah Crevits. Mr Crevits was classified White and Mrs Crevits Coloured. When their daughter, Aziyade, was born, the couple decided to register her as a Belgian citizen, rather than Coloured as South African law dictated. Their daughter was born in a maternity ward for Blacks after Mrs Crevits had been refused permission to have Aziyade in the

White section of the local hospital. Because of the law that segregated residential places, Mr and Mrs Crevits and their daughter were forced to live in a Coloured township near Potchefstroom.

These are a few instances of a long and incredibly complicated history and politics of social relationships in general and close 'mixed' relationships specifically. There is a recent and steadily growing body of empirical and theoretical work being undertaken into 'mixed' relationships (e.g. Dayile, 1998; Ratele, 1998b; Ratele, 2002; Stacey, 1998; Woodward, 1999). This sort of work is called for, given the recent apartheid *and* national liberation discourses of sameness/difference generally, but particularly because of past laws such as the *Prohibition of Mixed Marriages Act* and the *Immorality Act*. Such work should be seen as part and parcel of the body of investigations into social, political, cultural, as well as economic relations between racial and ethnic groups (see Foster & Nel, 1991). In spite of this growing interest, though, there is relatively little local social psychological work that examines inter-relationships (from the impersonal to the most intimate kind) among Coloureds, Indians/Asians, and Blacks (see Bodiba, nd.; Duncan, 1993; van der Ross, 1979).

There are a number of reasons for this state of affairs. I will delve into them later on in the chapter. But one of the main reasons has to do with the notion of 'race' (see Part II of this volume), and thus that of 'race mixing'. These notions in turn beg the questions: Are there such things as *pure, natural, biological* identities (see Parts II and III of this volume)? Is there such a thing as 'mono-raciality'? Another reason has to do with the fact that apartheid did not expressly proscribe sexual and marital relations between 'non-White' groups (people of colour). Still another reason has to do with the hesitancy on the part of critical scholars to look at the political, cultural, and social psychological anxieties that inhere in what Henry Louis Gates jnr terms intra-racial disparities (Gates & West, 1996). I will talk about these intra-group differences, but in relation to intra- and inter-group and inter-personal similarities. In other words, I will show that differences and sameness are part of a *dynamic and an unstable structure, the line between the two shifting over time and from place to place.* It is against this somewhat sparse, although historically fertile, ground that this chapter looks at 'mixed' relations, using Coloured–Black relationships as one of the examples around which our discussion revolves.

The chapter begins by looking at a defining element of inter-personal relationships – intimacy. I look at how intimacy is defined, while at the same time making a tentative gesture at the conditions that produce some relationships as 'mixed', as well as how we are to understand this. This leads to a discussion of how we, as individuals, increasingly use intimacy to define who we are as well as who we are not. I then go on to how relationships are not just private matters but bring the public and the personal together. This is followed by a consideration of how 'race' mixing came to be seen as dirty, impure, undesirable, pathological, and even criminal. The question here is whether it is possible to have an '(ab-)normal' relationship in an '(ab-)normal' society. Next I turn to look at relationships over and against the notion of identity as sameness/difference. Following this, I look at two discourses that (de-)stabilise this very sameness/difference network and each other. Last, and as paradoxical as it may seem, I suggest that at certain moments different is not equal to 'different' and 'the same' is not always 'the same'.

Box 12.1 Laying down the law

The Prohibition of Mixed Marriages Act, No. 55 of 1949

1.(1) As from the date of commencement of this Act *a marriage between a European and a non-European may not be solemnized, and any such marriage solemnized in contravention of the provisions of this section shall be void and of no effect.* Provided that

    (a) any such marriage shall be deemed to be valid, if –

        (i) it has been solemnized in good faith by a marriage officer, and neither of the parties concerned, or any other person in collusion with one or the other them, has made any false statement relating to the said marriage amounting to a contravention of section *four;* and

        (ii) any party to such marriage *professing to be a European or a non-European,* as the case may be, is in *appearance obviously* what he professes to be, or is able to show, in case of a party professing to be a European, that he *habitually consorts* with Europeans as a European, or in the case of a party professing to be a non-European, that he habitually consorts with non-Europeans as a non-European;

    (b) where any such marriage has been solemnized in good faith by a marriage officer, any children born or conceived of such marriage before it has been declared by a competent court to be invalid, shall be deemed to be *legitimate* (Statutes of the Union of South Africa, 1949:616; *own emphases*).

(Mis-)understanding intimacy

Intimacy is a central element in personal relationships. Intimacy is not sexual intercourse, although it is increasingly used as a euphemism for the latter. Broadly speaking, intimacy refers to close familiarity or union and to our innermost qualities. Intimacy is also used as a polite term for sex (Brown, 1993). Thus, while intimate relationships are substitutable with close personal relationships (see, for example, Ickes & Duck, 2000b), thereby referring to a wide array of relational practices covering the spectrum from parent–child dyads, sibling relationships, friendships, to romantic attraction and love, our attention will be focused on the sexually intimate relationship.

However, there is not one single kind of sexual intimacy. The sort of intimacy I am talking of here, with which we are familiar from television soap operas originating from the United States of America (such as *The Bold and the Beautiful*), and from here (such as *Generations*), may be called *disclosing intimacy*. This is a specific sort of closeness, of knowing, and of loving between individuals. 'The emphasis is on mutual disclosure, constantly revealing your inner thoughts and feelings to each other. It is an intimacy of self rather than an intimacy of the body, although completeness of intimacy of the self may be enhanced by bodily intimacy' (Jamieson, 1998:1). It is important to stress that this is a specific and historically recent understanding of intimate relationships, being part of the same cloth as recently formulated understandings of selfhood and identities (e.g. Hall, 1996; Harré, 1989; Rose, 1989; Rose, 1996). What this ultimately implies is that, when looking at relationships in general and 'mixed' ones in particular, we cannot stop at *what we are told they are*, but must examine how they come to be viewed the way they are. For instance, we must seek to understand why certain relationships, as opposed to others, come to be viewed as 'normal' while others are thought of as 'strange' or 'unusual' ('mixed'). In other words, we must go beyond showing the *presentness*, the here-and-now-ness, of these relationships and examine how they come to be spoken of in the way that they are.

> *Disclosing intimacy:* This is a specific sort of closeness, of knowing, and of loving between individuals. It emphasises mutual disclosure and revealing your inner thoughts and feelings to another.

A fuller understanding of relational life is one that accounts for the *historical, social, economic, political, and cultural coordinates* that *produce* some relationships as 'mixed' and others as 'pure' (although the term 'pure' may itself remain unarticulated and implicit). Accounting for the histories, social coordinates, economies, politics, and cultures of inter-personal and inter-group relations also functions to purposefully *dis*locate or *mis*understand current, taken-for-granted knowledge about these relations. While the coordinates of inter-personal relationships go much further and wider than what I indicate, my account exemplifies them by pointing to the work of the colonial legislators (in the 1920s – see Box 12.2), and the apartheid legislators (from the late 1940s to the 1980s – see Boxes 12.1, 12.3, and 12.4) in influencing and conditioning our understandings of relationships. All of this is part of developing a critical stance with regard to our histories, our present conditions, our cultures, our society, and our selves; in this case, undertaken by focusing on how ruling and dominant ideas, such as those of 'mixing', and thus of 'inter-raciality', 'inter-ethnicity', 'inter-faith', 'multi-culturalism', and so on, are not as obvious, innocent, or normal as they may at first appear.

The idea that we have to keep watch over knowledges or to dis-locate our own understandings is urged, among others, by the fact that Coloured–Black relationships, for instance are characterised by clashing views of Coloureds and Blacks as similar on one hand, and different on another. That is to say, at one moment you might hear one person saying Coloureds and Africans are part of a single group, and at the next moment you might hear it said that Coloureds and Blacks are different. In fact, you might have heard the view that Coloureds are not Blacks. An interesting aspect of this is that these conflicting viewpoints may be expressed in one locale, or more interestingly, by a single group of associates. To differing extents and at various moments then, Coloureds and Blacks are seen and interacted with as separate and distinct from each other, or as sharing commonalities and part of one group (see for example, Alexander, 1985; Biko, 1996; Lewis, 1987; van der Ross, 1979). Since we cannot fully discuss relationships without talking of identities, and before turning to other influences that motivate a wilful mis-understanding of notions of identities and 'mixing', let us look at how identity is related to intimacy.

Intimacy and identities

We cannot talk of relationships without talking of identities, because intimacy and identities are closely related.

We cannot talk of relationships without talking of identities, because intimacy and identities are closely related. Identities beg the question of difference (Meintjies, 1993). An individual establishes an identity in relation to other individuals and social groups with whom she or he is similar and to whom she or he belongs, and from others from whom she or he is different and does not belong (Howitt, 1989; Tajfel, 1982). That is also to say identities and differences are relational achievements (Gergen, 2002). In another way, one's intimate relationships are implicated in the constitution of who one is, but also who one is not. This is the centre of what I talk about later when I turn to the difference/sameness network.

Box 12.2 Deceiving one another for immoral purposes

The *Immorality Amendment Act*, No. 21 of 1950, was an amendment of Act No. 5 of 1927. The Act of 1950 was itself amended several times. But one of the main aims of the *Immorality Act*, 'to prohibit illicit carnal intercourse between Europeans and natives' (Statutes of the Union of South Africa, 1927:4), remained unchanged through the years. And nothing was altered between the 'twenties and the 'fifties regarding how unlawful carnal relations were defined. In substituting 'for section *seven* of the early Act' section 3 of the later Act states that, '*illicit carnal intercourse means carnal intercourse other than between husband and wife*' (Statutes of the Union of South Africa, 1950:217). This definition

is the same as the one in the principal Act (see Statutes of the Union of South Africa, 1927:6).

The first important change introduced by the 1950 Act is the replacement of the label 'natives'. This change was part of a bigger move by apartheid legislators to bring some 'order' and consistency in viewing their subjects. This, it must be noted, is a change that would keep evolving and transforming over the years. In the 1950 law, then, 'natives' were no longer to be regarded as natives but rather as 'non-Europeans'.

The second change that the Afrikaner law makers brought to His Majesty's project had to do with the 'defence of charge':

2. The following section is hereby inserted in the principal Act after section *two*:

2*bis*. It shall be a sufficient defence to any charge under section *one* or section *two* if it is proved to the satisfaction of the court or jury before whom the charge is brought that the person so charged at the time of the commission of the offence had reasonable cause to believe that the person with whom he or she committed the offence was a European if the person so charged is a European, or a non-European if the person so charged is a non-European (Statutes of the Union of South Africa, 1950:217).

In a debate on the Amendment Bill, Sam Khan, in a serious but mischievous tone, would say to the minister responsible:

The Minister must take this into account that today, littered through our statute book, there are *many conflicting definitions of a European*, and the result is that a person may be deceived. A person may be a European in terms of one definition and not a European in terms of another definition. A person may be registered as a European voter, and yet a non-European under this law, and that may give rise to an inference on the part of another person as to his or her race. It is for that type of case that I would like to ask the Minister whether before the third reading he will not go more carefully into the matter and whether some additional safeguard could not be introduced apart from the safeguard which has been moved by the hon. Member for Greenpoint' (Union of South Africa, 1950:3813; own emphases).

One establishes an identity in relation to other individuals and groups whom one feels are similar and belongs with, but at the same time, in relation to *other others* one feels are different from oneself.

It is remarkable that there is so little social psychological work locally on sexually intimate relationships because they are one of the most intuitively important sites for investigating reconstructions of identities and interpersonal and inter-group plots. Intimate relationships have serious implications for the self and the stories individuals tell themselves and tell others (see Murray, 1989). In fact, as we have said, intimacy connotes innermost nature or inward quality (Brown, 1993), as when a person says, 'my most intimate self'. When people tell others about their lives, one of the things they are likely to refer to is their sexual love relationships, in the narrower sense: their lover, partner, wife, husband. A person's relationships are used to give meaning to her or his life story.

> Sexual intimacy has increasingly become central to the way many people have come to give meaning to their inter-personal and social life.

As sexual intimacy has increasingly become central to the way many people have come to give meaning to their inter-personal lives and social world, the last few decades have seen a virtual explosion of material – films, television shows, self-help books, magazines – on this sort of intimacy. This increased importance of sexual intimacy and love to people's lives is not benign. One of the consequences of the cultural reproduction of intimacy is that it has become important in defining our sexual identities, practices, and relationships. It has also become equally important in defining other parts of our lives having little to do with sexual love or to being gay or straight. That is to say, having or not having sex, having or not having a certain relationship – found in the colloquial query, 'Who is she going out with?' Or the seemingly innocent, 'Are you married?' – also have favourable or unfavourable consequences in the development of meaning individuals give to their lives (not just to their sexual lives). What people call themselves, what happens between individuals, what people do, and the kinds of sexual relationships they establish, maintain or terminate, become the source of other identities and associations that get formed or rejected.

This can be linked to what constructionist and rhetorical social scientists have argued about in discussing the re-production of psychological and social life. Kenneth Gergen (1995), for example, has said that what we take to be true of things like mind or consciousness, of self or personality, of motivation and emotions, in fact finds its origins within relationships. John Shotter (2000), taking his cue from Wittgenstein, uses the terms *relationally-responsive activity* or *joint action* to talk about similar things. He interprets Wittgenstein as arguing that:

> we owe our very being as the kind of individuals we are to our embedding in a ceaseless stream of spontaneously responsive, living, bodily activity going on between the others and the othernesses in our surroundings, intrinsically relating us to them – I will call it relationally-responsive activity or joint action ... Not only do we owe what stable forms of life we live between us to their continual reproduction in this stream of spontaneously responsive activity, but also,

strangely, whatever possibilities that there are for their development and change (Shotter, 2000:2).

Lancaster (1997) has also argued that identity is a matter of locating and stabilising a self by way of the detour of the other. This is another way of saying that individuals need other people in relation to whom they define themselves, and get to know themselves, since identities are not natural, fixed 'things', but rather shifting productions that need other identities against which to 'fix' themselves so as to be understood. Identities work with other identities to hold each other in a more or less stable relation. A self, that is to say, is always established in relation to other selves.

Intimate relationships are therefore central to self-definition and, as we shall see presently, to group identities and inter-group differences. So we know that one of the relationships within which racial identification originates is the intimate relationship. Conversely, one of the relational sites from which sexual intimacy is produced is that of 'race'. A racialised identity such as Coloured, or Black, or White is defined here as a relational site within which we develop our understandings of certain signs and signifiers, like skin colour, ancestry, language, history, or ideology.

> Intimate relationships are central to self-definitions as they are to group identities and differences.

The public and intimate relations

I have suggested that intimate relationships have consequences that extend to extra-individual issues. Pierre Choderlos de Laclos, who wrote the novel on which the 1980s movie *Dangerous Liaisons* was based, is reported to have said that the world could be spared much pain if people were a little more careful about the misery that is often caused by a single dangerous intimacy. Laclos may have had in mind some of the unfavourable social implications, in addition to the favourable social ones, that attend intimacy (see Jamieson, 1998). For example, close relationships in the wider sense are an important training ground in social cohesion and group solidarity. But these relationships are equally useful tools to those who are desirous of maintaining power, in shoring up hierarchies, reproducing divisions, teaching who to hate, who is the outsider, what good people look like, who is the stranger, who is a possible friend, and so forth. In short, relationships from those early years of our lives are a good breeding ground for developing both positive and negative goals, love and hatred, racism and colour-blindness, division and unity. The apartheid legislators realised this early on. A lot more than the usual reconstructions of meaning takes place in this arena. Stories about who is part of us and who is 'other' are thick on this ground. As for the private and the public consequences, they reach even farther.

In a certain intriguing way 'mixed' relations bring the two outcomes we referred to (the favourable and unfavourable effects of relationships) together spectacularly. 'Mixed' relations link quite closely those large extra-individual discourses with the private moments between intimates. But this is no mere linking of the private and public, which anyhow happens with any close relationship. Relationships that are given the label 'mixed' link society and individuals, the cultural and subjective, the public and the private in ways 'unmixed' relationships rarely ever do. 'Mixed' relationships get to be seen as a (display of) confrontation between groups, and between the couple and the society that sees them as coming from different groups. Rather than being viewed as simply two people together, the existence of these relationships in racist societies becomes a larger, representative issue, and is looked upon as confronting the society's do's and don'ts, pushing the envelope of socially sanctioned desirability, legitimacy and propriety.

> Relationships that are given the label 'mixed' link society and individuals, the cultural and subjective, the public and the private in ways 'unmixed' relationships rarely ever do.

'Mixed' couples connect and willy-nilly act out a tightly wound complex of difference/sameness, exhibiting the politics of desire, sexuality, gender, 'race', culture, class, and history. What this implies also is that relationships such as marriages or close friendships, which are supposed to be driven by love or other socially or culturally valued emotions and sentiments, have a subtext. For example, films like *Guess Who's Coming to Dinner* (White people and Black people brought together by love) and *Pretty Woman* (an upper-class business man meeting and falling in love with a nice prostitute) and the interracial marriages in the local soap opera *Isidingo* (and the drama *Molo Fish*) have these purposes. In these scenarios, relationships are used not just to bring lovers together, but also to challenge existing prejudices or to establish new ideas about Blacks (Blackness) and Whites (Whiteness) (*Guess Who's Coming to Dinner*), to overturn stereotypes about businessmen and prostitutes (*Pretty Woman*), and to reconcile cultures, traditions, and 'races' (*Isidingo*).

Marriage, however, as with other intimate relations, can also be used to sow hatred, widen divisions, and prop up hierarchies. While intimacy can and is used to shape what individuals learn about home, 'us', insiders, it is also a fantastic aid for teaching whom not to trust, who is the outsider, part of 'them', the other. Narratives about who is not part of us (as opposed to who is), are thick around close relationships. Whereas the examples in the above paragraph show a little of what is hidden or glossed over when we think of close relationships (parents who would discourage their children from dating across the racial divide, friends who construct an outsider as a prostitute and not worth their company, the clash of traditions and customs, and so on), the television scenes of swastika-bearing young White children with their mothers and fathers in khaki apparel in Ventersdorp perhaps make it far clearer. Besides the obvious display of a certain political affiliation, families in uniform illustrate the point that close relationships (the family) are usable as part of the tools in trying to sustain power inequalities, social castes, classes, and divisions. Perhaps the important point to take note of is that the act of calling a relation-

> While intimacy can and is used to shape what individuals learn about home, 'us', insiders, it is also a fantastic aid for teaching whom not to trust, who is the outsider, part of 'them', the other.

ship 'mixed', against questions of permissible relations, is to pull public and private discursive practices close together, into each other, one against another. Calling a relation 'mixed' is in this respect a decisive epistemic act of violence. To say a person is involved in a 'mixed' relationship is not simply to name a set of practices but, more crucially, to pass judgement and construct a practice as socio-pathologic and illegitimate.

Rather than being seen as simply two people together, relationships that are called 'mixed' in racist societies confront the society's ideas of do's and don'ts, what is desirable and what not, what is acceptable and what not.

We have indicated that what we come to see as desirable or undesirable, good or bad, proper or improper, moral or immoral, 'mixed' or pure, and legitimate or illegitimate relational practice is not just the result of what is here-and-now, but that these binaries are produced by particular historical, economic, political and cultural conditions. A telling instance is that in October of the year in which the *Immorality* and the *Mixed Marriages Acts* were repealed, 1985, the Nederduitse Gereformeerde Kerk 'reversed a previous policy decision that racially-mixed marriages were "undesirable"' (South African Institute of Race Relations, 1987). The highest body of that church found and released a statement that the Bible did not actually prohibit 'mixed' marriages. Still, the church 'felt that different social circumstances, philosophies, and world views, as well as cultural, socio-economic, and other factors could create serious tensions in mixed marriages' (*ibid.*).

It is especially with the help of this understanding – which buttresses the fact that identity and other relational social and personal practices are historically embedded, culturally, economically and politically constructed, and discursively produced – that it becomes easy to see how a particular inter-personal relationship can be, and is, more than just a simple sum of those individuals involved, as hypothesised in balance, exchange, or equity theories (see for example Ickes & Duck, 2000b; Rusbult, 1980). It is actually never possible to come up with a sum of the elements of a relationship that make it always good or not, happy or sad, workable or not. Psychologists, then, can never say with absolute certainty that a young beautiful poor woman will always want to marry a rich man, or that a pretty young Coloured female will desire a handsome young Coloured male. Despite the fact that the above implies that intimacy is a moving, continual, and a permanently re-constructive (dialogical) effort towards meaning, knowledge of self and other, calling certain relationships 'mixed' means the embrace of identity as primordial, static, and imposed or ascribed without negotiation. Certain relationships, that is, are marked by society as undesirable, or bad, or improper, or immoral, or pathological because *the parts are said not to fit together, period!*

Socio-pathic relations and the orderly society

To speak of 'mixed' relations is to call attention to an error, at least an outlier, a social psychological deviation. Calling intimate relationships 'mixed', as we intimated, is part of a pathologising and criminalising socio-biological discourse (see Ellison & de Wet, 2002; Hook, 2002). This discourse suggests that there are *pure* relationships (for, it suggests, elsewhere, there are pure bodies, pure cultures, pure 'races', pure identities). It then prescribes that mixing with people who are unlike you in *a specified respect* is contaminating your body, your culture, your 'race', yourself. (However, the discourse also says intimacy with persons who are *like* you in a specified respect contaminates your body, your culture, your 'race', yourself.) When one says *this is a 'mixed couple,'* one signals the bringing together of things that are opposed to one another 'in nature', 'authentically'. One of the primary things this 'hailing' of the 'mixed' couple does is that it leaves the great majority of relations unhailed and unnamed. At the same time, there is an implicit meaning that what has been brought together is unnatural, unclean and insupportable, diseased and illicit.

Some examples should make this clearer. One does not call a relationship between an Black male and a Black female, or even that between two Black females (although the latter is also historically socially pathologised and legally criminalised), *a Black relationship*. Or, on seeing a young Coloured woman and young Coloured man, one does not usually say, 'those two, they are having *a Coloured relationship*'. Such statements would be deemed ridiculous. A relationship between people of the same 'race' group has no name and stays unspoken in the racial register because it is commonplace, average, everyday. These relationships remain unhailed because they are 'normal' (in a racist or

> Calling certain relationships 'mixed' is part of a pathologising and criminalising socio-biological discourse.

> A relationship between people of the same 'race' group has no name and stays unspoken in the racial register because it is commonplace, average, everyday.

racialising world). In this respect, 'normal' things are of course those things in the racial landscape that we 'expect' to see – for example, a Coloured male and a Coloured female.

But you may have noted that whereas the relationship between the two Black women has no 'race' name, it has a sexual name. This is one instance in which an apparent sameness is remarked on. (But, of course, this apparent sameness is itself different. I turn to the idea of sameness/difference presently.) Yet, we should note that the fact that the sexual name of a relationship is visible derives from the same source that draws attention to a close relationship between a Black woman and a Coloured man. Our histories and cultures have made us notice two Black females acting 'too intimately' with one another, because they have taught us to take note of differently 'raced' individuals with each other. Both kinds of relationship have been pathologised and criminalised by the intertwined network of social, economic, scientific, legal, and political regulations.

I earlier noted that when we say a relationship is 'mixed' we are seeing and calling attention to the stake of the public and of communities in personal and private matters. Dubow (1995: 181) has said that the narrative of the danger of mixing was acute precisely 'because it operated in the private arena as well as the public arena; it linked anxieties relating to sexuality, the family and the individual with the broader concerns of race'. The term 'mixed' is thus inspired by segregationist ideologies, sexual biological essentialism, begs questions of normality, and revives ideas of miscegenation (see Butchart, 1998; Dubow, 1995;

A relationship between two black people has no race name.

Gilman, 1985). Colonial and apartheid legislators seem to have known this when they deployed the word 'mixed'. That is also to say, even if apartheid legislators had not explicitly outlawed but simply pointed out 'mixed' marriages they would have, by that discursive act, brought home the idea of what are and what are not permissible marital relations, what is and what is not a 'normal' family. The act of saying some relations are 'mixed' (thus indicating that there are others that are not 'mixed') tends to stigmatise them, bringing to our attention how individuals should think of their private lives. One of the reasons this is so is because when we point and say '*so-and-so is in a "mixed relationship"*' we are re-producing and dramatising the narrative of difference/sameness, saying something not just about the couple but about our selves and our desires, our society's politics, our economy, and our culture.

It is true that *any* social relationship is capable of linking and theatricalising this story of sameness/difference, that all relationships have the potential to dramatically change social, cultural, and political plots (see for example, Gergen, 1995; 2002; Shotter, 2000; Shotter, nd.). In a relationship, an individual continually constructs and reconstruct himself or herself, the other person, and hence the relationship itself. The usual way to say it is to note that *people change*. What is unsaid here, however, is that relationships have a potential to and in fact do change individuals' emotions, activities, and knowledge. In other words, people are changed in or by their relations to other people. Shotter calls this 'the responsive order' (2000:2), and observes that this is because of the dialogical structuring of our relations both with respect to each other and the others around, a process that begins its appearance as soon as a second living human being responds to the activities of a first (Shotter 2000; Shotter, nd.).

As I have suggested, sexually intimate relationships, perhaps because of their privileged positioning in contemporary society and culture, are more capable than other kinds of relations to structure and alter our being and relating practices. More than other kinds of relations, intimate ties have implications for the individual, the partners, and the family, as well as for those not directly involved in the relationship, including the community and political society.

But this picture of 'purified', normalised and 'mixed', pathologised relations and the discourse of difference/sameness leaves out a few other important things. One of these is that social, economic, and cultural politics are rarely ever stationary. Contrary to popular belief, apartheid was not static, and more importantly, never uniformly bad to Black people or always good to all White people. The policy of apartheid was not born fully formed. It developed over time and underwent several alterations. There were several deliberate and unforeseen changes the country went through. Apartheid was favoured by some Black people and seen as evil by a few White people. So when we look at the (ab-)normalisation of what was labelled 'mixed' relations and the (dis-)orderliness of apartheid society we have to bracket (at certain points) many of the assumptions that we have inherited from that history. Much of that history presumed that identities are given, ascribed by the physical body, and that they are for life, permanent and obvious. Yet, as I have just said, it must be recognised that despite this assumption apartheid discourse itself was not seamless. It was characterised by change, sometimes turning against itself. In a debate in the apartheid parliament in 1950 on a Bill introduced by the government to amend the law on inter-racial sexual relations, the communist member of parliament Sam Khan cleverly remarked that the minister of justice's intended changes would not be sufficient to cover the case of a person who is deceived into believing that the person with whom the offence is committed belongs in the same group. Under the *Immorality Act* it was sufficient defence for the accused person to show that he or she had reasonable cause to believe that the person with whom the accused had illicit carnal intercourse was of the same 'race' as him or her (see Box 12.1).

Under another piece of apartheid legislation, any woman, including a White woman, who married or cohabited with either a Black or a Coloured man, was transformed in law to become a Black or Coloured. This was part of a peculiar logic and reasoning that makes it not only necessary, essential, but near impossible not to question the normality and truth of apartheid, and to seek to (mis-)understand its prescriptions about identities and relationships. As illustrated here, the language of apartheid was a language in the service of madness or at least an absurdity. Perhaps it was a half-madness, by which I mean that apartheid was not totally abnormal because it was also a normalising, protecting discourse. It was out to safeguard – ostensibly for everyone, but really on behalf of Whites – the purity of 'races'.

Sameness/difference in intimate relationships

But, somebody might ask, what about the obvious things like skin colour, like the way people speak, where one grew up. These things make a difference don't they? And what about culture, traditions, place of birth: don't these things show that people are different and therefore should keep to those who are like them? Do these things not affect the chances of a relationship being successful? The answer is yes, they do. But the question that goes hand in hand with this and which should be asked, is: Why do they?

In its obsessive, and some would say, paranoid need to *categorise* people as belonging to this or that 'race', colonialism and apartheid maintained that this was to be based not on what the person claimed to be, or could be, or any other hypothetical situation. A person's racial identity and population group was to be based on *appearance* and what others claimed the person to be, which was called *general reputation* (see Box 12.1). But, regarding appearance, we have to bear in mind that *appearance as identity* or *appearance as difference* only makes sense from a certain discursive angle, within a particular ideology. It is from this angle that we learn to see appearance in certain ways. In the same moment we are 'blinded' or 'disabled' to see it in other ways.

When we consider reputation as identity it actually contradicts the apartheid schema on so many points that it is surprising it formed part of how people were defined. Reputation comes out of habit. We are not born with habits. They are 'unnatural', socially acquired, things. One acquires a habit from doing stuff in a particular way, living in a certain way among a given group; that is, going about one's life. For instance, it does not come naturally to people to eat with chopsticks, to talk with a Cape Flats accent, to dance well, and so on. People learn from those around them. They are taught by society and culture to *see* certain things and to be blind to others (as important). Thus the need to classify people into 'racial' and ethnic categories is what assigns importance to appearance and reputation. Such things as brown hair, or a light complexion, or having green eyes, then become critical in social relationships. Differences or sameness based on such things as skin colour, hair, accent and surnames get to be all-important because they are made so by a regime and discourse preoccupied with 'race' and not because they are naturally significant markers of identity. Identifying marks, whether one has a European- or African-sounding last name, and of course skin colour, have been given special 'value' and therefore can be re-evaluated.

But note that, notwithstanding appearance, general acceptance, and when and where these become significant, under apartheid a person who voluntarily admitted to being Coloured or Black (or a White woman who married a Coloured or Black man) could not be classified as White. In other words, irrespective of how White a person looked or how he or she was treated by White neighbours, friends, colleagues, hypothetically if the person said he or she was not White, that person could not be classified as White. In addition, a person could not be regarded as both Coloured and Black at the same time, or Coloured and White at the same time. To illustrate the ludicrousness of the law of apartheid, let's take an example. Let us say a son was born of a White father and Coloured mother. The son looks lighter than his mother. Because of certain political or other kinds of decisions by one or both of the parents the son grows up to be generally accepted as White. However, later, because of certain political or other kinds of decisions, the son, grown into an adult man, claims for himself a Black African identity. As a heterosexual man he then meets, is attracted to, and ends up getting married to a Coloured woman. How do you imagine the development of the way of life of such a person? We can't really say for sure. But if it is possible that the son did not encounter too many difficulties in getting to be a White-looking Black man, what we know is that there are immense and complex problems he will have to confront thanks to the existent regime of 'race' and its inflexibility that prevents movement between identities (see de la Rey, 1997; Meintjies, 1993; Sunde & Bozalek, 1993).

In a similar vein, a woman known to be Coloured by others might not '*feel*' (by which I suggest that emotions are important to identities) or call herself Coloured, depending on her politics. It is in this caveat, where parentage, racial politics, politics of everyday life, and the often ignored emotions surrounding identity play a role, that the roots of the shorthand phrase 'so-called', which is sometimes applied to Coloureds, will be found. Not a straightforward thing to begin with, identity (Coloured, like Black, like African, not forgetting, White and European) multiplies and shifts and fragments as a person may call himself or herself other, 'unofficial' or 'generally unacceptable' names and things. If we ignore such things as the extent of an individual's project of positioning, of self-description and the emotional investment in establishing and affirming an identity (especially in the face of the schema of apartheid where one's identity and group membership were based almost wholly on appearance and reputation), we are likely to go on missing a lot of what goes into identification and relationships.

Given all this, someone may ask: Why do we continue to depend on the racial categories when interacting with others? Why can't people just go beyond appearance? For some people, especially in the post-apartheid, post-Truth-and-Reconciliation-Commission landscape, the issue of 'race' will be increasingly incidental. This may be seen as a way to wean ourselves from a dependence on 'race' discourse, as well as being a way to get beyond its uncomfortable histories and politics. The need to forget history may be motivated by an evasion of the unequal conditions in our country. However, this evasion, like the pervasive social and economic inequities, may well have been generated by South Africa's racist past. Such evasion is attributable to social-psychological repression and inhibition. For many people, keeping quiet about 'race' is an apparently easier way to deal, or more precisely, not to deal, with a discomfiting subject that could get them into trouble (Billig, 1998; Page, 1996). So the answer to the question of why people continue to factor in skin colour, accent, hair texture, and complexion is that appearance continues to matter (West, 1995), and, as we all know, it is not only how we look, racially, that makes the difference. People battle to get beyond 'race' because it is not that easy to forget history: the history of racial sameness/difference is embedded in the present social and economic structures.

Having said this we should reiterate that the notion of sameness/difference is not as easy as it appears. In point of fact, it is rather elusive. And, in addition to issues of racial identities and distinctions on their own, there is always a need to pay attention to how 'race' intersects with sexuality, class, and gender, and how their overlapping trajectories render inter-personal relationships ever more complex. Focusing on appearance or reputation, on marks of identity and difference, often shows itself to be an over-simplification. When looking at 'mixed' inter-personal relationships we need to pay attention to the multiple discursive practices which structure or go into constructing these relationships and the individuals 'inside' them, as well as those looking at them from the 'outside'. Of course, the structuring effects of these discourses are not restricted only to 'mixed' relationships. I now turn to two of these discourses to explore the possible ways in which they structure(d) intimacy.

Box 12.3 Socio-pathic acts

According to the Minister of Law and Order, Mr Louis Le Grange, a total of 929 persons had been arrested, 829 charged, 733 brought to trial, 221 acquitted, and 527 found guilty in terms of section 16 of the *Immorality Act* of 1957 from the date of the Act's inception to the date of its repeal on 19 June 1985. The Ministry of Law and Order could not explain the discrepancy between the total of people brought to trial and the numbers acquitted and found guilty. Mixed-race couples continued to face hardships despite the repeal of the *Prohibition of Mixed Marriages Act* of 1949 in 1985. In Johannesburg two children of a mixed marriage between a white man, Mr MA Roux, and his Coloured wife, Rona, were refused permission to attend the Whites-only Malvern Primary School in Belgravia – despite their having been allowed to live in a White group area by permit.

In March, 1985, a White store owner in Kirkwood (near Port Elizabeth), Mr Jack Salter, who had had his trading licence revoked by the Kirkwood municipality because he was married to a Coloured woman, won a supreme court case to have the licence renewed. The municipality had revoked the trading licence because, it said, his wife's Coloured classification automatically made him a Coloured person. He was thus barred from trading in a White group area. The judge, Mr Justice NW Zietsman, ruled that it had not been proved that Mr Salter was not White. He also found that Mr Salter could not be reclassified as a member of another race group unless the procedure laid down in the *Population Registration Act* had been followed.

A Cape Town man, Mr Albertus Smit, was found guilty in July of contravening the *Group Areas Act* of 1966 by living with his Coloured common-law wife of 12 years in a White group area. Mr Smit was under the impression that the area, Maitland, was a 'grey' area, where mixed-race couples could live together. The magistrate said, 'you were born in South Africa and should have known better.'

In a similar case, Mr Johannes Meintjies appeared in court for allowing his Coloured common-law wife to live with him in a White group area. He was subsequently found guilty. The magistrate, Mr MJC Tolken, cautioned and discharged the couple, saying that he had no power to change the law, only to apply it (South African Institute of Race Relations, 1987:8–9).

(De)stabilising discourses

I have headed this section '(de)stabilising discourses'. By this I mean that discourses such as those we inherit from the histories of our society, cultures, and political economies are usually both stabilising and destabilising at once. But, someone may ask, what are they precisely, these (de)stabilising discourses, and how can they be both stabilising and destabilising at the same time? Take a movement such as the Black Consciousness Movement (BCM) as an example. In defining Blacks as inclusive – incorporating Coloureds, Indians/Asians, and Blacks (by which I mean the people variably classified 'native' and 'African' by the apartheid regime) – the BCM was both redefining Blackness and bringing and holding together those who were historically oppressed, economically oppressed, and culturally subjugated (Biko, 1996). It was, in short, erecting and stabilising the currents of Black revolt; the oppressed, unequivocally people of colour, were united in their suffering and could therefore unite in the eradication of oppression.

But, at the same time, owing to how it conceived of Blackness, in saying there was no difference between the various socio-political groups that constitute people of colour, the BCM also concealed the instability of the category of Blackness itself. To say there are no differences between Indians/Asians, Coloured and Black Africans is to gloss over things. It is true that the BCM was intent on disrupting the segregationist discourse, and it could therefore be argued that it was necessary to hide certain doubts, anxieties, ambivalences and ambiguities regarding identities. It could then be said that when the movement set out to challenge the view of Blacks as essentially different from Coloureds it had to efface some of these uncertainties. This is precisely why the Black liberation movement is seen as a social and political *strategy* to destabilise the apartheid differentiation between Coloureds and Blacks. Intentions and strategy notwithstanding, the point is, the BCM inserted its own version of differences and defined its own kind of samenesses in the social and political landscape, thus shifting the fulcrum of difference and sameness that applied to South Africans.

By the same token, the discourse of separate 'races' was intended to naturalise and normalise what is socially or culturally, and hence arbitrarily, essential to a group and groups of people. What was then inessential was marked as different, unnatural, deviant. It is in this way that historical, economic, cultural and political discourses were, and indeed are, both stabilising and destabilising. The implication for those who step outside of the limits of a particular discursive world, the possible relations one cannot and can have, and the kind of person one is allowed to have relations with, and even the kind of being one can or cannot be, can well be imagined. In this regard, Foucault (1979) reminds us that discourse not only transmits and produces power, but also undermines and exposes it, making it possible to thwart it.

Among a host of impulses found in the history of South Africa there are then two in particular that urge the interrogation of the constructed difference between, or sameness of, Coloured and Black subjects. These impulses, it must be understood, are not simply about 'race'. More significantly, they are the formative background, the very social and discursive foundation, to reading 'mixed' and 'mixing' of identities and relationships. Investigating identities of Coloured–Black partners, and the relationships themselves, studying the discourses of sameness and difference which get produced, must be read against these historical impulses which continue to affect everyday exchanges, personal relationships, individual lives, inter-group processes, and cultural-psychological functioning. The role of history cannot be exaggerated with regard to how the identities of individuals and groups living within South Africa (which includes what came to be known as the Bantustan homelands, which were supposed to be outside South Africa) were formed to begin with (Moosa *et al.*, 1997; Stevens & Lockhat, 1997).

The first of the historical impulses is the racial classifications of apartheid. That classifying individuals as part of this or that 'population group' has had particular effects in respect of identification is well known. For example, the *Race Relations Survey* used to report on 'population and race classification' which included 'race' reclassification and matters related to the *Immorality* and *Prohibition of Mixed Marriages Acts*. Reports are that in the 1980s some 1 000 people were seeking reclassification yearly, and between 1983 and 1990 about 7 000 individuals had their race changed. In 1983 it is reported that the Department of Internal Affairs dealt with 1 189 reclassification applications, of which 997 were approved; in 1986 there were 1 642 and 1 102 went through (South African Institute of Race Relations, 1984; 1987). It must be noted that the greatest number of reclassification applications were from being classified Black to Coloured, and from Coloured to White. Only a small number wanted to be reclassified Black (Christopher, 1994; see also Chapter 5, this volume).

Of course racial reclassification of people did not operate independently. This programme was tied to other discursive moves of the White government of apartheid. For instance, the government wrote 'race' into the physical spaces (segregating living areas), the economic conditions (reserving jobs for Whites, not allowing 'non-Whites' to own certain businesses or, in certain areas, instituting preferential employment policies for certain 'races', etc.), into moral spaces (different churches for different 'races'), and into private and sexual lives (making inter-racial sex illegal). Given such a far-reaching policy it is not surprising that these public/private spaces continue to be defined, lived, spoken about, erected, and contested along racial lines. It is not difficult, then, to imagine that, for example, living in a space designated Coloured or Black or White, continuing to live surrounded by people who look like you, and interacting mostly with 'your own kind', can have a certain effects on the identities of those who live in and through these racialised spaces. It is easy to see why a 'race' discourse continues to be employed by the erstwhile subjects of apartheid law in personal, economic, social, and political life. These discourses continue to influence whom we choose to associate with, befriend, love, marry, or have sex with.

The second historical impulse is tied to the definition of the term 'Black' given to us by the BCM to include, formally, Black Africans, Indians/Asians, and Coloureds (Biko, 1996). As described earlier, the BCM defined Black as that collectivity that bore the brunt of White discrimination and oppression. This definition was important in many respects. For our purposes here, though, its importance is in serving as a counter-explanation to the powerful, legal impulse of apartheid's classificatory system. The BCM helped to redefine important aspects of identity and to redraw the constructed division between Coloureds, Indians/Asians and Black Africans. It re-directed debate towards the differences and violence that inhabited the boundary between Whites and people of colour. Also, it is crucial to recognise that the rhetoric of Black power was not only limited to organised political work. It would spread to influence, open up, and provide an alternative way for Coloured, Indian/Asian, and Black African people (that is, all people of colour) to experience, struggle with, negotiate, (re)construct, and make sense of their individual identities and intimate relationships against the background of the discursive structure of apartheid.

Consequences of conflicting discourses

What are the consequences of these conflicting historical efforts to (de)stabilise identities? In order to adequately respond to this question we must take note of the fact that efforts to hold identities in place are dogged by the idea that identities fit into neatly defined categories and tightly bound groups. The problem that such efforts sooner or later face is that categories and groups do not stay the same forever. Insofar as the social, political and economic circumstances with regard to which categorising and grouping was done change over time, the membership of categories and groups is also likely to shift. In other words, as circumstances change, notions of who is 'us' and who is 'them', who is 'in' and who 'out', also alter. Or, as a society is transformed and politics takes a different direction, who can be part of a group and who cannot gets reassessed.

However the problem of identity arises most sharply when others wish to change the way groups are drawn or when they challenge they manner identities themselves are thought of. Attempts to (re)define and (re)group identities are thus always struggles over and for people's bodies and minds. Definitions, as part of discourses, mobilise for subscribers and seek out supporters.

Common element between (de)stablising discourses

There is one commonality between the two impulses of sameness/difference worth noting. It is important to observe that there are similar difficulties attached to the BCM definition of 'Black' and the apartheid definition 'White'. This becomes especially apparent when addressing Black–Coloured relationships. Although they transmit, give off, or result in *divergent* social identities and political practices, what is common to both impulses is their *will-to-name*. In other words, although there was a difference between identity categories defined by apartheid legislators and executed by the 'race' classification board, and the identity categorisations contained in the writings of the Black consciousness philosophy, the element common to both was the political desire to name 'them' and 'us'. Proponents of both seem to have a need to define, classify and reclassify people. There is of course no way we can equate apartheid's objectifying 'race' regime and the movement for national freedom. Nevertheless, there is a tendency in both to essentialise identities, to think of people in freeze-frame, to reduce complexities and processes. This is invariably what definitions of identities tend towards: they hold practices in a time and a place, while they try to recruit people, while they seek support and endorsement.

So both the 'race' classifications of apartheid and the definition of Blackness of the BCM had essentialist tendencies, albeit *to varying degrees*. Both wanted people to subscribe to them and they each had their supporters. So what? One consequence of these different discourses for Coloured–Black relationships might be that a Coloured individual will imagine and engage in a relationship with a Black individual as with a *racial* other (because the individual thinks of himself or herself and others as part of essentially different 'races'), as opposed to an inter-*cultural* or inter-*ethnic* or inter-*class* one. (It is important of course to note that discourses of 'race' and racism incorporate cultural and ethnic discourses of difference into those of physical attributes and genetic predispositions (see for example, Chapter 4, this volume). But another Coloured individual, accessing another discourse, might construct a relationship between him- or herself and a Black individual as one of absolute identification thanks to common membership or belonging to the same group. For those involved, such a relationship may not be thought of as inter-racial. Yet another possibility is that a Coloured–Black relationship may be spoken of as a relationship of different (or similar individuals) even though the character of this difference (or similarity) may remain unexplained, or be hard to explain, or be explained with the help of everyday language: for instance, a person would say 'they are different because of where they grew up' (or, 'they are the same because they both have green eyes').

The point is that even when Black–Coloured relationships might be seen as 'mixed' or 'unmixed' relationships, the identity constructions of the individual actors in these relationships and the representations of the relationships are always already dislocated and dislocating, even if these relations are seen as between two *racially* or *otherwise* different (or similar) people. Owing to these discourses, these relationships need to find new ways of being conducted and spoken about. They encourage us to think about the lives of the 'mixed' couples as insiders, and our own lives as outsiders, in new ways. All of this leads from the idea that given the historical impulses we have noted, the fact that there are inter-racial relationships is a challenge to those historical impulses (Woodward, 1999). And the fact that there can be Black–Coloured intimate relations that are not constructed as inter-racial doubles up the challenge. Close relations between people of different 'races' (or cultures) disrupt the stereotype of keeping to one's own kind and disturb the division of the world into outsiders and insiders; that is also to say, close relations between people of supposedly of different 'kinds' redraw or redefine what is a 'kind', what is 'normal', what is 'legitimate'.

When is difference not different and similarity not the same?

It is important not to interpret this as saying Coloured–Black relationships, as is the case with any relationships, are relations of a special or better type. A 'mixed' relationship is not 'naturally' a special, better type of relationships, as much as relating to one's kind is neither natural nor superior. The object has been to show how 'mixed' relations are, shall we say, 'mixed-up', marked, and illegitimised by historical, socio-psychological, and cultural economies. Put differently, there are no natural, pure, *a priori* lawful relations. Moreover, what is lawful may not be just. 'Mixed' relations might have been unlawful under apartheid, but this does not mean that they were unjust, wrong, bad.

It is crucial to stress the many-sidedness of the point here: for example, on one side, we cannot exhaust what can be said about 'mixed' couples because there are as many 'types' of these relations as there are couples; on another side, the originality of any relational situation, and so the complexity of 'mixed' types of relationships does not make them superior, weird, or inferior. There is a third side: overlapping the notions that these relationships are simply too much trouble – as traditional 'common-sense' has it in respect of 'mixed' relationships generally – our most important relationships, including those with our parents, always have 'trouble' as element of them.

Without over-generalising, there is a possible way out of the identity quandary in which many people find themselves. The primary thing to realise is that the quandary is an artifact of the destabilising impulses I have traced. The traces of apartheid, to put it differently, can be found on most of our bodies, in our minds, in our identities, and in our relationships. Having recognised this fact, one invariably proceeds to acknowledging that someone who was known as Coloured is likely to be different *in some way* from a Black person in our country. Relationships, are inevitably pulled in different directions because people always access different stories and languages about themselves. '*In some way*' signals that the assumed difference or sameness between Coloureds and Blacks is not simply taken to be exactly that written into South African life by apartheid ideologues, or mobilised by the liberation movement, or, for that matter, presented by the mass media (see Chapter 4, this volume). It suggests a yet-to-be-specified, less simple, less stereotypical, and less obvious sameness or difference. It is a sameness that acknowledges difference, and a difference that incorporates similarities. The difference/ sameness between Blacks and Coloureds is of this kind: suggestive of textured lives, nuanced identities, and moments full of contradictory impulses. Also crucial to state is that these contradictions are not unwelcome. In fact, contradictions may be at the core of individual growth. In challenging essentialist conceptions of identity and bounded belonging, Paul Gilroy (1997:303) reminds us that the tense relationship between sameness and difference affords insights into how socio-political life should be organised: 'We should try to remember that the thresholds between sameness and difference are not fixed; they can be moved; and that identity making has a history, even though its historical character is often concealed.'

Paul Gilroy reminds us that 'the thresholds between difference and sameness are not fixed, that they are mobile, and that identity making has a history, even though it is often concealed'.

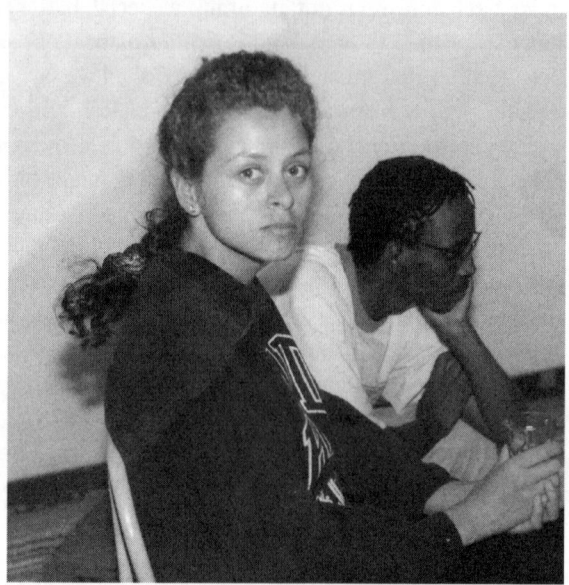

The major implication of saying partners in Coloured–Black relationships are similar and different in some yet-to-be-defined way, implies, therefore, that we can't merely say, 'All right then, the Coloured is racially or culturally different from the Black because of what happened in the history of this country ... whatever, we get the point, so can we go home now?' I am not promoting dismissiveness and apathetic acceptance. We also can't just say, 'We have always said there is no Coloured, we have always insisted that Coloured people are Black African, Coloured identity is a myth' (see van der Ross, 1979). The problem is that some 'mixed' couples and families may continue to face difficulties despite a denial of difference. Many of these problems were and still are generated largely by the destabilising collective and personal histories, intolerant cultures, and a racist society. Part of trying to overcome these, which in turn is an aspect of the move to overcome regressive notions of difference/sameness, is to work to dislocate our current understandings of relationships. This is something that Diran Adebayo (1996) tried to do in *Some Kind of Black*. That is, it *may* be possible to get beyond the problems and difficulties, at least ontologically, by reminding ourselves how reductionistic racialised identities are, how they dangerously over-simplify the heterogeneity and nuanced character of 'Colouredness', 'Blackness', and 'Whiteness'.

> ### Box 12.4 Mixed reactions on the repeal of 'mixed' relations
>
> The government said that as of 19 April 1986, six people were serving prison sentences under section 16 of the *Immorality Act* of 1957. Once this section was repealed, the authorities would consider taking steps in terms of section 69 of the *Prisons Act* of 1959 regarding their release. Section 69 allows the state president to release a prisoner or remit his/her sentence if he considers it expedient to do so. On 19 June 1986, section 16 of the *Immorality Act* and the *Prohibition of Mixed Marriages Act* of 1949 were repealed. Reaction to the move was mixed, several organisations labelling it 'window dressing'. Dr Nthato Motlana, who was the president of the Soweto Civic Association, said, 'We are not interested in the repeal of these laws. We want effective participation in the running of our country.' The Azanian People's Organisation and the United Democratic Front also dismissed the changes as cosmetic. The Progressive Federal Party welcomed the repeal of the laws, but their member, Mrs Helen Suzman, warned that South Africans should not bluff themselves that the government had embarked on the road to reform. A Gallup poll revealed that 51% of whites interviewed approved of the measure. A delegate at the Conservative Party's Transvaal congress in August called mixed-marriage couples 'murderers of their nations'. The deputy minister of constitutional development and planning, Mr Piet Badenhorst, said that in marriages between a white man and black woman the children would be classified 'Cape coloured'. In marriages between a white woman and black man the children would adopt the race of the father, except in case of an African father, in which case the children would be classified 'Cape coloured'. Children would attend schools of the group in which they had been classified, he said. Permits could be issued on application to mixed couples in which one member was white to live in white areas and for their children to attend white schools (South African Institute of Race Relations, 1986:4–5).

Conclusion

In this chapter I have sought to convey an understanding of 'mixed' relationships in general and Black–Coloured intimate relations specifically. I did this by looking at the ways in which relationships and identities are constructed and made normal or abnormal in history, culture, politics, and social life. I have argued that a thorough analysis of Black–Coloured intimate relationships is one that looks at the complex network of sameness/difference. In order to navigate this complex network, though, and so as to preclude oneself from thinking of the two persons in a relationship as simply different from each other or simply part of the same group, one has to keep check of one's understanding of identity categorisations. In this instance, this applies particularly to the terms 'Coloured(ness)', 'Black(ness)' and 'White(ness)'. Against the background of the paranoid, (de)stabilising segregationist discourse of apartheid and the discourse accessed by the national liberation movement, I have shown that when approaching identities and relationships referred to as 'mixed', there is always a need to understand the productiveness of the 'race names' we give ourselves and others. The principal motive here is to convey the need to be critical of many of the things we have come to take for granted.

It is important to end by reiterating that I have not said that it is a bad or good thing when an individual prefers others who look like him or her, and associates largely with his or her 'kind'. I have not said that 'mixed' relations are preferable or, conversely, to be avoided, across racial lines. Those who engage in 'mixed' relationships, I have said, are not a 'special' breed of people, inasmuch as Black men involved with Black women or White men with White women are engaged in neither natural nor superior intimate relationships. The crux of the problem behind this chapter has been the way 'mixed' relationships have been constructed and portrayed. My problem has been with the fact that colonialism and apartheid said people *must not* intimately associate with, desire, or marry those who did not look like them in appearance or who were not identified as part of their group by the state; and that those who did associate with, desire, or wish to marry others outside the determined parameters were putting themselves at considerable risk (of being hauled before a court and sent to gaol as *mad criminals, deviants,* even *perverts*).

Exercises for critical engagement

1   Find two articles in magazines or newspapers about intimate relationships. One of the articles should be the story of a relationship between two racially similar people, and the other should be the story of a 'mixed' couple. In the story you have found on a racially similar couple, try to identify for yourself some of differences between the couple that the writer constructs as insignificant. In the story you have found on a 'mixed' pair, identify some of similarities between the couple that the writer constructs as insignificant.

2   Find three stories about 'mixed' relationships in magazines, or newspapers, or from your older family members, or family friends, or from law reports. One story should be from before 1949, one from the period between 1950 and 1985, and the last should not be older than five years. The story from the middle period may be taken from foreign media. Compare the relationships from the three periods. What differences or similarities can you see in how the couples are characterised? What are some of the discourses employed in talking about the relationships? Also try to think about what is left unsaid in the stories you hear or read.

Recommended reading

Gilroy, P. (1997). 'Diaspora and the detours of identity'. In Hall, S. & K. Woodward (Eds.) *Identity and Difference*, pp. 276–330. London: Sage.

Ickes, W. & S. Duck (Eds.) (2000). *The Social Psychology of Personal Relationships*. Chichester: John Wiley & Sons.

Jamieson, L. (1998). *Intimacy: Personal Relationships in Modern Societies*. Cambridge: Polity Press.

Murray, K. (1989). 'The construction of identity in the narratives of romance and comedy'. In Shotter, J. & K. Gergen (Eds.) *Texts of Identity*, pp. 176–205. London: Sage.

Statutes of the Union of South Africa (1927). *The Immorality Act*, No. 5 of 1927. Pretoria: Government Printer.

Statutes of the Union of South Africa (1949). *The Prohibition of Mixed Marriages Act*, No. 55 of 1949. Pretoria: Government Printer.

Statutes of the Union of South Africa (1950). *The Immorality Amendment Act*, No. 21 of 1950. Pretoria: Government Printer.

Sexualities and Masculinities: Histories and Future Possibilities

PART FOUR

Lesbianism

Cheryl Potgieter

OUTCOMES

After having studied this chapter you should be able to:

- explain the essentialist and social constructionist perspectives on sexuality and lesbian identity
- explain various viewpoints as to what is understood by the term 'lesbian'
- debate whether or not lesbianism is foreign to African societies
- provide a historical perspective on the changing construction of lesbianism within psychology internationally, and
- trace the trends in psychological research on lesbianism in South Africa.

IN DOCUMENTING trends and silences in psychology in South Africa between 1948 and 1988, Mohammed Seedat (1992:xvi) highlights the manner in which a certain 'oppressive discourse historically informed' theoretical viewpoints and choice of research topics. Some of the theoretical and research subjects that received little priority within the discipline include social and cultural issues, psychologies of oppression, psychologies of women, and perhaps least of all, sexuality. The paucity of theoretical and research studies regarding sexuality is 'understandable' given that sexuality is traditionally one of the most taboo aspects of our condition (Levett, 1988). Where sexuality has received attention, the premise seems to have been that heterosexuality is the only or 'normal' sexuality and the focus of studies has been on heterosexual behaviours and identities. On the other hand, where homosexuality has received attention, the limited number of studies has been biased towards white gays and, to a lesser extent, white lesbians (Chan, 1989; Greene, 1994; Potgieter, 1997).

About this bias Berman has said that 'apartheid, and the privileges of whites in South Africa, have given disproportionate exposure to the presence of the white gay and lesbian community' (Berman, 1993:xx). She points out that this exposure has not been always positive but in fact contributed 'to the

Some of the theoretical and research subjects that have received little priority within the discipline of psychology include social and cultural issues, psychologies of women, and sexuality.

belief held by many black South Africans that homosexuality is an un-African, white, Western phenomenon' (*ibid.*). It should be noted that these biases in favour of White gays and White lesbians are not confined to this country. For example, Hill (1987:215) has noted that 'within the comparatively small amount of published studies on female homosexuality, the samples tend to be exclusively white, predominantly well educated, and upwardly mobile. Thus, in this marginalised area of research, black gay people's experiences and specifically black gay women's experiences have been rendered invisible.'

Essentialism refers to the assumption or ideas of essences or inner determinations of individuals and society. Predominantly used to refer to notions of biological, genetic and instinctual difference (also referred to as biological determinism), essentialist theories assume that people's identities, personalities, behaviours, and so on, are determined by inner and inborn aspects of themselves.

The aim of this chapter is to look at the ways in which lesbianism has been studied and constructed, especially in African societies. At the same time it sets out to challenge the silences on lesbianism within social psychology. To be sure, this is probably one of the very few texts in psychology in South Africa that devotes one whole chapter to the issue of lesbianism. I begin by looking at two general perspectives on thinking about sexuality. I then look at the historical and social emergence of lesbianism. Next I turn to the debates around how to define lesbianism. Because same-sex relations have tended to generate a great deal of debate, next I look at whether or not they are not un-African. The chapter ends by looking at international and local work on lesbianism.

How sexuality has been studied: Essentialist and constructionist perspectives

Essentialism takes various approaches to the study of sexuality. However, general beliefs held by essentialists would be that human behaviour is natural, and human behaviour is predetermined by genetic, biological or physical mechanisms. Sexuality is therefore seen as something that is fixed and not subject to change (Szesnat, 1997; Vance, 1989). Essentialists hold that human behaviours which are similar in form are the same across time and culture. These behaviours are a consequence of human drives, instincts or tendencies. As Szesnat (1997) points out, human beings would, in the essentialist view, have an in-built sexual essence. This internal essence would include a natural predisposition to a particular sexual orientation, which would be shaped differently by various material circumstances (environments), which accounts for the variety of sexual behaviours in different societies.

Essentialists generally assume that the categories 'homosexual' or 'heterosexual' are indicative of intrinsic differences within the individual. They would view homosexuality as a human attribute that varies from one person to another and from one culture to another, but they would argue that it is an intrinsic quality, just as heterosexuality is an intrinsic quality. When looking at *sexual identity*, essentialists would argue that being gay or lesbian is part of the innermost core of being human. Sexual identity is seen as given and something that shapes 'what we really are' (Weeks, 1986, 1987). As regards the related but more recent concept of *sexual orientation*, essentialist theorists would most likely look for culture-independent, objective and intrinsic properties that determine sexual orientation. The assumption would be that the categories of gay and lesbian are reflective of natural, intrinsic, unchanging and real differences (Epstein, 1987).

People like Jeffrey Weeks, who can be called a *social constructionist*, have a different view of sexuality. Weeks has argued that sexual identity 'is not a destiny but a choice' (1987:46). He says sexuality is intricately related to social and cultural relations. But like essentialist theories, constructionism is not a unitary and singular approach. As Vance (1989:19) points out, social constructionists 'show a gradual development of the ability to imagine that sexuality is constructed'. She uses the work of Katz (1976) to illustrate that there are different degrees of social constructionism. For example, in his earlier work, Katz documented the lives of gays and lesbians in earlier centuries. His work acknowledged that sexual acts like sodomy, as reported in documents of the seventeenth century, might not be equivalent to present-day homosexuality. He labelled same-sex acts of previous centuries as evidence of gay or lesbian persons. In his later work these 'sexual' acts were not evidence of gay or lesbian persons but rather were jumping-off points for a whole series of questions about the meanings of

Radical social constructivists argue that there is no essential, undifferentiated sexual impulse, sex drive or lust which resides in the body but rather that sexuality is constructed by culture and history.

these acts to the people who engaged in them and to the culture and time in which they lived (Katz, 1983). This example illustrates that there are various degrees of social construction, and that work which is labelled as social constructionist may have elements of essentialism. Vance (1989) states that this is evidenced in the work of many others (see Potgieter & Fredman, 1997). Therefore, within the constructionist movement, there are what we might call middle-ground constructionist and radical constructionists. Radical constructionists argue that there is no essential, undifferentiated sexual impulse, sex drive or lust which resides in the body due to physiological functioning and sensation. Radical constructionists say the sexual impulse itself is constructed by culture and history. In this case, an important constructionist question concerns the origins of these impulses, since they are no longer assumed to be intrinsic or, perhaps, even necessary.

The position of radical constructionism contrasts with more middle-ground constructionist theory (see Fredman & Potgieter, 1996; Katz, 1976). The latter implicitly accepts an inherent sexual impulse. This inherent impulse is what is then constructed in terms of acts, identities, community and object choice. The contrasts between middle-ground and radical positions make it evident that constructionists may well have arguments among each other, as well as with essentialists. Each degree of social construction points to different questions and assumptions when studying sexuality, possibly even to different methods and thus different answers.

Vance (1989) suggests that certain characteristics capture what we could term the minimum conditions or, alternatively, points of departure of social constructionism. These are that sexuality is a social construct, not a category independent of society and culture, and not objectively definable in every historical context. Categories and concepts employed in different cultures and historical periods are thus not objective, universal notions, but represent socio-cultural attempts to organise human experience. Social relations in all their diversity (even within a single culture) significantly shape the human experience, organisation and perception of sexuality. For the social constructionist there is no necessary or 'given' relationship between a particular pattern of sexual behaviour and the taking on of a particular pattern of sexual identity. What is crucial are the meanings individuals ascribe to their feelings, activity and relationships (see Gergen, 1985; Vance, 1989).

The historical and social emergence of 'lesbian'

Where does lesbianism come from? Is a lesbian here a lesbian there a lesbian everywhere and forever? Various writers have asked the question: 'When, how and why did the lesbian "emerge" or the term "lesbian" develop?' The terms 'lesbian' as well as a 'sexualised lesbian identity' were first used towards the end of the nineteenth century to label certain behaviours (Wolfe & Penelope, 1993). The reason for such labelling may have been to control and stigmatise women and particularly their sexual behaviour (see Chapter 12, this volume). Thus behaviour that had always taken place was now branded with negative connotations. Faderman (1981) and Jeffreys (1985) suggest that this labelling came about at this particular point in history because of the increasing possibility that women could live independently of men. They argue that this was as a result of the nineteenth-century women's liberation movement that threatened male hegemony and the institution of marriage that bound women to men in mandatory heterosexuality. The anxiety propelling this labelling was that 'if [women] gained all the freedom that feminists agitated for, what would attract them to marriage? Not sex drive, since women were not acknowledged to have one' (Faderman, 1981:237). For the male psyches threatened by economically independent and politically active women, the sexology theories which labelled certain sexual behaviour as deviant emerged at a convenient time to popularise arguments that a woman's desire for independence meant that she was not a 'real' woman.

A consequence of this negative labelling was that space was created for the law, the medical professions, religion, the media and culture to control women (Faderman, 1981; Wolfe & Penelope, 1993). Another consequence of the label was a radical alteration of public discourse around sexuality. Wolfe & Penelope (1993) assert that this labelling coincided with the first wave of women's liberation. Women were 'getting out of control', challenging patriarchy and thus needed to be controlled. Faderman (1981) further suggests that the development of the sexualised lesbian identity constituted a concerted effort on the part of sexologists to divide women, thus severing emotional and affectional bonds which bind all women against men. Thus, the sexologists were applying what could be seen as a 'divide and rule' strategy.

But Jeffrey Weeks (1986; 1987) does not agree totally with Faderman's viewpoint about the reasons for the social shifts or what they reflected. He argues that the emergence of homosexual identities was a product of struggle against prevailing norms. He asserts that sexologists were confronted by a new reality: people appearing in courts for certain behaviour (homosexual activity), and these people presenting themselves to the sexologists 'for help, largely as a result of a new politically motivated zeal to control manifestations of sexual desire' (Weeks, 1986:34). The definition of homosexuality (or lesbianism) as a 'distinct perversion' was an endeavour to, in some way, deal with the new reality. According to Weeks, it 'produced an inevitable response in the urge to self-definition' (*ibid.*; see also Chapter 8, this volume). Disagreement notwithstanding, what is clear from this discussion is that at a particular point in Western history, sexual activity began to define a certain type of individual (the lesbian, the gay, the bisexual, and so on).

So what is lesbianism?

Defining identities in general and sexual identities specifically, as I have suggested, is not as easy as it may appear at first. So I will look at which behaviours or relationships are excluded and which included in the category of lesbian. You will have noted by now that as with many concepts in social psychology, social science, and society in general, certain scholars and activists may prefer one definition while others will opt for another. You yourself may prefer one way of looking at an issue while your brother or sister may look at it differently and your friend may opt for a third way still.

The dominant assumption about sexuality is that persons can be slotted into certain sexual compartments: heterosexual, homosexual, bisexual and asexual. Together with this is the assumption that people are heterosexual until, in a manner of speaking, they are proven otherwise. Heterosexuality, in other words, is the dominant idea of sexuality (see Chapter 14).

Together with the dominant assumption that individuals can be slotted into sexual compartments – heterosexual, homo-sexual, bisexual – it is generally assumed that people are heterosexual until they are proven otherwise.

According to Golden (1987), when a person's *conduct* corresponds to one of these categories (heterosexual, homosexual, bisexual and asexual), it is assumed that the person embraces a sexual *identity* to match or complement the behaviour. Also, it is assumed that a person who engages in heterosexual sexual behaviour will assume a heterosexual identity – that is, the person would define herself as heterosexual. The same correlation between homosexual behaviour and identity is assumed. For example, Greene says 'those [women] who consider that their primary romantic/sexual attractions are to women are considered lesbian' (1994:389).

However, some writers have cautioned that the relationship between sexual behaviour and sexual identity is not that simple. They claim that sexuality is a fluid 'variable', and it should be seen as one part of a larger identity that is itself not static (Golden, 1987; Weeks, 1987). It should be clear then that in keeping with the notion that the category of lesbian is constructed in relation to the specific historical conditions, no consensus about the 'exact' definition of a lesbian is possible. In this regard, Clarke (1981:129) remarks that 'there is no one kind of lesbian, no one kind of lesbian behaviour, and no one kind of lesbian relationship ... Not all women who are involved in sexual-emotional relationships with women call themselves lesbians or identify with any partic-ular lesbian community'. Clarke has said that she only identifies a woman as lesbian when she says she is. What is significant in this definition is persons involved in same-sex relationships may not assume a gay or lesbian identity. Classifying lesbians purely by their engagement in same-sex erotic activity is assuming that a lesbian has 'something' (perhaps an instinct or inner charac-teristic) that makes her lesbian without her even knowing it (Kitzinger, 1987; Wolfe & Penelope, 1993).

In support of the above, in her interviews with college women, Golden (1987) found that many women identify as lesbian although they had been or were currently involved in a heterosexual alliance. In addition Weeks (1986; 1987) points out that certain individuals who identify as gay or lesbian and are part of the gay and lesbian community abstain from homosexual erotic activity. This again illustrates that the presence or absence of 'homosexual behaviour' does not automatically correspond to an identity.

The 'lesbian feminist' Adrienne Rich (1979:225) states 'before any kind of feminist movement existed, or could exist, lesbians existed: women who love women, who refused to comply with behaviour demanded of women'. African American feminists have also drawn on the 'women who love women' construction of the lesbian (see Cornwell, 1983; Lorde, 1984; 1988). Audre Lorde (1988:248), an African American 'lesbian feminist' said that 'when I say I am a Black Lesbian, I mean I am a woman whose primary focus of loving, physical as well as emotional, is directed to women'. Rich has proposed that instead of using the term 'lesbianism', thought should be given to a '*lesbian continuum*'. Highlighting the fact that trans-culturally and trans-historically women have been fundamentally committed to other women in diverse ways, she uses the term 'lesbian continuum' to refer to these experiences, though, at the time, there may have been no cultural conception of lesbianism (Rich, 1980).

This viewpoint has not been without its critics. Ferguson *et al.* (1981), for example, have asserted that defining lesbianism in this way erroneously over-looks the significance of sexual feelings and behaviour. Ferguson (1982:155) offers the following alternative definition: 'A lesbian is a woman who sees herself as centrally involved with a community of self-identified lesbians, whose sexual and erotic–emotional ties are primarily with women, and who is

'When I say I am a Black Lesbian, I mean I am a woman whose primary focus of loving, physical as well as emotional, is directed to women,' Audre Lorde (1988:248), an African American feminist said.

herself a self-identified lesbian.' Without de-emphasising the role of sexual behaviour, she argues that her definition includes both celibate and bisexual women as lesbians, as long as they identify themselves as lesbian.

Another group of feminists argue that lesbian is an identity which is not simply reducible to homosexual sexual practices. Lesbians thus need to come out, identify as lesbians and work actively against heterosexism and patriarchy (Jeffreys, 1990; 1993; Kitzinger, 1987). It could be argued that one of the limitations of this approach is that it excludes and denies the existence of those women whose sexual and affectional preferences are for other women but who do not identify as lesbians.

Zimmerman (1993) suggests that one way of answering this question would be to decide how inclusively or exclusively lesbianism is defined. Here it is suggested that women who define themselves as lesbian are lesbian, that is, self-identification will decide the issue. Others also suggest that this identifying title be confined to women who acknowledge that their sexual experience is predominantly with other women, although they might not use the word 'lesbian' to define themselves. This would prevent women who engage in heterosexual activity from being included, as well as men who, for whatever reason, might label themselves lesbian.

In Southern Africa, especially with regard to Black women, the issue of self-identified lesbian communities and self-identified lesbians is a bit more complicated (see Gay, 1985; Kendall, 1999; Potgieter, 1997; 2003). Firstly, many Black lesbians in Southern Africa are not part of 'self-identified lesbian communities' and, secondly, many do not label themselves lesbian although the majority of their sexual and emotional experiences are with women.

If nothing else two things are clear from this section. First, the question 'what or who is lesbian?' is not one that can be resolved easily or in absolute terms. Second, even feminists have not achieved consensus on the issue. What or who a homosexual is, just like what or who a heterosexual is, is defined differently by different theorists, researchers, and activists, just as it has been described differently over history and in different societies and cultures. This, then, leads us to look at how lesbianism has been viewed in African culture.

Un-African sexual practices and identities?

An argument that has been used by individuals and groups who have a history of opposing racial oppression, but who do not support the rights of gays and lesbians, is that homosexuality is un-African. Homosexuality is said to part of a corrupt Western society (Potgieter, 1997). This argument was put forward by a leading human rights lawyer in the defence of Winnie Madikizela-Mandela (the ex-wife of the former president of the country, Nelson Mandela) in a case in which she was accused of murdering a youth activist. The defense lawyer argued that she had in fact attempted to rescue the youth from his involvement with a White Methodist minister. The defence used homophobic rhetoric, linking homosexuality to *paedophilia* and in turn, foreign White culture. The defence argued that gay and lesbian sexual orientations are not found in Black culture *per se*, and that the same-sex practices of Black men and women can be explained by these people having been 'tainted' by homosexuality from 'White culture' (see Holmes, 1994).

The rhetoric of homosexuality being un-African has also been constructed by two prominent African politicians, namely former Pan Africanist Congress politician Khoisan X (previously known as Benny Alexander) and Zimbabwean president Robert Mugabe. In an interview with the Cape Town-based newspaper, *South*, Khoisan X was quoted saying, 'homosexuality is un-African. It is part of the spin off of the capitalist system. We should not take the European leftist position on the matter. It should be considered as a whole from our own Afrocentric position' (*South*, 13–17 June 1992). Mugabe has not been as 'subtle' in his public discourse regarding homosexuality. He has equated homosexuality with immorality, condemning it as 'an abhorrent Western import' and has said he finds it 'extremely outrageous and repugnant that such immoral and repulsive organisations should have any advocates' (*Mail & Guardian*, 4–10 August 1995).

Although the Constitution prohibits discrimination on the basis of sexual orientation, certain laws have not changed automatically and have had to be challenged. The most recent challenge was to recognise the legitimacy of children born to a lesbian couple by means of artificial insemination. The court ruled that Section 5 of the *Children's Status Act* (1987) was unconstitutional and that same sex partners who had children as a result of donated sperm or ovum be recognised as parents of legitimate children (see *Mail & Guardian*, www.mg.co.za [last accessed 26 March 2003]). An earlier case had legalised adoption of children by same-sex couples. The outcome of this case was successful. On the other side of things, same-sex marriages are presently still not legally recognised. This could probably be challenged within the next year, or alternatively, the law may be amended. Constitutional and legal changes are a starting point, but as psychology students we know that attitudes and ideologies do not automatically change when the law changes.

Historical accounts of female same-sex affiliations have been suppressed or overlooked by individuals who were documenting life in African societies and cultures. In addition, the issue of language or terminology presents a difficulty. Homosexual activity without persons labelling themselves as 'homosexual' is still commonplace, something which has been supported by research (Potgieter, 1997). As I have indicated, the label 'homosexuality', and thus what some would argue is the social construction of 'the homosexual', can only be traced to a relatively recent period in history and to a particular social, political, and cultural milieu.

In line with the general bias in sexuality research, scholarly work that has investigated homosexuality in various African societies has tended to pay attention to mainly male homosexuality (Potgieter, 1997). For example, anthropologist Evans-Pritchard (1970) documented the institution of 'boy wives' for military men among the Azande in Sudan. Parallel institutions or customs between women have not been emphasised. Judith Gay's study of 'mummy–baby' games among Basotho girls in Lesotho is an exception. According to Gay (1985), young girls start these games when they are still at primary (grade) school. In a mummy–baby relationship, an older girl acting as 'mummy' develops an intimate association with a younger one ('the baby'). Generally, the mummy presents gifts to the baby, who reciprocates by obeying and respecting the mummy. The two share both emotional and informational exchanges. Although Gay's study is the most in-depth one, Kendall (1999) has reported on evidence of similar female–female relationships in Lesotho. In her paper 'Women in Lesotho and the (Western) construction of homophobia', Kendall (1999) provides an account of woman marriage and general affectional relationships between women. However, this group of women are not labelled as 'lesbian' or anything else in this particular society.

A form of same-sex union that may be peculiar to African cultures is the institution of 'female husbands' or 'woman marriage'. The institution is not paid much attention except by Krige (1974) and Krige and Krige (1943). South African examples cited by Krige (1974) include: woman marriage among the Lovedu in the Northern Province, an institution by which it is possible for a woman to give bride wealth for, and marry, another woman; the rain queen Mojaji, who was known to have a number of wives; woman marriage among the Venda, although she says details about this tradition are limited; and, woman marriage amongst the Zulu (however, there is no information about how these marriages functioned within the society).

Two examples of Zulu woman marriages mentioned by Krige were told to her by a South African university professor who had collected the 'stories' in 1955: 'another case was that of an old widow with an only daughter, Nozinayitha ... The daughter courted and married a girl and found an unrelated man to act as "bull" (genitor)'; 'Councillor Musothsha Magwazi of the Court of Paramount Chief Cyprian from Nhlophenkulu Methodist Mission, Nongoma, told of a girl who came to his father to ask for a genitor for a wife she was going to marry' (Krige, 1974:27 & 28). The early British administration in Natal frowned upon woman-marriage, and women had to get past the White administrators to continue this tradition. Because colonial regulations required registration of each Zulu marriage and would not countenance a female husband, it became Zulu practice to register the genitor as the husband and the female husband as witness (ibid.:28).

These examples of same-gender relationships in South Africa show that the idea that homosexuality is un-African and a Western import is untenable. Just as other customs were 'tabooed' and outlawed by colonialists, the same could be said for institutionalised homosexuality within indigenous societies in South Africa.

An example of same-sex female relationships in African society is the story of Ifeyinwa Olinke. She lived in nineteenth-century Nigeria. Ifeyinwa Olinke was an industrious woman in a community where most of the entrepreneurial opportunities were seized by women, who thereby come to control much of the Igbo tribe's wealth. Ifeyinwa Olinke was overshadowed by her less prosperous male husband. As a sign of her prosperity and social standing, Ifeyinwa Olinke herself became a female husband to other women. Her epithet, Olinke, referred to the fact that she had nine wives. However, Amadiume argues that she was not lesbian. It could be argued that this writer sees homosexuality in a negative light, thus denies it. But we should be wary of forcing these relationships into the Western dichotomy of homosexual vs heterosexual (Amadiume, 1987:48–9).

There have been recent accounts which hold that 'female homosexuality' is an indivisible part of present-day Black South African society. Chan-Sam (1994) documents verbatim an interview with Bongi, a 24-year-old woman from Soweto who attended a boarding school for Black girls in the rural town of Nelspruit. Bongi recounts the tradition of 'amachicken' amongst the girls at the school:

> So you will be friends and share things. Very often this friendship can allow you to hold hands, kiss, talk in whispers: because you are sweethearts or sweeties. Sometimes it is called *amachicken* … The *amachicken* are the younger girls who are looked after by the older ones. Many *amachicken* share rooms with the older girls. I myself had a sweetie, but my heart was broken when she had to leave school. She was very good to me. She was very tender in love … she (the sweetheart) asked me if I was a lesbian. And that was the first time I heard the word. She said she didn't mind being friends with me, but if I was a lesbian she would be scared of me … but if we were *amachicken* she wouldn't mind (Chan-Sam, 1994:186–7).

This account is similar to one documented by Gay (1985). What is significant is that Bongi was not familiar with the label or identity of 'lesbian', and her *amachicken* would only continue the relationship if she was not 'lesbian'. This is indicative of the negative image which 'lesbian' conjures up. At the time of the interview Bongi was active in a gay and lesbian organisation and identified herself as lesbian.

Chetty (1994), drawing on a 1955 newspaper report, documents the life of a Black woman ('Coloured' under apartheid South Africa classification) who lived the life of a lesbian gangster in the 1950s. Gerti Williams, known as John

Williams, lived the life of a man for five years. The biographical account documents how she took on the role of what she assumed was 'a real man'. She also clearly states that she did not want to be a woman. The following excerpt from Chetty (1994:129) illustrates the identity which she assumed:

> All my gang are men, and the only feeling any regular man would have. But to be with the silly creatures all the time and to listen to their foolish chatter, I would never be able to bear. If I cannot be in the company of men, I would rather be dead. My earnest prayer each night is that God would be merciful to me and change me completely into a man. If it could be done by any operation, I would gladly risk it as no pain could be too severe if it meant the fulfilment of my desire … What is the end going to be, I don't know. There is no hope of marriage for us, and the raising of a family which I yearn for. We will have to spend the rest of our lives living like this, unless God is merciful and … lets me become a whole man.

The image of the lesbian as a man is reflected in the language used to refer to lesbians. They are referred to as '*man-vrou*' (man-woman) (Lewis & Loots, 1994). The women interviewed for the study stated that they were commonly referred to as '*nongayindoda*', which also means man-woman. Lewis and Loots remark that '… due to the silence surrounding lesbians, the homosexual subculture tended to be restricted to males' (1994:144). 'Derise' and 'Trish', two Coloured women interviewed by Lewis and Loots, said the only public images of homosexuality they had access to were gay men. They felt that lesbianism is not commonly spoken about as a result of the hostility of their families. Their discourse was thus silenced and 'led them to perpetuate their own silence in order to avoid discrimination and challenge' (Lewis & Loots, 1994:144).

Mention has also been made of lesbian *sangomas* (Gevisser, 1994). Chan-Sam (1994) interviewed a lesbian sangoma; she had another sangoma as a partner. These examples serve to underline the point that although same-sex unions are known to exist in African societies, they may not necessarily be labelled lesbian as they often are in a Western context. The terminology used to provide examples of 'homosexuality' in non-Western societies is completely inappropriate for the 'phenomena'. Scholars have argued that using these Western labels, even when modified, could obscure more than they clarify (Lancaster, 1987; Potgieter, 2003; Wekker, 1999). The point to be stressed is that there is ample information that negates the discourse that same-sex female relations are un-African, non-existent or an import of decadent Western society.

International trends in psychological research on lesbians

I have suggested that, to understand present trends in psychological research on lesbians, an historical perspective is important. The following section provides an overview of the changing conceptions of homosexuality internationally over the past five decades. The final section focuses on psychological research in South Africa. The overview is simplified and you are referred to Potgieter (1997) for a much more detailed and in-depth discussion.

Homosexuality as a sickness

During the 1930s, the dominant view amongst psychologists was that homosexuality was a sickness. Empirical support for this essentialist view came in the form of clinical case studies that traced the antecedent conditions which resulted in homosexual symptoms. In the early 1930s, two related studies were published. These studies provide an illustration of how the classic essentialist conception of homosexuality was translated into scientific prescriptions about sexual practices.

During the 1930s, the dominant view amongst psychologists was that homosexuality was a sickness.

The first study was conducted by psychologists Terman and Miles (1936). In order to validate their test of masculinity–femininity (M-F), Terman and his co-researcher included a sample of male homosexuals. The purpose was to demonstrate how a group of individuals with reputed cross-gender identification would compare with the general, 'normal' population. Terman went on to determine the cause of the homosexuality. He concluded that although biological factors could play some role, psychological conditioning played a major role. He saw the homosexual as a person who had failed to achieve and maintain adult heterosexual modes of sexual expression, and who was unable to meet the responsibility of establishing and maintaining a home (which involved the rearing of children).

Psychological research on female homosexuality echoed the sentiments of Terman. Research portrayed the homosexual female as sick, someone who had 'bad' child-rearing experiences, and lacking the ability to take on adult responsibilities. Caprio (1954), in research based on data from patients, prostitutes and fictional stories, concluded that his (lesbian) subjects were pathological. These findings were generalised to all lesbians, describing them as 'emotionally unstable and neurotic' individuals who needed to be recognised as 'sick and immature' women leading lives that 'ultimately result in frustration and loneliness' (Caprio, 1954:304). Two years later Bergler (1956) described lesbians as masochists, suffering from oral regression whose lesbianism was a result of unresolved weaning problems. Thus, most of the psychological literature of this period described lesbianism as a form of immaturity, an ego deficit, a narcissistic condition, or developmental delay. During the period between 1939 and 1960, *Psychological Abstracts* cite 22 articles that mention lesbianism. The majority of these articles suggest 'curing' homosexuality through psychoanalysis or shock therapy (Sang, 1989).

Homosexuality de-pathologised

Kinsey and his colleagues' *Sexual Behaviour in the Human Male* was followed by his *Sexual Behaviour in the Human Female*. Both texts presented statistics indicating that a large percentage of the population had homosexual experiences. The books also took the position, very controversial for the time, that homosexuality was a healthy expression of sexuality. A few years later, and influenced by Kinsey's ideas, research surfaced comparing heterosexual women with homosexual women. Many of these studies reported that lesbians are as 'psychologically adjusted' and 'healthy' as their heterosexual counterparts (Armon, 1960; Hopkins; 1969; Saghir & Robins, 1971; Seigelman, 1972; Thompson *et al.*, 1971). Armon's was the first comparison study published. She used projective measures to test psychoanalytic theories about lesbians, specifically examining the areas of dependency, conception of the feminine and masculine role, disparagement of men and confusion and conflict in sexual identification, and inter-personal relations. Armon found no significant differences between lesbian and heterosexual women, and thereby concluded that homosexuality should not be considered a clinical entity (1960). A number of studies reported that lesbians and heterosexual women share the same psychological characteristics (Adelman, 1980; Beach, 1980; LaTorre & Wendenberg, 1983). Adelman (1980), for example, found that lesbians meet the same developmental challenges as heterosexuals, and thus the notion of homosexuality as an abnormal or arrested development had to be questioned.

It should be stressed that the psychological literature is reflective, to a certain extent, of the social and the cultural mood. The period around 1970 is significant. Throughout the 1960s and 1970s articles were published that de-pathologised lesbianism. In 1973 the American Psychiatric Association removed homosexuality from its list of psychiatric disorders. In North America, 1969 marks the beginning of the contemporary gay/lesbian liberation movement, which was initiated by the Stonewall 'riots' in New York City. This was the first time that gay men and lesbians responded to police harassment and publicly defended their rights (Blumenfeld & Raymond, 1989).

It can be argued that the classical essentialists as well as Kinseyan essentialists both promoted the *medicalisation* of sexuality. Medicalisation refers to two inter-related processes. First, certain behaviours or conditions are given medical meaning, defined in terms of health and illness. Second, medical practice becomes a vehicle for eliminating or controlling problematic experiences that are defined as deviant (Kitzinger, 1987). This was definitely the case with homosexuality – homosexuals were first defined as sick, and then as just as healthy as heterosexuals.

A popular method used to de-pathologise lesbianism was first to identify heterosexual women as the norm ('regular healthy women'), and then to minimise the differences between lesbian and non-lesbian women. The 'normality' of lesbians was then demonstrated. The significant and instrumental psychological research undertakings since Kinsey have dissolved or minimised the differences between lesbian and heterosexual women

(Kitzinger, 1987). This is certainly true if one reviews research of the period (see Kingdom, 1979; LaTorre & Wendenberg, 1983; Muckler & Phelan, 1979; Saghir & Robins, 1971).

It has to be recognised that while this approach has certain shortcomings, it has been important in depathologising lesbianism. However, by depathologising lesbianism through the minimisation of difference, some of the important aspects of lesbian experience may have been overlooked or, in a sense, 'covered up'. These arguments highlight the 'new' medicalisation of homosexuality. However, Kitzinger, while highly critical of this research, recognises that it has achieved certain gains.

Homophobia as sickness

In this phase the shift has been towards research that focuses on 'the sick heterosexual' who cannot accept homosexuality, as well as the homosexual who suffers from internalised homophobia if s/he does not accept her/his homosexuality. Persons who cannot accept homosexuality are labelled 'homophobes' and are seen to be suffering from homophobia. Homophobes have an 'irrational fear or dread of homosexuals' (MacDonald, 1976). In Kitzinger's view, the sick homosexual is replaced with the sick homophobe. She sees this as another diagnostic reversal regarding homosexuality – the medicalised, pathologised discourse still being prevalent, albeit in a new form (Kitzinger, 1987).

The lesbian who cannot accept her homosexuality would, in this paradigm, be encouraged to make use of psychological services like individual counselling. During this phase the most important role for the psychological profession is the treatment of ego-dystonic homosexuality, commonly referred to as 'self-hatred' or internalised homophobia (Gatrell, 1984). Other researchers have also raised problems with the term 'homophobia'. Most researchers have criticised it for its male bias and its victimisation of individual 'homophobes' while ignoring societal structures (Plummer, 1981).

But many psychological researchers are not as critical of the 'homophobic diagnosis'. This is evidenced by the large number of scales and studies which have been devised to diagnose homophobia (see MacDonald & Games, 1974; Smith, 1971; Weinberg, 1972). Herek (1994:207) describes the popularity of this research: 'the literature of homophobia now comprises hundreds of published papers'.

South African psychological research on homosexuality

Many authors maintain that 'the specific societal context has a very significant influence upon social scientists' (Chesler, 1976:60; see also Billig, 1976; Essed, 1987). As such, it is important to provide an overview of the societal context in which psychology developed in South Africa to fully comprehend the lack of

In 1957 the government passed the *Sexual Offences Act*, which was intended to 'eliminate immoral behaviour' (RSA, 1957). 'Immoral behaviour' included sex between different 'races' (as defined by the apartheid state), prostitution, cruising, and immoral or indecent acts committed by a man older than 19 years with a man younger than 19. Initially, sexual acts between women were not constituted as crimes. However, in 1988 the Act was extended to outlaw 'immoral or indecent acts between women and girls under 19'. The media contributed to legitimising and entrenching the homophobic scare in its coverage of the first case under the extended legislation with the headlines like: 'Women who prey on girls' (*Sunday Times*, 19 November 1989).

It is interesting to note that sexual activity between two women has never been outlawed in South Africa. This may be a further illustration of the marginalisation of women, as well as denial that women could do without men. Lesbians, according to apartheid laws, were a mere figment of the imagination. There was no evidence that lesbianism is being practised in such a way that it in itself justifies criminal sanctions' (South African Parliament, House of Assembly, 1969. *Debates*. Col. 4803).

The role that psychologists and psychiatrists played in justifying the legal construction of homosexuality in South Africa is clear if one focuses on evidence provided by them to the courts and/or certain government commissions as well as the amount of value attached to that evidence. The following extract highlights the point: 'It must be noted that the evidence [regarding homosexuality] was submitted by the most eminent authorities in this field in South Africa, including professors from the well known universities and the government departments' (South African Parliament, House of Assembly, 1969. *Debates*. Col. 4804).

Various police officers also looked to the psychological profession for assistance. The South African psychological study by Liddicoat (1956) was frequently referred to. The conclusion reached was that homosexuality was usually the result of a personality or genetic abnormality. However, it could not be excused and, with the necessary psychological intervention, spiritual guidance, and a ban on the sale of certain sexual objects, this social evil could be eradicated. They felt that even the 'most hard-baked homosexual' would give anything to live a normal life; given that 'help was at hand', it was felt 'that the existing statutory sanctions should remain' (South African Parliament, House of Assembly, 1969. *Debates*. Col. 4804).

Psychologists who provided evidence in a memorandum to the 1968 Parliamentary Select Committee investigation into homosexuality argued that homosexuality was a sickness and that homosexuals could be 'cured' with spiritual and psychological intervention. In spite of this, they said that individuals should be held responsible for their behaviour. Although it was not logically sound, this evidence was used to argue for the criminalisation and prosecution of homosexuals. Psychologists did not publicly (or in any other way) question this criminalisation.

The absence of any kind of opposition to the criminalisation of homosexuality by psychologists is not surprising if one notes that 'psychology's roots, development, form and practices are all informed by the dominant legacy of apartheid' (Seedat, 1992:50). Seedat (*ibid*.) notes that racist and oppressive political ideology and practices influenced and framed the 'thinking, practice and roles' of a large number of South African psychologists.

research in South African journals on male and female homosexuality. In reviewing South African research, I will show how the homosexual has also been presented as sick, in need of help, and committing a sin. It will also become clear as to how this research has historically failed to include the experiences of the Black people.

As far as it has been possible to determine, up until late 1996 no article on female homosexuality had been published in an official psychology journal. In 1996, Blyth and Straker's piece on intimacy, fusion and frequency of sexual contact in lesbian couples became the first article to be published. But one must note that, in 1984, Theron published an article on the differences of opinion towards the American Psychiatric Association's decision to delete homosexuality from its list of psychiatric disorders. Theron argued that the decision was controversial because homosexuality had been accepted as abnormal in psychiatric circles for more than one hundred years. In addition to creating differences of opinion among professionals, this decision created a dilemma for the psychotherapist who was now faced with the decision to 'either try to change his [sic] homosexual client's sexual orientation or to help him [sic] to accept it' (Theron, 1984:106). The article further argued that the different perspectives on homosexuality should be critically assessed. Yet, while the writer seemed to support the notion that homosexuality was not abnormal, this is not stated explicitly. Whether the paucity of articles on both male and female homosexuality can be attributed to a complete absence of manuscripts on the topic, or the unwillingness of journals and other publications to publish such submissions, is unclear. It is probably a combination of both of these factors.

Early research

As early as the early 1950s, the first theses and dissertations about homosexuality were completed, mainly at Afrikaans universities. In 1951, Loedolff's study drew attention to the possible dangers of homosexuality and recommended treatment intervention that would lead to homosexuals being 'cured'. He stressed that treatment was necessary for lesbians and gay men, because he erroneously believed that homosexuals were sexually attracted to children and were therefore dangerous to society (Loedolff, 1951).

In 1956 Liddicoat completed a dissertation which Blyth (1989) commends as presenting a balanced view of homosexuality. However, both Loedolff (1951) and Liddicoat (1956) ignored the experiences of Black people. It is also significant that both these research reports were used as evidence in the 1968 Parliamentary Select Committee investigation into homosexuality referred to earlier.

Botha (1975) argued for a compassionate and patient attitude towards homosexuals, and for the treatment of homosexuality on the basis of Christian beliefs. However, his sample consisted only of White men. One wonders if his argument would have been similar had he focused on or included Black men. Given the attitudes of the psychological profession and the state towards Black people at the time – money would probably not have been spent on researching them on the grounds that they are 'beyond help' – these arguments for compassion and patience could be seen as representing a kind of faith in the redemption of Whites.

This is wholly consistent with the established views of the state, according to which the homosexual was deemed sick, a threat to the South African Christian society, and a result of faulty personality factors. Despite arguments that homosexuality should be criminalised, most officials were not in favour of imposing heavy prison sentences on gay men. At the same time, Black people in general and certain White activists were being given the heaviest prison sentences possible.

Researchers such as Jacobs (1975), Kotze (1974) and Prinsloo (1973), all working from the 'homosexuality as pathology or deviance' model, focused on gaining insight into the phenomenon and hopefully eventually 'curing' the White gay South African male. Once cured, this male would, in keeping with the logic and rationale of the time, take his rightful role in building a nation that reflected the principles and aims of the apartheid regime.

Woolfson (1975) conducted research on aetiological and personality factors of homosexual behaviour in women. This work was used by White activists in Natal in the 1980s to campaign for an end to the repression of homosexuals (Gevisser, 1994).

Between the 1950s and the 1980s, there was not much research on lesbians or lesbianism. Redlinghuys (1978) and Cronje (1979) both made comparisons between lesbians and heterosexual women, and both studies suggested that 'disturbed' roles within the family and generally problematic family relationships were contributing variables to female homosexuality. Once again, the experiences of Black women were overlooked in these studies.

More recent studies: 1980s–1990s

From the mid-1980s, more liberal, gay-affirmative research has been completed at historically White liberal universities. Some research focused on lesbians and their children and challenged court decisions that deemed lesbians to be unsuitable mothers – for instance Tucker's (1986) study. Blyth (1989) explored the identities presented by gay women. Knight (1989) contributed to affirmative research with a focus on female couples. These research projects were completed at the University of Cape Town and the University of Witwatersrand respectively, two of the country's historically White English universities. Although this research can only make a positive contribution to building a gay rights culture in South Africa, the experiences of Black women were not a part of these studies. Blyth (1989) recommends that the experiences of Black gay women be researched and documented to create a more accurate context for understanding sexual orientation.

A sociological study was published by Schurink (1981), which investigated the lifestyles of a group of lesbians. One of the conclusions was that lesbians have a high self-image as well as a high level of self-acceptance. Once again, however, the research was based on interviews with White lesbians.

The early 1990s saw a few psychology theses on homosexuality. For example, Tarrant (1992) examined the attitudes of 15 psychologists towards homosexuality and their approaches to therapy with gay clients. She found that most of these practitioners did not view homosexuality as being patho- logical *per se*, but there was a general lack of familiarity with the more recent literature and findings in the field. While these psychologists did not condone discrimination against gay men and women in any way, an active role for combating heterosexism was not advocated. The move towards gay-affirma- tive models of psychotherapy, which has occurred in other parts of the world, was not reflected in the attitudes of the research group. Tarrant's study (1992) does not indicate how many of the therapists interviewed were male and how many female, nor does it indicate how many of the participants were White and how many Black. Tarrant's (1992) research also does not refer to or demonstrate an awareness of the race, gender and class differences amongst gays and lesbians and their diverse experiences. These issues cannot be over- looked if we are serious about addressing the racism, heterosexism, and class bias in research, intervention models, as well as in university curricula that are used in the training of future psychologists.

In 1996 the first academic article focusing on Black lesbians was published by Potgieter in *Psychological Perspectives on Lesbian and Gay Issues*. The following year the same author completed a doctoral dissertation in psychology focusing on the lives of Black South African lesbians. The disserta- tion was the first South African, feminist social constructionist academic study in the area of lesbian psychology which was done by a Black woman.

It is fair to say that issues pertinent to gay and lesbian South Africans, particularly Black gays and lesbians, are still not part of the mainstream within South African academia. Although articles regarding lesbian and gay issues have been published in alternative South African journals (for example, *Agenda*) there remains a deafening silence regarding these topics in main- stream psychology journals, especially considering that articles have been published in South African sociology journals (for example, Duckitt, 1984; Kritzinger & Van Aswegen, 1994; Schulze, 1991).

Conclusion

This chapter has attempted to highlight the silences around issues of homo- sexuality within the discipline of psychology. Given that many debates centre on issues of essentialism and social constructionism, I have devoted some discussion to these two viewpoints and then moved on to when the term 'lesbian' emerged as well as why. The question of who or what is lesbian was also discussed. The discourse which argues that homosexuality is un-African was countered by providing evidence of homosexuality in African cultures and societies. The chapter gave an overview of how psychology has constructed homosexuality. The final sections looked at international and South African psychology regarding homosexuality.

Exercises for critical engagement

1   Write an essay in which you critically overview the changing conceptions of homosexuality over the past five decades. In your answer you could look at conceptions both internationally and in South Africa.

2   'I am lesbian' does not have a homogeneous meaning. Illustrate the point by referring to the various understandings of the 'identity'.

3   Lesbianism and male homosexuality are not un-African. Write an essay supporting the latter part of the statement.

Recommended reading

Blackwood, E. & S. Wieringa (Eds.) (1999). *Female Desires: Same-sex Relations and Transgender Practices Across Cultures.* New York Columbia.

Gevisser, M & E. Cameron (Eds.) (1994). *Defiant Desire: Gay and Lesbian Lives in South Africa.* Johannesburg: Ravan.

Potgieter, C. (1997). 'From apartheid to Mandela's Constitution: Black South African lesbians in the nineties'. In Green, B. (Ed.) *Ethnic and Cultural Diversity Among Lesbians and Gay Men,* pp. 88–116. Thousand Oaks, California: Sage.

Heterosexuality 14

Tamara Shefer

OUTCOMES

After having studied this chapter you should be able to:

- understand the current context of heterosexual practices in local communities through a review of the literature

- see the critical role that gender and other forms of power inequality such as age, class and 'race' play in heterosexual relationships

- look critically at what picture of men, women and heterosex is being promulgated in the literature, and

- reflect on what is required towards creating more equitable heterosexual relationships.

THIS CHAPTER explores the practices of heterosexuality in contemporary South Africa as they are portrayed within current research and literature. The chapter highlights how heterosexuality has received little critical attention, particularly within psychology, as it has been assumed to be normal and natural. More recently, however, due to the efforts of feminism, and the global imperative to address the HIV/AIDS pandemic, heterosexual practices have come under scrutiny. The chapter discusses heterosexual sexuality (heterosex) within five main themes drawn from the literature: gender and power inequalities in sexual relationships; male power and women's lack of negotiation in sexual relationships; coercive and violent practices in sexuality; the developmental and social context of masculinity and femininity in understanding heterosexual power relations; and the impact of HIV/AIDS on heterosex. The chapter also presents a critical discussion of some of the more negative implications of the current ways in which gender and heterosex are presented in the literature.

Heterosexuality under scrutiny

Jabu was shortlisted as a candidate for the Masters in Clinical Psychology Programme. At the interview he felt that it was important to identify himself as gay when asked if he had anything that he would like to share about himself. None of the heterosexual candidates, however, identified themselves in relation to their sexual orientation.

- What does this experience tell you about heterosexuality?
- What comes to mind when you think about sex?
- Why is it that when we think about sex, we immediately assume that it refers to sex between men and women?
- Why is it that when we think about sex, we immediately assume that it refers to heterosexual penetration?

Heterosexuality has historically been a silent partner to its binary opposite, homosexuality. Like Whiteness in respect of Blackness, or 'man' in relation to 'woman', the normative identity is always assumed to be unproblematic. The institution of heterosexuality has been idealised, romanticised and naturalised, while in many cultures homosexuality remains a marginalised, pathologised and stigmatised sexual orientation. Thus, as many have pointed out, heterosexuality has been relatively untouched and untheorised across most disciplines (Kitzinger & Wilkinson, 1993; Richardson, 1996). Yet, over the last few decades, heterosex has been increasingly problematised. Feminist work since the 1960s, and the urgency of the HIV/AIDS pandemic since the 1980s, have seen an increasing global focus on exploring sexuality between men and women. It has been widely argued and empirically illustrated that heterosexuality (as both institution and ideology) is a central site for the production and reproduction of gender power inequalities, with women having little power to assert their needs or negotiate for their safety or pleasure (see, for example, Holland *et al.*, 1990; 1991; Jeffreys, 1990; Kitzinger & Wilkinson, 1993; MacKinnon, 1989; Rich, 1980; Richardson, 1996; Vance, 1984). Furthermore, it has now been well recognised that central to understanding the barriers to challenging HIV/AIDS through safe sex practices are the taken-for-granted sexual practices and sexual identities of the two genders.

> Heterosexuality (as both institution and ideology) is a central site for the production and reproduction of gender power inequalities, with women having little power to assert their needs or negotiate for their safety or pleasure.

Given the high rate of HIV infection in sub-Saharan Africa and the fact that heterosexual relations are the primary mode of infection in these countries, research on (hetero-) sexuality has accelerated over the last decade in South Africa. As a consequence we now know quite a lot about the gender power inequalities that manifest in heterosexual relationships in local South African contexts.

As a discipline, psychology has been fairly silent on the issue of heterosexuality, at least with respect to theorising power inequalities in heterosexual

practices. While sexual development has been theorised in
psychology, from psychodynamic
theory to social constructionism,
much of the work has focused on
the development of (heterosexual) identity or on topics such
as inter-personal sexual attraction as in traditional social
psychology. Much of this work
has assumed heterosexuality as a
normative outcome of sexual
development and psychology has
been criticised for pathologising
homosexuality (see, for example,
Butler, 1990a, 1990b). There is a
growing body of critical feminist
psychological work that has
begun exploring such dynamics
(e.g. Wilkinson & Kitzinger,
1993).

Feminist work has shown that heterosexuality is a central site for the reproduction of gender power inequalities, with women largely having little power to assert their needs or negotiate for their safety or pleasure.

Gender and power inequalities in sexuality

At an international level, there is a large body of work in disadvantaged countries that views gender inequality and women's sexual and economic
subordination as central to HIV infection and women's reproductive health
generally (e.g. McFadden, 1992; Schoepf, 1988; Seidel, 1993; WHO, 1994).
With the *feminisation of poverty*, particularly evident in Africa, women,
through the intersection of economic and gender power inequalities, are especially vulnerable to HIV infection.

Such dynamics clearly play a significant role in the South African context
too. The economic context, cultural prescriptions and gender power inequalities all intersect to create barriers for women in the negotiation of heterosex,
and the imperative for women to be involved in sexual relationships for
economic gain has been illustrated (NPPHCN, 1995; Simbayi *et al.*, 1999;
Strebel, 1993). Furthermore, the colonial heritage of poverty, war and physical
dislocation (such as migrant labour systems) have been found to further
impact on women's ability to protect themselves from HIV infection. In South
Africa, as with the rest of Africa, the impact of the migrant labour system on
the spread of HIV has been illustrated (see, for example, Hunt, 1989;
Campbell, 2001; Campbell *et al.*, 1998).

Feminisation of poverty:
Poverty affects women more than it does men, and women globally are poorer than men. In Africa and other third world contexts, the majority of women are poor as a conse-quence of the colonial heritage and due to international gender inequalities. In South Africa Black, working-class women have historically been at the bottom of the economic hierarchy, occupying the lowest earning and most undervalued positions.

The articulation of gender with age and class positions young, poor women as particularly vulnerable to HIV infection and sexual abuse. South African studies illustrate that young women frequently get involved with older men for access to money and/or status (NPPHCN, 1995; Varga & Makubalo, 1996). Similarly, there is some anecdotal evidence that men are seeking younger women to have sex with in order to avoid sexually transmitted illnesses, which may be contributing to coercive sexual practices (Simbayi *et al.*, 1999). Another current example of the overlap between age and gender in South Africa and elsewhere in the region has been the rape of young girls and babies, which has been presented in the media as resulting from the apparently widely accepted belief that sex with virgins is a way of curing or protecting against HIV/AIDS (LoveLife, 2000; Vetten & Bhana, 2001).

Psychology has been fairly silent on the issue of heterosexuality, especially with regard to theorising power inequalities in heterosexual relations.

Male power and women's lack of negotiation in sexual relationships

In the search for understanding the vast barriers to 'safe' sexual practices, much research has highlighted the inequitable nature of 'normal' heterosexual relationships. It has been fairly widely reported that even if women have knowledge about HIV/AIDS or wish to protect themselves against pregnancy, they frequently are unable to successfully negotiate this (Shefer, 1999; Strebel, 1992; 1993; Varga & Makubalo, 1996).

On the other hand, traditional gender roles together with or outside of socio-economic factors clearly play a significant role as barriers to safe sex practices. The central role that cultural practices of gender power inequality play in creating barriers to the negotiation of safe and equitable heterosex has been increasingly theorised and researched in an international context. Similarly in South Africa, a number of key studies have highlighted the way in which gender power relations manifest in the negotiation of heterosex (see, for example, Miles, 1992; Shefer, 1999; Strebel, 1993). These studies show how women's lack of negotiation is strongly associated with socialised sexual practices where it is expected of women to be passive, submissive partners, while men are expected to initiate, be active and lead women in the realm of sexuality (Shefer, 1999; Varga & Makubalo, 1996). Men are viewed as in control of relationships and sexuality. Much of this is related to the cultural constructions of male and female sexuality. A number of qualitative studies highlight a popular construction of male sexuality as overwhelmingly strong, urgent and uncontrollable (Shefer & Ruiters, 1998; Shefer & Foster, 2001; Strebel, 1993). This

Heterosex: This term is used to refer to sexual practices between men and women. In most popular culture we simply use the term sex to refer to heterosex. This however assumes that all sexual activity takes place between men and women, and ignores homosexual sexuality.

has elsewhere been named the '*male sexual drive discourse*' (Hollway, 1989) that seems to play an important role in women's lack of negotiation in heterosex.

'Male sexual drive discourse' refers to the construction of men as highly sexual and always ready for sex (Hollway, 1989).

Emerging from the assumption that men are highly sexual is the construction of the domain of sexuality as masculine and a male preserve. Women are viewed as 'asexual', and therefore 'strangers' to matters related to sexuality. Women are understood to be waiting on men to 'show them the ropes'. They are expected to be focused on relationships and 'love', and sexuality is only legitimised for them if attached to these. A number of authors, both internationally and locally, emphasise the lack of a positive discourse on female sexuality – in other words, women do not appear to be able to express or view their sexuality or their sexual desires and pleasures as positive (Holland *et al.*, 1991; Hollway, 1995; 1996; Lesch, 2000; Shefer & Foster, 2001; Shefer & Strebel, 2001). Thus, there is an increasing call for the articulation of women's voices in the realm of sexuality. It is asserted that if women cannot 'say yes' to sexuality, and 'own' their sexuality and sexual desires, then they certainly cannot assertively 'say no' and negotiate what they desire in their sexual relationships with men.

Linked to the above is the reported pervasiveness of the traditional *double standard* where men are encouraged to actively pursue sexuality and take multiple partners (NPPHCN, 1995; Wood & Foster, 1995). On the other hand, women are punished for being sexually active, and constructed as 'loose' and promiscuous. Even having knowledge about sexuality, and admitting to having had sexual experience, appears to be taboo for women (Shefer, 1999).

Studies show how women's lack of negotiation in heterosexual relationships is associated with socialised sexual practices where it is expected of women to be passive partners and men are expected to be active.

A focus on condom use, in particular, has highlighted the problematic dynamics of heterosexual negotiation. In South Africa, studies show how condoms are generally not viewed positively by either men or women, are frequently seen as symbolising a lack of trust or infidelity, are seen as 'unmacho' by men and unromantic by women and contrary to their traditional female role ('women who carry condoms are promiscuous') (see, for example, Abdool Karim *et al.*, 1992a; Abdool Karim *et al.*, 1992b; Abdool Karim, *et al.*, 1992c; Lesch, 2000; Strebel, 1993; Varga & Makubalo, 1996; Wood & Foster, 1995). It is also more than evident from empirical findings that men's sexuality is privileged in decisions regarding condoms, with women fearing the loss of their partners, anxious about their men not enjoying sex with a condom, and fearing that a request for condoms will be interpreted as a lack of trust in the men or as an admission of their own infidelity (Bremridge, 2000; Campbell *et al.*, 1998; Shefer, 1999; Strebel, 1993; Wood & Foster, 1995). While there is a definite increase in calls for women-centred methods of protection against HIV infection (e.g. female condom and spermicides) in South Africa (e.g. Rees, 1998), there is little research on the efficacy of such methods and there is much resistance to these methods (Richards, 1996; Strebel & Lindegger, 1998).

Discourse on condom use also highlights the traditional prescriptions for female sexuality within the *whore-madonna dichotomy*. Qualitative research in South Africa, mirroring international literature (e.g. Waldby *et al.*, 1993), shows how men distinguish between 'clean' and 'unclean' women (Bremridge, 2000; Shefer, 1999; Wood & Foster, 1995), in which 'unclean' women constitute those who step outside prescribed feminine sexuality ('promiscuous' women and prostitutes). Condom use is therefore constructed by both men and women as inappropriate in long-term relationships where faithfulness is assumed. Clearly condoms are not neutral objects, but embody stigmas, which may differ from context to context and from one relationship to another, but nonetheless reflect dominant discourse on gendered power relations and serve to inhibit negotiations around 'safe sex'.

Excerpts from focus groups with UWC psychology students talking about heterosex

The 'male sexual drive' discourse:
It is no use us hiding away or ... denying it ... Men have got a very powerful urge ... sexual urge ... more than women have ... that is nature ... (Female participant)

Sex as a male domain:
I think that the men actually consider sex as a man's thing and not a woman thing ... Like if they get satisfied, then that's fine ... (Female participant)

Woman as passive and asexual:
Nice girls don't initiate ... and are passive (Female participant)

Male participant 1: What actually embarrasses men [is] ... if a lady is too active sexually they tend to label that lady. They tend to say ...

Male participant 2: ... that she's a bitch.

Male participant 3: Sometimes it's just her fear of exposing her knowledge about sex, especially during that first time. If she did during the first time, she could give him the wrong impression about her ... being a bitch.

Whore-madonna dichotomy:
If you change boyfriends from this one this month and next month another one, then you'll be labelled a bitch ... But if you have a steady affair for a long time, then you will be respectable ... (Female participant)

Culture and gender roles:
Male participant (following discussion of 'double standards'): I would think that maybe it's ... it's our culture [agreement from other men]

Female participant: But you cannot blame *the culture* all the time!

Male participant: What ... who said that men should be approaching the women? Nobody knows. But it is a fact ... it is what always happens ... in fact everyone knows that a man should do the proposal ... (Mixed group of participants)

Source: Shefer, 1999

While cultural constructions are found to play a huge role in the reproduction of unequal sexual practices, some authors are more critical of the way in which 'culture' may be used as a way of excusing problematic male behaviour and male power in sexual relationships (Shefer, 2002; Shefer *et al.*, 1999; Shefer & Foster, 2001). These authors point out how notions of 'tradition' and 'culture' are frequently used to rationalise and legitimise such practices as the 'double standard' (discussed earlier) and male promiscuity (based on notions of historical polygamy), as well as male lack of responsibility for contraceptives and safe sex practices.

Feminist writers have pointed out how notions of 'tradition' and 'culture' are frequently used to rationalise and legitimise double standards, male promiscuity, as well as male lack of responsibility for safe sex practices.

Coercive and violent practices

Given the high rate of violence against women in South Africa, much attention has been paid to this problem over the last decade. There has been a proliferation of research in South Africa on violence against women, and an increasing focus on the links between violence and heterosexuality and HIV/AIDS infection. Sexual violence against women and girls, whether by known or unknown rapists, is widespread. Coercive sexual practices and abuse have been increasingly reported in studies exploring heterosexual negotiations and practices. In this respect, girls and women are clearly more vulnerable to HIV/AIDS and other infection, as well as unwanted pregnancies. It has become apparent that for South African communities, violence and heterosex are inextricably interwoven (Shefer *et al.*, 2000). A recent spate of research among adolescents and children has revealed that their sexual experiences are bound up with violence and coercion (Buga *et al.*, 1996; NPPHCN, 1995; Richter, 1996; Varga & Makubalo, 1996; Wood *et al.*, 1996; Wood & Jewkes, 1998).

Reporting having sex against their will
- 28 per cent of Black, Coloured and Indian/Asian urban youth (Richter, 1996)
- 71 per cent of adolescent Black women in peri-urban Cape Town (Maforah in Wood *et al.*, 1996)

Coercive sexual practices
- A study in the rural Eastern Cape found that the most frequently cited reasons for women beginning sexual activity were coercion by a partner (28 per cent), and 'peer pressure' (20 per cent) (Buga *et al.*, 1996)
- A CIETafrica survey (in Vetten & Bhana, 2001) in Greater Johannesburg found that 27 per cent of young women and 32 per cent of young men did not see forced sex with someone they know as sexual violence
- When asked to write down the first experience that comes to mind when thinking about heterosex 22 per cent of UWC psychology students wrote of their own or others' experiences of violence and coercion, and a further 21 per cent spoke of issues of male power and women's lack of control (Shefer, 1999)

Everyday coercive practices in heterosex are also found to be common, particularly in interactions involving older men who are in more powerful social positions, and young women. Thus it is not only overt sexual violence that is commonplace. Rather, more subtle forms of coercion and pressure appear to be endemic to heterosexual relationships. Discourses of love and romance play a significant role in sexual coercion. This appears to be particularly salient for girls or women who speak of 'giving in' to male pressure for sex because of 'love', commitment and fear of loss of the relationship (Shefer, 1999; Varga & Makubalo, 1996; Wood *et al.*, 1996). In these studies, it is evident that girls' sexuality is constructed as responsive to and in the service of male sexuality. Even when young women are aware of power inequalities and double standards within discourses of love and sexuality, there appears to be little space for resistance given peer pressure and male violence (Wood *et al.*, 1996). A number of South African studies also highlight the widespread nature of coercive sexuality or unprotected sexuality linked to economic factors such as poverty, financial dependence, and job security (e.g. Jewkes & Abrahams, 2000; Vetten & Dladla, 2000).

> Discourses of love and romance play a significant role in sexual coercion.

A growing body of research is beginning to establish a strong link between violence against women and HIV/AIDS (see Vetten & Bhana, 2001 for a review). One of the significant areas hinges around condom usage in safe sex practices. Violence plays a role in negotiations around condoms, with women speaking of the fear and actual experience of angry or violent responses if they insist on condom use (Strebel, 1992; 1993; Varga & Makubalo, 1996; Shefer *et al.*, 2000). The link between violence and HIV/AIDS also emerges around the disclosure of HIV status, and attempts to practise safe sex by HIV-positive women. Although mostly anecdotal, there is evidence of male violence following women's disclosure of their HIV status in South African communities (Mthembu, 1998; Vetten & Bhana, 1991).

Developmental and social contexts of masculinity and femininity in understanding heterosexual power relations

This is still a fairly poorly subscribed area of research (Shefer, 1998), but there is wide acknowledgement, as elaborated below, of the significance of early gender development to heterosexual behaviour. Social and sexual inequalities that are powerfully implicated in young people's constructions of sexuality, love and relationships, are promulgated during childhood and adolescence.

> Social and sexual inequalities that are powerfully implicated in young people's constructions of sexuality, love and relationships, are promulgated during childhood and adolescence.

With respect to girls, some of the salient issues are related to puberty and the beginnings of their menstruation. One central thread is the lack of knowledge and access to reliable and constructive information that young people, at all corners of the globe, have through the process of their development. Young women in particular appear to lack basic knowledge about their bodies, reproductivity and sexuality (Bassett & Sherman, 1994; Bhende, 1995; Uwakwe *et al.*, 1994; Vasconcelos *et al.*, 1995). This lack of knowledge appears to be reinforced by global moralising and gendered discourses on female sexuality, where virginity and sexual naivety are prescribed for girls (Weiss *et al.*, 1996). Thus, even if women have sexual knowledge, they face social pressure to maintain an image of innocence, particularly with men, who may interpret knowledge as past sexual activity (as mentioned earlier). Consequently, it is very difficult for women to protect themselves against sexually transmitted infections (STIs) and AIDS, given that such measures will imply 'the outward appearance of an active sexual life which is not congruent with traditional norms of conduct for adolescent girls' (*ibid.*:9). In this way, dominant constructions of femininity act to decrease women's power in the negotiation of heterosex.

In the South African context, both historical and contemporary studies point to the protective construction of girls as sexually vulnerable to 'dangerous' male sexuality at the onset of menstruation (Lesch, 2000; Mager, 1996; Shefer, 1998). Practices of forcing and placing girls immediately on contraception, and warnings against boys and men are apparently common in many South African communities. In this way, young girls are taught of their passivity and vulnerability to men or boys and their menstruation is constructed as a negative, dangerous transition (Shefer, 1998; 1999). As a consequence young women are often unprepared for sexual relationships, lacking not only useful knowledge but also a positive sexual identity (Thomson & Scott, 1991).

Boys, on the other hand, appear to be socialised positively into their 'manhood', with puberty signifying a transition to active (hetero-)sexuality.

Nonetheless, manhood appears to be rigidly associated with heterosexuality and the ability to be sexual with multiple women. Thus, those who do not conform or are not successful in this realm may be punished or stigmatised. Alternative sexualities, either homosexual or those resistant to traditional macho masculinity, are still not well tolerated in South African communities. For men and boys, the feminist argument of the close ties between hetero-sexual and masculine identity are borne out by empirical studies. For example, when asked what it means to be a boy, a 12-year-old boy replied '... to have sex with a woman' (NPPHCN, 1995:35). The female answer from a 14-year-old girl is similarly stereotyped and makes no mention of sex: 'To be a mother ... to have a husband and to look after children' (*ibid.*:36).

Manhood appears to be rigidly associated with heterosexuality and the ability to be sexual with multiple women.

While masculinity studies have been fairly marginalised in South Africa, there is clearly a growing emphasis on understanding the role of masculinities in contemporary South Africa (see, for example, Morrell, 2001), including a focus on the masculine in heterosexual relationships (e.g. Dunbar Moodie, 2001; Shefer & Ruiters, 1998).

The impact of HIV/AIDS on heterosex

Few studies specifically focus on this, yet through using such a lens to look at contemporary findings it is evident that more work is needed to explore the impact of HIV/AIDS on heterosex. One would expect that the increased focus on heterosex and the attempt to popularise information on HIV/AIDS and safe sex practices would facilitate a move to more equitable sexual practices. Earlier studies have however found that in spite of increased knowledge and awareness, there has been little evidence of a change in gender power relation-ships in heterosexual practices (e.g. Perkel *et al.*, 1991). On the other hand, more recent calls for the inclusion of issues of gender relationship and specific skills of negotiation and assertiveness within educational and lifeskills inter-ventions may lead to more concrete changes in this area. More research is required, in particular evaluation studies on interventions that are currently in process.

Early studies around HIV/AIDS found that in spite of increased knowledge and awareness, there was little evidence of a change in gender power relationships in heterosexual practices.

Some pointers to a more negative impact of HIV/AIDS on heterosex include the now widely publicised 'virgin rape' phenomenon, mentioned earlier. The widespread belief that having sex with a virgin or with a young woman may lead to a cure for HIV/AIDS appears to have particular salience in Southern Africa (LoveLife, 2000). Although there is no proof that such a belief has lead to an increase of child sexual abuse, a number of sensationalised media cases have certainly established such a link in the public eye. Further-more, it stands to reason, as has been reported elsewhere, that the attempt to escape HIV/AIDS may lead to an increase in sexual practices between older men and younger women or girls. More research is clearly needed in this area to establish whether there is a more definitive relationship between HIV/AIDS and child sexual abuse.

Another area where HIV/AIDS may be impacting negatively on heterosex centres on the *stigmatisation* of HIV/AIDS and other STIs (Ratele & Shefer, 2002; Simbayi *et al.*, 1999). The continued silencing and stigmatisation of STIs in South African communities is believed to perpetuate unsafe sex practices, with men and women afraid to reveal their status and rather risk infecting their partners. Some studies even report a vindictive promiscuity among those who are infected in order to 'punish' others (Simbayi *et al.*, 1999). Also, given reports of violent retribution from male partners when women reveal their HIV status, mentioned above, it is expected that they may resist disclosure and avoid the insistence on safe sex out of fear of male violence.

Critical evaluation of contemporary findings on heterosexuality

The proliferation of research and the educational emphasis on heterosexual relationships is extremely important. It may even be argued that, disastrous as it is, the HIV/AIDS epidemic has opened up a significant space for challenging gender inequality as it manifests in heterosexual relationships, as well as gender roles and inequality more broadly. On the other hand, there are also problems and potential concerns with the way in which heterosexual relationships are currently viewed.

In relation to women, it is arguable that while it is important to highlight women's lack of negotiation in heterosex, the dominant picture of women emerging is that of inevitable victims of male power. Nobody would argue against the significance of acknowledging women's lack of power in heterosex, but it is also important that we do not inadvertently reproduce the dominant stereotype of women's passivity. Contemporary feminist writers have begun challenging the way in which feminist theories on heterosexuality have historically constructed power as the inherent preserve of (all) men, and women as inevitably disempowered victims of male power (Hollway, 1995; Jackson, 1996; Smart, 1996). Smart (1996), for example, speaks of a conflation of the penis with the phallus, in which she maintains all power is seen as male, and all males are seen as having access to power. She argues that both of these are problematic assumptions, given a post-modern understanding of the multiple, contextual and fluid nature of power. In this way, while most feminists distance themselves from biological determinism, she argues that power and gender are inadvertently essentialised, globalised and decontextualised.

What is probably most problematic about the continued emphasis on women's vulnerability, passivity and powerlessness, is that this emphasis serves to silence the many times that women *do* resist male power and *do* challenge men. Furthermore, the stereotyped image of women is ultimately

Contemporary feminist writers have begun challenging the way in which feminist theories on heterosexuality have historically constructed power as the inherent preserve of (all) men, and women as inevitably disempowered victims of male power.

What is probably most problematic about the continued emphasis on women's vulnerability, passivity and powerlessness, is that this emphasis serves to silence the many times that women do resist male power and do challenge men.

reproduced, with no space given to alternative images and discourses of women as strong, assertive and powerful agents. Importantly, as mentioned, the predominant picture of women remains one of asexual victims of male desires, and women's own sexual desires and a positive female sexuality are seldom represented in the literature.

The flipside of women being constructed as inevitable victims is the reproduction of the stereotype of men as inevitably powerful and controlling in relation to women in heterosexual relationships. While some authors have pointed out the salience of a 'male sexual drive' discourse in talk on heterosex, the literature itself appears to reproduce this stereotype. Clearly there is a silence around alternative ways of being men. There is very little literature that highlights men's resistance to traditional masculinity, or speaks of men's vulnerability to women and their difficulties with hegemonic masculinity. In some research, fragments of male vulnerability and the pressure on men to conform to hegemonic masculinity are beginning to emerge (see, for example, Shefer & Ruiters, 1998. See also Chapter 15, this volume). Nonetheless, there is still little work that gives a voice to the different ways of being men, and offers alternative and more nuanced versions of maleness in heterosexual relationships.

Finally, it is significant to note that while heterosexuality continues to be the normative sexual practice, idealised and romanticised in the public eye, the literature on heterosexuality overwhelmingly presents a picture of an oppressive, inequitable and often violent institution. While this has been an important step in the struggle towards gender equality, it is problematic that heterosexuality is presented as a homogeneous, unitary and singular experience in the literature. The literature appears to assume only one way of being heterosexual, and presents heterosexuality as an institution that inevitably reflects and reproduces power imbalance. Furthermore, most work seems to accept a construction of heterosex as centred on penetrative sexuality, again reproducing, rather than challenging, the social stereotypes of what heterosex is. As with masculinities, alternative pictures and experiences of heterosexuality and heterosex are silenced and/or marginalised. It could be argued that if we are not presented with alternative images and discourses on heterosex, there is no way in which we can challenge the current oppressive context of heterosexual relationships.

> While heterosexuality continues to be the normative sexual practice, idealised and romanticised in the public eye, the literature on heterosexuality overwhelmingly presents a picture of an oppressive, inequitable and often violent institution.

Conclusion

For the most part, the current picture of heterosex emerging from research in South Africa, as it is globally, is one imbued with much negativity. We have seen how heterosex is interwoven with gender power inequality, in which both men and women are engaged in reproducing the traditional roles of masculinity and femininity. It has become evident that such roles and power inequality between men and women mean that they do not negotiate sexuality very successfully or equitably. Given the dangers associated with heterosex, including unwanted pregnancies, STIs and HIV/AIDS, the opportunity for men and women to negotiate their sexual practices safely is an imperative. Yet, by all accounts there are major barriers, related to the power inequalities of gender, class and age that stand in the way of open and equitable sexual negotiation.

It is important to begin to expose different experiences of heterosex and developing new ways of thinking about relations between women and men.

On the other hand, we need to be cautious about the way in which the current focus on heterosexuality may itself perpetuate this problematic pattern of behaviours. Given this negative picture of heterosex, it is evident we need to find ways to create new identities and ways of relating sexually as men and women. This means that we need to move beyond criticising and highlighting the inequities of heterosex to also exploring the alternatives and resistances to this dominant mode of relationship. Thus, while we need to be cautious of denying the problematic reality of heterosexuality for many women (and men), and the way in which it currently facilitates women's vulnerability to HIV/AIDS, STIs and unwanted pregnancies, we also need to allow for the development of an alternative picture of men, women and heterosex. It is important to begin exposing different experiences of heterosex and developing new ways of thinking and talking about the sexual relationships between men and women. An important way of doing this involves highlighting the margin-alised experiences and voices on sexuality, such as those of men who resist taking power and control in heterosex, and of women who resist passivity and have positive experiences of their sexuality with men. We need to begin docu-menting some of the experiences which contradict our 'normal' image of men and women – such as men who enjoy affection without sex, and examples of women's strength and agency in resisting male power in heterosex. Men need to be encouraged to admit to their vulnerability in sexual relationships, just as women need to begin to assert their sexual desires and own their sexuality. Finally, we need to be able to expose images of a positive heterosexuality as well. In order to challenge the current problematic context of heterosex, we need to be able to imagine a more equitable and mutually enjoyable experience.

Exercises for critical engagement

1   Reflect on your own growing up as a girl or boy. What were the messages you received about your gender and sexual identity?

2   Think about your community and how it responds to a woman who initiates a sexual relationship. How does this differ for a man who does? Why is this so?

3   What are the barriers to safe sex practices in your community? What do you think would facilitate safe sex practices?

4   Do you agree with the statement: 'If women could express their own desires for sexuality, they would be better equipped to say "no" when they don't want sex'?

5   How do you think other forms of inequality impact on gender inequalities in sexual relationships? Think of some examples from your own community.

Endnote

1   Also see the section entitled *The impact of HIV/AIDS on heterosex* for a critical comment on this perception.

Recommended reading

Butler, J. (1990). *Gender Trouble: Feminism and the Subversion of Identity.* New York: Routledge.

Foucault, M. (1981). *The History of Sexuality, Vol. 1: Introduction.* Harmondsworth: Penguin Books.

Richardson, D. (Ed.) (1996). *Theorising Heterosexuality.* Milton Keynes: Open University Press.

Segal, L. (1994). *Straight Sex: Rethinking Heterosexuality and the Politics of Pleasure.* London: Virago.

Shefer, T. (1999) *Discourses of Heterosexual Negotiation and Relation.* Unpublished doctoral thesis, University of the Western Cape, Cape Town.

Wilkinson, S. & C. Kitzinger (Eds.) (1993). *Heterosexuality: A Feminism and Psychology Reader.* London: Sage.

Historical Representations of 'Race', Masculinity and Homosexuality

15

Lindsay Clowes

OUTCOMES

After having studied this chapter you should be able to:

- explain what a gendered discourse is
- understand some of the ways in which discourses around race are shaped by discourses around gender
- identify some of the discursive strategies by means of which homosex has been constructed as deviant and dangerous in the South African media in the past, and
- identify some of the discursive strategies by means of which heterosex has been constructed as normative in the South African media in the past.

THE ESTABLISHMENT of homosexuality as deviant and dangerous in the South African media has been a process where the interactions between Western morality, twentieth century legal and medical *discourses* and traditional discourses of silence around sexual affairs have served to marginalise certain urban and, to a lesser extent, rural men. These discourses have provided a framework and a backdrop against which, for example, *Drum* magazine constructed an unambiguously heterosexual urban masculinity. But if urban heterosexuality was *hegemonic*, it was not *monolithic*, and within its confines there were conflicts and tensions around intersections with other *identities*. This chapter explores the discourses around the intersecting identities of race, masculinity and homosexuality through a case study of *Drum* magazine. In its efforts, for example, to 'discourage any moral looseness' (*Drum*, April 1955), certain aspects of the relationships between both rural and urban men and women were ignored, disparaged and dismissed, while others were endorsed and applauded. Grafting a long tradition of a Western heterosexism (that, for the most part, worked against women) onto changing rural practices (that tended to privilege men), inequalities in the gendered relationships between urbanising Black men and women were established as both normal and normative in the pages of the magazine. At the same time, given the wide variety of racially defined groups inhabiting the South African social and political landscape in the middle to late twentieth century, along with the struggle for national liberation, inequalities between men were widespread. As represented in *Drum*, responses to these inequalities were articulated in discourses around race, sexuality, manhood and nationalist struggle that were themselves gendered in such a way as to marginalise homosexual masculinity.

South Africa and *Drum* in the 1950s

The first edition of the *African Drum*, later to become simply *Drum*, appeared on South African streets in March 1951. Owned and edited by White men, the magazine was largely written by Black men (unlike other South African publications aimed at Black audiences). Within the year *Drum* had established a solidly increasing circulation with a primarily urban Black male audience, and by the following year was claiming to articulate 'the authentic voice of non-Europeans in Africa' (*Drum*, November 1953). Developing, by the mid-1960s, into five separate editions produced in five different locations around Africa, the magazine was enormously influential. It was, according to one analyst, 'one of the most popular magazines in Anglophone Africa in the 1960s and 1970s' (Mutongi, 2000:1). Wole Soyinka records that the 'average Nigerian reader' of the mid-1950s 'was weaned on *Drum*' (Soyinka, 1988:168). The focus of this chapter, though, is on the South African version of *Drum*, which produced world class photographers in the persons of Peter Magubane and Bob Gosani, and employed as journalists men who subsequently became household names through their work. Henry Nxumalo – Mr *Drum* himself – was joined by Todd Matshikiza, Arthur Maimane, Can Themba, Casey Motsisi, Bloke Modisane, Ezekiel Mpahlele, Lewis Nkosi, Nat Nakasa, Stan Motjuwadi, as well as many others.

This chapter is drawn from my doctoral dissertation, which explored the changing ways in which *Drum* magazine constructed masculinities between 1951 and 1984, when the magazine changed ownership. In the early years of the magazine men were portrayed entering beauty contests, regularly replaced women in advertisements for baby food, and were constructed as men through their concern with their appearance, their intimate relationships with parents, wives and children, and through their close connections with the home. This changed over time, and later versions of the magazine saw men constructed as beings with few ties to the home or to the women and children supposedly in those homes. No longer admitted to beauty contests, men were primarily constructed in relation to non-kin men such as employers and colleagues.

Underpinning this study is an understanding of the media in which they are seen as socialising agents, as influential interpreters of reality through the power wielded by editors, owners and writers over meaning and significance, through the privileging of 'one version of reality over another' (Burstyn, 1999:22). There is much debate about the extent to which the values of the popular press dominate or control the ways in which we understand the world, although there is broad agreement that the media does not have free rein to impose its own versions of reality onto a gullible and unwitting public. But as Stuart Hall (1997:356) has noted:

> [T]he more one accepts that how people act will depend in part on how the situations in which they act are defined ... the less one can assume either a natural meaning to everything or a universal consensus on what things mean – then, the more important, socially and politically, becomes the process by means of which certain events get recurrently signified in particular ways.

As magazines – and the people who make them – are products of particular social and historical landscapes, they inevitably reflect the gendered and racialised contexts in which they themselves are made. This ultimately shapes the version finally offered to consumers. This study takes a feminist postmodern position that our understanding of the material world does not pre-exist language, but is constructed through it. While readers themselves construct meaning through their engagement with the texts, the range of available meanings is framed by language and genre as well as the social and historical context. 'Reality itself is written within cultural systems,' according to Ferber, and in terms of relations of power and dominance. What is at stake is which and whose 'narrative structure will prevail in the interpretation of events in the social world' (Ferber, 1999:7). See also Chapter 4 in this volume for a discussion of media representations of race, and for an early, but very clear discussion about how the mass media influences our understanding of reality see Herman and Chomsky (1988).

The gendered discourses produced by these men need to be understood against a complex context in which particular and specific assumptions about male sexuality existed. While it is necessary to identify these assumptions in order to attempt to understand their location, it is also necessary to acknowledge my own assumptions and understandings. My position is that the relationship between gender and sexuality is neither straightforward nor one-dimensional. Stein (1999) has pointed to the complexities surrounding accounts of human sexuality, and the fierce debates that are raging in the academy: it is not the place of this chapter to attempt to resolve these issues. Suffice it to say that for the purposes of this discussion I have assumed that sexual desire is inborn, but that the expression and direction of that desire is both culturally and historically specific. As Stein has so eloquently observed, sexual norms and practices differ according to time and place. He points, for example, to contemporary Latin American men who have intercourse with other men and yet have no difficulty identifying themselves as heterosexual, providing that they themselves are not penetrated (Murray & Roscoe, 1998; Stein, 1999). Closer to home, Kendall (in Murray & Roscoe, 1998:230) argues

It has been argued that Basotho women define sexual activity in such a way that makes lesbianism linguistically inconceivable – not that lesbian sex doesn't take place, but it isn't considered 'sexual' (Kendall, in Murray & Roscoe, 1998).

that Basotho women 'define sexual activity in such a way that makes lesbianism linguistically inconceivable – not that [lesbian sex] doesn't take place, but it isn't considered "sexual".' Sexual norms and practices not only differ from place to place, though, they also change over time. There seems to be agreement in the academy, for instance, that the *stigmatisation* of homosexuals as aberrant and deviant (where deviance equalled a threat) in the West took place only in the middle to late nineteenth century (Tosh, 1994). By the 1950s and 1960s, Western understandings of male sexuality had changed little since the biomedical discourses of the mid-nineteenth century had *pathologised* certain kinds of sexual practices and sexual preferences, and it was this discourse that underpinned *Drum's* representations of male sexuality.

Homosexual acts, furthermore, were established as criminal. Drawing on the traditions of both Roman and Dutch law that discriminated against homosexuals, the South African legal system has, according to Judge Edwin Cameron, 'never treated lesbians and gays kindly'. 'Only male/female sex acts which were directed to procreation were permitted. All other sexual acts – whether between men or between a man and a woman – were cruelly punished' (Cameron, 1994:91). In a society where even acts between consenting heterosexual couples could be criminalised, individuals involved in same-sex relationships were unlikely to draw attention to themselves. Overall then, in mid-twentieth century White South Africa at least, the conceptualisation of homosexuality as dangerously deviant had long been hegemonic (Cameron, 1994; Murray, 1998).

There is, however, a great deal of evidence to suggest that at least some elements within Southern African Black society took a far more casual approach to sexual affairs between men. Homosexual relationships – what were widely known as 'mine marriages' between older and younger men – had a long history in the compounds in and around Johannesburg (Achmat, 1993; Breckinridge, 1998; Dunbar Moodie, 1994; 1988; Harries, 1990). As Junod put it at the turn of the century, '[t]he immense majority of the Natives themselves do not consider this sin as of any importance at all. They speak of it with laughter' (Junod in Dunbar Moodie, 1994:125). Murray and Roscoe (1998) have collected a series of texts suggesting that the apparent absence of homosexual desire in Africa was more the product of Western *ethnocentric* discourse than it was an accurate description of African sexual practices. At the same time, however:

> Sensitised by missionaries and Western education, defensive in the face of stereotypes of black hypersexuality, and resentful of sexual exploitation in colonial institutions, the first generation of postcolonial Africans was extremely reluctant to discuss the subject of homosexuality (Murray & Roscoe, 1998:xvi).

Perhaps, as well, Black South Africans 'placed a strong taboo upon the open discussion of [all] sexual matters', constructing what Epprecht and others have described as a 'culture of discretion', a claim given substance by Epprecht's (1998:636) observation that there are 'no explicit terms for homosexuality or discrete homosexual acts in Shona' (see also Kendal, 1998; Shire, 1994). Given these factors, then, it is hardly surprising that the Black male writers who wrote eagerly and authentically about aspects of urban township life – and who strongly objected when their ability to do so was threatened – seemed less able and less willing to write about other kinds of experiences.

While *Drum's* version of urban masculinity was clearly established in opposition to ideas and practices around urban and rural femininity, it was also constructed in the context of continuing and escalating attempts by the White state to deny urban Black men a voice (Epprecht, 1998:642). As Kimmel has said '[m]anhood is demonstrated for other men's approval ... Masculinity is a *homosocial* enactment' (Kimmel, 1994:128), and a great deal of evidence suggests that apartheid was understood by Black men as a project aimed at denying their manhood. By the 1950s, colonialism had long been understood as an assault on men's masculinity. As one 'Pondo gentleman' reported in the 1930s, '[t]imes long ago were good. Everything is bad now. We pay taxes. Long ago men were not white men's women' (Berger in Barnes, 1999:176). In 1959, Robert Sobukwe, leader of the newly formed Pan Africanist Congress, certainly understood apartheid in this way, declaring that Europeans 'conceive[d] of the African people as a child nation, composed of Boys and Girls' (Sobukwe, 1959:7). In their objections to the early *Drum*, several Black informants had made the same connection. 'Africans have been kept and reared and taught like babies', declared one reader. '[A]ll we ask is to be treated like men' (*Drum*, August 1951).

> While *Drum's* version of urban masculinity was clearly established in opposition to ideas and practices around urban and rural femininity, it was also constructed in the context of continuing and escalating attempts by the White state to deny urban Black men a voice.

Drum's images of manhood fed into (and was fed by) discourses around nationalist struggle in which a hegemonic White heterosexual masculinity attempted to deny manhood to Black men. In the context of similar White supremacist discourse in the United States, Ferber has noted that 'what it means to be a man is intimately tied up with race ... race and gender identity are absolutely inseparable ... the construction of one depends upon the other' (1999:119). In a context where manhood was intimately linked to heterosex, and where homosexuality was understood as a 'violation of masculinity', a recognition by *Drum* that some Black men preferred men might have undermined the implicit argument that Black men's heterosexuality *demonstrated* manhood, a demonstration that pointed wordlessly but articulately to the futility and misguidedness of the apartheid project. Thus the magazine emphasised over and over again that it was via sexual liaisons with *women* that males – both Black and White – became men. Through its images of women *and* other men, the magazine presented a vision of heterosexual urban manhood that was predicated on the continuing (and often violent) subordination and marginalisation of both women and homosexual men.

> *Drum's* images of manhood fed into (and was fed by) discourses around nationalist struggle in which a hegemonic White heterosexual masculinity attempted to deny manhood to Black men.

These assumptions meant that, in speaking (as it repeatedly claimed) for all Black men, *Drum* barely recognised the existence of male voices expressing a preference for men. Although the magazine's self-declared aim was 'to be the voice of those who have no voice' and its task 'to put forward the views and feelings of those who have no constitutional method to express their views, and often no outlet for their feelings but a cry' (*Drum*, July 1958), it was primarily heterosexual voices that were expressed by *Drum*. Although homosexual Black men were amongst those who had 'no constitutional method to express themselves', their voices and views remained almost entirely hidden. Overall, drawing on Western biomedical discourse, itself emerging from a Judeo-Christian framework that had long labelled homosexuality as deviant (in the context of a South African legal system that defined homosexual acts as criminal), a 'heterosexual assumption' underpinned *Drum*'s approach (Alwood, 1996:8). Combined with pressure from the apartheid state, the financial imperatives inherent in publishing a magazine in a capitalist economy, the need for authenticity (given an audience conceived to be largely urban, largely male, predominantly Black and almost entirely straight), this perspective served to construct a complex *dialectic*. This dialectic shaped both the magazine and its audience in particular ways, and served to establish heterosexuality as hegemonic almost by default. In essence, the magazine's model was underlain by *essentialist* assumptions that heterosexuality was ordained by God and given substance by biology, and that maleness, masculinity and heterosexuality were interchangeable terms.

Drum and homosex from the 1950s

Yet there were traces of other possibilities. While men's desire for men or women's desire for women was almost entirely invisible and unmentionable in the early *Drum*, there were hints of alternative – and unacceptable – desires in later volumes of the magazine. Between 1951 and the departure of editor Anthony Sampson in 1955, there were just four extremely brief, and largely indirect, allusions to homosexuality and none at all to lesbianism. One of the more direct mentions came in an article arguing that 'adverse' changes in sexual behaviour were linked to urbanisation: '[h]omosexuality is another evil which is spreading among Africans in cities' (*Drum*, February 1954).

The same volume saw Manalil Gandhi, earlier jailed for 50 days as a result of his participation in the Defiance Campaign, complain about conditions in prisons. Apart from beatings and poor food, Gandhi alleged that in order to prove they were not smuggling tobacco, prisoners were required to undress and jump up and down before turning to bend down and expose their anuses to prison guards. Despite this, however, 'a good deal' of tobacco entered the jail, with prisoners going to 'the extent of selling their body, mind and soul for it' (*Drum*, February 1954). Other evidence supports Gandhi's observation, suggesting that homosexual relations were widespread in South African jails in the middle of the twentieth century. Mopeli Paulus had been sentenced to twelve months' hard labour in Pretoria in 1951 for his alleged participation in the Witzieshoek Rebellion of 1950. In his autobiography, Paulus noted that '[t]here is everything in the world in jail – things that seem unimagineable – even rape'. 'You must,' noted Paulus more matter-of-factly later on, 'play to the desires of the place you are in' (*Drum*, February 1955). Others jailed in the 1950s remembered similar events. In his memoirs some thirty years later, Godfrey Moloi took care to distance himself from such activities, noting that '[s]ome of the younger boys would do the most immoral acts just for a cigarette' whilst in jail. While hardened criminals had 'brides', '[b]oys of my age, some of whom I knew very well, had to fall victims to the sodomites to survive' (Moloi, 1987:136, 151, 156).

Evidently sexual pairings between men in jail were relatively common. But when Mr *Drum* himself, Henry Nxumalo, contrived to be jailed in order to establish the validity of Gandhi's story of conditions in jail not a word was said about sexual relations between men. Although the focus of Nxumalo's article was on the requirement that prisoners strip naked, *nothing* was said of Gandhi's allegation that the purpose of this was to eliminate the smuggling of tobacco for which prisoners would be willing to sell their 'body, mind and soul'. Homosexual relations in jail, or anywhere else for that matter, were neither investigated nor commented upon: a stony silence surrounded this aspect of urban existence. What troubled the writers at *Drum* was the requirement that uncircumcised boys were stripped alongside circumcised men, thus offending both. It was enough, it seemed, to make the point that prison regulations themselves demanded 'that searching ... be conducted with due regard to decency and self respect' (*Drum*, March 1954).

It was several years later that another reader drew *Drum*'s attention to the 'scandalous' homosexual relationships in the mining compounds surrounding Johannesburg. Stephen Tau of Benoni expressed his deep concern that:

> [s]ome men in the compounds 'marry' other men and treat them as their wives. The unfortunate fellow who falls into such a bad habit never returns home. He goes on treating his man as a queen until he is without shoes ... Having no money and a home to go to, they move into the locations and get to work for Shebeen queens who pay them with skokiaan. I hope this kind of thing will come to a quick end (*Drum*, June 1961).

Drum, though, was not interested in pursuing this line of enquiry, choosing not to respond to Tau's observations. But despite the lack of response another reader raised the matter again in 1963. 'I couldn't believe that men could "marry" other men on the mines until I saw this myself, happening right in front of my eyes. What can be done about this disgrace to African people? Is there no way to stop it?' But no reporter was sent to investigate, and *Drum's* response was merely to confirm that these shocking practices did indeed exist: 'It DOES happen. It IS a disgrace. The only way to put an end to it is for miners to be allowed to live normal family lives' (*Drum*, February 1963).

For *Drum*, it seemed, there was no question that these 'disgraceful' practices were the result of apartheid policies that limited the right of women to be in town: homosex was not an option that any Black man would choose if there was a woman available. And *any* woman it seemed would do. *Drum's* position was made very clear at the end of 1964, when a young man asked the magazine's advice:

> I am 32, have a good job and own a car. But I have no girlfriend because I simply hate women. My mother is very concerned about this and has often pleaded with me to have a girlfriend. She has even promised to maintain any girl I may choose. My mother's fear, which she has expressed to close members of the family, is that I am not normal. I am quite normal. My problem is that I just can't face the idea of going to bed with a woman. The very sight of women disgusts me. What should I do to allay the fears of my mother?

'If you are not kidding, then you must be queer' responded *Drum* bluntly. 'It is difficult to believe that you are normal.' Giving little thought to the happiness of a woman in such a relationship, *Drum* went on to remonstrate that '[e]ven men who have been known to harbour intense hatred for women have been known to have a woman in their life.' Finally the hapless reader was instructed to 'give the matter more serious thought – at least for the sake of your poor mother. Or do you hate her too?' (*Drum*, December 1964).

Discourses of 'race', gender and sex

But as the years moved on, as White editors and Black writers came and went, and as restrictions over what could be printed were tightened up in the context of apartheid, a small space emerged in which *Drum* seemed to acknowledge an alternative to heterosex. It was in the context of an increasingly hostile political environment, alongside a change of editor, that *Drum* first began to recognise in print that a few readers were unwilling to align themselves to the magazine's version of a masculinity defined through monogamous and/or polygamous heterosexuality. Perhaps, though, this recognition was intimately connected to the escalating attempts by the White state to deny Black manhood. If Black men's claim to manhood was, like White men's, predicated on heterosexuality, then (conceiving masculinity to be relational to other masculinities) homosexual masculinity – or something like it – was a *necessary* oppositional category.

Masculinities

Masculinity is imagined here to be a complex and multi-faceted identity that is actively and creatively produced by men through the inter-secting relationships with other identities, such as those of sexuality, race, class and ethnicity in each particular historical and cultural context. In the sense that each man has to construct his own masculinity there are multiple masculinities, where each specific version can be seen as a vital point of intersection of different forms of power, stratification, subjective identity formation and desire. Yet the different versions of masculinity emerging from the changing confluence of these intersections are neither equivalent in terms of power, status and privilege, nor are they fixed. They take on power in relation to women and 'other', less valued, forms of masculinity. While, for example, the masculinity embodied and practiced by White middle-class heterosexual Western men is not monolithic, it currently dominates those masculinities embodied and performed by, for example, Black and/or gay men.

Thus the discourse that was to emerge around male sexuality in *Drum* was intrinsically shaped by the discourse of race. Retief (1994:100) has noted that '[t]here is a long history that remains as yet unwritten of the repression and regulation of sexuality by the apartheid state ... far from being a political irrel-evancy, sex has been an important area of concern for successive generations of National Party governments'. Sexual policing, argues Retief, went hand in hand with racist legislation aimed at 'keeping the white nation sexually and morally pure so that it had the strength to resist the black communist onslaught' (*ibid.*). According to Epprecht (1998: 642), the 'racially charged context of [Zimbabwe's] nationalist struggle' worked to reduce the possibilities for admitting and tolerating sexual ambiguities. Of American White suprem-acists, Ferber has argued persuasively that '[i]t is an understatement to claim that white supremacy is obsessed with interracial sexuality ... Far more than a lurid preoccupation, the obsession with interracial sexuality is part of the process of boundary maintenance essential to the construction of race and gender identity' (Ferber, 1999:6). Similar constructions existed in South Africa, tying race and gender identities together in a complex web of mutually constructed meanings.

From the perspective of the men who made *Drum*, the attempt to speak with an adult Black male voice in a racist society, where Black men were conceived of as 'boys', was best achieved by closely aligning Black men's sexu-ality with that of White men. At the same time, perhaps *Drum*'s silences with regard to alternatives to heterosex constituted a recognition that acknowl-edging Black homosexual relationships would have reflected badly on Black people in general, as further evidence of their rampant and uncivilised sexu-ality. If being a man in the 'modern' world meant penetrative intercourse with women only, then any claim to adulthood for Black men would presumably have to foreground Black men's heterosexuality.

Images of non-heterosexual men first appeared in *Drum* in early 1955, with the arrival of a new editor, Sylvester Stein. The first signs of this were evident in September, with the publication of both photographs and a report of a performance of the 'All Male Non-European Revuette and Minstrel Show'. Taking place in Cape Town, almost 900 miles from Johannesburg, the stars of the show were Coloured as opposed to Black South Africans. Entitled 'The Moffees Can Can' this supposed 'review' made almost no mention of the show itself, preferring to focus almost entirely on the 'Moffees' who were the 'star attractions' and who, it was carefully explained, were female impersonators (*Drum*, September 1955).

The journalists' unease with such gender bending is clear, reinforcing Butler's observation that drag performances, such as those of the 'moffies' (*Drum* used both spellings), destabilise the 'distinctions between the natural and the artificial, depth and surface, inner and outer through which discourses about genders almost always operate', thus bearing the potential to undermine normative heterosexuality (Butler, 1990:viii). Taking care to ensure that the word 'girls' went into inverted commas almost every time it was used, the writer described how '(Joey) Costello led her energetic and versatile girls – er – boys Yvonne, Linda, Carmen and Piper, through some ... entertaining can-can dances' (*Drum*, September 1955). Although not a word was said about the sexual preferences of these 'female impersonators', and readers were left to draw their own conclusions, it was clear (the term 'moffie' had long been used to label men displaying 'feminine' behaviour) that these were likely to be men who desired men (de Waal in Gevisser, 1994:x).

A few months later, the Coloured 'moffies' were back in the news when an unidentified *Drum* photographer attended a 'moffie drag'. The photographer – evidently an experienced drag goer – was surprised to find White 'moffies' in attendance. A photograph of a mixed race couple caught White Dolores as she 'applie[d] with ticklish finger some makeup to the face of Ada' (*Drum*, October 1956). For 'average' Black readers the message was clear – 'moffies' were either Coloured or White, way out of the ordinary, an exotic spectacle far removed from 'normal' lives. Thus, far from undermining normative masculine hetero-sexuality, as Butler suggests, in this particular case such images served to reinforce it: by burlesquing women's conduct, the 'moffies' left their audience in no doubt that they were actually male. At the same time shifting, rather than eliminating, the racial discourse, Black manhood was set up in opposition to an effeminate Coloured manhood.

After this brief appearance in 1955 and 1956 such images disappeared from the magazine until 1959. An explanation of these renewed absences may lie in the passage of the *Immorality Act* of 1957, an attempt by the White state to consolidate restrictive and oppressive legislation around an individual's choice of sexual partner. But while the Act contained several provisions criminalising homosexual relations, it was the criminalisation of certain heterosexual acts between White and Black that captured the public's, the state's and *Drum's* imagination. Black South African men had experienced a century or more of lessons teaching them to control their 'natural' hetero-sexual desire for White women. In the context of apartheid, Black men's heterosexuality represented a performance of gender *and* race: a performance that kept them in the arms of Black, not White women. White men in contrast had long been able to prove their manhood through intercourse with women of all races. But for an apartheid state bent on separate development, such intercourse, along with homosexual relations, was anathema. Yet in the light of the state's attempts to police a *variety* of sexual desires and sexual liaisons, *Drum's* focus was narrowly and firmly on inter-racial heterosexual relations. If White men could demonstrate manhood through sexual intercourse with Black women, so too presumably, could Black men. Given the context of a racialised nationalist struggle, there was thus a great deal of media mileage to be had from exposing the hypocrisy surrounding inter-racial heterosexual affairs between resourceful White men and resourceless Black women.

The 'moffies' returned briefly in 1959 when *Drum* covered another of the 'moffie drags', again establishing the 'moffies' (Coloured men in far away Cape Town) as exotic and alien. Quoting the host, Madame Costello, complaining about the previous party, when 'skollies' had gatecrashed and people 'were smoking dagga in my place', the report is structured in such a way as to empha-sise the unreliability and instability of the 'moffies'. The article starts with Madame Costello's reluctance ever to hold another party: 'I swore then I would never give another drag'. It ends with her making the same remarks about the present party: 'I'll never have another drag in my place ... Never! I swear it!' Further developing its image of 'moffies' as exotic, spectacular and decidedly 'abnormal', as improperly gendered males, *Drum* declared that 'everyone of the 40 or so people ... was a man – or at any rate male'. While the younger 'moffies' 'would have attracted a lot of male glances in any company', the older ones 'looked a little grotesque' and by the end of the evening 'looked tired and lonely and very pathetic' (*Drum*, January 1959). If only they had chosen 'normal' lives, the subtext seemed to say, these males would be neither tired, lonely nor pathetic.

By the end of the 1950s it had become increasingly difficult to 'put forward the views and feelings of those who have no constitutional method to express their views' – no matter that these views and feelings (as mediated by the producers of *Drum*) were narrowly conceived to represent those of the silent and very straight majority (*Drum*, July 1958). The 'moffies' of Cape Town, however, remained newsworthy and, when female drum majorettes were to be incorporated into the Coon Carnival for the first time in January 1962, *Drum* contrasted Yvonne de Carlo, a 'moffie' who had lead the carnival every year since 1950, with the leader of the majorettes, Elizabeth Miller. The first words introducing de Carlo to readers described her fluttering eyelashes, and effectively established her as different, affected and 'feminine'. In contrast, 'Miss Western Province 1961', the wholesome Elizabeth Miller and her team, were to provide Yvonne with 'tougher competition than ever before ... for 34 lusty, busty high stepping girls will be out in their satin suits and peaked caps'. The last word over who would prove to be the most popular was allocated to Miss Miller: 'A girl is a girl ... I don't know what a Moffie is – and I hate to think' (*Drum*, January 1962).

When the 'moffies' of Cape Town elected a new Queen, *Drum* provided nearly two pages of coverage of the event. Present at the nightclub where the affair took place 'were about 60 moffies, a cluster of real men and one or two pukka women. Oh, yes – there was the odd young boy as well.' The 'spectacle' and its dangers were hinted at by playing with the ambiguity of the term 'twist' further on:

> When the moffies weren't busy electing a new queen they were twisting – in fact it was the most twisted party I've seen. Men in dresses twisted with men in dresses, men in dresses danced with men in pants, and men in dresses twisted with little boys. And men in dresses DIDN'T twist with women in dresses (*Drum*, January 1964).

Discourses of danger, deviance and difference

It was just a few months after this, in April 1965, that *Drum* became a supplement to the weekly *Golden City Post*. But even with its substantially reduced pages and text, *Drum* continued to print stories and pictures of the 'moffies', advertising these stories in the supplement to increase sales of the newspaper. When *Drum* was relaunched as an independent monthly magazine three years later in 1968, a more robust coverage of sexual matters added sex education to the focus on inter-racial liaisons and 'moffies'.

The first edition after the three-year hiatus observed that 'the loudest squeals came from 'Cape Town's 500 or so moffies' when new legislation against homosexuals meant 'offenders being jailed for up to three years'. Noting that 'moffies' could be seen either as 'figures of a fun, a shrill if somewhat distasteful joke', or as 'a menace to public good and hand-flapping exhibitionists of moral decay', the magazine reinforced constructions of moffies as deviant, different and dangerous. Pointing to the 'heartache behind the frills and fun', *Drum* emphasised the tragedy of the 'truths' it was about to reveal – the 'real face of the moffie world'.

> Behind the gay and devil-may-care image ... lies the heaving anxiety of their hearts to live a full and proper life ... Socially they are misfits. Normal men find them amusing from a distance but repulsive at close quarters. Normal women, on the other hand, are initially shocked by their feminine behaviour (*Drum*, April 1968).

The notion of 'abnormality' resurfaced again in a series on sex education which made very clear what was and what was not acceptable. In 'Sex: the shadows over happiness, problems in childhood and later', homosexuality was the main 'problem' identified (*Drum*, November 1968). This 'problem', explained *Drum*, was generally connected to an individual's upbringing, and it was over-protective single mothers who were largely to blame when sons 'turned' into homosexuals. And this was tragic as 'the life of a homosexual is generally not a happy one', and although 'homosexual people can be helped to lead normal lives as ordinary men and women through psychiatric treatment ... surgery is quite useless and cannot help a homosexual to become a normal person' (*Drum*, November 1968). Although it was only much later on that *Drum* was to spell out its view that 'moffies and lesbians, in most cases, were not born that way' (at the same time making explicit its conflation of moffies with all male homosexual identities), the idea that homosexual behaviour was forced upon easily moulded youngsters or a choice forced upon men through the absence of women had long underpinned *Drum's* representations of 'moffies'.

The dangers of homosexual desire, this time conflated with paedophile desire, were displayed for readers yet again in December 1969 when it was revealed that '[t]he sex maniac who slew small boys' had emerged from a 'broken' home and had been sexually assaulted by a man when he was 13 years of age. Implying that homosexuality was infectious, and that homosexual males were all potential molesters and murderers of small boys, *Drum* noted 'Achmat was behind bars, inevitably for sodomy' by the age of 18. After serving his time Achmat's release saw his 'perversion' take 'an even more sinister twist' when 'not satisfied with merely slaking his lust for children of his own sex, he had the urge to kill them as well' (*Drum*, December 1969). Juxtaposed against images of 'moffies', readers were offered constructions of homosex that ranged from tragic to deadly.

Given such images it is understandable that silences around homosexual relationships extended to the magazine's problem and correspondence pages too. Early on there was no one, apparently, either in need of advice about (or willing to acknowledge) homosexual desire in these pages. The vast bulk of the letters finding their way into print came from women complaining about men, or men complaining about women. For the most part such letters expressed an understanding of sexual relationships premised upon an unconditional acceptance of heterosexual relations between men and multiple female partners as the norm.

Different contexts, different discourses

In contrast, versions of *Drum* that were produced to the north of South Africa contained far more letters about homosexual relationships. 'About an eighth of the letters printed ... addressed this topic, often inquiring whether or not homosexual relationships were socially or culturally accepted' (Mutongi, 2000:16). Mutongi argues that, in the mid-1960s, there was a degree of tolerance of what he defines as 'situational' or 'temporary' homosexuality in East, West and Central African copies of *Drum*, but the moment there was any indication that these relationships might be stable or long term, the magazine's response was much more negative, immediately talking of disease and psychiatrists, criminality and social outcasts. It could be argued that this relative tolerance was connected to a context in which the future was full of hope. This was a context marked by the ending of nationalist struggles and the establishment of majority rule, rooted in an emphasis on development and located in the post-World War II era of unparalleled economic growth. In the absence of a racialised struggle for masculinity it may be that a small space briefly opened up in which to articulate other possibilities for manhood.

Back in South African versions of *Drum*, though, such letters and such possibilities were scarce, with individuals expressing any variety of male-to-male desire presented as dangerous and perverted predators. In contrast, *intersexed* individuals were conceived of quite differently, constructed instead as the hapless victims of their own biology. In a society where one's gender identity (and thus sexual desire) was directly tied to the possession (and appearance) of specific bodily parts, such individuals had a serious problem. 1959 saw farm worker John Samson make *Drum* headlines after 'Doctors declared him to be a woman' (*Drum*, October 1959). Another article told the story of a young man who developed breasts in his early twenties, and had been found to possess ovaries. His several attempts at suicide were represented by *Drum* as the natural response of a man whose 'soul was ripped to shreds' by his own biology, but who could reclaim normality through surgery. 'He had to become a woman to live. The alternative was death' (*Drum*, November 1968; August 1969; December 1972; August 1974).

By the beginning of the 1970s, and having drawn on a long tradition constructing the homosexual as a *patriarchal* scapegoat, *Drum* had established a powerful discourse of homosexuality (read 'moffies') as both deviant, dangerous and 'other' (Stein, 1999; Tosh, 1994). And having established such images, *Drum* spent the next five years almost entirely silent about homosexual affairs. This silence may be attributed in large part to the demolition and forced removals taking place in Cape Town's District Six, which had been the source of most of *Drum*'s stories about 'moffies'. It was in December of 1970, for example, that *Drum* recorded that Eugene Fritz, better known as Kewpie, 'socialite, ballet dancer, cabaret and strip tease artist' was 'brimful of plans and enthusiasm for her new hairdressing salon in Kensington' (*Drum*, December 1970). Nearly all of the magazine's stories about homosexual men had been about cross-dressers like Kewpie, men who had lived in District Six, as it was in this cosmopolitan area that 'moffies' had lived in relative openness. 'Gay dances, drag shows, and Mardi Gras incorporating cross-dressing were part of the Cape flavour in the 1950s and 1960s' (Isaacs & McKendrick, 1992:93). At least one social commentator has argued that District Six had to be demolished precisely because it permitted such goings on. 'The mixing of the races was discouraged', says Oswald Mtshali, 'because it was believed to be a cause of *miscegenation*. Places like District Six were regarded as breeding grounds for homosexuality. The "moffies" were pilloried and treated with contempt. In the Black areas these "outcasts" were rare' (Mtshali in Stein & Jacobsen, 1986:16). Whatever the accuracy of Mtshali's views, the declaration in 1966 of District Six as a White area under the *Group Areas Act* signalled the beginning of the end of an era for the 'moffies'. As forced removals gradually dispersed Kewpie and others to a variety of locations around the Cape Flats, alongside changes in the clubs, hotels and architecture of the foreshore, the easy proximity that had facilitated this particular lifestyle came to a gradual end.

It was only towards the end of 1976 that the Cape Town 'moffies' reappeared briefly in *Drum*. But, in the '[g]ay world of the moffee hairdresser', an article that focused on Kewpie's Kensington salon, life was revealed to be anything but gay. Identified as a 'breed apart', joined only by that 'common bond of loyalty and that special affinity found among comrades in affliction', the moffies were separate 'from the true male and true female in the Cape community'. None of 'nature's sex indecisions' as the reporter put it, 'are truly happy and most seek escape. Self deception is common with drugs and liquor playing no small part. Ninety per cent would welcome a sex change operation and only today's prohibitive cost prevents wholesale surgery tomorrow' (*Drum*, October 1976).

A distinction was made between 'moffies' and gay men for the first time a few months later in a story about the 'moffies' of Johannesburg. But with the collapse of the Cape Town scene, reports about individuals claiming unorthodox sexualities all but vanished from the pages of *Drum*. Instead, the magazine focused on the never-ending supply of heterosexual contraventions of the *Immorality Act*. As with earlier cases deemed newsworthy by *Drum*, and reflecting official statistics across the country, most of these involved White men and Black women. If White women were entering into liaisons with Black men, there was, apart from the story of Regina Brookes in the mid-1950s, no record of this in the pages of *Drum*, suggesting that the magazine had little interest in publicising competition between Black and White men over White women. In the context of apartheid South Africa, heterosexual practice that empowered Black men also kept them in their place, which was in the arms specifically of *Black* women.

The intersections between apartheid, racism and competing masculinities and sexualities, as they were played out in the pages of *Drum*, worked to disadvantage those unable or unwilling to claim allegiance to the dominant heterosexuality. On the one hand, there was *Drum*'s tension-filled relationship with the apartheid state, which increasingly endeavoured to restrict what was written and published as part of a much broader attempt to construct and maintain a subordinate Black masculinity. Heightened efforts by the state to control public discourses can be read as an increasingly intense aspect of the extreme competition between racially defined (and unequally resourced) rival masculinities. As hooks says, '[s]ince competition between males is sanctioned within male-dominated society, from the standpoint of white patriarchy, black masculinity must be kept "in check." Black males must be made subordinate in as many cultural arenas as possible' (1995:99). And given the importance of heterosexuality to twentieth-century notions of manhood and masculinity, what better cultural arena than that of sexuality to challenge and resist claims and counterclaims to manhood?

Thus, if apartheid was an ideology and a set of practices that attempted to deny manhood to Black men, *Drum*'s resistance to that ideology was premised on demonstrating Black men's claim to a manhood that, like White manhood, was defined through sexual intercourse with women. But this claim, while perhaps understandable given the wider socio-historical context of hegemonic heterosexuality and apartheid, also compromised the magazine's claim to speak for all those who had no voice. *Drum*'s representations of 'normal' heterosexual masculinity in opposition to 'deviant and dangerous' homosexual masculinity was signalled and symbolised through portrayals of Coloured men in drag in distant Cape Town. All 'real' (i.e. heterosexual men), the sub-text read, were created equal and should receive similar treatment in law and society. Thus, while *Drum* fought for the right for Black men to be seen as men, its offer of proof focused on heterosexual affairs, illustrating again and again how 'men will be men'.

Same-sex desire between men in the Black community thus remained almost entirely invisible in the pages of *Drum* between 1951 and 1984, when the magazine's ownership changed. The stories, for example, of Black men's sexual affairs with men in the mines and prisons around Johannesburg remained unwritten. In contrast, intersexed people of all races were both acknowledged and permitted to speak, with long and detailed reports about their experiences predominantly in their own words (*Drum*, August 1969; November 1975; August 1977). Homosexual men (and women), on the other hand, could not so easily blame their biology, and while intersexed individuals were permitted at least some kind of voice, homosexual men were not. Reports about men who laid claim to homosexual identities tended to be in the third person, their words mediated by the journalists and sub-editors who shaped the final product. Thus the Coloured drag queens of Cape Town saw words put into their mouths, words that helped construct them (and condemn them) as outcasts on the very margins of South African society. When *Drum* did write about these kinds of unorthodox sexualities, it did so by representing men who desired men as males who were *not* men, as an exotic spectacle, as 'moffies', and as such defined as 'sex deviates', 'nature's jokes' and a 'breed apart' – the result of nature's 'flight of fancy' (*Drum*, January 1959; April 1968; October 1976; February 1977). Thus, despite its belief in its own efforts to 'speak for those who have no voice' and its willingness to provoke the apartheid state, where alternatives to heterosexuality were concerned, the pages of *Drum* were infused with the same kind of homophobic and racialised discourse as that emanating from the White heterosexist racists it elected to challenge.

Exercises for critical engagement

1 How much choice do you think the writers at *Drum* had about representing homosexual men as deviant and dangerous?
2 Examine a contemporary magazine and think firstly about how much coverage it gives to homosexual lives, and secondly what kind of coverage it provides.
3 Examine a contemporary magazine and see how many allusions to hetero- sexual lives you can find. Some things to look out for: text or pictures showing couples; pictures of men or women with wedding rings, or in pairs; issues around parenting, marriage; who the cookery pages are addressed to; who is assumed to be cooking for whom; stories about dating, and who is dating whom; the kinds of problems raised on the problem pages, etc. Think very carefully about what is *not* featured.

Recommended reading

Epprecht, E. (1998). 'The "Unsaying" of indigenous homosexualities in Zimbabwe: Mapping a blindspot in an African Masculinity'. *Journal of Southern African Studies*, 24(4): 631–651.

Ferber, A. (1999). *White Man Falling*. Lanham: Rowman & Littlefield.

Gevisser, M. & E. Cameron (1994). *Defiant Desire: Gay and Lesbian Lives in South Africa*. Braamfontein: Ravan.

Murray, S. & W. Roscoe (Eds.) (1998). *Boy-Wives and Female Husbands*. New York: St Martin's Press.

Mutongi, K. (2000). 'Dear Dolly's advice: Representations of youth, courtship, and sexualities in Africa, 1960–1980'. *International Journal of African Historical Studies*, 33(1):1–23.

Shire, C. (1994). 'Men don't go to the moon: Language, space and masculinities in Zimbabwe'. In Cornwall, A. & N. Lindisfarne (Eds.) *Dislocating Mascu- linity: Comparative Ethnographies*, pp. 147–158. London: Routledge.

Stein, E. (1999). *The Mismeasure of Desire: The Science, Theory, and Ethics of Sexual Orientation*. New York: Oxford University Press.

Psychology and the Political, the Social and Leadership

Political Leadership in the Context of Reconciliation

16

Shahnaaz Suffla & Mohamed Seedat

OUTCOMES

After having studied this chapter you should be able to:

- define and describe the following in your own words
  - political leadership
  - psycho-cultural interpretation of leadership
  - social capital
  - transformational leadership
  - warrior-style leadership
  - negotiation
  - reconciliation
  - interactive leadership style
- discuss the prerequisite challenges that characterised South Africa's reconciliation process, and
- explain the role of South African transformational political leadership in promoting reconciliation.

I N RECENT South African history, different political and civic leaders and their organised constituencies appear to have exercised their agency in diverse ways in relation to the process of reconciliation. Political leadership, operating within a transforming context, and characterised by vision, pragmatism, integrity and moral authority appears to have been instrumental in creating social consent and shifting former antagonists to peaceful engagement and dialogue. Drawing on the experiences and contributions of specific political and civic figures, and scrutinising the dominant discourse surrounding a specific national tragedy, we argue that the formalised processes of reconciliation are predicated on the early interventions of transformational political leadership.

South Africa's Truth and Reconciliation Commission (TRC) has been both criticised for its limitations, as well as hailed as a powerful symbol and instrument of healing and reconciliation, and as one that has served to centralise the ideals of non-racialism, national unity and peace building (e.g. Hamber & Mofokeng, 2000; Posel & Simpson, 2002). A discussion of the strengths and weaknesses of the TRC is not within the scope of this chapter. Instead, it is argued that preparations for reconciliation typically precede the establishment of statutory bodies such as the TRC.

It is worth noting that, within the South African context, the concept of reconciliation remains complex and contested. Notwithstanding the debates, reconciliation generally refers to a complex psycho-social and political process focused on encouraging antagonists to dialogue around contentious issues with a view to arriving at sufficient consensus about the basis of the conflict and its solution. Integral to peace-building and peace-keeping mechanisms such as the TRC, reconciliation also involves the acknowledgement of hurt perpetrated in the cause of oppression and/or liberation. It includes statements of regret and apology, reparation for victims, and a willingness to work towards peace and social justice. In this sense, reconciliation is also connected to forgiveness and the restoration of relationships and, importantly, begins with a spirit of constructive engagement followed by substantive and concrete measures to ensure that the parties remain reconciled.

The roots of the reconciliation process in South Africa may be traced back to earlier historical events. When the *Promotion of National Unity and Reconciliation Bill* was promulgated, it formalised a 17-member commission with the intent of facilitating a truth and recovery process aimed at reconciliation with the past. Its mandate, as a statutory agent of national unity and reconciliation, was to establish as complete a picture as possible of the nature, causes and extent of past gross human rights violations, to provide reparation and rehabilitation to victims of abuse, to grant amnesty to perpetrators of human rights abuses who offered full disclosure about the crimes they had committed, to formulate a set of recommendations to the president with respect to the creation of institutions conducive to a stable and fair society and measures to prevent future human rights violations, and to compile a report publicising the work and findings of the TRC. To assist with these objectives, the legislation established three committees within the TRC: the Committee on Human Rights Violations, the Committee on Amnesty and the Committee on Reparation and Rehabilitation.

To fulfil its mandate the TRC conducted public hearings across the country to listen to stories of victims and perpetrators of human rights abuses. The hearings were seen to contribute to the formation of a shared public space in which different voices could be heard and silences broken, in which victims could be affirmed and their dignity restored, and became the subject of extensive media dissemination. Thus, the TRC formalised the reconciliation process in that it made reconciliation a public issue and institutionalised the associated roles of transformational leadership.

In this chapter we intend to examine the roles of political leaders who operate from within organised political structures to promote reconciliation in periods of conflict and transition to peace. Our analysis is based on a recognition of the connection between socio-political processes and the practice of leadership and, against this backdrop, is specifically focused on a scrutiny of transformative leadership functioning within a transforming context. Following Samuels (1996:81), we seek to encourage 'deep reflection on the great political issues of the day and on politics itself so that a recognition can emerge that there really is no divide between the spiritual and the social, between the private and the public, between the inner life and the world of politics'. This position maintains that a concern for the social and political acknowledges the political history of groups and individuals and the connection between politics, psychological transformation and social identity. Our intention is organised around a very specific aim. We seek to examine the role of civic and political leadership in the reconciliation process in South Africa. We do so drawing from relevant theories on political leadership, focusing on the leadership functions called into play during the transition process, and the challenges posed to leaders in forging reconciliation between Black and White South Africans.

In reviewing the historical record of events leading up to and following the country's first democratic election process, we will focus on specific events of national significance. From the onset we wish to acknowledge that a variety of broader political processes and factors may have converged to create opportunities for visionary political leaders to exercise their agency and transformative styles of leadership (e.g. internal unrest, international sanctions, the increasing impact of economic globalisation, changing configurations of social contexts in Africa, etc.). However, we regard the examination thereof as interesting subject matter for a separate analysis, and restrict our chapter to the stated aims. We therefore begin our analysis with a consideration of one specific national tragedy, the assassination of Chris Hani, by way of illustrating the role of early political leadership in reconciliation. Although by no means the earliest evidence of reconciliation, Hani's death presents a powerful expression of the impetus given to social transformation by historical events that unfolded in South Africa's political arena.

The death of Chris Hani: Tragedy and hope

Chris Hani's involvement in resistance politics spanned a period of about three decades. He joined the military wing of the African National Congress (ANC)

The former Chief of Staff of Umkhonto we Sizwe and General Secretary of the South African Communist Party, Chris Hani, behind Nelson Mandela, was assassinated on 10 April 1993 while peace and reconciliation were being negotiated.

– Mkhonto we Sizwe (MK) – in 1962, was elected to the ANC executive in 1974, became Chief of Staff of MK in 1987, and was elected as General Secretary of the South African Communist Party (SACP) in 1991. In 1991 he was also named as the front-runner to Thabo Mbeki for the ANC's deputy presidency, but withdrew in favour of a compromise candidate, Walter Sisulu. He was widely tipped in political circles as a successor to ANC president, Nelson Mandela; his fame and popularity were thus perceived to be second only to that of Nelson Mandela.

Hani was assassinated on 10 April 1993, just as multi-party negotiations were sharply focused on peace and reconciliation, and with it the prospect of democracy in the country. In the aftermath of Hani's assassination the front page of *The Weekly Mail*, a national weekly newspaper, gave voice to the deep emotions evoked by Hani's brutal murder. Angry and grieving Black South Africans said:

'The people are very angry ... You can't kill a leader of the people and not expect nothing to happen.'

'No more peace, no more peace!'

'Kill us, kill us, we are already dead!'

'The people are shattered into a thousand pieces, everyone is just running with his own little piece of hatred.'

'This is a message for De Klerk ... things must move quickly.'

(*The Weekly Mail*, 16–22 April 1993)

On another page of the same newspaper, a journalist quoted White South Africans as saying:

'I cried when Dr. Verwoed died and I'm gonna celebrate tonight'.

'I'm crying about the brutal and senseless murder of a man who wanted negotiations for black and white South Africans ...'

'This is a war we're involved in ... he's one of the enemy and we wiped him out. This is a racial war and there's only going to be one winner'.

(*The Weekly Mail*, 16–22 April 1993)

The same journalist concluded that while few Whites could see the political dangers in the murder of a high-profile and popular Black leader, most could only express their ill-defined unease and fear (*The Weekly Mail*, 16–22 April 1993).

Hani's death served to underline the fragility of negotiations between the ANC and the National Party (NP), and appeared to accelerate the constitutional process at multi-party talks which had been going on for nearly three years. Hani's death, the most serious crisis that faced South Africans since the initiation of negotiations, forced political leadership from both sides of the spectrum to act swiftly and decisively. However, *The Weekly Mail* (16–22 April 1993) reported that while the ANC leadership, and particularly Nelson Mandela, attempted to address the fears and anger of the entire country, both Black and White, some members of the NP resorted to according blame to the ANC leadership for what it saw as the ANC's failure to control the militant mood of the masses in the period following Hani's murder. *The Weekly Mail* (*ibid.*) described the response of the NP as a reversion to old-style strategies to minimise the fears of its White constituency. Some saw de Klerk's decision to declare further unrest areas and to control rallies as potentially fuelling the conflict provoked by the tragedy. Yet other political analysts observed that de Klerk would in this instance have no choice but to assume a clear position on negotiations. Nonetheless, in spite of the strains between the negotiating partners, Hani's death and the intense anger that it evoked for Black South Africans underscored the reality that there was no alternative to negotiations and urgent transformation in the country. Within a week of the assassination, the ANC had insisted that as a matter of urgency an election date be set (sealed just two weeks after the murder), that a Transitional Executive Council be established, and that an interim constitution be negotiated. *The Weekly Mail* (23–29 April 1993) observed that 'there was something intensely political about Hani's death where a death mirrors the political life of an entire nation', thus highlighting the reality that the country needed a political settlement urgently.

As political analysts hypothesised that Hani's murder was a desperate attempt by White supremists to sabotage negotiations and to slow down progress towards elections, and questioned whether the ANC and NP would survive the crisis, *The Weekly Mail* (16–22 April 1993) reported on ANC president Nelson Mandela's two statesmanlike national television broadcasts, in which he attempted to skilfully employ Hani's murder to allay the fears of a racial war and to call for a non-racial South Africa: 'Mandela stood there, a symbol of national unity …'. Tokyo Sexwale, ANC Pretoria-Witswatersrand-Vereeniging (PWV) chairperson, explained, 'Leadership shows itself by going ahead of its followers during a moment of crisis, uncertainty and confusion' (*The Weekly Mail*, 23–29 April 1993). Jeremy Cronin, SACP member, in later years attributed the responses of the ANC leadership to 'the strategic intelligence and maturity of the ANC–alliance leadership' (Cronin, 1999). He suggested that the responses of the ANC leadership carried echoes of Hani's own declaration that 'we will defend ourselves resolutely, but we will not contribute to a spiral of violence' (*ibid.*). In scrutinising the role of leadership during this crisis, *The Weekly Mail* (23–29 April 1993) concluded that 'the

ANC emerged with the moral authority of the leadership of the nation. Even most whites know that now.'

It has been argued that given that most South Africans have been the victims of the tragedy and brutality of apartheid, space within which to collectively identify with this history and share in the experience of reclaiming individual memories is crucial to the process of reconciliation and reparation (Gobodo-Madikizela, 1995). Hani's funeral served as a powerful moment for South Africans across the spectrum to mourn the tragedy of apartheid, and the individual and collective losses of the past. In this instance, leadership showed itself to be attuned and responsive to the importance of offering their respective constituencies the space for emotional catharsis. Thousands of people, mainly Black South Africans, assembled at the First National Bank (FNB) stadium in Johannesburg on the day of the funeral; they were described as 'disciplined, mourning and dignified' (*The Weekly Mail*, 23–29 April 1993). It was the first funeral of a Black political leader to be televised nationally, and as such, the media served to perform an influential role in reinforcing the reconciliatory role of leadership and supporting the discourse of reconciliation that characterised the responses of leadership to the tragedy at the time. For example, in his televised tribute to Hani, Archbishop Desmond Tutu referred to the assassinated political leader as 'a man of peace, a man of justice and reconciliation, a man for negotiation' (SABC, 1993). Tutu's speech at the FNB stadium delivered a strong plea for peace, reconciliation and unity:

> His death is not a defeat, his death is our victory. We, all of us, black and white, all of us are going to live in peace, and justice, and friendliness in this country. And so, dear friends, we commit ourselves, each one of us, we commit ourselves to discipline, we commit ourselves to peace, we commit ourselves to negotiation and reconciliation. Nobody can stop us on our march to victory ... no guns, nothing. Nothing will stop us for we are moving to freedom ... we will be free, all of us black and white together' (SABC, 1993).

Thus, Hani's funeral came to epitomise both loss and despair, as well as hope and promise; it captured the mood of the majority of South Africans.

Hani's death and funeral placed the accent on the emotional depth of feelings generated in situations of social conflict, and the consequent need for peace-making efforts to address divergent interests beyond the cognitive level. Mack, for instance, argues that parties must come to recognise the connection between past losses and present fears, and to engage in collective mourning and reconciliation. He adds that the cycle of victimisation and vengeance often evoked in such situations can be fractured by the attitude of healing and transcending conflict, when opponents 'do a great deal of listening to the telling of history, especially of each group's hurts and its version of where responsibility has lain' (Mack in Ross, 1995:537). Others, too, have proposed that for the purposes of brokering enduring peace there can be no moving beyond loss without the experience of mourning for groups as well as individuals, for example, through public ceremonies and memorials imbued with psychological significance.

Theoretical considerations on the role of political leadership

In this section we attempt to critically discuss the conciliatory roles of South African political and civic leadership in the context of existing knowledge on political leadership. We will explore the constructs of political leadership as they are observed to have manifested in South Africa's reconciliation process. The literature on political leadership contains a wide variety of perspectives regarding what leadership is and how it is (or should be) conducted. Over the last twenty years, studies of leadership have included, for example, perspectives on the leadership styles of high-profile political figures within the international political community (e.g. Kaarbo & Hermann, 1998), the character and personality of political leaders (e.g. Immelman, 1993), and leadership and gender (e.g. Adler, 1996). However, a detailed review of this literature is beyond the scope of the present chapter. Suffice to mention that *leadership style* is defined as the multiple ways in which leaders relate to those around them, whether constituents or other leaders, how they structure interactions, and the norms, rules and principles that they utilise to guide such interactions (Kaarbo & Hermann, 1998). *Political leadership,* specifically, is defined as a social structure, or specifically as a structure of power and influence in society, and as a role that formulates a strategic vision for a populace, or any of it social sub-systems, and of determining the means by which the vision would be realised (Balogun, 1997).

Features of transitional leadership

It has been argued that in the context of mutually exclusive political ideologies and visions, the process towards reconciliation calls for leaders to be realistic and visionary; defined as 'the ability (vision) to consider existing realities as transformed possibilities' (Keren in Liebenberg, 1993:43). Liebenberg (1993) proposed that constructive engagement in democratisation and reconciliation demands transformational leadership from the political agents of change. According to Burns (in Lowe & Galen Kroeck, 1996), the transformational leader is one who articulates a vision of the future that can be shared with his or her group, and who engages with others in such a manner that the leader and the follower raise one another to a higher level of motivation and morality. The transformational leader seeks opportunities in the face of risk, is less likely to support the status quo, and attempts to raise the level of consciousness about the importance of valued outcomes by, for example, focusing on the needs of the collective. This style of leadership encourages follower autonomy within the overlay of the leader's vision, and thus strives to empower the masses. Unlike the warrior model of leadership (Nice, 1998), which emphasises that leadership is inseparably related to conflict and opposition, the transformational style asserts that results are more important than the methods used to achieve them, and lays emphasis on exploiting the vulnerabilities of others; the transformational leader seeks to uplift rather than exploit followers, is attuned to the moral dimension of conflict, and sees the opportunity for improving peoples' lives. In offering the descriptions above, it is acknowledged that leadership style may be dynamic and thus transform in relation to socio-political processes.

The qualities ascribed to the transformational leader call to mind the many powerful descriptions accorded to Nelson Mandela for his role in South Africa's transformational process. For example:

> This country was fortunate to have a leader of Nelson Mandela's calibre to take it through the rapids of transition. And his policy of reconciliation was appropriate ... All South Africans, victors and vanquished, those who assumed the reins of power and those who lost them, needed assurance that they all had a stake in the future. His steady hand was meant to apply balm to bruised egos and to counsel the new elite to exercise power with caution. He succeeded magnificently (*Financial Mail*, 17 December 1999).

> Few people in recorded history have been the subject of such high expectations; still fewer have matched them; Mandela has exceeded them ... any other nation would consider itself privileged to have his equal as its leader ... (*The Mail & Guardian*, 24 December 1998–7 January 1999).

> ... the world moral leader, the greatest statesman of the century ... (*Management Today*, September 1999).

> ... breathtaking magnanimity and willingness to forgive ... a potent agent for reconciliation (Tutu, 2000:59).

Transformational leadership appears to bear a close resemblance to charismatic leadership. A crucial aspect of the political process in South Africa prior to transformation involved the articulation of a clear political vision and change. Lowe and Galen Kroeck (1996) argue that such challenges call for charismatic leadership whereby the charismatic leader formulates and articulates a vision, effectively communicates a sense of mission, and instills pride, faith and respect amongst his or her followers. These processes are seen to engender trust in the leader and involvement in the mission, and to attest to the leader's commitment to the cause and his or her concern for the collectivity (Shamir, 1994). The leader's emotional and motivational effects on followers are also seen to be an important component of charisma.

For leaders driven by a vision of peace, as opposed to the need for power, status or acclaim, solving problems and achieving causes is highly salient, and mobilisation and effectiveness of political strategy feature prominently in their progression towards their goals. This, according to Renshon (1992), involves good judgment in the political arena, or the capacity to discern the essential nature of the problem, the potential avenues of response and their implications, and a sense of the means by which these might be accomplished. The quality of this analysis, reflection, and ultimately insight inform the making of politically consequential decisions, which directly affect a nation's physical and political integrity, and socio-economic well-being. Etheridge (1992:497) elaborates that the fullest expression of wisdom and good judgment in politics is *statesman-ship*, 'enduring decisions that restructure systems so that, for the long term, the world begins to work better for everyone'. A statesman – like Nelson Mandela for instance – is able to do more than select from limiting and pre-existing choices, but seeks newly forged agreements in the forms of coalitions, norms or policies which may sculpt a hopeful future from a history characterised by conflict and deep societal cleavages. Moskop (1996) also relates good judgment to prudence, or practical wisdom, which involves the psychological capacity to bring varied types of information to bear on the decision-making process. He argues that a more *comprehensive leadership approach* combines issues of political means and ethical ends, as well as personal skills and environmental constraints. It is highly probable then that a great measure of prudence within South African political leadership contributed to shifting the political environment towards reconciliation.

Prerequisite challenges

As increasing attention and concern focused on South Africa's political arena in the 1980s and 1990s, questions were being raised as to what conditions would provide the motivation for political leaders to respond to the conflict in this deeply divided society (du Toit, 1989), and cautions were being issued that the actions of South Africa's political leadership could make all the difference between degeneration into civil war and transformation to sustainable democracy (Liebenberg, 1993). Accordingly, qualitative and sustained responses to political reform challenges were demanded from the ruling NP and the ANC-led opposition, these representing the most prominent and significant but by no means the only political parties to participate in the transformation process, and being the ones that appeared to receive the most institutional and international support. The reality facing political leaders was that there was little option to resolving the conflict but to search for a bargained resolution, and thereby to effect society's transition to democracy. According to Balogun (1997), democracy is not likely to come about unless leadership becomes relevant to democratisation and governance reform. A number of political analysts have concluded that the particular leadership style that leaders adopt and the quality of political leadership ultimately shapes the way in which they deal with political crises and conflicts and, in turn, the future of an entire nation (e.g. du Toit, 1989; Kaarbo & Hermann, 1998). Accordingly, South African political leadership prepared to engage in a political style that would shift from adversarial politics to negotiation politics.

Negotiation has been defined as a process by which two or more parties attempt to resolve perceived incompatible goals without resorting to the use of violence (Carnevale & Pruitt in Garling *et al.*, 2000). Garling *et al.* (2000) understand negotiation to be a critical tool in diplomacy, defined as the use of peaceful means to prevent or resolve conflict. Certainly, in South Africa, the very real possibility of violence appeared to motivate leadership, both within the NP and the ANC, to cooperate, negotiate and bargain with one another, and thereby to assume a more reconciling orientation. The politics of negotiation in South Africa were complex and wide-ranging. Bargaining about bargaining included discussions on what was considered to be negotiable and what was not; preliminary bargaining focused on a constitutional formula for the country, preconditions for negotiations (for example, the unbanning of political organisations, press freedom, etc.), and the review of political strategies historically implemented by both sides in response to the conflict; and substantive bargaining involved agreement on one specific settlement from the range of possible settlements to which both parties agreed, that is, a shift to multiparty democracy (du Toit, 1989).

On 2 February 1990, F.W. de Klerk announced the unbanning of the ANC and the Pan African Congress (PAC), and committed his government to an election based on a universal franchise. This heralded the closure of the insurrectionary phase of the political transition process, and a new phase characterised by a strategic environment that evoked fresh challenges for transformation through cooperation and negotiation between the ruling elite and the liberation movement. Constitutional negotiations were the centrepiece of this phase. However, against the rhetoric of bargaining and negotiation and the politics of negotiation and compromise between the political leaders, leaders were challenged to prepare their respective constituencies for negotiation and dialogue prior to the formalisation of statutory promulgations, and to de-legitimise violence as a means of change or maintaining the status quo. This function implies a shift in discourse that de-emphasises the rhetoric of combat and focuses on reconciliation instead. For example, in response to the need to address white fears of transformation and reconciliation, in 1992 the NP held a referendum to test the feelings of its constituency on proposed power-sharing with Black South Africans. Additionally, to legitimise the need for compromise from constituencies, the media came to play a particularly important and educative role by stressing values such as tolerance, cooperation, negotiation and conciliation, and in providing information to the public. Brett (2000), in drawing from research on culture and negotiation, argues that, since the values and norms shared by members of a social group, and the economic, social, political and religious institutions that influence group members can impact on negotiations, successful negotiation outcomes point to the value of information sharing between groups, available means for searching for information, and the motivation to search for information. That is, if negotiators remain motivated to search for information on which to construct consensus, and communicate information to their constituencies, then tensions inherent to negotiations can be minimised. Liebenberg (1993) supports the notion of an interactive leadership style, which he refers to as a type of visionary political leadership that is in constant interaction with its followers, co-leaders and adversarial leaders, and which seeks to maintain and enhance bottom-top and top-bottom communication.

Psycho-cultural interpretation theory offers an interesting framework within which to understand the challenges that faced political leadership during South Africa's transition process. Psycho-cultural interpretation theory refers to a fusion of contemporary ideas about human development with an anthropological emphasis on shared culture to explain the origin and development of shared worldviews, which in turn offers explanations of motivations for social and political action (Ross, 1995). It articulates an important set of connections between individual developmental processes and collective behaviour. Ross (*ibid.*) explains that in situations of ethnic conflicts, deep-rooted threats to identity and security fears serve as a powerful obstruction which prevents groups from addressing the competing interests or ideologies which divide them. Conflict management proposals that follow from this theory begin with an acceptance of each party's interpretation of the conflict. Specific peace-making proposals then attempt to modify or lower the salience of mutual fears and threats adversaries hold in order to facilitate a process whereby parties can begin to develop integrative and reconciliatory solutions which address their substantive differences, thereby increasing the chances of developing a mutually acceptable solution. At the simplest level, this is involved when leaders or diplomats engage in 'talks about talks'. This framework emphasises issues of trust, security and identity as the primary sources of the anxiety that is experienced by parties in situations of conflict and reconciliation, and emphasises attempts to lower communal anxiety. Ross (*ibid.*) cites, as an example of this, de Klerk's 1990 decision to release Nelson Mandela from prison, to recognise the ANC, and to negotiate an end to White rule in South Africa, framing the example as an illustration of de Klerk's attempt to break down the deep distrust between White and Black South Africans, and to thereby facilitate progress in negotiations. Ross (*ibid.*) correctly cautions that given the constraints often facing political leaders, dramatic efforts of single leaders need to be supported by additional institutionalised and informal diplomatic attempts to solve conflict and encourage reconciliation.

Similarly, Sullivan and Transue (1999), in their review of the psychological underpinnings of democracy, highlight that the development of democratic political institutions depends critically upon political tolerance and inter-personal trust between group members. Since levels of political tolerance have been shown to be directly influenced by perceptions of threat, they argue that the manner in which political leadership and the information environment, that is the media, portray groups with differing ideological orientations will accordingly have a direct influence on citizens' expression of, and internalisation of, political tolerance. Inter-personal trust is seen to be important to the extent that it supports transitional processes and democratic values. Sullivan and Transue (*ibid.*) link the issue of trust to the concept of social capital, which refers to 'features of social organisation, such as trust, norms, and networks, that can improve the efficiency of society by facilitating coordinated action' (Putnam in Sullivan & Transue, 1999:644). The presence of social capital within a society is seen to enhance the notion of the collectivity.

Furthermore, research has shown that leaders who are more responsive to the context have been found to demonstrate higher levels of empathy to their environment, are interested in how relevant constituencies are viewing events and in soliciting their support. For these leaders, flexibility, political timing and consensus building are conceptualised as important leadership tools in the process of reconciliation (Kaarbo & Hermann, 1998). Leaders who are attuned to the political processes unfolding within their environment are reported to be more pragmatic and open to information and cues emerging from their environment. Such leaders are responsive to information that is both discrepant and supportive of the options being pursued, seeking political insights into the voices and experiences of both their followers and adversaries. They emphasise co-alignment with significant role players towards a consensus position that would facilitate reconciliation.

As alluded to earlier in the chapter, it is recognised that leadership style needs to be understood in the context of broader social processes. An important idea, though, is the argument that transformative leaders in the South African context demonstrated the insight to interpret and respond to the socio-political cues encouraging reconciliation. Given the range of choices available to them, these leaders opted for a negotiated political settlement. This position may have failed to satisfy all, but it helped to dismantle institutionalised racism. Thus, the preceding discussion illustrates that individual leaders chose to take advantage of the transforming currents within South Africa's socio-political arena, and to galvanise the collective with vision and pragmatism.

Conclusion

The TRC was obviously the main institutionalised mechanism for considering gross human rights violations, for supporting a new democratic order, and for the promotion of healing and reconciliation. Although current political leadership has acknowledged that a key component of the process of reconciliation and nation building involves major socio-economic transformation (*Management Today*, September 1999), the TRC has nonetheless, despite its limitations, served as a powerful medium for different groups to recognise the contemporary consequences of a shared past and, importantly, for serving as a prerequisite for enduring reconciliation and peace. However, in our chapter, we have argued that the formalised processes of reconciliation are predicated on the early interventions of transformational political leadership that needs to be credited for having demonstrated a certain degree of insight, prudence and vision to capture and accommodate early opportunities for promoting reconciliation, as illustrated in the instance of Chris Hani's death. Many commentators are of the opinion that the ideology, policies and political strategies of the ANC have from the very onset favoured reconciliation, non-racial democracy and nation building.

Exercises for critical engagement

1   'Lasting reconciliation is contingent on unconditional forgiveness.' Form two groups and debate the merits of such a view. In articulating respective views, the two debating groups should clearly define their understanding of reconciliation and unconditional forgiveness. A third group can be selected to observe and note patterns of communication and leadership styles that emerge during the debate.

2   Select two contemporary political leaders of your choice who represent two different leadership styles. Describe their respective styles and illustrate examples to substantiate your descriptions.

Recommended reading

De la Rey, C. (2001). 'Reconciliation in divided societies'. In Christie, D.J., Wagner, R.V. & D.D. Winter (Eds.) *Peace, Conflict and Violence: Peace Psychology for the 21st Century*, pp. 251–261. New Jersey: Prentice-Hall.

Garling, T., Kristensen, H., Backenroth-Ohsaka, G., Ekehammar, B. & M.G. Wesselles (2000). *International Journal of Psychology* (Special Issue – Diplomacy and Psychology), 35(2).

Knox, C. & P. Quirck (2000). *Peace Building in Northern Ireland and South Africa: Transition and Reconciliation*. New York: St Martin's Press.

Mandela, N. (1995). *Long Walk to Freedom*. London: Little Brown & Co.

Wilmot, J. & L. van der Vijver (2001). *After the TRC: Reflections on Truth and Reconciliation*. Athens, Ohio: Ohio University Press.

17

Street Life and the Construction of Social Problems

Vuyisile Mathiti

OUTCOMES

After having studied this chapter you should be able to:

- discuss the limitations of the distinction made between children of the streets and children on the streets
- describe the state of the quality of life of street children
- critically discuss the theoretical perspectives used in understanding how social problems are constructed
- discuss how discontinuities in socialisation affect identity formation, and
- explain three models used when planning interventions for street children.

THE PRESENCE of an ever-increasing number of street children is generating concern. This concern is informed by their low position on the power ladder relative to other interest groups in South Africa. But they constitute an important social group. Despite difficulties in determining the exact number of street children, attempts to derive estimates continue. Agnelli (in Chetty, 1997) estimates that there are 30 million street children world-wide. A significant proportion of this number – seven to eight million – is found in Brazil (Dimenstein, 1991). In Vietnam, the number of street children is estimated at 2 000 (Barr, 1995). The figure of 4 000 in Rwanda is thought to have increased due to an influx of people to Kigali after the 1994 war (Spry-Leverton, 1996). Swart (in Donald & Swart-Kruger, 1994) estimated the presence of over 10 000 street children in South Africa. That the number of street children has increased since Swart's estimates, seems reasonable.

The first part of this chapter will examine conceptual problems in defining street children. The second part offers an overview of the state of the quality of life of street children. The third part looks at how social problems are constructed. The context used to explore theoretical approaches to the construction of social problems is street life. Implications for identity formation are examined.

Children *of* the streets and children *on* the streets

Although the use of the concept of street child is credited to a newspaper article in 1957, the first known record of street children in South Africa was in the form of a report published in 1917 by the Society for the Protection of Child Life (Peacock in Hansson, 1991). The scientific community developed interest much later in the phenomenon of street children. According to Scharf *et al.* (1986) the first research findings on the phenomenon of street children were published in 1986, even though the work for that study had started a few years earlier. It was not until the late 1980s that the phenomenon that is known world-wide as 'street children' began to arouse interest in some sections of the public and academic community (Hansson, 1991).

The term 'street children' is one coined by outsiders (Hansson, 1991). The children to whom the concept is applied have a different nomenclature. For example, according to Scharf *et al.* (1986) and Swart (1990), in Johannesburg and Durban they call themselves *malunde* (those of the streets) and *malalapipe* (those who sleep in the pipes), whereas in Cape Town they call themselves *strollers* (those walking on the streets).

When defining the concept of street children, a distinction is often made in the literature between children *on* the streets and children *of* the streets. This distinction, first introduced by Ennew (in Scharf *et al.*, 1986), seems to have universal acceptance (Barr, 1995; Dimenstein, 1991; Richter, 1988; Scharf *et al.*, 1986; Smith, 1996; Swart, 1990). According to Richter (1988:7), children *on* the streets are defined as those 'go into urban areas in order to earn or beg money and who then return home. These children contribute all or most of their earnings to their families. Importantly, children on the street are attached to, and integrally involved with, their families.' Children *of* the streets, on the other hand, are defined as those '... who have abandoned (or have been abandoned by) their families, schools and immediate communities, before they are 16 years of age, and drifted into a nomadic life' (*ibid.*). It is for the latter group that the term 'street children' has been reserved.

The distinction used to categorise the experiences of an increasing number of children who are making a living on the streets is artificial, convenient and spurious. According to Richter (1988), children on the streets return home and contribute most or all of their earnings to their families, whereas children of the streets have no contact with their families. However, this distinction is problematic. A noteworthy proportion of street children has contact with family and does not sleep on the street permanently. For example, some of the children in a study conducted by Mathiti (2000) maintained contact with their families despite being considered children of the street. They reported visiting their families once in a month or once in two months. This contradicts an important criterion that children of the streets do not maintain contact with their families.

In response to the inadequacies of this distinction, Smith (in Hansson, 1991) introduced the concepts of full-time and part-time street children. These concepts no longer use the criterion of sleeping on the streets as a distinguishing factor. They instead use relative time spent on the street. Children of the streets will be those who are on the streets full-time whereas children on the streets will be those who are on the streets part-time.

The activity pattern of most street children defies this methodical categorisation. Although the children in a study by Mathiti (2000) were living at shelters, few (4 per cent) reported sleeping on the streets occasionally, 38 per cent were regularly involved in income-generating activities, and 68.8 per cent had access to educational services, and many still returned home for short periods. Some of the children reported that some members of their families visited them at the shelters. Hansson (1991) also noted this activity pattern, which clearly contradicts the currently accepted distinction between children on the streets and children of the streets. After a review of studies conducted by Smith and Keen, Hansson noted that most of the females who were strolling (engaging in activities that characterise street children) part-time showed different activity patterns at different times.

> During term-time, they strolled after school, or at times truanted in order to stroll during school time, but generally they returned home at night to sleep. At weekends and during school vacations, however, they typically strolled and slept on the streets at night (Hansson, 1991:7).

If we were to accept the distinction between children of the streets and children on the streets, this would mean, for example, that children on the streets would be defined as such during the week and differently during school vacations and weekends. This is an untenable proposition indeed. Hansson (1991) further noted that although 71 per cent of the females interviewed by Smith strolled full-time, 35 per cent had intermittent contact with their families, and that only a few of the females who were on the streets claimed to contribute their earnings directly to their families. This pattern further contradicts the current distinction between children of the streets and children on the streets.

A further problematic aspect of this distinction is that it promotes the neglect of the needs of the children on the streets. That these children have to earn an income is seldom denounced as an inadmissible pursuit.

It can be argued that children on the streets are more vulnerable to chronic abuse and neglect than children of the streets because the possibility of getting help is better for the latter than the former group. Nonetheless, that these children have to provide for their own and their families' needs is a flagrant violation of both their rights and moral precepts. The majority of South African children, especially street children, are disappointed with the adult community, given the pervasive nature of the violation of their rights. Experiences such as physical and sexual abuse, neglect, abject poverty, HIV/AIDS and family violence reinforce their perception that an adult-dominated world is indifferent, pernicious and untrustworthy. Escaping this domination is perceived as a desirable goal and when attained, a significant achievement.

The quality of life of street children

An analysis of the condition of street children suggests that they experience social, health, emotional and educational difficulties (see the box below). Some of their difficulties include the distressing realities of increasing separation from their families and loss of access to basic facilities such as health, education and recreation (UNICEF, 1986). Their social, health, physical, emotional and educational difficulties have been well documented (Barrette, 1995; Bourdillon, 1995; Cockburn, 1994; Donald & Swart-Kruger, 1994; Smith, 1996; Swart, 1990).

Ben (not his real name) is a quiet 12-year-old youngster. His parents divorced four years ago when he was eight years old. He has not seen nor spoken to his father since the divorce. His mother remarried when he was ten years old. His relationship with his stepfather can be described as stormy. He believes that his stepfather does not like him and he says he does not like him either. According to Ben, his stepfather treats him differently to his two siblings. For example, he does not shout at them or call them names. His mother has tried to intervene in order to improve his relationship with his stepfather. He has expressed displeasure with the lack of a relationship with his paternal relatives.

He has expressed a wish to stay with his uncle, but his mother refused. That the mother is unemployed means that the family has to rely on his stepfather to meet their needs. According to Ben, it is rare for the family to have three meals per day. Sometimes they have to do with one meal per day. As a result, he started stealing money to buy food. He admitted that he stole money from his stepfather and uncle a few times. His uncle caught him on one occasion and had a serious talk with him about the consequences of theft. He decided to go to the city to beg for money and food. He could no longer attend school and was sad to drop out of school because he will no longer be a doctor (a dream he has cherished since he was six). Although he says it is tough on the streets and that he does not like it, he says it is better than staying with his stepfather. He says he misses his mother and siblings and cries when he misses them. His greatest wish is to have a relationship with his father.

Donald and Swart-Kruger (1994) have observed that these children face emotional problems such as loss of relationship with an adult caregiver, anxiety and depression. They have to deal with feelings of being unloved, unwanted and rejected (Cockburn, 1991; Swart, 1990). The lack of nurturance contributes to emotional insecurity, self-blame, and warped development of a sense of relating to and engaging with others. That unmet affectional and dependency needs are acutely experienced by street children is shown in a study conducted by Richter (in Donald & Swart-Kruger, 1994), where she found that street children displayed higher than normal rates of enuresis, regressive behaviour, anxiety and depression.

Street children are socially marginalised and rejected by many segments of society (Smith, 1996). They constantly face violence, harassment and abuse. On the whole, they are exploited and victimised social reprobates whom society loves to hate. Police brutality is not an uncommon experience for many street children. Besides the antagonism, hostilities and violence they face, they also experience hunger, cold, sexual abuse and sexually transmitted diseases (Chetty, 1997).

A study by Jansen et al. (1990) documented the effects of glue sniffing by street children. They had multiple deficits, which included visual-spatial diffi-culties, visual scanning problems, language problems, motor coordination, memory and concentration deficits. These cognitive deficits are related to a number of factors, such as the use of various drugs. A number of studies have highlighted the use of drugs by street children (Chetty, 1997; Cockburn, 1995; Donald & Swart-Kruger, 1994). For example, in her study in Durban, Chetty (1997) found that most of the street children smoked dagga (23.3 per cent) followed by glue sniffing (22.8 per cent), benzine sniffing (16.6 per cent) and use of alcohol (16.6 per cent). There were also children sniffing petrol (16.1 per cent) and inhaling paint thinners (7.8 per cent). It seems as if dagga, glue and alcohol are some of the drugs most widely used by street children. These drugs are sometimes used to provide a cushioning effect against hunger, cold, illness, fear and insecurity (Chetty, 1997). A study by Richter (in Moran, 1994) suggests that approximately 30 per cent of the street children who experiment with solvents become chronic users.

A compromise in their sense of safety is another source of vulnerability. These children are exposed to cold, rain and storms. Often they do not have sufficient protective clothing. They are also at risk of pedestrian traffic acci-dents, particularly after glue-sniffing episodes (Donald & Swart-Kruger, 1994). That so many children are neglected and uncared for by their families, commu-nities and government is a flagrant violation not only of their rights, but also of moral and religious precepts (Chetty, 1997). Despite a review of existing literature suggesting that street children are 'at-risk children', many of them have survived the harsh realities of their environments. The resilience displayed by these children has given rise to a pervasive paradox between the evidence of developmental vulnerabilities across social, emotional, cognitive and physical areas of development, on the one hand, and the evidence of tenacity, resourcefulness and ingenuity, on the other (Chapman, 1997; Donald & Swart-Kruger, 1994).

Even though they face multiple stressors, such as malnutrition and undernutrition, illness, injuries, anxiety, social rejection, violence and lack of protective clothing, some of these children are able to overcome these adversities. Although the mechanisms of protection and preservation used by these children are not yet fully understood, 'research findings on the whole support the notion that young people are potentially resilient and that ... they have the capacity to resist being overwhelmed by [their experiences] in the long term' (Smith, 1996:94). Mathiti (2000) observed that social support, however limited, was a mitigating factor.

Developmental implications of a poor quality of life

Emotional development

Donald and Swart-Kruger (1994) assert that the greatest emotional risk most street children face is the loss or lack of an adequate relationship with an adult figure. Due to disappointment with the primary caregiver, most of the street children have adopted a sceptical, disengaging way to relate to adult figures. They experienced disappointment with their primary caregivers for their inability or unwillingness to meet their affectional and dependency needs. High levels of physical (50 per cent) and sexual (17 per cent) abuse by the primary caregivers were reported by Cockburn (in Chapman, 1997). In terms of Erickson's theory (in Meyer *et al.*, 1997), the loss of a relationship with an adult figure has profound implications for trust, shame, guilt, inferiority and identity confusion. Successful resolution of these developmental tasks contributes to healthy psychological functioning. Failure to resolve these tasks can lead to a sense of mistrust, low self-esteem, identity confusion and social alienation. Unsuccessful resolution of these tasks can predispose street children to serious psychological and social problems.

Against the background of these emotional developmental risks, and as mentioned earlier, street children are more likely to develop anxiety, depression, enuresis and regressive behaviour (Richter in Donald & Swart-Kruger, 1994). The results of a study by Richter (in Chapman, 1997) showed that street children who have retained some links with their families showed more emotional disturbance than those who have broken off completely. Even though the reasons for this finding are not entirely clear, it is hypothesised that the conditions that motivated the children to leave home resurface when they meet their families. They are exposed to unremitting circumstances. The perception that their primary caregivers show unwillingness to change their 'old ways' can be experienced as demoralising and can contribute to feelings of anger, bitterness and resentment. This finding has implications for programme development in that programme developers must assess the family environments before the children are reconnected with their families. However, groups of street children have supported each other physically and emotionally. The group is important in ensuring the satisfaction of affectional needs.

Social development

Street children face rejection from many segments of society. They face violence, harassment and marginalisation. They are outcast. Their position as 'social rejects' is likely to put a positive social identity and feelings of self-worth at risk. This is likely to lead to 'victim identity' (Donald & Swart-Kruger, 1994:172).

Generally, street children are exploited and victimised reprobates whom society loves to hate.

Their clothing and unkempt appearance are factors that contribute to premature judgements by people. The rejection that results from such judgements reinforces the street children's negative self-perception. Although these children often have contact with people who evaluate them negatively, they avoid these contacts and seek people whose evaluations are anticipated to be positive. Consequently, their social contact becomes circumscribed. Their *affiliation needs* are often not met given the constraints imposed on their social contacts, and the group is often regarded as a resource to satisfy psychological needs. The fluid and erratic nature of the composition of groups and relationships is likely to negatively affect the establishment of permanent relationships and the benefits that flow from these (Donald & Swart-Kruger, 1994).

Street life as a social problem: Theoretical perspectives

This section focuses on two theoretical perspectives, namely, the positivist and constructionist, that help to explain the social position of street children and the implications for identity formation.

Positivist perspective

According to Stefan (1993:2), *positivism* suggests that 'social problems are conditions that can be objectively identified as having some intrinsic harmful effects'. From this perspective, a social problem is considered as an individual, group, condition or activity that is apparently troublesome, threatening or perilous. A significant element of a social problem is its high public risk value.

According to Chetty (1997), the incarceration of street children is partly motivated by their public nuisance value. Their unkempt appearance, tendency to beg for food and money and sleeping on the streets undermine the efforts of city managers to build 'marketable brands' and can hasten neighbourhood decline. This perception is racially inspired (see Chapter 5, this volume). Furthermore, the possibility that they will beg from tourists is regarded as a problem in that it might annoy the tourists or even 'scare' them away. This has the potential to undermine the local economy. From the positivist perspective, street children are regarded as a social problem because they can delimit local economic growth and threaten environmental health. The assistance of the police is often solicited to deal with this 'social problem' because it threatens law and order.

Furthermore, a street life is considered a social problem because it is considered to be inconsistent with societal norms that expect children to be under parental care and supervision. The constitutionally guaranteed rights in the *Bill of Rights* (The Constitution, 1996) and the United Nations' (1993) *Convention on the Rights of the Child* (CRC) document the provisions that should be made for children. When these provisions are not met, the condition of the intended recipient is regarded as a social problem. This perception is motivated by a desire to protect the individual from him- or herself and to protect society. In this way, social order and balance can be maintained.

Children's rights

SECTION 28 (South African Constitution)

1. Every child has a right
    a. to a name and nationality;
    b. to family care or parental care, or to appropriate alternative care when removed from the family environment;
    c. to basic nutrition, shelter, basic health care services and social service;
    d. to be protected from malnutrition, neglect, abuse or degradation;
    e. to be protected from exploitative labour practices;

> f. not to be required or permitted to perform work or provide services that
>   i) are inappropriate for a person of that child's age; or
>   ii) place at risk the child's well-being, education, physical or mental
>   health or spiritual, moral or social development;
> g. not to be detained except as a measure of last resort, in which case, in
>   addition to the rights a child enjoys under sections 12 and 35, the child
>   may be detained only for the shortest appropriate period of time, and
>   has the right to be
>   i) kept separately from detained persons over the age of 18 years; and
>   ii) treated in a manner, and kept in conditions, that take account of the
>   child's age
> h. to have a legal practitioner assigned to the child by the state, and at
>   state expense, in civil proceedings affecting the child, if substantial injus-
>   tice would otherwise result; and
> i. not to be used directly in armed conflict; and to be protected in times of
>   armed conflict.
> 2. A child's rights are of paramount importance in every matter concerning the
>   child.
> 3. In this section 'child' means a person under the age of 18 years.

Constructionist perspective

Some authors have expressed dissatisfaction with the positivist perspective. Stefan (1993:2) has observed that 'not all apparently dangerous, threatening or troublesome conditions are considered social problems, while other unimportant issues have become major concerns for the media and society'. Mills (1978:19) put it succinctly when he stated that 'not child labour but comic books, not poverty but mass leisure are at the centre of concern'. The dissatisfaction has led to the consideration of social problems as the result of social constructionism (Blummer, 1971). In other words, the social constructionist's perspective suggests that a phenomenon or condition is conceived and defined as a social problem rather than objectively determined to be one.

In line with a constructionist perspective on social problems, Schneider (in Stefan, 1993) believes that the claims and claim-making activities, and not the objective condition, constitute a social problem. In other words, social problems are what people claim they are and are not defined in terms of their truthfulness. Schneider maintains that a situation or phenomenon will be considered a social problem if it is viable, which is to say, functional for those with power on their side. A difficulty or abnormality needs to be usable and valuable once it has been defined as a social problem. What makes a successful problem would be the viability rather than the validity of claims (Schneider, 1985). This view is also shared by Anderson (in Stefan, 1993:3) who observed that 'for a certain situation to be regarded as a "problem" rather than a mere "condition" or "the way things are", there must be some reason or interest in creating it'.

The operation of divergent and conflicting interests, intentions and objectives results in the construction of a plethora of contesting problems that compete for attention and recognition as legitimate social problems (Blummer, 1971). Entry into the arenas of public discourse is a selective process involving conflict over recognition, confirmation and rejection of claims (Hilgartner & Bosk in Stefan, 1993). The success with which an issue enters the arena of public discourse and consequently transforms into a social problem, is also influenced by its 'credentials' and legitimation (Blummer, 1971). The rise to prominence of a social problem will invite the attention of government agencies, social action groups, political campaigns, news media and the academic community. The notability of a problem helps to create ameliorative conditions.

Media discourse plays a significant role in the construction of social problems. The process of news selection, emphasis on expert opinions and objective reporting means the content of media discourse is not reflective of divergent views but promotes the opinions of politicians, experts and government officials. The emphasis on authoritative views promotes a single definition of a social problem (Stefan, 1993).

Perhaps the greatest emotional risk most street children face is the loss or lack of an adequate relationship with an adult figure.

The viability criterion in defining social problems was met for child abuse to be defined as a social problem. Stefan (1993) observed that until 1988 child abuse and child sexual abuse were virtually unknown in South Africa except to a small esoteric group of paediatricians in Durban. The following year, in 1989, the issue of child abuse was useful in supporting the government's election campaign. Prior to the election, the police invited media representatives to offer coverage to the campaign to clamp down on crime by and against children. Stefan observed that 'during late 1989 and 1990 the coverage of child sexual abuse declined somewhat, but the issue was taken by secondary media such as popular, professional and academic magazines' (*ibid.*: 11). From a constructionist perspective, street life has remained out of public discourse and attention because, unlike child abuse, it is not usable. It cannot be used during election campaigns due to the negative public perception and social stereotyping of street children. The socially ascribed status of 'adult-child' also

means the issue of street existence cannot compete with other children's issues. It cannot compete in the 'social problem's marketplace' against issues such as malnutrition, HIV/AIDS orphanage, abuse and neglect because it is considered to affect 'adult-children' as opposed to affecting children.

Another explanation for the entry of social problems into social discourse is the migration of an issue from a large centre to the periphery (Stefan, 1993). An issue of concern emerges in a large cultural centre and then moves to the perimeter. The sexual abuse of children *as a social problem* emerged in the United States in the 1960s, was diffused to Britain and other remote locations such as South Africa in the 1980s (Stefan, 1993). To aid the dispersion process, the group that occupies the highest strata often appropriates more power to itself. The media, wittingly or unwittingly, plays a crucial role in the dispersion process. For example, the South African public received an increasing number of reports on international concern about sexual abuse of children in the late 1980s (Robertson in Stefan, 1993). The media has treated street children with 'benign neglect'. In those instances that street children received media coverage, their representation was negative. They were often portrayed as violent, beggars or criminals.

Viewed in this light, street life has remained outside the arenas of public discourse because of the lack of power of claim-makers to diffuse it to the centre (decision-makers in national and international communities). In South Africa, the position of powerlessness has often been underlined by racial considerations (see Chapter 4). That an overwhelming number of street children come from the historically disadvantaged communities serves to disempower and undermine efforts to make street life part of the socio-political programme and public speeches and debates. The complex intersection of being a Black (a low social class) child (a low social class) who lives on the streets (a low social class) foils the entry of a street life in public discourse. Street life has been envisaged as a 'Black thing' considering that for a long time the South African media have been predominantly White-owned with a significant White audience (again, see Chapter 4).

Street life is also a gendered experience. Although it is accepted that females comprise a small minority of the street children in South Africa (Richter, 1988; Scharf et al., 1986), some commentators believe that this under-representation reflects gender construction. For example, Hansson (1991) believes that the way in which the phenomenon of street children is defined reflects the typical experience of males. Females are excluded because their activity patterns do not fit the male-inspired definition of what it is to be a child. Consequently, an erroneous conclusion is reached that there are fewer females than males. One of the unfortunate consequences of under-representing the number of female street children is the neglect of their needs. Unlike their male counterparts, they are perceived to be in less need of assistance. This gendered perception has led to fewer programmes and facilities for this group.

> The predicament of the street girl is far more intricate due to her condition of abandonment and to her nature as a woman. In the streets she is more exposed to the consequences brought about by the role of women in society ... she is subject to the consequences of premature maternity, of abandonment and prostitution (Paulo Freire cited in Barrette, 1995:39).

The age restriction (females under 16 years of age) is a criterion that serves to exclude a large proportion of female street children. Fifty per cent of the sample in a study conducted by Smith and Keen were over the age of 16 (Hansson, 1991). Their finding suggests that females tend to start a street existence at a later age (in their early teens) than do males (10 years of age). Most of the female street children are soon disqualified because of age considerations. The choice of 16 years as the cut-off point is viewed with suspicion considering that the legal age marking adulthood is 18 years. That males start a street life earlier is an advantage that helps them to gain street experience and subsequently, status and power (Chetty, 1997). The lack of experience means that females do not meet an important requirement that would afford them status and authority.

A further gendered and devalued perception is that female street children are prostitutes. This identity attracts disgust and condemnation from society. The absence of low-risk, income-generating activities for females is considered as one of the possible antecedent factors. Parking cars, which is a relatively low-risk income-generating activity, is male-dominated. The territorial behaviour of males in this area is considered a defence mechanism against competition. This leaves females with a few high-risk alternatives, such as selling sexual services. Due to the possibility of assault and arrest, this activity is performed in less public places (Hansson, 1991). The male-dominated nature of a street existence has led to constructions that reflect male experience to the exclusion of female experience.

Discontinuity in socialisation and social identity

According to Erikson (in Meyer *et al.*, 1997), experiences at each life stage are an effective preparation for the next. The continuity in the socialisation process provides smooth transitions from one stage to another. The family, as a primary *socialisation* agent during the formative years, plays a crucial role in helping children learn skills and attitudes that enhance their social participation. The learned behavioural patterns prepare children to respond effectively to familial and societal demands at subsequent phases. Experiences of such continuities enable clarity of *social roles* and social integration.

However, a street life is marked by discontinuities that lead to social isolation and rejection. This rupture in socialisation is punctuated by a depressed quality of life experienced by street children (Chetty, 1986; Dimenstein, 1991; Mathiti, 2000; Smith, 1996; Swart, 1990). The ascribed 'adult-child' status serves to promote the discontinuities that are encountered. This status involves the display of both child and adult behavioural patterns. In other words, a child is expected to engage in normal child behaviours, and to shift his or her behavioural repertoire in the direction of adulthood. In a study on the quality of life of street children, Mathiti (2000) observed that one of the significant recreation and leisure activities of the street children was playing with toys. Recreation and leisure activities were undertaken after the execution of adult responsibilities such as searching for employment (mainly as parking attendants) and food. These discontinuities suggest that their role as children has been redefined in quite a radical way. As a result, the previously established childhood rhythms and patterns of engaging with the social world have been disrupted. Consequently, role confusion and fragmented identities are experienced. The production and recognition of the fragmented identity, 'adult-child', is problematic indeed. The fragmented identities and a constricted social network serve to undermine the development of a strong and normative sense of relating to self and others.

A number of studies have shown that street children have constricted social networks (Apteker, 1994; Bourdillon, 1995; Chetty, 1994; Dimenstein, 1991; Smith, 1996). The police are one of the few social institutions with which they have frequent contact. This contact has often been described as violent and brutal (Chetty, 1997). Besides the police, street children have limited, if any, contact with schools. The circumvention of their sense of belonging created poor and inadequate identification with their communities.

The view that individual identity is a product of self-construction is problematic in the context of fragmented identities, because it discounts the role of social context in identity formation. The negative collective identity of street children is seen as a product of social construction. Their identity is therefore constructed and situated in a flow of social discourses (see Chapter 6 on how apartheid, considered an extension of colonialism, appropriated the means and resources for a positive identity). Some of the discourses involve their low position on the social ladder. Their low social class relative to other groups does not evoke honour and pride. Their powerlessness further serves to entrench their low social class with the resultant negative public perception and *stereotyping*. Their unkempt appearance, unconventional survival strategies, abandonment of family and status as a public nuisance reinforce this perception. Exposure to socially sustained negative discourses inevitably shapes the way street children look at and constitute themselves. Loneliness

> Studies have shown that street children have constricted social networks, with the police one of the few social institutions with which they have fequent contact.

and rejection therefore facilitate the formation of a negative collective identity. However, tensions have been observed in this regard. The street children have resisted the imposed identities by their rejection of the name 'street children'. In a study conducted in Hillbrow, Swart (1990) noted that most of the children rejected the label of 'street children' and suggested various possible alternative names.

Although it has been argued in this section that identity is socially constructed and situated, this thesis should not be construed as support for *social determinism*. Identity is not viewed as a complete reflection of social circumstances but of the dynamic tensions within individuals and among contending social discourses.

The consequences of devalued identities

The person who is *stigmatised* is a person whose social identity calls his or her full humanity into question (Ratele & Shefer, 2002; Tajfel & Turner, 1979). The perception of others is that this person is marginal, secondary (at best), flawed and impaired. Such people are often the targets of negative stereotypes. In this section I examine the consequences of devalued identities for well-being, minority status and identification.

Well-being

There is a paucity of research examining the influence of group membership on well-being. According to Mathiti (2000), well-being is used in a rather broad sense to include a variety of temporary emotional states or moods (e.g. happiness, anxiety, depression), as well as more stable positive or negative feelings (such as self-acceptance and self-esteem). It can be assumed, from a theoretical perspective, that membership in a minority group with a devalued identity may be associated with negative feelings. First, membership in this group can attract negative reactions such as stigmatisation, social isolation and violence. The literature is replete with these experiences on the part of street children (Chetty, 1997; Richter, 1988; Swart, 1990). They can lead to negative emotions and ultimately undermine the emotional well-being of the street children. Second, the internalisation of devalued images can lead to undesirable psychological and behavioural consequences such as poor self-esteem, feelings of rejection and detrimental personality and value changes. Third, given that personal feelings of worth depend on the social evaluation of the *in-group* with which a person is identified, self-hatred and feelings of worthlessness tend to arise from membership of an outcast group (Tajfel & Turner, 1979). Fourth, members of groups that are devalued and are relatively small are disadvantaged when they need to solicit validations from *many* similar others (*ibid.*).

As a result, members of minority groups may feel less secure than members of majority groups. Although research findings examining the influence of group *status* and size on well-being are contradictory, there is also new evidence which confirms that, at least under some conditions, members of low-status minority groups differ in well-being from members of high-status majority groups (Tajfel & Turner, 1979).

Minority status

Tajfel and Turner (1979) have argued that membership of a group constitutes distinct social-psychological states for members, and members of minority groups generally find themselves in cognitive-affective crossfire.

Tajfel and Turner (1979) maintain that membership of a minority group and membership of a majority group each constitute distinct socio-psychological situations for the particular member. Unlike majority members, minority members typically find themselves in what they call cognitive-affective cross-fire. On the one hand, being a small figure (minority) against a large (majority) makes membership of that group salient and members cannot forget their affiliation to such groups. They are reminded of their membership in a minority group by word or deed. As a result, their membership of this group becomes a central aspect for the minority (more so than for the majority). Furthermore, minority membership entails risks and stressful experiences that may be unknown to members of the majority group. The risks, which often lead to negative affective experiences, are increased if the image of the minority is devalued. Compared to majority members, there are strong forces pushing minority members towards their group or keeping them in it, while at the same time there are stronger affective forces pulling them away. As a result, minority members experience internal conflict. According to Tajfel and Turner (*ibid.*), they may opt for individual or group strategies. Individual strategies may involve dis-identification with or exit from their group. Assertive inter-group behaviour can be a possible collective strategy.

Identification

The impact of the group status is often moderated by the strength of the ties of the individual with the group. A review of experimental work on the effects of relative group status on the degree to which individuals identify with their groups shows that low group status generally results in lower levels of identification than high group status (Tajfel & Turner, 1979). This has been explained from a social identity perspective. According to this perspective, people are likely to resist membership or involvement with a low-status group because this may diminish the possibility of their achieving a positive social identity (*ibid.*). Decreasing the level of identification may help members to experience less negative emotions that may ensue as a result of membership in a lower status group.

Models of intervention

Intervention programmes have been motivated by the observation that street life impacts negatively on street children's health. Health is seen in a broad sense as a state of complete physical, mental and social well-being, and not merely the absence of disease or infirmity (World Health Organisation in Parmenter, 1994). These programmes suggest that many street children could be helped to overcome the effects of their harsh environments.

According to Cockburn (1995), intervention programmes can be divided into three broad approaches, namely, containment, cure and prevention. The *containment* approach usually occurs in closed institutions where correctional measures are applied. She believes that this approach is costly and ineffective. The second approach, *cure*, involves weaning children away from street life and gradually introducing them to mainstream society (see also Schurink, 1993). This approach is sometimes termed rehabilitative because it puts emphasis on resocialising the street child. The third approach, *prevention*, is aimed at preventing the occurrence of the street child phenomenon by attempting to identify the root cause of the problem (see Rapholo, 1996).

An assessment of these approaches by Cockburn (1995), Rapholo (1996) and Smith (1996) suggests that the containment approach is the least effective approach, the prevention approach the least explored, and the curative or rehabilitative approach the most moderately promising of the three. According to Cockburn (1993), the success or failure of these intervention programmes is partly dependent on the skills and training of service providers. Her advocacy of the use of trained service providers is borne out by the success of pilot projects using trained street workers in the Cape Town area. Chetty (1997) also shares this view. In an exploratory investigation of the street child phenomenon in Durban, she found that:

> the majority of service providers had not proceeded beyond matriculation level, and that they advocated largely punitive measures in respect of street children ... Most agreed that street children were likely to become hardened criminals. Some of the reasons given in support of this statement were that the children refused to listen, they isolated themselves from the community (Chetty, 1997:177–178).

These views suggest that the service providers concerned did not really understand street children, and demonstrate the critical importance of professional, trained workers. Their perceptions, which leaned towards hard options, were inconsistent with the sympathy and understanding expected of them. This divergence is unhealthy for any intervention programme.

Conclusion

The phenomenon of a street existence is a complex one. The tendency is to treat those on and of the streets as an insignificant minority of problematic

Health:
A state of complete physical, mental and social well-being and not merely the absence of disease.

Containment approaches are used in closed institutions where correctional measures are applied.

Curative approaches involve weaning children away from street life and gradually introducing them to mainstream society.

Preventative approaches are aimed at preventing the occurrence of the street child phenomenon by attempting to identify the root cause of the problem.

children. It has been argued in this chapter that street children constitute a significant social group that has, unfortunately, not been part of public debate. Their depressed quality of life is a source of concern. They are considered a social problem for reasons that do not promote their interests. The negative public perception has engendered a devalued negative identity.

Exercises for critical engagement

1 Provide a critique of the media coverage of street children in South Africa in the last few months to see how street children have been represented.
2 What are some of the factors that could explain the high representation of Black, male children on the street?
3 Discuss factors that put the development of a positive social identity for street children at risk.
4 Compare and contrast the positivist and constructivist approaches to street life.
5 With reference to street children, discuss three possible consequences of a devalued identity.
6 It has been suggested that street children have utilised effective coping mechanisms to deal with the harshness of their situation. Discuss some of the coping strategies used by the street children.
7 The aim of most intervention programmes for street children is often to reunite them with their family. Do you think this should be the aim of most or all interventions? Motivate your answer.
8 You have been appointed to a by the government commission into the investigation of the phenomenon of street children. Write a five-page report of the most significant findings and recommendations of your commission.

Recommended reading

Barrette, M. (1995). *Street Children Need Our Care*. Pretoria: Kagiso Publishers.

Chetty, V. (1997). *Street Children in Durban: An Exploratory Investigation*. Pretoria: Human Sciences Research Council.

Donald, D. & J. Swart-Kruger. (1994). 'The South African street child: Developmental implications'. *South African Journal of Psychology*, 24(4):196–174.

Swart, J. (1990). *Malunde: The Street Children of Hillbrow*. Johannesburg: Witwatersrand University Press.

Understanding and Preventing Violence

18

Garth Stevens, Mohamed Seedat &
Ashley van Niekerk

OUTCOMES

After having studied this chapter you should be able to:

* understand the historical location and importance of violence as a social phenomenon and as an object of social inquiry

* describe a range of social scientific perspectives and definitions of violence

* explain a range of psychological paradigms and definitions of violence, and

* critically apply the public health model as a health science framework within which violence can be described, analysed, theorised and prevented through various forms of social action.

Looking back: Violence as endemic to South Africa

THE PARTICULAR form and expression of contemporary South African society has undoubtedly been influenced and shaped by its violent history of racism and oppression. For the social scientist, locating current manifestations of violence within their ideological, historical and material contexts is therefore critical if comprehensive understandings of such manifestations are to be generated alongside appropriate forms of social action aimed at preventing them. Such a critical social analysis allows for scrutiny of the ways in which violence has mutated over time and in different social contexts, its various points of genesis within social formations, its cyclical impacts and residual effects on all sectors of society, and an ability to historically understand and develop interventions to address current manifestations of violence in South Africa. This is particularly important as we strive to develop scientific approaches that can make relevant contributions to the overall health, psychosocial well-being and development of the population, in ways that move beyond scientific rhetoric to concrete social action.

The endemic nature of violence within the history of South Africa was already evident in the period of initial 'discovery' and conquest that was premised on colonial expansion and slavery as far back as the mid 1600s (Banton, 1988; Callinicos, 1987; Miles, 1989). This was followed by concerted efforts to penetrate the interior of South Africa for a range of social and economic reasons, and was accompanied by wars of dispossession, slavery and indentured labour (Callinicos, 1987). These genocidal, controlling and exclusionary practices were most frequently justified through scientific racism and notions of 'bringing civilisation to African heathens' (Miles, 1989). Throughout this period, racism increasingly became institutionalised through the legislative processes, thereby enabling the development of White privilege through Black economic and social exploitation. The result was the emergence of an increasingly polarised society that facilitated the growth of White-owned and -controlled local and regional economies within Southern Africa. These processes and outcomes were further entrenched in the pre-apartheid years as economic independence from colonial powers was pursued, and the necessity to formalise 'racial' exploitation became an economic imperative. It ultimately culminated in the institutionalisation and legalisation of racism in the 1948 apartheid policy that advocated 'racial' segregation and separate development, and furthermore ensured White privilege through the legal, social, economic, political and military control of Blacks (Alexander, 1985; O'Meara, 1983; Terreblanche & Natrass, 1990; Wolpe, 1988).

While the effects of state-sanctioned violence have been well documented (see for example, Cooper, 1990; Duncan, 1991; Letlaka-Rennert, 1990; Reynolds, 1989; Straker 1992), it also spawned a history of resistance, counter-violence and liberatory politics. Examples of this counter-violence were most notably found in the anti-colonial uprisings amongst Blacks, the armed struggle waged by various elements within the liberation movement, and the range of historical uprisings that occurred throughout the turbulent years of apartheid. Despite the eventual formation of a 'non-racial' democracy in 1994 and the dismantling of the apartheid state apparatus, the social and psychological effects of prolonged repression and counter-violence also became readily apparent, even in post-apartheid South Africa (see for example, Dawes & Donald, 1994; Duncan & Rock 1994; Richter, 1994). Bulhan (1985:131) emphasises the historical connections between violence, oppression and racism, and argues that a 'situation of violence is essentially a cauldron of violence. It is brought into existence and maintained by dint of violence. This violence gradually permeates the social order to affect everyday living. In time, the violence takes on different guises and becomes less blatant and more integral to institutional as well as interpersonal reality.'

Living with the fallout: Violence in contemporary South Africa

The ongoing socio-economic inequities, social fragmentation, and individual socialisation patterns have been asserted as amongst the spectrum of causal agents complicit in the persisting prominence of violence in South African society (Butchart *et al.*, 2000). Despite the political and social reform that characterises present-day South Africa, violence has indeed continued to permeate our everyday realities. Violence remains a major cause of death, disability and psychic trauma, and prevails as a significant area of attention for the social scientist. While the impact of globalisation on South African economic policy and its negative effects on the living standards of the majority of South Africans may also be construed as a violent consequence (Bond, 1994; 2000), the more overt manifestations of contemporary violence tend to be dominated by intra- and inter-personal forms of violence that are not as overtly politicised as they were during the apartheid era.

The ongoing socio-economic inequalities have been seen by researchers and theorists as part of the spectrum of causal agents complicit in the persisting prominence of violence in South African society.

The violence epidemic

Annually more than two million people around the world die as a result of injuries arising from violent acts (WHO, 2001) and by the year 2020 injuries will be the second largest contributor to the global burden of disease. This pattern is likely to be emphasised in sub-Saharan Africa, due to the anticipated concentration of wars, regional conflicts and inter-personal violence (Murray & Lopez, 1996). Presently, wars are one of the leading injury-related causes of death in Africa (WHO, 2001).

In South Africa, data from the National Injury Mortality Surveillance System (NIMSS) shows homicide to be the major cause of death as a result of injury, accounting for approximately 46 per cent of all the cases recorded in the NIMSS. Firearms and sharp objects are the main external causes of death (Burrows *et al.*, 2001). Similarly, non-fatal injuries presenting at sentinel health facilities appear to be dominated by inter-personal acts of violence within South Africa (Peden & van der Spuy, 1998).

For those who survive the immediate effects of a violent assault, their injuries often result in permanent disability. While violence and the associated injury patterns vary across gender, age, region and income groups, the overall impact is tremendous human suffering, serious social consequences (e.g. heightened levels of perceived threat and fear), and a significant economic burden to families, communities and the country (e.g. loss of income amongst victims and their dependents, skewed patterns of health expenditure, etc.). In addition, violence is also often associated with a wide range of health and psychosocial problems (Bergman, 1992; Farrington, 1991; UNAIDS, 1999; WHD, 1997), such as eating and sleeping disorders, mental illness, unwanted pregnancies and sexually transmitted diseases (e.g. HIV/AIDS). Central to this cursory overview of violence in South Africa today is the fact that it remains a significant psycho-social and health priority requiring vital description, analysis, theorising and social intervention.

Making sense: Perspectives and definitions of violence

There is a range of ways to define and understand violence. One method is to frame its definition according to commonly identified key components. These components include, amongst others, the nature of the relationship between victim and perpetrator (e.g. intimate–stranger violence); the form of discipline that examines violence (e.g. psychology); the broader paradigm into which violence is inserted as a phenomenon (e.g. social constructionism); and the 'essential nature' of the violence (e.g. child abuse). While at present there is still no single broadly accepted typology of violence, the WHO Task Force's classification (WHO, 1996) provides a useful reference point. It distinguishes between three types of violence (see box below).

Types of violence

The WHO Task Force (WHO, 1996) distinguishes between three types of violence:
- *Inter-personal violence* encompasses violent behaviours that occur between individuals, but are not planned by any social or political groups in which they participate. It occurs in many forms, and can be grouped into three categories according to the victim-perpetrator relationship:
  - family and intimate violence (mainly child abuse and violence against women, but may also include violence against vulnerable groups such as the elderly and the disabled if this occurs in a family setting)
  - violence among acquaintances (e.g. in a social setting between 'friends')
  - stranger violence (e.g. homicide by a perpetrator unknown to the victim).

Violence between acquaintances and strangers also includes: workplace violence (including health-care institutions and prisons); violence in schools (including bullying); community-based violence (that does not further the aims of a formally defined group or cause); youth violence (that does not further the aims of a formally defined group or cause); sexual violence between strangers or acquaintances; and crime-related violence.

- *Self-directed violence* involves intentional and harmful behaviours directed at oneself. Suicide represents the most severe type of self-inflicted violence. Other types of self-inflicted violence include suicide attempts, and behaviours where the intent is self-destructive, but not lethal (e.g. self-mutilation).
- *Organised violence* is violent behaviour planned to achieve the specific objectives of a social or political group. It includes political violence involving carefully executed efforts to intimidate an opposing political faction violently. Genital mutilation of women and men in the name of religious and cultural rites of passage might also be considered a form of organised violence. As a last example, war is the most highly organised form of violence as it is often waged in a strictly regimented manner by military organisations specifically trained in undertaking violence.

In the following sections we highlight definitions derived from disciplines that take violence as their subject matter as well as the paradigms into which violence is inserted, and examine the consequent implications for prevention. These perspectives are by no means an attempt to provide an exhaustive account of discipline-specific approaches to violence. We illustrate the most prominent definitions that provide some indication of varied emphases that are often placed on the understandings and prevention of violence as a social phenomenon.

Paradigmatic approaches to violence within psychology

Degenaar (1980) provides a broad social scientific definition of violence in suggesting that it is an extreme force willfully carried out against a person, violating that person because it does not show respect for his or her intrinsic value. This definition highlights three key dimensions, namely, the intentionality behind the violence, the extreme force that violates the victim's integrity, and a value that is ascribed to the victim (Olivier, 1991). One psychological definition suggests that it involves the 'application of force, action, motive or thought in such a way (overt, covert, direct or indirect) that a person or group is injured, controlled or destroyed in a physical, psychological or spiritual sense' (van der Merwe, 1989:16).

Even though these definitions differ with regard to the exact description of what constitutes violence, the similarities can clearly be found in the relational nature of violence as well as the emphasis on psychic, intra-personal and subjective consequences for the victim(s). This section highlights such differences and contestations within psychology, by examining varied paradigms into which violence may be inserted and the implications for prevention efforts.

Individualistic approaches

Throughout the history of psychology, the study and understanding of violence and conflict have been central, particularly within social psychology.

Individualistic
approaches to
violence view it as
having an essentially
intra-psychic basis.

Psycho-dynamic
views of violence
describe it as the
conscious
manifestation of
unconscious wishes,
drives, and fantasies
due to poor
defensive mecha-
nisms within the
personality structure
to repress the
unconscious
impulses.

The *individualistic* approaches tended to view violence as having an essentially intra-psychic basis. In South Africa, from as early as the 1890s through until the 1960s, psycho-dynamic approaches (with strong 'racialised' overtones) dominated understandings of violence (Butchart *et al.*, 2000). Common to psycho-dynamic approaches, violence was viewed as the conscious manifestation of unconscious wishes, drives and fantasies due to poor defense mechanisms within the personality structure and an inability to repress these unconscious impulses (Freud, 1938). At other points, violence was viewed as a specific deficit within the psychological constitution of individuals who were unable to control aggressive impulses due to heightened levels of frustration. This hypothesis also assumed that the root of violence laid in the inability of individuals to contain such levels of frustration within their personality structures (Dollard *et al.*, 1939). Others focused on specific authoritarian personality formations and configurations to explain the prevalence of violence in specific populations. This approach suggested that due to particular familial and parenting styles, children internalise a rigid and domineering style of relating, thereby promoting the development of authoritarianism and even the enactment of violence (Adorno *et al.*, 1950; see also Chapter 3, this volume). Despite Bandura's (1977) attempts to infuse the individualistic approaches with an appropriate social context within which individuals learn through modelling the social behaviour of others, these approaches have by and large been consistently critiqued for the lack of historical, social and ideological content in their analyses of violence. The assumption that violence is essentially rooted in the personality and learning processes of individuals implicitly directs social scientists towards individualistic methods of prevention and control. In South Africa, adherents of this approach envisaged the individual's mind as the primary object of violence prevention interventions (Butchart *et al.*, 2000). This approach does not account for the fact that violence occurs as a relational phenomenon in a specific time, space and context, and that the personal experiences and actions of individuals interact with temporal, spatial and contextual events and processes that are in turn shaped by broader historical, ideological and material conditions. Furthermore, it has often been criticised for pathologising victims and sustaining oppressive socio-political structures (*ibid.*).

Group relations

In response to the limitations of the individualistic approaches, some theorists attempted to locate the study of violence within the context of *group* dynamics and relations. Here specifically, Sherif's (1966) *Realistic Conflict Theory* attempted to account for inter-group conflict as the result of competition between groups for scarce resources. Gurr (1970) went even further to suggest that even in the absence of an objective scarcity in resources, when groups perceive themselves to be relatively deprived in relation to other groups, they tend to experience heightened levels of resentment and discontent, which may in fact result in violence being enacted at an inter-group level. In South Africa, the 1960s saw a similar shift in the conceptualisation of violence as a legitimate tactic of political struggle between the apartheid state and its opponents (Butchart *et al.*, 2000). A further approach that had attempted to examine the connection between individuals and groups within situations of group, crowd or collective violence can be found in deindividuation theory (Festinger *et al.*, 1952). Proponents of this theory essentially argued that within the context of collective violence, individual psyches tend to become less resistant to a group norm, and within this context, individuals tend to lose their individualised controls and subject themselves to the norm of the group. The anonymity generates a sense of safety and diffusion of responsibility that may encourage collective acts of violence that might not have been enacted had the individuals not been in the presence of the group (Foster & Durrheim, 1998). Many of these approaches made significant contributions to social psychology in their identification of group processes as being much more than the mere sum of individual psychological processes within groups. They also provided useful beginnings for social scientists to explore group conflicts. However, they too failed to provide a thorough analysis of why violence resulted within some groups and not in others, and how the salient causes related to group and/or collective violence are delimited by historical, material, ideological and cultural processes prevailing within the social context at that particular time.

> Realistic conflict theory accounts for inter-group conflict as the result of competition between groups for scarce resources.

> Deindividuation theory argued that within the context of collective violence, individual psyches tend to become less resistant to a group norm, and within this context, individuals tend to lose their individualised controls and subject themselves to the norm of the group.

Individual–social interactions

During the 1960s, an imperative for mainstream, experimental social psychology was to develop a theoretical position that allowed for the incorporation of both individual and group functioning within a single framework. Tajfel's (1981) *Social Identity Theory* seemingly provided an answer to the problem of individual–social dualism that had plagued psychology. This approach argued that all individuals simultaneously occupy positions within a range of individual and group identities, and that depending on the social context of interaction, these identities either become less or more salient. It therefore provided an analysis of the complexity and range of individual and group interactions that may at times be consistent and/or contradictory. In a recent South African application, Bornman (1998) explores a number of group–individual factors reported to exacerbate conflict amongst groups differentiated according to perceived ethnic, 'racial' or class membership, including group identification, the experience of relative deprivation, and conformity to group norms. However, despite attempts to link identities to the enactment of

> Social Identity Theory argues that all individuals simultaneously occupy positions within a range of individual and group identities, and that depending on the social context of interaction, these identities either become less or more salient.

violence through this approach, it failed to identify why group or individual identities become more or less salient within the social context at a given point in time and why violence is enacted at some points and not at others. Foster (1991) argued that an analysis of ideology in these studies was notably absent, and that the use of these analyses in understanding violence and conflict needed to be augmented with an examination of the role of ideology.

From contextual theories to social constructionism

In developments that were occurring relatively independently of this process, several theorists attempted to provide a more contextually sound view of violence through looking at historical, ideological and material social contexts of violence production. Fanon (1968) and Mannoni (1962) adopted approaches that attempted to understand violence within the framework of colonial oppression, racism and violence. They argued that the social conditions of structural, vertical violence gave rise to the generation of intra-personal, inter-personal and collective counter-violence. Others, such as Bulhan (1985), also focused on the social factors that constrained human development and ultimately resulted in violence amongst marginalised groups within oppressive contexts beyond colonial social formations. These approaches were more *sociogenic* in their understandings of violence and implicitly started to incorporate what we today know as the paradigm of *social constructionism*. They incorporated the idea that all psycho-social phenomena are representations that are constructed by and through the contexts from which they emerge. They therefore started to focus not only on social, but historical, material and ideological antecedents of violence. A recent South African example of this analysis is provided by Butchart *et al.* (2000). By extension, contextual approaches link violence prevention interventions to political and ideological processes that are aimed at fundamental and revolutionary social transformation.

> Sociogenic approaches have argued that the social conditions of structural, vertical violence give rise to the generation of intra-personal, inter-personal and collective counter-violence.

Postmodern developments

In recent years, an increasingly strong perspective has been to move beyond the frameworks of modernity and to view violence as more than being essentially derived from the structures of personalities, economic systems, political systems and so forth. *Postmodern* frameworks argue that the idea of violence simply being socially constructed is restrictive, and rather focuses on the individual's subjective experiences of social encounters within these historically, ideologically, materially, culturally and temporally specific contexts. The aim is therefore not to generate a single fundamental 'truth' or definition pertaining to violence, but rather to deconstruct understandings, social actions and cultural expressions related to violence and to generate understandings unique to its relational location in time and space (Curran *et al.*, 1996).

> Postmodern frameworks focus on the individual's subjective experiences of social encounters with the aim of deconstructing understandings, social actions and cultural expressions related to violence and to generate understandings unique to its relational location in time and space.

The above-mentioned paradigms have facilitated robust debate within psychology as to the description, analysis and theorising of violence, but the critical component of translation into relevant social action has most frequently been implied or even arbitrarily disconnected from such description, analysis and theorising. In many instances, violence prevention has been the exclusive domain of psychotherapists, or has been relegated to the fringes of community psychology, participatory action research, development work and social activism. However, the endemic nature of violence and its deleterious effects in many contexts is increasingly challenging researcher–practitioners to address violence comprehensively and concretely through prevention initiatives.

Related perspectives and definitions

The range of psychological approaches reflected above does not, however, constitute the only formulations of violence. An array of broader social scientific and health approaches to violence have also made significant contributions to understanding violence and its prevention in South Africa. We outline a selection of some of the more prominent contributions below.

Sociological perspectives and definitions

The sociological approach to violence broadly suggests that violence is not necessarily exerted by an individual but by social structures, created and/or perpetuated by custom or by law (Degenaar, 1980). Within this approach, these structures invariably curtail the freedoms of subjects or discriminate unjustly against certain sections of the population. This is premised on classical sociological theory that suggests that violence is a form of social deviance through which individuals and/or groups react to restrictive social control inherent to these social structures (Durkheim, 1998; Weber, 1969). Sociological understandings of violence clearly de-emphasise the role of the individual in the perpetration of violence and instead insist on the importance of analysing social structures in the origination and perpetuation of violence, and the subsequent transformation of these social structures in the prevention and control of violence. Such structural violence shows itself when resources and powers are unequally shared and are the property of a restricted number who use them not for the good of all, but for the domination of the less favoured. Furthermore, this form of violence causes harm through the inflexibility and rigidity of rules within the social structure in dealing with difference. Through gender, 'race', and class studies, we have become much more aware in recent years of the harm that can be caused without any given perpetrator, but by the existence of policies and rules that do not allow for differences.

> The sociological approach to violence broadly suggests that violence is not necessarily exerted by an individual but by social structures, created and/or perpetuated by custom or by law.

Criminological perspectives and definitions

Generally within criminology, violence is construed as the intentional and violent violation of law that is committed without defense or justification, and is sanctioned by the state as criminal, with the implicit consequence of enforcement and punishment through deterrence, incapacitation and incarceration (Keseredy & Schwartz, 1996). This approach generally emphasises the importance of individuals and/or groups and their intentional acts of violence which contravene social codes as embodied within the legal system (Smit & Cilliers, 1998). While criminologists certainly recognise the impact of social factors on the generation of violent behaviour, there is often a focus on the individual and/or group experiences of such social factors. In addition, psychological responses to these social contexts are frequently focused upon to construct understandings of the patterns of causation associated with violence. Furthermore, the response to violence within criminology tends to be underscored by processes and mechanisms that ensure minimal behavioural deviance amongst the population in relation to the law, thus the focus on deterrence and punishment.

Health perspectives and definitions

Recent years have seen a growing number of researchers, practitioners and decision-makers in the field of violence prevention and control locating violence within a health paradigm (Butchart et al., 2000; Kruger et al., 1998). Within this framework, violence is viewed as the 'intentional use of physical force or power, threatened or actual, against oneself or another, or against a group or community, that either results in or has a high likelihood of resulting in injury, death, psychological harm, maladjustment or deprivation' (WHO, 1996:3–4). This definition clearly focuses on violence as a significant social phenomenon, which impacts on morbidity, mortality and future risk factors that may negatively influence the overall population health status. The mainstream conceptualisation of violence and its prevention within this framework concentrates on the identification of patterns of intentional violence, the study of causal pathways and risks, and the elimination or minimisation of such risks. While social antecedents are certainly considered as risk factors within this framework as well, the dominant understanding of violence is constructed as an impingement on satisfactory health status. However, recent years have seen an increasing modification of this framework to accommodate for resilience factors and also to embrace an asset-based approach, as well as to incorporate both social–scientific and bio–medical methods into its application (Butchart & Kruger, 2001; Stevens et al., in press).

The following section attempts to looks at one possible framework for violence description, analysis, theorising and social action directed at its prevention. In so doing, it endeavours to transcend disciplinary boundaries and to allow for truly scholarly interactions (Billig, 1988) that promote greater collaboration across disciplinary, methodological and theoretical boundaries. This is particularly critical, given the complex causal pathways and constructed meanings of violence that may necessitate the broadest possible range of health and social–scientific inputs to comprehensively prevent and control this social phenomenon.

Re-committing to social action: Adapting the public health approach

The increased utilisation of the public health approach in violence prevention (WHO, 2001), and its adaptation for use within communities in South Africa, are relatively well-documented features (see for example Butchart, 1996; Butchart & Kruger, 2001; Butchart *et al.*, 1996; Emmett & Butchart, 2000; Kruger *et al.*, 1998; Seedat, 1995). The following section provides the conceptual basis for reinterpreting a classic public health approach, and the manner in which this facilitates interdisciplinarity, methodological pluralism, theoretical diversity, community empowerment, and sectoral and inter-sectoral coalition-building.

As separate frameworks for research and intervention in the area of violence prevention, health and social scientific approaches are frequently driven by differing epistemologies, ontologies, methodologies and theoretical understandings. Because the public health model was initially developed in the context of high-income countries, a central challenge is therefore to determine its value and appropriateness for South Africa and other low-income countries. Given that large urban areas have complex causal relationships linked to violence, and the fact that this complexity increases with the decrease in income (Mohan, 1996), this framework cannot simply be transposed to the South African context. The public health framework essentially argues that many of the principles that are utilised with communicable and non-communicable diseases can also be applied to the control and prevention of violence (Butchart, 1996). Within the public health approach, violence is not only preventable, but its consequences and impact can also be contained. The public health approach recognises the psycho-social, neurological, physiological and cognitive components of violence. It views violent behaviour as a consequence of the interaction between environmental, socialisation and behavioural factors evident at the level of populations (Butchart, 1996). The utility of the public health approach is threefold. Firstly, it offers a four-step logic, representing an interactive process to focus on the *magnitude and causes* of violence (step 1 and step 2). In step 3, the focus is on developing and testing prevention interventions and in step 4 implementation of *what works* on a large scale (see Figure 18.1).

The public health approach views violence as a consequence of the interaction between environmental, socialisation and behavioural factors evident at the level of populations.

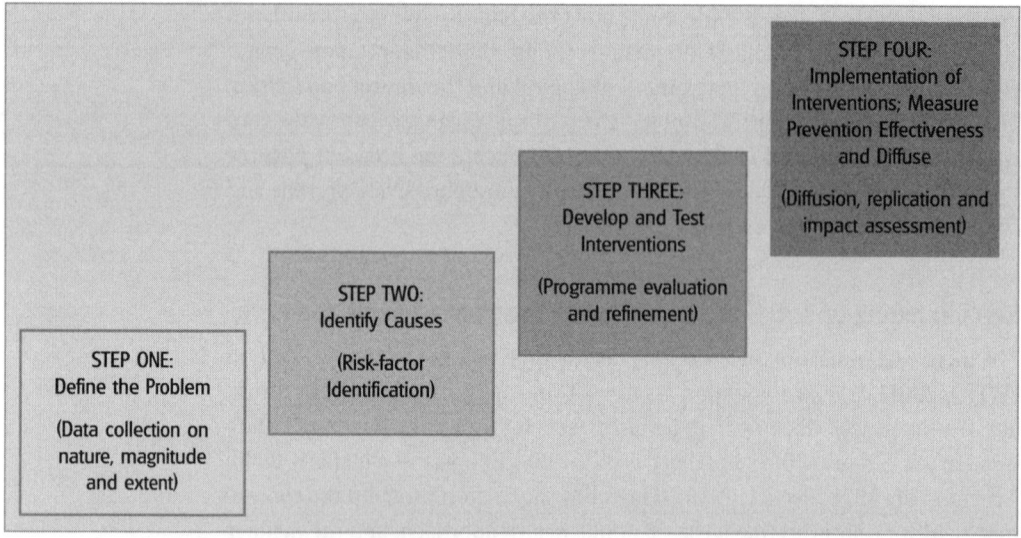

Figure 18.1
The public health
model

Secondly, the public health approach allows for an analysis of violence and the development of appropriate preventative interventions across two dimensions (Haddon & Baker, 1981). The first dimension, based on the idea that violent injuries are events located in time, divides violence into three stages: pre-event, event and post-event. The second dimension argues that violence is determined by both risk and resiliency factors (e.g. age, gender, physical strength, psycho-social skills), agent factors (e.g. perpetrator and weapon) and environmental factors (e.g. lack of socio-economic opportunities).

Thirdly, the public health approach accommodates for conscious interdisciplinarity (e.g. criminology, economics, psychology, urban planning, history) and cross-sectoral perspectives (e.g. health, criminal justice, transport, housing, NGOs, business) in our attempts to study violence and its magnitude, causes and prevention. Below we examine some of the benefits of the public health approach as one potential framework through which research can be translated into concrete action in the area of violence prevention.

Public health: A four-step logic

One of the more useful aspects of the public health approach and its application to addressing violence is in the basic four-step logic that it employs. This logic can be found in some form or another in most social-scientific and health-related disciplines, and therefore facilitates interdisciplinary approaches to understanding and preventing violence. Below, this four-step process is outlined, and we examine the manner in which it may contribute to holistic research and programme design that encourages the translation of research data into concrete practice.

Figure 18.2
Figure research and prevention utilising public health logic

PROBLEM ⟶ RESPONSE			
STEP ONE: Define the Problem (Data on nature, magnitude & extent) Collective needs assessment (Accessing, co-construc- tion and description of community needs)	STEP TWO: Identify Causes (Risk-factor identification) Identify indigenous causal models (Elicit organic explana- tions and resilience factors)	STEP THREE: Develop and Test Interventions (Programme evaluation and refinement) Generate/evaluate Community responses (Action-reflection research)	STEP FOUR: Implementation of Interventions; Measure Prevention Effectiveness and Diffuse (Diffusion, replication and impact assessment) Social action for social change (Social mobilisation) Methodologies utilised

METHODOLOGIES UTILISED
• Focus groups/
  interviews
• Rapid participatory
  appraisals
• Descriptive content
  analyses
• Surveillance
  (epidemiological)
• Surveys
	• Multivariate analyses
	• Case-control and case-
	  crossover studies
	• Thematic and
	  Discursive analyses
	• Participatory action
	  research
		• Participatory action
		  research
		• Illuminative program
		  evaluation
		• Evaluation research
		• Control studies
		• Cost-analyses
			• Trend monitoring
			• Evaluation research
			• Materials development
			  and documentation
			• Formal and informal
			  training
			• Advocacy and lobbying
			  strategies
			• Promoting social
			  movements
			• Media utilisation
			• Interdisciplinary
			  collaborations and
			  theoretical diversity

INTERDISCIPLINARY COLLABORATIONS AND THEORETICAL DIVERSITY
• Biostatisticians
• Psychologists
• Criminologists
• Sociologists
• Anthropologists
• Epidemiologists
• Historians
• Economists
• Health workers
• Community-based
  knowledge brokers
  and key stakeholders
	• Biostatisticians
	• Psychologists
	• Criminologists
	• Sociologists
	• Anthropologists
	• Epidemiologists
	• Historians
	• Economists
	• Health workers
	• Targeted community
	  roleplayers
		• Psychologists
		• Criminologists
		• Sociologists
		• Anthropologists
		• Historians
		• Economists
		• Health workers
		• Existing service
		  deliverers
		• Recipients, community
		  intervention roleplayers
		  and boader
		  community
			• Biostatisticians
			• Psychologists
			• Criminologists
			• Sociologists
			• Anthropologists
			• Epidemiologists
			• Historians
			• Economists
			• Health workers
			• Lobbyists and
			  advocates
			• Materials and media
			  specialists
			• Broader community
			• Policy- and decision-
			  makers
			• Multiple targets

PROBLEM			RESPONSE
MULTIPLE TARGETS • Women • Youth • Children • Income-defined groups • 'Racially'-defined groups • Other at-risk and high-risk groups, behaviors and environments	• Women • Youth • Children • Income-defined groups • 'Racially'-defined groups • Other at-risk and high-risk groups, behaviors and environments	• Women • Youth • Children • Income-defined groups • 'Racially'-defined groups • Other at-risk and high-risk groups, behaviors and environments	• Women • Youth • Children • Income-defined groups • 'Racially'-defined groups • Other at-risk and high-risk groups, behaviors and environments • Intervention levels
INTERVENTION LEVELS • Individual • Familial or household • School and workplace • Service delivery sites • Community • Provincial • National	• Individual • Familial or household • School and workplace • Service delivery sites • Community • Provincial • National	• Individual • Familial or household • School and workplace • Service delivery sites • Community • Provincial • National	• Individual • Familial or household • School and workplace • Service delivery sites • Community • Provincial • National

Magnitude: What is the problem?

In this step, the public health model examines the *how, when, where,* and *what* of violence. Thus, violence can be described in relational terms, including information on the number of cases, demographic characteristics of victims and perpetrators, the victim–perpetrator relationship, the mechanisms of violent injury, the involvement of products such as handguns and alcohol, and the temporal and geographical characteristics of violent incidents. Surveillance systems, as an example of routine sources of quantitative data, provide timely information on the who, what and when of violence, and inform population-based studies that are used to assess risks, triggers, and causes of violence. In addition, qualitative analyses may also be utilised to provide and augment information on specific populations that may be at risk of specific forms of violence, thereby promoting methodological pluralism (Stevens *et al.*, in press).

Risks, triggers and causes: What are the determinants?

Risk factor identification looks at the why of violence. Risk factors are factors that are shown to increase the possibility of exposure or experience of violence. In a study of risk factors we are interested, for instance, in the relationship between violence and variables such as age, gender, gun ownership, alcohol abuse, and inequalities in power. These and other such risk factors are often associated with both violent perpetration and violent victimisation. Risk factors are sometimes specific to certain types of violence. For example, ease of access to firearms increases the risk of homicide and violence between acquaintances and strangers.

Once we understand risk factors and the micro-, meso- and macro-causes, we can design specific prevention programmes to reduce violence and violent behaviour. For example, programmes may be targeted at young males, as they are a high-risk group for perpetrating and experiencing inter-personal violence. Other programmes target access to firearms or alcohol legislation, yet others focus on employment or empowerment activities to address inequalities in gender and wealth.

Within the public health approach we determine the risks, triggers, and causes of violence through analysis secured through routine information systems (e.g. injury and violence surveillance systems) or population based quantitative and qualitative studies (e.g. case control studies, cross-sectional studies, discursive analyses, etc.). Given public health's multi-disciplinary orientation, a feminist perspective may be introduced to understand how, for instance, patriarchy, gender inequality, and poverty contribute to femicide. Similarly, those interested in uncovering the discourses underlying our social constructions of violence may introduce critical theory to conduct an archival and historical analysis with a view to producing alternative explanations of violence. Likewise, researchers focusing on 'race' or ethnicity may place the accent on 'racialised' patterns of socio-political, economic and geographical exclusion in their explanations of violence and associated prevention measures. This step basically allows us to take a multi-disciplinary understanding as to the causes of violence, including all of the discipline-specific and paradigmatic approaches referred to above. At a theoretical level, contextual social analyses complement more technical analyses of specific determinants, risks and triggers prior to, during and after violent events. Violence can therefore be addressed at a macro-level as well as at the levels of individuals, families and communities. This allows for the possibility of moving beyond the restrictive definitions of violence that are situation- and event-specific (Haddon & Baker, 1981), to include political and ideological components that help to contextualise this phenomenon (Bulhan, 1985). This form of inter-disciplinarity is not only desirable, but imperative for a comprehensive understanding of the complex underpinnings of violence that are located within the subjective, cultural, ideological, material and historical realms that help to constitute social realities.

Develop and test interventions: What works?

Problem definition, risk factor analysis and the determination of causes help us to understand violence in relational terms, illuminating the association between people, products and the environments that promote the contexts of violence. Such understandings should then enable the design, implementation and evaluation of intervention programmes. In this step we are interested in the study of *what works*. Programmes may assume a singular or multiple focus (e.g. youth violence, child abuse, family violence), targeting one or more at-risk environments (e.g. schools, recreational facilities), or risk factors (e.g. poverty, life styles), and one or more at-risk groups (e.g. children, young men, the elderly, etc.).

An example of a schools-based violence prevention programme

Inter-personal violence disproportionately involves young people as both victims and perpetrators of violence. Of particular concern is the proliferation of violence and injuries within schools. Prevention of schools-based violence and injury is therefore a public health and educational priority. School violence is affected by levels of violence in communities and the broader society.

Safe schools programmatic summary

- Assessment, monitoring, surveillance and evaluation.
- Behaviour, conduct and discipline codes.
- Staff and student training.
- Student leadership and responsibility.
- Parental participation.
- After-school safety activities.
- Crisis management strategies.
- Broader community involvement.
- Environmental design.
- Policy formulation, adoption and implementation.

Interventions may also be directed at different parts in the chain of causation of violence and therefore interventions are also categorised under the *four Es*: Education, Environmental change, Engineering, and Enforcement.

The four Es of public health interventions

Education: Aimed at changing individual skills, knowledge, and beliefs.

Environmental: Aimed at modifying physical and social spaces that place people at risk of violence.

Engineering: Aimed at reducing risk by improving the safety of dangerous products.

Enforcement: Involves the development and enforcement of legal measures and practices that prevent violence.

Interventions may furthermore be classified as *passive* or *active* depending on the level of activity required of the group or individual being targeted. Whereas *active interventions* require deliberate action from the targeted group/individual (e.g. community mobilisation against firearm proliferation), passive measures require no individual action (e.g. policy formulation and enforcement that attempts to address violence at national, regional and international levels). This could conceivably incorporate strategies aimed at regional disarmament, demilitarisation and the development of more equitable global economic policies. Within the public health approach, prevention programmes may therefore assume varying intensities, focus on different target groups, target various settings including geographical locations, and socio-economically stratified groups.

Implement interventions: How is it done and what is its impact?

The fourth and final step in the public health model deals with implementation vis-à-vis those good practices that have been shown to be effective. Typically, good practice initiatives, including demonstration programmes, are utilised to inform public health policy and practice on violence prevention and containment. Institutional and funding support is vital for the adoption of known and evaluated good practices on a large scale. In short, focusing on *how do you do it?* addresses the translation of effective programmes into wide-scale prevention policy and practice. It should also consciously involve two additional Es, namely *Evaluation* and *Empowerment.* Here, the public health approach structurally incorporates the necessity for programme evaluation to assess the overall impact of such of programmes. In addition, it can also actively encourage the inclusion of communities in the prevention of violence through participatory processes that facilitate self-reliance, self-determination, ownership and empowerment to control the outcome of their everyday realities.

From the above, it becomes apparent that the public health framework can be utilised as a structural logic to ensure that research in the form of description, analysis and theorising is translated into conscious forms of evidence-led and evaluated social action. This adapted framework represents a matrix through which to engage in violence prevention work, and simultaneously accommodates for theoretical diversity, methodological pluralism, inter-disciplinarity and varied scientific philosophies (see Figure 18.2). It also allows for evidence-led interventions to be structured across micro-, meso- and macro-levels; with universal, targeted and specified populations and environments; and at primary, secondary and tertiary levels. However, it is important to note that this adapted matrix is not underpinned by a generic scientific neutrality that automatically accommodates for diverse philosophical foundations of science, but rather, that it allows for the conscious co-existence of varying ontologies, epistemologies and methodologies in the prevention of violence.

This is particularly important to emphasise, given the erroneous belief that the public health model is in and of itself an all-encompassing and scientifically neutral framework to accommodate for a range of diverse perspectives. The key element in this process is therefore the *conscious* introduction of alternative and complementary perspectives of science and their application to the resolution of violence as an obstacle to health, psycho-social well-being and social development.

Looking ahead

In conclusion, we argue that violence is a preventable social phenomenon and is not an intractable social problem or an inevitable part of the human condition. The wide variation in the form and extent of violence among and within populations over time suggests that violence is the product of complex, yet modifiable, subjective and social factors.

Within the public health approach, health and social science researchers and practitioners have an important role to play in providing a vision and leadership in the establishment of national social programmes and policies for violence prevention. This becomes an even more desirable prospect when one considers that it may occur within the context of inter- and intra-sectoral coalition-building, multi-disciplinary theorising, methodological eclecticism and a philosophy of empowerment. In so doing, the public health logic provides important entry points for researchers and practitioners to reflexively consider as they dynamically engage in processes related to describing, analysing, theorising and preventing violence.

Exercises for critical engagement

1   *Violence in South Africa constitutes a significant historical and current psychosocial and health priority.* Please discuss and substantiate your argument in relation to this statement.

2   Describe the main types of violence as defined by the WHO (1996).

3   Describe and critically discuss one psychological definition of violence.

4   Describe the main features and limitations of the individualistic, group relations, individual–group, contextual and postmodern psychological approaches to understanding violence.

5   Describe the key contributions and limitations of the sociological, criminological, and health perspectives on violence.

6   Provide a critical discussion of the public health approach to violence prevention.

Recommended reading

Bornman, E., van Eeden, R. & M. Wentzel (Eds.) (1998). *Violence in South Africa: A Variety of Perspectives*. Pretoria: HSRC.

Bulhan, H.A. (1985). *Frantz Fanon and the Psychology of Oppression*. New York: Plenum Press.

Butchart, A. & J. Kruger (2001). 'Public health and community psychology: A case study in community-based injury prevention'. In Seedat, M., Duncan, N. & S. Lazarus (Eds.) *Theory, Method and Practice in Community Psychology: South African and Other Perspectives*, pp. 215–241. Cape Town: Oxford University Press.

Emmett, T. & A. Butchart (Eds.) (2000). *Behind the Mask*. Pretoria: HSRC Publishers.

Foster, D. & J. Louw-Potgieter (Eds.) (1991). *Social Psychology in South Africa*. Johannesburg. Lexicon Publishers.

Stevens, G., Seedat, M., Swart, T. & C. van der Walt (2003). 'Promoting methodological pluralism, theoretical diversity and interdisciplinarity in a multi-levelled violence prevention initiative in South Africa'. *Journal of Prevention and Intervention in the Community*, in press.

Bibliography

Abdool Karim, S.S., Abdool Karim, Q., Preston-Whyte, E. & N. Sankar (1992). 'Reasons for lack of condom use among high school students'. *South African Medical Journal*, 82:107–110.

Abdool Karim, Q., Preston-Whyte, E. & S.S. Abdool Karim (1992). 'Teenagers seeking condoms at family planning services: Part I. A user's perspective'. *South African Medical Journal*, 82:356–359.

Abdool Karim, Q., Abdool Karim, S.S. & E. Preston-Whyte (1992). 'Teenagers seeking condoms at family planning services: Part II. A provider's perspective'. *South African Medical Journal*, 82:360–362.

Aboud, F. (1987). 'The development of ethnic self-identification and attitudes'. In Phinney, J. & M. Rotheram (Eds.) *Children's Ethnic Socialisation: Pluralism and Development*, pp. 32–35. Newbury Park: Sage.

Aboud, F.E. & S.R. Levy (1999). 'Are we ready to translate research into programs?' *Journal of Social Issues*, 55(4):621–625.

Abraham, M. (2000). *Speaking the Unspeakable. Marital Violence among South Asian Immigrants in the United States*. New Brunswick: Rutgers University Press.

Abrahams, N., Jewkes, R. & R. Laubsher. (1999). *'I Do Not Believe in Democracy in the Home.' Men's Relationships With and Abuse of Women*. Tygerberg: CERSA (Women's Health) Medical Research Council.

Abrahams, Y. (2000). *Colonialism, Dysfunction and Dysjuncture: The Histiography of Sarah Baartman*. Unpublished doctoral thesis, University of Cape Town.

Achmat, Z. (1993). '"Apostles of civilised vice": "Immoral practices" and "unnatural vice" in South African prisons and compounds, 1890–1920'. *Social Dynamics*, 19(2):92–110.

Adam, H. (1995). 'The politics of ethnic identity: Comparing South Africa'. *Ethnic and Racial Studies*, 18(3):457–475.

Adebayo, D. (1996). *Some Kind of Black*. London: Virago.

Adelman, M. (1980). *Adjustment to Aging and Styles of Being Gay: A Study of Elderly Gay Men and Lesbians*. Unpublished doctoral dissertation, University of California, Berkeley.

Adler, M. (1996). 'Skirting the edges of civilisation: Two Victorian women travelers and "colonial spaces" in South Africa'. In Darian-Smith, E., Gunner, L. & S. Nuttall (Eds.) *Text, Theory, Space: Land, Literature and History in South Africa and Australia*, pp. 83–98. London: Routledge.

Adler, N.J. (1996). 'Global women political leaders: An invisible history, an increasingly important future'. *Leadership Quarterly*, 7(1):133–161.

Adorno, T.W., Frenkel-Brunswik, E., Levinson, D.J. & R.N. Sanford (1950). *The Authoritarian Personality*. New York: Harper.

Agence France-Presse (1998). 'South African players face sanction over racism claims'. *Internet Sports Features Page*: www.afp.com/english (accessed 6 May 1998).

Alessandri, A.C. (Ed.) (1999). *Frantz Fanon: Critical Perspectives*. London: Routledge.

Alexander, N. (1985). *Sow the Wind: Contemporary Speeches*. Johannesburg: Skotaville.

Alexander, N. (1992). 'National liberation and socialist revolution'. In A. Callinicos (Ed.) *Between Apartheid and Capitalism*, pp. 114–136. London: Bookmarks.

Alexander, N. (1996). *Towards a National Plan for South Africa: Report of the Language Plan Task Group (LANGTAG)*. Pretoria: Department of Arts and Culture, Science and Technology.

Alexander, N. (2001). 'Language politics in South Africa'. In Bekker, S., Dodds, M. & M. Khosa (Eds.) *Shifting African Identities*, Vol. 2, pp. 141–152. Pretoria: Human Sciences Research Council.

Allport, G. (1954). *The Nature of Prejudice*. Reading: Addison-Wesley.

Allport, G.W. (1968). 'The historical background of modern social psychology'. In Lindzey, G. & E. Aronson (Eds.) *The Handbook of Social Psychology*, Vol. 1, 2nd Edition, pp. 1–80. Reading: Addison-Wesley.

Alwood, E. (1996). *Straight News: Gays, Lesbians, and the News Media*. New York: Columbia University Press.

Amadiume, I. (1987). *Male Daughters, Female Husbands: Gender and Sex in an African Society*. London: Zed Books.

ANC (African National Congress) (2000). 'Stereotypes steer the news'. Submission to the HSRC Inquiry into Racism in the Media. *Rhodes Journalism Review*, 19:21.

Anderson, K. (1997). 'Gender, status, and domestic violence. An integration of feminist and family violence approaches'. *Journal of Marriage and the Family*, 59:655–669.

Anzieu, D. (1985). *Le Moi Peau* [The Ego Skin]. Paris: Dunod.

Apteker, L. (1994). 'Street children in the developing world: A review of their condition'. *Cross-Cultural Research*, 28(3):195–224.

Armon, V. (1960). 'Some personality variables in overt female homosexuality'. *Journal of Projective Techniques and Personality Assessment*, 24:292–309.

Arnold, M. (Ed.) (1979). *Steve Biko: Black Consciousness in South Africa*. New York: Vintage.

Aronson, E. (1984). *The Social Animal*, 4th Edition. New York: W.H. Freeman & Company.

Aronson, E., Stephan, C., Sikes, J., Blaney, N. & M. Snapp (1978). *The Jigsaw Classroom*. Beverley Hills: Sage.

Artz, L. (2001). 'Policing the Domestic Violence Act: Teething troubles or system failure'. *Agenda*, 47:4–13.

Ashcroft, B. Griffiths, G. & H. Tiffin (Eds.) (1995). *The Post-colonial Studies Reader*. London & New York: Routledge.

Atkinson, D., Morten, G. & D.W. Sue. (1983). *Counselling American Minorities*. Dubuque, Iowa: W. C. Brown.

Bakare-Yusuf, B. (2003). '"Yorubas don't do gender": A critical review of Oyerunke Oyewumi's *The Invention of Woman: Making African Sense of Western Gender Discourses'*. *African Identities* (in press).

Baker, P.L. (1997). 'And I went back: Battered women's negotiation of choice'. *Journal of Contemporary Ethnography*, 26(1):55–74.

Balier, C. (1988). *Psychanalyse des Comportements Violents*. Paris: PUF.

Balogun, M.J. (1997). 'Enduring clientelism, governance reform and leadership capacity: A review of the democratisation process in Nigeria'. *Journal of Contemporary African Studies*, 15(2):237–260.

Bandura, A. (1977). *Social Learning Theory*. New Jersey: Prentice-Hall.

Banton, M. (1988). *Racial Consciousness*. London: Longman.

Banyard, V.L. & S.A. Graham-Bermann (1993). 'Can women cope? A gender analysis of theories of coping with stress'. *Psychology of Women Quarterly*, 17:303–318.

Barnes, T. (1999). *We Women Worked so Hard: Gender, Urbanization and Social Reproduction in Colonial Harare, Zimbabwe, 1930–1956.* Portsmouth: Heinemann.

Baron, R.A. & D. Byrne (1981). *Social Psychology,* 3rd Edition. Boston: Allyn and Bacon.

Baron, R.A. & D. Byrne (1997). *Social Psychology,* 8th Edition. Boston: Allyn and Bacon.

Barr, C. (1995). 'Saigon's street kids stand up for themselves'. *The Child Care Worker,* 13(8).

Barrette, M. (1995). *Street Children Need Our Care.* Pretoria: Kagiso Publishers.

Barthes, R. (1964). *Critique et Véréte.* Paris: Seuil.

Bassett, M. & J. Sherman (1994). 'Female sexual behaviour and the risk of HIV infection: an ethnographic study in Harare, Zimbabwe'. *Women and AIDS Program Research Report Series.* Washington DC: International Center for Research on Women.

Beach, B. (1980). *Lesbian and Non-lesbian Women: Profiles of Development and Self-actualization.* Unpublished doctoral dissertation, University of Iowa.

Bekker, S. (2001). 'Identity and ethnicity'. In Bekker, S., Dodds, M. & M. Khosa (Eds.) *Shifting African Identities,* Vol. 2, pp. 1–6. Pretoria: HSRC.

Benokraitis, N.V. & Feagin, J.R. (1995). *Modern Sexism: Blatant, Subtle and Covert Discrimination.* Englewood Cliffs, New Jersey: Prentice Hall.

Benson, S. (1997). 'The body, health and eating disorders'. In Woodward, K. (Ed.) *Identity and Difference,* pp. 121–181. London: Sage Publications/The Open University.

Bergler, E. (1956). *Homosexuality: Disease or Way of Life?* New York: Collier Boales.

Bergman, L. (1992). 'Dating violence among high school students'. *Social Work,* 37(1):21–27.

Berman, K. (1993). 'Lesbians in South Africa: Challenging the invisibility'. In Krouse, M. & K. Berman (Eds.) *The Invisible Ghetto: Lesbian and Gay Writing from South Africa,* pp. xvii–xxi. Johannesburg: COSAW Publishing.

Bertelsen, E. (2000). 'Race, class and other prejudices'. *Rhodes Journalism Review,* 19:19–20.

Bertoldi, A. (1998). 'Oedipus in (South) Africa? Psychoanalysis and the politics of difference'. *American Imago,* 55(1):101–134.

Bhabha, H.K. (1994). *The Location of Culture.* London & New York: Routledge.

Bhende, A. (1995). 'Evolving a model for AIDS prevention education among underprivileged adolescent girls in urban India'. *Women and AIDS Program Research Report Series.* Washington DC: International Center for Research on Women.

Biko, S. (1978). *I Write What I Like.* Randburg: Ravan Press.

Biko, S. (1988). *I Write What I Like.* London: Penguin.

Biko, S. (1996). *I Write What I Like.* London: The Bowerdean Publishing Company.

Billig, M. (1976). *Social Psychology and Intergroup Relations.* London: Academic Press.

Billig, M. (1988). 'Methodology and scholarship in understanding ideological explanation'. In C. Antaki (Ed.) *Analysing Everyday Explanation,* pp. 199–215. London: Sage Publications.

Billig, M. (1998). 'Rhetoric and the unconscious'. *Argumentation,* 12:199–216.

Bion, W. (1962). *Learning from Experience.* London: Heinemann.

Bion, W. (1963). *Elements of Psychoanalysis.* London: Heinemann.

Blumenfeld, W. & D. Raymond. (1989). *Looking at Gay and Lesbian Life.* Boston: Beacon Press.

Blummer, H. (1971). 'Social problems as collective behaviour'. *Social problems,* 18:298–306.

Blyth, S. (1989). *An Exploration of Accounts of Lesbian Identities.* Unpublished Master's thesis, University of Cape Town.

Blyth, S. & G. Straker (1996). 'Intimacy, fusion and frequency of sexual contact in lesbian couples'. *South African Journal of Psychology,* 26(4):253–256.

Bobo, L. (1988). 'Group conflict, prejudice, and the paradox of contemporary racial attitudes'. In Katz, P.A. & D.A. Taylor (Eds.) *Eliminating Racism. Profiles in Controversy,* pp. 85–114. New York: Plenum Press.

Bodiba, L.J. (nd.). *The Coloured-African Divide in the Western Cape: A Legacy of Apartheid.* Unpublished paper.

Bograd, M. (1990). 'Feminist perspectives on wife abuse: An introduction'. In Yllö, K. & M. Bograd (Eds.) *Feminist Perspectives on Wife Abuse*, pp. 11–26. Newbury Park: Sage.

Bograd, M. (1999). 'Strengthening domestic violence theories: Intersections of race, class, sexual orientation, and gender'. *Journal of Marital and Family Therapy*, 25(3):275–289.

Boloka, G. (2000). 'Not yet uhuru'. *Rhodes Journalism Review*, 19:35.

Bond, P. (1994). 'RDP versus World Bank'. *International Viewpoint*, 257:16–17.

Bond, P. (2000). *Elite Transition*. London: Pluto Press.

Boonzaier, F. (2001). *Woman Abuse: Exploring Women's Narratives of Violence and Resistance in Mitchell's Plain.* Unpublished Master's thesis, University of Cape Town.

Bornman, E. (1998). 'Group membership as determinant of violence and conflict: The case of South Africa'. In Bornman, E., van Eeden, R. & M. Wentzel (Eds.) *Violence in South Africa: A Variety of Perspectives*, pp. 85–116. Pretoria: HSRC.

Bornman, E. (1999). 'The individual and the group in the social, political and economic context: Implications for South Africa'. In Bekker, S. & R. Prinsloo (Eds.) *Identity? Theory, Politics, History*, Vol. 1, pp. 39–66. Pretoria: Human Sciences Research Council.

Botha, A.H. (1975). *Pastorale Sorg aan die Homoseksuele Mens.* Unpublished doctoral dissertation, University of Pretoria.

Bourdillon, M. (1995). 'The children on our streets'. *The Child Care Worker*, 13:12–13.

Bowlby, J. (1988). *A Secure Base: Parent-child Attachment and Healthy Human Development.* New York: Basic Books.

Bozzoli, B. (1987). *Class, Community and Conflicts.* Johannesburg: Ravan Press.

Brah, A. (1996). *Cartographies of Diaspora: Contesting Identities*, London: Routledge.

Brah, A. (2000). 'Difference, diversity, differentiation'. In Back, L. & J. Solomons (Eds.) *Theories of Race and Racism: A Reader*, pp. 431–446. London: Routledge.

Braude, C. (1999). *Cultural Bloodstains: Towards Understanding the Legacy of Apartheid and the Perpetuation of Racial Stereotypes in the Contemporary South African Media.* Parktown: SAHRC.

Brecker, C. (1994). 'Left faces new challenge'. *International Viewpoint*, 257:6–12.

Breckinridge, K. (1998). 'The allure of violence: Men, race and masculinity on the South African goldmines, 1900–1950'. *Journal of Southern African Studies*, 24(4):669–693.

Bremridge, C. (2000). *Constructions of Male Adolescent Sexuality: An Exploratory Study in a Coloured, Rural Community.* Unpublished Master's thesis, University of Stellenbosch.

Brett, J. (2000). 'Culture and negotiation'. *International Journal of Psychology*, 35(2):97–104.

Brown, L. (Ed.) (1993). *The New Shorter Oxford English Dictionary on Historical Principles.* Oxford: Clarendon Press.

Browne, A. (1987). *When Battered Women Kill.* New York: Free Press.

Browne, A. (1997). 'Violence in marriage: Until death do us part'? In Cardarelli, A.P. (Ed.) *Violence between Intimate Partners: Patterns, Causes, and Effects*, pp. 48–69. Boston: Allyn and Bacon.

Buga, G., Amoko, D. & D. Ncayiyana (1996). 'Sexual behaviour, contraceptive practice and reproductive health among school adolescents in rural Transkei'. *South African Medical Journal*, 86(5):523–527.

Bulhan, H.A. (1979). 'Black psyches in captivity and crisis'. *Race and Class*, 20(3):243–261.

Bulhan, H.A. (1980a). 'Frantz Fanon: The revolutionary psychiatrist'. *Race & Class*, 21(3):251–271.

Bulhan, H.A. (1980b). 'Dynamics of cultural in-betweenity: An empirical study'. *International Journal of Psychology*, 15:105–121.

Bulhan, H.A. (1985). *Frantz Fanon and the Psychology of Oppression*. New York: Plenum Press.

Bulhan, H.A. (1992). 'Imperialism in studies of the psyche'. In Nicholas, L. (Ed.) *Psychology and Oppression*, pp. 1–34. Johannesburg: Skotaville.

Bundy, C. (2000). 'The beast of the past'. In James, W. & D.P. van der Vijver (Eds.) *After the TRC: Reflections on Truth and Reconciliation in South Africa*, pp. 9–20. Cape Town: David Phillip.

Burrows, S., Bowman, B., Matzopoulos, R. & A. van Niekerk (2001). *A Profile of Fatal Injuries in South Africa 2000*. Tygerberg: Medical Research Council.

Burstyn, V. (1999). *The Rites of Men: Manhood, Politics and the Culture of Sport*. Toronto: University of Toronto Press.

Busch, A. (1999). *Finding Their Voices: Listening to Battered Women Who've Killed*. New York: Kroshka Books.

Butchart, A. & J. Kruger (2001). 'Public health and community psychology: A case study in community-based injury prevention'. In Seedat, M., Duncan, N. & S. Lazarus (Eds.) *Theory, Method and Practice in Community Psychology: South African and Other Perspectives*, pp. 215–241. Cape Town: Oxford University Press.

Butchart, A. (1996). 'Violence prevention in Gauteng: The public health approach'. *Acta Criminologica*, 9(2):5–15.

Butchart, A. (1998). *The Anatomy of Power: European Constructions of the African Body*. Pretoria: Unisa.

Butchart, A., Nell, V. & M. Seedat (1996). 'Violence in South Africa: Its definition and prevention as a public health problem'. In Seager, J. & C. Parry (Eds.) *Urbanisation and Health in South Africa*, pp. 1–41. Tygerberg: Medical Research Council.

Butchart, A., Terreblanche, M., Hamber, B. & M. Seedat (2000). 'Violence and violence prevention in South Africa: A sociological and historical perspective'. In Emmett, T. & A. Butchart (Eds.) *Behind the Mask*, pp. 29–54. Pretoria: HSRC.

Butler, J. (1990a). *Gender Trouble: Feminism and the Subversion of Identity*. New York: Routledge.

Butler, J. (1990b). 'Gender trouble, feminist theory, and psychoanalytic discourse'. In Nicholson, L.J. (Ed.) *Feminism/Postmodernism*, pp. 324–340. New York and London: Routledge.

Butler, J. (1993). *Bodies That Matter*. New York: Rouledge.

Butulia, U. (2000). *The Other Side of Silence: Voices from the Partition of India*. London: Hurst and Company.

CAL (Cape Action League). (1987). *Introduction to 'Race' and Racism*. Cape Town: CAL.

Callaghan, N., Hamber, B. & S. Takura (1997). *A Triad of Oppression: Violence, Women, and Poverty*. Johannesburg: South African NGO Coalition.

Callinicos, L. (1987). *Working Life 1886–1940*. Johannesburg: Ravan Press.

Cameron, E. (1994). '"Unapprehended felons": Gays and lesbians and the law in South Africa'. In Gevisser, M. & E. Cameron (Eds.) *Defiant Desire: Gay and Lesbian Lives in South Africa*, pp. 89–98. Braamfontein: Ravan.

Camilleri, C. (1990). 'Identité collective et gestion de la disparité culturelle: essai d'une typologie' [Collective identity and the management of cultural disparity: Towards a typology]. In Camilleri, C., Kasterszein, J., Lipiansky, M.E., Malewska-Peyre, H., Taboada-Leonetti, I. and A. Vasquez (Eds.) *Stratégies Identitaires*, pp. 85–110. Paris: PUF.

Campbell, C. (1995). 'Identity and difference'. *Agenda*, 4:45–63.

Campbell, C. (2001). 'Going underground and going after women: Masculinity and HIV transmission amongst black workers on the gold mines'. In Morrell, R. (Ed.) *Changing Men in Southern Africa*, pp. 275–286. Pietermaritzburg: University of Natal Press.

Campbell, C., Mzaidume, Y. & B. Williams (1998). 'Gender as an obstacle to condom use: HIV prevention amongst commercial sex-workers in a mining community'. *Agenda*, 39:50–57.

Campbell, J. (1992). 'If I can't have you, no one can: Power and control in homicide of female partners'. In Radford, J. & D. Russel (Eds.) *Femicide: The Politics of Woman Killing*, pp. 99–113. New York: Twayne/Gale Group.

Campbell, J.C., Miller, P., Cardwell, M.M. & A. Belknap (1994). 'Relationship status of battered women over time'. *Journal of Family Violence*, 9(2):99–111.

Caprio, F.S. (1954). *Female Homosexuality: A Psychodynamic Study of Lesbianism*. New York: Citadel Press.

Carby, H. (1987). *Reconstructing Womanhood: The Emergence of the Afro-American Woman Novelist*. New York: Oxford University Press.

Cario, R. (1997). *Les Femmes Résisten au Crime*. Paris: L'Harmattan.

Carrim, N. (2000). 'Critical anti-racism and problems in self-articulated forms of identities'. *Race, Ethnicity and Education*, 3(1):25–44.

Caute, D. (1970). *Frantz Fanon*. New York: Viking Press.

Césaire, A. (1995). *Notebook of a Return to My Native Land*. Newcastle-upon-Tyne: Bloodaxe Books.

Chan, C. (1989). 'Issues of identity development among Asian American lesbians and gay men'. *Journal of Counseling and Development*, 68(1):16–20.

Chan-Sam, T. (1994). 'Profiles of black lesbian life on the Reef'. In Gevisser, M. & E. Cameron (Eds.) *Defiant Desire: Gay and Lesbian Lives in South Africa*, pp. 186–192. Johannesburg: Ravan Press.

Chapman, M.D. (1997). *The Group Psychotherapeutic Effects of Human Modelling Psychotherapy on the Self-esteem of Street Children Identified as Having Low Self-esteem*. Unpublished Master's dissertation, University of North-West.

Chesler, M.A. (1976). 'Contemporary sociological theories of racism'. In Katz, P.A. (Ed.) *Towards the Elimination of Racism*, pp. 21–72. New York: Pergamon.

Chetty, D. (1994). 'Lesbian gangster: the Gertie William story'. In Gevisser, M. & E. Cameron (Eds.) *Defiant Desire: Gay and Lesbian Lives in South Africa*, pp. 128–133. Johannesburg: Ravan Press.

Chetty, V.R. (1997). *Street Children in Durban: An Exploratory Investigation*. Pretoria: HSRC.

Chipkin, I. (2002). *The South African Nation*. Unpublished manuscript.

Christian, B. (2000). 'Black feminism and the academy'. In Back, L. & J. Solomons (Eds.), *Theories of Race and Racism: A Reader*, pp. 462–472. London: Routledge.

Christopher, A.J. (1994). *The Atlas of Apartheid*. London: Routledge.

Clark, D. (1993). '"With my body I thee worship": The social construction of marital sex problems'. In Scott, S. & D. Morgan (Eds.) *Body Matters*, pp. 22–34. London: The Falmer Press.

Clarke, C. (1981). 'Lesbianism: An act of resistance'. In Moraga, C. & G. Anzaldua (Eds.) *This Bridge Called My Back: Writings by Radical Women of Color*, pp. 128–137. Massachusetts: Persephone Press.

Cockburn, A. (1991). 'Street children: Victims of multiple abuses'. Paper presented at the South African Society for the *Prevention of Child Abuse and Neglect Conference*, Durban, nd.

Cockburn, A. (1994). 'Who cares? Sexual abuse and the street child'. *The Child Care Worker*, 12(7):11–12.

Cockburn, A. (1995). 'Looking after street children: A model indigenous to South Africa'. Paper presented at the *Tenth Biennial Conference of the National Association of Child Care Workers*. Cape Town, nd.

Collins, A. (2001). 'How the social psychologist got his facts: A postcolonial tale'. *Psychology in Society*, 27:53–60.

Collins, P.H. (1990). *Black Feminist Thought: Knowledge, Consciousness and the Politics of Empowerment*. New York: Routledge.

Connell, R. (1995). *Masculinities*. Cambridge: Polity Press.

Cooper, S. (1990). 'The violence of apartheid on the family'. *University of the Western Cape Psychology Resource Centre Bulletin*, 1(1):2–3.

Cornwell, A. (1983). *Black Lesbian in White America*. Tallahassie, Florida: Naiad.

Cronin, J. (1999). 'We're right here, in the South – Chris Hani's legacy': www.sacp.org.za/pr/press/1999/nw0411.htm (accessed 6 June 2000).

Cronjé, C.J. (1979). *Lesbinisme: Etiologie in Psigodinamika*. Unpublished Master's thesis, Rand Afrikaans University, Johannesburg.

Curran, J., Morley, D. & V. Walkerdine (Eds.) (1996). *Cultural Studies and Communications*. New York: Halstead Press.

Dangor, Z., Hoff, L.A. & R. Scott (1996). *Woman Abuse in South Africa: An Exploratory Study*. Johannesburg: Nisaa Institute for Women' Development.

Das, A. (1996). 'Language and body: Transactions in the construction of pain'. *Daedelus*, 125(1):67–92.

Davis, F.J. (1992). *Who is Black? One Nation's Definition*. Pennsylvania: Pennsylvania State University Press.

Davis, K. (Ed.) (1997a). *Embodied Practices: Feminist Perspectives on the Body*. London: Sage Publications.

Davis, K. (1997b). '"My body is my art": Cosmetic surgery as feminist utopia?' *The European Journal of Women's Studies*, 4(1):23–37.

Dawes, A. & D. Donald (Eds.) (1994). *Childhood and Adversity*. Cape Town: David Phillip.

Dawes, A. (1994). 'The emotional impact of political violence'. In Dawes, A. & D. Donald (Eds.) *Childhood and Adversity*, pp. 177–199. Cape Town: David Phillip.

Dayile, N.M. (1998). *The Representation of Inter-ethnic/Racial Life Stories*. Unpublished Honours Research Project, Women and Gender Studies, University of the Western Cape, Cape Town.

De Beer, A.S. (1997). 'Mass communication in society: Pervasive images and images of our time'. In de Beer, A.S. (Ed.) *Mass Media for the Nineties: A South African Handbook of Mass Communication*, pp. 5–25. Pretoria: van Schaik.

De la Rey, C. (1991). 'Intergroup relations: Theories and positions'. In Foster, D. & J. Louw-Potgieter (Eds.) *Social Psychology in South Africa*, pp. 26–53. Johannesburg: Lexicon.

De la Rey, C. (1997). 'South African feminism, race and racism'. *Agenda*, 32:6–10.

De Waal Malefijt, A. (1976). *Images of Man: A History of Anthropological Thought*. New York: Knopf.

Degenaar, J.J. (1980). 'The concept of violence'. *Politikon*, 7(1):14–27.

Derrida, J. (1978). *Writing and Difference*. London: Routledge.

Descartes, R. (1968). *Discourse on Method and the Meditations*. London: Penguin Books.

Diederichs, P. (1997). 'Newspapers: The fourth estate'. In de Beer, A.S. (Ed.) *Mass Media for the Nineties: A South African Handbook of Mass Communication*, pp. 71–100. Pretoria: van Schaik.

Dimenstein, G. (1991). *Brazil. War on Children*. London: Latin America Bureau.

Dobash, R.E. & R. Dobash (1979). *Violence against wives: A Case against Patriarchy*. New York: The Free Press.

Dobash, R.P., Dobash, R.E., Wilson, M. & M. Daly (1992). 'The myth of sexual symmetry in marital violence'. *Social Problems*, 39(1):71–85.

Dolby, N.E. (2000). *Constructing Race: Youth, Identity and Popular Culture in South Africa*. New York: State University of New York Press.

Dollard, J., Doob, L.W., Miller, N.E., Mower, O.H. & R.R. Sears (1939). *Frustration and Aggression*. New Haven: Yale University Press.

Donald, D. & J. Swart-Kruger (1994). 'The South African street child: Developmental implications'. *South African Journal of Psychology*, 24(4):169–174.

Dovidio, J.F. & S.L. Gaertner (1986). *Prejudice, Discrimination and Racism*. London: Academic Press.

Du Bois, W.E.B. (1995). *W.E.B du Bois Reader*. New York: H. Holt.

Du Toit, P. (1989). 'Bargaining about bargaining: Inducing the self-negating prediction in deeply divided societies – the case of South Africa'. *Journal of Conflict Resolution*, 33(2):210–230.

Dubow, S. (1995). *Illicit Union: Scientific Racism in South Africa*. Johannesburg: Witwatersrand University Press.

Duckitt, J.H. (1984). 'Attitudes of white South Africans toward homosexuality'. *South African Journal of Sociology*, 15(2):89–93.

Duffy, A. (1995). 'The feminist challenge: Knowing and ending the violence'. In Mandell, N. (Ed.) *Feminist Issues: Race, Class and Sexuality*, pp. 152–184. Scarborough, Canada: Prentice Hall.

Dunbar Moodie, T. (2001). 'Black migrant mine labourers and the vicissitudes of male desire'. In Morrell, R. (Ed.) *Changing Men in Southern Africa*, pp. 297–315. Pietermaritzburg: University of Natal Press.

Dunbar Moodie, T. with Ndatshe, V. & B. Sibuyi (1988). 'Migrancy and male sexuality on the South African goldmines'. *Journal of Southern African Studies*, 14(2):228–256.

Dunbar Moodie, T. with V. Ndatshe. (1994). *Going for Gold: Men, Mines & Migration*. Berkeley: University of California Press.

Duncan, N. & B. Rock (1994). *Inquiry into the Effects of Public Violence on Children: Preliminary Report*. Sandton: Goldstone Commission.

Duncan, N. & B. Rock. (1995). 'South African children and public violence: Quantifying the damage'. *Psychology Resource Centre Occasional Publication Series*, No. 9. University of the Western Cape, Cape Town.

Duncan, N. & C. de la Rey (2000). 'Racism: A psychological perspective'. Paper presented at the South African Human Rights Commission's *National Conference on Racism and Related Forms of Intolerance*, Sandton, 30 September–2 October.

Duncan, N. (1991). 'The black family and child development'. *Psychology Quarterly*, 2(1):2–5.

Duncan, N. (1993). *Discourses of Racism*. Unpublished doctoral dissertation, University of the Western Cape, Cape Town.

Duncan, N. (1996). 'Discourses on public violence and the reproduction of racism'. *South African Journal of Psychology*, 26(3):172–182.

Duncan, N. (2001). 'Discourses on race and racial difference'. Paper presented at the meeting of the *Second Biannual Congress of the International Academy of Intercultural Research*, Mississippi, 18–22 April.

Duppong, K. (1999). *Intimate Partner Homicide: The Role of Gender Equality and Type of Intimate Relationship.* Unpublished doctoral thesis, Southern Illinois University, Carbondale.

Durkheim, E. (1998). 'Functions of crime'. In Macionis, J.J. & N.V. Benokraitis (Eds.) *Seeing Ourselves: Classic, Contemporary and Cross-cultural Readings in Sociology*, pp. 150–152. New Jersey: Prentice-Hall.

Durrheim, K. (1999). 'Research design'. In Terre Blanche, M. & K. Durrheim (Eds.) *Research in Practice.* Cape Town: University of Cape Town Press.

Edley, N. & M. Wetherell (1995). *Men in Perspective: Practice, Power and Identity.* London: Prentice Hall.

Edwards, J. & L. McKie (1997). 'Women's public toilets: a serious issue for the body politic'. In K. Davis (Ed.) *Embodied Practices: Feminist Perspectives on the Body*, pp. 135–149. London: Sage Publications.

Eiguer, A. (1998). *Clinique Psychanalytique du Couple.* Paris: Dunod.

Eiguer, A., Ruffiot, A. & Associates (1984). *La Thérapie Psychanalytique du Couple.* Paris: Dunod.

Ellison, G. & T. de Wet (2002). '"Race", ethnicity and psychopathology of social identity'. In Hook, D. & G. Eagle (Eds.) *Psychopathology and Social Prejudice*, pp. 139–149. Cape Town: University of Cape Town Press.

Ellsberg, M., Caldera, T., Herrera, A., Winkvist, A. & G. Kullgren (1999). 'Domestic violence and emotional distress among Nicaraguan women. Results from a population-based study'. *American Psychologist*, 54(1):30–36.

Emmett, T. & A. Butchart (Eds.) (2000). *Behind the Mask.* Pretoria: HSRC Publishers.

Epprecht, E. (1998). 'The "Unsaying" of indigenous homosexualities in Zimbabwe: Mapping a blind spot in an African masculinity'. *Journal of Southern African Studies*, 24(4):631–651.

Erasmus, Z. (2000). 'Hair Politics'. In Nuttall, S. and C. Michael (Eds.) *Sense of Culture: South African Culture Studies.* London: Oxford University Press.

Erikson, E.H. (1963). *Childhood and Society.* New York: Norton.

Erikson, E.H. (1968). *Identity: Youth and Crisis.* New York: Norton.

Essed, P. (1986). *The Dutch as Everyday Problem.* Amsterdam: CRES Publications.

Essed, P. (1987). *Academic Racism.* Amsterdam: CRES Publications.

Etheridge, L.S. (1992). 'Wisdom and good judgment in politics'. *International Society for Political Psychology*, 13(3):497–516.

Evans, I. (1990). 'The racial question and intellectual production in South Africa'. *Perspectives in Education*, 11:21–35.

Evans-Pritchard, E.E. (1970). 'Sexual inversion among the Azande'. *American Anthropologist*, 72:1428–1434.

Ewing, C. (1990). 'Psychological self-defence: A proposed justification for battered women who kill'. *Law and Human Behaviour*, 14(6):579–594.

Eyber, C., Dyer, D. & R. Versveld (1997). *Resisting Racism. A Teacher's Guide to Equality.* Cape Town: TLRC & IDASA.

Faderman, L. (1981). *Surpassing the Love of Men: Romantic Friendship and Love Between Women from the Renaissance to the Present.* New York: William Morrow.

Fanon, F. (1968) [1961]. *Toward the African Revolution.* New York: Grove.

Fanon, F. (1968). *The Wretched of the Earth*. New York: Grove Press.

Fanon, F. (1970) [1959]. *A Dying Colonialism*. New York: Grove.

Fanon, F. (1986) [1952]. *Black Skin, White Masks*. London: Pluto.

Fanon, F. (1990) [1963]. *The Wretched of the Earth*. London: Penguin.

Farrington, D.P. (1991). 'Childhood aggression and adult violence: Early precursors and later-life outcomes'. In Pepler, D.J. & K.H. Rubin (Eds.) *The Development and Treatment of Childhood Aggression*, pp. 5–29. New Jersey: Lawrence Erlbaum Associates.

Feldman, A. (2000). 'Violence and vision: The prosthetics and asthetics of terror'. In Das, V., Kleinman, A., Ramphele, M. & P. Reynolds (Eds.) *Violence and Subjectivity*, pp. 46–78. Berkeley: University of California Press.

Ferber, A. (1999). *White Man Falling*. Lanham: Rowman & Littlefield.

Ferguson, A. (1982). 'Patriarchy, sexual identity and the sexual revolution'. *Agenda*, 28:48–53.

Ferguson, A., Zita, J. & K. Addelson (1981). 'On compulsory heterosexuality and lesbian existence: Defining the issues'. *Signs*, 7:158–199.

Festinger, L., Pepitone, A. & T. Newcomb (1952). 'Some consequences of deindividuation in a group'. *Journal of Abnormal and Social Psychology*, 47:38–389.

Fiffer, S.S. & S. Fiffer (Eds.) (1999). *Body*. New York: Avon Books.

Finchilescu, G. & G. Nyawose (1998). 'Talking about language: Zulu students' views on language in the new South Africa'. *South African Journal of Psychology*, 28(2):53–61.

Finn, J. (1985). 'The stresses and coping behavior of battered women'. *Social Casework: The Journal of Contemporary Social Work*, 51:341–349.

Fleury, R.E. (2000). 'When ending the relationship does not end the violence: Women's experiences of violence by former partners'. *Violence Against Women*, 6(12):1363–1383.

Foster, D. (1991a). 'Introduction'. In Foster, D. & J. Louw-Potgieter (Eds.) *Social Psychology in South Africa*, pp. 3–23. Johannesburg: Lexicon Publishers.

Foster, D. (1991b). *On Racism: Virulent Mythologies and Fragile Threads*. Inaugural lecture, University of Cape Town.

Foster, D. (1991c). 'Social influence I: Ideology'. In D. Foster & J. Louw-Potgieter (Eds.) *Social Psychology in South Africa*, pp. 345–391. Johannesburg: Lexicon Publishers.

Foster, D. & E. Nel (1991). 'Attitudes and related concepts'. In Foster, D. & J. Louw-Potgieter (Eds.) *Social Psychology in South Africa*, pp. 121–167. Isando: Lexicon Publishers.

Foster, D. & J. Louw-Potgieter (Eds.) (1991). *Social Psychology in South Africa*. Johannesburg: Lexicon Publishers.

Foster, D. & K. Durrheim (1998). 'Crowds, psychology and crowd control'. In Bornman, E., van Eeden, R. & M. Wentzel (Eds.) *Violence in South Africa: A Variety of Perspectives*, pp. 117–146. Pretoria: HSRC.

Foucault, M. (1973). *The Order of Things*. New York: Random House.

Foucault, M. (1979). *Discipline and Punish*. Harmondsworth: Penguin.

Foucault, M. (1980). 'Power/knowledge'. In Gordon, C. (Ed.) *Power/Knowledge: Selected Interviews and other Writings by Michel Foucault, 1972–1977*. New York: Pantheon Books.

Foucault, M. (1981). *The History of Sexuality, Vol 1: Introduction*. Harmondsworth: Penguin.

Franchi, V. (1999). *Approche Clinique et Sociocognitive des Processus Identitaires et de la Représentation de Soi en Intercultural* [A Clinical and Intercultural Study of the Construction of Identity at the Interface of Cultural Affiliations]. Unpublished doctoral thesis. Nanterre: Laboratoire IPSE, University of Paris X.

Franchi, V. 2000. 'Positioning of self at the intersection of differing acculturation discourses, cross-cultural study of identity strategies among youth schooled in Paris'. Paper presented at the *15th Congress of the International Association for Cross-Cultural Psychology*, Pultusk, Poland, 16–21 July.

Franchi, V. & A. Andronikof-Sanglade (1998). 'Debating interpretive frameworks for conceptualizing self, identity and culture: The case of French-born youth of second generation immigrant descent, schooled in France'. Paper presented at the *25th International Conference of Cross-Cultural Psychology*, Bellingham, USA, 4–8 August.

Franchi, V. & A. Andronikof-Sanglade (2001). 'Intercultural identity structure of second generation French women of African descent'. In Bekker, S., Dodds, M. & M. Khosa (Eds.) *Shifting African Identities*, Vol. 2, pp. 115–132. Pretoria: Human Sciences Research Council.

Franchi, V. & T.M. Swart (2003). 'From apartheid to affirmative action: The use of 'racial' markers in past, present and future articulations of identity among South African students'. *International Journal of Intercultural Relations*, 27:209–36.

Frankenberg, R. (1993). *White Women, Race Matters: The Social Construction of Whiteness*. Minneapolis: University of Minneapolis Press.

Freud, S. (1912). 'On the universal tendency to debasement in the sphere of love'. *Standard Edition XI*, pp. 179–190. London: Hogarth Press.

Freud, S. (1913). 'Totem and taboo'. *Standard Edition XIII*, pp. 1–161. London: Hogarth Press.

Freud, S. (1914). 'On narcissism: An introduction'. *Standard Edition XIV*, pp. 73–102. London: Hogarth Press.

Freud, S. (1918). 'The taboo of virginity'. *Standard Edition XI*, pp. 193–208. London: Hogarth Press.

Freud S. (1921). 'Group psychology and the analysis of the Ego'. *Standard Edition XVIII*, pp. 65–143. London: Hogarth Press.

Freud, S. (1922). 'Some neurotic mechanisms in jealousy, paranoia and homosexuality'. *Standard Edition XVIII*, pp. 221–232. London: The Hogarth Press.

Freud, S. (1932). 'Femininity'. *Standard Edition XXII*, pp. 112–135. London: Hogarth Press.

Freud, S. (1938). *The Basic Writings of Sigmund Freud*. New York: Modern Library.

Frye, M. (1992). 'Oppression'. In Andersen, M.L. & P. Hill Collins (Eds.) *Race, Class and Gender*. Belmont, California: Wadsworth.

Fuss, D. (1994). 'Interior colonies: Frantz Fanon and the politics of identification'. *Diacritics*, 24(2):20–42.

Garling, T., Kristensen, H., Backenroth-Ohsako, G., Ekehammar, B. & M.G. Wessells (2000). 'Diplomacy and psychology: Psychological contributions to international negotiations, conflict prevention, and world peace'. *International Journal of Psychology*, 35(2):81–86.

Gartner, R., Dawson, M. & M. Crawford (2001). 'Woman killing: Intimate femicide in Ontario, 1974–1994'. In Russel, D. & R. Harmes (Eds.) *Femicide in Global Perspective*, pp. 147–165. New York: Columbia University.

Gates, H.L. Jr & C. West (1996). *The Future of the Race*. New York: Alfred A. Knopf.

Gatrell, N. (1984). 'Combating homophobia in the psychotherapy of lesbians'. *Women and Therapy*, 3:13–29.

Gavey, N. (1996). 'Women's desire and sexual violence discourse'. In Wilkinson, S. (Ed.) *Feminist Social Psychologies. International Perspectives*, pp. 51–65. Buckingham: Open University Press.

Gavey, N. (1997). 'Feminist poststructuralism and discourse analysis'. In Gergen, M.M. & S.N. Davis (Eds.) *Toward a New Psychology of Gender*, pp. 49–60. New York: Routledge.

Gay, G. (1985). 'Implications of the selected models of ethnic identity development for educators'. *Journal of Negro Education*, 54:43–55.

Gay, J. (1985). '"Mummies and babies" and friends and lovers in Lesotho'. *Journal of Homosexuality*, 2(3–4):97–116.

Gergen, K. & M. Gergen (1981). *Social Psychology*. New York: Harcourt Brace Jovanovitch.

Gergen, K. (1973). 'Social psychology as history'. *Journal of Personality and Social Psychology*, 26:309–320.

Gergen, K. (1995). 'Social construction and the transformation of identity politics': www.swarthmore.edu/SocSci/kgergen1/text8.html (accessed 10 August 2001).

Gergen, K. (1996). 'Social psychology as social construction: the emerging vision': www.swarthmore.edu/SocSci/ kgergen1/ (accessed 10 August 2001).

Gergen, K. (2002). 'From identity to relational politics'. In Holzman, L. & J. Morss (Eds.) *Postmodern Psychologies, Social Practice, and Political Life*, pp. 130–150. New York: Routledge.

Gergen, K.J (1985). 'The social constructionist movement in modern psychology'. *American Psychologist*, 40:266–275.

Gevisser, M. (1994). 'A different fight for freedom'. In Gevisser, M. & E. Cameron (Eds.) *Defiant Desire: Gay and Lesbian Lives in South Africa*, pp. 14–73. Johannesburg: Ravan Press.

Giesbrecht, N. & I. Sevcik (2000). 'The process of recovery and rebuilding among abused women in the conservative evangelical subculture'. *Journal of Family Violence*, 15(3):229–248.

Gillespie, C. (1989). *Justifiable Homicide: Battered Women, Self-defense, and the Law*. Colombus: Ohio State University Press.

Gilman, S. (1985). *Difference and Pathology: Stereotypes of Sexuality, Race, and Madness*. New York: Cornell University Press.

Gilroy, P. (1994). *The Black Atlantic: Modernity and Double Consciousness*. Cambridge, Massachusetts: Harvard University Press.

Gilroy, P. (1997). 'Diaspora and the detours of identity'. In Hall, S. & K. Woodward (Eds.) *Identity and Difference*, pp. 276–300. London: Sage.

Gilroy, P. (2000). *Between Camps: Nations, Cultures and the Allure of Race*. Cambridge, Massachusetts: Harvard University Press.

Gobodo-Madikizela, P. (1995). 'Remembering and the politics of identity'. *Psychoanalytic Psychotherapy in South Africa*, 3:57–62.

Goldberg, D.T. (1988). *The Social Formation of Racist Discourse*. Unpublished paper.

Golden, C. (1987). 'Diversity and variability in women's sexual identities'. In The Boston Lesbian Psychologies Collective (Eds.) *Lesbian Psychologies: Explorations and Challenges*, pp. 18–34. Urbana and Chicago: University of Illinois Press.

Gondolf, E. & E. Fisher (1988). *Battered Women as Survivors: An Alternative to Treating Learned Helplessness*. Lexington: DC Heath & Co.

Gordon, L.R., Sharpley-Whiting, T.D. & R.T. White (Eds.) (1996). *Fanon: A Critical Reader*. London: Blackwell.

Gore, J.P., Miller, J.P. & J. Rappaport (1999). 'Conceptual self as normatively oriented: The suitability of past narrative for the study of cultural identity'. *Culture and Psychology*, 5(4):371–398.

Govinden, D.B. (1997). '"Dominion to rule": The abuse of women in Christian homes'. *Journal of Constructive Theology*, 3(2):23–38.

Greene, B. (1994). 'Lesbian women of color: Triple jeopardy'. In Comas-Diaz, L. & B. Greene (Eds.) *Women of Color: Integrating Ethnic and Gender Identities in Psychotherapy*, pp. 389–427. New York: Guildford.

Greer, G. (1999). *The Whole Woman*. London: Doubleday.

Gregg, N. (1993). '"Trying to put first things first": Negotiating subjectivities in a workplace organizing campaign'. In Davis, K. & S. Fisher (Eds.) *Negotiating at the Margins: The Gendered Discourses of Power and Resistance*, pp. 172–204. New Brunswick: Rutgers University Press.

Gross, L. (1995). 'Out of the mainstream: Sexual minorities and the mass media'. In Dines, G. & J.M. Humez (Eds.) *Gender, Race and Class in Media*, pp. 61–69. Thousand Oaks: Sage.

Grosz, E. (1994). *Volatile Bodies: Toward a Corporeal Feminism*. Bloomington: Indiana University Press.

Guillais, J. (1986). *La Chair de l'Autre*. Paris: Orban.

Gurr, T.R. (1970). *Why Men Rebel*. Princeton: Princeton University Press.

Haddon, W. & S. Baker (1981). 'Injury control'. In Clark, D. & C. MacMahon (Eds.) *Preventive and Community Medicine*, pp. 109–140. Boston: Little Brown and Company.

Haffajee, F. (1998). 'Wanted: A woman newspaper editor'. *Tribute*, (March):40–45.

Haj-Yahia, M.M. (2000). 'Wife abuse and battering in the sociocultural context of Arab society'. *Family Process*, 39(2):237–255.

Halford, W.K., Sanders, M.R. & B.C. Behrens (2000). 'Repeating the errors of our parents? Family-of-origin spouse violence and observed conflict'. *Family Process*, 39(2):219–235.

Hall, G.S. (1919). 'Some possible effects of the war on American psychology'. *Psychology Bulletin*, 16:48–9.

Hall, S. (1995). 'The white of their eyes'. In Dines, G. & J.M. Humez (Eds.) *Gender, Race and Class in Media*, pp. 18–22. Thousand Oaks: Sage.

Hall, S. (1996). 'Introduction: Who needs "identity"?' In Hall, S. & P. du Gay (Eds.), *Questions of Cultural Identity*, pp. 1–17. London: Sage.

Hall, S. (1996). 'The question of cultural identity'. In Hall, S., Held, D., Hubert, D. & K. Thompson (Eds.) *Modernity: An Introduction to Modern Societies*, pp. 595–634. Cambridge, Massachusetts: Blackwell.

Hall, S. (1997). 'The rediscovery of "ideology": Return of the repressed in media studies'. In Boyd Barret, O. & C. Newbold (Eds.) *Approaches to Media*, pp. 354–364. London: Arnold.

Hallowell, A.I. (1955). *Culture and Experience*. Philadelphia: University of Pennsylvania Press.

Hamber, B. & T. Mofokeng (Eds.) (2000). *From Rhetoric to Responsibility: Making Reparations to the Survivors of Past Political Violence in South Africa*. Johannesburg: Centre for the Study of Violence and Reconciliation.

Hampton, R.L., Vandergriff-Avery, M. & J. Kim (1999). 'Understanding the origins and incidence of spousal violence in North America'. In Gullotta, T.P. & S.J. McElhaney (Eds.) *Violence in Homes and Communities: Prevention, Intervention, and Treatment*, pp. 39–70. Thousand Oaks: Sage.

Hanmer, J. (1996). 'Women and violence: Commonalities and diversities'. In Fawcett, B., Featherstone, B., Hearn, J. & C. Toft (Eds.) *Violence and Gender Relations: Theories and Interventions*, pp. 7–21. London: Sage.

Hansonn, D. (1991). *We the Invisible Face: A Feminist Analysis of the Conception of 'Street Children' in South Africa*. Cape Town: University of Cape Town Press.

Harré, R. (1989). 'Language games and the texts of identity'. In Shotter, J. & K. Gergen (Eds.) *Texts of Identity*, pp. 20–35. London: Sage.

Harré, R. (1998). *The Singular Self: An Introduction to the Psychology of Personhood*. London: Sage.

Harries, P. (1990). 'Symbols and sexuality: Culture and identity in the early Witwatersrand mines'. *Gender & History*, 11(3):318–336.

Henriques, J., Hollway, W., Urwin, C., Venn, C. & V. Walkerdine (1984). *Changing the Subject.* New York: Methuen.

Herek, G. (1994). 'Assessing heterosexuals' attitudes toward lesbians and gay men'. In Greene, B. & G. Herek (Eds.) *Lesbian and Gay Psychology: Theory, Research and Clinical Applications*, pp. 206–228. Thousand Oaks, California: Sage.

Herman, E. & N. Chomsky (1988). *Manufacturing Consent: The Political Economy of the Mass Media.* New York: Pantheon.

Hill, M. (1987). 'Child-rearing attitudes of black lesbian mothers'. In The Boston Lesbian Psychologies Collective (Eds.) *Lesbian Psychologies: Explorations and Challenges*, pp. 215–226. Urbana and Chicago: University of Illinois Press.

Hoff, L.A. (1990). *Battered Women as Survivors.* London: Routledge.

Holland, J., Ramazanoglu, C. & S. Scott (1990). 'Sex, risk, danger: AIDS education policy and young women's sexuality'. *Women Risk and Aids Project (WRAP)*, Paper 1. London: Tufnell Press.

Holland, J., Ramazanoglu, C., Scott, S., Sharpe, S. & R. Thomson (1991). 'Pressure, resistance, empowerment: Young women and the negotiation of safer sex'. *Women Risk and Aids Project (WRAP)*, Paper 6. London: Tufnell Press.

Hollway, W. (1989). *Subjectivity and Method in Psychology: Gender, Meaning and Science.* London: Sage.

Hollway, W. (1995). 'Feminist discourses and women's heterosexual desire'. In Wilkinson, S. & C. Kitzinger (Eds.) *Feminism and Discourse: Psychological Perspectives*, pp. 86–105. London: Sage.

Hollway, W. (1996). 'Recognition and heterosexual desire'. In Richardson, D. (Ed.) *Theorising Heterosexuality*, pp. 91–108. Milton Keynes: Open University Press.

Holmes, R. & S. Holmes (1994). *Murder in America.* Thousand Oaks: Sage.

Holmes, R. (1994). '"White rapists made coloureds (and homosexuals)": The Winnie Mandela trial and the politics of race and sexuality'. In Gevisser, M. & E. Cameron (Eds.) *Defiant Desire: Gay and Lesbian Lives in South Africa*, pp. 284–294. Johannesburg: Ravan Press.

Holtzworth-Munroe, A. (2000). 'A typology of men who are violent toward their female partners: Making sense of the heterogeneity in husband violence'. *Current Directions in Psychological Science*, 9(4):140–143.

Hook, D. (2002). 'Introduction: A "social psychology" of psychopathology". In Hook, D. & G. Eagle (Eds.) *Psychopathology and Social Prejudice*, pp. 1–18. Cape Town: University of Cape Town Press.

hooks, b. (1990). *Yearning: Race, Gender and Cultural Politics.* Boston: South End Press.

hooks, b. (1995). *Killing Rage: Ending Racism.* New York: Penguin.

hooks, b. (1995). 'Doing it for Daddy'. In Berger, M., Wallis, B. & S. Watson (Eds.) *Constructing Masculinity*, pp. 98–106. New York: Routledge.

Hoosen, S. & A. Collins (2001). 'Women and AIDS: how discourses of gender and sexuality affect safe sex behaviour'. *Journal of the Islamic Medical Association of South Africa*, 8(3):62.

Hopkins, J. (1969). 'The lesbian personality'. *British Journal of Psychiatry*, 115:1436.

Horne, S. (1999). 'Domestic violence in Russia'. *American Psychologist*, 54(1):55–61.

Hotaling, G.T. & D.B. Sugarman (1986). 'An analysis of risk markers in husband to wife violence: The current state of knowledge'. *Violence and Victims*, 1(3):101–124.

Howitt, D. (1989). *Social Psychology: Conflicts and Continuities – An Introductory Textbook.* Milton Keynes: Open University Press.

Hunt, S.W. (1989). 'Migrant labour and sexually transmitted diseases: AIDS in Africa'. *Journal of Health and Social Behaviour,* 30:353–373.

Hydén, M. (1994). *Woman Battering as Marital Act. The Construction of a Violent Marriage.* Oslo: Scandinavian University Press.

Hydén, M. (1999). 'The world of the fearful: Battered women's narratives of leaving abusive husbands'. *Feminism & Psychology,* 9(4):449–469.

Ickes, W. & S. Duck (Eds.) (2000a). *The Social Psychology of Personal Relationships.* Chichester: John Wiley & Sons.

Ickes, W. & S. Duck (2000b). 'Personal relationships and social psychology'. In Ickes, W. & S. Duck (Eds.) *The Social Psychology of Personal Relationships,* pp. 1–8. Chichester: John Wiley & Sons.

IMF (International Monetary Fund) (2000). *International Statistics.* Bloomberg: IDEA-global.com.

Immelman, A. (1993). 'The assessment of political personality: A psychodiagnostically relevant conceptualisation and methodology'. *International Society for Political Psychology,* 14(4):725–741.

Isaacs, G. & B. McKendrick (1992). *Male Homosexuality in South Africa: Identity Formation, Culture and Crisis.* Cape Town: Oxford University Press.

Jackson, S. (1996). 'Heterosexuality and feminist theory'. In Richardson, D. (Ed.) *Theorising Heterosexuality,* pp. 21–38. Milton Keynes: Open University Press.

Jackson, S. (2001). 'Happily never after: Young women's stories of abuse in heterosexual love relationships'. *Feminism & Psychology,* 9(4):449–469.

Jacobs, M. (1975). *Conditioned Aversion Applied to the Treatment of Homosexuality and Compulsive Ruminations.* Unpublished Master's thesis, University of the Witwatersrand, Johannesburg.

Jacobs, T. & F. Suleman (1999). 'Breaking the silence: A profile of domestic violence in women attending a community health centre.' Health Systems Trust: www.hst.org.za/research/violence/ (accessed 5 October, 2000).

Jamieson, L. (1998). *Intimacy: Personal Relationships in Modern Societies.* Cambridge: Polity Press.

Jansen, J. (Ed.) (1991). *Knowledge and Power in South Africa: Critical Perspectives across the Disciplines.* Johannesburg: Skotaville.

Jansen, P., Richter, L.M., Griesel, R.D. & J. Joubert (1990). 'Glue sniffing: A description of social, psychological and neuropsychological factors in a group of South African street children'. *South African Journal of Psychology,* 20(3):150–158.

Jeffreys, S. (1985). *The Spinster and her Enemies: Feminism and Sexuality 1880–1930.* Oxford: Pandora.

Jeffreys, S. (1990). *Anticlimax: A Feminist Perspective on the Sexual Revolution.* London: The Women's Press.

Jeffreys, S. (1993). *The Lesbian Heresy: A Feminist Perspective on the Lesbian Sexual Revolution.* Australia: Spinifex Press.

Jennings, J. & C. Murphy (2000). 'Male–male dimensions of male–female battering: a new look at domestic violence'. *Psychology of Men and Masculinity,* 1(1):21–29.

Jensen, V. (1996). *Why Women Kill: Homicide and Gender Equality.* London: Lynne Rienner.

Jewkes, R. & N. Abrahams (2000). *Violence against Women in South Africa: Rape and Sexual Coercion.* Pretoria: Crime Prevention Research Resources Centre, CSIR.

Jewkes, R., Penn-Kekana, L., Levin, J., Ratsaka, M. & M. Schrieber (1999). *'He Must Give Me Money, He Mustn't Beat Me'. Violence against Women in Three South African Provinces.* Tygerberg: CERSA (Women's Health) Medical Research Council.

Johns, L. (1995). 'Racial vilification and ICERD in Australia'. *Murdoch University Electronic Journal of Law*, 2(1): www.murdoch.edu.au/elaw/indices/title/johns21_abstract.html (accessed 17 April 2003).

Johnson, A.D. (1994). *Journey Magazine*, Spring. New York: Rochester.

Johnson, H. (1996). *Dangerous Domains: Violence Against Women in Canada.* Toronto: Nelson Canada.

Jones, J.M. (1986). *Prejudice and Racism.* London: Addison-Wesley.

Jones, J.M. (1997). *Prejudice and Racism*, 2nd edition. New York: McGraw-Hill.

Julien, I. (Director) (1996). *Frantz Fanon: Black Skin, White Masks.* Arts Council of England, BFI/K Films, UK.

Kaarbo, J. & M.G. Hermann (1998). 'Leadership styles of prime ministers: How individual differences affect the foreign policymaking process'. *Leadership Quarterly*, 9(3):243–263.

Kane, T.A. & P.K. Staiger (2000). 'Male domestic violence'. *Journal of Interpersonal Violence*, 15(1):16–29.

Katz, J. (1976). *Gay American History: Lesbians and Gay Men in the USA.* New York: Crowell.

Katz, P.A. & D.A. Taylor (Eds.) (1988). *Eliminating Racism: Profiles in Controversy.* New York: Plenum Press.

Katz. J. (1983). *Gay/Lesbian Almanac.* New York, Harper & Row.

Kendall (1998). '"When a woman loves a woman" in Lesotho: Love, sex and the Western construction of homophobia'. In Murray, S. & W. Roscoe (Eds.) *Boy-Wives and Female Husbands*, pp. 223–241. New York: St. Martins Press.

Kendall, K. (1999). 'Women in Lesotho and the (Western) construction of homophobia'. In Blackwood, E. & S. Wieringa (Eds.) *Female Desires: Same Sex Relations and Transgendere Practices Across Cultures*, pp. 157–178. New York: Columbia University Press.

Keseredy, W. & M. Schwartz (1996). *Contemporary Criminology.* New York: Wadsworth.

Khmelkov, V.T. & M.T. Hallinan (1999). 'Organizational effects on race relations in schools'. *Journal of Social Issues*, 55(4):627–645.

Kimmel, M. (1994). 'The contemporary "crisis" of masculinity in historical perspective'. In Brod, E. (Ed.) *The Making of Masculinities: The New Men's Studies*, pp. 120–138. Boston: Allen & Unwin.

Kingdom, M.A. (1979). 'Lesbians'. *Counseling Psychologist*, 8(1):44–45.

Kirkwood, C. (1993). *Leaving Abusive Partners.* London: Sage.

Kitzinger, C. (1987). *The Social Construction of Lesbianism.* London: Sage.

Kitzinger, C. & S. Wilkinson (1993). 'Theorizing heterosexuality'. In Wilkinson, S. & C. Kitzinger (Eds.) *Heterosexuality: A Feminism and Psychology Reader*, pp. 1–32. London: Sage.

Klaaren J. & J. Ramji (2001). 'Inside illegality: Migration policing in South Africa after apartheid'. *Africa Today*, 48(3):35–47.

Klein, M. (1946). 'Notes on some schizoid mechanisms'. In *Envy and Gratitude and Other Works 1946–1963.* London: Hogarth Press.

Knight, S. (1989). *Towards an Understanding of an Invisible Minority.* Unpublished Master's thesis, University of the Witwatersrand, Johannesburg.

Koss, M. (1994). *No Safe Haven: Male Violence Against Women at Home, at Work, and in the Community.* Washington DC: American Psychological Association.

Kotze, C.G. (1974). *'n Diepteigologiese Ondersoek na die Verskynsel van Homoseksuele Gedrag*. Unpublished doctoral dissertation, University of Pretoria.

Kozu, J. (1999). 'Domestic violence in Japan'. *American Psychologist*, 54(1):50–54.

Krige, E.J. (1974). 'Women-marriage with special reference to the Lovedu – its significance for the definition of marriage'. *Africa*, 44(11):11.

Krige, E.J., & J.D. Krige (1943). *The Realm of a Rain Queen*. London: Oxford University Press.

Kritzinger, A. & F. van Aswegen (1994). 'Problems associated with stigmatization: The case of lesbianism'. *South African Sociological Review*, 5(1):83–98.

Krog, A. (1998). *Country of My Skull*. Johannesburg: Random House.

Kruger, J., Butchart, A., Seedat, M. & A. Gilchrist (1998). 'A public health approach to violence in South Africa'. In Bornman, E., van Eeden, R. & M. Wentzel (Eds.) *Violence in South Africa: A Variety of Perspectives*, pp. 399–424. Pretoria: HSRC.

Kuper, L. (1974). *Race, Class and Power: Ideology and Revolutionary Change in Plural Societies*. London: Duckworth.

Lancaster, R.N. (1987). 'Subject honor and object shame: The construction of male homosexuality and stigma in Nicaragua'. *Ethnology*, 27:111–125.

Lancaster, R.N. (1997). 'Guto's performance: Notes on the transvestism of everyday life'. In Lancaster, R.N. & M. di Leornado (Eds.) *The Gender Sexuality Reader*, pp. 558–570. New York: Routledge.

LaTorre, R. & K. Wendenburg (1983). 'Psychological characteristics of bisexual, heterosexual and homosexual women'. *Journal of Homosexuality*, 9(1):87–97.

Laville, R. (2000). 'An anthropology of race'. *Rhodes Journalism Review*, 19:9.

Legassick, M. (1980). 'The frontier tradition in South African historiography'. In Marks, S. & A. Atmore (Eds.) *Economy and Society in Pre-industrial South Africa*, pp. 44–79. London: Longman.

Lelyveld, J. (1987). *Move Your Shadow: South Africa, Black and White*. London: Abacus.

Lempert, L. B. (1996). 'Women's strategies for survival: Developing agency in abusive relationships'. *Journal of Family Violence*, 11(3):269–289.

Lesch, E. (2000). *Female Adolescent Sexuality in a Coloured Community*. Unpublished doctoral dissertation, University of Stellenbosch.

Letlaka-Rennert, K. (1990). 'Soweto street children: Implications of family disintegration for South African psychologists'. In Nicholas, L.J. & S. Cooper (Eds.) *Psychology and Apartheid*, pp. 100–114. Cape Town: Vision Publications.

Levett, A. (1988). *Psychological Trauma: Discourses of Childhood Sexual Abuse*. Unpublished doctoral thesis. University of Cape Town.

Lewis, G. (1987). *Between the Wire and the Wall: A History of South African 'Coloured' Politics*. Cape Town: David Phillip.

Lewis, J. & F. Loots (1994). '"Moffies en manvroue": Gay and lesbian life histories in contemporary Cape Town'. In Gevisser, M. & E. Cameron (Eds.) *Defiant Desire: Gay and Lesbian Lives in South Africa*, pp. 140–157. Johannesburg: Ravan Press.

Liddicoat, R. (1956). *Homosexuality: Results of a Survey Related to Various Theories*. Unpublished doctoral dissertation, University of the Witwatersrand, Johannesburg.

Liebenberg, I. (1993). *Transition from Authoritarian Rule to Democracy in South Africa: The Role of Political Leadership and Some Strategies to Attain Democracy*. Unpublished Master's thesis, University of the Western Cape, Cape Town.

Lockhat, R. & A. van Niekerk (2000). 'South African children and mental health: A history of adversity, violence and trauma'. *Ethnicity and Health*, 5(3/4):291–302.

Loedolff, J.J. (1951). *Homosexualiteit: 'n Sosiologiese Studie.* Unpublished Master's thesis, University of Pretoria.

Lorde, A. (1984). *Sister Outsider.* Trumansberg, New York: The Crossing Press.

Lorde, A. (1988). *A Burst of Light.* London: Sheba Feminist Publishers.

Louw-Potgieter, J. (1988). 'The authoritarian personality: An inadequate explanation for inter-group conflict in South Africa'. *Journal of Social Psychology,* 128(1):75–87.

Louw-Potgieter, J., Kamfer, L. & R.G. Boy (1991). 'Stereotype reduction workshop'. *South African Journal of Psychology,* 21(4):219–224.

LoveLife (2000). *Hot Prospects, Cold Facts.* Cape Town: Colorpress.

Lowe, K.B. & K. Galen Kroeck (1996). 'Effective correlates of transformational and transac-tional leadership: A meta-analytic review of the MLQ literature'. *Leadership Quarterly,* 7(3):385–425.

Lui, M. (1999). 'Enduring violence and staying in marriage: Stories of battered women in rural China'. *Violence against Women,* 5(12):1469–1492.

MacDonald, A. & R. Games (1974). 'Some characteristics of those who hold positive and negative attitudes toward homosexuals'. *Journal of Homosexuality,* 2(1):3–10.

MacDonald, A. (1976). 'Homophobia: Its roots and meanings'. *Homosexual Counselling Journal,* 3:23–33.

Macdonell, D, (1987). *Theories of Discourse.* Worcester: Basil Blackwell.

Macey, D. (2000a). *Frantz Fanon: A Life.* London: Granta.

Macey, D. (2000b). *The Penguin Dictionary of Critical Theory.* London: Penguin Books.

MacKinnon, C. (1989). *Toward a Feminist Theory of the State.* Harvard: Harvard University Press.

Mager, A. (1996). 'Sexuality, fertility and male power'. *Agenda,* 28:12–24.

Malepa, M. (1990). 'The effects of violence on the development of young children in Soweto'. *Centre for Intergroup Studies Occasional Papers,* No.13. Cape Town: Centre for Inter-group Studies.

Mama, A. (1995). *Beyond the Masks. Race, Gender and Subjectivity.* London: Routledge.

Mama, A. (1996). *The Hidden Struggle. Statutory and Voluntary Sector Responses to Violence Against Black Women in the Home.* London: Whiting & Birch.

Mandaza, I. (2000). 'White heroes & bêtes noires'. *Rhodes Journalism Review,* 19:23.

Mandaza, I. (2001). 'Southern African identity: A critical assessment'. In Bekker, S., Dodds, M. & M. Khosa (Eds.) *Shifting African Identities,* Vol. 2, pp. 133–140. Pretoria: HSRC.

Mandela, W. (1985). *Part of My Soul.* London: Penguin.

Manganyi, N.C. (1973). *Being-Black-in-the-World.* Johannesburg: Skotaville.

Manganyi, N.C. (1981). *Looking through the Keyhole.* Johannesburg: Ravan Press.

Mannoni, O. (1962). *Prospero and Caliban: The Psychology of Colonisation.* New York: Praeger.

Marais, H. (1998). *South Africa: Limits to Change – The Political Economy of Transition.* London: Zed Books.

Marcia, J.E. (1966). 'Development and validation of ego identity status'. *Journal of Personality and Social Psychology,* 3:551–558.

Marcia, J.E. (1980). 'Identity in adolescence'. In Adelson, J. (Ed.) *Handbook of Adolescent Psychology,* pp. 159–187. New York: Wiley.

Markus, H. & D. Oyserman (1989). 'Gender and thought: The role of the self-concept'. In Crawford, M. & M. Hamilton (Eds.) *Gender and Thought,* pp. 100–127. New York: Springer-Verlag.

Markus, H. & E. Wurf (1987). 'The dynamic self-concept: A social psychological perspective'. *Annual Review of Psychology*, 38:299–337.

Markus, H. (1977). 'Self-schemas and processing information about the self'. *Journal of Personality and Social Psychology*, 35:63–78.

Markus, H., & A.R. Herzog (1991). 'The role of the self-concept in ageing'. In K.W. Schaie (Ed.) *Annual Review of Gerontology and Geriatrics*, Vol. 11. New York: Springer-Verlag.

Markus, H., & S. Kitayama (1991). 'Culture and the self: Implications for cognition, emotion and motivation'. *Psychological Review*, 98:224–253.

Markus, H., Cross, S., & E. Wurf (1990). 'The role of the self system in competence'. In Sternberg, R.J. & J. Kolligian, Jr (Eds.) *Competence Considered*, pp. 205–25. New Haven, Connecticut: Yale University Press.

Marquard, L. (1957). *South Africa's Colonial Policy.* Johannesburg: South African Institute of Race Relations.

Martin, D. & M. Wilson (1988). *Homicide.* New York: Aldine de Gruyter.

Mathiti, V. (2000). *The Quality of Life of Street Children in Pretoria: An Exploratory Study.* Unpublished Master's dissertation, University of Pretoria.

Matshazi, N.S. (1996). *Magona's Autobiography: A Recognition of the Interconnectedness of Race, Class, and Gender in the Lives of Black South African Women.* Unpublished Master's thesis, University of the Witswatersrand, Johannesburg.

May, J., Woolard, I. & S. Klasen (2000). 'The nature and measure of poverty and inequality'. In J. May (Ed.) *Poverty and Inequality in South Africa: Meeting the Challenge*, pp. 19–50. Cape Town: David Phillip.

Mbeki, T. (1998). 'I am an African'. In *Africa: The Time has Come. Selected Speeches.* Cape Town: Mafube Publishing.

Mbembe, A. (2002). 'African Modes of Self-Writing'. *Public Culture*, 14(1):239–273.

McCloskey, L.A. (1996). 'Socioeconomic and coercive power within the family'. *Gender & Society*, 10(4):449–463.

McCulloch, J. (1983). *Black Soul White Artifact: Fanon's Clinical Psychology and Social Theory.* Cambridge: Cambridge University Press.

McDougall, W. (1908). *An Introduction to Social Psychology.* London: Methuen.

McFadden, P. (1992). 'Sex, sexuality and the problems of AIDS in Africa'. In Meena, R. (Ed.) *Gender in Southern Africa: Conceptual and Theoretical Issues*, pp. 157–195. Harare: SAPES.

McGrath, J.E. (1970). *Social Psychology: A Brief Introduction.* London: Holt, Rinehart, Winston.

McWhirter, P.T. (1999). 'La violencia privada. Domestic violence in Chile'. *American Psychologist*, 54(1):37–40.

Meintjies, S. (1993). 'Dilemmas of difference'. *Agenda*, 19:37–44.

Memmi, A. (1982). *Le Racisme.* Brassière Saint-Amand: Gallimard.

Mercader, P., Houel, A. & H. Sobota (2003). *Crime Passionnel, Crime Ordinaire.* Paris: Presses Universitaires de France.

Meyer, W.F., Moore, C. & H.G. Viljoen (1997). *Personology: From Individual to Ecosystem.* Johannesburg: Heinemann.

Mhlambo, M.G. (1993). *Violence as an Impediment in the Actualisation of the Psychic Life of the Child in Education: A Psycho-pedagogic Perspective.* Unpublished Master's thesis. University of Zululand, Durban.

Mhone, G., Humber, J.L., Gault, R.T., & D. Mokhobo (1998). 'Affirmative action – Is South Africa heading down a route which many African Americans are re-thinking?' *CDE Debate,* No. 10.

Miles, L. (1992). 'Women, AIDS, power and heterosexual negotiation: A discourse analysis'. *Agenda,* 15:14–27.

Miles, R. (1989). *Racism.* London: Routledge.

Miles-Doan, R. (1998). 'Violence between spouses and intimates: Does neighbourhood context matter?' *Social Forces,* 77(2):623–645.

Milgram, S. (1963). 'Behavioural study of obedience'. *Journal of Abnormal and Social Psychology,* 67:371–378.

Milgram, S. (1974). *Obedience to Authority.* New York: Harper & Row.

Mills, C.W. (1978). *The Sociological Imagination.* Harmondsworth: Penguin.

Mills, S.W. (2001). 'Intimate femicide and abused women who kill'. In Russel, D. & R. Harmes (Eds.) *Femicide in Global Perspective,* pp. 71–87. New York. Columbia University.

MMP (Media Monitoring Project) (1999). *The News in Black and White: An Investigation into Racial Stereotyping in the Media.* Parktown: SAHRC.

Mohan, D. (1996). 'Control of injuries in large cities: Dealing with plurality and complexity'. *Karolinska Institute Summary of International Congress, Safe Communities: The Application to Large Urban Environments,* Dallas, Texas, 14–26 November.

Mohanty, C.T. (1988). 'Under Western eyes: Feminist scholarship and colonial discourses'. *Feminist Review,* 30:61–89.

Mokoe, A. (2000). 'Beating the black drum'. *Rhodes Journalism Review,* 19:15.

Moloi, G. (1987). *My Life,* Vol. 1. Johannesburg: Ravan Press.

Mona, V. (1999). 'Racism in the fourth estate'. *Tribute,* (January):57–59.

Moore-Gilbert, B. (1997). *Postcolonial Theory: Contexts, Practices, Politics.* London & New York: Verso.

Moosa, F., Moonsamy, G. & P. Fridjohn (1997). 'Identification patterns among black students at a predominantly white university'. *South African Journal of Psychology,* 27(4): 256–260.

Moran, C.T. (1994). *Coping Strategies and Personality Traits in Street Children: An Exploratory Study.* Unpublished Master's dissertation, University of Natal, Durban.

Morgan, D. & S. Scott (1993). 'Afterward: Constructing a research agenda'. In Scott, S. & D. Morgan (Eds.) *Body Matters,* pp. 135–139. London: The Falmer Press.

Morrell, R. (Ed.) (2001). *Changing Men in Southern Africa.* Pietermaritzburg: University of Natal Press.

Moscovici, S. (1972). 'Society and theory in social psychology'. In Israel, J. & H. Tajfel (Eds.) *The Context of Social Psychology: Critical Assessment,* pp. 17–68. London: Academic Press.

Moskop, W.W. (1996). 'Prudence as a paradigm for political leaders'. *International Society for Political Psychology,* 17(4):619–642.

Motsei, M. (1993). *Detection of Woman Battering in Health Care Settings: The Case of Alexandra Health Clinic.* Johannesburg: Centre for Health Policy.

Motsemme, N. (1999). *Voices of Loss and Voices of Nation: The Truth and Reconciliation Commission and Women's Testimonies.* Unpublished Master's thesis, University of Sussex, Falmer.

Motsemme, N. (2002). 'Gendered experiences of Blackness in post apartheid South Africa'. *Social Identities,* 8(4):647–673.

Motz, A. (2001). *The Psychology of Female Violence*. Philadelphia: Taylor and Francis.

Mouton, J. (1996). *Understanding Social Research*. Pretoria. Van Schaik.

Mthembu, P. (1998). 'A positive view'. *Agenda*, 39:26–29.

Muckler, B. & G. Phelan (1979). 'Lesbian and traditional mothers' responses to adult response to child behaviour and self-concept'. *Psychological Reports*, 44(3):880–882.

Murray, C.J.L. & A.D. Lopez (Eds.) (1996). *The Global Burden of Disease*. Boston: Harvard University Press.

Murray, K. (1989). 'The construction of identity in the narratives of romance and comedy'. In Shotter, J. & K. Gergen (Eds.) *Texts of Identity*, pp. 176–205. London: Sage.

Murray, S. (1998). 'Sexual politics in contemporary Southern Africa'. In Murray, S. & W. Roscoe (Eds.) *Boy-Wives and Female Husbands*, pp. 243–254. New York: St. Martin's Press.

Murray, S. & W. Roscoe (Eds.) (1998). *Boy-Wives and Female Husbands*. New York: St Martin's Press.

Mutongi, K. (2000). 'Dear Dolly's advice: Representations of youth, courtship, and sexualities in Africa, 1960–1980'. *International Journal of African Historical Studies*, 33(1):1–23.

Nast, H.J. & S. Pile (Eds.) (1998). *Places Through the Body*. London: Routledge.

Ndebele, N. (1991). *Rediscovery of the Ordinary: Essays on South African Literature and Culture*. Johannesburg: Cosaw.

Neil, W. (1999). *Understanding Domestic Homicide*. Boston: North-Eastern University Press.

Neisser, U. (1988). 'Five kinds of self-knowledge'. *Philosophical Psychology*, 1(1):35–59.

Nell, V. & F. van Staden (1988). 'An affirmative action prospectus for South African universities'. *South African Journal of Psychology*, 84:19–22.

Nice, D.C. (1998). 'The warrior model of leadership: Classic perspectives and contemporary relevance'. *Leadership Quarterly*, 9(3):321–332.

Nicholas, L.J. & S. Cooper (Eds.) (1990). *Psychology and Apartheid*. Johannesburg: Vision Publications.

Nix, J. (1998). 'To protect and abuse: An exploratory study discussing intimate partners of police as victims of domestic abuse'. *Centre for the Study of Violence and Reconciliation, Seminar*, No. 4: www.wits.ac.za/csvr/papers/papnix.htm (2 August 2001).

Nodoba, G. (2002). 'Many languages, different cultures. The effects of linguicism in a changing society'. In Duncan, N., Gqola, P., Hofmeyer, M. *et al.* (Eds.) *Discourses on Difference, Discourses on Oppression*, pp. 331–358. Plumstead: CASAS Book Series.

Norval, A.J. (1996). *Deconstructing Apartheid Discourse*. London: Verso.

NPPHCN (National Progressive Primary Health Care Network) (1995). *Youth Speak out for a Healthy Future: A Study on Youth Sexuality*. Braamfontein: NPPHCN/UNICEF.

Ntshangase D.K. (1993). *The Social History of Iscamtho*. Unpublished Master's thesis, University of the Witwatersrand, Johannesburg.

Nurius, P.S., Furrey, J. & L. Berliner. (1992). 'Coping capacity among women with abusive partners'. *Violence and Victims*, 7(3):229–243.

Nuttall, S. (2000). 'Telling "free" stories? Memory and democracy in South African autobiography since 1994'. In Nuttall, S. & C. Coetzee (Eds.) *Negotiating the Past: The Making of Memory in South Africa*, pp. 75–88. Cape Town: Oxford University Press.

Nuttall, S. (2001). 'Subjectivities of Whiteness'. *African Studies Review*, 24(2):115–40.

O'Meara, D. (1983). *Volkskapitalisme*. Braamfontein: Ravan Press.

O'Neill, D. (1998). 'A post-structuralist review of the theoretical literature surrounding wife abuse'. *Violence against Women*, 4(4):457–490.

Oetting, E.R., & F. Beauvais (1991). 'Orthogonal cultural identification theory: The cultural identification of minority adolescents'. *Journal of the Addictions*, 25(5A & 6A): 655–85.

Olivier, J. (1991). 'The South African Police: Managers of conflict or party to the conflict'. *Centre for the Study of Violence and Reconciliation Seminar*, No. 1, Johannesburg.

Oyewumi, O. (1997). *The Invention of Woman: Making African Sense of Western Gender Discourses*. Minneapolis: University of Minnesota Press.

Oyserman, D. (1993). 'The lens of personhood: Viewing self and others in a multicultural society'. *Journal of Personality and Social Psychology*, 65(5):993–1009.

Page, C. (1996). *Showing My Color: Impolite Essays on Race and Identity*. New York: Harper-Collins.

Parker, I. (1989). *The Crisis in Modern Social Psychology – and How to End It*. London: Routledge.

Parker, I. (1999). 'Introduction: varieties of discourse and analysis'. In Parker, I. & The Bolton Discourse Network (Eds.) *Critical Textwork. An Introduction to Varieties of Discourse and Analysis*, pp. 1–12. Buckingham: Open University Press.

Parmenter, T.R. (1994). 'Quality of life as a concept and measurable entity'. *Social Indicators Research*, 33:9–46.

Passerini, L. (1992). *Memory and Totalitarianism*. Oxford: Oxford University Press.

Peden, M. & J. van der Spuy. (1998). 'The cost of treating firearm victims'. *Trauma Review*, 6(2):4–5.

Perilla, J.L., Bakeman, R. & F.H. Norris (1994). 'Culture and domestic violence: The ecology of abused Latinas'. *Violence and Victims*, 9(4):325–339.

Perkel, A., Strebel, A. & G. Joubert (1991). 'The Psychology of AIDS Transmission: Issues for Intervention'. *South African Journal of Psychology*, 21(3):148–152.

Petrik, N.D., Petrik Olson, R.E. & L.S. Subotnik (1994). 'Powerlessness and the need to control. The male abuser's dilemma'. *Journal of Interpersonal Violence*, 9(2):278–285.

Pettigrew, T. (1958). 'Personality and sociocultural factors in intergroup attitudes: A cross-national comparison'. *Journal of Conflict Resolution*, 2:29–42.

Phinney, J.S. (1990). 'Ethnic identity in adolescents and adults: Review of research'. *Psychological Bulletin*, 108:499–514.

Pickel, B. (1996). *Ethnicity and Ethnic Awareness in the Former Coloured Areas*. Unpublished research report. Cape Town: Human Sciences Research Council.

Pityana, S.M. (1992). 'The role and place of research and intellectual discourse in the reproduction of social relations of racial domination in South Africa'. *Development South Africa*, 9:481–486.

Plummer, K. (1981). 'Homosexual categories: Some research problems in the labelling perspective of homosexuality'. In Plummer, K. (Ed.)*The Making of the Modern Homosexual*, pp. 53–75. London: Hutchinson.

Posel, D. & G. Simpson (Eds.) (2002). *Commissioning the Past: Understanding South Africa's Truth and Reconciliation Commission*. Johannesburg: Witwatersrand University Press.

Posel, D. (2001). 'Race as common sense'. *African Studies Review*, 44(2):87–114.

Potgieter, C. (1997). 'From apartheid to Mandela's constitution: Black South African lesbians in the nineties'. In Greene, B. (Ed.) *Ethnic and Cultural Diversity Among Lesbians and Gay Men*, pp. 88–116. Thousand Oaks, California: Sage.

Potgieter, C. (2003). 'Black South African lesbians: Discourses on motherhood and women's roles'. *Journal of Lesbian Studies,* in press.

Potgieter, C. & L. Fredman (1997). 'Childhood sexuality'. In de la Rey, C., Duncan, N., Shefer, T. & A. Van Niekerk (Eds.) *Contemporary Issues in Human Development: A South African Focus*, pp. 99–109. Halfway House: International Thomson Publishing.

Prinsloo, S.W. (1973). *'n Vergelykende Persoonlikeheidstudie Tussen 'n Groep Passiewe Homoseksuele en 'n Kontrole Groep*. Unpublished Master's thesis, University of Pretoria.

Profitt, N.J. (2000). *Women Survivors, Psychological Trauma, and the Politics of Resistance*. New York: The Haworth Press.

Ramphele, M. (1995a). *Across Boundaries: The Journey of a South African Leader*. New York: Feminist Press.

Ramphele, M. (1995b). *A Life*. Cape Town: David Phillip.

Ramphele, M. (2000). 'Teach me how to be a man: An exploration of the definition of masculinity'. In Das, V., Kleinman, A., Ramphele, M. & P. Reynolds (Eds.) *Violence and Subjectivity*, pp. 102–119. Berkeley: University of California Press.

Rapholo, J.C. (1996). *The Self-concept of Street Children Compared to that of Placement Children*. Unpuplished Master's dissertation, University of Natal, Durban.

Ratele, K. & T. Shefer (2002). 'Stigma in the social construction of sexually transmitted diseases'. In Hook, D. & G. Eagle (Eds.) *Psychopathology and Social Prejudice*. Cape Town: UCT Press.

Ratele, K. (1998a). 'The end of the black man'. *Agenda*, 37:60–64.

Ratele, K. (1998b). 'Relating to whiteness: Writing about the black man'. *Psychology Bulletin*, 8(2):35–40.

Ratele, K. (2002). 'Interpersonal relationships around race'. In Duncan, N., Gqola, P.M., Hofmeyer, M., Shefer, T., Malunga, F. & M. Mashige (Eds.) *Discourses on Difference, Discourses on Oppression*, pp. 371–406. Cape Town: Centre for Advanced Studies of African Society.

Read, A. (Ed.) (1996). *The Fact of Blackness: Frantz Fanon and Visual Representation*. Seattle: Bay Press.

Redlinghuys, J.L. (1978). *'n Psignodinamiese Ondersoek na die Verskynsel van Lesbinisme Binne 'n Gesinstruktuur*. Unpublished Master's thesis, University of Pretoria.

Rees, H. (1998). 'The search for female-controlled methods of HIV prevention'. *Agenda*, 39:44–49.

Renshon, S.A. (1992). 'The psychology of good judgment: A preliminary model with some application to the Gulf War'. *Political Psychology*, 13(3):477–495.

Retief, G. (1994). 'Keeping Sodom out of the lager'. In Gevisser, M. & E. Cameron (Eds.) *Defiant Desire: Gay and Lesbian Lives in South Africa*, pp. 99–111. Braamfontein: Ravan.

Reynolds, P. (1989). *Childhood in Crossroads*. Cape Town: David Phillip.

Rhodes Journalism Review (2000). *Racism in the Media*. Grahamstown: Rhodes University.

Rich, A. (1979). *On Lies, Secrets, and Silences: Selected Prose 1966–1978*. New York: W.W. Norton.

Rich, A. (1980). 'Compulsory heterosexuality and lesbian existence'. *Signs*, 5(4):631–660.

Richards, C.C. (1996). 'Female condom acceptability study'. *Women's Health News*, 18:23.

Richardson, D. (1996). 'Heterosexuality and social theory'. In Richardson, D. (Ed.) *Theorising Heterosexuality*, pp. 1–20. Milton Keynes: Open University Press.

Richie, B.E. & V. Kanuha (1997). 'Battered women of color in public health care systems'. In Zinn, M.B., Hondagneu-Sotelo, P. & M. Messner (Eds.) *Through the Prism of Difference: Readings on Sex and Gender*, pp. 121–129. Boston: Allyn and Bacon.

Richter, L. (1994). 'Economic stress and its influence on the family and caretaking patterns'. In Dawes, A. & D. Donald (Eds.) *Childhood and Adversity*, pp. 28–50. Cape Town: David Phillip.

Richter, L. (1996). *A Survey of Reproductive Health Issues among Urban Black Youth in South Africa*. Unpublished final grant report for the Society for Family Health.

Richter, L.M. (1988). *Street Children. The Nature and Scope of the Problem in Southern Africa*. Report no. 88–02. Pretoria: Institute for Behavioural Sciences, University of South Africa.

Rose, N. (1989). 'Individualizing psychology'. In Shootter, J. & K. Gergen (Eds.) *Texts of Identity*, pp. 176–205. London: Sage.

Rose, N. (1996). 'Identity, genealogy, history'. In Hall, S. & P. du Gay (Eds.) *Questions of Cultural Identity*, pp. 1–17. London: Sage.

Rosenberg, S. (1990). 'Une stratégie de recherche pour l'analyse structurale et fonctionnelle de l'identité de la personne' [A research strategy for the structural and functional analysis of personal identity]. *Psychologie Française*, 35(1):51–57.

Rosenthal, D. (1987). 'Ethnic identity development in adolescents'. In Phinney, I.S. & M.S. Rotherman (Eds.) *Children's Ethnic Socialisation, Pluralism and Development*, pp.156–179. Newbury Park, California: Sage.

Ross, E.A. (1908). *Social Psychology: An Outline and a Source Book*. New York: Macmillan.

Ross, F. (1996). 'Existing in secret places: Women's testimony in the first five weeks of public hearings of the Truth and Reconciliation Commission'. Paper presented at the *Faultiness Conference*, Cape Town, 25–26 July.

Ross, M.H. (1995). 'Psychocultural interpretation theory and peacemaking ethnic conflicts'. *International Society for Political Psychology*, 16(3):523–543.

RSA (Republic of South Africa) (1957). *Sexual Offences Act*, No. 23 of 1957. Pretoria: Government Printer.

RSA (Republic of South Africa) (1969). *Immorality Amendment*, No. 57 of 1969. Pretoria: Government Printer.

RSA (Republic of South Africa) (1986). *Hansard Debates of the House of Assembly*. (A) 2q col 28, (A) 7q col 664, 20 March. Cape Town: The Government Printers.

RSA (Republic of South Africa) (1987). *Hansard Debates of the House of Assembly*. (A) 3q col 162, 19 February. Cape Town: The Government Printers.

Rusbult, C.E. (1980). 'Commitment and satisfaction in romantic associations: A test of the investment model'. *Journal of Experimental and Social Psychology*, 16:172–186.

Russel, D. & R. Harmes (Eds.) (2001). *Femicide in Global Perspective*. New York: Columbia University.

SABC (South African Broadcasting Corporation) (1993). *Chris Hani: 1942–1993* (video recording). Johannesburg: SABC.

Saghir, M.T. & E. Robins (1971). 'Male and female homosexuality: Natural history'. *Comparative Psychiatry*, 12:503–510.

Samuels, A. (1996). 'The politics of transformation/the transformation of politics'. *International Journal of Psychotherapy*, 1(1):79–89.

Sang, B. (1989). 'New directions in lesbian research, theory and education'. *Journal of Counseling and Development*, 68:92–96.

Sansome. L. (1997). 'The new Blacks from Bahia: Local and global in Afro-Bahia'. *Social Identities*, 3(4):457–93.

Sasaki, B. (1998). 'Reading silence in Joy Kogawa's *Obsan*'. In Fisher, J. & E. Silber (Eds.) *Analysing a Different Voice*, pp. 117–140. Oxford: Rowan and Littlefield.

Saul, J.S. (1986). 'Introduction: The revolutionary prospect'. In Saul, J.S. & S. Gelb (Eds.) *The Crisis in South Africa*, pp. 9–52. New York: Monthly Review Press.

Saunders, D.G. (1990). 'Wife abuse, husband abuse, or mutual combat? A feminist perspective on the empirical findings'. In Yllö, K. & M. Bograd (Eds.) *Feminist Perspectives on Wife Abuse*, pp. 90–113. Newbury Park: Sage.

Scharf, W., Powell, M. & E. Thomas (1986). 'Strollers: Street children of Cape Town'. In Burman, S. & P. Reynolds (Eds.) *Growing up in a Divided Society: The Context of Childhood in South Africa*. Johannesburg: Ravan Press.

Schiebinger, L. (Ed.) (2000). *Feminism and the Body*. Oxford: Oxford University Press.

Schneider, J.W. (1985). 'Social problem theory: The constructionist's view'. *Annual Review of Sociology*, 11:209–229.

Schoepf, B.G. (1988). 'Women, AIDS and economic crisis in Central Africa'. *Canadian Journal of African Studies*, 22(3):625–644.

Schornstein, S.L. (1997). *Domestic Violence and Health Care: What Every Professional Needs to Know*. Thousand Oaks: Sage.

Schulman, N. (1995). 'Laughing across the color barrier: In living color'. In Dines, G. & J.M. Humez (Eds.) *Gender, Race and Class in Media*, pp. 438–444. Thousand Oaks: Sage.

Schulze, S (1991). 'Homoseksuele identiteitsvorming by 'n groep Suid-Afrikaanse mans'. *South African Journal of Sociology*, 22(3):78–83.

Schurink, W. (Ed.) (1993). *Street Children*. Pretoria: Human Sciences Research Council.

Schurink, W.J. (1981). *Gay-Vroue: 'n Sosiologiese Verkenning van die Leefwyse van 'n Aantal Lesbieërs aan die Hand van Outobiografiese Sketse*. Pretoria: HSRC.

Sears, D.O. (1988). 'Symbolic racism'. In Katz, P. and D. Taylor (Eds.) *Eliminating Racism. Profiles in Controversy*, pp. 53–84. New York: Plenum Press.

Seedat, M. (1990). 'Programmes, trends and silences in South African psychology'. In Nicholas, L. & S. Cooper (Eds.) *Psychology and Oppression*, pp. 23–49. Johannesburg: Vision/Madiba Publications.

Seedat, M. (1995). 'Creating safe communities in the context of reconstruction and development: The Centre for Peace Action'. *Psychosocial Research and Practice*, 2:27–32.

Seedat, M.A. (1992). *Topics, Trends and Silences in South African Psychology, 1948–1988*. Unpublished doctoral thesis, University of the Western Cape, Cape Town.

Seepe, S. (1998). *A Critical Look at the South African Media*. Unpublished article, University of Venda, Thohoyandou.

Seidel, G. (1993). 'Women at risk: Gender and AIDS in Africa'. *Disasters*, 17(2):133–142.

Seigelman, M. (1972). 'Adjustment of homosexual and heterosexual women'. *British Journal of Psychiatry*, 120:479.

Sennet, J. & D. Foster (1996). 'Social identity: Comparing white English-speaking South African students in 1975 and 1994'. *South African Journal of Psychology*, 26(4):203–11.

Shamir, B. (1994). 'Ideological position, leaders' charisma, and voting preferences: Personal vs. partisan elections'. *Political Behaviors*, 16(2):265–287.

Sharp, J. (1997). 'Non-racialism and its discontents: A post-apartheid paradox'. Paper presented at the *Conference on Identity, Theory, Politics and History*, Human Sciences Research Council, Pretoria, 3–4 July.

Shefer, T. (1998). '"Girl's stuff": Stories of gender development in a local context'. *Psychology Bulletin*, 8(2):1–11.

Shefer, T. (1999). *Discourses of Heterosexual Negotiaton and Relation*. Unpublished doctoral thesis, University of the Western Cape, Cape Town.

Shefer, T. (2000). 'Discourses of culture in students' talk on heterosex'. Paper presented at the conference *Discourses on Difference and Oppression*, University of Venda, Makhado, 20–22 July.

Shefer, T. (2002). 'Discourses of culture and difference in the construction of heterosex'. In Duncan, N., Gqola, P., Hofmeyer, M., Shefer, T., Malunga, F. & M. Mashige (Eds.) *Discourses on Difference, Discourses on Oppression: Centre for Advanced Studies of African Society (CASAS) Book Series,* No. 24, pp. 427–441. Cape Town: CASAS.

Shefer, T. & A. Strebel (2001). 'Re-negotiating sex: Discourses of heterosexuality among young South African women students'. *Journal of Psychology in Africa,* 11(1):38–59.

Shefer, T. & D. Foster (2001). 'Discourses on women's (hetero)sexuality and desire in a South African local context'. *Culture, Health and Sexuality,* 3(4):375–390.

Shefer, T. & K. Ruiters (1998). 'The masculine construct in heterosex'. *Agenda,* 27:39–45.

Shefer, T., Potgieter, C. & A. Strebel (1999). 'Teaching gender in psychology at a South African university'. *Feminism and Psychology,* 9(2):127–133.

Shefer, T., Strebel, A. & D. Foster (2000). '"So women have to submit to that..." Discourses of power and violence in student's talk on heterosexual negotiation'. *South African Journal of Psychology,* 30(2):11–19.

Sherif, M. & C.W. Sherif (1969). *Social Psychology.* Evanston & London/Toyko: Harper & Row/John Weatherill, Inc.

Sherif, M. (1966). *Group Conflict and Co-operation.* London: Routledge & Kegan Paul.

Sherif, M., Harvey, O., White, B., Hood, W. & C. Sherif (1961). *Intergroup Conflict and Cooperation: The Robber's Cove Experiment.* Norman: University of Oklahoma, Institute of Group Relations.

Sherlock, J. (1993). 'Dance and the culture of the body'. In Scott, S. & D. Morgan (Eds.) *Body Matters,* pp. 35–48. London: The Falmer Press.

Shilling, C. (1997). 'The body and difference'. In Woodward, K. (Ed.) *Identity and Difference,* pp. 63–120. London: Sage Publications/The Open University.

Shire, C. (1994). 'Men don't go to the moon: Language, space and masculinities in Zimbabwe'. In Cornwall, A. & N. Lindisfarne (Eds.) *Dislocating Masculinity: Comparative Ethnographies,* pp. 147–158. London: Routledge.

Shotter, J. (2000). 'At the boundaries of being: Refiguring our intellectual lives together.' Draft paper of plenary address given at the *Psychology 2000 Congress,* Joensuu, Finland, 1 September: www.pubpages.uhn.edu/~jds/Finland.htm

Shotter, J. (nd.). 'Wittgenstein and the everyday: From radical hiddenness to "nothing is hidden" from representation to participation': www.pubpages.uhn.edu/~jds/JMB.htm

Simbayi, L., Strebel, A., Wilson, T., Andipatin, M., Msomi, N., Potgieter, C., Ratele, K. & T. Shefer (1999). *Sexually Transmitted Diseases in the South African Public Health Sector.* Unpublished report compiled for the National Department of Health. University of the Western Cape, Cape Town.

Skutnabb-Kangas, T. (1990). 'Legitimating or deligitimating new forms of racism: The role of researchers'. *Journal of Multilingual and Multicultural Development,* 11(1/2):77–99.

Slovo, J. (1989). *The South African Working Class and the National Democratic Revolution.* London: South African Communist Party.

Smart, C. (1996). 'Collusion, collaboration and confession: On moving beyond the heterosexuality debate'. In Richardson, D. (Ed.) *Theorising Heterosexuality,* pp. 161–195. Milton Keynes: Open University Press.

Smit, B. & C. Cilliers (1998). 'Violence and the criminal justice system'. In Bornman, E., van Eeden, R. & M. Wentzel (Eds.) *Violence in South Africa: A Variety of Perspectives*, pp. 201–226. Pretoria: HSRC.

Smith, C.S. (1996). *The Life-world of Street Children in the Durban Metropolitan Area*. Unpuplished doctoral thesis, University of Pretoria.

Smith, G. (2000). 'From suffering in silence, to drawing strength from the margins'. *Agenda*, 46:34–41.

Smith, K.T. (1971). 'Homophobia: A tentative personality profile'. *Psychological Reports*, 29:1091–1094.

Smith, T.B., & C.R. Stones (1999). 'Identities and racial attitudes of South African and American adolescents: A cross-cultural examination'. *South African Journal of Psychology*, 29(1):23–9.

Smitherman-Donaldson, G. & T. van Dijk (1988). *Discourse and Discrimination*. Detroit: Wayne State University Press.

Sobukwe, R. (1959). *Opening Address to the Africanist Inaugural Convention*. Karis Carter Collection, UCT 2:DP1:30/1. Cape Town: University of Cape Town.

Sole, K.E. (1993). *Authority, Authenticity and the Black Writer: Depictions of Politics and Community in Selected Fictional Black Consciousness Texts*. Unpublished doctoral thesis, University of the Witswatersrand, Johannesburg.

Solomon, R.C. (1988). *Continental Philosophy since 1750: The Rise and Fall of the Self*. Oxford: Oxford University Press.

Sonking, D. (1985). *The Male Batterer*. New York: Springer.

South African Human Rights Commission (SAHRC) (2000). *Faultlines: Inquiry into Racism in the Media*. Parktown: SAHRC.

South African Institute of Race Relations (1984). *Race Relations Survey 1983, Volume 37*. Johannesburg: South African Institute of Race Relations.

South African Institute of Race Relations (1986). *Race Relations Survey 1985*. Johannesburg: South African Institute of Race Relations.

South African Institute of Race Relations (1987). *Race Relations Survey 1986, Part 1*. Johannesburg: South African Institute of Race Relations.

Soyinka, W. (1988). *Art, Dialogue and Outrage*. Ibadan: New Horn Press.

Speake, J. (Ed.) (1979). *A Dictionary of Philosophy*. London: Pan Books.

Spears, R. & I. Parker (1996). 'Marxist theses and psychological themes'. In Parker, I. & R. Spears (Eds.) *Psychology and Society: Radical Theory and Practice*, pp.1–17. London: Pluto Press.

Spry-Leverton, J. (1996). 'Lessons in survival for children of war'. *Child and Youth Care*, 14:11–13.

Squire, C. (1998). 'Women and men talk about aggression: An analysis of narrative genre'. In Henwood, K., Griffin, C. & A. Phoenix (Eds.) *Standpoints and Differences. Essays in the Practice of Feminist Psychology*, pp. 65–90. London: Sage.

Stacey, M. (1998). 'Mixed blessings: Experience of mixed race couples in South Africa'. *Psychology Bulletin*, 8(2):41–46.

Stark, E. & A. Flitcraft (1996). *Women at Risk. Domestic Violence and Women's Health*. Thousand Oaks: Sage.

Statutes of the Union of South Africa (1927). *The Immorality Act*, No. 5 of 1927. Pretoria: Government Printer.

Statutes of the Union of South Africa (1949). *The Prohibition of Mixed Marriages Act*, No. 55 of 1949. Pretoria: Government Printer.

Statutes of the Union of South Africa (1950a). *The Immorality Amendment Act*, No. 21 of 1950. Pretoria: Government Printer.

Statutes of the Union of South Africa (1950b). *The Population Registration Act*, No. 30 of 1950. Pretoria: Government Printer.

Steenveld, L. (2000a). 'Defining the undefinable'. *Rhodes Journalism Review*, 19:11.

Steenveld, L. (2000b). 'Cricket's infamous coolie creeper'. *Rhodes Journalism Review*, 19:25.

Steenveld, L. (2000c). 'Equality and expression'. *Rhodes Journalism Review*, 19:26.

Stefan, S. (1993). 'Power of discourse and discourse of power in making an issue of sexual abuse in South Africa: The rise and fall of social problems'. *Critical Arts*, 7(2):1–18.

Stein, E. (1999). *The Mismeasure of Desire: The Science, Theory, and Ethics of Sexual Orientation*. New York: Oxford University Press.

Stein, P. & R. Jacobsen. (1986). *Sophiatown Speaks*. Johannesburg: Junction Avenue Press.

Stevens, G. & R. Lockhat (1997). '"Coca-cola kids" – Reflections on black adolescent identity development in post-apartheid South Africa'. *South African Journal of Psychology*, 27(4):250–55.

Stevens, G. (1996). *The 'Racialised' Discourses of a Group of Black Parents and Adolescents in a Western Cape Community*. Unpublished Master's thesis. University of the Western Cape, Cape Town.

Stevens, G. (1997). *Understanding 'Race' and Racism: A Return to Traditional Scholarship*. PRC Occasional Publications Series. Bellville: University of the Western Cape.

Stevens, G., Seedat, M., Swart, T. & C. van der Walt (2003). 'Promoting methodological pluralism, theoretical diversity and interdisciplinarity in a multi-levelled violence prevention initiative in South Africa'. *Journal of Prevention and Intervention in the Community*, in press.

Steyn, M.E. (2002). *'Whiteness Just isn't What it Used to Be'. White Identity in a Changing South Africa*. New York: State University of New York Press.

Stout, K. (1992). 'Intimate femicide, an ecological analysis'. *Journal of Sociology and Social Welfare*, 19(3):29–50.

Straker, G. (1992). *Faces in the Revolution*. Cape Town: David Philip.

Straker, G. (1992). *Faces in the Revolution*. Cape Town: David Phillip.

Strebel, A. & G. Lindegger (1998). 'Power and responsibility: Shifting discourses of gender and HIV/AIDS'. *Psychology in Society*, 24:4–20.

Strebel, A. (1992). '"There's absolutely nothing I can do, just believe in God": South African women with AIDS'. *Agenda*, 12:50–62.

Strebel, A. (1993). *Women and Aids: A Study of Issues in the Prevention of HIV Infection*. Unpublished doctoral thesis, University of Cape Town.

Strebel, A., & G. Lindegger (1998). 'Power and responsibility: shifting discourses of gender and HIV/AIDS'. *Psychology in Society*, 24:4–20.

Sullivan, J.L. & J.E. Transue (1999). 'The psychological underpinnings of democracy: A selective review of political tolerance, interpersonal trust, and social capital'. *Annual Review of Psychology*, 50:625–650.

Sunde, J. & V. Bozalek, V. (1993). '(Re)searching difference'. *Agenda*, 19:29–36.

Swart, J. (1990). *Malunde: The Street Children of Hillbrow*. Johannesburg: Witwatersrand University Press.

Swart, T.M. (2001). *A Study of Identity Articulations among University-attending Students in South Africa*. Unpublished Master's dissertation. Johannesburg: University of the Witwatersrand.

Swartz, L. & A. Levett. (1989). 'Political repression and children in South Africa: The social construction of damaging effects'. *Social Science and Medicine,* 28:741–750.

Szesnat, H. (1997). 'The essentialist-social constructionist debate and biblical research'. In Germond, P. & S. de Gruchy (Eds.) *Aliens in the household of God,* pp. 270–294. Cape Town: David Philip.

Tajfel, H. (1959). 'Quantitative judgement in social perception'. *British Journal of Psychology,* 10:16–29.

Tajfel, H. (1972). 'Introduction'. In Israel, J. & H. Tajfel (Eds.) *The Context of Social Psychology: Critical Assessment,* pp.1–13. London: Academic Press.

Tajfel, H. (1981). *Human Groups and Social Categories.* Cambridge: Cambridge University Press.

Tajfel, H. (1982). *Social Identity and Intergroup Relations.* Cambridge: Cambridge University Press.

Tajfel, H. & C. Fraser (Eds.) (1978). *Introducing Social Psychology.* Middlesex: Penguin.

Tajfel, H. & J. Turner (1979). 'An integrative theory of inter-group conflict'. In Austin, W. & S. Worchel (Eds.) *The Social Psychology of Inter-group Relations.* California: Brooks/Cole.

Tambo, A. (1987). *Preparing for Power: Oliver Tambo Speaks.* London: Heinemann.

Tarrant, S. (1992). *Psychotherapy with Gay Clients: Therapeutic Approaches of Clinical Psychologists in Durban.* Unpublished Master's thesis, University of Durban Westville, Durban.

Terman, L. & C. Miles (1936). *Sex and Personality: Studies in Masculinity and Feminity.* New York: McGraw-Hill.

Terre Blanche, M. & K. Durrheim (1999). 'Histories of the present: Social science research in context'. In Terre Blanche, M. & K. Durrheim (Eds.) *Research in Practice: Applied Methods for the Social Sciences,* pp. 1–16. Cape Town: University of Cape Town Press.

Terre Blanche, M., Bhavanani, K. & D. Hook (Eds.) (1999). *Body Politics: Power, Knowledge & the Body in Social Sciences.* WITS: Histories of the Present Press.

Terreblanche, S. & N. Nattrass (1990). 'A periodisation of the political economy from 1910'. In Nattrass, N. & E. Ardingon (Eds.) *The Political Economy of South Africa,* pp. 6–23. Cape Town: Oxford University Press.

Terreblanche, S. & N. Nattrass (1990). 'A periodisation of the political economy from 1910'. In Nattrass, N. & E. Ardington (Eds.) *The Political Economy of South Africa,* pp. 6–23. Cape Town: Oxford University Press.

Therborn, G. (1980). *The Ideology of Power and the Power of Ideology.* London: Verso.

Theron, A. (1984). 'Meningsverskil rondom die Amerikaanse Psigiatriese Vereniging se besluit om homoseksualiteit as psigopatologiese versteuring te skrap'. *South African Journal of Psychology,* 14(3):106–112.

Thomson, R. & S. Scott (1991). 'Learning about sex: Young women and the social construction of sexual identity'. *Women Risk and Aids Project (WRAP),* Paper 4. London: Tufnell Press.

Thompson, J.B. (1984). *Studies in the Theory of Ideology.* Cambridge: Polity Press.

Thompson, J.B. (1990). *Ideology and Modern Culture.* Cambridge: Polity Press.

Thompson, N., McCandless, R. & B. Strickland (1971). 'Personal adjustment of male and female homosexuals and heterosexuals'. *Journal of Abnormal Psychology,* 78(2):237–240.

Thornton, R. (1996). 'The potentials and boundaries in South Africa: Steps towards a theory of social change'. In Webner, R. & T. Ranger (Eds.) *Postcolonial Identities in Africa.* London: Zed Books.

Tiefenthaler, J. & A. Farmer (2000). 'The economics of domestic violence'. In Park, Y.J., Fedler, J. & Z. Dangor (Eds.) *Reclaiming Women's Spaces: New Perspectives on Violence Against Women and Sheltering in South Africa*, pp. 177–199. Johannesburg: Nisaa Institute for Women's Development.

Tosh, J. (1994). 'What should historians do with masculinity? Reflections on nineteenth-century Britain'. *History Workshop Journal*, 38:179–202.

Tucker, C. (1986). *A Medico-legal Examination of Homosexual Women and Their Children: Ethical Considerations and the Role of the Clinical Psychologist*. Unpublished Master's thesis, University of Cape Town.

Turner, B.S. (1984). *The Body and Society*. New York: Basil Blackwell.

Tutu, D. (2000). 'No future without forgiveness'. *Essence*, 30(9):58–60.

UNAIDS. (1999). *Trends in HIV Incidence and Prevalence: Natural Course of the Epidemic or Results of Behavioural Change?* UNAIDS/99.12 E. Geneva: UNAIDS.

UNICEF (1986). *Approaches to Improving the Lives of Working Children and Street Children*. New York: UNICEF.

Union of South Africa (1950). *Debates of the House of Assembly (Hansard) Third Session Tenth Parliament, 20 January–24 June. Vol. 71*. Cape Town: Unie-Volkspers.

United Nations (1993). *The United Nations' Convention on the Rights of the Child*. Geneva, United Nations.

United Nations (2000). *International Convention on the Elimination of all Forms of Racial Discrimination*: www.unhchr.ch (accessed 6 October).

United States Department of Justice (1996). *Violence by Intimates*. Federal Bureau of Investigations Supplementary Homicide Reports (SHR): 1976–1996.

Uwakwe, C.B.U., Mansaray, A.A. & G.O.M. Onwu (1994). *A Psycho-educational Program to Motivate and Foster AIDS Preventative Behaviors among Female Nigerian University Students*. Unpublished final technical report, Women and AIDS Research Program. Washington DC: International Center for Research on Women.

Valentine-Daniel, E. (2000). 'Mood, moment, and mind'. In Das, V., Kleinman, A., Ramphele, M. & P. Reynolds (Eds.) *Violence and Subjectivity*, pp. 333–366. Berkeley: University of California Press.

Van der Merwe, H.W. (1989). *Pursuing Justice and Peace in South Africa*. New York: Routledge.

Van der Ross, R.E. (1979). *Myths and Attitudes: An Inside Look at the Coloured People*. Cape Town: Tafelberg.

Van der Walt, C. Franchi, V. & G. Stevens (2003). 'The South African Truth and Reconciliation Commission: "Race", historical compromise and transitional democracy'. *International Journal of Intercultural Psychology*, 27:251–67.

Van Dijk, T. (1987). *Communicating Racism. Ethnic Prejudice in Thought and Talk*. Newbury Park: Sage.

Van Dijk, T. (1987). *Communicating Racism*. Newbury Park: Sage.

Van Dijk, T. (1989). 'Structures and strategies of discourse and prejudice'. In van Oudenhoven, J.P. & T.M. Willemsen (Eds.) *Ethnic Minorities. Social Psychological Perspectives*, pp. 115–138. Amsterdam: Swets & Zeitlinger.

Van Dijk, T. (1990). 'Discourse and inequality'. Unpublished keynote address presented at the *International Communication Association Conference*, Dublin, 25–30 June.

Van Dijk, T. (1991). *Elite Discourse and the Reproduction of Racism*. Amsterdam: University of Amsterdam.

Van Zyl, S. (1998). 'The Other and other Others: Post-colonialism, psychoanalysis and the South African question'. *American Imago*, 55(1):77–100.

Vance, C. (1989). 'Social construction theory: problems in the history of sexuality'. In Altman, D., Vance, C., Vicinus, M. & J. Weeks (Eds.) *Homosexuality, Which Homosexuality?*, pp. 13–34. London: GMP Publishers.

Vance, C.S. (1984). 'Pleasure and danger: Toward a politics of sexuality'. In Vance, C.S. (Ed.) *Pleasure and Danger: Exploring Female Sexuality*, pp. 1–27. Boston: Routledge.

Varga, C. & L. Makubalo (1996). 'Sexual non-negotiation'. *Agenda*, 28:31–38.

Vasconcelos, A., Neto, A., Valenca, A., Braga, C., Pacheco, M., Dantas, S., Simonetti, V. & V. Garcia (1995). 'Sexuality and AIDS prevention among adolescents from low-income communities in Recife, Brazil'. *Women and AIDS Program Research Report Series*. Washington DC: International Center for Research on Women.

Vetten, L. (1999). 'Violence Against Women in Metropolitan South Africa: A Study on Impact and Service Delivery'. *Institute for Security Studies Monograph Series,* No. 41: www.wits.ac.za/csvr/pubsgend.htm (28 September, 2000).

Vetten, L. (2000). 'Gender, race and power dynamics in the face of social change. Deconstructing violence against women in South Africa'. In Park, Y.J., Fedler, J. & Z. Dangor (Eds.) *Reclaiming Women's Spaces. New Perspectives on Violence Against Women and Sheltering in South Africa*, pp. 47–80. Johannesburg: Nisaa Institute for Women's Development.

Vetten, L. & J. Dladla (2000). 'Women's fear and survival in inner-city Johannesburg'. *Agenda*, 44:70–75.

Vetten, L. & K. Bhana (2001). *Violence, Vengeance and Gender: A Preliminary Investigation into the Links Between HIV/AIDS and Violence Against Women in South Africa.* Johannesburg: The Centre for the Study of Violence & Reconciliation.

wa Machwofi, N. (1998). *On Capitalism, Ethnic Dominance and Racism: The Elite Media and the 'Million Man March'*. Kenosha: University of Wisconsin-Parkside.

waThiong'o, N. (1986). *Decolonising the Mind: The Politics of Language in African Literature.* London: James Currey.

Waldby, C., Kippax, S. & J. Crawford (1993). '*Cordon sanitaire:* "clean" and "unclean" women in the AIDS discourse of young heterosexual men'. In Aggleton, P., Davies, P. & G. Hart (Eds.) *AIDS: Facing the Second Decade*, pp. 29–39. London: Falmer Press.

Waldman, L. (1995). '"This house is a dark room". Domestic violence on farms in the Western Cape'. *African Anthropology*, 11(2):60–81.

Walker, L. (1979). *The Battered Woman.* New York: Harper and Row.

Walker, L. (1984). *The Battered Woman Syndrome.* New York: Springer.

Walker, L. (1989). *Terrifying Love: Why Battered Women Kill and How Society Responds.* New York: Harper & Row.

Walker, L.E. (2000). *The Battered Woman Syndrome*, 2nd Edition. New York: Springer.

Watts, C., Osam, S. & E. Win (1995). *The Private is Public. A Study of Violence Against Women in Southern Africa.* Harare: Women in Law and Development in Africa (WiLDAF).

Weber, M. (1969). *Max Weber on Law and Economy in Society.* Harvard: Harvard University Press.

Weedon, C. (1987). *Feminist Practice and Poststructuralist Theory.* Oxford: Blackwell Publishers.

Weeks, J. (1986). *Sexuality.* London: Ellis Horwood.

Weeks, J. (1987). 'Question of identity'. In Caplan, P. (Ed.) *The Cultural Construction of Sexuality*, pp. 31–51. London: Tavistock.

Weinberg, G. (1972). *Society and the Healthy Homosexual*. New York: St Martin's Press.

Weinreich, P. (1989a). 'Variations in ethnic identity: Identity Structure Analysis'. In K. Leibkind (Ed.) *New Identities in Europe: Immigrant Ancestry and the Ethnic Identity of Youth*, pp. 41–75. London: Gower.

Weinreich, P. (1989b). 'Conflicted identifications: A commentary on Identity Structure Analysis concepts'. In K. Leibkind (Ed.) *New Identities in Europe: Immigrant Ancestry and the Ethnic Identity of Youth*, pp. 219–36. London: Gower.

Weinreich, P., Chung, L.L., & M.H. Bond (1991). 'Ethnic stereotyping and identification in a multicultural context: "Acculturation", self-esteem and identity diffusion in Hong Kong Chinese university students'. *Psychology and Developing Societies*, 8(1):107–67.

Weiss, E., Whelan, D. & G.R. Gupta (1996). *Vulnerability and Opportunity: Adolescents and HIV/AIDS in the Developing World*. Washington DC: International Center for Research on Women.

Wekker, G (1999). '"What's identity got to do with it?" Rethinking identity in the light of the Mati work in Suriname'. In Blackwood, E. & S. Wieringa (Eds.) *Female Desires: Same-sex Relations and Transgender Practices Across Cultures*, pp. 119–139. New York: Columbia University Press.

West, C. (1992). 'Black Leadership and the Pitfalls of Racial Reasoning'. In Morrison, T. (Ed.) *Race-ing Justice and En-gendering Power: Essays on Anita Hill, Clarence Thomas, and the Constructions of Social Reality*. New York: Pantheon.

West, C. (1995). *Race Matters*. New York: Vintage.

Westlund, A. C. (1999). 'Pre-modern and modern power: Foucault and the case of domestic violence'. *Signs: Journal of Women in Culture and Society*, 24(4):1045–1066.

Wetherell, M. & J. Potter (1988). 'Discourse analysis and the identification of interpretative repertoires'. In Antaki, C. (Ed.) *Analyzing Everyday Explanations*, pp. 168–183. London: Sage.

Wetherell, M. (Ed.) (1996). *Social Psychology: Identities, Groups and Social Issues*. London: Sage.

Whitfield, C. (2000). 'Words and wounds'. *Rhodes Journalism Review*, 19:30.

Whitlock, G. (1996). 'A "White-Souled State": Across the "South" with Lady Barker'. In Darian-Smith, E., Gunner, L. & S. Nuttall (Eds.) *Text, Theory, Space: Land, Literature and History in South Africa and Australia*, pp. 65–80. London: Routledge.

WHO (World Health Organisation) (1994). *Women and AIDS: Agenda for Action*. Global Programme on AIDS. Geneva: World Health Organisation.

WHO (World Health Organisation) (1996). *Violence: A Public Health Priority*. EHA/SPI/POA.2. Geneva: World Health Organisation.

WHO (World Health Organisation) (2001). *Proceedings of WHO Meeting to Develop a Five-year Strategy*. Unpublished document WHO/NMH/VIP/01.04. Geneva: Department of Injuries and Violence Prevention, World Health Organisation.

Wiegman, R. (1995). *American Anatomies: Theorising Race and Gender*. Durham: Duke University Press.

Wilkinson, S. & C. Kitzinger (Eds.) (1993). *Heterosexuality: A 'Feminism & Psychology' Reader*. London: Sage.

Williams, P. & L. Chrisman (Eds.) (1994). *Colonial Discourse and Post-colonial Theory*. New York: Columbia University Press.

Williams, P.J. (2000). 'Race and rights'. In Back, L. & J. Solomons (Eds.) *Theories of Race and Racism: A Reader*, pp. 410–425. London: Routledge.

Williams, R. (1997). 'Texts and discourses'. In de Beer, A.S. (Ed.) *Mass Media for the Nineties. A South African Handbook of Mass Communication*, pp. 341–362. Pretoria: van Schaik.

Wilson, F. & M. Ramphele (1989). *Uprooting Poverty*. Cape Town: David Phillip.

Wilson, M. & M. Daly (1992). 'Till death us do part'. In Radford, J. & D. Russel (Eds.) *Femicide: The Politics of Woman Killing*, pp. 83–93. New York: Twayne/Gale Group.

Winnicott, D. W. (1965) [1963]. 'The development of the capacity for concern'. In *The Maturational Processes and the Facilitating Environment: Studies in the Theory of Emotional Development*, pp. 73–82. New York: International Universities Press.

Winnicott, D.W. (1960). *Le Processus de Maturation Chez l'Enfant* [The process of development in the child]. Paris: Payot.

Winnicott, D.W. (1965) [1958]. 'The capacity to be alone'. In *The Maturational Processes and the Facilitating Environment: Studies in the Theory of Emotional Development*, pp. 29–36. New York: International Universities Press.

Winnicott, D.W. (1965) [1960]. 'The theory of the parent-infant relationship'. In *The Maturational Processes and the Facilitating Environment: Studies in the Theory of Emotional Development*, pp. 37–55. New York: International Universities Press.

Winnicott, D.W. (1965) [1962]. 'Ego integration in child development'. In *The Maturational Processes and the Facilitating Environment: Studies in the Theory of Emotional Development*, pp. 56–63. New York: International Universities Press.

Woelz-Stirling, N.A., Kelaher, M. & L. Manderson (1998). 'Power and the politics of abuse: Rethinking violence in Filipina-Australian marriages'. *Health Care for Women International*, 19:289–301.

Wolfe, S. & J. Penelope (1993). 'Sexual identity/textual politics: Lesbian decomposition'. In Wolfe, S. & J. Penelope (Eds.) *Sexual Practice, Textual Theory: Lesbian Cultural Criticism*, pp. 1–24. Cambridge, Massachusetts: Blackwell.

Wolpe, H. (1975). 'The theory of internal colonialism: The South African case'. In Oxaal, I., Barnett, T. & D. Booth (Eds.) *Beyond the Sociology of Development*, pp. 229–252. London: Routledge and Kegan Paul.

Wolpe, H. (1988). *Race, Class and the Apartheid State*. Addis Ababa: Organisation for African Unity.

Women's Health and Development (WHD) (1997). *Violence Against Women. A Priority Health Issue*. Geneva: Family and Reproductive Health, World Health Organisation.

Wood, K. & D. Foster (1995). '"Being the Type of Lover ...": Gender-differentiated reasons for non-use of condoms by sexually active heterosexual students'. *Psychology in Society*, 20:13–35.

Wood, K. & R. Jewkes (1998). *'Love is a Dangerous Thing': Micro-dynamics of Violence in Sexual Relationships of Young People in Umtata*. Tygerberg: Medical Research Council.

Wood, K. & R. Jewkes (2001). '"Dangerous" love. Reflections on violence among Xhosa township youth'. In Morrell, R. (Ed.) *Changing Men in Southern Africa*, pp. 317–336. Pietermaritzburg: University of Natal Press.

Wood, K., Maforah, F. & R. Jewkes (1996). *Sex, Violence and Constructions of Love among Xhosa Adolescents: Putting Violence on the Sexuality Education Agenda*. Tygerberg: Medical Research Council.

Woodward, W. (1999). 'Disturbing difference: Some literary representations of inter-racial relationships in the "new" South Africa'. Paper presented at the *Utrecht University–*

University of the Western Cape UNITWIN Colloquium, University of the Western Cape, Cape Town.

Woolfson, L. (1975). *Aetiological and Personality Factors Relating to Homosexual Behaviour in Adult Females*. Unpublished Master's thesis, University of South Africa, Pretoria.

Worchel, S., Cooper, J. & G.R. Goethals (1988). *Understanding Social Psychology*, 4th Edition. Chicago: The Dorsey Press.

Wyrick, D. (1998). *Fanon for Beginners*. London & New York: Writers and Readers.

Yllö, K. & M. Bograd (Eds.) (1990). *Feminist Perspectives on Wife Abuse*. Newbury Park: Sage.

Young, R. (1990). *White Mythologies: Writing History and the West*. London: Routledge.

Zahar, R. (1969). *Frantz Fanon: Colonialism and Alienation*. New York & London: Monthly Review Press.

Zaman, H. (1999). 'Violence against women in Bangladesh: Issues and responses'. *Women's Studies International Forum*, 22(1): 37–48.

Zarkov, D. (1997). 'Sex as usual: Body politics and the media war in Serbia'. In Davis, K. (Ed.) *Embodied Practices: Feminist Perspectives on the Body*, pp. 110–127. London: Sage Publications.

Zimbardo, P.C. (1974). 'On the ethics of intervention in human psychological research: With special reference to the Stanford prison experiment'. *Cognition*, 2:243–256.

Zimmerman, B. (1993). 'What has never been: An overview of lesbian feminist criticism'. In Wolfe, S. & J. Penelope (Eds.) *Sexual Practice, Textual Theory: Lesbian Cultural Criticism*, pp. 33–54. Cambridge Massachusetts: Blackwell.

Zur, J.N. (1998). *Violent Memories: Mayan War Widows in Guatemala*. Oxford: Westview Press.

Index

Note: Page numbers in italics refer to figures